INSTANT SYNONYMS AND ANTONYMS

Compiled by

Donald O. Bolander, B.S., M.A.
Director of Education, Career Institute

Dolores D. Varner

Elliott Pine

5,100 Main Word Entries

52,000 Synonyms

31,000 Antonyms

Published by

CAREER INSTITUTE

1500 Cardinal Drive   Little Falls, New Jersey 07424

Instant Synonyms and Antonyms

a quick, handy reference guide especially prepared for

Authors	High School and
Teachers	College Students
Executives	Reporters
Clergymen	Speakers
Editors	Copywriters
Secretaries	Businessmen
Librarians	Parents
Correspondents	Speechwriters

and for everyone in any occupation or activity who wants
to express their thoughts clearly and forcefully by
using just the right word at the right time.

1980 Edition
ISBN 0-911744-06-1

© Copyright 1970 by
CAREER INSTITUTE, INC.
Library of Congress Catalog No. 75-113518
Printed in the United States of America

SA80-1

Purpose of This Book

The effective speaker and writer knows there is real power in words, and he uses this power by selecting just the right words to convey the precise meaning and effect he wants. The purpose of this book is to give you an instant reference guide to help you select words that will add vigor, color, and preciseness to all you say or write.

This dictionary contains 5,100 main word entries with 52,000 synonyms and 31,000 antonyms. For a main idea or word, the synonyms give you a wide choice of other words of similar meaning; whereas, the antonyms give you a selection of words with opposite meanings.

For example, take the key synonym, "abandon": You will find "abandon" listed alphabetically—along with the following synonyms and antonyms:

abandon, desert, forsake, quit, relinquish, leave, reject, surrender, yield, resign, repudiate, discontinue, sacrifice, vacate, forswear, withdraw, abdicate. *Antonyms*, undertake, pursue, cherish, keep, maintain, uphold, adopt, support, occupy, retain.

The *antonyms* immediately follow the *synonyms*. You find both in one quick operation—a great help when you want to *clarify* by using *contrast*.

With this handy word-reference volume at your elbow you need never again worry about making embarrassing "word mistakes," overworking tired words, or just plain dull writing! As you use this little volume you'll also be automatically enlarging your vocabulary. You will add "sparkle" and interest to everything you write and say.

A

abaft, aft, astern, behind, rear. *Ant.* forward, front, ahead.

abandon, desert, forsake, quit, relinquish, leave, reject, surrender, yield, resign, repudiate, discontinue, sacrifice, vacate, forswear, withdraw, abdicate. *Ant.* undertake, pursue, cherish, keep, maintain, uphold, adopt, support, occupy, retain.

abandoned, deserted, forsaken, shunned, left, discontinued, cast off, despised, scorned, relinquished, abdicated, repudiated, vacated, surrendered; wicked, corrupt, dissolute, degraded, immoral, impure, sinful. *Ant.* cherished, upheld, defended, maintained, supported, adopted; pure, chaste, moral, innocent, virtuous, holy, unstained.

abase, disgrace, shame, lower, degrade, confound, mock. *Ant.* respect, honor, praise, cherish, elevate, dignify, glorify, extol, uplift, exalt.

abash, disconcert, discourage, discompose, confuse, bewilder, shame, confound, humble, humiliate, mock, embarrass, mortify, crush. *Ant.* encourage, hearten, praise, embolden, uphold, cheer, buoy, stimulate, rally.

abate, lower, lessen, decrease, diminish, moderate, mitigate, reduce, restrain, slacken, assuage, alleviate. *Ant.* enlarge, increase, prolong, extend, amplify, foment, intensify, enhance.

abatement, reduction, lessening, diminution, decrease, subsidence, moderation. *Ant.* increase, augmentation, enlargement.

abbreviate, shorten, lessen, condense, reduce, curtail, abridge, contract. *Ant.* lengthen, increase, extend, distend, enlarge, expand.

abbreviation, abridgment, contraction, abstraction, shortening, curtailment. *Ant.* enlargement, expansion, extension, increase, augmentation.

abdicate, resign, abandon, forsake, give up, renounce, quit, relinquish, surrender. *Ant.* hold, maintain, retain, remain, claim, defend, assert.

abdomen, belly, stomach, middle, paunch.

aberration, deviation, irregularity, variation, divergence, distortion, insanity, eccentricity, peculiarity, anomaly, lapse, perversion.

abet, aid, help, stimulate, assist, encourage, incite, instigate, promote, uphold, support. *Ant.* discourage, impede, obstruct, frustrate, baffle, resist, confound, hinder, dissuade, deter.

abeyance, suspension, inaction, dormancy, indecision, suppression, reservation, adjournment. *Ant.* operation, enforcement, renewal, action, revival, exercise.

abhor, hate, loathe, detest, despise, abominate, dislike, execrate, scorn. *Ant.* love, cherish, esteem, like, desire, enjoy, admire, approve, relish.

abhorrent, hateful, odious, detestable, shocking, offensive, repulsive, loathsome, repellent. *Ant.* delightful, enjoyable, admirable, likable, pleasing.

5

abide, live, stay, sojourn, inhabit, dwell, reside, tarry, stop, lodge, remain; bide, bear, endure, tolerate. *Ant.* go, move, depart, leave; shun, resist, reject, despise.

ability, capacity, capability, skill, understanding, aptitude, efficiency, attainment, knowledge, talent. *Ant.* ignorance, limitation, stupidity, incompetency.

abject, base, mean, servile, low, humble, groveling, contemptible, pitiful, ignoble, inferior, absurd. *Ant.* exalted, magnificent, imposing, noble, proud, excellent.

able, qualified, capable, strong, competent, efficient, fitted, skillful, effective. *Ant.* ineffective, infirm, feeble, weak, delicate.

abnormal, unusual, unnatural, aberrant, irregular, odd, erratic, anomalous. *Ant.* normal, usual, standard, customary.

abode, residence, quarters, lodging, dwelling, habitation, house, home.

abolish, abrogate, annul, nullify, invalidate, revoke, destroy, quash, cancel, extinguish. *Ant.* establish, institute, continue, confirm, promote, legalize, restore.

abominable, detestable, horrible, odious, disgusting, hateful, loathsome, repugnant, revolting, vile, infamous. *Ant.* lovable, enjoyable, likable, sweet, alluring, pleasant, pleasing.

abortive, vain, useless, ineffective, futile, fruitless, miscarrying, ineffectual. *Ant.* effectual, productive, efficacious, successful, fruitful.

abound, teem, flourish, overflow, swell, swarm, flow. *Ant.* be rare, be scarce, want, lack, need.

about, concerning, around, nearby, nearly, approximately, regarding. *Ant.* remote, afar, separated, distant.

above, over, overhead, higher, superior, preceding. *Ant.* below, low, inferior.

abrasion, attrition, erosion, grinding, rubbing, wearing.

abridgment, condensation, digest, epitome, synopsis, analysis, compendium, abstract, summary, precis. *Ant.* enlargement, addition, extension.

abroad, overseas, away, outside, out, forth. *Ant.* domestic, at home.

abrogate, annul, repeal, abolish, cancel, revoke, void, nullify, quash, negate, vacate. *Ant.* ratify, establish, approve, sanction.

abrupt, sudden, impetuous, steep, precipitate, quick, sheer, hasty, brusque, short. *Ant.* gradual, deliberate.

abscond, run away, flee, hide, depart, leave, retreat, bolt, disappear, slip away, withdraw. *Ant.* remain, stop, stay, endure, abide, continue.

absent, missing, away, nonexistent, void, truant, blank, withdrawn. *Ant.* present, attending, existing, remaining, here.

absolute, perfect, thorough, total, supreme, entire, unrestricted, complete, unconditional, despotic, arbitrary, imperative, tyrannous, authoritative, positive, dogmatic, commanding, pre-emptory, autocratic, unlimited. *Ant.* mild, humble, meek, docile, yielding, gentle, submissive, lowly, insufficient, part, contingent, complaisant, accountable, responsible, limited, lenient, tractable.

absolve, pardon, release, exonerate, clear, forgive, cleanse, acquit, overlook, exempt, liberate, set free, discharge. *Ant.* bind, accuse, charge, impeach, convict, compel, obligate, condemn, blame, incriminate.

absorb, imbibe, engross, assimilate, incorporate, consume, merge, exhaust, engulf, swallow. *Ant.* disgorge, emit, disperse, eject, dissipate, exude, spew.

abstinence, abstention, continence, self-denial, temperance, fasting, frugality, self-control, abstaining, self-restraint, sobriety, forbearance. *Ant.* excess, greed, self-indulgence, intemperance, gluttony.

abstract, excerpt, select, steal, remove, separate, discriminate, appropriate, divert, detach, eliminate, withdraw, distract, take away. *Ant.* restore, fill up, strengthen, unite, increase, conjoin, complete, combine, add, repair, mend, expand, insert.

abstracted, absent-minded, engrossed, removed, withdrawn, heedless, careless, absorbed, oblivious, negligent, preoccupied. *Ant.* alert, attentive, thoughtful, prompt, wide-awake, intent.

abstruse, profound, abstract, difficult, subtle, recondite, esoteric. *Ant.* plain, obvious, clear, open.

absurd, stupid, ridiculous, unreasonable, preposterous, senseless, foolish, silly, nonsensical, inconsistent, ill-advised, crazy, false, ludicrous, chimerical, erroneous, wild, mistaken, inconclusive, infatuated. *Ant.* rational, sound, undeniable, reasonable, wise, true, logical, sensible, solemn, incontestable, indisputable, substantial, infallible, incontrovertible, unquestionable, established, demonstrable, certain, demonstrated.

abundant, plentiful, profuse, copious, opulent, flowing, lavish. *Ant.* rare, scarce.

abuse, *v.* ill-use, defame, ill-treat, violate, damage, injure, malign, disparage, harm, slander, scandalize, vilify, depreciate, misuse, reproach, wrong, persecute, molest, aggrieve, oppress, desecrate, ruin, prostitute; *n.* opprobrium, vituperation, scorn, ill-usage, reproach, disgrace, ignominy, dishonor, infamy, slander, blame, humiliation, contempt. *Ant.* praise, eulogize, favor, vindicate, conserve, applaud, shield, defend, cherish, protect, preserve, commend, uphold, benefit, respect, approve, honor, sustain; praise, commendation, approval, sanction, respect, regard, panegyric, applause.

academic, learned, literary, scholastic, scholarly, lettered, pedantic, collegiate, theoretical, formal. *Ant.* ignorant, illiterate, practical.

accede, assent, concur, consent, agree. *Ant.* protest, denounce, refuse, dissent.

accelerate, hurry, dispatch, expedite, hasten, quicken, speed up, facilitate. *Ant.* retard, obstruct, hinder, defer, postpone, resist.

accentuate, stress, heighten, intensify, emphasize, exaggerate, underline, affirm. *Ant.* moderate, minimize, subdue.

accept, receive, get, assent, take, gain, concur, acquire, admit, acknowledge, agree. *Ant.* refuse, dispute, reject, discard, deny, renounce, disagree, decline.

acceptable, pleasing, welcome, agreeable. *Ant.* disagreeable, unwelcome, annoying.

accessory, ally, aide, abettor, companion, assistant, helper, henchman, colleague, partner, accomplice, follower. *Ant.* opponent, enemy, betrayer, principal.

accident, casualty, happening, contingency, misfortune, mishap, misadventure, hazard, chance, disaster, calamity. *Ant.* plan, provision, calculation, purpose, ordinance, law, fate, decree, intention, certainty, appointment, necessity.

acclaim, cheer, honor, applaud, praise, laud, extol, glorify. *Ant.* jeer, dishonor, revile, berate.

accommodate, serve, adjust, arrange, harmonize, oblige, furnish, conform, adapt, supply, fit, reconcile, fashion. *Ant.* impede, stop, unsuit, disarrange, hinder, obstruct, embarrass, prevent, limit.

accompany, attend, conduct, follow, escort, convoy, join, chaperon. *Ant.* leave, desert.

accomplish, perform, achieve, execute, complete, fulfill, do, attain, consummate, realize, carry out, effect, succeed, manage, perfect, discharge. *Ant.* fail, nullify, block, undo, deter, forsake, frustrate, disappoint, abandon, relinquish.

accomplishment, attainment, fulfillment, qualification, performance, completion, skill, art. *Ant.* defeat, frustration, failure, unfulfillment.

accord, *v.* allow, agree, admit, acquiesce, harmonize, concede, give, assent, grant, permit. *Ant.* refuse, disallow, contend, challenge, oppose, disagree, relinquish, controvert, dispute, question, argue, antagonize.

accord, *n.* agreement, acquiescence, harmony, unison, reconciliation. *Ant.* disagreement, refusal, opposition, dissension, strife.

accost, salute, assail, greet, speak to, address, approach, solicit, recognize. *Ant.* shun, avoid, ignore, scorn, evade.

account, narrative, description, detail, report, statement, charge, explanation, bill, reckoning.

accountable, answerable, amenable, liable, censurable, responsible. *Ant.* irresponsible, untrustworthy, blameless, unreliable.

accounting, settlement, reckoning, computation, bill, auditing, tallying, scoring.

accrue, accumulate, increase, grow, gain, result, gather, become a legal right, yield.

accumulate, amass, pile, accrue, stack, add, collect, gather, hoard, bring together, assemble, aggregate. *Ant.* scatter, dissipate, divide, disperse, spend, squander, waste, lessen, dwindle.

accumulation, collection, aggregation, heap, concentration, stock, mass, store. *Ant.* dispersion, separation, scattering, dissipation, division.

accurate, correct, trustworthy, particular, certain, exact, precise, sure, right, authoritative, reliable. *Ant.* erroneous, questionable, doubtful, mistaken, wrong, false, untruthful, uncertain, vague, erring, astray, unreliable, inaccurate.

accuse, blame, charge, censure, incriminate, denounce, implicate.

accustom, familiarize, acclimatize, harden, inure, addict, train, habituate.

achieve, do, accomplish, fulfill, attain, conquer, execute, perform, act, effect, get, win, gain, administer, succeed. *Ant.* fail, ignore, neglect, fall down, retreat, forsake, abandon, relinquish, lose.

achievement, attainment, feat, exploit, deed, accomplishment, performance, act, action, fulfillment, completion, execution. *Ant.* loss, neglect, cessation, failure, negligence, injury, misfortune, defeat, forfeiture, waste.

acid, sour, stinging, bitter, tart, pungent, sharp, acrid. *Ant.* bland, mild, smooth, sweet.

acknowledge, admit, allow, concede, confess, believe, accept, grant, recognize, endorse, profess, subscribe, declare, uphold, certify. *Ant.* refuse, decline, deny, ignore, repudiate, renounce, disown.

acquaint, inform, tell, notify, enlighten, announce. *Ant.* deceive, misrepresent, mislead, falsify.

acquaintance, familiarity, intimacy, cognizance, experience, association, knowledge, esteem. *Ant.* unfamiliarity, inexperience, ignorance, strangeness.

acquire, get, procure, reach, achieve, obtain, secure, collect, gain, earn, inherit, attain, win, master. *Ant.* lose, fail, forfeit.

acquit, forgive, pardon, free, absolve, discharge, clear, liberate, release, exculpate, repay, exonerate. *Ant.* convict, keep, hold, condemn, bind, defeat, doom, convince, repudiate, reprove, blame, censure, disapprove, denounce.

acrimony, tartness, acerbity, bitterness, sharpness, harshness, anger, asperity, irascibility, malevolence, severity, malignity, acridity, causticity. *Ant.* amiability, mildness, smoothness, complacency, gentleness, suavity, kindness, tenderness, sweetness, courtesy, flattery, politeness.

act, *v.* perform, enact, simulate, do, make, play, operate, effect, execute, continue, accomplish, transact, enforce, achieve, administer, consummate, persevere, perpetrate; *n.* action, feat, deed, exercise, work, operation, movement, accomplishment, execution, proceeding, exploit, transaction, performance, achievement, effect. *Ant.* refrain, hesitate, halt, abstain, give up, cease, stop, discontinue; cessation, inertia, rest, stoppage, repose, inaction, indolence, quiescence, inactivity, immobility, quiet.

9

action, achievement, deed, engagement, feat, battle, exploit, accomplishment, motion, exercise, operation, agency, work, activity, behavior, performance, business. *Ant.* inertia, sluggishness, inaction, inactivity, repose, idleness.

active, alert, busy, spry, supple, quick, sharp, brisk, sprightly, agile, hustling, industrious, lively, energetic, diligent, vigorous, wide-awake, expeditious, mobile, restless, ready, prompt, nimble. *Ant.* inactive, dull, slow, indolent, idle, heavy, stupid, quiet, inert, quiescent.

activity, exercise, business, quickness, vigor, motion, action, alertness, agility, readiness, liveliness, sprightliness, progress, swiftness, speediness, progressiveness. *Ant.* inactivity, idleness, dullness, laziness, sluggishness, inertia, stupidity.

actual, real, genuine, certain, positive, certified, confirmed, factual, undoubted, existent, reliable, authentic, sure. *Ant.* doubtful, false, fictitious, mythical, unreliable, legendary, feigned, pretended, unreal.

acumen, insight, discernment, keenness, sharpness, penetration, acuteness, shrewdness, accuracy, perspicacity, sagacity, wisdom, intelligence. *Ant.* dullness, stupidity, moroseness, obtuseness, insensibility, apathy, sluggishness, slowness.

acute, sharp, keen, trenchant, penetrating, intense, astute, smart, shrewd, quick, critical, poignant, pointed. *Ant.* obtuse, chronic, dull, stupid.

adapt, suit, accommodate, fit, conform, arrange, harmonize, settle, proportion, set, attune, regulate, modify, adjust. *Ant.* confuse, misfit, misplace, disarrange, disturb, displace, misapply, disorder, dismember, derange, dislocate.

add, enlarge, extend, increase, append, attach, augment, amplify, adjoin, affix, annex. *Ant.* subtract, diminish, reduce, decrease, lessen, withdraw, remove, deduct.

addicted, attached, dedicated, accustomed, devoted, habituated, disposed, prone, inclined, predisposed, given. *Ant.* averse, opposed, unaccustomed, indisposed, reluctant, disinclined.

addition, increase, supplement, codicil, appendage, increment, annexation, adjunct. *Ant.* subtraction, decrease, lessening, loss, diminution, shrinkage, withdrawal.

address, *v.* speak to, approach, accost, hail, salute, greet, acclaim, court, woo, apostrophize; *n.* speech, oration, appeal, discourse; tact, dexterity, ability, skill, deportment, politeness, demeanor, manners, adroitness, discretion. *Ant.* overlook, ignore, avoid, elude, shun, pass; rudeness, clumsiness, awkwardness, stupidity, folly, fatuity.

adept, skillful, artful, accomplished. *Ant.* awkward, crude, unskilled.

adequate, suited, adapted, satisfactory, sufficient, suitable, equal, fit, fitted, fitting, enough, able, commensurate, competent, ample, capable, qualified. *Ant.* inadequate, unsuitable, unqualified, useless, unfit, insufficient, incompetent, wanting, lacking.

adhere, stick, cling, unite, cleave, attach, fasten, join. *Ant.* separate, loosen, disunite, unfasten, disjoin.

adherent, follower, disciple, votary, partisan, comrade, backer, supporter, accessory. *Ant.* opposer, adversary, deserter.

adhesive, sticky, glutinous, gummy, cohesive, viscous, viscid, waxy, tenacious, gelatinous. *Ant.* inadhesive, loose, separable, apart, free, separated.

adjacent, adjoining, near, bordering, close, nigh, next, beside, contiguous, neighboring, abutting, conterminous, attached. *Ant.* far, distant, away from, beyond, detached, separate, disconnected.

adjournment, postponement, prorogation, discontinuance, dissolution, consummation, respite. *Ant.* beginning, commencement, continuity, prolongation, continuance.

adjunct, addition, appendage, complement, appurtenance, auxiliary, dependency. *Ant.* subtraction, removal, lessening, disjunction.

adjust, regulate, accommodate, settle, fit, adapt, organize, classify, conform, prepare, straighten. *Ant.* disarrange, confuse, scatter, disorganize, disorder, derange.

administer, minister, execute, distribute, govern, manage, furnish, control, conduct, superintend, discharge, supply, regulate, provide, give, dose. *Ant.* fail, neglect, deny, restrain, refuse, oppose, nullify, forego, withhold.

admirable, worthy, attractive, captivating, enticing, astonishing, striking, wonderful, surprising, excellent, good, alluring, praiseworthy, desirable. *Ant.* unworthy, ordinary, mediocre, uninviting, contemptible, despicable, disgusting, censurable, shameful.

admiration, wonder, appreciation, deference, estimation, approbation, praise, encomium, applause, regard, respect, approval, surprise, amazement, gratification, esteem, pleasure. *Ant.* hatred, hate, detestation, disregard, contempt, disapproval, distrust, denunciation, dissatisfaction, disgust, aversion, dislike, loathing, antipathy, repugnance.

admire, appreciate, approve, praise, extol, honor, respect, esteem, love, adore, look at. *Ant.* blame, ridicule, detest, execrate, scorn, dishonor, abhor, vilify, abominate, dislike, belittle.

admissible, worthy, proper, confirmed, suitable, right, passable, fair, permissible, just, allowable, probable, likely, possible, agreeable, justified, justifiable, permitted, sanctioned, warranted, attested, approved. *Ant.* unworthy, unsuitable, wrong, unfair, unlikely, unjust, false, irrelevant, foreign, absurd, ridiculous, applicable, illegitimate, inadmissible.

admission, admittance, acknowledgment, allowance, confession, concession, access, entrance fee, approach. *Ant.* denial, rejection, refusal, repudiation, disallowance, expulsion, repulsion.

admit, allow, permit to enter, open for, acknowledge, avow, suffer, grant, assent, welcome, receive, concede, confess, own, tell, induct, matriculate. *Ant.* deny, refuse, shut, dismiss, repulse, dissent, dispute, repel, confute, reject, eject, expel, debar, oust.

11

admonish, warn, advise, counsel, censure, forewarn, caution, rebuke, reprimand, dissuade, exhort. *Ant.* approve, applaud, praise, compliment, commend.

adolescence, youth, immaturity, minority, teen-age, puberty. *Ant.* adulthood, maturity.

adopt, assume, embrace, choose, appropriate, accept, espouse, pass, approve. *Ant.* reject, repulse.

adore, worship, venerate, love, extol, praise, honor, glorify. *Ant.* mock, despise, execrate, detest, hate, curse.

adorn, ornament, beautify, garnish, embellish, illustrate, decorate, gild. *Ant.* deform, deface, spoil, mar, disfigure, damage, tarnish.

adroit, slick, skilled, skillful, dexterous, proficient, clever, expert, artful, ready. *Ant.* unskilled, awkward, dense, dull, maladroit.

adult, of legal age, mature, grown-up, ripe. *Ant.* immature, juvenile, adolescent.

adulterate, debase, pollute, defile, corrupt, alloy, muddle, confuse. *Ant.* purify, clarify, refine, improve, free.

advance, go onward, proceed, improve, continue, progress, heighten, promote, accelerate, exalt, allege, increase, rise, lend, supply. *Ant.* recede, turn, stop, yield, return, withdraw, hesitate, stand, halt, retrogress.

advancement, promotion, progression, progress, gain, improvement, proficiency, preferment, elevation, enhancement, forwardness, superiority. *Ant.* retrogression, deterioration, descent, decline, return, reversion, retreat, stoppage, degeneration.

advantage, benefit, profit, assistance, help, gain, interest, good, utility, expediency, superiority, success, victory. *Ant.* obstacle, loss, hindrance, handicap, incumbrance, restriction.

advantageous, beneficial, gainful, profitable, useful, helpful, good, favorable, assisting, expedient, convenient. *Ant.* unfavorable, harmful, injurious, profitless, retarding, deleterious.

adventure, excitement, event, enterprise, circumstance, trip, undertaking, expedition, affair, transaction, venture, trial, experiment, engagement. *Ant.* isolation, passiveness, inaction, avoidance, stillness, inertness, inactivity.

adversity, misfortune, calamity, accident, ill-luck, disaster, distress, obstacle, misery, opposition, antagonism. *Ant.* help, aid, encouragement, assistance, favor, fortune, cooperation, approval.

advertisement, notice, ad, proclamation, announcement, commercial message.

advice, counsel, guidance, suggestion, exhortation, opinion, charge, instruction, directions, admonition, injunction, lesson, caution, warning. *Ant.* misinformation, misdirection, deception, betrayal, misrepresentation.

advise, counsel, direct, acquaint, apprise, tell, inform, admonish, warn, instruct, suggest, show. *Ant.* lead astray, pervert, betray, deceive, dissemble, trick, delude, pretend, feign.

advocate, support, maintain, champion, recommend, favor, promote, advance, forward, plead. *Ant.* attack, oppose, protest.

affable, friendly, courteous, mild, gracious, urbane, complaisant, suave, civil, pleasing, benign. *Ant.* impolite, surly, haughty, disdainful, arrogant.

affair, incident, event, concern, duty, business, occasion, liaison, amour, happening.

affectation, pretension, mannerism, pose, artificiality, insincerity, pompousness, unnaturalness, air. *Ant.* artlessness, naturalness, naivete, simplicity.

affection, love, friendship, goodwill, attachment, friendliness, fondness, kindness, tenderness, solicitude. *Ant.* dislike, unkindness, ill-will, aversion, animosity, antipathy.

affiliate, join, merge, combine, associate, connect, ally. *Ant.* separate, disjoin, divide.

affirm, assert, state, aver, declare, insist, depose, propose, claim, warrant, say, swear, vow, maintain, assure. *Ant.* deny, nullify.

affliction, misfortune, tribulation, distress, trouble, sorrow, suffering, adversity, injury, woe, misery, disaster, anguish, wretchedness. *Ant.* relief, comfort.

affluent, wealthy, opulent, rich, abounding, plenteous. *Ant.* poor, destitute, impecunious, penniless, needy.

affray, fight, battle, controversy, conflict, combat, quarrel, struggle, contest, brawl, riot, fracas.

affront, insult, irritate, provoke, taunt, vex, annoy, exasperate, tease, aggravate, offend. *Ant.* please, appease, satisfy, mollify, assuage.

afraid, timid, alarmed, terrified, terror-stricken, frightened, fearful, cowardly, timorous, apprehensive, anxious. *Ant.* fearless, valiant, gallant, courageous, valorous, bold, brave, intrepid, heroic, confident, undaunted, undismayed, venturesome, collected, audacious.

aged, old, senile, hoary, ripe, mellow, elderly, antiquated, doddering, superannuated, decrepit. *Ant.* young, vigorous, unripe.

agent, operator, performer, doer, promoter, mover, actor, factor, consignee, functionary, means, deputy, representative, instrument. *Ant.* chief, principal, originator, employer, inventor, master.

aggravate, worsen, irritate, heighten, intensify. *Ant.* improve, help, cure, soothe, relieve.

aggregate, mass, collection, total, sum, whole. *Ant.* individual, particular, unitary, part.

agitate, shake, move, provoke, rouse, perturb, excite, arouse, impel, drive, convulse, disturb, actuate, trouble, bother, annoy, fluster, stir. *Ant.* calm, soothe, quiet, lull, still.

agony, pain, suffering, distress, torment, affliction, trial, torture, anguish, misery. *Ant.* happiness, health, peace, comfort.

agree, concur, approve, consent, accept, assent, admit, acquiesce, accede, accord, unite, join, harmonize. *Ant.* protest, oppose, contradict, differ, dissent, disagree, contend, dispute.

agreeable, pleasant, pleasing, enticing, loving, charming, inviting, acceptable, ready, willing. *Ant.* disagreeable, unpleasant, discordant, contentious, incongruous.

aid, help, advance, foster, promote, relieve, abet, encourage, assist, succor, uphold, support, advocate, back. *Ant.* injure, impede, block, hinder.

aim, goal, mark, object, endeavor, intention, aspiration, inclination, determination, end, design, tendency, purpose. *Ant.* aimlessness, oversight, thoughtlessness, carelessness, heedlessness, neglect.

air, manner, look, demeanor, mien, style, appearance, carriage, behavior, fashion, bearing.

alacrity, speed, swiftness, activity, briskness, celerity, eagerness, readiness, quickness, liveliness, animation, sprightliness, agility, vivacity, cheerfulness, promptness, alertness. *Ant.* apathy, slowness, reluctance, indolence, indifference, unwillingness, dullness, aversion, disinclination.

alarm, terror, fright, fear, consternation, panic, dread, affright, apprehension. *Ant.* security, peace, confidence, assurance.

alert, active, lively, prompt, brisk, ready, wide-awake, watchful, prepared, vigilant. *Ant.* heavy, dull, slow, drowsy, sluggish, lethargic, inattentive, inobservant.

alien, strange, opposed, hostile, distant, foreign, inappropriate, inapplicable, contradictory, unlike, irrelevant, contrasted, contrary, conflicting, unconnected, extraneous. *Ant.* akin, alike, relevant, corresponding, appropriate, proper, apropos, native, friendly.

alike, identical, kindred, homogeneous, similar, analogous, uniform, equal, equivalent. *Ant.* unlike, distinct, heterogeneous, different, dissimilar, opposite.

alive, animate, existent, live, breathing; active, vivacious, subsisting, living, lively, quick, alert, animated. *Ant.* dead, inanimate, lifeless, deceased; spiritless, dull, morose.

allay, soothe, pacify, calm, mollify, tranquilize, quiet, compose, alleviate, appease, relieve. *Ant.* arouse, excite, agitate, stir, rouse, provoke, kindle.

allege, aver, state, adduce, assert, asseverate, assign, introduce, say, produce, claim, maintain, offer, quote. *Ant.* deny, dissent, object, protest, repudiate, disagree, negate.

allegiance, loyalty, duty, submission, homage, subjection, devotion, obedience, faithfulness, fealty. *Ant.* dissatisfaction, disloyalty, treason, treachery.

alleviate, mitigate, lessen, abate, moderate, soften, assuage, relieve, remove, lighten. *Ant.* increase, intensify.

alliance, union, fusion, confederation, federation, coalition, partnership, confederacy, league, compact. *Ant.* hostility, enmity, discord, separation, secession, disunion, war.

allot, give, grant, distribute, assign, apportion, award, divide, yield, ordain, determine, allocate, dispose, arrange, design, hand over, concede. *Ant.* withhold, retain, keep, confiscate, reject, deny, refuse, disallow, confuse, shuffle.

allow, permit, assent, authorize, empower, license, yield, sanction, grant, let, consent, concede, admit, tolerate. *Ant.* deny, forbid, disallow, prohibit, refuse, protest, disapprove.

alloy, combine, amalgamate, adulterate, debase, mix, impair, lessen. *Ant.* purify, clear.

allure, lure, entice, coax, draw, attract, decoy, cajole, inveigle, win, captivate, tempt, persuade, seduce, invite, lead, wheedle, charm, fascinate, enchant, bewitch. *Ant.* repel, warn, threaten, dissuade, discourage.

alone, solitary, single, unaccompanied, isolated, desolate, lonely, only, sole. *Ant.* together, accompanied.

alter, change, transform, metamorphose, vary, modify, moderate, regulate, qualify, shift, diversify. *Ant.* keep, retain, preserve, continue, maintain.

alternative, option, preference, choice, pick, election. *Ant.* compulsion, obligation.

always, constantly, ceaselessly, ever, perpetually, eternally, forever. *Ant.* at no time, never.

amalgamation, union, blend, compound, mixture, combination, consolidation, merger. *Ant.* separation, division.

amass, heap, hoard, store, accumulate, collect, gather, pile, aggregate. *Ant.* disperse, disburse, squander, scatter, spend, waste, expend, distribute, dissipate, dole.

amateur, nonprofessional, beginner, learner, neophyte. *Ant.* professional, scholar, master.

amazement, surprise, wonder, bewilderment, admiration, confusion, astonishment, awe. *Ant.* indifference, steadiness, coolness, composure, calmness.

ambiguous, equivocal, vague, indefinite, obscure, indistinct, indeterminate. *Ant.* clear, explicit, lucid, definite.

ambition, aspiration, goal, end, striving, attempting, competition, desire, attainment, eagerness. *Ant.* indifference, nonfulfillment, laziness, satisfaction, contentment.

amend, improve, purify, better, correct, reform, rectify, change, mend, repair. *Ant.* harm, debase, impair, spoil, corrupt, blemish, deteriorate.

amiable, gentle, agreeable, pleasing, good-natured, kindly, lovable, affectionate, winning. *Ant.* dour, peevish, morose, quarrelsome, ill-humored, surly, rude.

among, amid, amidst, between, interspersed. *Ant.* separate, alone, disparate.

amorous, loving, affectionate, ardent, erotic, passionate, tender, fond. *Ant.* cool, cold, frigid, loveless.

amplify, enlarge, increase, unfold, magnify, extend, develop, widen, expand, dilate, augment. *Ant.* reduce, condense, epitomize, summarize, curtail, abridge.

amuse, entertain, engross, cheer, beguile, gladden, please, titillate, divert, interest. *Ant.* bore, tire, annoy.

analogy, likeness, similarity, resemblance, correspondence. *Ant.* unlikeness, dissimilarity.

analysis, dissection, separation, classification, segregation. *Ant.* synthesis, combination, assembly.

15

ancestry, lineage, parentage, blood, stock, race, pedigree, descent, line, family.

ancient, old, aged, obsolete, dated, archaic, antiquated, antique. *Ant.* new, modern.

anger, ire, wrath, temper, peevishness, indignation, resentment, fury, rage, scorn, displeasure, passion, madness, irritation, vexation, petulance, exasperation, impatience, animosity. *Ant.* good nature, mildness, gentility, calmness, smoothness, clemency, forbearance, jollity, patience, placidity, pleasantness.

anguish, distress, suffering, pain, affliction, sorrow, torment, worry, woe, misery, grief, anxiety, pang. *Ant.* comfort, joy.

animate, enliven, rouse, vivify, encourage, activate, cheer, vitalize, quicken, inspire. *Ant.* kill, deactivate, discourage.

annihilate, exterminate, kill, obliterate, destroy, abolish, nullify, annul, eliminate, extirpate, extinguish, eradicate. *Ant.* preserve, save.

announce, tell, communicate, expound, promulgate, advertise, make known, blazon, notify, publish, say, broadcast, proclaim, give out, declare, circulate, state, report, reveal. *Ant.* conceal, suppress, hold, refrain.

annoy, trouble, harry, vex, irritate, plague, harass, irk, fret, pester, bother, molest. *Ant.* aid, soothe, please.

answer, reply, acknowledge, respond, retort, rejoin, rebut, confute. *Ant.* ask, question.

antagonism, antipathy, discord, enmity, animosity, opposition, conflict, rancor, hostility, dissension. *Ant.* harmony, agreement, accord.

anticipation, expectancy, presentiment, hope, foreboding, forecast, forethought, apprehension, foretaste, expectation. *Ant.* doubt, fear, wonder, surprise, sensation, amazement.

antipathy, hatred, aversion, opposition, detestation, repugnance, abhorrence, repulsion, antagonism. *Ant.* liking, admiration, love, respect, regard, approval, approbation.

antique, ancient, superannuated, quaint, old-fashioned. *Ant.* new, recent, modern.

anxiety, anguish, misgiving, care, concern, foreboding, worry, dread, apprehension, trouble, disquiet, fretting, fear, perplexity. *Ant.* ease, calmness, tranquility, peace, contentment.

appall, horrify, dismay, terrorize, alarm, daunt, frighten, shock. *Ant.* comfort, console, calm, assure.

apathy, unconcern, unfeelingness, indifference, passiveness, phlegm, lethargy, impassibility, tranquility, insensibility, sluggishness, immobility. *Ant.* care, sensitiveness, emotion, passion, frenzy, fury, disturbance, distress, sympathy, susceptibility.

apology, excuse, supplication, plea, defense, justification, evasion, acknowledgment, confession, pretext. *Ant.* accusation, censure, disapprobation.

apparent, evident, manifest, obvious, clear, plain, visible. *Ant.* unclear, hidden, uncertain, doubtful, dubious, equivocal.

appeal, call, apply, request, invoke, plead, pray, ask, beg, beseech, entreat, supplicate. *Ant.* deny, disclaim, retract, refuse, revoke, renounce, recall.

appearance, arrival, coming, advent; aspect, look, guise, semblance, form, demeanor, presence. *Ant.* departure, leaving, absence.

appease, mollify, allay, pacify, assuage, calm, conciliate, soothe. *Ant.* irritate, roil, annoy, tease, provoke, aggravate, incite.

applause, acclaim, approval, approbation, commendation, clapping, cheering, bravos. *Ant.* disapproval, disapprobation, jeers.

appoint, name, designate, choose, select, set, allot, direct, command, assign, ordain. *Ant.* dismiss, remove, recall, withdraw, cancel, nullify.

appetite, craving, desire, liking, disposition, relish, longing, thirst, inclination, zest, proneness, proclivity, propensity, passion, lust, impulse. *Ant.* aversion, distaste, dislike.

apportion, allot, dispense, assign, dole, distribute, mete, allocate, share, ration. *Ant.* withhold, monopolize.

appraise, set a value on, estimate, evaluate, survey, consider.

appreciate, comprehend, value, esteem, realize, thank. *Ant.* disparage, depreciate.

approach, near, arrive, approximate, equal, attempt, accost. *Ant.* leave, depart.

appropriate, *v.* take, assign, assume, arrogate, usurp, seize; *adj.* opportune, suitable, becoming, proper, fitting, applicable. *Ant.* give, bestow; unsuitable, unfitting, inept.

approve, endorse, accept, sanction, confirm, commend, countenance, ratify, justify, validate. *Ant.* disapprove, censure, reject.

approximation, approach, likeness, nearness, propinquity, similarity, neighborhood, resemblance, contiguity. *Ant.* remoteness, variation, distance, difference.

ardent, passionate, eager, earnest, intense, enthusiastic, keen, warm, fervid. *Ant.* cold, lukewarm, indifferent.

arid, dry, barren, sterile, desert-like. *Ant.* moist, damp, rainy.

argue, dispute, wrangle, debate, differ, discuss. *Ant.* ignore, agree, overlook, harmonize.

arraign, accuse, indict, charge, prosecute, cite, censure. *Ant.* free, discharge, exonerate.

arrange, adjust, compare, assort, classify, group, range, set, sort, marshal, array, dispose, harmonize. *Ant.* confuse, disturb, disorder, disarrange.

arrest, halt, stop, apprehend, seize, capture, delay, check. *Ant.* release, activate.

arrive, come, reach, emerge, attain, land, appear. *Ant.* disappear, depart, go, leave.

arrogant, insolent, proud, haughty, disdainful, overbearing. *Ant.* humble, meek, servile.

artifice, ruse, stratagem, trick, machination, wile, guile, maneuver, contrivance, finesse. *Ant.* candor, innocence, honesty, frankness, openness, ingenuousness, sincerity.

ascend, climb, mount, rise, advance, progress, scale, soar, leap. *Ant.* descend, decline.

ascetic, austere, abstemious, rigid, stern, self-denying. *Ant.* luxurious, sensuous, voluptuous, dissolute.

ask, question, request, petition, pray, demand, solicit, supplicate, beg, beseech, appeal, apply for. *Ant.* answer, refuse, command, reject, deny, claim, insist.

aspire, seek, crave, hope, long, desire, yearn, sigh. *Ant.* disdain, give up on.

assault, attack, rape, invasion, charge, onslaught. *Ant.* surrender, defense.

assemble, collect, congregate, combine, gather, convoke, meet, unite, join, convene, compile, muster, levy. *Ant.* disperse, scatter.

assent, agree, accept, concur, consent, allow, concede, recognize, ratify, acquiesce, approve. *Ant.* reject, disapprove.

assert, declare, state, insist, avow, allege, affirm. *Ant.* reject, deny, controvert.

associate, ally, combine, confederate, conjoin, link, unite, league, connect, attach, couple, affiliate. *Ant.* part, disassociate, separate, sever, disunite.

assort, sort, separate, arrange in order, classify, distribute, rank. *Ant.* jumble, disarrange, mix, mingle.

assume, take, appropriate, adopt, put on, affect, arrogate. *Ant.* put off, doubt, relinquish.

assurance, confidence, assertion, boldness, self-reliance, arrogance, self-confidence, effrontery, trust, assumption, presumption. *Ant.* doubt, shyness, distrust, dismay, fear, trepidation, misgiving, timidity, confusion, hesitancy.

astonish, surprise, perplex, amaze, astound, frighten, startle. *Ant.* bore, calm.

astute, clever, smart, crafty, keen, cunning, artful, sharp, subtle, shrewd, perspicacious, penetrating, knowing. *Ant.* dull, ignorant, stupid, obtuse.

attach, fasten, associate, seize, allocate, secure, stick, fix, unite, join, connect, conjoin, affix, annex, adjoin, add, append, combine. *Ant.* sever, disunite, remove, detach, disjoin, separate.

attachment, tie, bond, love, friendship, esteem, devotion, respect, regard, tenderness, estimation, affinity, affection. *Ant.* alienation, enmity, dislike.

attack, assail, assault, violate, seize, infringe, encroach, charge, besiege, combat, beset, encounter *Ant.* protect, defend, sustain, shelter.

attain, get, gain, accomplish, master, win, obtain, secure, achieve, grasp, procure, acquire, earn, compass, reach. *Ant.* give up, abandon, surrender, fail, miss.

attempt, effort, attack, trial, endeavor, essay, undertaking, experiment. *Ant.* certainty, success.

attention, application, notice, intentness, study, concentration, care, diligence, observation, circumspection, heed. *Ant.* neglect, disregard.

attraction, charm, fascination, magnetism, pull, lure, enticement, allure, affinity. *Ant.* repulsion.

audacity, boldness, rashness, presumption, arrogance, effrontery, impudence, brazenness. *Ant.* meekness, mildness, gentility, forbearance, restraint, timidity, humility.

austere, rigid, rigorous, acrimonious, severe, stern, harsh, cruel, unrelenting, sharp, strict, exacting. *Ant.* mild, kind, gentle, meek.

authentic, true, real, legitimate, authoritative, veritable, accredited, genuine, reliable, trustworthy, certain, accepted. *Ant.* disputed, unauthorized, counterfeit.

authority, control, prestige, right, rule, sovereignty, jurisdiction, dominion, mastery, title, supremacy, power, command.

auxiliary, helper, confederate, ally, aid, assistant. *Ant.* adversary, opponent, opposer, competitor, rival.

average, mean, normal, ordinary, median, medium, common, usual, mediocre, standard. *Ant.* unusual, extraordinary, exceptional.

aversion, antipathy, dislike, repugnance, hatred, opposition. *Ant.* liking, care, affection, love, attachment, fondness.

avoid, shun, escape, evade, dodge, forbear, eschew, elude. *Ant.* seek, meet, encounter, face.

awaken, arouse, excite, stir up, stimulate. *Ant.* put to sleep, quiet, calm, stupefy.

award, honor, reward, bestow upon, recognize, adjudge, allot. *Ant.* withhold, withdraw, reject.

aware, alert to, awake, cognizant, conscious of, lively. *Ant.* unaware, unconscious of.

away, absent, gone, aside, off, far, not near, distant. *Ant.* near by, close, present, here.

awe, dread, impressiveness, fear, reverence, veneration, solemnity, respect. *Ant.* familiarity, poise, equanimity, calmness.

awkward, ungainly, unhandy, rough, maladroit, gawky, uncouth, shuffling, clumsy, bungling, unskillful. *Ant.* adroit, clever, handy, dexterous, skillful, graceful, apt, artful.

axiom, rule, proposition, maxim, aphorism, proverb, adage, precept, apothegm. *Ant.* nonsense, paradox, absurdity, sophism, contradiction.

B

backward, toward the rear, behind, in reverse order, retrogressive, retarded, dull, stupid. *Ant.* forward, to the front, intelligent, ahead.

bad, wicked, evil, rotten, false, spurious, disgusting, wrong, vile, corrupt, ill, base, abandoned, vicious, abominable, detestable.

baffle

    Ant. good, right, worthy, competent, benevolent, true, honest, just, sincere, beneficial, advantageous, profitable, virtuous, reputable, upright, propitious.

baffle, confound, defeat, elude, circumvent, balk, counteract, cheat, disconcert, outwit, foil, thwart, frustrate. *Ant.* support, assist, aid, abet, help.

balance, equilibrium, stability, harmony, symmetry, proportion, poise. *Ant.* unbalance, disproportion.

banal, trite, hackneyed, flat, inane, fatuous, vapid, commonplace, ordinary, stereotyped. *Ant.* original, exciting, fresh, new.

banish, exile, put out, proscribe, ostracize, expatriate, expel, oust, dismiss, debar. *Ant.* repatriate, forgive.

barbarous, savage, barbaric, uncouth, rude, brutal, untamed, cruel, inhuman, uncivilized, atrocious. *Ant.* civilized, humane, cultured, courteous, graceful, gentle, refined.

barren, unproductive, sterile, desolate, empty. *Ant.* fertile, full of life, productive, fecund.

barrier, bulwark, bar, prohibition, obstacle, rampart, restriction, hindrance, blockade, obstruction. *Ant.* admittance, thoroughfare, opening, entrance, passage.

base, vile, degraded, inferior, shameful, worthless, mean, corrupt, low, vulgar, contemptible, despicable, unworthy, dishonorable, ignoble. *Ant.* superior, majestic, grand, exalted, high-minded, noble, moral.

basic, fundamental, principal, primary, indispensable, essential, vital. *Ant.* extra, additional, secondary.

batter, beat, mar, smash, belabor, thrash, dent, bruise, pummel, pound, disfigure, destroy, demolish. *Ant.* protect, secure, treat gently, cover, screen.

bear, carry, produce, convey, transport, support, sustain, suffer, maintain, endure, yield, undergo. *Ant.* evade, shun, dodge, cast aside, avoid, refuse.

beat, strike, flog, batter, castigate, spank, pommel, bruise, belabor, cudgel, thrash, crush, whip, hit; overcome, excel, defeat, conquer. *Ant.* defend, guard, protect, help, assist; relinquish, surrender.

beautiful, handsome, nice, fine, pretty, good-looking, lovely, elegant, fair, enticing, splendid, captivating, attractive, graceful. *Ant.* ugly, repulsive, homely, offensive.

becoming, decent, proper, befitting, comely, congruous, neat, fitting, suitable, worthy, decorous, graceful, seemly. *Ant.* unbecoming, improper, ill-fitting, unsuitable, indecorous, displeasing, unfitting, unseemly.

before, forward, ahead, sooner, prior, earlier. *Ant.* after, behind, later, afterward.

beg, beseech, implore, petition, pray, solicit, crave, entreat, ask, supplicate. *Ant.* give, bestow, favor, grant, concede, remunerate, reward, assist, cede

beginning, origin, source, start, rise, inception, commencement, spring, opening, fountain, outset, inauguration. *Ant.* end, finish, goal, completion, conclusion, consummation.

behavior, deportment, bearing, manners, breeding, conduct, action, demeanor, management, attitude, tactics, strategy, policy.

bend, deflect, influence, mold, turn, flex, contort, curve, twist, crook, divert. *Ant.* straighten.

benefit, favor, advantage, kindness, service, civility, utility, profit, blessing. *Ant.* injury, harm, hurt, handicap, hindrance, obstacle, disadvantage.

benevolence, beneficence, humanity, kindness, benignity, tenderness, bounty, almsgiving, kindheartedness, charity, goodwill, sympathy, generosity, liberality, philanthropy, kindliness, munificence, unselfishness. *Ant.* malevolence, hatred, ill will, envy, selfishness, malignity, unkindness.

between, intermediate, amid, among. *Ant.* away from, separate.

beyond, far, farther, distant, above, superior, yonder, over, more. *Ant.* near, here, close by.

bigoted, intolerant, narrow-minded, hidebound, prejudiced, blind, obstinate, opinionated. *Ant.* tolerant, open-minded.

bind, tie, fasten, secure, hitch, shackle, moor, restrain, restrict, obligate. *Ant.* unbind, unloose, free, untie, loose, unfasten, unchain, release.

bitter, acrid, sour, disagreeable, distasteful, sharp, biting. *Ant.* sweet, pleasant, agreeable.

blame, censure, condemn, upbraid, reproach, reprove, condemn, reprehend, accuse. *Ant.* praise, laud, thank, exalt, commend, applaud, exculpate, exonerate.

blank, bare, void, vacant, unfilled, empty, barren. *Ant.* occupied, filled.

bleak, bare, chilly, chilling, wild, unsheltered, dismal, dull, dreary, gloomy, damp, cold, desolate. *Ant.* sunny, cheerful, pleasant, serene, comforting, warm, mild, balmy.

blemish, flaw, fleck, mark, stain, spot, defect, fault, smirch, stigma, imperfection, taint, deformity, disfigurement, defacement, disgrace, dishonor, tarnish, blot. *Ant.* ornament, embellishment, decoration, adornment.

blind, sightless, unseeing; careless, stupid, heedless, obtuse, dense, dull-witted. *Ant.* sharp-eyed, farsighted, cunning, penetrative, shrewd, quick, keen.

bliss, gladness, happiness, joy, blessedness, rapture. *Ant.* sadness, sorrow, pain.

blithe, merry, jolly, animated, joyful, cheerful, gay, vivacious, light-hearted, effervescent. *Ant.* sad, dull, morose.

blot, blacken, smudge, dirty, soil, foul, stain, smirch, blotch, erase, cancel, expunge. *Ant.* whiten, purify, wash, cleanse, restore, record.

blow, box, rap, stroke, cuff, knock, buffet, lash, stripe, hit, cut, thump, concussion, disaster, calamity, misfortune. *Ant.* caress, embrace, good fortune.

bluff, gruff, rough, bold, inconsiderate, impolite, brazen, brusque, rude, unmannerly, discourteous, blustering, coarse, uncivil, blunt, outspoken, abrupt, open, frank, daring. *Ant.* polite, refined, genial, kindly, courteous, urbane, reserved, gracious, civil, suave, agreeable, pleasant.

blunt, obtuse, bluff, harsh, dull, forthright, rough, stolid, direct. *Ant.* subtle, tactful, polite, suave.

boast, brag, flourish, exult, vaunt, bluster. *Ant.* speak modestly.

bold, brave, courageous, fearless, determined, intrepid, undaunted, dauntless, daring, valiant, venturesome, adventurous, audacious, stout-hearted, impudent, rude. *Ant.* timid, shy, timorous, gentle, meek, backward.

border, brim, edge, brink, trimming, margin, rim, boundary, verge, confine, frontier, limit, termination, extremity, end. *Ant.* center, region, interior, territory, inside.

bore, weary, tire, fatigue, annoy; drill, tunnel, burrow, pierce. *Ant.* amuse, interest.

borrow, take temporarily, adopt, imitate, obtain. *Ant.* lend, return, pay off.

bound, circumscribe, limit, define, confine, measure, curb, restrict, compel, leap, jump, spring, skip, recoil, check, impel, restrain, coerce. *Ant.* enlarge, extend, loosen, liberate.

boundary, limit, border, terminal, brink, margin, frontier, termination. *Ant.* inside, interior.

brave, fearless, heroic, gallant, bold, valiant, chivalrous, undaunted, courageous, venturesome, adventurous, dauntless, chivalric, firm, hardy, plucky. *Ant.* cowardly, timid, shrinking.

break, crack, smash, shatter, sever, shiver, crush, burst, split, rend, fracture, rive, rupture, demolish, destroy, tear, batter, subdue, curb, violate, infringe, separate. *Ant.* mend, join, unite.

bright, brilliant, flashing, lustrous, shining, scintillating, luminous, radiant, shiny, sunny, glittering, sparkling, glossy, shimmering, beaming, dazzling, incandescent, burning, glistening, glorious, cheery. *Ant.* dark, obscure, shady, cloudy, threatening, gloomy, murky.

brilliant, bright, glowing, luminous, scintillating, splendid, effulgent, shining, radiant, dazzling, glorious; highly intelligent. *Ant.* dull, dark; stupid.

brim, edge, border, verge, rim, lip, top, brink, line, margin, outline. *Ant.* center, interior.

bring, carry, bear, fetch, convey, induce, adduce, produce, import, attract, cause, draw, move, conduct, transmit, transfer, sustain, transport. *Ant.* leave, pass up, relinquish, refuse, abandon, give up.

brittle, fragile, weak, delicate, breakable, frail, thin, slender, tenuous. *Ant.* tough, strong, unbreakable, resistible, durable.

broad, wide, extensive, large, ample, clear, open, comprehensive, general, spacious, liberal, open-minded, liberal-minded. *Ant.* narrow, illiberal, contracted, conservative.

build, construct, erect, put up, frame, raise, found, make, establish, manufacture. *Ant.* destroy, demolish, pull down, dismantle, raze, overturn, ruin, overthrow.

burn, set on fire, incinerate, oxidize, cremate, consume, ignite, char, brand, singe, kindle, cauterize, scorch, blaze. *Ant.* cool, subdue, smother, put out, stifle, extinguish.

business, occupation, profession, calling, work, duty, transaction, trade, barter, avocation, concern, craft, vocation, commerce, job, trading, pursuit, art, handicraft, matter, affair, employment. *Ant.* avocation, hobby, inactivity, unemployment.

but, except, notwithstanding, save, yet, still, though, unless, more-over, provided, barely, besides, that, and, only, however, merely, nevertheless, just, further, furthermore.

buy, purchase, acquire, procure, secure, obtain, negotiate, shop, bribe. *Ant.* vend, transfer, sell, market.

byword, proverb, saying, apothegm, maxim, adage, aphorism, precept, oddity.

C

cabal, faction, combination, gang, junta; intrigue, plot, conspiracy.

cabalistic, recondite, occult, secret, obscure, mystical, esoteric. *Ant.* plain, open, aboveboard.

cajole, coax, inveigle, wheedle, lure, blandish, beguile. *Ant.* repel, repulse.

calamity, disaster, misfortune, mishap, mischance, distress, misery, woe, affliction, adversity, sorrow, trouble, grief, tribulation, trial, sadness. *Ant.* benefit, comfort, blessing, happiness, joy, profit, favor, prosperity, advantage.

calculate, estimate, enumerate, reckon, rate, consider, weigh, count, number, account, compute, appraise, sum up, value. *Ant.* guess, assume.

call, exclaim, scream, yell, shout, roar, clamor, cry (out), utter, shriek, invite, ejaculate, command, demand, address, speak, telephone, proclaim, convoke, name, summon, term, designate, rally, assemble, invoke. *Ant.* listen, refrain, stifle, smother, restrain, conceal, be still.

calling, occupation, business, profession, vocation, trade, art, craft. *Ant.* hobby, amusement, avocation.

callous, unfeeling, careless, indifferent, careless, insensible, unsusceptible, hard, dull, obdurate, indurated. *Ant.* feeling, tender, soft, compassionate, merciful, clement, pitying, gracious, sympathetic.

calm, cool, quiet, collected, unruffled, reserved, undisturbed, serene, self-possessed, tranquil, dispassionate, placid, sedate, gentle. *Ant.* ruffled, rough, boisterous, agitated, excited, angry, inflamed, fierce, furious, violent, roused, stormy.

calumny, defamation, slander, libel, detraction, lying, backbiting, falsehood, foulness, aspersion, distortion, evil-mindedness, scandal, uncharitableness. *Ant.* charity, commendation, praise, goodwill, friendliness, kindness, benevolence, sympathy.

cancel, quash, annul, abolish, remove, erase, rescind, expunge, postmark, repeal, nullify, efface, delete, revoke, obliterate, vacate, void, wipe out, rub off. *Ant.* approve, sustain, uphold, maintain, record, confirm, continue, establish, ratify.

candid, truthful, sincere, impartial, frank, unbiased, fair, honest, open, simple, artless, ingenuous, naive, straightforward, aboveboard. *Ant.* intriguing, artful, shrewd, sly, wily, tricky, insincere, designing.

candor, frankness, sincerity, fairness, truthfulness, impartiality, openness. *Ant.* deception, falsehood, double-dealing, unfairness, partiality, deceit, artifice, trick, guile, fraud, ruse, stratagem, finesse.

canon, standard, rule, law, ordinance, regulation, formulary, precept, criterion, schedule.

capable, able, competent, fitted, suitable, qualified, adequate, equal, efficient, skillful, impressive, susceptible. *Ant.* incompetent, unqualified, unskillful, unable, inefficient, incapable, unfit.

capacity, volume, expanse, size, magnitude, content, faculty, aptness, ability, genius, skill, gift. *Ant.* smallness, impotence.

caper, gambol, bound, prank, antic, cut-up, romp.

capital, principal, primary, first, paramount, important, chief, best, major, leading, essential, excellent, prime, fine, splendid, vital, first-rate, serious, fatal. *Ant.* secondary, unimportant, poor, low-grade.

capricious, odd, changeable, crotchety, fanciful, freakish, whimsical, fickle, wayward, vacillating, idiosyncratic. *Ant.* staid, steadfast, constant, staunch, dependable.

captivate, enchant, bewitch, charm, enthrall, fascinate, entrance, enslave. *Ant.* repel, disillusion, disgust, displease, offend.

captivity, bondage, confinement, slavery, servitude, imprisonment, subjection. *Ant.* freedom, independence, liberty, liberality, license.

capture, grasp, catch, take, seize, arrest, apprehend, snare, trap. *Ant.* free, release, lose.

cardinal, principal, leading, fundamental, capital, chief, central, main, essential, vital, necessary. *Ant.* lesser, minor, negligible, insignificant.

care, attention, concern, solicitude, heed, anxiety, watchfulness, forethought, wariness, precaution, perplexity, prudence, caution, trouble, vigilance, worry, circumspection, charge. *Ant.* neglect, carelessness, negligence, disregard, heedlessness, omission, oversight.

career, progress, way, course, walk, pursuit, line, sphere, business, experience, occupation, profession, vocation, calling. *Ant.* torpor, inactivity, idleness, inaction, sloth, inertia, indolence, stupor.

careful, cautious, meticulous, attentive, vigilant, watchful, prudent, wary, mindful, scrupulous. *Ant.* careless, unconcerned, negligent, thoughtless.

caress, pet, pamper, embrace, fondle, cuddle, flatter, kiss, salute, hug. *Ant.* spurn, forsake, neglect, abandon, buffet, insult, annoy, provoke, irritate, exasperate, displease, aggravate, tease.

caricature, exaggeration, travesty, parody, imitation, misrepresentation, burlesque, farce, ridicule, mimicry. *Ant.* truth, reality, fact, exactitude, precision, accuracy, naturalness.

carnage, slaughter, butchery, massacre, destruction, blood, havoc, bloodiness.

carnal, earthy, fleshly, concupiscent, lascivious, vulgar, worldly, lustful, sensual, physical. *Ant.* spiritual, chaste, ethereal, intellectual.

carping, caviling, faultfinding, captious, hypercritical, disparaging, pedantic.

carriage, walk, pace, mien, manner, gait, deportment, demeanor, bearing, behavior.

carry, transport, convey, bear, move, take, remove, transmit, bring, lift, support, sustain.

cartel, monopoly, trust, pool, syndicate, combination.

case, instance, contingency, occurrence, situation, event, example, circumstance, subject, condition.

cast, pitch, shy, throw, hurl, fling, heave, direct, propel, sling, toss.

caste, rank, race, class, lineage, blood, order, descent, ancestry.

casual, haphazard, fortuitous, contingent, careless, cursory, chance, accidental, heedless, negligent, random, incidental. *Ant.* formal, deliberate, planned, premeditated.

casualty, chance, accident, hazard, disaster, calamity, misfortune, adversity, mishap. *Ant.* good fortune, prosperity.

cataclysm, catastrophe, upheaval, disaster, flood, convulsion, misfortune, calamity.

catastrophe, misfortune, calamity, disaster, misadventure, mishap, mischance, misery, revolution, visitation, affliction, cataclysm, blow. *Ant.* blessing, benefit, prosperity, favor, success, comfort, privilege, happiness, pleasure.

catch, grasp, capture, clasp, seize, snatch, grip, take, clutch, secure, apprehend, comprehend, entrap, discover, overtake. *Ant.* lose, give up, miss, let go, restore, fail, release, cast aside, throw away.

category, class, heading, grade, group, division, concept, rank, form, genus, denomination, order.

catharsis, purge, purification, cleansing.

cause, agent, origin, source, spring, causation, fountain, designer, antecedent, originator, object, reason, inducement, condition, precedent, power, motive, determinant, occasion. *Ant.* outcome, effect, result, consequence, development, end, fruit, issue, outgrowth, product.

cautious, watchful, wary, careful, prudent, circumspect, attentive, discreet, thoughtful, calculating. *Ant.* incautious, careless, rash, impetuous, headstrong, unthinking, heedless, hasty.

cavity, hollow, hole, depression, cave, excavation, concavity, opening. *Ant.* mound, hill, prominence, projection, protuberance, elevation, swelling, convexity.

cease, terminate, quit, stop, finish, end, refrain, conclude, desist, halt, withdraw, discontinue. *Ant.* begin, commence, start, enter upon, initiate, continue.

cede, yield, grant, relinquish, surrender, deliver, accord, assign, transfer, convey. *Ant.* win, gain, receive.

celebrate, keep, observe, commemorate, praise, extol, solemnize, glorify, honor. *Ant.* forget, neglect, overlook, ignore, disregard, dishonor, violate, profane, despise.

celebration, observance, commemoration, glorification, merrymaking, festivity, gaiety, frolic, hilarity, joviality, merriment. *Ant.* grief, sadness, solemnity, sorrow, mourning, wailing, lamentation, depression, melancholy.

celerity, speed, quickness, rapidity, swiftness, alacrity, haste. *Ant.* slowness, sluggishness.

celestial, unearthly, heavenly, divine, angelic, supernal, ethereal, holy. *Ant.* mortal, infernal, hellish, earthly.

censure, criticism, reprimand, blame, reproach, reprehension, rebuke, remonstrance, reproof, stricture, condemnation. *Ant.* praise, commendation, approval, endorsement, recommendation, sanction, approbation, confirmation, ratification.

center, midpoint, nucleus, focus, heart, middle, core, hub, midst, axis. *Ant.* rim, edge, periphery.

ceremony, rite, ritual, solemnity, protocol, formality, observance, form.

certain, sure, unquestionable, incontrovertible, undeniable, reliable, unfailing, indisputable, secure, infallible, real, true, undoubted, indubitable. *Ant.* wavering, unreliable, uncertain, dubious, vague, doubtful, faltering, ambiguous, questionable, equivocal, obscure.

certify, testify, declare, assure, inform, attest, demonstrate, prove, avouch, aver, vouch, acknowledge, state. *Ant.* deny, depreciate, repudiate, disown, discredit, censure, reject, negate, contradict, counteract.

chagrin, mortification, vexation, shame, humiliation, discomposure, disappointment, dismay, confusion. *Ant.* delight, rapture, exultation, triumph, rejoicing, gladness.

chain, series, row, sequence, succession, string, progression, set, course.

challenge, demand, question, defiance, invitation, trial, obstacle, opportunity. *Ant.* agreement, acceptance, victory.

hance, fate, fortune, risk, casualty, hazard, luck, accident, venture, random. *Ant.* design, intention, certainty, aim, plan, purpose, scheme, assurance, stability.

hange, alteration, variation, mutation, innovation, transformation, novelty, transmutation, metamorphosis, modification, transition, vicissitude, revolution, deviation, reverse, renewal, regeneration, exchange, conversion. *Ant.* firmness, permanency, fixedness, constancy, steadiness, steadfastness, changelessness, stability, duration, certainty, durability.

haos, disorder, confusion, shambles, snarl, disorganization. *Ant.* harmony, system, order, method.

haracter, personality, reputation, constitution, disposition, nature, temperament, temper, estimation, repute, spirit, symbol, species, standing, record, mark, letter, type.

haracteristic, personality, singularity, peculiarity, individuality, distinction, manners, specialty, attitude, bearing, idiosyncrasy, trait, mark, attribute, quality, property, feature, indication, sign, trace.

harge, accuse, indict, tax, score, ascribe, assess, burden, attack, command, exhort.

harity, beneficence, benefaction, philanthropy, alms, giving, bounty, altruism, generosity. *Ant.* selfishness, stinginess, ill will.

harlatan, mountebank, quack, fraud, cheat, humbug, impostor, faker, pretender.

harming, entrancing, captivating, bewitching, fascinating, delightful, enchanting, enrapturing, winning, ravishing, irresistible, attractive, pleasing, alluring. *Ant.* disgusting, repellent, disagreeable, offensive, unpleasant.

hase, pursue, hunt, hound, seek, trail, track, tail, shadow, stalk. *Ant.* avoid, elude, lose.

haste, pure, virtuous, simple, modest, innocent, incorrupt, immaculate, unstained, uncontaminated, unaffected, undefiled, neat, trim, uncorrupted, classic. *Ant.* unchaste, lewd, wanton, lascivious, lustful, corrupt, defiled.

hasten, humble, subdue, humiliate, purify, soften, try, correct, refine, discipline, afflict. *Ant.* encourage, uplift, embolden, assist, help, benefit, cheer, animate, inspirit, stimulate, comfort, succor.

hastise, punish, reprove, reprimand, discipline, correct, chasten, castigate, reprehend, whip, afflict. *Ant.* forgive, comfort.

heap, inexpensive, inferior, low-priced, mean, common, shabby, worthless, petty, valueless, contemptible, despicable. *Ant.* dear, valuable, costly, priceless, expensive, worthy, precious.

heat, hoodwink, deceive, victimize, swindle, beguile, defraud, dupe, fool.

heck, curb, bridle, hinder, impede, repress, counteract, moderate, restrain, inhibit, control, obstruct, stop, stay, slacken, reduce. *Ant.* aid, help, assist, encourage, expedite, allow, accelerate, release, speed, quicken, license, instigate, indulge, hasten, hurry, liberate.

27

cheerful, gay, merry, sprightly, joyous, spirited, buoyant, happy, lively, bright, sunny, blithe, joyful, enlivening. *Ant.* dull, weary, stupid, sad, unhappy, dolorous, melancholy, gloomy, dejected, cast-down, sorrowful, mournful, morose, heavy-hearted.

cherish, indulge, nourish, encourage, nurture, nurse, harbor, shelter, treasure, protect, cheer, comfort, value, cling to, hold dear. *Ant.* abandon, renounce, relinquish, give up, repudiate, forsake, desert, cast off, leave, denounce, discourage.

chicanery, duplicity, fraud, intrigue, trickery, subterfuge, deception, machination. *Ant.* honesty, fair dealing.

chief, supreme, principal, capital, prime, leading, paramount, first, main, cardinal, essential, predominant, pre-eminent. *Ant.* minor, secondary.

choice, option, selection, alternative, election, volition, determination; excellent. *Ant.* choiceless, voteless; inferior, poor, second-rate.

chivalrous, valiant, heroic, courteous, gallant, knightly, courageous, generous, brave, high-minded, spirited, valorous. *Ant.* cowardly, fearful, terror-stricken, timorous, timid, contemptible, base, rude, mean, unmannerly, petty, shy.

choleric, angry, testy, petulant, irascible, wrathful, cranky, cross, fiery. *Ant.* calm, cool, nonchalant, placid.

choose, pick, select, cull, collect, adopt, elect, prefer, arrange, remove, separate. *Ant.* dismiss, refuse, reject, discard, repudiate, disclaim, decline, cast out, leave, throw aside.

chronic, persistent, settled, rooted, confirmed, inveterate, constant, established. *Ant.* occasional, temporary.

circle, clique, society, coterie, set, class, companions.

circumference, perimeter, compass, ambit, periphery, circuit, girth, bounds, boundary, border.

circumlocution, redundance, verbiage, diffuseness, pleonasm, wordiness, periphrasis, verbosity, tediousness. *Ant.* conciseness, plainness, condensation, terseness, compactness, compression.

circumscription, confinement, enclosure, limitation, boundary, fencing. *Ant.* openness, freedom.

circumspect, careful, wary, heedful, discreet, judicious, observant, cautious, prudent, vigilant. *Ant.* bold, audacious, foolhardy, careless.

circumstance, incident, fact, accompaniment, situation, occurrence, point, detail, item, event, particular, position.

circumvent, balk, thwart, frustrate, prevent, check, foil, forestall, outwit. *Ant.* help, aid.

cite, call, summon, name, arraign, adduce, mention, quote, notify, warn, invite, convoke. *Ant.* hush, ignore, disregard, neglect, be silent.

civil, polite, courteous, affable, urbane, gracious, refined, mannerly, debonair, suave, civic, civilized. *Ant.* rude, boorish, ill-mannered, churlish.

28

claim, maintain, assert, contend, advance, affirm, allege, demand, ask, require. *Ant.* deny, release.

clamor, noise, shouting, uproar, din, outcry, hullabaloo, hubbub, blare, tumult. *Ant.* quiet, peace, silence.

clandestine, secret, private, hidden, covert, furtive, surreptitious, stealthy, concealed. *Ant.* open, clear, aboveboard, forthright.

clarify, make clear, purify, cleanse, make plain, explain, refine. *Ant.* muddle, muddy, diffuse, complicate.

clash, conflict, differ, contend, disagree, quarrel, collide, dispute. *Ant.* agree, concur, accept, accord.

class, rank, order, degree, standing, grade, caste, coterie, genus, clan, circle, set, clique, division, category, kind, group.

classic, standard, chaste, elegant, simple, clean-cut, trim, neat, model, first-rate, refined, Greek, Roman, antique, pure. *Ant.* modern, mixed, baroque, unclassical, barbaric.

clean, pure, unadulterated, unmixed, cleansed, purified, spotless, stainless, untarnished. *Ant.* dirty, filthy, adulterated, defiled, foul, mixed, impure, besmirched, tarnished, spotted, stained.

clear, bright, vivid, lucid, transparent, pure, sunny, apparent, plain, limpid, perspicuous, unmistakable, unequivocal, manifest, free, evident, obvious, guiltless, distinct, explicit, definite, straightforward. *Ant.* shaded, obscure, dark, opaque, shadowy, muddy, dim, ambiguous, mysterious, gloomy, unintelligible, vague, turbid.

clever, able, skillful, expert, bright, dexterous, apt, adroit, capable, smart, talented, intelligent, sharp, ingenious, intellectual, keen, quick, quick-witted. *Ant.* dull, stupid, slow, awkward, clumsy, thick-witted, ignorant.

climax, culmination, apex, vertex, peak, summit, acme, zenith.

cling, adhere, grasp, persist, stick, cleave, embrace. *Ant.* release, let go, loosen.

clog, jam, choke, stop, obstruct, encumber, impede, block, hamper, congest. *Ant.* unblock, clear, free.

cloister, monastery, priory, abbey, nunnery, convent, seclusion, retirement, isolation, meditation, solitude.

close, *adj.* near, intimate, neighboring, immediate, adjoining, contiguous, adjacent, attached; *v.* shut, stop, bar, occlude, plug, trap, seal, fence in, make tight, end, complete, finish. *Ant.* away, far, beyond, detached; open, unclose, release, begin.

clumsy, awkward, cumbersome, ponderous, maladroit, unwieldy, heavy, bungling, incompetent, inept. *Ant.* dexterous, adroit, clever, facile.

clutch, grasp, seize, grip, grapple, cling to, embrace. *Ant.* release, free, give up.

coagulate, congeal, clot, clobber, set, curdle, thicken. *Ant.* thin out, dilute, dissolve.

coalition, combination, alliance, conspiracy, confederacy, compact, league, union, treaty. *Ant.* separation, difference, bickering.

coarse, rough, gross, unpolished, vulgar, unrefined, indelicate, inelegant, crude, harsh, rude, impure, bawdy. *Ant.* delicate, fine, refined, dainty, choice.

coax, wheedle, flatter, invite, cajole, persuade, inveigle, entice, fawn. *Ant.* repulse, scoff, scorn, reproach, deride, taunt, delude, insult.

cogent, convincing, forcible, valid, potent, powerful, urgent, strong, sound, effective, persuasive. *Ant.* unconvincing, weak, invalid, ineffective.

cohesion, consolidation, cementing, coagulation, concretion, integration, coherence.

coincide, concur, agree, correspond, synchronize, harmonize, collude, match, equal, accord, tally, square. *Ant.* differ, disagree, diverge, deviate, clash.

cold, frigid, wintry, very cool, freezing, icy, frosty, bleak, chilly, indifferent, unconcerned, unfeeling, distant, reserved, forbidding, passionless, apathetic. *Ant.* warm, glowing, fiery, ardent, fervid, hot, genial, enthusiastic, zealous, eager, affectionate, animated, excited.

collaborate, cooperate, collude, concur, combine, join, unite; conspire, connive. *Ant.* disagree.

collapse, fall down, cave in, subside, faint, fail. *Ant.* recover, rise, revive, rally.

collateral, subordinate, related, secondary, concurrent, dependent, allied. *Ant.* principal, chief, main.

colleague, partner, associate, coadjutor, collaborator, companion, ally, confederate. *Ant.* opponent, enemy, foe, antagonist.

collect, receive, obtain, get, assemble, accumulate, gather, amass, congregate, convene, muster, aggregate, summon, gain, reap. *Ant.* scatter, strew, dissipate, disperse, throw away, break up, divide, spread, disseminate, apportion, dispense, distribute, allot, partition, share, assign.

collision, impact, clash, contact, meeting, encounter, shock, conflict, clashing, concussion. *Ant.* concurrence, concord, harmony, agreement.

colloquial, familiar, informal, dialectal, conversational. *Ant.* formal, correct, standard.

collusion, conspiracy, craft, deceit, complicity, connivance.

color, paint, tinge, tint, redden, blush, flush, dye, stain.

colossal, huge, immense, gigantic, enormous, vast, mammoth, tremendous, prodigious. *Ant.* tiny, small, little, miniature.

comatose, torpid, faint, drowsy, stuporous, lethargic, unconscious. *Ant.* awake, alert, active, lively.

combat, battle, struggle, fight, contest, duel. *Ant.* peace, accord, agreement, surrender, compromise, truce.

combination, union, association, confederacy, league, alliance, party, faction, mixture, blend. *Ant.* separation, detachment, division, partition, dissolution.

combustion, burning, oxidation; disturbance, violence, rioting.

ome, arrive, attain, proceed, advance, near, reach. *Ant.* depart, go, leave.

omely, handsome, pretty, prepossessing, graceful, pleasing, seemly, agreeable, beautiful, nice. *Ant.* ugly, plain, unattractive, coarse, uninviting.

omfort, console, solace, help, support, encourage, succor, aid, assist, alleviate, cheer, assuage, relieve, allay. *Ant.* aggravate, sorrow, trouble, annoy, irritate, provoke, afflict, bother, torment, torture, vex.

omfortable, cheerful, satisfied, pleasant, genial, cheery, well-off, contented, snug, warm, commodious, convenient, agreeable, cozy, sheltered, protected. *Ant.* uncomfortable, discontented, miserable, unhappy, neglected, forsaken, abandoned.

omic, funny, diverting, farcical, ludicrous, humorous, amusing, witty, droll. *Ant.* sober, solemn, tragic.

command, order, injunction, control, mandate, precept, authority, power, requisition, charge, behest. *Ant.* countermand, revocation, contradiction.

ommemorate, solemnize, celebrate, recall to mind, keep, observe, honor, memorialize. *Ant.* forget, neglect, disdain, dishonor.

ommence, begin, initiate, institute, found, inaugurate, start, cause, introduce, establish, originate. *Ant.* end, cease, finish.

ommend, praise, recommend, approve, cite, extol, laud. *Ant.* disapprove, censure, admonish, reprimand, rebuke.

omment, remark, explanation, note, observation, interpretation, gloss, exposition.

ommerce, trade, industry, business, intercourse, traffic.

ommingle, mix together, blend, unite, join, fraternize, amalgamate. *Ant.* separate, divide, segregate.

ommiseration, compassion, pity, sympathy, condolence, empathy, *Ant.* indifference, coldness, callousness.

ommission, appointment, authority, duty, power, errand, function, warrant, committee, delegation, board.

ommit, trust, entrust, confide, promise, delegate, relegate, assign, consign, entrust, do, enact, transact, act, perpetrate, discharge, perform, imprison. *Ant.* desist, stop, cease, wait, keep from, be inactive, idle, rest, stand still.

ommodious, suitable, comfortable, useful, fit, appropriate, roomy, expedient, advantageous, accommodating, convenient. *Ant.* unsuitable, uncomfortable, unfavorable, confined, cramped, inconvenient.

ommodity, goods, articles, materials, stock, wares, merchandise, possessions, property, belongings, assets, chattels.

ommon, ordinary, habitual, mutual, public, low, frequent, usual, customary, mean, vulgar. *Ant.* rare, unusual, scarce, superior, infrequent, peculiar, valuable, cultured, refined, extraordinary, uncommon, high, excellent, noble, aristocratic.

commotion, excitement, agitation, tumult, perturbation, confusion, turmoil, skirmish, disturbance. *Ant.* calmness, quietness, peace, placidity, tranquility, repose, rest, stillness.

communicate, write, convey, announce, promulgate, impart, tell, state, publish, divulge, disclose, reveal, enlighten, make known. *Ant.* conceal, suppress, withhold, keep silent.

communion, fellowship, concord, agreement, intercourse, harmony, conversation, union, brotherhood, friendship, association, sacrament, relationship. *Ant.* separation, division, discord, disunion, enmity, antagonism, hostility, disagreement, contention.

communism, Marxism, socialism, anti-capitalism, communalism, Bolshevism. *Ant.* capitalism, democracy.

community, district, neighborhood, section, region, area, locality.

commute, travel; exchange, substitute, interchange, reduce.

compact, dense, thick, pressed, close, solid, condensed, packed, concentrated. *Ant.* loose, slack, diffuse, thin.

companion, associate, consort, comrade, friend, mate, follower, fellow. *Ant.* stranger, enemy, opponent, antagonist, foreigner, alien, outsider.

company, assembly, meeting, assemblage, partnership, party, band, throng, gathering, congregation, convention, multitude, crowd, conclave, conference, association, collection, convocation, group, host. *Ant.* loneliness, privacy, solitude, seclusion, dispersion, diffusion, dissemination, distribution.

compare, contrast, match, liken, balance, test. *Ant.* differentiate, vary, modify.

compassion, mercy, sympathy, commiseration, kindness, tenderness, pity. *Ant.* cruelty, hatred, severity, injustice, tyranny, persecution, indifference.

compatible, harmonious, accordant, suitable, agreeable. *Ant.* incompatible, quarrelsome, inharmonious.

compel, force, enforce, coerce, constrain, oblige, necessitate, drive, make, influence. *Ant.* balk, bar, hamper, thwart, impede, baffle, prevent, obstruct, block, check, stop, delay, deter, oppose.

compensation, remuneration, recompense, indemnity, consideration, satisfaction, amends, reciprocity, return, reward, emolument, advantage, profit, gain, benefit. *Ant.* loss, deprivation, damage, forfeiture, confiscation, penalty, fine.

competent, able, skillful, capable, proficient, adequate, sufficient, efficient. *Ant.* incompetent, inept, inadequate.

complacent, contented, assured, smug, satisfied, conceited, stuffy. *Ant.* dissatisfied, restless, uneasy.

complain, grumble, whine, fret, nag; remonstrate, repine, regret, grieve, deplore. *Ant.* praise, applaud, sanction, commend, recommend, approve, confirm.

complement, supplement, counterpart, entirety, whole.

complete, *adj.* full, replete, finished, all, entire, whole, total, perfect; *v.* execute, consummate, accomplish, terminate, effectuate, end, conclude, finish, realize, achieve. *Ant.* incomplete, lacking deficient, defective, missing, wanting, short, imperfect; halt, cease, abandon, forsake, neglect, withdraw, forget, ignore.

complex, involved, entangled, abstruse, complicated, heterogeneous, composite, obscure, intricate, confused, mingled, conglomerate, manifold, multiform, compound. *Ant.* easy, simple, direct, single, obvious, clear, plain, uniform, homogeneous, evident, apparent, discernible.

compliment, praise, congratulate, laud, felicitate, flatter, sanction, endorse, confirm, please, adulate, soothe, gratify. *Ant.* censure, minimize, lessen, lower, criticize, blame, reprehend, stigmatize, disparage, denounce, reproach, upbraid.

comply, accede, conform, obey, assent, agree, concur, yield, submit, coincide, approve, acquiesce, consent. *Ant.* refuse, reject, deny, decline, disobey, oppose, disclaim, spurn, repudiate.

compose, form, make, fashion, arrange, write, formulate, draw up, construct, constitute; allay, smooth, calm, pacify, comfort, quiet. *Ant.* break, scatter, disarrange, destroy, ruin, annul, disperse; agitate, excite, arouse, discompose.

compound, complex, composite, combined, mixed, conglomerate, heterogeneous, complicated. *Ant.* simple, elemental, single, pure, absolute, unmixed.

comprehend, understand, grasp, comprise, include, embrace, know, see, perceive, encompass, contain, involve, apprehend, conceive, discern. *Ant.* exclude, misunderstand, misapprehend, mistake, err, blunder, misinterpret, misconceive.

compress, reduce, squeeze, crowd, condense, constrict, press, digest, consolidate, abridge. *Ant.* stretch, extend, swell, expand, rarefy, increase.

comprise, comprehend, contain, encompass, include, embrace, consist, cover, involve. *Ant.* lack, want, fail, fall short, exclude, reject, except.

compromise, adjustment, arrangement, conciliation, accommodation, settlement, arbitration, agreement, concession. *Ant.* altercation, disagreement, strife, dispute, dissension, quarrel, disputation, controversy, contest.

compulsion, constraint, restraint, necessity, urgency, obligation, coercion, force. *Ant.* freedom, freewill, independence, entreaty, petition, license.

compute, reckon, figure, calculate, count, enumerate, tally. *Ant.* guess, estimate, conjecture, surmise.

conceal, hide, secrete, screen, dissemble, mask, disguise, protect, bury, cover, shroud, seal, camouflage. *Ant.* uncover, open, reveal, expose, lay bare, disclose, discover, divulge, betray.

concede, assent, yield, permit, acquiesce, allow, grant, surrender, admit, acknowledge, relinquish. *Ant.* deny, refuse, differ, dissent, disagree, dispute, contradict, repudiate, protest, reject.

conceit, egotism, vanity, pride, self-esteem. *Ant.* humility, modesty, meekness, diffidence.

conceive, imagine, devise, think, realize, visualize; become pregnant.

concise, compact, short, brief, pointed, pithy, crisp, terse, succinct, laconic, condensed. *Ant.* diffuse, redundant, wordy, repetitive.

conclusion, end, finish, termination, determination, consequence, result, inference, deduction, decision, opinion, resolution. *Ant.* preface, beginning, prelude, introduction, preamble, commencement, start.

concrete, tangible, solid, real, specific, firm, particular, actual, hard, material, definite. *Ant.* abstract, ideal, immaterial, intangible.

concur, agree, join, unite, combine, certify, endorse, approve, assent, consent, coincide. *Ant.* disagree, differ, disapprove, argue, reject, dispute, dissent, object, oppose.

condemn, convict, doom, denounce, disapprove, reprove, blame, censure, reprobate, sentence. *Ant.* approve, exonerate, absolve, praise, pardon, acquit, discharge, release, free, forgive, clear, set free.

condone, forgive, remit, allow, excuse, pardon, disregard, overlook, absolve. *Ant.* condemn, punish, forbid.

conduct, *v.* direct, guide, transact, handle, manage, regulate, govern, lead, behave, act; *n.* behavior, deportment, management, air, demeanor, guidance, regulation, manners, bearing, attitude. *Ant.* abandon, forsake, desert, refuse, resign, leave, quit, relinquish, retire (from), renounce, forego.

confederate, ally, accomplice, partner, accessory, associate, supporter, colleague. *Ant.* enemy, opponent, opposition.

confer, talk, discuss, compare, converse; consult, deliberate; give, donate, grant, bestow.

confess, disclose, concede, certify, allow, admit, acknowledge, own, recognize, accept, avow. *Ant.* conceal, cover, disguise, disavow, repudiate, deny, secrete, veil, disown.

confident, sure, sanguine, positive, assured, dauntless, bold, certain. *Ant.* dubious, despondent, apprehensive, uncertain.

confine, limit, enclose, bound, restrict, circumscribe, bind, imprison, detain. *Ant.* free, release, unfetter, expand.

confirm, prove, establish, approve, corroborate, sanction, settle, attest, ratify, assure, sustain, uphold, support, affirm, validate, endorse, substantiate, strengthen. *Ant.* upset, annul, cancel, void, abrogate, overthrow, shatter, weaken, destroy, unsettle, shake, contradict, oppose.

confiscate, seize, commandeer, take, appropriate. *Ant.* return, give back, restore.

conflict, strife, encounter, combat, contest, dissension, war, struggle, contention, duel, battle, fight, engagement. *Ant.* peace, repose, tranquility, calmness, quietness, harmony, concord.

confusion, discomfiture, disarrangement, disorder, jumble, turmoil, muddle, chaos, clutter. *Ant.* order, system, method, sense.

confute, refute, disprove, confuse, defeat, confound, dismay. *Ant.* prove, attest, verify, demonstrate, confirm, affirm, endorse.

conjecture, guess, theory, speculation, presumption, inference, surmise, assumption, hypothesis, supposition, fancy, conception. *Ant.* certainty, fact, truth.

conjoin, join, connect, unite, associate, combine, affix, attach, adjoin, connect. *Ant.* sever, remove, detach, disconnect, disjoin, separate, disunite, discard.

conquer, overpower, overthrow, subdue, overcome, prevail, vanquish, defeat, crush, master, subjugate, rout, discomfit, humble, down, quell, checkmate, reduce, surmount. *Ant.* yield, succumb, forfeit, surrender, fail, lose, retreat, cede.

conscientious, scrupulous, careful, honest, just, upright, trusty, incorruptible, exacting, strict. *Ant.* dishonest, corrupt, unjust.

conscious, aware, sensible, awake, percipient, certain, informed, sure, cognizant, apprised, assured. *Ant.* insensible, ignorant, unaware, unconscious, cold, impassive, indifferent, unfeeling, senseless.

consent, accede, agree, assent, comply, yield, allow, permit, concur, approve, acquiesce, accept, concede. *Ant.* refuse, deny, disagree, withdraw, withhold, disapprove, dissent, differ, prevent, demur, object.

consequence, result, outgrowth, effect, end, issue, product, fruit, upshot, sequel, outcome. *Ant.* cause, origin, beginning, source, preparation, commencement, inception, rise, start.

consider, meditate, weigh, deliberate, ponder, examine, reflect, contemplate, regard. *Ant.* ignore, dismiss, pass, forget, neglect, abandon.

considerate, kind, charitable, solicitous, cautious, prudent, serious, sympathetic, unselfish, meditative. *Ant.* uncharitable, unkind, unfeeling, mean, harsh, neglectful, disrespectful, selfish, haughty, repressive, scornful, imperious.

consideration, attention, thought, reflection, friendliness, kindness, forethought, motive, prudence, caution, care, watchfulness, heed, pay, recompense, money, value. *Ant.* disregard, neglect, default, thoughtlessness, negligence, carelessness, heedlessness, omission, failure.

consign, deliver, send, remit, ship, delegate, commit, condemn, devote. *Ant.* receive, hold, retain.

consistent, consonant, accordant, harmonious, regular, uniform, equable, same, undeviating. *Ant.* inconsistent, varying, incongruous, incompatible, unsuitable, disagreeing.

console, comfort, gladden, support, ease, sympathize (with), cheer, encourage, rouse, solace, inspire, freshen, invigorate. *Ant.* depress, sadden, grieve, trouble, wound, disturb, annoy, censure, scold, dispirit, lower, condemn, blame, discouarge, dishearten.

consolidate, unite, combine, affiliate, merge, solidify, fuse, compact, harden, thicken, condense, compress. *Ant.* sever, disjoin, separate, thin (out), melt, disperse.

conspicuous, visible, plain, outstanding, open, eminent, celebrated distinguished, famous, notable, obvious, illustrious, prominent well-known, commanding. *Ant.* unseen, secret, hidden, concealed unknown, humble, obscure, covered.

constancy, firmness, steadiness, fixedness, stability, steadfastness resolution, permanence, reliability, faithfulness, loyalty, unchanging, reliability, sameness. *Ant.* inconstancy, fickleness, wavering variability, changeableness, fluctuation, vacillation, mutability instability, unsteadiness, capriciousness.

consternation, alarm, terror, horror, panic, fear, astonishment, dismay, wonder, surprise, amazement. *Ant.* tranquility, quietness peacefulness, calm, repose, stillness, rest.

constrain, compel, force, prevent, oblige, urge, repress, press, drive restrain, confine. *Ant.* ask, request, beg, cajole, flatter, implore coax, plead, supplicate.

constrict, compress, shrink, squeeze, cramp, tighten, limit, bind hamper. *Ant.* expand, untie, release, free, loosen.

construct, erect, make, build, compose, form, fabricate, produce *Ant.* demolish, break, destroy, overthrow, ruin, annihilate, raze dismantle.

consummate, *v.* complete, finish, fulfill, perfect, accomplish; *adj* absolute, intact, achieved, executed, excellent, best, supreme. *Ant* neglect, leave unfinished; incomplete, unfinished, second rate.

consume, use up, eat, absorb, waste, destroy, exhaust, annihilate corrode, squander, spend, devour, imbibe, swallow. *Ant.* hoard accumulate, collect, gather, store.

contaminate, pollute, infect, corrupt, taint, stain, soil, debase vitiate, deprave, spoil, defile, poison. *Ant.* purify, ameliorate enhance, freshen, brighten, elevate, dignify, exalt, heal, cure.

contemplate, consider, study, meditate, muse, ponder, reflect, view intend. *Ant.* neglect, disregard, discard, reject.

contempt, scorn, disdain, disparagement, mockery, derision, neglect slight, slur, disregard, disrespect. *Ant.* regard, respect, praise admiration, affection, applause, approval, endorsement, sanction approbation.

contemptible, vile, abject, cowardly, mean, base, despicable, pitiful worthless, depraved, degraded, scurrilous, degenerate, despised *Ant.* good, worthy, respectable, decent, loved, brave, courageous honorable, admired, gracious, pleasing, obliging.

contend, battle, fight, engage, compete, contest, dispute, struggle combat, cope, oppose, vie, grapple, strain, maintain. *Ant.* cede abandon, cease, stop, halt, leave, desert, quit.

contention, strife, altercation, contest, struggle, controversy, feud conflict, quarrel, animosity, bitterness, enmity, variance, discord disagreement, competition. *Ant.* affection, regard, benevolence goodwill, amity, friendliness, respect, consideration, kindness sympathy.

contentment, satisfaction, happiness, acceptance, serenity, ease, joy, *Ant.* misery, sadness, dissent, regret, discomfort.

contest, *n.* battle, conflict, controversy, altercation, struggle, engagement, feud, dispute, argument, competition, match, race; *v.* debate, object, oppose, dispute, argue, defend, battle, fight, contend, question. *Ant.* peace, calm, quietness, tranquility, repose, stillness, rest; agree, stop, abandon, retire, forsake, give up, resign, relinquish.

continual, continuous, perpetual, constant, incessant, uninterrupted, unceasing, unvarying, invariable, unbroken, regular, persistent, steady, ceaseless, unremitting. *Ant.* intermittent, interrupted, broken, uncertain, checked, stopped, finished, concluded.

continuance, continuation, prolongation, extension, duration, production, existence. *Ant.* stoppage, arrest, impediment, hindrance, obstruction, finish.

continue, persist, persevere, maintain, sustain, advance, proceed, go on. *Ant.* stop, halt, cease, finish, complete, end, desist.

contract, *n.* covenant, agreement, stipulation, compact, engagement, promise, obligation, guarantee, pledge, liability, cartel, bargain, convention, pact; *v.* abbreviate, shorten, diminish, decrease, shrink, abridge, narrow, lessen, condense, reduce, incur, assume. *Ant.* enlarge, expand, lengthen, stretch, spread, extend, increase, amplify, dilate.

contradict, oppose, deny, resist, impugn, correct, rectify, retreat, recant, recall, demur, disclaim, resist, contravene, refute, dispute. *Ant.* agree, acquiesce, endorse, confirm, approve, sign, seal, vouch, verify, sanction, guarantee, accept.

contrary, opposite, unlike, counter, adverse, dissimilar, opposed, conflicting, contradictory, antagonistic. *Ant.* like, similar, alike, resembling, homogeneous, correspondent, harmonious, suitable, agreeing.

contrast, difference, opposite, contrariety, converse, contradiction, divergence, antithesis, incongruity, incompatibility, variation, disparity, dissimilarity, diversity. *Ant.* agreement, similarity, likeness, uniformity, sameness, conformity, homogeneity, unity, identity, equality, copy.

contravene, contradict, oppose, interpose, nullify, annul, thwart, obstruct, void, defeat, hinder. *Ant.* coincide, concur, agree, assist, approve, assent, consent, harmonize.

contribute, give, share, add (to), subscribe, donate, help, supply, assist, cooperate, aid, furnish, befriend, benefit, favor. *Ant.* shun, ignore, neglect, harm, injure, denounce, counteract, oppose, disapprove, withhold.

contrivance, appliance, apparatus, construction, device, invention, mechanism, design; ruse, trick, scheme, plot, plan.

contrive, invent, make, frame, form, plan, design, devise, scheme, arrange, plot, project, execute. *Ant.* destroy, ruin, wreck, waste, abolish, disrupt, overthrow, topple, demolish, smash.

control, guide, direct, restrain, hold, check, govern, rule, repress, prevent, coerce, command, dominate, regulate, manage. *Ant.* give up, abandon, resign, ignore, relinquish, retire, renounce, leave, quit, forsake.

controversy, argument, discussion, debate, dispute, quarrel, contention, altercation, bickering, wrangling. *Ant.* agreement, peace, quietness, forbearance, restraint, patience.

convalesce, recover, rally, improve, revive, recuperate. *Ant.* die, regress, fail, falter.

convene, meet, collect, gather, congregate, muster, convoke, assemble. *Ant.* disperse, adjourn, scatter.

convenient, fit, handy, accessible, ready, easy, adapted, available, fitted, suited, opportune, commodious. *Ant.* unsuitable, inopportune, inconvenient, useless, inaccessible, inexpedient.

conventional, customary, accepted, orthodox, usual, formal, social, ordinary, stipulated, prevalent. *Ant.* unconventional, informal, extraordinary, foreign, strange, irregular, unusual.

convergence, conjunction, meeting, confluence, approach, concourse, assemblage, focal point. *Ant.* divergence, division, disjunction.

conversation, talk, speech, palaver, discussion, interview, discourse, communication, communion, conference, intercourse, chat, parley, colloquy, dialogue.

convert, alter, adapt, turn (from), change, metamorphose, resolve, transform, transmute, transfigure, modify, appropriate. *Ant.* let be, fix, endure, remain, retain, maintain, persist, keep.

convey, carry, move, shift, impart, communicate, inform, transfer, transport, transmit, remove, bear, give, change, sell. *Ant.* hold, keep, retain, preserve, accomplish.

convince, persuade, clarify, influence, induce, satisfy, sway, move, affect, touch. *Ant.* dissuade, warn, deprecate.

convivial, festive, hospitable, gay, jolly, merry, cordial, sociable, jovial. *Ant.* dismal, solemn, staid, severe.

convoke, convene, assemble, call, gather, summon, muster, collect. *Ant.* dismiss, dissolve, discharge, adjourn, disband, disperse, scatter, separate.

convolution, wave, twist, curl, involution, sinuosity, coil, winding, line, circumvolution. *Ant.* straight line, level surface, uncurved.

convoy, escort, accompany, attend, watch over, protect, support. *Ant.* desert, leave, neglect, ignore.

cool, *adj.* frigid, frosty, wintry, calm, gelid, fresh, shivery, indifferent, unfeeling, apathetic, distant, unresponsive, cold; *v.* refrigerate, freeze, harden. *Ant.* warm, glowing, sultry, sunny, kind, responsive, feeling, warm-hearted; melt, thaw.

cooperate, aid, assist, help, work with, combine, fraternize, connive, plan, perform, relieve, support, second, approve, endorse, promote, forward, encourage. *Ant.* hinder, obstruct, retard, delay, encumber, handicap, impede, disturb, annoy, prevent.

cordial, hearty, sincere, amicable, kindly, earnest, pleasant, warm, genial, friendly, gracious. *Ant.* cool, unfriendly, indifferent, hostile, inhospitable.

corporeal, bodily, corporal, in the flesh, material, physical. *Ant.* incorporeal, not material, spiritual.

corpulent, fat, plump, fleshy, beefy, stout, portly, obese. *Ant.* thin, slender, weak.

correct, reform, improve, repair, remedy, reprove, amend, rectify, chastise, punish. *Ant.* coddle, pamper, indulge, soften.

correlation, reciprocation, likeness, correspondence, similarity. *Ant.* unlikeness, divergence, difference, disparagement.

corroborate, confirm, certify, endorse, approve, sanction, support, back, assure, affirm. *Ant.* reject, deny, refute, disprove, disallow, oppose, disclaim, contradict.

corrupt, base, low, debased, contemptible, mean, lewd, demoralized, impure, infected, depraved, perverted, rotten, tainted, vitiated, unsound. *Ant.* clean, pure, wholesome, sound, noble, exalted, pure-minded, high, decent, honorable.

corruption, swindling, graft, perversion, rottenness, putrefaction, decay, baseness, depravity, degradation, infamy, vice, wickedness, guiltiness, criminality. *Ant.* honesty, uprightness, soundness, integrity, morality.

counsel, advise, admonish, inform, apprise, acquaint, recommend, suggest, warn, instruct, guide. *Ant.* conceal, withhold, misinform.

count, number, calculate, score, enumerate, compute, figure, total, reckon. *Ant.* guess, estimate.

counterfeit, bogus, false, sham, spurious, forged, fraudulent, dishonest. *Ant.* real, true, genuine.

courage, bravery, valor, fearlessness, intrepidity, boldness, firmness, fortitude, spirit, daring, hardihood, heroism, gallantry, mettle, pluck, determination, dauntlessness. *Ant.* cowardice, weakness, fear, timidity.

courteous, polite, suave, civil, mannerly, obliging, bland, agreeable, affable, urbane, well-mannered, polished, cultivated, refined, attentive. *Ant.* impolite, discourteous, pompous, unmannerly, rough, rude, overbearing, dictatorial, uncivil.

covert, hidden, clandestine, surreptitious, furtive, secret, concealed, underhand, sly, disguised. *Ant.* overt, open, candid, frank, public, unconcealed.

covetousness, avarice, cupidity, desire, craving, wish, greed, envy, miserliness. *Ant.* liberality, benevolence, munificence, generosity.

cowardly, timid, shy, timorous, effeminate, weak, afraid, sissy, spiritless, chicken-hearted. *Ant.* bold, courageous, daring, dauntless.

credible, believable, reliable, plausible, reasonable, probable, trustworthy. *Ant.* incredible, improbable, unbelievable.

crime, transgression, sin, misdemeanor, wickedness, outrage, vice, immorality, misdeed, infringement, depravity, felony, violation, offense. *Ant.* virtue, goodness, honor, uprightness, innocence, benignity, benevolence.

criminal, *adj.* vile, vicious, wicked, abominable, immoral, sinful, wrong, iniquitous, unlawful, illegal, felonious, culpable, blamable, guilty, nefarious; *n.* delinquent, offender, malefactor, felon, culprit, convict. *Ant.* upright, honest, good, moral, honorable, innocent, undefiled, faultless, virtuous, sinless, pure, blameless, legal, lawful, right, meritorious, just.

criterion, test, standard, rule, model, norm, fact, proof, measure, law, principle, opinion. *Ant.* guess, conjecture, possibility, fancy, supposition, probability, chance.

crooked, bent, curved, angular, zig-zag, winding, wry, deformed, bowed; deceitful, lawbreaking, dishonest, fraudulent, criminal. *Ant.* straight, right, regular, direct; upright, law-abiding, honest, respectable, moral.

cruel, barbarous, brutal, merciless, ferocious, savage, inhuman, pitiless, cold-blooded, harsh, sadistic. *Ant.* kind, considerate, feeling, gentle, merciful, compassionate, charitable.

cultivate, develop, tend, train, educate, farm, work, grow, raise, civilize, refine, pursue, foster. *Ant.* deteriorate, neglect, depress.

culture, education, learning, experience, knowledge, development, civilization, manners, refinement, scholarship, cultivation, propagation, breeding. *Ant.* ignorance, stupidity, boorishness, wildness, pretension, illiteracy, vulgarity.

curious, inquisitive, interesting, examining, inquiring, meddling, prying. *Ant.* incurious, dull, indifferent.

cursory, hasty, superficial, careless, desultory, slight. *Ant.* thorough, complete, perfect, painstaking, meticulous.

custom, fashion, habit, manner, practice, usage, precedent, rule, mores, convention, wont. *Ant.* irregularity, deviation, difference, departure, divergence.

cynical, sneering, contemptuous, pessimistic, distrustful, petulant, testy, satirical, doubtful. *Ant.* hopeful, believing, calm, pleasant, good-natured.

D

dainty, nice, delicate, particular, choice, sweet, fine, refined, pretty, fastidious, rare, exquisite, elegant, pure, soft, tender, pleasing. *Ant.* sour, bitter, tasteless, unpleasant, disgusting, coarse, harsh, gross, repellent, inferior.

dally, trifle, idle, coquet, dawdle, delay, linger, toy, prolong, caress, philander, flirt, fondle. *Ant.* hurry, be attentive.

dam, block, stop, impede, suppress, choke, clog, obstruct, hamper, hinder, bar. *Ant.* open, release, unblock.

damage, *n.* injury, detriment, spoilation, loss, evil, wrong, disadvantage, misfortune; *v.* harm, mar, impair, wound, spoil, hurt. *Ant.* benefit, advantage, award, recompense, reward, boon, profit, favor; repair, improve, mend, enhance, perfect.

damn, curse, condemn, punish, anathematize, execrate, denounce, ban, banish. *Ant.* bless, cherish, praise, exalt, favor, promote, benefit, magnify.

danger, peril, jeopardy, risk, hazard, venture, exposure, chance, precariousness, defenselessness, insecurity, menace. *Ant.* safety, preservation, certainty, sureness, carefulness, confidence, care, security.

daring, bold, brave, adventurous, intrepid, fearless, courageous, stout-hearted, audacious, defiant, impudent, obtrusive. *Ant.* shy, modest, retiring, bashful, timid, diffident, cowardly, chicken-hearted, afraid.

dark, obscure, dim, dismal, shadowy, murky, gloomy, opaque, black, somber, shady, swarthy, dusky, overcast, clouded, mysterious, sinister. *Ant.* light, transparent, bright, vivid, clear, manifest, plain, visible, apparent, evident, distinct, illumined, brilliant, lucid.

daunt, intimidate, discourage, scare, frighten, dishearten, dismay, terrify, appal. *Ant.* encourage, assist, aid, help, embolden, succor, stimulate, animate, incite.

dazzle, confound, daze, impress, overpower, blind, astonish, amaze, bewilder, astound. *Ant.* darken, befog, dampen.

dead, deceased, defunct, lifeless, inanimate, extinct, perished, gone, obsolete, departed. *Ant.* alive, live, living, existent, continuing, existing, being, enduring, animate.

deadly, fatal, mortal, destructive, destructful, poisonous, noxious, virulent. *Ant.* invigorating, stimulating, preservative, energizing, wholesome, animating, strengthening.

deal, *n.* agreement, affair, racket, transaction, conspiracy; *v.* distribute, allot, give, barter, allocate, apportion, share, mete. *Ant.* take, keep, retain, hold, receive.

dear, costly, expensive, exorbitant, valuable, high-priced, scarce, precious, beloved, cherished. *Ant.* cheap, low-priced, common, inexpensive, worthless, valueless, despised.

death, expiration, end, decease, demise, extinction, dissolution. *Ant.* life, existence, being, entity.

debase, impair, demean, humble, dishonor, corrupt, taint, shame, adulterate, abase, contaminate, disgrace, pervert. *Ant.* elevate, enhance, lift, improve.

debauch, corrupt, pervert, debase, defile, degrade, pollute, seduce, adulterate, contaminate.

debonair, buoyant, jaunty, gracious, lively, sprightly, gay, elegant, urbane. *Ant.* clumsy, awkward, maladroit.

debris, rubbish, rubble, trash, wreckage, litter, remains, sediment, detritus, ruins.

debt, liability, charge, deficit, obligation, arrears, debit. *Ant.* asset, overage, excess.

decay, decline, deterioration, disintegration, decadence, putrefaction, degeneracy, spoilage, decomposition, corruption, rot. *Ant.* vigor, growth, germination, development, strength, healthiness, force, vigorousness.

deceit, falseness, deception, duplicity, fraud, trickery, hypocrisy, untruth, sham, guile, cunning, treachery, imposition, delusion, artifice. *Ant.* truth, truthfulness, honor, honesty, uprightness, openness.

deceive, delude, dupe, lie to, be dishonest with, cheat, outwit, trick, mislead, circumvent, defraud, beguile, entrap. *Ant.* advise, aid, counsel, help, succor, assure, be truthful, be candid, be frank.

decent, respectable, decorous, modest, chaste, seemly, befitting, proper. *Ant.* improper, lewd, obscene.

deception, equivocation, lie, falsehood, fabrication, prevarication, trickery, duplicity, delusion, craft, cunning, dishonesty, fraud, deceitfulness, dissimulation. *Ant.* candor, honesty, square-dealing, openness, simplicity, veracity, sincerity, truthfulness, frankness.

decide, determine, conclude, settle, adjudicate, terminate, resolve. *Ant.* delay, hesitate, postpone, defer, wait, procrastinate.

decision, determination, conclusion, outcome, result, verdict, finding, judgment, resolution. *Ant.* vacillation, procrastination, delay, deferment, postponement, indetermination, indefiniteness.

declaration, avowal, statement, utterance, affirmation, profession, proclamation. *Ant.* silence, denial, retraction.

decline, deteriorate, lessen, retrogress, fail, decay, ebb, wane, waste, decrease, diminish. *Ant.* increase, improve.

decompose, rot, crumble, decay, disperse, disintegrate, putrefy. *Ant.* grow, increase, multiply, improve.

decorum, seemliness, form, etiquette, sedateness, propriety, dignity. *Ant.* license, indecency, impropriety.

decoy, lure, tempt, mislead, entice, beguile, entrap. *Ant.* lead, reveal, show, guide.

decrease, abate, lessen, diminish, decline, wane, narrow, reduce, curtail, minimize, subtract, reduce, shrink, contract. *Ant.* grow, dilate, extend, swell, enlarge, increase, develop, widen, expand, add.

decree, *v.* decide, direct, ordain, order, prescribe, command, determine, dictate, sentence, judge; *n.* judgment, edict, ordinance, law, order.

decry, disparage, derogate, criticize, condemn, depreciate, discredit, censure. *Ant.* praise, magnify, exalt, extol, acclaim, approve.

dedicate, devote, consecrate, apportion, set apart, offer, hallow, sanctify, bless, enshrine, give. *Ant.* alienate, misapply, misuse, desecrate, misconvert.

deduce, infer, reason, judge, derive, deem, suppose, assume, think, presume, conclude, believe.

deed, act, action, perpetration, commission, achievement, exploit, accomplishment, feat, performance. *Ant.* omission, failure.

deep, profound, low, below, beneath, abysmal, bottomless, subterranean, submerged; abstruse, learned, designing, scheming, low-toned, artful, insidious, contriving, penetrating. *Ant.* shallow, superficial, ignorant, unintelligent, unintellectual, flighty, artless, frivolous.

deface, disfigure, deform, injure, mark, mar, blemish, damage, mutilate, spoil, erase, obliterate, impair, destroy, maim. *Ant.* beautify, bedeck, adorn, decorate, grace, embellish, ornament, deck, array.

defame, revile, besmirch, charge, accuse, slander, traduce, detract, vilify, malign, backbite, misrepresent, debase, degrade, harm, scandalize. *Ant.* praise, laud, exalt, boost, eulogize, extol, endorse, commend, approve, glorify.

default, *v.* lapse, fail, forfeit, omit, neglect, defect; *n.* defection, blame, censure, shortcoming, delinquency, incompleteness. *Ant.* perfection, advantage, carefulness, completeness, accuracy, vigilance, satisfaction, supply, observance.

defeat, nonsuccess, failure, repulse, downfall, frustration, rebuff, overthrow, subjugation, beating, extermination, whipping, threshing, destruction. *Ant.* success, victory, mastery, advantage, conquest, triumph, security, supremacy, attainment, ascendancy.

defect, imperfection, flaw, fault, spot, blemish, shortcoming, scar, want, omission, drawback, deficiency, weakness, incompleteness, impediment. *Ant.* advantage, improvement, perfection, completeness, faultlessness, excellence.

defend, guard, protect, shelter, shield, insure, save, safeguard, secure, cover, justify, plead, fortify. *Ant.* desert, abandon, leave, abdicate, quit, forsake, resign, relinquish, renounce, surrender.

defense, vindication, plea, excuse, safeguard, apology, bulwark, fortress, guard, protection, shelter, shield, justification. *Ant.* desertion, capitulation, surrender, betrayal, abandonment, flight, yielding.

defer, put off, delay, postpone, adjourn, procrastinate, prolong, protract, hinder, retard, restrain, suspend, break up, dissolve. *Ant.* expedite, hasten, accelerate, advance, forward, further, quicken, stimulate, force.

deficient, inadequate, incomplete, wanting, scarce, lacking, short, defective, imperfect. *Ant.* adequate, sufficient, enough, ample, perfect, satisfactory.

defile, pollute, corrupt, taint, stain, soil, sully, infect, befoul, spoil, contaminate, debauch, seduce. *Ant.* clean, cleanse, wash, purify, disinfect, sanctify, glorify.

define, fix, settle, determine, ascertain, describe, limit, elucidate, decide, explain, interpret. *Ant.* mix, confuse, tangle, derange, distort, twist.

definite, fixed, determinate, clear, specified, definitive, bounded, exact, limited, circumscribed, certain, precise, positive. *Ant.* indefinite, uncertain, vague, undefined, unbounded, indeterminate, unlimited, inexact, indistinct.

definition, explanation, exposition, meaning, significance, determination, elucidation, description, restriction, specification, translation, rendering, commentary, interpretation. *Ant.* nonsense, confusion, vagueness, absurdity.

deflate, empty, reduce, exhaust; humble. *Ant.* inflate, raise, blow up, fill; praise, flatter.

deflect, turn, swerve, avert, divert, deviate, twist, diverge. *Ant.* strike, hit.

deform, distort, injure, disfigure, cripple, spoil, contort, mar, deface, impair. *Ant.* improve, beautify, perfect, repair.

deformed, malformed, crippled, disjointed, distorted, disfigured, misshapen, twisted, unsightly, unseemly. *Ant.* shapely, graceful, symmetrical, well-formed, well-built, regular.

defraud, cheat, dupe, swindle, trick, rob, deceive, delude, overreach, beguile, hoodwink, gull, fool, deprive, inveigle. *Ant.* befriend, assist, contribute, support, help, remunerate, return, requite, repay.

defray, meet, liquidate, pay, bear, quit, clear, settle, satisfy, adjust, discharge. *Ant.* repudiate, refuse, disown, embezzle, disclaim, deny, abjure.

deft, adroit, nimble, dexterous, assured, skillful, adept, clever, agile, handy, expert. *Ant.* awkward, clumsy, ungainly, inept, maladroit.

defy, challenge, oppose, scorn, provoke, slight, disobey, flout, spurn, dare, brave. *Ant.* agree (with), obey, surrender (to), accept.

degenerate, deteriorate, decline, demoralize, corrupt, worsen, decay, debauch, debase, sink. *Ant.* improve, ameliorate.

degradation, baseness, meanness, abasement, dishonor, disgrace, debasement, degeneracy, vice, humiliation, decline, removal, dismissal. *Ant.* honor, elevation, exaltation, reward, admiration, superiority, ascendancy.

degree, grade, extent, measure, quality, order, station, rank, stage, mark, class, division, space, interval, step, distinction, testimony, honor, qualification. *Ant.* space, mass, numbers, size.

dejection, depression, despondency, melancholy, gloom, heaviness, sadness, discontent, sorrow, despair, pensiveness. *Ant.* cheer, joy, delight, merriment, laughter, hilarity, gaiety, exhilaration.

delay, defer, postpone, protract, prolong, procrastinate, put off, linger, loiter, dally, retard, hesitate, halt, hinder. *Ant.* forward, advance, speed, accelerate, hasten, expedite, dispatch.

delectable, delightful, toothsome, savory, pleasant, delicious, agreeable, gratifying, luscious, palatable. *Ant.* offensive, nauseating, repulsive, loathsome.

deleterious, harmful, injurious, hurtful, pernicious, deadly, lethal, damaging, noxious, poisonous, destructive. *Ant.* helpful, advantageous, beneficial, healthful, salutary.

deliberate, *v.* study, consider, weigh, ponder, estimate, reflect, consult, meditate, contemplate, regard, examine; *adj.* careful, cautious, intentional, purposed, studied, judged, unhurried, thoughtful, considered, pondered, weighed, reasoned, cool, prudent, slow. *Ant.* pass over, reject, repudiate, disclaim, discard, spurn; hurried, hasty, sudden, rash, careless, unconsidered, unintentional, imprudent.

delicate, frail, fragile, tactful, weak, sickly, feeble, soft, gentle, fastidious, dainty, fine, refined, slender, tender, compassionate, nice. *Ant.* rough, rude, indelicate, coarse, vulgar, boisterous, robust, mean, depraved.

delicious, sweet, palatable, pleasing, luxurious, choice, delightful, luscious, dainty, exquisite, tasteful, appetizing, gratifying, savory. *Ant.* sour, bitter, unpalatable, distasteful, disagreeable, unsavory, nauseous, coarse.

delightful, agreeable, pleasing, satisfactory, gratifying, pleasant, enjoyable, glad, alluring, merry, inspiring, pleasurable. *Ant.* sorrowful, sad, mournful, wearisome, painful, miserable, melancholy, troublesome, depressing, distressing, disappointing.

delirium, madness, mania, raving, wandering, lunacy, aberration, frenzy, dementia, insanity, hallucination. *Ant.* sanity, normality, reason, saneness, steadiness, regularity.

deliver, convey, bring (to), liberate, rescue, hand over, give, save, pronounce, release, cede, redeem, transmit, discharge, surrender. *Ant.* hold, retain, confine, restrain, capture, betray, bind, limit, restrict, imprison.

delusion, error, hallucination, illusion, fallacy, fantasy, deception, misconception, chimera, phantom. *Ant.* reality, fact, certainty, actuality, truth, substance, materiality.

demand, request, solicit, charge, ask, levy, order, seek, supplicate, require, want, beg, beseech, crave, implore. *Ant.* tender, present, offer, give, grant, reply.

demeanor, air, bearing, behavior, appearance, attitude, manner, conduct. *Ant.* misbehavior, unmannerliness.

demented, mad, insane, crazy, maniacal, irrational, lunatic, deranged, frenzied. *Ant.* sane, rational, normal, lucid, reasonable.

demise, death, decease, end, transfer, conveyance, alienation. *Ant.* birth, non-alienation.

demolish, raze, destroy, overturn, level, ruin, wreck, dismantle, devastate. *Ant.* build, rebuild, improve, embellish, uphold, better, mend, produce, repair, restore, construct.

demonstration, show, presentation, exposition, exhibition, evidence, explanation, proof, induction, deduction, substantiation, consequence, conclusion, certainty, manifestation, corroboration, verification. *Ant.* misrepresentation, falsification, concealment, distortion, mysticism, confusion.

demoralize, corrupt, confuse, disconcert, disorganize, discourage, undermine, pervert, incapacitate. *Ant.* encourage, organize, exalt, hearten, inspire, invigorate.

demur, object, except, shy, hesitate, balk, waver, pause, vacillate, dissent, scruple, disapprove. *Ant.* agree, accept, assent, consent.

demure, modest, staid, prim, sedate, diffident, coy, decorous, shy, prudish, sober. *Ant.* indecorous, impudent, shameless, wanton.

denote, signify, mean, express, intend, mark, imply, specify, connote, indicate.

denounce, condemn, accuse, indict, blame, charge, decry, curse, arraign, scold, censure, reprimand, reprehend, reprove, reproach. *Ant.* praise, commend, applaud.

dense, thick, solid, massive, compact, concentrated, impenetrable, substantial, close, compressed. *Ant.* thin, rare, scattered, open, sparse.

deny, contradict, refuse, oppose, disown, disclaim, reject, repudiate, renounce, withhold, gainsay. *Ant.* acknowledge, confess, reveal, concede, grant, affirm, confirm, agree, accede, assent, attest, admit.

depart, leave, quit, decamp, set out, retire, go, withdraw, vanish, vary, deviate, desert, decease, die. *Ant.* remain, stay, tarry, stop, wait, linger, abide, dwell, continue.

dependent, contingent, relying, relative, consequent, conditional, reliant, subject, collateral. *Ant.* absolute, unconditional, free, independent, categorical, underived.

depict, delineate, portray, picture, sketch, draw, describe, paint, illustrate, represent. *Ant.* confound, confuse, caricature, distort.

deplete, drain, empty, exhaust, weaken, lessen, diminish. *Ant.* fill, augment, increase, enlarge, strengthen.

deplore, regret, lament, mourn, complain, grieve, deprecate, fret, sorrow, cry (for). *Ant.* rejoice, delight, boast, cheer, triumph, revel.

deportment, conduct, demeanor, behavior, air, manner, carriage, style, form, comportment, bearing, mien.

deposit, place, lay down, put (in bank), hoard, pay (as pledge), save; precipitate, settle. *Ant.* withdraw; erode.

depravity, corruption, degeneracy, depravation, deterioration, sinfulness, wickedness, immorality. *Ant.* goodness, virtue, honor, purity, nobleness, integrity, uprightness, morality, justice.

deprecate, disapprove, regret, deplore, protest, condemn. *Ant.* commend, endorse, approve.

depreciate, undervalue, underrate, lower, decry, detract, disparage, decrease, despise, denounce. *Ant.* increase, raise, recommend, praise, commend, approve, extol, exalt, magnify.

depress, sink, lower, abase, dispirit, humble, deject, degrade, debase, humiliate, disgrace, discourage. *Ant.* upraise, cheer, console, comfort, praise, encourage, urge, stimulate.

depression, business decline, hard times, misery, gloom, poverty, sorrow, unhappiness, humiliation, abasement, dejection, melancholy. *Ant.* business boom, joy, happiness, cheer, lightheartedness, comfort, satisfaction, contentment, elevation.

46

deprive, strip, bereave, despoil, take, rob, abridge, debar, divest, depose, dispossess, separate. *Ant.* give, add, confer, help, assist, present, restore, return, repay, replace, enrich, supply, endow.

derelict, *adj.* abandoned, wrecked, neglected; delinquent, negligent; *n.* vagrant, tramp, bum, outcast.

derision, scorn, contempt, irony, sarcasm, ridicule, mockery, insult, disregard, disrespect, disdain, slur, slight. *Ant.* flattery, respect, regard, reverence, adulation.

derivation, origin, source, rise, root, cause, beginning, foundation, fountain, nucleus, commencement, spring. *Ant.* end, extinction, termination, result, resultant, consequence, issue, outgrowth, effect, conclusion.

derogatory, deprecatory, lessening, detracting, disparaging, defamatory, belittling. *Ant.* praising, lauding, helping, favoring.

descent, declivity, slope, decline, degradation, fall, slant, extraction, debasement, origin, lineage, pedigree, ancestry, genesis. *Ant.* ascent, climb, elevation, ascension, mounting, rise, upgrade.

describe, delineate, portray, define, depict, illustrate, explain, set forth, recite, picture, relate, recount, characterize, narrate, express, represent. *Ant.* misrepresent, caricature, distort, twist, exaggerate, falsify, confuse, lie, deceive.

desecrate, profane, secularize, pervert, pollute, abuse, misuse, violate, defile, debase. *Ant.* sanctify, purify, cleanse, consecrate, hallow.

desert, *n.* wasteland, wilderness; reward, due, merit; *adj.* forsake, abandon, secede, abdicate, quit, leave. *Ant.* field, pasture, oasis, garden; penalty, punishment, retribution; remain, stay, continue, dwell, abide, wait.

deserve, merit, win, earn, have right to, be worthy of. *Ant.* unworthy of, undeserving.

design, delineation, sketch, contrivance, object, picture, drawing, diagram, pattern, decoration, plan, project; intention, aim, end, scheme, purpose.

designate, choose, name, specify, indicate, appoint, select, characterize, denominate, signify.

designing, tricky, astute, cunning, crafty, underhanded, wily, sly, scheming, unscrupulous. *Ant.* open, frank, naïve, candid, honest.

desirable, acceptable, pleasing, wanted, enviable, delightful, proper, valuable, profitable, judicious, beneficial, advisable, worthy. *Ant.* undesirable, bad, hurtful, baneful, injurious, harmful, noxious, evil, detrimental.

desire, longing, yearning, craving, wish, affection, ambition, zeal, eagerness, ardor, propensity, coveting, concupiscence, inclination. *Ant.* repulsion, disgust, dislike, opposition, aversion, distaste, antagonism, abhorrence, detestation.

desist, cease, stop, discontinue, forbear, abstain, drop, relinquish, quit. *Ant.* continue, persevere, endure, wait, hold, carry on, keep on, retain.

desolate, abandoned, deserted, forgotten, bereaved, forsaken, lonely, solitary, alone, forlorn, uninhabited, waste, dreary, dejected, inhospitable, unpeopled, comfortless, miserable, secluded, wild, bare, bleak, dismal. *Ant.* pleasant, enjoyable, inhabited, populated, full, teeming.

despair, hopelessness, desperation, discouragement, despondency, sadness, depression, dejection. *Ant.* hope, ambition, courage, trust, expectation, confidence, cheerfulness, faith, expectancy, encouragement, elation, anticipation, assurance.

desperate, reckless, foolhardy, mad, careless, bold, audacious, rash, furious, determined, hopeless, critical, extreme, irretrievable, frantic. *Ant.* calm, confident, hopeful, peaceful, quiet, contented, satisfied, secure, cautious.

despicable, low, mean, base, contemptible, lying, cowardly, abject, vile, worthless, depraved, pitiful, scurrilous, corrupt, shameless. *Ant.* high, noble, exalted, decent, respectable, worthy, virtuous, upright, honest, honorable, pure, praiseworthy.

despise, condemn, denounce, hold in contempt, dislike, scorn, spurn, disdain, detest, deride, abhor, abominate, loathe. *Ant.* cherish, love, applaud, extol, praise, commend, recommend, admire.

despondent, depressed, melancholy, low, disheartened, dejected, sad, despairing. *Ant.* buoyant, ebullient, happy, satisfied, lighthearted, elated.

despotic, arbitrary, autocratic, arrogant, absolute, cruel, tyrannical. *Ant.* limited, constitutional.

destination, objective, purpose, intention, design, fate, doom, point, location, goal, end, port, bourn, terminus.

destiny, fate, decree, doom, judgment, fortune, lot, end, predetermination, predestination, condition, chance, portion, necessity, conclusion, finality. *Ant.* will, volition, choice, freedom.

destitution, indigence, lack, poverty, want, privation, distress, need, beggary, pauperism, penury. *Ant.* riches, wealth, luxury, plenty, abundance, affluence, security, profusion, prosperity, opulence.

destroy, ruin, demolish, extirpate, consume, terminate, overthrow, raze, devastate, kill, obliterate, dismantle, dispel, annihilate, ruin, slaughter, exterminate. *Ant.* construct, build, restore, replace, adorn, renew, embellish, upraise, repair, refresh, revive, create, invigorate, fabricate, strengthen, resuscitate.

destruction, ruin, desolation, devastation, extirpation, fall, havoc, cataclysm, obliteration, extinction, annihilation, extermination, eradication, demolition, subversion, downfall, overthrow, abolishment. *Ant.* restoration, replacement, renewal, recovery, revival, restitution, reparation, reinstatement.

desultory, cursory, rambling, abnormal, flighty, loose, irregular, discursive, wandering, superficial, unsettled, erratic. *Ant.* firm, steady, regular, methodical, unalterable, fixed, permanent, stable, determined, constant.

detach, separate, withdraw, disunite, disconnect, disengage, untie, remove, unfasten, loosen, sever, part, disjoin. *Ant.* unite, bind, join, combine, connect, merge, coalesce, adhere, couple, attach, link.

detail, *v.* tell, relate, itemize, report, narate, appoint, assign, particularize, describe; *n.* portion, part, particular, item, specification, trifle, article, account, recital, description, narrative. *Ant.* conceal, hide, cover, withhold, stifle, suppress, evade, reserve; whole, entirety.

detain, keep, restrain, repress, check, withhold, stay, stop, hinder, curb, prevent, limit, delay, hold back, retain, bar, confine. *Ant.* free, release, liberate, let go, deliver.

detect, expose, discover, unearth, uncover, catch, identify, unmask, determine, disclose, perceive, espy, ferret out, ascertain, apprehend. *Ant.* miss, fail, blunder, mistake, overlook, pass by, omit.

deter, warn, stop, dissuade, discourage, restrain, prevent, hinder, frighten, disincline. *Ant.* encourage, advise, foster, persuade, promote, incite, induce, support, influence, stimulate, instigate, urge.

deteriorate, decay, decompose, disintegrate, wear, corrode, erode, rot, rust, atrophy, collapse, mold, oxidize, discolor, wane, ebb, recede, decline, retrogress. *Ant.* improve, renew, refurbish.

determine, decide, ascertain, settle, resolve, fix, limit, define, find out, conclude, end, bound, specify, restrict, affect, influence. *Ant.* doubt, waver, hesitate, vacillate, falter.

determined, decided, firm, unalterable, immovable, stable, fixed, resolute, willful, stubborn, unwavering. *Ant.* wavering, undecided, vacillating, uncertain, irresolute, inconstant, fluctuating.

detest, hate, loathe, abhor, despise, dislike, abominate, execrate. *Ant.* like, prefer, love, admire, esteem, respect, appreciate, prize.

detour, deviation, side road, digression, by-pass. *Ant.* direct route, highway.

detraction, slander, defamation, calumny, backbiting, aspersion, disparagement, vilification, libel, diminution, depreciation, derogation. *Ant.* praise, respect, flattery, adulation, admiration, eulogy, applause, commendation, recommendation.

detriment, hurt, harm, loss, deterioration, damage, bane, injury, evil, disadvantage, impairment, inconvenience, wrong. *Ant.* gain, profit, advantage, interest, benefit, help, assistance, utility, favor, augmentation, improvement.

devastate, ruin, demolish, desolate, wreck, sack, strip, waste, pillage, despoil. *Ant.* enrich, renew, restore, replenish, furnish, produce, upbuild, embellish, cultivate, refresh, benefit, preserve.

develop, uncover, unfold, disclose, evolve, mature, grow, cultivate, amplify, enlarge, exhibit, disentangle, unravel, extend. *Ant.* repress, shorten, conceal, circumscribe, narrow, hide, compress, lessen, confine.

development, project, expansion, growth, improvement, subdivision, maturity, evolution, disclosure, unfolding. *Ant.* degeneration, decline, lack of progress.

deviate, deflect, digress, turn, stray, wander, swerve, depart from, divert, shift, shunt. *Ant.* direct, straight, unswerving, directly, straightforward, persevere, continue.

device, artifice, contrivance, invention, machine, gadget, design; machination, ruse, expedient, plan, scheme, stratagem.

devise, bequeath, will, arrange, make, contrive, plan, invent, prepare, concoct. *Ant.* disarrange, muddle, fumble.

devoid, void, wanting, destitute, unendowed, unprovided, without, lacking, bare, empty. *Ant.* full, complete, possessing, furnished, replete, supplied, equipped, abundant, sufficient, adequate.

devolve, fall (upon), be handed down, convey, commission, consign, deliver, depute, authorize, alienate.

devote, dedicate, consign, assign, apportion, apply, appropriate, set apart, allot, attend, study. *Ant.* waste, squander, misapply, misuse, misappropriate, pervert.

devotion, consecration, piety, zeal, ardor, devoutness, religiousness, sincerity, earnestness, adherence, observance, intensity. *Ant.* apathy, carelessness, heedlessness, indifference, neglect.

devour, consume, eat greedily, waste, destroy, gorge, swallow (up), wolf, gobble, bolt, prey upon. *Ant.* vomit, disgorge.

devout, pious, religious, zealous, reverent, fervent, sincere, earnest, godly, righteous, moral, devotional. *Ant.* irreligious, ungodly, unrighteous, irreverent, impious, unholy, secular, worldly.

dexterity, art, ability, expertness, aptness, aptitude, facility, skill, adroitness, deftness, readiness, cleverness, handiness. *Ant.* awkwardness, clumsiness, unskillfulness, blundering, ineptitude, inaptitude.

diagram, drawing, plan, plat, map, chart, blueprint, sketch, outline.

dialect, provincialism, accent, idiom, jargon, vernacular, patois. *Ant.* standard speech, official language.

dictate, prompt, suggest, speak, direct, command, order, instruct, prescribe, tell, say, advise, warn, decree. *Ant.* beg, plead, ask, implore, importune, follow, echo, repeat, obey, answer.

dictatorial, imperious, domineering, arbitrary, arrogant, dogmatic, overbearing, tyrannical, haughty. *Ant.* submissive, acquiescent, retiring, bashful, modest, subservient, obsequious, passive, docile.

diction, style, expression, choice of wording, vocabulary, language, verbiage, phraseology.

dictionary, lexicon, wordbook, glossary, vocabulary, reference.

dictum, pronouncement, judgment, maxim, decision, statement, saying, command.

die, expire, depart, cease to live, decay, perish, decease, demise, wither, decline, vanish, recede, pass away, pass on, sink, wane. *Ant.* begin, live, move, remain, last, endure, exist, continue, survive, grow, flourish.

die, matrix, mold, stamp, form, punch, thread cutter, block, cube, perforator, prototype.

difference, separation, disagreement, dissent, discord, distinction, variety, estrangement, deviation, inequality, dissimilarity, variation, divergence, inequality, disparity, unlikeness, discrepancy, discrimination, diversity. *Ant.* agreement, similarity, consent, assent, concurrence, accord, harmony, amity, uniformity, unity, congruity.

different, various, varying, differing, heterogeneous, divers, unlike, manifold, distinctive, diverse, separate, distinct, discordant. *Ant.* similar, like, concordant, resembling, correspondent, harmonious, homogeneous, same.

differentiate, distinguish, discriminate, isolate, particularize, contrast. *Ant.* confuse, mingle, group.

difficult, hard, intricate, involved, arduous, obscure, perplexing, laborious, troublesome, unyielding, unmanageable, rigid, puzzling, enigmatical, obscure, trying, confused, complicated, complex, unaccommodating. *Ant.* easy, simple, yielding, complacent, light, lucid, tractable, calm, tranquil, free, unconcerned, smooth, plain, pleasant.

difficulty, quarrel, contention, argument, obstruction, impediment, dispute, obstacle, perplexity, trouble, problem, worry, annoyance, loss, embarrassment, discouragement, anxiety, distress, dilemma, complication, intricacy, entanglement, oppression. *Ant.* comfort, ease, facility, pliancy, flexibility, pleasure, contentment, felicity, satisfaction, gratification.

diffident, timid, shy, hesitant, bashful, modest, shrinking. *Ant.* bold, brazen, brash.

diffuse, discursive, wordy, copious, dispersed, protracted, scattered, tedious, tiresome, prolonged, verbose, repetitive. *Ant.* confined, limited, restricted, brief, short, abbreviated.

diffusion, dispersion, spreading, circulation, propaganda, scattering, distribution, broadcasting. *Ant.* collection, restriction, suppression.

digest, transform, assimilate, ponder, order, arrange, absorb, prepare, weigh, shorten, abridge, condense, classify. *Ant.* confound, complicate, derange, expand.

dignify, exalt, elevate, prefer, ennoble, decorate, adorn, promote, advance, revere, honor, proclaim, extol, magnify, glorify, award. *Ant.* condemn, stultify, degrade, shame, disgrace, calumniate, detract, slander, slur, insult, belittle, humble, humiliate, abase, demean, lower.

dignity, decorum, propriety, magnificence, grace, nobility, decency, elegance, worth, station, greatness, repute, eminence, stateliness, majesty. *Ant.* degradation, lowliness.

digression, deviation, excursion, divergence, departure, rambling, detour. *Ant.* directness, straightness, perseverance.

dilapidated, crumbling, decayed, deteriorating, depreciating, going to ruin, sagging. *Ant.* renewed, rebuilt, refinished.

dilate, stretch, widen, broaden, expand, swell, enlarge, extend, open, spread, increase. *Ant.* shorten, condense, contract, compress, abridge, reduce, abstract, lessen, repress, limit.

dilatory, tardy, procrastinating, dawdling, lagging, slow, unwilling, late, reluctant. *Ant.* brisk, sharp, quick, ready, willing, eager, active, zealous, enthusiastic, intense, fervid.

dilemma, quandary, doubt, problem, fix, predicament, difficulty, plight, perplexity. *Ant.* escape, solution, freedom, advantage.

diligence, care, assiduity, attention, earnestness, keenness, alertness, quickness, heed, industry, perseverance, application, carefulness, intensity. *Ant.* sloth, laziness, dullness, languor, ennui, carelessness, lethargy, apathy, unconcern, indifference, neglect, indolence, slowness, inactivity.

dilute, weak, thin, watery, reduced. *Ant.* strong, full strength, concentrated, rich, thick.

dim, obscure, blurred, shadowy, shaded, gloomy, misty, indefinite, indistinct, clouded, dull, mysterious, faint, opaque. *Ant.* clear, bright, brilliant, glossy, distinct, burnished.

dimension, size, area, bigness, amplitude, bulk, extent, capacity, magnitude, measurement.

diminish, lessen, reduce, contract, compress, curtail, abate, impair, retrench, decrease, minimize, lower, degrade, shorten, dwindle, shrink, wane, abridge. *Ant.* increase, enlarge, magnify, widen, expand, extend, swell, prolong, protract, lengthen, amplify, dilate.

din, uproar, hubbub, racket, clamor, clatter, noise, clangor, clash. *Ant.* quiet, silence.

dingy, dirty, soiled, discolored, dusky, dim, grimy, dark, murky, sordid, faded. *Ant.* clean, spotless, immaculate, colorful, glossy, bright.

diplomatic, tactful, politic, artful, adroit, calm, cool, courteous, clever. *Ant.* rude, rash, tactless, artless, blunt.

direct, conduct, lead, guide, manage, contrive, order, dispose, sway, regulate, adjust, govern, head, supervise, show, train, control, influence, demonstrate, explain, teach, inform, instruct, aim, point, usher. *Ant.* deceive, delude, mislead, misguide, lead astray, beguile, diverge, reflect.

direction, way, goal, course, line, bearing, address, aim, inclination, end, tendency, guidance, management, government, leadership, superintendence, control, order, command, instruction. *Ant.* misdirection, deviation, misinstruction.

disability, unfitness, incapacity, inability, weakness, decrepitude, impotence, incompetence, infirmity, defect, feebleness, uselessness, powerlessness, inadequacy, disqualification, forfeiture. *Ant.* fitness, ability, power, capability, efficacy, potentiality, force, strength, capacity, suitableness, effectiveness, adaptability, qualification, recommendation.

disadvantage, detriment, hurt, hindrance, difficulty, prejudice, drawback, check, harm, evil, stumbling block. *Ant.* advantage, gain, benefit, profit, aid, help, assistance, interest, utility, service.

disaffect, disdain, alienate, dislike, estrange, disorder, make disloyal. *Ant.* attract, increase (affection of).

disagree, differ, dissent, contend, dispute, quarrel, vary, clash, fight, combat, oppose, argue. *Ant.* agree, concur, consent, acquiesce, coincide, accept, harmonize.

disappear, vanish, withdraw, go away, dissolve, fade, depart, melt, evaporate, cease. *Ant.* appear, materialize.

disappoint, frustrate, thwart, betray, baffle, defeat, foil, deceive, delude, balk, fail, vex, mortify. *Ant.* satisfy, assist, cooperate, succor, help, please, relieve, support, befriend.

disapproval, depreciation, dislike, odium, disapprobation, censure, condemnation, blame, disparagement. *Ant.* approval, sanction.

disaster, calamity, misfortune, mischance, mishap, misadventure, catastrophe, adversity, cataclysm, tragedy, evil. *Ant.* fortune, advantage, blessing, benefit, privilege, prosperity, happiness.

disband, disperse, demobilize, dissolve, break up. *Ant.* assemble, unite, mobilize.

disburse, expend, pay, distribute, spend, settle. *Ant.* collect, receive, deposit, save, retain.

discard, eliminate, discharge, scrap, dismiss, repudiate, divorce, reject, shed, abandon, cancel. *Ant.* adopt, embrace, retain, keep, seek.

discern, perceive, observe, see, descry, behold, recognize, distinguish, discriminate, understand, discover, look, know, espy, detect. *Ant.* overlook, disregard, slight, neglect.

discharge, dismiss, fire, project, shoot, retire, perform, expel, emit, release, acquit, clear, free, settle, pay. *Ant.* load, hire, imprison.

discipline, order, method, government, regulation, chastisement, rule, training, punishment, instruction, drill, organization. *Ant.* confusion, chaos, disorder, rebellion, mutiny, disturbance, misrule, irregularity, derangement, misgovernment.

disclaim, deny, reject, disallow, abandon, disavow, repudiate, disown. *Ant.* accept, admit, recognize, own, claim.

disclose, unfold, reveal, tell, unveil, uncover, inform, utter, divulge, discover, unmask, betray, acknowledge, concede, grant, declare, open. *Ant.* hide, conceal, withhold, cover, veil, deceive, disguise, secrete, mask.

discontent, uneasiness, frustration, dissatisfaction, restlessness, disappointment, disillusionment, vexation. *Ant.* content, peace, satisfaction.

discord, confusion, disturbance, disharmony, quarreling, disagreement, dissension, contention, strife, clash, rupture, dissonance, variance, animosity, harshness, wrangling, difference. *Ant.* good will, harmony, peace, concord, agreement, agreeableness, amity, cooperation, accordance, congruity, union.

discount, reduction, allowance, deduction, rebate, loss, drawback, refund. *Ant.* increase, increment, premium, rise.

discourse, talk, confer, argue, declaim, debate, lecture, dissertate, expatiate, discuss, converse.

discourteous, unmannerly, forward, uncivil, impolite, boorish, ill-mannered, unpolished, abusive, ungracious, impudent, vulgar, rude, disrespectful. *Ant.* polite, mannerly, refined, courteous, civil.

discover, disclose, invent, descry, detect, discern, expose, ascertain, find, contrive, uncover, manifest, realize, reveal, unearth, elicit, *Ant.* hide, mask, conceal, secrete, screen, disguise, bury, cover, cloak, suppress.

discredit, disgrace, shame, defame, libel, stigmatize, disparage, disbelieve, doubt, impeach. *Ant.* credit, praise, laud, commend.

discreet, cautious, thoughtful, judicious, wary, prudent, sensible, discerning, careful, wise, circumspect, serious, attentive, watchful, considerate. *Ant.* indiscreet, incautious, reckless, imprudent, unwary, foolish, rash, injudicious, unrestrained, blind, heedless, hasty, foolhardy, precipitate, thoughtless, incautious, unguarded.

discrepancy, difference, variance, disagreement, contrariety, inconsistency. *Ant.* agreement, accordance, harmony, concurrence.

discretion, carefulness, sagacity, wariness, caution, thoughtfulness, judgment, tact, finesse, prudence, foresight, circumspection. *Ant.* recklessness, imprudence, rashness, foolishness, thoughtlessness, heedlessness.

discrimination, acuteness, prudence, caution, perception, foresight, forethought, care, heed, vigilance, discernment, circumspection, acumen, sagacity, differentiation, shrewdness, distinction, insight. *Ant.* foolhardiness, rashness, dullness, shortsightedness, recklessness, imprudence, carelessness, negligence.

discuss, argue, debate, dispute, controvert, comment, explain, talk, converse, confer, examine, analyze, wrangle.

disdain, contempt, scorn, contumely, arrogance, scornfulness, pride, superciliousness, haughtiness, derision. *Ant.* admiration, respect, praise, laudation, encouragement, flattery, esteem, favor, support.

disease, malady, sickness, ailment, complaint, disorder, infirmity, illness, morbidity, infection, attack, seizure, stroke, fit, decay, convulsion, deterioration, unhealthiness, affliction, indisposition, affection, unsoundness. *Ant.* health, soundness, virility, vigor, strength, forcefulness, robustness, sturdiness.

disengage, loose, free, clear, extricate, release, withdraw, detach, disentangle, liberate, separate, unravel, loosen. *Ant.* bind, tie, tighten, fasten, ensnare, entangle, attach, unite.

disfigure, mutilate, spoil, injure, distort, blemish, mar, damage, deform, deface. *Ant.* restore, repair, decorate, adorn.

disgrace, dishonor, shame, odium, reproach, ignominy, disfavor, disrepute, infamy, opprobrium, scandal, baseness, humiliation. *Ant.* honor, exaltation, elevation, reputation, respect, renown, dignity, esteem, self-respect.

disguise, change, mask, conceal, dissemble, camouflage, feign, hide, pretend, screen, make-up, cover, veil. *Ant.* open, unmask, bare, strip, uncover, reveal.

disgust, loathing, abomination, abhorrence, distaste, dislike, hatred, aversion, repugnance, detestation, nausea, revulsion, resentment. *Ant.* liking, admiration, reverence, approval, approbation, favor, commendation, respect, esteem, fondness, desire.

dishonest, deceitful, untrustworthy, crooked, corrupt, false, untrue, perfidious, fraudulent, lying, unscrupulous, cheating. *Ant.* upright, honest, scrupulous.

disloyal, faithless, unfaithful, disaffected, perfidious, unpatriotic, subversive, traitorous. *Ant.* loyal, true, faithful, worthy.

dismal, gloomy, sad, melancholy, dark, dingy, cheerless, somber, dreary, doleful, direful, sorrowful, dolorous, dreadful, unhappy, unfortunate, horrid, horrible, depressing. *Ant.* joyful, glad, gay, cheerful, pleasant, bright, hopeful.

dismantle, take apart, take down, strip, unrig, raze, demolish. *Ant.* assemble, build, construct, raise.

dismay, dread, horror, awe, alarm, fright, fear, discouragement, consternation, apprehension, misgiving, trepidation, anxiety. *Ant.* intrepidity, assurance, courage, boldness, unconcern, confidence, presumption, venturesomeness.

dismiss, discharge, discard, repudiate, decline, refuse, reject, repel, suspend, bounce, remove, depose, fire, expel, banish, spurn. *Ant.* retain, keep, hold, preserve, maintain, secure, engage, employ, hire, continue.

disobey, defy, rebel, transgress, disregard, violate, ignore, resist, infringe. *Ant.* obey, accept, submit.

disorder, irregularity, tumult, confusion, disarrangement, bustle, riot, disturbance, illness, sickness, indisposition, disorganization, turbulence, lawlessness, anarchy. *Ant.* order, regularity, neatness, arrangement, conformity, regulation, method, system, vigor, health.

disorderly, irregular, confused, disheveled, tumultuous, chaotic, unruly, lawless, unrestrained. *Ant.* regular, neat, disciplined, calm, trim, orderly, law-abiding.

disparage, belittle, lower, underestimate, depreciate, asperse, decry, traduce, deprecate, discredit, dishonor, underrate, defame, undervalue. *Ant.* praise, eulogize, acclaim, commend, laud, approve, flatter, recommend, compliment, sanction.

dispatch, send, transmit, expedite, hasten, accelerate, speed, conclude, perform, kill. *Ant.* hold, retain, slow.

dispel, scatter, disperse, dissipate, disseminate, spread, dismiss, strew, banish, rout, dissolve. *Ant.* collect, gather, assemble, recall, convene, increase, amass, accumulate, aggregate, garner.

dispense, sell, dole out, allot, apportion, assign, distribute, apply, execute, administer, carry out, excuse, exempt, release. *Ant.* retain, keep back, absorb, take in.

disperse, scatter, sow, distribute, dissolve, strew, dispel, separate, disseminate, fade, diffuse, spread, dissipate. *Ant.* assemble, collect, gather, concentrate.

displace, misplace, disarrange, confuse, mislay, disturb, derange, unsettle, jumble, mix, eject, dismiss, discharge, depose, unseat, dispossess, uproot, displant, remove, dislodge, crowd out. *Ant.* arrange, assort, classify, adjust, dispose, place, sort, array, group.

display, *v.* expose, show, exhibit, unfold, open, parade, flaunt; evince, manifest; *n.* exhibition, show, layout, array, demonstration, ostentation, flourish; manifestation. *Ant.* conceal, suppress, hide, veil, cover, secrete, cloak, disguise, camouflage, withhold, curtain.

displease, annoy, vex, disturb, tease, anger, provoke, disappoint, disgruntle, antagonize, gall, offend, disgust, dissatisfy, pique, rile, irritate, exasperate, torment, tantalize, harass, mortify, taunt, plague, chagrin, bother, worry, trouble, pester. *Ant.* calm, please, satisfy, mollify, tranquilize, quiet, allay, appease, pacify, soothe, lull, compose, assuage, conciliate, propitiate, reconcile, delight, gratify, humor.

dispose, arrange, place, locate, order, regulate, settle, bestow, give, adjust, classify, adapt, conform. *Ant.* disarrange, disorder, hold, retain, displace, secrete, disturb, dislodge, conceal, secure, cover.

disposition, nature, temperament, character, inclination, make-up, personality, leaning, proclivity, temper, tendency, bent, bias; disposal, adjustment, control.

dispute, argument, disagreement, quarrel, debate, estrangement, controversy, discussion, contention, contest, conflict, altercation, denial, questioning, difference, feud, variance, dissension, discord. *Ant.* agreement, harmony, unison, concurrence, unity, accord, concession, amity.

disqualify, render unfit for, remove from contention, disable, bar, incapacitate, disenfranchise, prohibit. *Ant.* qualify, accept, fit.

disreputable, disgraceful, despicable, ignoble, shameful, infamous, discreditable, dishonorable, shady, unworthy, scandalous, vulgar, base, low, shocking. *Ant.* reputable, respected, honorable.

disrespectful, disparaging, discourteous, contemptuous, irreverent, rude, uncivil, impious, insolent, flippant, insulting, impertinent, impolite, derisive. *Ant.* respectful, courteous.

dissatisfaction, discontent, disappointment, dislike, disgruntlement, displeasure, uneasiness, malcontentment, distaste, disapproval, disapprobation, discomfort. *Ant.* satisfaction, pleasure, relief, contentment, happiness, gratification, recompense, compensation, amends.

dissect, anatomize, examine, cut up, analyze. *Ant.* assemble, synthesize.

dissent, disagree, differ, vary, dispute, contend, except, conflict, object, disclaim, condemn, oppose, disapprove, censure. *Ant.* agree, coincide, credit, approve, join, concur, commend, endorse, sanction, ratify, confirm, authorize, allow, assent.

dissertation, lecture, tract, thesis, discourse, study, essay, theme, composition, commentary, sermon, homily.

dissipate, waste, spread, squander, lavish, scatter, diffuse, debauch, disperse. *Ant.* accumulate, save, absorb, concentrate, conserve.

dissolute, loose, licentious, abandoned, bad, vicious, evil, libertine, rakish, lewd, lascivious, profligate, corrupt, wanton, dissipated, impure, depraved, obscene, unchaste. *Ant.* pure, virtuous, moral, temperate, good, unstained, chaste, virginal, uncontaminated, incorrupt, immaculate, undefiled.

dissolve, melt, divide, render, thaw, evanesce, separate, disappear, disintegrate, disorganize, fade, vanish, destroy, evaporate. *Ant.* concentrate, assemble, unite.

distant, remote, apart, far, afar, separated, separate, removed, indifferent, cool, cold, aloof, haughty, shy, faint, indistinct. *Ant.* near, adjacent, close, neighboring, nigh, convenient, affectionate, warm, friendly, kind, sympathetic.

distasteful, repugnant, disagreeable, displeasing, unsavory, objectionable, disgusting, obnoxious, loathsome, nauseating, offensive, repellent, unpalatable, repulsive. *Ant.* agreeable, pleasing, welcome, savory, delectable.

distend, expand, dilate, stretch, inflate, swell, blow up, grow, tumefy. *Ant.* contract, narrow, shrink, constrict.

distinction, eminence, superiority, note, rank, elevation, separation, discrimination, discernment, difference, penetration, acuteness, acumen, judgment, clearness. *Ant.* mediocrity, sameness, meekness, inferiority, humility, lowliness, abjectness, amalgamation, indifference, mixture, combination.

distinguished, eminent, illustrious, famous, great, conspicuous, renowned, celebrated, well-known, noted, prominent, glorious, noble, brilliant. *Ant.* obscure, lowly, humble, ordinary, common, unpretentious, unknown, unassuming, unobtrusive, unpretending.

distort, twist, deform, gnarl, mangle, pervert, disfigure, contort, deface, impair, bend, falsify, slant, misshape, misconstrue. *Ant.* straighten, balance, align, explain.

distract, perplex, bewilder, confuse, derange, disorder, puzzle, daze, confound, mystify, embarrass, mislead. *Ant.* assure, placate, please, embolden, mitigate, assuage, pacify, calm, reassure, allay, soften, compose, conciliate.

distress, suffering, pain, trouble, grief, misery, agony, perplexity, misfortune, adversity, calamity, catastrophe, danger, need, hardship, misadventure, unhappiness, wretchedness, sorrow. *Ant.* pleasure, comfort, gratification, satisfaction, joy, gaiety, hilarity, revelry, festivity.

distribution, allotment, dispensation, deal, division, arrangement, partition, dole, apportionment, classification, disposal. *Ant.* collection, maintenance, preservation, hoard, storage, retention, storing.

distrust, doubt, suspicion, misgiving, uncertainty, disbelief. *Ant.* trust, confidence, belief.

disturb, discompose, annoy, unsettle, trouble, worry, vex, confuse, derange, agitate, arouse, rouse, distress, bother, disarrange, disorder, displace, disconcert, unbalance. *Ant.* pacify, quiet, calm, soothe, soften, arrange, mollify, allay, still, appease, conciliate, compose, reconcile, tranquilize.

disuse, discontinuance, abolition, cessation, abrogation, abolishment, intermission, obsolescence, neglect, abandonment. *Ant.* use, continuance, continuation, continuity, prolongation, repetition, extension, production.

divergent, deviating, disagreeing, varying, incomparable, contrary, differing, diverse, branching, separating. *Ant.* convergent, similar, parallel, identical.

diverse, different, divergent, varying, multiform, separate, differing, dissimilar. *Ant.* same, like, similar, identical.

divest, disrobe, denude, unclothe, peel, uncover, deprive, bare, strip, undress. *Ant.* clothe, dress, invest, cover, restore (property).

divide, part, separate, distribute, disunite, sunder, sever, disjoin, bisect, disconnect, detach, disengage, dissolve, partition, assign, allot, split, apportion. *Ant.* join, unite, attach, connect, annex, add, append, combine, couple, link, tie, fasten, bind.

divine, holy, sacred, heavenly, angelic, godlike, consecrated, devoted, dedicated, venerable, sanctified, spiritual. *Ant.* evil, diabolical, wicked, profane, blasphemous, devilish, impious, low, base.

division, separation, detachment, compartment, section, partition, portion, difference, discord, disunion, share, allotment, department. *Ant.* union, unity, accord, agreement, uniformity, indivisibility, singleness, oneness, concord.

divulge, reveal, inform, describe, relate, disclose, impart, betray, tell, communicate, discover, show, uncover, unveil. *Ant.* conceal, secrete, cloak, veil, hide, disguise, dissemble, prevaricate, retain.

do, execute, perform, accomplish, transact, finish, make, produce, execute, work, enact, complete, achieve, effect, commit, fulfill, realize, transact, consummate, perpetrate, act, discharge. *Ant.* fail, neglect, avoid, miss, spoil, defeat, frustrate, ruin, destroy, undo, idle, tarry, hesitate, procrastinate, defer, put off.

docile, obedient, meek, mild, gentle, quiet, submissive, manageable, tractable, pliant, pliable, tame, compliant, yielding, amenable. *Ant.* stubborn, unyielding, resolute, determined, dogged, willful, obstinate, intractable, inflexible, firm, opinionated, disobedient, obdurate, headstrong, refractory.

doctrine, belief, dogma, precept, teaching, principle, tenet, gospel, propaganda, rule, proposition, opinion, theory, religion, creed, faith, persuasion, conviction, cult. *Ant.* heresy, schism, unbelief, heterodoxy, error, falsehood, disbelief, infidelity, skepticism.

document, writing, archive, record, deed, notation, paper, script, manuscript.

dodge, evade, elude, escape, avoid, side-step, equivocate, quibble. *Ant.* near, approach, face, meet, encounter, confront.

dogmatic, positive, immovable, unchangeable, opinionated, dictatorial, imperious, peremptory, overbearing, authoritative, doctrinal, arrogant, domineering. *Ant.* uncertain, wavering, doubtful, ambiguous, skeptical, hesitating, equivocal, dubious, hesitant, unsettled, fluctuating, vacillating, indecisive.

dole, allotment, alms, apportionment, benefit, gratuity, pittance, division.

domestic, tame, domesticated, gentle, internal, household, native, home. *Ant.* wild, untamed, foreign, savage.

domicile, home, abode, dwelling, residence, habitation, apartment, accommodations, lodging, quarters.

dominant, controlling, predominant, commanding, ruling, prevailing, imperious, aggressive, governing, imperative, lordly, despotic, authoritative, overbearing, domineering. *Ant.* humble, obscure, subordinate, unassuming, backward, retiring, bashful, modest, reserved, non-aggressive, reluctant.

dominion, authority, ascendancy, jurisdiction, government, control, sway; territory, region, district, empire, commonwealth, country. *Ant.* subjection, service, bondage, submission, inferiority, subjugation, dependency.

donation, grant, gratuity, endowment, benefaction, benefit, gift, bequest, bounty, contribution, charity, alms, present, provision, subscription.

done, ended, finished, achieved, completed, executed, concluded, solved, performed, consummated, over. *Ant.* incomplete, raw, unfinished, inchoate, partial.

double, *n.* counterpart, twin, duplicate, understudy, stand-in; *v.* duplicate, repeat; enlarge; *adj.* dual, twofold, duplex, twin, paired, coupled, bipartite. *Ant.* single, lone, unique.

doubt, distrust, disbelief, dubiousness, agnosticism, concern, qualm, quandry, question, incredulity, unbelief, skepticism, suspicion, uncertainty, scruple, misgiving, perplexity, indecision, suspense, hesitancy, irresolution, hesitation, mistrust. *Ant.* faith, trust, fidelity, confidence, belief, credence, conviction, reliance, assurance, certainty, dependence.

dowry, property right, endowment, portion, share, gift, dot, dower.

draft, *v.* draw, sketch, delineate; call up, conscript, impress; *n.* check, money order, bill of exchange, letter of credit; wind, breeze.

draw, pull, haul, drag, attract, describe, sketch, inhale, move, bring, convey, tow, tug, allure, write, infer, deduce. *Ant.* repel, repulse, alienate, reject, rebuff, estrange.

drawback, hindrance, limitation, defect, flaw, injury, allowance, detriment, discount, rebate, allowance. *Ant.* advantage, benefit, premium, extra.

dread, fear, horror, terror, panic, fright, awe, dismay, alarm, consternation, apprehension, trepidation, anxiety, timidity, misgiving, cowardice. *Ant.* boldness, bravery, intrepidity, calmness, courage, confidence.

dream, fantasy, illusion, imagination, vision, fancy, conceit, trance, romance, hallucination, nightmare, reverie, chimera, deception, delusion, fallacy. *Ant.* reality, substance, verity, certainty, fact, realization, actuality, truth, existence, solidity, materiality.

dress, clothes, attire, apparel, garments, costume, raiment, habit, frock, gown, uniform, vestments, robes, habiliments, appearance, array. *Ant.* undress, disarray, bareness.

drift, *n.* tendency, tenor, end, meaning, objective, inference, purport, result, intent, scope; bearing, direction, course; *v.* advance, float, wander, move, heap up, be carried, stray, deviate (from course).

drill, *n.* discipline, exercise, instruction, study, practice, repetition, training; boring tool; *v.* bore, perforate, puncture.

drive, guide, steer, control, conduct, thrust, impel, urge, direct, ride, push, compel, propel, resist, coerce, actuate, incite, force, hurl, hammer, move, instigate, press, stimulate, encourage. *Ant.* check, stop, retard, discourage, hinder, halt, curb, restrain, lead, repress, entice, attract, induce, incline, tug, tow, drag, haul.

drop, drip, trickle, dribble, percolate, emanate, plunge, collapse, faint, fall, descend, droop, give up, cease, terminate, relinquish, abandon, stop. *Ant.* empty, flood, flow, evaporate, rise, squirt, splash, sprinkle, pour, continue, pursue.

drown, inundate, swamp, immerse, engulf, submerge, overwhelm, perish, plunge, deluge, suffocate, muffle, overpower, overflow, sink. *Ant.* rescue, save, preserve, extricate, deliver, recover, float, raise.

drug, *n.* medicine, narcotic, specific, pharmaceutical, dope, biological, compound, extract, anesthetic; sedate, narcotize, anesthetize, knock out, desensitize.

dry, arid, parched, stale, barren, sear, moistless, thirsty, watertight, dull, tedious, uninteresting, meagre, juiceless, vapid, prosy, hard, jejune, severe, cynical, sneering, sarcastic. *Ant.* wet, moist, damp, soggy, soaked, oozing, watery, saturated, muddy, humid, dripping, juicy, interesting.

dubious, doubtful, wavering, hesitant, unclear, equivocal, unsure, suspicious, unreliable, unsettled, problematical, uncertain, questionable, reluctant. *Ant.* certain, sure, definite, positive.

dull, stupid, stolid, doltish, insensate, half-witted, blunt, tedious, uninteresting, dim, dark, obtuse, prosy, dry, lifeless, witless, senseless, heavy, insipid, commonplace, dismal, gloomy, vapid, sad. *Ant.* lively, sprightly, witty, sharp, quick, keen, interesting, humorous, spirited, vivacious, active, smart, brainy, intelligent.

dumbness, muteness, speechlessness, aphonia, voicelessness. *Ant.* talkativeness, volubility.

duplicate, *n.* facsimile, likeness, replica, tracing, copy, reproduction, transcript, counterpart, twin; *v.* redo, repeat, copy, trace, reproduce. *Ant.* original, pattern, prototype, example, archetype, model.

duplicity, guile, artifice, fraud, deceit, dishonesty, hypocrisy, perfidy. *Ant.* honesty, simplicity, guilelessness, openness.

durable, lasting, permanent, strong, hard, constant, continuing, abiding, changeless, enduring, remaining. *Ant.* passing, fleeting, transitory, vanishing, impermanent, perishable, ephemeral, short, temporary.

duress, compulsion, constraint, confinement, captivity, coercion.

duty, office, function, responsibility, accountability, obligation, right, business, province, calling, service, employment, task, charge, allegiance. *Ant.* irresponsibility, disloyalty, falsehood, betrayal, faithlessness, treachery, inconstancy, perfidiousness, deceit, unfaithfulness.

dwelling, home, abode, residence, domicile, quarters, habitation, house, accommodations, apartment, flat.

dwindle, diminish, decrease, lessen, narrow, contract, drop, fall, taper, wane, fade, melt, shrink, decline, reduce, curtail, shorten, abridge. *Ant.* increase, grow, multiply, add, augment, enlarge, dilate, swell, extend, widen, spread, expand.

dye, stain, imbue, color, infuse, tinge, pigment, tint. *Ant.* bleach, fade.

E

eager, earnest, enthusiastic, ardent, fervent, keen, anxious, zealous, desirous, intent, impatient, yearning, longing, vehement, glowing, burning, intense, ablaze, avid, athirst, ambitious, solicitous, hot, importunate, impetuous, impassioned, forward. *Ant.* diffident, retiring, heedless, cool, apathetic, calm, phlegmatic, uninterested, purposeless, slow, stolid, dispassionate, unconcerned, indifferent, careless, unmindful, unmoved.

earnings, profits, income, allowance, salary, wages, remuneration, reward, commission, stipend, pay, emolument, interest. *Ant.* costs, expenses, losses.

earnest, ardent, serious, eager, sincere, solemn, grave, zealous, urgent, warm, importunate, fervent, weighty, sober, thoughtful, sedate, intense, determined, forceful, decided, resolute, steady, firm. *Ant.* trifling, frivolous, light, careless, negligent, heedless, inattentive, inconsiderate, insincere, thoughtless, unconcerned, capricious, regardless.

earthly, mundane, worldly, profane, temporal, carnal, sordid, base, material, global, earthy. *Ant.* spiritual, heavenly, incorporeal, immaterial.

ease, comfort, quietude, repose, tranquility, security, calmness, convenience, peace, serenity, restfullness, easiness, satisfaction, consolation, solace, expertness, facility, readiness. *Ant.* worry, sorrow, discomfort, irritation, disquiet, annoyance, unrest, strife, turmoil, vexation, perplexity, difficulty, uneasiness, effort.

easy, light, comfortable, indulgent, facile, gentle, smooth, unconcerned, effortless, simple, elementary, unanxious, secure, composed, manageable, flexible, pliant. *Ant.* hard, difficult, puzzling, involved, complex, intricate, arduous, laborious, troublesome, severe, oppressive, complicated, entangled, perplexed, onerous, exhausting, trying.

ebb, recede, wane, dwindle, abate, sink, lessen, retire, decay, fall, retreat, decline. *Ant.* flow, wax, improve, revive, increase, climb.

eccentric, odd, queer, wayward, abnormal, strange, anomalous, particular, singular, aberrant, irregular, deviating, unusual, quaint, fantastic, quizzical, outlandish, crotchety, cranky, erratic. *Ant.* regular, normal, orderly, customary, plain, ordinary, usual, formal, natural, common, conventional, steady, firm, constant, fixed, uniform.

economical, saving, sparing, thrifty, frugal, careful, provident, close, penurious, chary, watchful, circumspect, low, moderate, reasonable, inexpensive. *Ant.* liberal, squandering, wasteful, generous, careless, bounteous, free, munificent, improvident, expensive.

ecstasy, joy, delight, rapture, rejoicing, ebullience, transport, exultation, bliss, merriment, triumph, revelry, ravishment, gratification, glorification, excitement. *Ant.* trouble, sorrow, worry, doldrums, hypochondria, despair, pessimism, hopelessness, unhappiness.

eddy, *v.* swirl, whirl, spin, reverse; *n.* whirlpool, maelstrom. *Ant.* still, calm.

edge, border, brink, boundary, side, verge, margin, brim, rim, ring, periphery, circumference, extremity, butt, tip; sharpness, keenness. *Ant.* surface, area, space, interior, center, extension; bluntness, thickness, dullness.

edict, decree, proclamation, order, command, law, statute, writ, manifesto, announcement, judgment, ordinance, mandate, public notice.

edifice, building, structure, house, skyscraper.

edit, correct, arrange, digest, select, adapt, reduce, trim, change, compile, compose, revise, rectify, issue, publish.

education, schooling, training, culture, learning, information, study, cultivation, reading, instruction, teaching, literacy, background, indoctrination, edification, discipline, knowledge, development, refinement, enlightenment, scholarship. *Ant.* ignorance, miseducation, misinstruction, stupidity, illiteracy.

eerie, weird, strange, supernatural, peculiar, grotesque, fantastic, odd, curious, uncanny. *Ant.* natural, normal, usual.

efface, expunge, obliterate, wipe, blot, cancel, erase, annul, destroy. *Ant.* keep, retain, confirm, renew, approve, strengthen.

effect, *n.* consequence, result, execution, event, issue, outcome, end, finish, consummation, inference, conclusion, decision, deduction, determination, validity, completion; *v.* accomplish, operate, execute, realize, achieve, finish, fulfill, conclude, do, perform, consummate. *Ant.* cause, beginning, commencement, origin, foundation, source; fail, neglect, cease, abandon, omit, quit, leave, overlook.

effective, efficient, serviceable, efficacious, operative, useful, potent, fruitful, trenchant, conducive, talented, adequate, productive, capable, competent, yielding, resultant. *Ant.* inoperative, useless, inefficient, inadequate, incapable, fruitless, weak, incompetent, nonproductive.

effeminate, delicate, womanish, feminine, unmanly, unvirile, odd, childish, queer, sissy, soft. *Ant.* manly, masculine, virile, robust.

effervescent, bubbling, fermenting, boiling, volatile, buoyant, gay, frothy, hilarious, gleeful. *Ant.* flat, staid, sober, sedate.

efficiency, ability, capability, capableness, proficiency, orderliness, effectiveness, fitness, power, capacity, competency, qualification, knowledge, suitability, adaptability, thoroughness, completeness. *Ant.* inability, incompetency, incapacity, inadequacy, weakness, impotence, powerlessness, helplessness, ignorance.

effort, exertion, application, endeavor, trouble, essay, toil, labor, trial, strain, work, pains, attempt, energy. *Ant.* ease, neglect, failure.

egotistic, vain, boastful, conceited, inflated, bombastic, self-centered, proud, ostentatious, affected, showy, self-important, egocentric, narcissistic, pretentious, pompous. *Ant.* retiring, reserved, meek, unobtrusive, humble, modest, unostentatious, diffident, bashful, shy, timid, deferent, shrinking, submissive, unassuming.

elaborate, gaudy, showy, ostentatious, decorated, garnished, complex, detailed, complicated, intricate, elegant, imposing, polished, ornamented, embellished, refined, perfected, beautified. *Ant.* ordinary, plain, common, general, usual, simple, regular, normal, unrefined.

elapse, expire, go away, pass, glide, vanish, lapse, intervene. *Ant.* remain, stay, stand still.

elastic, resilient, pliant, buoyant, stretchable, ductile, supple, limber, rubbery, springy, lithe, adaptable, extensible, flexible. *Ant.* rigid, tense, inflexible, stiff.

elated, animated, exultant, delighted, ecstatic, exhilarated, high-spirited, exalted, enraptured, enlivened, gleeful, cheered. *Ant.* depressed, gloomy, downhearted, low, saddened, disappointed.

elect, choose, opt, resolve, call, select, take, judge, ordain, decide on, prefer, settle, pick. *Ant.* reject, cancel, recall, refuse.

elegant, polished, refined, well-formed, pleasing, graceful, lovely, luxurious, opulent, elaborate, polite, pleasant, agreeable, courteous, sophisticated, handsome. *Ant.* crude, awkward, uncouth, repellent, slovenly, inelegant, rude, rough, coarse, unrefined, ungraceful, rustic, simple, common.

eject, banish, dismiss, discharge, dispossess, oust, expel, dislodge, remove, evict, exile, emit, propel, cast out, discard. *Ant.* accept, establish, fix, settle, sanction, place, confirm, retain, approve, authorize, allow, countenance, appoint.

elementary, primary, basic, physical, natural, component, constituent, rudimentary, simple, uncompounded, unmixed, pure, easy, undeveloped, plain, unaffected, not difficult. *Ant.* difficult, compound, collective, aggregate, complex, involved, mixed, complicated, hard, abstruse, composite, heterogeneous, confused, intricate, advanced, secondary.

elevate, raise, hoist, heighten, promote, elate, glorify, exalt, honor, magnify, dignify, advance, lift, erect, buoy, improve, respect, revere, esteem. *Ant.* lower, deprecate, denounce, despise, shame, depress, disgrace, condemn, disdain, spurn.

elicit, evoke, wrest, bring forth, prompt, extort, extract, draw, educe. *Ant.* repress, suppress.

eliminate, expel, dislodge, cancel, oust, proscribe, banish, abolish, abrogate, exterminate, efface, obliterate, expunge, delete, void, expurgate, eradicate, slough, liquidate, censor, excise, extirpate, uproot, pluck, discharge, remove, eject, excrete, displace. *Ant.* replace, restore, include, receive, hold, maintain, retain, keep, preserve, accept, ratify.

eloquence, oratory, rhetoric, expression, oration, declamation, style, ability, diction, speech, voice, talent, appeal, fluency, wit. *Ant.* dullness, silence, stuttering, stammering, slowness, hesitancy.

elucidate, explain, illustrate, interpret, expound, clarify, illuminate. *Ant.* obscure, mystify, darken, becloud, confuse, distract.

elude, dodge, shun, avoid, foil, baffle, escape, evade, parry, mock, frustrate, equivocate, escape, eschew. *Ant.* seek, invite, court, dare, encounter, meet, confront, solicit, ask, allure, attract, draw, entice, inveigle.

emanate, issue, spring, exhale, radiate, come, emerge, proceed, stem, originate, flow, arise. *Ant.* withdraw, sink, return.

embarrass, perplex, entangle, distress, trouble, annoy, discomfit, nonplus, abash, encumber, puzzle, disconcert, hamper, obstruct, confuse, involve, complicate, bewilder, distract, harass, worry, plague, vex, confound, tease, mystify, bother. *Ant.* please, help, assist, encourage, inspire, extricate, comfort, cheer, exhilarate, invigorate, urge, impel, stimulate, promote, liberate, simplify, expedite, facilitate, gladden.

embellish, adorn, decorate, exaggerate, enrich, deck, beautify, ornament, illustrate, garnish. *Ant.* injure, despoil, spoil, mar, tarnish, simplify, destroy, obliterate, disfigure, deteriorate, deface.

embezzle, steal, forge, pilfer, appropriate, misappropriate, purloin, peculate, misuse, filch, misapply, defalcate, falsify, plunder, rob, swindle, cheat, defraud. *Ant.* reimburse, pay back, make good, recompense, return, satisfy, remunerate, balance, compensate, indemnify.

emblem, symbol, figure, image, token, sign, attribute, representation, type, memento, mark, brand, trademark, reminder, keepsake, souvenir, medal, miniature, character, device, motto, logotype, design.

embody, incorporate, contain, integrate, embrace, comprehend, comprise, include, concentrate, codify, systematize. *Ant.* exclude, disperse, disintegrate.

embrace, clasp, encircle, squeeze, press, caress, surround, accept, hug, comprehend, contain, espouse, subscribe to, adopt, seize, cling to. *Ant.* neglect, ignore, release, exclude, reject, miss, lose, shun, evade.

emergency, crisis, strait, dilemma, conjuncture, necessity, exigency, pressure, urgency, embarrassment, perplexity, state, quandary, casualty, difficulty, importunity, tension, distress, compulsion, obligation. *Ant.* rescue, deliverance, solution, habit, normality, regularity, stability, routine, conventionality.

emigrate, migrate, leave, quit, abandon, egress, escape, move, depart. *Ant.* remain, stay, dwell, reside.

eminent, distinguished, well-known, prominent, famous, celebrated, conspicuous, noted, illustrious, foremost, exalted, superior, supreme. *Ant.* obscure, unknown, humble, modest, diffident, lowly, unpretentious, retiring, petty, paltry, insignificant, run-of-the-mill.

emissary, agent, messenger, investigator, go-between, representative, mediator, deputy, factor, substitute, commissioner, intermediary, proxy, delegate, spy, scout, secret agent, envoy, legate, nuncio, ambassador, diplomat, plenipotentiary.

emit, exhale, discharge, vent, breathe forth, open, utter, report, publish, evaporate, express, issue. *Ant.* contain, retain, keep in, stifle, withhold, conceal, repress, suppress, stop, smother, restrain, refrain.

emotion, sensation, impression, feeling, response, reaction, passion, sensibility, inspiration, sentiment, empathy, mood, presentiment. *Ant.* apathy, impassivity, insensibility, dispassion.

empathy, understanding, compassion, appreciation, sensitivity, commiseration, comprehension, insight, sympathy, affinity. *Ant.* unfeelingness.

emphatic, strong, determined, forceful, forcible, earnest, insistent, pointed, impressive, positive, important, solemn, consummate, energetic, effective, affecting, cogent, potent, irresistible. *Ant.* weak, vacillating, wavering, timid, uncertain, hesitating, bland, diffident, shy, fearful, sensitive, reserved, shrinking, modest, unwilling, reluctant, bashful.

employment, work, business, vocation, avocation, job, career, use, hire, service, engagement, calling, occupation, trade, pursuit, craft, office, profession. *Ant.* idleness, unemployment, inactivity, laziness, weariness, ennui, languor.

empower, grant, authorize, commission, license, sanction, delegate, permit, warrant, depute, commit, entrust, appoint, countenance, approve, confirm, allow, ratify. *Ant.* dismiss, reject, banish, abandon, revoke, disenfranchise, disqualify.

empty, hollow, bare, unfilled, unoccupied, unfurnished, vacant, void, devoid, unreal, vacuous, destitute, unsatisfactory, weak, stupid, silly, senseless, ignorant, hungry, fasting, barren, meaningless, fruitless, foolish. *Ant.* full, filled, replete, occupied, complete, inhabited, tenanted, entire, adequate, sufficient, sated, abundant, satisfied, copious, wise, thoughtful, erudite.

emulation, competition, imitation, rivalry, controversy, contention, jealousy, strife, contest, envy, antagonism, striving, earnestness, struggle, ambition. *Ant.* differentiation, lethargy, negligence, sluggishness, carelessness, inactivity, heedlessness, apathy, unconcernedness.

enable, empower, authorize, allow, permit, sanction, let. *Ant.* disallow, remove, prevent, oppose.

enchant, charm, fascinate, enrapture, enthrall, captivate, bewitch, ravish, attract, allure, entice. *Ant.* disenchant, disillusion, free, repel, disgust, offend, displease, dissatisfy, disappoint.

encircle, encompass, surround, enfold, wrap, circumscribe, ring, span, loop, embrace, gird. *Ant.* free, loosen, release, unwrap, throw off.

encomium, citation, tribute, praise, laudation, glorification, eulogy, eulogium, commendation, panegyric. *Ant.* denunciation, censure, condemnation, disapprobation, blame, reprehension, vilification, disapproval.

encompass, encircle, surround, gird, beset, enclose, hem in, invest, environ, include, envelop.

encounter, attack, conflict, engagement, onset, assault, combat, battle, action, meeting, skirmish, assailment, invasion, inroad, charge, clash, collision, impact, concussion. *Ant.* avoidance, agreement, truce, concord, conformity, harmony, union, evasion, retreat, peace.

encourage, urge, sanction, support, foster, cherish, animate, inspirit, embolden, cheer, incite, advise, stimulate, impel, instigate, goad, enliven, exhilarate, inspire, comfort, approve, spur. *Ant.* deject, discourage, dispirit, dampen, depress, dishearten, dissuade, deter, mock, deride, distract, confuse, humble, humiliate, denounce.

encroach, infringe, trespass, enter upon, intrude, invade, poach, transgress, infract, violate. *Ant.* shun, keep off, avoid, eschew, dodge, evade, elude, recede, retire, withdraw.

encumbrance, burden, hindrance, drawback, drag, clog, lien, weight, mortgage, impediment, difficulty, obstacle, load. *Ant.* advantage, help, assistance, incentive, alleviation, unburdening, aid, succor, stimulus, stimulant.

end, *n.* aim, object, goal, completion, upshot, conclusion, termination, purpose, result, expiration, close, extremity, terminal, boundary, finish, limit, issue, death, consequence, ambition; *v.* cease, stop, close, wind up, quit, terminate, break off, settle, conclude, desist, leave, relinquish, die. *Ant.* beginning, origin, commencement, start, rise, cause, source, spring, initiation, inception, opening, outset, inauguration, foundation; begin, start, commence, initiate, originate, institute, inaugurate, enter upon, introduce, set out, set up, establish, found.

endanger, peril, imperil, expose, jeopard, jeopardize, hazard, risk, venture, chance. *Ant.* guard, keep from harm, protect, watch, cover, hide, conceal, secure, defend.

endeavor, attempt, try, essay, undertake, exert, aim, strive, attack, contend, struggle, wrangle, contest, labor, work, aspire, apply. *Ant.* idle, rest, cease, shun, give up, quit, stop, trifle, discard, ignore, put off, procrastinate, postpone, defer, delay.

endless, eternal, everlasting, incessant, perpetual, interminable, unlimited, continuous, uninterrupted, infinite, constant, ceaseless, boundless, imperishable. *Ant.* transient, ephemeral, passing, transitory.

endorse (also spelled **indorse**), ratify, sign, subscribe, back, assist, sanction, confirm, guarantee, recommend, support, authorize, warrant, secure, attest, corroborate. *Ant.* reject, disavow, refuse, oppose, disparage, censure, denounce, admonish, disapprove, protest, deprecate.

endowment, benefit, benefaction, gift, provision, empowerment, bequest, grant, gratuity, donation, bounty, capacity, attainment, qualification, natural gift, mentality, ability, genius, talent. *Ant.* damage, loss, detriment, injury, harm, drawback, confiscation.

endurance, strength, fortitude, forbearance, submission, resignation, patience, persistence, diligence, continuance, duration, continuation, tolerance, allowance, inconvenience, firmness, coolness, perseverance, courage, stamina, restraint, resistance. *Ant.* yielding, surrender, weakness, tiredness, breakdown, faltering, succumbing.

enemy, foe, rival, antagonist, adversary, attacker, opponent, falsifier, calumniator, competitor, slanderer, vilifier, defamer, defiler, predator, traducer. *Ant.* friend, benefactor, helper, assistant, adviser, well-wisher, backer, supporter, comrade, ally, companion, associate, confidant, adherent, coadjutor, upholder, accomplice, protector, guardian, accessory.

energetic, industrious, effective, aggressive, dynamic, enterprising, forcible, powerful, vigorous, potent, lusty, strong, determined, mighty, cogent, active, diligent. *Ant.* weak, vacillating, puny, unsteady, wavering, fluctuating, hesitant, inadequate, inactive, lazy, idle, slow, sluggish, spiritless.

energy, strength, vitality, vim, vigor, power, force, activity, endurance, effectiveness, capacity, momentum, efficacy, capability, potentiality, power, robustness, toughness, lustiness, vehemency, puissance, potency, efficiency, output, zeal, push. *Ant.* weakness, uncertainty, vacillation, hesitancy, idleness, laziness, ennui, weariness, tiredness, apathy, negligence, inactivity, fatigue, heaviness, sluggishness, dullness, indolence.

enervate, debilitate, weaken, enfeeble, impair, weary, reduce, sap, injure, attenuate, paralyze, soften, daze. *Ant.* strengthen, buoy up, invigorate, energize, animate, encourage, inspirit, cheer, enliven, incite, exhilarate.

enforce, compel, coerce, persuade, constrain, strain, drive, exert, execute, exact, require, urge, oblige, force, necessitate, press, impel. *Ant.* neglect, disregard, restrain, omit, drop, dodge, abandon, slight, overlook, dismiss, default, leave, quit, forego, renounce, give up.

enfranchise, give right, enable, release, emancipate, free, empower, license, qualify. *Ant.* disenfranchise, revoke (license), disqualify.

engage, employ, hire, busy, occupy, enlist, allure, incite, attract, entertain, engross, accept, retain, reserve, attack, participate, use, commission, charter, appoint, delegate, authorize, depute, ordain, constitute, mesh with (gears). *Ant.* dismiss, discharge, displace, release, reject, remove, oust, eject, put out, cancel, shun, banish, discard, expel, refuse, decline, dislodge, disengage.

engagement, betrothal, espousal, plighting, pledge, obligation, consenting, bond, compact, appointment, encounter, commitment, battle.

engender, breed, cause, excite, create, generate, incite, occasion, procreate, reproduce. *Ant.* kill, destroy, dampen.

engrave, etch, carve, chisel, cut into, impress, sculpture, lithograph.

engrossed, absorbed, busy, engaged, taken up, monopolized, fascinated, rapt, captivated, filled up, enamored, bewitched. *Ant.* repelled, inattentive, dissatisfied, oblivious, negligent, uncaring.

engulf, absorb, swallow up, bury, drown, submerge, imbibe, entomb, overwhelm, sink, swamp, deluge, inundate, overflow, overcome, fill up.

enhance, increase, augment, magnify, raise, intensify, advance, elevate, heighten, swell, aggravate. *Ant.* diminish, reduce, lower, assuage, shrink, degrade.

enigmatic, baffling, inscrutable, puzzling, mysterious, vague, cryptic. *Ant.* clear, plain, open, obvious, explicit.

enjoin, order, ordain, appoint, admonish, direct, prescribe, dictate, instruct, advise, counsel, exhort, enforce, forbid, stop, require, halt, charge, command, debar, prevent, prohibit, preclude, inhibit, interdict, hinder. *Ant.* permit, allow, submit.

enjoyment, pleasure, gratification, satisfaction, indulgence, voluptuousness, delight, hedonism, happiness, rapture, comfort, charm, liking, joy, gladness, ecstasy, exultation, triumph. *Ant.* abhorrence, sorrow, grief, misery, woe, sadness, calamity, affliction, worry, strife, unhappiness, toleration, dissatisfaction, discomfort, uneasiness, care.

enlarge, increase, extend, broaden, swell, augment, expand, dilate, magnify, grow, spread, amplify, lengthen, add, heighten, distend, protuberate. *Ant.* attenuate, diminish, lessen, reduce, curtail, lower, abate, decrease, abridge, contract, epitomize, shorten, abbreviate, prune, condense, compress.

enlighten, illumine, illuminate, inform, divulge, instruct, edify, tell, teach, impart, educate, train, direct, enjoin, persuade, acquaint, apprise, disclose, notify, advise, admonish, counsel, inculcate indoctrinate, communicate, reveal. *Ant.* confuse, delude, mislead, bewilder, obscure, darken, dim, perplex, embarrass, nonplus, disconcert, confound.

enlist, enter, register, enroll, interest, embody, incorporate, join, attract, employ, engage, hire, induce, procure, reserve, retain, obtain, get. *Ant.* dissuade, shun, avoid, discourage, withdraw, disband, prevent, restrain, deter, check, hold back, dishearten, constrain, leave, quit, demobilize.

enliven, cheer, vivify, quicken, exhilarate, inspire, animate, stir up, gladden, delight, gratify, please, rejoice, charm, satisfy, incite, encourage, comfort, rouse, indulge, arouse, excite, stimulate, brighten, refresh. *Ant.* sadden, dull, dampen, stupefy, cloy, pall, dim, darken, tire, weary, bore, fatigue, debilitate, jade, exhaust, bother, pester, stultify, harass, enervate.

enmity, hatred, malice, rancor, spite, animosity, malignity, illwill, antagonism, hostility, acrimony, malevolence, bitterness, dislike, opposition, unfriendliness, antipathy, aversion, detestation, spitefulness, grudge, pique, abhorrence, repugnance, disgust. *Ant.* friendship, friendliness, kindness, kindliness, agreement, regard, amity, sympathy, harmony, intimacy, affinity, attachment, fellowship, companionship, adherence, confidence, goodwill, benevolence, cordiality, cooperation, concordance, conformity, esteem, peace, brotherliness, love.

ennui, boredom, surfeit, tedium, languor, listlessness. *Ant.* vigor, enthusiasm, ebullience, buoyancy, energy, concentration.

enormous, gigantic, colossal, huge, immense, vast, prodigious, extraordinary, monstrous, amazing, elephantine, marvelous, mammoth, miraculous, astonishing, ponderous, excessive, atrocious, overwhelming, great, stupendous, wonderful. *Ant.* small, little, tiny, minute, insignificant, inconsiderable, light, trivial, petty, paltry, slight, trifling, dwarfish, imponderable, inconsequential, unimportant, diminutive.

enough, sufficient, plenty, abundant, adequate, full, complete, ample, copius, plenteous. *Ant.* scarce, lacking, wanting, needed, scant, deficient, bare, inadequate, insufficient.

enrage, anger, goad, tempt, exasperate, madden, infuriate, irritate, irk, incense, inflame, agitate, provoke, chafe, nettle, excite, craze. *Ant.* soften, mollify, soothe, calm, pacify, reconcile, conciliate, appease, compose, mitigate, moderate.

enrapture, enchant, charm, captivate, bewitch, fascinate, allure, enthrall, entrance, ravish, thrill, delight, enamor, please. *Ant.* repel, disgust, agitate, anger, annoy, shock, irritate, weary, tire, displease, offend, vex, pique, provoke.

enrich, supply, refine, endow, add, aggrandize, improve, embellish, adorn, develop, fertilize, cultivate. *Ant.* deplete, rob, reduce, take from, impoverish.

enroll, register, enlist, inscribe, subscribe, list, record, sign, fill out, enter, affix. *Ant.* discard, reject, abrogate, neglect, omit, pass over, repudiate, protest, cancel, deactivate, dismiss.

enter, join, penetrate, intrude, pierce, begin, insert, encroach, start, enroll, record, register, introduce. *Ant.* leave, go out, exit, vacate, emerge, depart, remove, withdraw.

enterprise, undertaking, venture, adventure, work, performance, endeavor, energy, scheme, risk, hazard, engagement, activity, action, business. *Ant.* inactivity, inaction, indolence, passiveness, sloth, unemployment.

entertainment, amusement, fun, merriment, enjoyment, pleasure, party, sport, cheer, delight, frolic, diversion, pastime, recreation, play, feast, banquet, picnic, dance, concert, social event, merry-making. *Ant.* gloom, sadness, boredom, weariness, listlessness, ennui, fatigue, drudgery, work, toil, depression, melancholy, labor.

enthusiasm, rapture, fervor, joy, transport, passion, ardor, vigor, devotion, excitement, vehemence, feeling, emotion, zeal, warmth, optimism, eagerness, frenzy, exhilaration, earnestness, intensity, fanaticism, ecstasy, hilarity, mirth, merriment, gaiety. *Ant.* dullness, tiredness, weariness, melancholy, ennui, pessimism, doubt, moroseness, coldness, indifference, lassitude, carelessness, apathy, lethargy, languor, wariness, calmness, dejection, calculation, caution, timidity, lifelessness, deadness.

entice, attract, draw, allure, charm, decoy, lure, wheedle, prevail upon, seduce, tempt. *Ant.* repel, disgust, reject, scare, frighten.

entrance, gate, door, doorway, gateway, inlet, ingress, entry, portal, opening, access, adit, approach, admission, admittance, accession, entree, introduction, penetration, passage, vestibule, initiation, commencement, beginning. *Ant.* outlet, exit, departure, withdrawal, exclusion, expulsion, rejection, refusal, emission, end, egress, recall.

entrap, catch, ensnare, decoy, lure, inveigle, entice, involve, allure, deceive, seduce, attract, entangle, catch, implicate, mislead, fool, beguile. *Ant.* warn, advise, admonish, counsel, aid, befriend, direct, guide, assist, help, free, release, clear, liberate, deliver, rescue.

entreat, beg, implore, supplicate, importune, ask, beseech, solicit, petition, request. *Ant.* demand, command, take, force, compel.

envelop, wrap, cover, enfold, surround, blanket, conceal, enclose, hide. *Ant.* reveal, unwrap, uncover, open.

envious, jealous, suspicious, resentful, cautious, watchful, covetous, displeased, invidious, malignant, malicious, odious. *Ant.* laudatory, helpful, charitable, well-disposed, pleased, benevolent.

environment, surroundings, culture, neighborhood, location, vicinity, background, setting, influences.

envoy, ambassador, commissioner, plenipotentiary, agent, nuncio, representative, legate, messenger.

ephemeral, transient, evanescent, momentary, fugitive, fleeting, transitory, temporary, passing, short, short-lived, vanishing, brief. *Ant.* long, long-lived, lasting, abiding, durable, enduring, permanent, perpetual, eternal, immortal, everlasting, endless, interminable.

70

epicurean, luxurious, gastronomic, sensual, voluptuous, sybaritic, fastidious, particular. *Ant.* ascetic, austere, puritanical, self-denying.

episode, incident, occurrence, event, happening, adventure, circumstance.

epithet, name, title, appellation, ascription, agnomen, invective, cognomen, eponym, patronymic, nickname, byword, sobriquet, denomination.

epistle, letter, missive, message, dispatch, note, communication, lesson, writing, rescript.

epitome, brief, abridgment, abstract, compendium, summary, digest, synopsis, precis, syllabus, synthesis, essence, abbreviation, contraction, condensation, curtailment, outline. *Ant.* enlargement, extension, expansion, development, distention, dilation, increase, addition, augmentation, increment.

equable, even, calm, uniform, unchanging, constant, equal, serene, steady, unruffled, regular. *Ant.* variable, changeable, fitful, fluctuating, spasmodic.

equal, equable, even, like, alike, invariable, uniform, same, unvarying, fair, just, equitable, adequate. *Ant.* unequal, unfair, unjust, unlike, changeable, variable, varying, disproportionate, disproportioned, ill-matched.

equanimity, composure, self-control, evenness, poise, serenity, calmness, balance. *Ant.* agitation, anxiety, perturbation, unevenness, disturbance, excitation.

equipment, apparatus, paraphernalia, gear, array, materiel, outfit, furnishings.

equitable, impartial, fair, unprejudiced, honest, objective, reasonable, just. *Ant.* inequitable, unfair, slanted, biased, injust, partial, disproportionate.

equivalent, tantamount, commensurate, equal, alike, same, similar, comparable, parallel, synonymous, identical, interchangeable, convertible, reciprocal, analogous, correspondent. *Ant.* different, unlike, unequal, unmatched, dissimilar.

equivocal, ambiguous, uncertain, indeterminate, indefinite, puzzling, doubtful, dubious, perplexing, enigmatic, obscure, indistinct, suspicious, questionable, involved, vague, ambivalent, cryptic, hazy, wavering, deceptive, fluctuating. *Ant.* clear, plain, obvious, lucid, distinct, transparent, evident, open, manifest, apparent, visible, unclouded, discernible, forthright, unequivocal, certain, indubitable.

eradicate, uproot, extirpate, exterminate, root out, destroy, decimate, annihilate, abolish, disperse, extinguish, nullify, devastate, kill, consume, remove. *Ant.* plant, beget, foster, propagate, instill, initiate, embed, settle, fix, stabilize, establish, institute, fortify, strengthen, secure, confirm.

erode, corrode, eat, wear, deteriorate, weather, abrade, gnaw, rub, destroy.

erotic, amorous, sexual, sensual, amatory, passionate, concupiscent, lustful, ardent, exciting, erogenous, carnal, libidinous, arousing. *Ant.* cold, frigid, spiritual, passionless, celibate, suppressed.

erratic, odd, strange, unruly, aberrant, eccentric, desultory, queer, peculiar, fluctuating, flighty, wandering, uncertain, capricious, unreliable, changeable. *Ant.* steady, sure, certain, rigid, regular, dependable, reliable, methodical.

error, blunder, mistake, oversight, omission, fallacy, fault, delusion, deviation, fall, slip, transgression, indiscretion. *Ant.* correctness, certainty, certitude, correction, precision, truth, accuracy.

erudite, learned, scholarly, knowing, cultured, enlightened, bookish, recondite, educated. *Ant.* unlettered, illiterate, common, ignorant, uneducated.

eruption, outbreak, rash, explosion, outburst, discharge, commotion, efflorescence.

escape, flee, fly, evade, break, defect, avoid, elude, decamp, abscond.

escort, guard, lead, convoy, conduct, protect, accompany, guide, chaperon, safeguard, usher, attend. *Ant.* abandon, leave alone, neglect, desert, maroon.

especially, chiefly, mainly, specially, particularly, principally, definitely, firstly, notably. *Ant.* generally, commonly, indefinitely, usually, loosely, ordinarily, normally.

espouse, embrace, assume, defend, adopt, betroth, marry. *Ant.* abandon, reject, abjure, forsake, divorce.

essay, dissertation, tract, treatise, attempt, effort, trial, venture, endeavor, paper, composition, article, thesis, disquisition, editorial, comment.

essential, necessary, fundamental, vital, substantive, basic, inherent, elemental, requisite, major, key, indispensable, intrinsic, characteristic. *Ant.* secondary, accessory, auxiliary, minor, subsidiary.

establish, confirm, institute, found, build up, verify, endow, confirm, ratify, fulfill, prove, set up, authorize, demonstrate, substantiate, fix, plant, carry out, settle, constitute, organize, determine. *Ant.* overthrow, topple, ruin, destroy, invalidate, disestablish, raze, tumble, replace, defeat, wreck, pull down, confuse, disprove, controvert, overcome, unsettle.

estate, property, land, goods, possessions, holdings, fortune, effects, interest, domain, inheritance; state, rank, condition, degree, station, position.

esteem, regard, respect, reverence, favor, appreciation, admiration, approbation, veneration, approval, commendation, honor, praise, sanction, deference, estimation. *Ant.* contempt, disregard, scorn, disrespect, contumely, disapprobation, disdain, derision, mockery, slight, insolence, insult, ridicule, reproach, abuse, abhorrence, antipathy, aversion, dislike, hatred.

estimate, compute, rate, appraise, appreciate, consider, esteem, prize, value, measure, calculate, weigh, reckon, number, count, assess, evaluate, think, reason. *Ant.* guess, disregard.

estrangement, abstraction, alienation, withdrawal, removal, diversion, transference, disaffection, disagreement, antagonism, separation, difference. *Ant.* union, bond, affinity, closeness, comradeship, friendship, partnership, coalition, agreement, attraction, alliance, combination, coalescence.

eternal, everlasting, unending, never-ending, perpetual, endless, infinite, boundless, deathless, immortal, continual, interminable, timeless, imperishable, unceasing, incessant, ceaseless, constant, enduring, permanent, undying. *Ant.* finite, ending, temporary, transitory, inconstant, ceasing, short, changeable, mutable, brief, fluctuating, variable, transient, evanescent, ephemeral.

ethical, moral, virtuous, righteous, good, principled, honest. *Ant.* unethical, corrupt, immoral, vicious, dishonest, unbecoming.

eulogize, praise, laud, compliment, celebrate, commend, applaud, extol. *Ant.* scorn, sneer at, degrade, demean, condemn, ignore.

evade, avoid, equivocate, prevaricate, dodge, lie, shuffle, shun, elude, trick, quibble, shift, cavil, mystify, dissemble, cover, conceal, deceive, pretend, confuse. *Ant.* acknowledge, approach, meet, testify, declare, face, confront, approach, encounter, clarify, explain, expound, elucidate, confess, illustrate, confirm, verify, prove.

evacuate, expel, empty, make vacant, clear, purge, scour, discharge, void, emit, leave, quit, retreat, relinquish, vacate, abandon, desert. *Ant.* fill, load, charge, stuff, enter, take over, occupy.

evaporate, dry, vaporize, disappear, dissolve, fade, vanish, evanesce, disperse, go away. *Ant.* condense, appear, sublimate, consolidate, crystallize.

evasive, elusive, avoiding, escaping, dodging, side-stepping, dishonest, lying, prevaricating, equivocating, quibbling. *Ant.* honest, direct, straight-forward, forthright.

evaluate, estimate, weigh, appraise, value, assess, calculate, rate, judge. *Ant.* guess, hazard.

even, level, plain, smooth, equal, clear, open, flat, uniform, regular, unbroken, tied, flush, peaceful, calm. *Ant.* uneven, rough, lumpy, jagged, ridged, rugged, broken, wrinkled, irregular, rugate, disparate, troubled, agitated, furrowed.

event, incident, fact, case, outcome, issue, result, consequence, milestone, circumstance, chance, episode, possibility, contingency, occurrence, fortune, sequel, accident, adventure, end, happening. *Ant.* origin, start, cause, antecedent.

evict, oust, expel, dispossess, debar, exclude, eject, deprive, discard. *Ant.* admit, accept, receive, welcome.

evidence, data, testimony, grounds, documentation, authority, facts, indication, premises. *Ant.* disproof, doubt, refutation, contradiction.

evident, clear, plain, open, distinct, manifest, public, obvious, patent, transparent, perceptible, visible, discernible, conspicuous, unmistakable, tangible, palpable, indubitable, glaring, overt, apparent, distinguishable, indisputable, incontrovertible. *Ant.* obscure, unknown, hidden, concealed, puzzling, occult, invisible, unseen, dark, impenetrable, questionable, impalpable, undiscovered, confused, imperceptible, covert, secret, intricate, perplexing, complex, involved.

evil, ill, harm, mischief, depravity, wickedness, sin, misfortune, corruption, crime, sinfulness, badness, immorality, vice, vileness, baseness, malignity, hatred, scandal, sorrow, woe, viciousness, calamity, wrong, pollution, contamination, depravation, lewdness, licentiousness, lasciviousness, wantonness, lustfulness, obscenity, profligacy. *Ant.* goodness, virtue, honor, uprightness, rectitude, respect, decency, reputation, nobleness, purity, wholesomeness, integrity, honesty, renown, esteem, chastity, justice, sinlessness, repute, fame, credit, estimation, worth, respectability, character, merit.

evince, show, evidence, reveal, indicate, prove, manifest, disclose, exhibit, display, demonstrate. *Ant.* conceal, repress, suppress, hide.

evoke, summon, rouse, excite, stimulate, elicit, educe, waken, arouse, provoke. *Ant.* silence, quiet, repress, squelch, stifle.

exact, right, correct, proper, particular, punctual, reliable, true, accurate, careful, methodical, precise, nice, definite, scrupulous, strict, prompt, timely, suitable, meet, appropriate, determinate, adapted, fitting, specific, rigorous, unequivocal, literal. *Ant.* inaccurate, approximate, wrong, false, untrue, unreliable, careless, inappropriate, unfitting, inexact, indeterminate, unsuitable, indefinite, variable, irregular, untimely, erroneous, loose, deceptive, incorrect.

exaggerate, magnify, amplify, heighten, enlarge, embellish, stretch, embroider, overdo, expand. *Ant.* minimize, lessen, shrink, reduce, understate, attenuate, depreciate.

exalt, ennoble, dignify, raise, promote, heighten, elevate, magnify, extol, glorify, praise, commend, recommend, advance, honor, laud, applaud. *Ant.* denounce, degrade, condemn, demean, despise, depose, accuse, charge, lower, impair, spurn, disdain, scorn, humble, humiliate.

examination, check-up, analysis, investigation, inquiry, search, research, scrutiny, inspection, inquisition, quiz, questioning, trial, test, assay.

example, model, pattern, ideal, archetype, type, sample, specimen, standard, warning, illustration, exemplification, precedent, prototype, design, mold, copy, original, representation, typical case.

exasperate, irritate, exacerbate, infuriate, anger, vex, incense, rouse, inflame, frustrate, aggravate, enrage, provoke, chafe, nettle, annoy. *Ant.* mollify, placate, conciliate, assuage, calm.

exceed, excel, overdo, outdo, overtax, surpass, exaggerate, outvie, outstrip, transcend, eclipse, surmount, top, outnumber, outrun, pass. *Ant.* lag, dally, dawdle, fail, loiter, linger, delay, saunter, tarry, be tardy, fall behind.

excellent, superior, peerless, admirable, estimable, surpassing, best, eminent, meritorious, valuable, prime. *Ant.* inferior, lesser, poor, neglible.

except, but, save, excepting, excluding, rejecting, exempting, barring, omitting. *Ant.* including, admitting, embracing.

exceptional, uncommon, extraordinary, unusual, scarce, rare, choice, novel, unique, singular, remarkable, unparalleled, incomparable, unprecedented, wonderful, marvelous. *Ant.* common, unexceptional, conventional, banal, ordinary, customary, usual, habitual, frequent, normal, general, regular, expected, wonted, accustomed.

excerpt, citation, extract, quote, selection, culling, abbreviation, clipping.

excess, profusion, over-abundance, extravagance, luxuriance, waste, lavishness, redundance, redundancy, surplus, superfluity, superabundance, exorbitance, overplus, plenty, prodigality, dissipation, gluttony, intemperance. *Ant.* lack, want, necessity, moderation, insufficiency, poverty, dearth, deficiency, defect, scantiness, need, failure, shortcoming, economy, frugality, inadequacy, hunger, distress, privation, indigence.

exchange, trade, swap, transfer, convert, substitute, barter, retort, sell, convert, reciprocate.

excite, rouse, activate, provoke, arouse, incite, awaken, stimulate, irritate, agitate, inflame, kindle, anger, induce, offend, aggravate, enrage, incense, chafe, exasperate, tease, annoy, worry, goad, taunt, mock. *Ant.* allay, pacify, deaden, soothe, soften, lull, quiet, repress, check, compose, assuage, appease, abate, alleviate, calm, subdue, reconcile, conciliate, mollify, mitigate, tranquilize, lessen, palliate, ameliorate, propitiate, moderate, ease, comfort.

exclamation, outcry, cry, call, interjection, utterance, declaration, statement, saying, speech, expletive.

exclude, prohibit, omit, boycott, prevent, debar, obviate, blackball, bar, ostracize, ban, veto, except, reject. *Ant.* admit, include, add, accept, welcome, enlist, incorporate.

excruciating, agonizing, racking, overwhelming, grueling, rending, tormenting, severe, intense, painful, extreme, acute. *Ant.* mild, soothing, comforting, pleasing.

excursion, jaunt, ramble, expedition, outing, trip, tour, journey, voyage, travel, digression, episode, divergence.

excuse, apology, defense, extenuation, pretext, vindication, reason, plea, explanation, alibi.

execrate, curse, objurgate, revile, imprecate, condemn, reprehend, abhor, damn, berate. *Ant.* praise, commend, laud, extol, applaud.

execute, fulfill, perform, do, direct, effect, accomplish, carry out, complete, achieve, consummate, enforce, administer, finish, gain, compass, win, attain, realize, sign, seal, render, reach, get, obtain, finish, kill. *Ant.* fail, fall short, omit, neglect, ignore, disregard, miss, forget, overlook, slight, undo, leave, abandon, give up, quit, relinquish, forego, resign, suspend, shirk, shelve.

exempt, free, clear, liberated, absolved, excused, privileged, irresponsible, unamenable, excluded, released, freed, undrafted, not liable, nonvulnerable, unrestrained, unbound, uncontrolled, untrammeled, unshackled, unchecked, unrestricted. *Ant.* nonexempt, liable, responsible, subject, accountable, obliged, bound, vulnerable, necessitated, answerable, amenable, constrained, restrained, checked, trammeled, shackled, confined, coerced, driven, compelled, commanded.

exercise, practice, exertion, employment, training, drill, application, use, performance, occupation, activity, action, act, enjoyment, operation. *Ant.* inactivity, rest, laziness, idleness, relaxation, slothfulness, inaction, sluggishness, repose, indolence, cessation.

exertion, effort, exercise, attempt, activity, labor, strain, struggle, trial, travail, toil, endeavor, work, grind, action. *Ant.* inaction, inactivity, quietness, laziness, idleness, sloth, lethargy.

exhausted, tired, wearied, wasted, consumed, spent, worn, worked out, drained, empty, fatigued, jaded. *Ant.* fresh, keen, ready, strong, restored, rested, forceful, refreshed, invigorated, vigorous, powerful, lusty.

exhibit, show, display, discover, demonstrate, reveal, manifest, offer, present, disclose, evince, flaunt. *Ant.* hide, conceal.

exhilarate, inspirit, enliven, cheer, gladden, stimulate, elate, rejoice, invigorate, thrill, spur. *Ant.* dull, depress, dampen, deject, suppress, repress, sadden, discourage.

exigency, emergency, necessity, crisis, difficulty, distress, demand, need, want, strait, urgency. *Ant.* normality, ordinariness, regularity.

exonerate, acquit, absolve, free, justify, relieve, discharge, release, restore, vindicate, clear, exempt, except. *Ant.* condemn, blame, find guilty, imprison, accuse, indict, charge, censure.

exorbitant, excessive, exceeding, extreme, expensive, inordinate, over-priced, oppressive, unreasonable, extravagant, unconscionable. *Ant.* reasonable, just, moderate, inexpensive, below cost, fair, low, normal, sensible.

expand, amplify, extend, augment, magnify, widen, spread, stretch, increase, dilate, enlarge, develop. *Ant.* shrink, contract, condense, abbreviate.

expect, await, contemplate, envision, anticipate, hope, foresee.

expedite, forward, advance, facilitate, accelerate, hurry, hasten, urge, quicken. *Ant.* delay, slow, retard, hinder, obstruct.

expedition, journey, trip, undertaking, mission, excursion, voyage, cruise, campaign, trek, safari, quest; alacrity, speed.

expel, evict, discharge, eject, banish, eliminate, remove, proscribe, oust, excrete. *Ant.* absorb, admit, take in, invite, accept.

expense, cost, price, payment, charge, outlay, expenditure, outgo, disbursement, value, sum, amount, upkeep, harm, debit, loss. *Ant.* profits, receipts, return, proceeds, revenue, product, income, gain, increase, accession, acquisition, emolument, perquisites.

experience, living through, feeling, encountering, meeting, enduring, background, suffering, seasoning, enjoying, testing, trial, wisdom, knowledge, sagacity, learning by doing. *Ant.* ignorance, lack of knowledge, greenness, rawness, immaturity.

experiment, proof, trial, examination, attempt, verification, test, practice, exercise, research, assay, endeavor, undertaking.

explain, interpret, elucidate, manifest, teach, expound, illustrate, translate, decipher, construe, unravel, unfold, solve, clarify, justify. *Ant.* perplex, complicate, involve, confuse, tangle, bewilder, confound, obcure, cloud, befuddle, mystify, confirm.

explicit, definite, express, plain, positive, clear, intelligible, evident, categorical, comprehensible, certain, precise, exact, determinate, absolute, obvious, manifest, distinct. *Ant.* indefinite, hazy, mixed, doubtful, confused, unintelligible, puzzling, vague, indeterminate, obscure, ambiguous, involved, equivocal, dubious.

expound, express, clarify, interpret, explain, analyze, present, state, elucidate, construe. *Ant.* cloud, obscure, confuse.

express, declare, signify, communicate, assert, tell, utter, denote, designate, represent, send, forward, dispatch. *Ant.* suppress, withhold, retain, repress, check, hold back, restrain.

exquisite, elegant, fine, rare, dainty, charming, appealing, perfect, responsive, consummate, matchless, precious, rich, poignant, intense, acute, choice, select, excellent, refined, polished, debonair, vintage. *Ant.* imperfect, valueless, ugly, crude, dull, vapid, poor, worthless, inferior, boorish, common, ordinary, unrefined.

extant, existent, surviving, existing, undestroyed, lasting, enduring, contemporary. *Ant.* departed, gone, destroyed, extinct.

extemporaneous, offhand, improvised, unpremeditated, ad lib, unplanned, extempory, unstudied, unprepared, impromptu, ready, informal. *Ant.* elaborated, premeditated, studied, written, read, recited, prepared, contrived, designed, formed, provided, planned, procured.

extend, reach, stretch, protract, increase, enlarge, lengthen, add, augment, amplify, expand, dilate, spread, elongate, attenuate, draw out, give, grant. *Ant.* contract, shorten, curtail, compress, narrow, abbreviate, decrease, abridge, epitomize, lessen, condense, cut down, reduce, hold back, retain.

external, outside, outer, exterior, superficial, extrinsic, foreign. *Ant.* internal, inside, intrinsic, within, domestic.

exterior, outside, surface, shell, skin. *Ant.* inside, interior, internal (part), core.

exterminate, annihilate, destroy, expel, extirpate, banish, uproot, remove, overthrow, abolish, decimate, kill, eradicate. *Ant.* foster, preserve, protect, cherish, nurture, keep, guard, secure, defend, propagate, plant, maintain, save, replenish, develop, colonize, breed, build up, beget.

extinguish

extinguish, abate, quench, abolish, destroy, obscure, kill, eradicate, extirpate, exterminate, annihilate, suppress, choke. *Ant.* light, ignite, kindle, enflame, enliven, animate, nurture, initiate, aid, release, secure.

extortionate, demanding, oppressive, inordinate, harsh, severe, stern, rapacious, exorbitant, grasping, exacting, squeezing, excessive, rigorous. *Ant.* moderate, reasonable, generous, magnanimous, gentle.

extract, educe, extort, eradicate, pull, obtain, draw, extirpate, elicit, remove, evoke, derive, distill. *Ant.* insert, introduce, instill, impregnate, interject, intervene.

extraordinary, unusual, rare, exceptional, marvelous, peculiar, particular, singular, uncommon, unwonted, special, inordinate, phenomenal, wonderful, egregious. *Ant.* common, usual, regular, normal, standard, customary, ordinary.

extravagant, lavish, profuse, immoderate, liberal, wasteful, prodigal, destructive, excessive, inordinate, extreme. *Ant.* parsimonious, economical, reasonable, stingy, close, close-fisted, penurious.

extreme, last, final, terminal, farthest, utmost, ultimate, greatest, rarest, remote, intensive, immoderate, extravagant, outermost, far, fanatical, maximum. *Ant.* moderate, medium, limited, calm, ordinary, steady, quiet, subdued, repressed, sober, dispassionate, near, nigh, adjacent.

extricate, liberate, deliver, free, unbind, unchain, disengage, loose, disentangle, release, unfasten, untie, let go, pull (out of), rescue, ransom, affranchise. *Ant.* tie, bind, chain, confine, imprison, incarcerate, entangle, restrict, circumscribe, fetter, retain, limit, restrain.

exuberant, overflowing, profuse, energetic, lavish, abundant, rank, prolific, luxuriant, copious, vigorous, wanton. *Ant.* sterile, austere, barren, needy, depleted.

exult, rejoice, enjoy, glory, swagger, vaunt, crow, boast, triumph, brag, bluster. *Ant.* wail, sorrow, mourn, grieve, deplore, lament, cry, moan, weep.

F

fabric, textile, cloth, dry goods, stuff, substance, material, structure, organization.

fabricate, construct, make, manufacture, frame, produce, compose, build, form, invent, devise, put together, plan, arrange, erect, forge, fake, feign, prevaricate, counterfeit. *Ant.* tear down, ruin, destroy, raze, wreck, shatter, disarrange, break, demolish, split, disintegrate, disrupt.

fabulous, legendary, mythical, untrue, fictitious, feigned, ridiculous, false, absurd, incredible, immense, wonderful, astounding, exaggerated, amazing, extraordinary. *Ant.* historical, proven, true,

78

testified, admitted, warranted, guaranteed, credible, known, ordinary, normal, simple, usual, general, common.

acade, front, affectation, false front, veneer, cover-up, ornamentation, appearance. *Ant.* base, character, sincerity.

ace, *n.* visage, countenance, outside, appearance, mien, presence, surface, front, exterior, physiognomy, feature; boldness, confidence, effrontery, impudence, ego, impertinence; *v.* meet, oppose, confront, defy, venture, dare, resist, challenge, brave, overlay, coat. *Ant.* interior, inside, back, rear; humility, backwardness, bashfulness; fear, retire, withdraw, slink, shrink, retreat, refuse, creep away, sneak, crouch.

acetious, jocular, jocose, merry, witty, humorous, funny, amusing, ironic, frivolous, pleasant, jesting, waggish, comical, laughable, droll. *Ant.* serious, solemn, morose, sad, melancholy, dull, stolid, phlegmatic, grave, formal, ceremonial, pensive, gloomy, somber, dejected, dignified.

acile, easy, ready, dexterous, artful, flexible, quick, skillful, clever, adroit, expert, apt, tactful, able, proficient, courteous, affable, agreeable, slippery, smooth. *Ant.* hard, difficult, laborious, slow, unskillful, clumsy, unhandy, awkward, plodding, arduous, toilsome, wearisome, tedious, rude, boorish, disagreeable.

acility, readiness, quickness, easiness, ease, dexterity, skillfulness, expertness, adroitness, proficiency, cleverness, ability, resource, convenience, civility, courtesy, affability. *Ant.* difficulty, slowness, unfitness, ineptitude, unsuitableness, clumsiness, awkwardness, unskillfulness, discourtesy, rudeness.

acsimile, copy, reproduction, photograph, picture, duplicate, pattern, replica, transcript. *Ant.* difference, distinction, diversity, dissimilarity, variation, modification, negative, opposite.

action, coterie, party, sect, set, combination, clique, cabal, circle, division, denomination, block, wing. *Ant.* unity, conformity, entirety, homogeneity.

actious, recalcitrant, rebellious, seditious, dissident, insubordinate, contentious. *Ant.* cooperative, united, helpful.

actitious, artificial, spurious, bogus, phony, counterfeit, affected, forced, synthetic, fabricated, sham, unnatural. *Ant.* genuine, authentic, real, bona fide, natural, spontaneous.

actor, agent, steward, bailiff, deputy, manager, representative, substitute, delegate, proxy, commissioner, vicar, attorney, actor, doer, element, part.

aculty, ability, aptitude, capacity, gift, talent, skill, knack, bent, function, right, means, authority. *Ant.* incompetence, inability, ineptness, incapacity.

ade, weaken, pale, dim, whiten, bleach, disappear, vanish, ebb, dwindle, taper off, wane, wither, deteriorate, blur, evanesce. *Ant.* sharpen, darken, strengthen, recover, improve, energize, enhance.

fail

fail, falter, abort, collapse, abandon, default, miss, omit, disappoint, desert, weaken, decline, leave, miscarry, abandon, neglect, drop, wither, fade, quit, forego, flounder. *Ant.* win, get, surpass, gain, capture, obtain, pass, discharge, deliver, recover, merit, earn, attain, procure, succeed, achieve, reach, accomplish, finish.

faint, weak, timid, faltering, worn, powerless, languid, feeble, worn out, weary, listless, pale, thin, faint-hearted, fatigued; unclear, indistinct, inaudible, soft. *Ant.* brave, courageous, bold, dashing, resolute, strong, unafraid, daring, fearless, adventurous, intrepid, hazardous, fresh, hearty, vigorous, sturdy, energetic; distinct, loud, clear.

fair, clear, sunny, dry, pleasant, equitable, unbiased, honest, frank, open, mild, impartial, candid, just, reasonable, moderate, civil, decent, nice, clean, pure, blond, pale, light (complexioned), handsome, pretty. *Ant.* wet, cloudy, threatening, showery, stormy, dark, rainy, rough, tempestuous, unjust, dishonest, partial, unfair, double-dealing, devious, unreasonable, ugly, unfavorable, repellent, dark (complexioned).

faith, creed, belief, trust, credence, assurance, confidence, conviction, piety, assent, tenets, fidelity, reliance, trust, doctrine, loyalty, fidelity. *Ant.* unbelief, misgiving, disbelief, infidelity, suspicion, incredulity, rejection, disloyalty, distrust, skepticism, doubt, denial, dissent, faithlessness, agnosticism.

faithful, true, loyal, constant, honest, straight, dependable, attached, honorable, trustworthy, firm, incorruptible, trusty, stanch, unwavering, unswerving, devoted, accurate, exact. *Ant.* capricious, fickle, uncertain, untrustworthy, untrue, unfaithful, unreliable, false, faithless, wavering, perfidious, treacherous, irresolute, unstable, variable, changeable, inconstant, vacillating, dishonorable, dishonest, disloyal, inaccurate, inexact, different.

fall, sink, tumble, descend, settle, lower, totter, drop, topple, droop, decline, plunge, lessen, abate, ebb, diminish, weaken. *Ant.* rise, ascend, climb, surmount, scale, tower, soar, improve, strengthen, advance, reach, attain.

fallacy, delusion, sophistry, illusion, fantasy, quibbling, casuistry, untruth, subterfuge, evasion, equivocation, flaw, misconception, error, mistake, misstatement, perversion, aberrancy. *Ant.* truth, sureness, fact, evidence, certainty, demonstration, axiom, proof, soundness, verity, surety, logic, reality, verification.

fallible, erring, inaccurate, faulty, untrustworthy, unreliable, awkward, ignorant, clumsy, sinful, careless, undisciplined. *Ant.* correct, reliable, trustworthy, perfect, unerring, capable, artful, knowing, infallible.

false, untrue, lying, erroneous, fallacious, spurious, bogus, mendacious, fabricated, sophistical, deceptive, mock, sham, counterfeit, incorrect, make-believe, pretended, illusory, unreal, dishonest, deceptive, misleading. *Ant.* true, correct, factual, valid, accurate, right, unassailable, established, confirmed, known, tested, pure, genuine, real, substantiated, honest, straight, axiomatic, just, legitimate, sanctioned, actual, certain.

falter, hesitate, doubt, stammer, stutter, waver, demur, weaken, flinch, shrink, vacillate, totter, hobble, slip, fluctuate, stagger, delay, pause, scruple, tremble, reel. *Ant.* persevere, continue, persist, demand, insist, pursue, stay, endure, remain, maintain, contend, drone, chatter, urge, press, incite, impel, stimulate, instigate, compel, encourage.

familiar, intimate, well-known, proverbial, informed, acquainted, common, customary, usual, informal, comfortable, unconstrained, unreserved, accessible, easy, approachable, casual, presuming, impudent, disrespectful. *Ant.* unfamiliar, unknown, new, strange, unacquainted, foreign, formal, reserved, distant, stiff, respectful, ceremonious, unapproachable, constrained.

famous, well-known, celebrated, illustrious, renowned, distinguished, noted, eminent, conspicuous, brilliant, glorious, noble, honorable. *Ant.* obscure, inconspicuous, unknown, humble, undistinguished, infamous, degraded, ignominious, dishonored, disgraced, shameful.

fanatical, bigoted, narrow-minded, prejudiced, illiberal, devoted, rabid, radical, extreme, domineering, credulous, superstitious, obstinate, unreasonable, zealous, stubborn, self-opinionated, unfair, biased, partial, obsessed, dogmatic. *Ant.* broad-minded, liberal, unprejudiced, impartial, just, dispassionate, nonpartisan, reasonable, rational, comfortable, tolerant, indulgent, forbearing, magnanimous, fair-minded.

fanciful, imaginary, capricious, fantastic, odd, queer, whimsical, freakish, fickle, changeable, fitful, unsteady, inconstant, grotesque, chimerical, imaginative, visionary, unreal, dreamy, fluctuating, creative, romantic, variable, vacillating, erratic, ideal. *Ant.* real, steady, constant, serious, firm, sincere, earnest, grave, practical, fixed, uniform, regular, undeviating, equable, steadfast, unchanging, resolute, determined, accurate, unalterable, invariable, sure, literal, sound, sensible, true, reasonable, calculated, ordinary, commonplace, solid, prosaic.

fancy, imagination, supposition, vagary, predilection, conception, mood, caprice, conceit, fondness, humor, whim, inclination, idea, belief, notion, image, ideal, dream. *Ant.* fact, reality, verity, truth, exactness, veracity, certainty, actuality, stability, accuracy, positiveness, precision, definiteness.

fantastic, fanciful, whimsical, queer, odd, capricious, vague, strange, imaginary, peculiar, wonderful, singular, amazing, unbelievable, wild, illogical, bizarre, quaint, uncommon, comical, eccentric, visionary, far-fetched. *Ant.* common, commonplace, customary, ordinary, usual, trite, regular, normal, conventional, hackneyed, serious, banal, logical, solemn, steady, fixed, constant, formal, precise, ceremonious.

far, distant, removed, away, remote. *Ant.* near, close, convenient, handy.

farcical, ludicrous, hilarious, foolish, absurd, extravagant, comic, ridiculous, droll, funny. *Ant.* sad, melancholy, tragic, sober.

farsighted, forward-thinking, clear-sighted, prepared, far-seeing, clairvoyant, level-headed, prudent, foresighted, judicious. *Ant.* rash, shortsighted, impractical, unthinking, injudicious, unprepared, imprudent.

fascinate, charm, enchant, beguile, bewitch, entrance, captivate, enamor, enrapture, attract, draw, enthrall, allure, entice, invite, enslave, overpower, ravish, delight. *Ant.* repel, disgust, displease, weary, fatigue, tire, horrify, anger, agitate, shock, frighten, appall, daunt.

fashion, *v.* shape, make, design, form, mold, plan, create, cast, sculpture, contrive, fabricate, manufacture, style; *n.* appearance, fad, manner, mode, vogue, smartness.

fast, quick, rapid, fleet, flying, speedy, expeditious, swift, nimble, accelerated, active, agile, alert, brisk, lively, wild, dissolute, dissipated, reckless, abandoned, secure, tight, permanent, lasting. *Ant.* slow, sluggish, tardy, dilatory, slothful, dull, heavy, settled, dull-witted, steady, plodding, solemn, quiet, virtuous, upright, model, exemplary, well-behaved, good, insecure, impermanent, loose.

fasten, bind, affix, link, connect, tie, attach, anchor, secure, lock. *Ant.* release, open, detach, untie, unfasten, loosen.

fastidious, delicate, finicky, fussy, dainty, particular, nice, meticulous, squeamish, choosy, critical. *Ant.* gross, boorish, uncritical, tasteless, indifferent.

fat, fleshy, beefy, brawny, portly, unwieldy, corpulent, stout, obese, unctuous, swollen, bulky, rich, well-to-do, wealthy, luxuriant. *Ant.* lean, thin, attenuated, slender, lithe, sinewy, slight, slim, graceful, poor, impoverished, indigent, penniless.

fatal, lethal, mortal, deadly, baleful, baneful, destructive, killing, murderous, pernicious. *Ant.* enlivening, vivifying, healthful, strengthening, invigorating, wholesome, nourishing, animating, vital.

fate, destiny, doom, lot, end, goal, death, luck, fortune, finish, predestination, chance, predetermination, consummation, fortune, misfortune.

fatigue, weariness, enervation, languor, exhaustion, debilitation, weakness, feebleness, dullness, faintness, deterioration, lassitude, heaviness, listlessness, tiredness. *Ant.* vigor, briskness, force, liveliness, keenness, alertness, vim, restoration, strength, energy, forcefulness, activity, sprightliness, spirit, vivacity.

fatuous, foolish, stupid, silly, idiotic, childish, dull, dense, dimwitted, ignorant. *Ant.* sensible, intelligent, bright, keen, clever, smart, knowledgeable, realistic.

fault, blemish, flaw, imperfection, misdeed, detriment, delinquency, misdemeanor, failing, slip, defect, drawback, weakness, omission, imperfection, responsibility, foible, error. *Ant.* advantage, help, assistance, gain, benefit, correctness, merit, perfection, soundness, blessing, favor, good, utility.

favorable, advantageous, kind, friendly, assisting, helpful, predisposed, auspicious, propitious, conducive, beneficial, convenient, useful, salutary, fair. *Ant.* unfavorable, disadvantageous, useless, opposed, hindering, hurtful, derogatory, harmful, injurious, unpropitious, detrimental, inconvenient, unfriendly.

fear, fright, terror, consternation, panic, horror, dismay, dread, trepidation, phobia, misgiving, tremor, alarm, awe, reverence, disquietude, apprehension, trembling, agitation, anxiety. *Ant.* bravery, courage, endurance, endeavor, resolution, heroism, valor, fortitude, intrepidity, fearlessness, gallantry, nonchalance, calm, security, unconcern.

feasible, workable, achievable, attainable, practical, practicable, possible. *Ant.* unfeasible, fantastic, impractical, visionary, unrealistic, foolish, inconceivable, unattainable.

feast, banquet, entertainment, treat, festival, festivity, repast, refreshment, carousal, merrymaking, barbecue, picnic. *Ant.* dearth, hunger, famine, fasting, abstinence, need, necessity, indigence, distress, scarcity.

feat, act, effort, deed, exploit, action, exertion, performance, exercise, execution, attainment, accomplishment, achievement, acquisition, maneuver. *Ant.* inaction, abstinence, idleness, failure, stagnation, unemployment, passiveness, laziness, sloth.

fecund, fertile, productive, prolific, yielding, fruitful, inventive, creative. *Ant.* sterile, barren, unfruitful, futile, unproductive, impotent.

fee, compensation, payment, wage, emolument, pay, bill, account, charge, cost, remuneration.

feeble, weak, puny, delicate, infirm, debilitated, frail, enervated, forceless, faint, languid, exhausted, decrepit, impaired, sickly. *Ant.* forceful, vigorous, strong, powerful, stout, robust, firm, hardy, solid, healthy, muscular, hearty, hale, sound.

feeling, sense, sensation, perception, emotion, susceptibility, sensibility, passion, excitement, consciousness, conviction, tenderness, sensitiveness, opinion, sentiment, sympathy, impression. *Ant.* insensibility, apathy, immobility, indifference, stolidity, stupidity, unfeelingness, impassiveness, lethargy, stoicism, unconcern, deadness, unconsciousness, numbness.

felicitate, congratulate, greet, compliment. *Ant.* sympathize (with), condole, discourage, dismay, reject.

felicity, bliss, rapture, ecstasy, joy, happiness, comfort, blessing, gladness, cheer, mirth, merriment, gaiety, gratification, pleasure, charm, delight, satisfaction, enjoyment, cheerfulness, joviality, frolic, hilarity, festivity, aptness, appropriateness. *Ant.* misery, unhappiness, dejection, sorrow, sadness, melancholy, grief, woe, misfortune, distress, despondency, loss, gloom, torment, worry, calamity, wretchedness, depression, dullness, inaptness, despair.

felonious, criminal, malignant, malicious, evil, depraved, underhand vile, villainous, traitorous, perfidious, malevolent, heinous, corrupt, harmful, noxious, injurious, wicked, perverse, base, vicious wrong. *Ant.* good, noble, praiseworthy, generous, commendable charitable, kind, decent, honorable, laudable, exalted, benevolent beneficent, remedial, helpful, worthy, meritorious, advantageous

feminine, womanish, womanly, womanlike, maidenly, chaste, female soft, tender, delicate. *Ant.* masculine, manly, male, virile, unfeminine, unwomanly, brave, strong, hardy.

ferment, seethe, boil, bubble, concoct, heat, roil, leaven, raise, stir fret, agitate, excite, embroil. *Ant.* calm, quiet, soothe, dampen cool, repress.

ferocious, fierce, savage, untamed, barbarous, wild, brutal, cruel sanguinary, ravenous, vehement, violent, unrestrained, bloodthirsty, murderous, merciless, pitiless, brutish, fearsome, frightful. *Ant.* mild, gentle, tame, docile, tractable, modest, quiet peaceful, tender, harmless, innocent, inoffensive, innocuous, soft manageable, susceptible, yielding, affectionate.

fertile, fruitful, prolific, plenteous, productive, luxuriant, fecund rich, teeming, abundant, plentiful, copious, exuberant. *Ant.* sterile, childless, barren, unproductive, unyielding, arid, jejune empty, fruitless, destitute, waste, unprofitable, useless, valueless

fervent, ardent, earnest, passionate, animated, glowing, fiery, hot vehement, enthusiastic, eager, intense, zealous, fanatical, rabid *Ant.* cool, chilly, impassive, phlegmatic, adverse, grudging, hesitant.

fetid, noisome, foul-smelling, putrid, mephitic, malodorous, rank stinking, repulsive. *Ant.* aromatic, fragrant, sweet-smelling, perfumed, balmy.

feud, quarrel, row, strife, enmity, bitterness, animosity, dissension hostility, dispute, controversy, brawl, affray, broil, antagonism vendetta, contest, altercation, wrangle, bickering, disagreement argument. *Ant.* peace, fraternity, brotherhood, friendliness, calm repose, tranquility, order, harmony, concord, love, confidence esteem, regard.

feudal, servile, subject, downtrodden, dependent, enslaved, vassal peasant. *Ant.* free, aristocratic, independent.

fever, temperature, heat, ardor, fire, agitation, excitement, mania frenzy, delirium, disease. *Ant.* calmness, coolness, health.

fiasco, debacle, catastrophe, failure, miscarriage. *Ant.* success completion, achievement, triumph, victory.

fickle, unreliable, uncertain, vacillating, variable, fanciful, unstable unsettled, inconstant, mutable, fitful, wavering, changeable, spasmodic, irresolute, unsteady, capricious, whimsical, unfixed, restless, purposeless, hesitant, volatile, wayward, shifting. *Ant.* steady, constant, settled, unchanging, resolute, persevering, firm determined, unshaken, fixed, steadfast, dependable, unswerving decided, definite, undeviating, regular, unwavering, faithful stanch, attached.

fiction, invention, myth, fable, story, creation, figment, romance, novel, legend, fabrication, epic, parable, allegory, falsehood, untruth, imagination, fancy. *Ant.* history, fact, reality, certainty, sureness, truth, verity, literalness, truthfulness, genuineness, authenticity, actuality, incident, occurrence, happening, event, circumstance, biography.

fictitious, false, untrue, feigned, spurious, counterfeit, imaginary, erroneous, fallacious, fabricated, sham, mendacious, fabulous, artificial, bogus, lying, fraudulent, untruthful, apocryphal, unreal, fanciful. *Ant.* true, proven, genuine, real, certain, authentic, veritable, reliable, official, recognized, factual, trustworthy, literal, authorized, exact, actual, positive, accurate, unquestioned, precise, correct, confirmed, guaranteed.

fidelity, conscientiousness, allegiance, fealty, trustworthiness, accuracy, constancy, integrity, faithfulness, devotion, loyalty, trueness, sincerity, steadfastness, obedience, resolution, adherence, support, devotedness, zeal, earnestness, ardor. *Ant.* unfaithfulness, treachery, chicanery, double-dealing, stratagem, falseness, trickery, perfidiousness, lying, disloyalty, insincerity, fluctuation, prevarication, vacillation, wavering, unsteadiness, inconstancy.

fidget, fret, fuss, worry, toss, twitch, jitter, chafe. *Ant.* rest, repose, relent, relax.

fiendish, devilish, malignant, infernal, malicious, atrocious, cruel, inhuman, diabolical, demoniac. *Ant.* angelic, benign, benevolent, kindly.

fierce, ferocious, enraged, violent, wild, fiery, brutal, barbarous, truculent, savage, passionate, angry, dangerous. *Ant.* gentle, mild, quiet, docile, soft, meek, placid, peaceful, tame, patient, kind, submissive, affectionate, harmless, tender, timid, innocent, inoffensive, innocuous.

fiery, fierce, passionate, unrestrained, vehement, ardent, spirited, mettlesome, fervid, impassioned, irascible, impetuous, choleric, angry, violent, furious, fanatical, inflamed, burning, enthusiastic, excited, intense, animated, vivacious. *Ant.* dull, phlegmatic, sluggish, moderate, subdued, monotonous, tiresome, uninteresting, flat, slow, prosy, commonplace, prosaic, vapid, cool.

fight, battle, contest, contend, dispute, brawl, clash, skirmish, box, wrangle, struggle, quarrel, strive.

figment, fiction, fantasy, falsehood, invention, fabrication, imagination. *Ant.* fact, reality, truth.

figurative, metaphorical, symbolic, allegorical, euphemistic, typical, representative, emblematical, florid, ornate, poetical. *Ant.* plain, straightforward, literal, honest, real.

figure, numeral, sum, amount, allegory, emblem, picture, symbol, type, metaphor, design, representation, character, outline, shape, form, appearance, construction.

file, arrangement, cabinet, drawer, chart, folder, line, row, column, list, index, catalog, record, dossier, rasp, tool.

fill, pack, pad, stuff, put, pour, load, swell, distend, feed, satisfy, complete, pervade, saturate, permeate, occupy, engage. *Ant.* empty, discharge, void, deplete, exhaust, drain, draw, use, remove, expend, waste, vacate, leave, scatter.

filter, strain, purify, clarify, separate, refine, sift, infiltrate, settle, screen.

final, last, extreme, decisive, terminal, ending, ultimate, definitive. *Ant.* opening, inceptive, embryonic, inaugural, first, continual, interim, unending, persistent.

financial, monetary, fiscal, pecuniary, sumptuary, budgetary.

find, meet, confront, ascertain, experience, detect, perceive, discover, furnish, observe, attain, recover, invent, procure, get, determine, reach, espy, discern, see, spy. *Ant.* lose, miss, fail, mislay, omit, forfeit, neglect, fall short, ruin, destroy, deprive of, abandon, block, thwart, misplace, prevent, overlook, forget, drop, forsake.

fine, *adj.* beautiful, attractive, choice, dainty, showy, rare, excellent, delicate, polished, good, courteous, refined, slender, minute, thin, admirable, nice, keen, suitable, exquisite, clarified, sharp, clear, smooth, small, pulverized, ground, elegant, handsome, subtle, pure, sensitive, slight, tenuous, splendid; *n.* penalty, forfeiture, forfeit, confiscation, sequestration, damage, amercement, cost, mulct, charge, loss, punishment. *Ant.* improper, coarse, clumsy, heavy, rude, thick, stout, awkward, blunt, rough, gross, indelicate, unrefined, vulgar, immodest, uncouth, brutish, bluff, indecorous, impolite, unbecoming, ignorant, churlish, surly, illiterate, rustic, insolent, impertinent, saucy, unpolished; reward, remuneration, recompense, indemnity, satisfaction, compensation, reimbursement, amends, requital.

finesse, tact, art, craft, cunning, strategy, duplicity, wiles, trickery, artifice, deception, skill, competence. *Ant.* openness, plainness, rudeness, honesty, clarity.

finish, end, completion, conclusion, close, termination, terminus. *Ant.* beginning, start, origin, source, initiation.

finite, limited, bounded, restricted, circumscribed, measurable, determinate. *Ant.* infinite, unbounded, eternal, endless.

firm, solid, strong, enduring, steadfast, steady, fixed, unyielding, tenacious, unfaltering, resolute, rugged, sturdy, stable, constant. *Ant.* weak, yielding, unsettled, loose, wobbling, defective, untied, deficient, unfastened, irresolute, wavering, unconnected, slack, unstable, disjointed.

fit, suitable, adapted, proper, appropriate, becoming, expedient, apt, adequate, apposite, congruous, competent, conformable, suited, correspondent, contrived, calculated, befitting, seemly, decorous, decent, pertinent, prepared, qualified. *Ant.* unfit, unsuitable, unfitting, ungainly, unseemly, untimely, amiss, misfitted, awkward, incongruous, ill-timed, inadequate, miscontrived, improper, miscalculated, misapplied, inappropriate, inexpedient.

fitful, spasmodic, capricious, intermittent, flickering, unstable, restless, uncertain, convulsive, variable, fickle, random, whimsical, desultory. *Ant.* steady, constant, uinform, even, certain, sure, fixed.

fix, determine, settle, establish, prepare, place, limit, fasten, bind, attach, locate, plant, secure, tie, apply, set, consolidate, decide, root, repair, correct, adjust, mend, restore. *Ant.* change, unsettle, weaken, unlock, unbolt, loosen, move, shake, disturb, unlatch, unfix, detach, disarrange, displace, free, neglect, ignore, corrupt, destroy.

flaccid, soft, flabby, weak, drooping, limber, lax, yielding, loose. *Ant.* firm, solid, strong, resisting, sturdy, steady, unyielding, tough, tenacious.

flag, decline, pall, sag, lag, languish, fail, droop, sink; signal, wave, gesture, indicate. *Ant.* restore, strengthen, rehabilitate, revive, reanimate; hide, disguise, sneak, lie low, lurk.

flagrant, glaring, atrocious, wicked, outrageous, infamous, gross, monstrous, rank. *Ant.* mild, restrained, moral.

flame, blaze, burn, light, ignite, flare. *Ant.* quench, extinguish.

flashy, garish, showy, meretricious, pretentious, flamboyant, gaudy, jazzy, ostentatious. *Ant.* sober, simple, quiet, subdued, natural, neat.

flat, dull, tasteless, insipid, depressed, heavy, unpleasing, dejected, spiritless, prostrate, fallen, horizontal, level, even, positive, low, absolute, plane, flush. *Ant.* sharp, acrid, bubbling, effervescing, lively, spirited, keen, frothy, raised, round, elevated, rough, uneven, hilly, rugged, mountainous.

flatter, praise, laud, exalt, fawn, cringe, extol, wheedle, blarney, cajole, caress, blandish, soothe, court, soften, placate, gratify, coax, please, satisfy, humor, entice. *Ant.* condemn, denounce, scorn, despise, mock, ignore, spurn, offend, displease, affront, taunt, disparage, belittle, anger, shock, annoy, ridicule, insult, scoff, disgrace, shame, abuse, jeer, sneer, deride.

flaunt, brandish, flourish, parade, blazon, display, advertise, expose, vaunt, flash. *Ant.* hide, conceal, disguise, cloak, retire, camouflage.

flavor, taste, gusto, savor, essence, relish, zest, aroma, spirit, soul, quality.

flawless, perfect, exact, whole, spotless, unmarred, immaculate, pure, impeccable, unblemished. *Ant.* imperfect, damaged, tainted, flawed, defective, disfigured.

fleeting, transient, transitory, evanescent, ephemeral, brief, short, flitting, temporary, passing, fugitive, vanishing, momentary. *Ant.* long, long-lived, enduring, lasting, constant, continual, fixed, unchanging, permanent, everlasting, unalterable, eternal, endless, perpetual.

flexible, pliant, supple, elastic, plastic, lithe, limber, yielding, pliable, bending, ductile, docile, tractable. *Ant.* stiff, unbending, inflexible, unyielding, stubborn, resistant, rigid, brittle, austere, obstinate, constrained, stern, rigorous, formal.

flicker, waver, fluctuate, flare, glint, quiver, shimmer, flutter. *Ant.* shine steadily, glow.

flimsy, thin, transparent, inane, poor, trifling, puerile, slight, weak, superficial, gauzy, shallow, unsubstantial, feeble, jerry-built. *Ant.* thick, solid, opaque, heavy, substantial, firm, strong, serious, sound, real, tough, unbreakable, stiff, tenacious, hard, durable.

flinch, shrink, wince, falter, recoil, cringe, blench, retreat, withdraw, run, cower. *Ant.* stand, face, confront, sustain, hold out.

fling, throw, heave, cast, pitch, chuck, toss. *Ant.* catch.

flippant, saucy, bold, impertinent, playful, pert, forward, glib, talkative, voluble, irreverent, careless, disrespectful. *Ant.* serious, respectful, reverent, reserved, quiet, courteous, retiring.

float, drift, fly, hover, wave, skim, sail, glide.

flock, group, herd, litter, hatch, pack, drove, brood, swarm, set, bevy, covey, lot, collection, company, throng, congregation, gathering. *Ant.* solitary (one).

florid, ornate, embellished, fancy, flowery, rhetorical, red-faced, ruddy, flushed, high-colored. *Ant.* simple, bland, straight-forward, unadorned, pale, pallid, pasty, colorless.

flourish, thrive, prosper, increase, accumulate, win, grow, triumph, lead, conquer, enlarge, boast, vaunt, twirl, wave, brandish, brag, shake. *Ant.* decay, diminish, weaken, decrease, sink, fall, lessen, decline, tumble, collapse, degenerate, deteriorate, pass, starve, wither, fade, die.

flout, scorn, disdain, spurn, jeer, mock, insult, ridicule, despise, sneer. *Ant.* revere, praise, esteem, respect.

flow, stream, issue, progress, float, run, course, glide, spout, gush, roll, move, pass, circulate. *Ant.* stop, stagnate, close up, check, prevent, cease, retard, cork, bottle up.

flower, bloom, blossom, expand, bud, burgeon, grow, mature, develop, open, unfold. *Ant.* droop, fade, flag, age, decline, sag, slip, wane, languish, die.

fluctuate, vacillate, waver, hesitate, digress, oscillate, deflect, sway, teeter, wander, detour, undulate, deviate, swerve, vary, veer, alter, change, vibrate, totter. *Ant.* stand, hold, remain, stay, persist, abide, stick, stop, cease, delay, postpone, decide.

fluent, flowing, liquid, moving, changing, changeable, voluble, glib, easy, smooth, ready, apt, expert, copious, prepared. *Ant.* slow, hesitant, stuttering, stammering, dull, prosy, unprepared, firm, heavy, dilatory, sluggish, still, motionless, inactive.

flurry, disturbance, agitation, hurry, bustle, squall, blow, commotion, hubbub, gust. *Ant.* quiet, calm.

flux, change, mutation, transition, flow, discharge, motion, activity, fluctuation. *Ant.* inactivity, constancy, fixity, stability.

fly, soar, hover, wing, skim, glide, ascend, rise, float, aviate, escape, flee, abscond. *Ant.* walk, remain, stay.

focus, center, centrum, concentration, limelight, cynosure.

foe, enemy, antagonist, adversary, attacker, opponent, combatant, hater, rival, competitor, defamer, vilifier, slanderer. *Ant.* friend, well-wisher, helper, assistant, companion, associate, adviser, ally, comrade, coadjutor, confidant, adherent.

foil, balk, check, circumvent, disappoint, thwart, defeat, frustrate. *Ant.* abet, advance, aid, further, assist, oblige, serve, promote.

folk, people, persons, individuals, family, group, crowd, race, nation, congregation, gathering, community, members, brotherhood, society, association, league.

follow, pursue, chase, accompany, succeed, copy, imitate, practice, ensue, use, conform, obey, chase, attend, observe, heed, mimic, understand, trace, track, trail. *Ant.* discard, reject, scorn, ignore, avoid, disregard, pass over, shun, elude, eschew, neglect, slight, abjure, misunderstand.

follower, pupil, attendant, servant, partisan, pursuer, adherent, disciple, successor, protege. *Ant.* enemy, antagonist, adversary, scorner, scoffer, objector, oppressor, rejecter, persecutor.

folly, foolishness, weakness, silliness, imbecility, absurdity, madness, imprudence, misconduct, fatuity, simplicity, weak-mindedness, shallowness. *Ant.* wisdom, prudence, sapience, knowledge, forethought, understanding, discernment, craftiness, judgment, cunning, artfulness, shrewdness, subtlety, astuteness, acuteness, wiliness, cleverness, ingenuity.

foment, encourage, abet, aid, excite, urge, instigate, promote, incite, stimulate, arouse. *Ant.* calm, dull, suppress, dampen, repress, discourage.

fondle, caress, pet, toy, cuddle, neck, nuzzle, stroke. *Ant.* reject, disdain.

fondness, affection, attachment, concern, love, kindness, regard, desire, devotion, ardor, liking, tenderness. *Ant.* aversion, hatred, dislike, antipathy, disgust, repugnance, enmity, opposition, spite.

fool, trick, deceive, cheat, delude, con, dupe, pretend, make believe, hoodwink, mystify. *Ant.* honor, respect, disabuse, clarify, authenticate.

foolhardy, rash, impetuous, incautious, headlong, precipitate, venturesome, reckless, headstrong, careless, thoughtless, regardless. *Ant.* cautious, prudent, thoughtful, watchful, careful, attentive, wary, calculating, discreet, guarded.

foolish, simple, silly, irrational, crazy, imbecile, brainless, ridiculous, nonsensical, absurd, preposterous, fatuous, witless. *Ant.* astute, wise, keen, thoughtful, cautious, careful, prudent, judicious, sagacious, discerning, sensible, circumspect, considerate.

forbear, abstain, refrain, pause, restrain, defer, avoid, desist, spare, delay, stop, cease, bear, tolerate, endure, suffer, stay. *Ant.* act, insist, accomplish, perform, do, persist, proceed, persevere, continue, pursue.

forbearance, patience, tolerance, leniency, fortitude. *Ant.* haste, impatience, intolerance, strictness.

forbid, prohibit, bar, restrain, oppose, preclude, interdict, obstruct, cancel, hinder, inhibit, prevent, deny, deprive, exclude. *Ant.* allow, sanction, encourage, recommend, commend, countenance, approve, authorize, order, command, abet, permit, confirm.

force, *n.* power, strength, energy, compulsion, coercion, duress, violence, vigor, might; organization, body, army, navy, aggregation, armament, troops, battalion, company, regiment, division, number; *v.* coerce, compel, drive, make, impel, necessitate, constrain, oblige, urge, incite, instigate, actuate, move, push, rush. *Ant.* weakness, uselessness, powerlessness, feebleness, debility, frailty, disability, inability, impotence, incapacity, incapability, incompetence, helplessness; restrain, obstruct, block, impede, hinder, hold, prevent, stay, check, repress, keep back, suppress, hamper, delay, retard, thwart.

foreboding, omen, premonition, worry, portent, dread, concern, presentiment, prediction, augury, prognostication, fear.

forecast, prediction, divination, prognostication, forethought, foresight, prescience, foreknowledge, foretoken, prognosis, estimate, foretelling, conjecture, prophecy, foreseeing, prevision, vaticination, augury. *Ant.* retrospect, recollection, reminiscence, retrospection, memory, hindsight.

forego, see **forgo.**

foreign, alien, strange, external, extraneous, extrinsic, outside, far, exotic, remote, distant, exterior, irregular, irrelevant, different, unnatural, unaccustomed, unknown. *Ant.* native, indigenous, near, regular, known, local, original, familiar, similar, like, accustomed, interior.

forerunner, herald, harbinger, predecessor, ancestor, precursor, forefather, scout, forebear, progenitor, pioneer, proclaimer, omen, vanguard, sign, warning. *Ant.* successor, descendant, disciple, follower, offspring, attendant, servant, dependent, trailer, sequel.

foresight, prescience, premeditation, forecast, forethought, preparation, foreknowledge, anticipation, prophecy, clairvoyance, carefulness, prognostication, economy, prudence. *Ant.* hindsight, impetuosity, rashness, ignorance, folly, carelessness, foolishness, wastefulness, waste, thoughtlessness.

forever, always, perpetually, everlastingly, eternally, continually, endlessly immortally, unremittingly. *Ant.* briefly, temporarily, shortly, fleetingly, transitorily.

forfeit, loss, fine, penalty, mulct, damages, amercement, relinquishment. *Ant.* gain, victory, profit, reward.

forge, construct, built, form, contrive, counterfeit, falsify, invent, fabricate, coin, produce, imitate, design, fashion, make, feign, trace, reproduce, duplicate, transcribe, copy.

forget, disregard, neglect, slight, overlook, omit, lose, ignore. *Ant.* recall, recollect, remember, reminisce.

forgive, except, excuse, acquit, absolve, remit, pardon, exempt, cancel, spare, clear, overlook, release, free, exonerate, exculpate. *Ant.* blame, impeach, arraign, charge, accuse, indict, retain, withhold, censure, discredit, retaliate, punish.

forgo, leave, resign, renounce, waive, relinquish, quit, desist, abstain, abandon. *Ant.* perform, fulfill, act, retain, keep, hold, accomplish, maintain, pursue, execute, undertake, continue, yield.

forgoing, antecedent, preceding, anterior, prior, former, previous, preliminary, precedent, antecedent, introductory. *Ant.* following, succeeding, subsequent, consequent, ensuing, posterior, behind.

forlorn, lonely, miserable, wretched, forgotten, forsaken, abandoned, helpless, depressed, solitary, alone, friendless, abject, deserted, destitute, bereft, deprived, comfortless, desolate, lonesome, dejected, cast down, pitiable. *Ant.* sociable, genial, communicative, merry, glad, gratified, happy, serene, gay, joyful, cheerful, delighted, animated, pleased, comfortable, satisfied, vivacious, exhilarated, blithe, sprightly, mirthful, lively, buoyant, spirited.

form, *v.* plan, devise, construct, fashion, mold, shape, make, constitute, organize, educate, frame, arrange, invent, produce, contrive, design, create, assemble, build, erect, compose, plot, figure; *n.* arrangement, appearance, outline, embodiment, formation, structure, conformation, sketch, representation, image, likeness, resemblance, state, condition, observance, ceremony, ritual. *Ant.* scatter, disarrange, wreck, ruin, destroy, devastate, dismantle, overthrow, demolish, revise, pull down, upset, damage, subvert, overturn, raze; irregularity, shapelessness, amorphism, deformity, monstrosity, distortion, mutilation, defacement.

formal, methodical, stiff, exact, precise, ritualistic, ceremonious, ceremonial, orderly, punctilious, official, systematic, pompous, impressive, solemn, functional, imposing, ministerial. *Ant.* ordinary, common, informal, casual, relaxed, normal, customary, usual, unconventional, habitual, normal, customary, comfortable, general.

former, foregoing, preceding, previous, anterior, antecedent, prior, before. *Ant.* later, after, succeeding, future, following, subsequent, latter, ensuing, consequential.

formidable, appalling, dreadful, impregnable, dangerous, terrible, menacing, impressive, awe-inspiring, shocking, tremendous, invincible, overwhelming, fearful, indomitable. *Ant.* inconspicuous, trivial, harmless, helpless, weak, feeble, despicable, contemptible, powerless, pleasant.

formulate, devise, frame, fabricate, concoct, express. *Ant.* hazard, guess, fumble.

forsake, fail, relinquish, quit, leave, drop, desert, abandon, forgo, renounce, disown, abjure, abdicate, resign. *Ant.* retain, remain, assist, aid, succor, persevere, continue, stay, sustain, nurture, comfort, help, claim, maintain, hold, keep, cherish.

forte, strong point, talent, skill, knack, genius, feature. *Ant.* incompetence, clumsiness, impotence.

forthwith, at once, right away, directly, instantly, immediately, *Ant.* never, shortly, eventually, later.

fortification, escarpment, breastwork, fortress, fort, blockhouse, trenches, castle, citadel, fastness, defenses, protection, parapet, bunker, wall, entrenchment, stronghold.

fortitude, resolution, heroism, endurance, courage, spirit, brawn, vigor, intrepidity, coolness, power, firmness, strength, patience, bravery, boldness, fearlessness, dauntlessness, enterprise, hardihood, forbearance, gallantry. *Ant.* cowardice, weakness, fear, spiritlessness, trepidation, fright, terror, timidity, panic, infirmity, consternation, enervation.

fortuitous, fortunate, contingent, incidental, random, accidental, casual, chance. *Ant.* deliberate, rehearsed, plotted, planned, arranged, calculated.

fortunate, successful, prosperous, auspicious, happy, lucky, satisfied, encouraging, propitious, providential, favorable, fortuitous, contented, advantageous. *Ant.* unhappy, dissatisfied, discontented, unlucky, unfortunate, miserable, adverse, untoward, ill-fated, jinxed, crushed, sorrowful, downcast, sad.

fortune, accident, end, goal, destiny, doom, luck, fate, chance, fortuity; judgment, determination; inheritance, wealth, riches, possession, property. *Ant.* misfortune, poverty, catastrophe, downfall, hardship.

forward, expedite, advance, encourage, promote, help, cultivate, favor, aid. *Ant.* discourage, impede, hinder, frustrate, stop, slow, hobble.

foster, favor, gratify, indulge, harbor, tend, nourish, nurse, encourage, cherish, promote, aid, please, humor, comfort, fondle, support. *Ant.* disregard, scorn, spurn, ignore, neglect, omit, overlook, shun, slight, leave, cast off, reject, disdain, abandon, discourage, hinder.

foul, offensive, polluted, tainted, defiled, impure, unclean, nasty, filthy, dirty, rotten, putrid, disgusting, fetid, decayed, diseased, tarnished, soiled, vitiated, contaminated, squalid, corrupt, fetid, decayed, diseased, carious, stinking, putrescent; obscene, coarse, vulgar, indecent, unfair, dishonest. *Ant.* undefiled, pure, clean, spotless, untainted, uncorrupted, untarnished, sterile, unsullied, immaculate, unblemished, fair, virgin, innocent, guileless, white, wholesome, gratifying, pleasing, speckless, good, becoming, just, honest, inviting, sound.

found, start, build, erect, originate, establish, institute, constitute, ground, plant, settle, raise, endow; cast, mold. *Ant.* destroy, raze, disestablish, terminate, dissolve.

foundation, substructure, origin, root, ground, basis, base, bottom, footing, understructure, rudiments, elements, groundwork, underpinning; establishment, endowment, institution. *Ant.* roof, dome, apex, crown, superstructure, arch, spire, tower, top, cupola, peak, pinnacle, vertex, summit.

fracas, quarrel, brawl, row, fight, disturbance, riot, uproar, dispute. *Ant.* peace, quiet, calmness, harmony, benignity.

fraction, percentage, section, part, segment, bit, piece, division, portion. *Ant.* whole, all, total, entirety.

fractious, fretful, peeved, peevish, testy, captious, cross, petulant, quick-tempered, snappish, waspish, pettish, perverse, irritable, touchy, refractory, bickering, quarrelsome, irascible. *Ant.* calm, mild, even-tempered, gentle, forbearing, meek, patient, enduring, unruffled, tranquil, agreeable, quiet, peaceful, tractable, cool, composed, self-possessed, dispassionate, undisturbed, placid.

fracture, rupture, rift, break, breach, crack, rent, split. *Ant.* union, juncture, conjugation.

fragile, weak, feeble, delicate, frail, brittle, infirm, breakable. *Ant.* hardy, robust, strong, tough, elastic, firm, vigorous, wiry, virile, resistant, unbreakable, coarse, thick, enduring, sinewy.

fragment, trimming, bit, scrap, piece, remnant, shard, fraction, chip, remainder, trace, residue. *Ant.* completeness, unity, entirety, sum, aggregate, total, all, whole.

fragrant, perfumed, sweet-smelling, aromatic, redolent, scented, spicy. *Ant.* stinking, noisome, malodorous, mephitic, noxious, foul, putrid.

frailty, infirmity, languor, feebleness, debility, weakness, foible, delicacy, imperfection, inability, puniness, lassitude, faintness. *Ant.* vigor, strength, vitality, hardiness, power, might, energy, ability, health, robustness, potency, puissance, lustiness, soundness.

frame, invent, fabricate, make, construct, fashion, form, build, compose, constitute, plan, devise, forge, mold, shape, contrive, adjust. *Ant.* destroy, ruin, scatter, wreck, cancel, demolish, raze.

franchise, patent, monopoly, license, right, vote, privilege, liberty, incorporation, suffrage, freedom, prerogative, charter, choice, voice. *Ant.* deprivation, serfdom, slavery, bondage, oppression, servitude, disaffirmation.

frank, candid, artless, sincere, open, familiar, easy, free, direct, honest, aboveboard, plain, ingenuous, straightforward. *Ant.* hypocritical, insincere, deceptive, secretive, dissembling, deceitful, reticent, indirect, dishonest, devious, cunning.

frantic, mad, distracted, frenzied, raving, raging, furious, violent, deranged, agitated, rabid, insane, delirious, crazy, wild, frenetic, berserk, overwrought, angry. *Ant.* peaceful, calm, quiet, meek, subdued, composed, tranquil, tractable, docile, collected, cool, kind, gentle, dispassionate, self-possessed.

fraternize, mingle, mix, affiliate, federate, consort, associate, concur, harmonize, intermingle, cooperate, unite, coalesce. *Ant.* disagree, quarrel, fight, argue, seclude, boycott, segregate.

fraud, cheat, deception, deceit, guile, duplicity, chicanery, artifice, imposture, circumvention, forgery, hoax, trickery, swindle, dishonesty, treachery, cheating. *Ant.* truth, integrity, honesty, good faith, justice, fairness, authenticity, sincerity, probity, frankness, equity, rectitude, right, conscientiousness.

fraudulent, deceitful, dishonest, counterfeit, false, wily, treacherous, fake, tricky, delusive, sham. *Ant.* honest, upright, valid, true, authentic.

freak, abnormality, monstrosity, vagary, whim, caprice, crotchet, humor, fancy, change, conceit, quirk, whimsy, inconstancy, unsteadiness, fickleness, sport, fluke, aberration, irregularity. *Ant.* normality, naturalness, conformity, perfectness, regularity, purpose, firmness, resolution, steadiness, honesty, steadfastness, constancy, resoluteness, resolve.

free, generous, liberal, bounteous, bountiful, munificent; frank, candid, artless, independent, familiar, open, unconfined, loose, unreserved, unrestricted, easy, clear, exempt, careless, footloose, unfettered, unobstructed, ingenuous, unencumbered, unattached, unconstrained, unrestrained; gratuitous, chargeless, gratis, costless. *Ant.* selfish, tight-fisted, enslaved, limited, confined, bound, restrained, incarcerated, compelled, barred, prevented, checked, curbed, suppressed, attached, detained, costly, restricted, dear, expensive, choice, chargeable, high-priced, expensive, scarce, precious, priceless.

freedom, independence, liberty, emancipation, frankness, openness, unrestrictedness, outspokenness, scope, latitude, license, unrestraint, liberality, privilege, exemption, franchise, prerogative, deliverance, right, advantage, self-government, immunity, boldness, familiarity, forwardness. *Ant.* serfdom, slavery, servitude, imprisonment, incarceration, confinement, bondage, subjection, submission, deprivation, dependence, subordination, abasement, restriction, restraint, captivity, drudgery, limitation, coercion, hindrance, compulsion, difficulty.

freight, cargo, shipment, burden, load, transportation, lading.

frenzy, rage, fury, derangement, mania, transport, aberration, madness, agitation, wildness, excitement, delirium. *Ant.* delight, rapture, ecstasy, calmness, sanity.

frequent, repeated, many, general, recurrent, numerous, continual, common, usual, recurring, regular, periodic. *Ant.* infrequent, rare, unusual, uncommon, irregular, sporadic, occasional.

frequently, regularly, often, usually, persistently, repeatedly. *Ant.* seldom, infrequently, rarely.

fresh, novel, new, recent, vivid, modern, natural, unused, vigorous, healthy, hardy, unwearied, young, green, raw, sweet; impertinent, bold, cheeky, flippant. *Ant.* trite, stale, hackneyed, shopworn, tired; courteous, respectful, deferential.

ret, gnaw, gall, chafe, corrode, agitate, disturb, rub, anger, vex, annoy, worry, fidget. *Ant.* soothe, please, soften, comfort, calm, smooth, placate, heal, ignore.

retful, cross, peevish, captious, irritable, worried, anxious, annoying, nagging. *Ant.* kind, calm-tempered, appeasing, soothing, easy-going, comforting, cheerful, relaxed.

riction, rubbing, attrition, traction, abrasion, erosion, grating, frication, sanding; disagreement, conflict, disharmony, discord. *Ant.* smoothness, lubrication; accord, unity, consensus, harmony, agreement.

riend, companion, associate, acquaintance, familiar, colleague, ally, comrade, advocate, benefactor, crony, pal, mate, adherent, coadjutor, partner, assistant, supporter, confidant. *Ant.* enemy, opponent, adversary, calumniator, vilifier, slanderer, foe, competitor, antagonist, rival.

riendly, conciliatory, favorable, sympathetic, helpful, kind, kindly, loving, sociable, neighborly, well-disposed, amicable, propitious, fond, affectionate, attentive, intimate, peaceable, brotherly, genial, agreeable, accessible, cordial, companionable, tender, affable, solicitous, hearty. *Ant.* unfriendly, unsociable, unkind, antagonistic, envious, ill-disposed, censorious, uncharitable, fault-finding, grouchy, combative, opposing, nagging, deceptive, treacherous, false, grudging, harmful, prejudicial, pernicious, cool, hostile, adverse, grumbling, disaffected, contentious, estranged, inimical, alienated, reserved, distant.

righten, terrify, dismay, intimidate, appall, daunt, scare, affright, browbeat, alarm, shock, abash, dishearten, dispirit, startle, threaten, hector, discourage, astound, horrify, depress. *Ant.* reassure, buoy up, encourage, strengthen, invigorate, relieve, vitalize, hearten, animate, inspirit, inspire, incite, gladden, exhilarate, enliven, cheer, impel, embolden, rouse, stimulate, excite, comfort, energize, urge.

rightful, terrible, shocking, calamitous, dire, alarming, dreadful, fearful, terrifying, awful, horrible, horrid, hideous, abominable, disgusting, detestable, ugly, appalling, astounding, direful, grim, ghastly, grisly, gruesome, loathsome. *Ant.* encouraging, heartening, pleasing, appealing, attractive, charming, fascinating, lovely, agreeable, handsome, beautiful, lovely, beguiling, inviting, admirable, delightful, gratifying, lovable, amiable.

rigid, ice-cold, arctic, chilling, cool; passionless, lifeless, reserved, inhibited, unresponsive, dull, rigid, formal. *Ant.* warm, temperate; amorous, ardent, fervid, responsive, uninhibited.

rill, decoration, ruffle, pleat, ruff; affectation, extravagance, inessential. *Ant.* necessity, essential, fundamental, heart.

ringe, border, edge, outskirts, boundary, edging, perimeter, tassel, flounce, trimming. *Ant.* interior, inside, center, heart, core.

frivolous, foolish, gay, playful, flippant; puerile, childish, indecorous immature, inconsequential, small, paltry, insignificant, inconsiderable, light, futile, little, shallow, petty, trifling, picayune vain, idle. *Ant.* wise, important, earnest, serious, weighty solemn, grave, mature, adult, sensible, thoughtful, formal, deep sound, salient, relevant, significant, essential, momentous, dignified, pertinent, applicable.

frolic, gambol, sport, frisk, romp, lark, caper, escapade, fun, prank revel.

front, forepart, van, anterior, facade, face, prow; brow, forehead; manner, mien, bearing. *Ant.* rear, back, astern, posterior.

frontier, boundary, limits, edge, hinterlands, borderland, new land wilderness. *Ant.* heartland, interior, center, inland, settlements.

frown, sulk, glower, scowl, glare, lower, disapprove. *Ant.* beam smile, shine, approve.

frugality, carefulness, economy, providence, conservation, thrift management, husbandry, parsimony, chariness, saving, miserliness, scrimping, providence, foresight, moderation, stinginess penuriousness. *Ant.* destruction, lavishness, waste, luxuriousness, liberality, extravagance, spending, prodigality, indulgence voluptuousness, wastefulness, superfluity, excess, profuseness squandering, gratification.

fruitful, plenteous, plentiful, productive, prolific, fertile, fecund luxuriant, rich, abundant, yielding, ample, copious, bountiful exuberant. *Ant.* empty, unproductive, barren, fruitless, futile childless, unprofitable, sterile, bare, unyielding, useless, arid impotent, ineffective, unsuccessful, exhausted, spent, depleted worn out, drained.

frustrate, balk, foil, defeat, disappoint, circumvent, nullify, bar baffle, confound, thwart, disconcert, hinder, stop, counteract prevent. *Ant.* encourage, accomplish, assist, help, cooperate support, aid, succor, satisfy, foster, befriend, forward, facilitate countenance, abet, stimulate.

fugitive, *n.,* deserter, runaway, truant, outcast, vagabond, refugee escapee; *adj.* ephemeral, elusive, fleeting, erratic, volatile. *Ant* prisoner, captive, convict, parolee; persistent, stable, obvious manifest, enduring.

fulfill, do, execute, perform, complete, effect, accomplish, comply satisfy, achieve, end, consummate, finish, realize, terminate discharge, effectuate, attain, enforce. *Ant.* neglect, fail, omit miss, disappoint, cease, quit, forsake, stop, abandon, resign withdraw, ignore, relinquish, forgo.

full, complete, replete, glutted, swollen, abounding, surfeited, sufficient, stocked, ample, whole, sated. *Ant.* incomplete, starved void, empty, unsatisfied, hungry.

fulminate, curse, denounce, menace, rage, swear, inveigh, rave thunder; explode, detonate. *Ant.* praise, support, defend, help appease, aid; defuse, dampen.

fulsome, excessive, gross, coarse, offensive, loathsome, nauseous, rank, sickening, displeasing, abhorrent, disgusting, detestable, odious, obnoxious. *Ant.* pleasant, pleasing, acceptable, suitable, agreeable, moderate, gratifying, delightful, satisfying, satisfactory, encouraging, comforting, soothing.

fun, *n.* enjoyment, merriment, frolic, amusement, diversion, gaiety, glee, entertainment, pleasantry, sport, play. *Ant.* sadness, dullness, melancholy, woe.

function, *n.* role, job, task, position, bailiwick, duty, office, business; *v.* work, do, serve, perform, operate, preside, moderate, officiate. *Ant.* unemployment, idleness; fail (to do), ignore, malfunction, misconduct, mismanage.

fundamental, principal, radical, essential, basic, chief, intrinsic, primary, indispensable, elemental. *Ant.* subordinate, superficial, secondary, auxiliary, dispensable.

fumble, err, blunder, miss, fail, botch, mismanage, misplay, stumble, stammer, feel, grope.

fume, fret, rave, rage, resent, bristle, bridle, seethe, storm, foam, chafe, bluster, curse; vaporize, smoke, fumigate, darken (wood). *Ant.* calm, subside, reconcile (oneself), stifle.

funereal, sad, solemn, somber, dark, sepulchral, dismal, woeful, black, death-like, lugubrious, grim. *Ant.* cheerful, happy, joyous, blithe, exuberant, animated, lively.

funny, humorous, ludicrous, diverting, comical, amusing, bizarre, droll, absurd, odd, ridiculous, laughable, witty. *Ant.* sober, grave, serious, melancholy, sad, humorless.

furious, dashing, angry, vehement, boisterous, violent, sweeping, impetuous, rolling, desperate, mad, fierce, raging, distracted, stormy, frantic, passionate, wild, ferocious, savage, turbulent, wrathful, frenzied, delirious, crazy, insane, infuriated, rabid, excited, inflamed, fuming, unbalanced, deranged. *Ant.* meek, mild, peaceful, quiet, cool, calm, kind, pleased, tranquil, pacific, satisfied, contented, unruffled, smooth, placid, composed, easy, undisturbed, dispassionate, self-possessed, suave, bland, affable, complaisant, gracious, moderate, polite, urbane.

furnish, supply, equip, give, yield, present, provide, purvey, cater, appoint, outfit, fit. *Ant.* dismantle, strip, denude, withhold.

furniture, equipment, fittings, apparatus, movables, supplies, furnishings, appointments.

further, promote, assist, support, advance, expedite, aid. *Ant.* hinder, frustrate, impede, delay, check, obstruct.

furtive, clandestine, sly, secret, covert, stealthy, surreptitious. *Ant.* aboveboard, forthright, open, overt.

fuse, merge, join, unify, anneal, unite, blend, amalgamate, meld, melt, dissolve, mix, coalesce, commingle, homogenize, intermingle, solder, braze, weld, combine, integrate. *Ant.* separate, cut, disperse, divide.

futile

futile, ineffective, vain, useless, fruitless, inefficient, ineffectual, valueless, unsatisfying, resultless, empty, idle, abortive, unavailing, trivial, trifling. *Ant.* satisfactory, effective, fruitful, productive, efficient, yielding, profitable, advantageous, lucrative, instrumental, gainful, beneficial, helpful, useful, conducive.

G

gaiety, cheerfulness, glee, happiness, animation, joy, good humor, hilarity, jollity, blithesomeness, merriment, joviality, mirth, vivacity; finery, glitter, flashiness, sparkle, show. *Ant.* sadness, dullness, unhappiness, misery, plainness, simplicity, drabness.

gain, profit, increase, acquire, earn, win, attain, obtain, realize, reap, get, accomplish, reach, procure, achieve, effect, secure, benefit, consummate. *Ant.* lose, miss, spend, expend, forfeit, waste, exhaust, squander, decrease, lavish, scatter, destroy, disperse, dissipate.

gait, walk, stride, step, pace, movement, canter, progress, rate.

galaxy, assemblage, company, cluster, group, collection, bevy, array, constellation.

gallant, chivalrous, brave, bold, courageous, heroic, intrepid, fearless, valiant, valorous, splendid, mighty, strong, undaunted, kind, noble, daring, attentive, courteous, high-minded, polite, affable, manly, urbane, high-spirited, stout-hearted, gay, showy, magnificent. *Ant.* timorous, cowardly, fearful, effeminate, soft, craven, dastardly, poor-spirited, mean, base, contemptible, rude, discourteous, ill-bred, unpolished, impolite, rough, churlish, ungentlemanly.

galling, chafing, annoying, vexatious, vexing, irritating, rubbing, nagging, excoriating, troublesome, provoking, teasing, worrying, distressing, tantalizing. *Ant.* soothing, emollient, consoling, mollifying, soft, assuaging, mitigating, allaying, improving, appeasing, comforting, satisfying.

gamble, risk, wager, bet, speculate, stake, hazard, play, chance, expose. *Ant.* invest, plan, safeguard, insure.

game, *n.* pastime, play, recreation, frolic, sport, diversion, fun, amusement, merriment, festivity, entertainment, spree, prank, lark, gambol, merrymaking, gaiety, adventure, venture, enterprise, scheme; *adj.* sporting, willing, daring, disposed, favorable, nervy, courageous, valiant. *Ant.* drudgery, work, toil, melancholy, sadness, labor, uneasiness, grief, sorrow; cowardly, unwilling, cautious, disinclined.

gamut, register, scope, extent, range, scale, compass.

gap, hollow, chasm, breach, chink, rift, crevice, cleft, cavity, hiatus, lacuna, space, passage, opening, interstice, vacancy, crack, hole, vacuity, aperture, fissure, orifice. *Ant.* fence, enclosure, barrier, bolt, rail, wall, barricade, obstacle, shield, defense, obstruction, stricture, impediment.

garment, clothing, attire, garb, dress, vestment, habiliment, robe, apparel, wrap.

garble, corrupt, distort, deface, misstate, misquote, mutilate, pervert, mix, muddle, scramble, falsify, misrepresent. *Ant.* quote, state, communicate, correct, edit, unscramble, clarify.

garish, ostentatious, showy, tawdry, dazzling, flashy, gaudy, glaring, blatant, vulgar, ornate, flamboyant. *Ant.* modest, sober, discreet, quiet, somber.

garner, collect, harvest, accumulate, hoard, store, deposit, husband, treasure, save, reserve. *Ant.* dissipate, spend, waste, strew.

garnish, adorn, embellish, decorate, deck, beautify, enhance, furnish, ornament, bedeck, array, strew, grace, trim. *Ant.* deface, spoil, disfigure, mar, impair, injure, strip, dismantle, destroy, raze, obliterate, erase, deteriorate, harm, damage, hurt.

garrulous, wordy, prolix, prattling, verbose, chattering, loquacious, talkative, bumptious, babbling, self-assertive. *Ant.* reserved, still, silent, taciturn, quiet, speechless, reticent, laconic, modest, pithy, retiring, restrained, terse, brief, melancholy, moody.

gather, accumulate, collect, meet, assemble, amass, congregate, pick, group, convoke, convene, muster, cull, herd, contract, marshal, pile, heap, store, acquire, attract, garner, summon, deduce, infer. *Ant.* spread, strew, scatter, disperse, disseminate, dissipate, apportion, dole, dispose, distribute, allot, dispense, deal, disband, diffuse, assign, adjourn, separate.

gauche, blundering, uncouth, awkward, inept, clumsy, unpolished, immature, clownish. *Ant.* deft, skillful, adroit, dexterous, mature, polished.

gaudy, glittering, tawdry, flashy, showy, gay, ornamented, adorned, alluring, garish, vulgar, cheap, tasteless, brilliant, dazzling, glaring, sparkling, frilly, bright, scintillating, shining, flashing, flamboyant, glistening, glossy. *Ant.* plain, refined, dull, simple, tasteful, somber, lustreless, solemn, ugly, uninteresting, tarnished, gloomy, dark, obscure, shaded, dusky, dismal, faded, colorless, dim, darkened, pale, rusty, withered, blanched.

gauge, measure, size, caliber, diameter, thickness, template, norm, standard, criterion, evaluation, calculation. *Ant.* guess, hazard, estimate.

gaunt, scraggy, emaciated, haggard, bony, meager, lank, skinny, attenuated, slender, thin, lean, spare, shriveled, hollow, empty, hungry, withered, shrunken. *Ant.* stout, fat, obese, heavy, robust, plethoric, gross, corpulent, plump, fleshy, brawny, portly, lusty, well-fed, well-developed, strong, hearty, hale, vigorous.

gay, blithe, lively, merry, hilarious, sportive, sprightly, frolicsome, showy, jovial, joyous, jolly, cheerful, buoyant, bright, happy, affable, vivacious, blithesome, convivial, festive, jocose, witty, comical, waggish, humorous, colorful, entertaining. *Ant.* dull, morose, grouchy, discouraged, listless, solemn, sullen, moody sulky, melancholy, unhappy, sour, spiritless, languid, splenetic gloomy, petulant, depressed, angry, cross, grim, crushed, color less, low-spirited, dejected.

gaze, gawk, gape, watch, stare, observe, peer, look. *Ant.* ignore disregard, overlook.

genealogy, descent, ancestry, stock, parentage, lineage, pedigree progeniture, family, history.

general, universal, common, widespread, comprehensive, inclusive commonplace, usual, prevalent, public, customary, generic, or dinary, normal, prevailing, frequent, everyday, popular, familiar habitual, unlimited, extensive, whole, all-embracing, indefinite conventional. *Ant.* particular, rare, limited, definite, infrequent circumscribed, unusual, uncommon, remarkable, unwonted, excep tional, extraordinary, singular, unique, individual, single, alone only, sole, specific.

generalization, analysis, deduction, conclusion, summary, summation axiom, popularization. *Ant.* specificity, uniqueness, exception particularization.

generally, chiefly, usually, ordinarily, commonly, mainly, princi pally. *Ant.* especially, particularly, rarely, seldom, infrequently occasionally.

generation, production, engendering, formation, race, breed, stock kind, reproduction, creation, procreation, children, family, age progeny, caste, era, span, period. *Ant.* wreckage, destruction breakdown, obliteration, dissolution, abolition.

generic, general, typical, ideal, characteristic, representative, com prehensive. *Ant.* particular, individual, special, peculiar.

generous, noble, beneficent, liberal, bountiful, honorable, charitable free, open-handed, munificent, open-hearted, high-minded, mag nanimous, chivalrous, unselfish, whole-hearted, forgiving. *Ant* selfish, miserly, closefisted, parsimonious, illiberal, sparing, pe nurious, stingy, uncharitable, avaricious, mean, sordid, greedy grasping, covetous, petty, rapacious.

genial, kind, cordial, pleasing, warm-hearted, pleasant, cheering hearty, merry, affable, jovial, outgoing, mild, courteous, inspir ing, complaisant, benign, gracious, urbane, polite, blithe, jolly convivial, cheerful, brotherly, fraternal, well-disposed, hospitable buoyant, sunny, congenial, joyful, lively, enlivening, joyous, spir ited, sprightly, animated. *Ant.* moody, dull, dolorous, gloomy inhospitable, sorrowful, grouchy, doleful, dismal, sulky, morose sullen, melancholy, petulant, peevish, solemn, cross, austere stern, grim, cranky, crusty, irritable, testy, surly, rough, per verse, eccentric, rude, dispiriting, fretful, pensive.

genius, brilliance, talent, expertise, adroitness, intellect, skill, bent brains, character, nature, adeptness, ability, disposition, gift capacity, power, aptitude, endowment, knack, leaning, quality, faculty, wisdom, astuteness, propensity, perspicacity, grasp, judgment, sagacity, discernment, acumen, wit. *Ant.* ignorance, witlessness, idiocy, folly, incapacity, silliness, imbecility, inability, moroseness, stupidity, foolishness, asininity, brainlessness, incompetence, stolidity, shallowness, obtuseness, fatuity, ineptitude, senility, ineptness, inaptitude, inaptness, irrationality, simplicity.

genteel, polished, polite, well-bred, urbane, refined, cultured, pleasing, graceful, fashionable, well-mannered, elegant, well-behaved, accomplished, courteous, kind, kingly, appropriate, stylish, congenial. *Ant.* rough, gruff, uncultured, unrefined, gross, coarse, dull, stupid, dense, thick, boorish, doleful, severe, sullen, surly, rugged, stern, harsh, stubborn, clownish, rustic, rude, ill-bred, dowdy, ill-mannered, censorious, captious, disagreeable, odious, repulsive, forbidding, repelling, repugnant.

gentle, kind, tender, mild, bland, placid, peaceful, docile, meek, soft, tame, soothing, suave, moderate, temperate, calm, benign, easy, pacific, serene, balmy, sweet, pleasing, yielding, light, genteel, tractable, compliant. *Ant.* uncultured, boorish, rough, coarse, uncouth, harsh, excessive, strong, rude, wild, barbarous, vulgar, unpolished, clownish, ill-tempered, gross, ill-mannered, uncivil, stormy, boisterous, ungracious.

genuine, veritable, real, unadulterated, tested, proven, unmixed, authentic, natural, true, frank, valid, unalloyed, unaffected, actual, right, legitimate, factual, sincere, honest, unquestionable, exact. *Ant.* meretricious, false, deceptive, questionable, unreal, unacceptable, adulterated, illegitimate, mixed, compounded, alloyed, jumbled, confused, blended, erroneous, misleading, fallacious, bogus, spurious, counterfeit, sham, assumed, mock.

germ, beginning, source, origin, embryo, bud, fount, sprout, sprig, root, offshoot, rudiment, principle, spore, microorganism, virus, microbe, element, bacterium, pathogen, seed. *Ant.* outgrowth, issue, end, fruit, conclusion.

germane, pertinent, related, fitting, relevant, apropos, cognate, appropriate, allied. *Ant.* irrelevant, unfitting, unrelated, inapplicable, inapposite.

germinate, sprout, bud, grow, shoot, develop, swell, vegetate, evolve, effloresce. *Ant.* die.

gesture, action, attitude, movement, motion, posture, carriage, pose, behavior, manner, bearing, deportment, conduct, signal, indication, sign.

get, procure, receive, obtain, achieve, attain, earn, gain, acquire, win, secure, capture, seize, learn, comprehend, grasp, propagate, arrive, reach, generate. *Ant.* relinquish, quit, leave, renounce, forgo, surrender, retract, withdraw, repudiate, desert, vacate, abjure, foreswear, forsake, release, lose, misunderstand, misconstrue, sacrifice, abnegate.

ghastly, hideous, wan, pallid, shocking, grim, deathly, cadaverous, ashen, spectral, ghostly, unearthly, unnatural, weird, uncanny, terrible, terrifying, horrible, grisly, frightful, dreadful, revolting, awe-inspiring. *Ant.* healthy, ruddy, pleasing, agreeable, nice, pleasant, beautiful, wholesome, rosy, fine, lovely, appealing, captivating, attractive, delightful, alluring, compelling, enticing, fascinating, strong, vigorous, blooming.

ghost, specter, vision, shadow, haunt, wraith, apparition, sprite, soul, spirit, goblin, image, phantom, banshee, fairy, appearance, delusion, hallucination. *Ant.* matter, substance, reality, body, materiality, substantiality, actuality, fact, essence, existence, being.

giant, monstrous, titanic, huge, enormous, large, immense, colossal, super, vast, gigantic, whopping. *Ant.* miniature, pygmy, tiny, little, minute, dwarf, puny, stunted, microscopic, infinitesimal.

gibe, jeer, flout, sneer, scoff, mimic, deride, taunt, mock, ridicule, harass, fool, chaff, tease, plague, vex, provoke, irritate, annoy, torment. *Ant.* exalt, praise, encourage, laud, foster, respect, applaud, inspirit, commend, animate, inspire, incite, forward, urge, elevate, instigate, impel, approve, sanction, support, advance, admire, recommend.

giddy, light-headed, light, dizzy, faint, vertiginous, mutable, unsteady, shaky, doddering, uncertain, thoughtless, unreliable, gay, flighty, romantic, careless, capricious, fanciful, chimerical, dazed, unbalanced, wild, irresponsible, frivolous, silly, vain. *Ant.* solemn, steady, serious, reliable, consistent, constant, firm, uniform, regular, calm, well-balanced, equable, level-headed, cool, grave, dependable, conservative, stable, earnest, sedate, sober, settled, attentive, careful, sensible.

gift, donation, present, largess, benefaction, gratuity, alms, endowment, bounty, bequest, legacy, provision, charity, munificence, bonus, boon, favor, bestowal, kindness, benevolence, liberality, support, maintenance, talent, knack, aptitude. *Ant.* privation, loss, deprivation, forfeiture, forfeit, penalty, detriment, confiscation, indemnity, sequestration, subtraction, disinheritance.

gigantic, immense, huge, enormous, colossal, prodigious, amazing, vast, monstrous, titanic, great, extensive, massive, mammoth, bulky, stupendous. *Ant.* dwarfish, small, little, short, minute, Lilliputian, abridged, contracted, diminutive, insignificant, inconsiderable, slight, emaciated, slender, wizened.

gimmick, gadget, contrivance, angle, point, device, trick, swindle, adjunct, fraud.

gird, secure, bind, strap, encircle, surround, fortify, support, endow, girdle, clothe, equip, invest, furnish, arm. *Ant.* loosen, untie, release, strip, divest.

girth, size, circumference, perimeter, outline, boundary, measure, cinch, dimensions, corpulence.

gist, pith, substance, essence, point, core, meaning, significance, basis, sense, crux, tenor, upshot.

give, confer, bestow, grant, donate, bequeath, furnish, yield, impart, convey, supply, present, deliver. *Ant.* deprive, take, bereave, dispossess, divest, strip, steal, seize, remove, withhold, retain, keep, rob, hold, receive, accept.

glad, cheerful, pleased, gratified, joyful, exulting, cheering, joyous, merry, happy, delighted, inspiring, content, jolly, blithesome, gay, pleasing, vivacious, lively. *Ant.* sorrowful, sad, peevish, cranky, melancholy, dejected, censorious, mournful, oppressed, heavy, depressed, dispirited, downcast, grieved, disapproving, pessimistic, grouchy, discouraged.

glamour, charm, fascination, allure, appeal, bewitchment, magic, enchantment, aura, spell, attraction. *Ant.* dullness, blandness, obscurity, lackluster.

glance, sight, peep, look, view, glimpse; graze, brush, touch.

glare, scintillate, glisten, coruscate, flash, shine, glitter, glimmer, reflect, flicker, gleam, glow, shimmer, beam, sparkle, twinkle, dazzle, radiate; stare, glower, frown, scowl.

glassy, smooth, vitreous, brittle, glabrous, polished, transparent, crystalline, limpid, dull-eyed, expressionless, glossy, translucent, lustrous, silken, bright. *Ant.* dim, lusterless, dull, opaque, obscure, rough, jagged, uneven, cloudy, rugged, tarnished.

gleam, flash, shine, shimmer, sparkle, glitter, ray, glint.

glee, merriment, joviality, gaiety, joyfulness, hilarity, mirth, joy, exhilaration, elation, jollity, sprightliness, liveliness, animation, vivacity, frolic, fun, cheerfulness. *Ant.* dullness, gloom, sadness, sorrow, melancholy, listlessness, depression, despondency, dejection, lamentation, wretchedness, unhappiness, abjection, grief.

glib, fluent, facile, voluble, vocal, articulate, smooth, urbane, suave, oily. *Ant.* faltering, stammering, quiet, inarticulate, implausible, shy, reticent, uncommunicative.

glisten, gleam, glitter, flash, scintillate, shine, sparkle, twinkle.

gloat, boast, rejoice, triumph, brag, crow, exult, revel, delight, flaunt. *Ant.* sympathize, condole, commiserate.

gloomy, dusky, clouded, dim, shady, dark; sad, cheerless, glum, low-spirited, down-hearted, downcast, dejected, oppressive, melancholy, funereal, depressed, heavy, dull, crestfallen, morose, depressing, moody, sorrowful, pensive, sullen, unhappy, miserable, pessimistic, discouraged, discontented. *Ant.* joyful, joyous, light-hearted, rejoicing, merry, buoyant, cheerful, satisfied, light, contented, happy, animated, uplifted, sparkling, blithe, sprightly, vivacious, exulting, lively, jolly, sunny, optimistic, glowing, clear, bright, serene.

glorify, magnify, exalt, extol, worship, praise, celebrate, adore, bless, honor, reverence, revere, esteem, venerate, idolize, appreciate, prize, value, elevate, commend, applaud, laud, exaggerate, flatter,

glorious

sanctify. *Ant.* abase, debase, lower, condemn, contemn, despise, mock, degrade, sully, humble, humiliate, shame, reproach, censure, disparage.

glorious, famous, renowned, illustrious, exalted, noble, distinguished, splendid, resplendent, admirable, celebrated, wonderful, brilliant, marvelous, wondrous, shining. *Ant.* infamous, disgraceful, shameful, odious, ignominious, opprobrious, heinous, wicked, scandalous, ridiculous, contemptible, flagrant, atrocious, modest, moderate.

glossy, shining, reflecting, even, smooth, polished, lustrous, glazed, sleek, velvety, elegant, refined, polite; specious, showy, deceptive, superficial. *Ant.* dull, lusterless, clouded, dimmed, unpolished, stained, sullied, soiled, tarnished, rough, ruffled, uneven; unrefined, uncouth; genuine, pure, valid, honest, scrupulous.

glow, burn, flush, light, blaze, radiate, flame, shine, gleam, flare. *Ant.* fade, die.

glum, morose, moody, dejected, surly, dismal, blue, sullen, gloomy, dispirited, low. *Ant.* lighthearted, happy, cheerful, joyous, gay, spirited, jaunty, buoyant.

glut, fill, cloy, stuff, gorge, surfeit, satiate, cram, deluge, flood, satisfy, devour, consume, overeat. *Ant.* abstain, fast, cease, restrain, reduce, subdue, forbear, relinquish, moderate, curb, diet, repress, deny, control.

glutinous, adhesive, gluey, viscous, gummy, sticky, cohesive, viscid. *Ant.* glueless, dry, clean, slippery, powdery.

gnarled, knotty, twisted, rugged, contorted, knotted. *Ant.* smooth, straight, plain, direct.

go, move, pass, proceed, disappear, begin, depart, walk, decamp, step, travel, stir, retire, leave, abscond, run, budge, retreat, withdraw, recede, desert, relinquish, abandon. *Ant.* come, become, arrive, appear, approach, enter, stop.

goad, prod, spur, pressure, impel, push, force, motivate, provoke, urge, prompt, jog. Ant. dissuade, deter, discourage, restrain, divert.

goal, aim, object, destination, end, ambition, intention; target, finish line, basket, end zone.

godly, righteous, devout, godlike, religious, pious, holy, reverent, humble, submissive, hallowed, devotional, moral, saintly, divine, consecrated, sinless, inviolate, pure, incorrupt, stainless, sacred, immaculate, celestial, devoted. *Ant.* ungodly, sinful, impious, profane, evil, bad, wicked, godless, irreverent, irreligious, unholy, unhallowed, heathen, sacrilegious, unsanctified, worldly, immoral, vile, corrupt, iniquitous, depraved.

gorge, satiate, glut, fill, stuff, sate, gobble, bolt, cram, surfeit. *Ant.* starve, fast, diet.

good, righteous, upright, benevolent, just, true, honest, virtuous, well-behaved, moral, chaste, pure, untainted, unspotted, sinless, incorrupt, fine, stainless, honorable, conscientious, sound, valid, serviceable, real, genuine, reputable, suitable, fit, proper, useful, propitious, appropriate, valuable, agreeable, satisfactory, strong, satisfying, pleasant, complete, reliable, health-giving, invigorating, gratifying. *Ant.* bad, evil, wicked, vile, sinful, depraved, impure, corrupt, disgraceful, dishonorable, unsound, dishonest, contemptible, vicious, debased, base, abandoned, abominable, foul, execrable, hateful, abhorrent, loathsome, odious, horrible, rotten, detestable, offensive, unsuitable, disagreeable, unpleasant, unhealthy, noxious, deleterious, injurious.

goodwill, patronage, prestige, advertising, standing, attitude, reputation, friendliness, favor, kindness, benevolence, zeal, ardor, earnestness. *Ant.* ill will, notoriety, bad repute, unfriendliness, unkindness.

goods, material, merchandise, property, effects, chattels, freight, ware, stock, belongings, commodities.

gorgeous, superb, grand, surpassing, stately, magnificent, glorious, splendid, great, resplendent, majestic, imposing, affecting, impressive, lavish, gay, brilliant, dazzling, attractive. *Ant.* plain, simple, unpretentious, unimpressive, ordinary, common, tawdry, dull, modest, lowly, customary, usual, unadorned, homely, insignificant, unimposing, commonplace, unattractive.

gossip, chatter, chitchat, scandal, hearsay, prattle, tattle, rumor, newsmongering, palaver. *Ant.* news, statement, announcement, publication, declaration, proclamation.

gossamer, feathery, sheer, light, cobwebby, ethereal, frothy, gauzy, diaphanous. *Ant.* heavy, substantial, solid, gross, coarse.

govern, rule, direct, control, moderate, command, manage, guide, curb, influence, mold, restrain, minister, reign, dictate, administer, conduct, supervise, dominate, regulate, oversee, lead, check, adjust, order, superintend. *Ant.* obey, assent, comply, yield, submit, accede, fulfill, perform, follow, agree to, cede, surrender, acquiesce, consent, conform, give way, permit, suffer, allow.

government, rule, order, law, authority, administration, sway, control, constitution, state, kingdom, republic, democracy, polity, sovereignty, empire, method, system, regulation, direction. *Ant.* anarchy, rebellion, confusion, revolution, chaos, lawlessness, mob rule, disorder, tumult, riot, turbulence, insubordination, mutiny, revolt, insurrection, resistance, sedition.

graceful, becoming, comely, handsome, beautiful, elegant, neat, fit, suitable, congruous, refined, pleasing, harmonious, tasteful, trim, flowing, smooth, fitting, seemly, clean, dexterous, nimble, proportioned, symmetrical, dignified, charming, unaffected, easy. *Ant.* awkward, uncouth, ungraceful, rude, vulgar, unpolished, undignified, boorish, slovenly, careless, loose, negligent, clumsy, rough, ungainly, unrefined, coarse, bungling, blundering, gawky, maladroit, unhandy, unskillful.

gracious, merciful, kind, beneficent, nice, benevolent, bland, mild, munificent, hospitable, amiable, tactful, congenial, courteous, thoughtful, compassionate, tender. *Ant.* rough, rude, domineering, coarse, vulgar, crude, harsh, unkind, cruel, rigorous, hard, severe, austere, exacting, stern, uninviting, ill-tempered, uncivil, inhospitable, discourteous, acrimonious, sarcastic, ironical.

grade, level, quality, rank, brand, step, stage, gradient, incline, slope. *Ant.* uniformity, sameness, gradelessness, level, plane.

gradual, slow, creeping, unintermittent, continuous, progressive, gradational, regular, step-by-step, inching, continual, perpetual, incessant. *Ant.* sudden, abrupt, unexpected, unanticipated, hasty, precipitent, intermittent.

graduate, end, finish, qualify; adapt, adjust, measure, regulate, proportion, calibrate.

graft, shoot, bud, scion, transplant; corruption, influence, booty, loot, bribe, rebate, favoritism, kickback.

grand, majestic, stately, dignified, exalted, lofty, splendid, gorgeous, superb, pompous, sublime, magnificent, grandiose, august, large, great, illustrious, imposing, ostentatious, striking, elegant, pretentious, showy, brilliant, impressive. *Ant.* inferior, low, ragged, tattered, threadbare, mean, menial, humble, pitiful, contemptible, poor, paltry, unpretentious, petty, trivial, trifling, insignificant, little, unimposing, ordinary, common, commonplace.

grandeur, majesty, stateliness, dignity, augustness, pomp, splendor, style, magnificence, greatness, loftiness. *Ant.* humility, simplicity, plainness, quietness, dullness, lowliness.

grandiloquent, pompous, grandiose, bombastic, turgid, inflated, declamatory, pretentious, rhetorical, oratorical, haughty. *Ant.* unpretentious, simple, plain, direct, unadorned, humble, servile, lowly.

grant, *n.* gift, reward, allocation, present, allowance, stipend, donation, benefaction, gratuity, endowment, concession, conveyance, bequest, contribution, privilege; *v.* permit, yield, concede, let, agree, accede, allow, give, bestow, confer, transfer, comply, concur, present, furnish. *Ant.* loss, deduction, decrement, detriment, damage, forfeiture, charge; refuse, withhold, deny, decline, repel, reject, rebuff, disavow, disclaim, disown, renounce, oppose, forbid.

graphic, forcible, powerful, telling, illustrative, pictorial, vivid, picturesque, descriptive, intelligible, explicit, clear, comprehensible, definite, lucid, striking, diagrammatic, detailed, distinct, precise, expressive. *Ant.* weak, obscure, confused, ambiguous, mixed, perplexing, unintelligible, uncertain, enigmatic, incomprehensible, doubtful, abstract, crytographic, jumbled, involved, complicated, complex, intricate, abstruse.

grapple, seize, clutch, catch, clinch, hug, hold, hook, clamp, cope, wrestle, contend, struggle, clasp, fasten; comprehend, understand, unite. *Ant.* release, unleash, loose, abandon, surrender, ignore, withdraw.

rasp, catch, clutch, seize, grip, retain, grapple, clasp, take, capture, apprehend, appropriate, comprehend, understand, perceive, infer, recognize, discern, deduce. *Ant.* lose, slip, liberate, free, release, unclasp, miss, loose, disengage, extricate; misinterpret, miscomprehend, misconstrue, misconceive, misunderstand.

rate, rasp, grind, rub, abrade, scrape, scratch, comminute, creak, pulverize; vex, irritate, jar, fret, annoy. *Ant.* comfort, soothe, please, placate.

rateful, thankful, appreciative, beholden, obliged, gratified; agreeable, pleasing, acceptable. *Ant.* ungrateful, thankless, unmindful, forgetful, unacknowledged, unrequited, unrewarded, heedless, careless, rude, abusive.

ratification, satisfaction, enjoyment, pleasure, delight, fulfillment, reward, comfort, happiness, contentment, compensation, choice, recompense, self-indulgence, voluptuousness, preference, favor, inclination, purpose, determination, indulgence. *Ant.* sacrifice, denial, asceticism, abstinence, fasting, pain, mortification, submission, humiliation, penance, vexation, chagrin, disappointment, suffering, forbearance.

ratify, indulge, humor, satisfy, please, delight, satiate, placate, pamper, yield, favor, comply, acquiesce, grant, flatter, coddle, pet, fondle, treat. *Ant.* displease, disappoint, pain, deprive, disgust, offend, vex, annoy, disturb, provoke, scoff, taunt, mock, pique, dissatisfy, ridicule, blame.

ratis, gratuitous, free, freely. *Ant.* costly.

ratitude, gratefulness, indebtedness, acknowledgement, thankfulness. *Ant.* ingratitude, thanklessness, discourtesy.

ratuitous, unprovoked, free, voluntary, spontaneous, groundless, unfounded, wanton. *Ant.* deserved, warranted, called-for, forced, earned, merited.

rave, serious, solemn, heavy, sober, important, momentous, sedate, weighty, staid, demure, thoughtful, earnest, intense, ponderous, consequential, critical. *Ant.* light, airy, volatile, buoyant, gay, capricious, flippant, vain, frivolous, thoughtless, trifling, unimportant, inconsequential, idle, trivial, nugatory, futile.

reat, big, large, huge, majestic, noble, vast, gigantic, grand, bulky, august, dignified, extensive, extraordinary, extended, powerful, wide, strong, unsurpassed, eminent, commanding, famous, famed, illustrious, celebrated, noted, distinguished, conspicuous, gallant, renowned, elevated, prominent, high, glorious, influential, brave, honorable, exalted, heroic, courageous, fearless, intrepid, valiant, daring, authoritative, stately, generous, magnanimous, chivalrous, high-minded, excellent, splendid. *Ant.* small, little, short, dwarfish, stunted, wizened, withered, diminutive, minute, petty, mean, low, contemptible, shallow, ordinary, common, pusillanimous, weak, powerless, ignorant, poor, unknown, plebian, infamous, evil, wicked, obtuse, dense, obscure, abject, base, beg-

greedy

garly, undignified, wretched, vulgar, ignoble, groveling, spiritless impotent, insipid, degraded, sordid, degenerate, servile, paltry menial, shameful.

greedy, avid, avaricious, ravenous, acquisitive, grasping, rapacious gluttonous, voracious, devouring, parsimonious, miserly, close grudging, sordid, mercenary, illiberal, stingy, covetous. *Ant* liberal, open-handed, generous, sharing, charitable, philanthropic prodigal, profuse, improvident, lavish, spendthrift, extravagant wasteful.

greet, hail, address, receive, welcome, accost, salute.

gregarious, social, convivial, neighborly, companionable, accessible friendly, amicable. *Ant.* inhospitable, unsociable, unfriendly.

grief, sorrow, sadness, tribulation, woe, regret, trial, affliction melancholy, vexation, mourning, misfortune, adversity, distress evil, calamity, catastrophe, misery, trouble, pain, bereavement failure, hardship, worry, anxiety, anguish. *Ant.* joy, gladness rejoicing, happiness, ecstasy, delight, gratification, satisfaction triumph, victory, merriment, exhilaration, pleasure.

grievance, complaint, wrong, affliction, burden, grief, trial, sorrow tribulation, injury, injustice, hardship. *Ant.* justice, happiness, joy, right, success, victory.

grievous, painful, afflicting, heavy, baleful, unhappy, woeful, sorrowful, oppressive, burdensome, distressing, weighty, serious lamentable, mortal, momentous, outrageous, heinous, calamitous *Ant.* light, trivial, venial, harmless, salutary, advantageous, innocuous, good, pleasant, pleasureable, gratifying, agreeable, comforting, beneficial.

grim, sullen, stern, austere, severe, sour, threatening, repellent dour, terrifying, forbidding, macabre, cranky, rigid, rigorous gloomy, ugly, desperate, resolute, intractable, sulky, cross, glum morose, inflexible, serious, ghastly, ruthless, gruesome, sinister threatening. *Ant.* pleasant, mild, bland, smiling, laughing, gay blithe, merry, suave, calm, agreeable, charming, winning, winsome, attractive, engaging, amiable, cordial, cheerful, buoyant light-hearted, enlivening, soothing, debonair, sunny, serene, jovial gleeful, inspiriting, mirthful, jocose.

grimace, affectation, frown, contortion, scowl, face, leer, squint smirk.

grind, crush, oppress, harass, tire, worry, annoy, afflict, tyrannize domineer, bully, inflict, dominate, override, overpower, trample coerce, overcome, burden, overwhelm, abrade, polish, whet, grate, reduce, pulverize, sharpen, masticate. *Ant.* lighten, relieve, help succor, encourage, comfort, solace, assist, alleviate, diminish mitigate, assuage, ameliorate, allay, soften, soothe, mollify, console, cheer, enliven, inspirit, refresh, roughen, blunt, dull.

grip, grasp, clasp, hold, clutch, seize, grab. *Ant.* release, loosen untie, relax, drop.

grisly, horrible, terrible, disgusting, sickening, loathsome, detestable, abhorrent, frightful, odious, repellent, forbidding, revolting, repugnant, abominable. *Ant.* pleasing, attractive, nice, beautiful, lovely, sweet, dainty, refined, alluring, charming, captivating, good-looking, agreeable, fascinating, personable.

grit, nerve, courage, fortitude, mettle, pluck, endurance, decision, spirit; sand, gravel, abrasive. *Ant.* cowardice, faintheartedness, timidity, reluctance, fear, fright.

grizzly, gray-haired, hoary, grizzled, gray, silvered.

groan, moan, lament, cry, sob, wail, grumble, sigh, growl, complain. *Ant.* cheer, rejoice, applaud, laugh, sing, chuckle.

grope, fumble, attempt, try, feel (one's way), finger, grapple, hesitate, search. *Ant.* comprehend, perceive.

gross, coarse, indelicate, rough, vulgar, obscene, lewd, impure, sensual; thick, monstrous, enormous, bulky, dense, fat, corpulent, large, unwieldy, obese, fleshy, ponderous, rude, low, vulgar, unbecoming, repulsive; total, whole. *Ant.* fine, delicate, comely, fair, refined, dainty, slender, thin, svelte, graceful, easy, appealing, attractive, choice, well-bred, handsome, proper, purified, moral, clean, intellectual, virtuous, spiritual, pure, chaste; net, modified, post-deduction.

grotesque, fantastic, misshapen, absurd, odd, unnatural, bizarre, incongruous, curious, startling, monstrous, strange. *Ant.* normal, usual, customary, typical, average.

ground, *n.* land, estate, property, section, part, surface, possession, place, region, habitat, locality, country, territory, origin, foundation, base, basis, support, cause, reason, evidence. *v.* establish, fix, settle, base, set; train, instruct, educate.

group, assembly, cluster, collection, order, class, assemblage, bunch, crowd, audience, company, throng, meeting, clique, set.

grovel, crawl, cringe, fawn, sneak, stoop, kneel, crouch, cower, beg, snivel, beseech, implore, wheedle, blandish, flatter, prostrate. *Ant.* command, order, control, govern, discipline, master, lead, rule, direct, dictate, spurn, despise, face, scorn, disdain, ridicule, deride, taunt, jeer, provoke, stand up (to).

grow, expand, swell, enlarge, increase, augment, wax, dilate, stretch, spread, develop, thicken, accumulate, extend, bud, burgeon, puff, amplify, inflate, tumefy, mature, germinate; plant, raise, breed, farm, nurture, sow, cultivate. *Ant.* decrease, diminish, lessen, detumesce, abate, reduce, lower, sink, wither, fade, fail, vanish, dwindle, droop, decline, etiolate, wizen, decay, stagnate, die; kill, destroy.

growth, development, expansion, increase, multiplication, extension, enlargement, advancement, accretion, proliferation. *Ant.* drop, decline, withering, failure, slippage, loss, death.

growl, grumble, snarl, mumble, complain, murmur, mutter, howl, groan, bemoan. *Ant.* purr, hum, sing.

grudge, spite, rancor, malice, hatred, aversion, pique, grievance, animosity, enmity, ill will, jealousy, malevolence, malignity, antagonism, antipathy, hostility, abhorrence, disgust, dislike, detestation, resistance, opposition, contrariety, maliciousness, resentment. *Ant.* goodwill, benevolence, friendliness, kindness, brotherliness, tenderness, benignity, generosity, sympathy, philanthropy, affection, admiration, graciousness, liberality, fondness, congeniality, agreement, accord, affinity.

gruesome, ghastly, hideous, ugly, grim, horrifying, fearful, grisly, repulsive, macabre, frightful, appalling. *Ant.* nice, pleasant, pretty, handsome.

gruff, abrupt, blunt, rugged, rough, bluff, sour, rude, unceremonious, short, coarse, snappish, cross, curt, morose, surly, churlish, stern, snarling, harsh, uncivil, acrimonious. *Ant.* free, easy, civil, pleasant, sunny, serene, courteous, polite, obliging, respectful, attentive, urbane, conciliating, affable, complaisant, gracious, benign, friendly, cheerful, genial, ready, kind.

guarantee, certify, testify, aver, vouch, attest, verify, declare, assure, endorse, secure, obligate, insure, guard, warrant, indemnify, support, confirm, affirm, assert, allege, avow, depose. *Ant.* deny, disown, decry, ignore, deprecate, condemn, censure, oppose, disclaim, reject, contradict, disaffirm, disprove, disavow, detract, disparage, depreciate, renounce.

guaranty, pledge, agreement, promise, surety, security, guarantee, warranty, assurance.

guard, watch, protect, guide, secure, defend, safeguard, keep, preserve, fortify, champion, treasure, shelter, shield, police, observe, superintend, supervise, tend, attend. *Ant.* neglect, forsake, abandon, disregard, desert, leave, quit, relinquish, withdraw, cease, stop, resign.

guardian, trustee, protector, advisor, bodyguard, keeper, insuror, foster parent, chaperon, sentry, warden.

guess, believe, surmise, reckon, assume, imagine, suppose, conjecture, opine, fancy. *Ant.* calculate, measure, know, ascertain.

guide, lead, direct, convey, shepherd, control, conduct, regulate, persuade, induce, order, dispose, command, contrive, manage, sway, train, educate, influence. *Ant.* mislead, release, abandon, ignore, disregard, quit, misguide, neglect.

guile, craft, cunning, artifice, duplicity, deceit, double-dealing, dishonesty, trickery, knavishness, fraud, wiliness, cleverness, artfulness, craftiness, astuteness, slyness, subtlety, dissimulation, chicanery, deception, rascality, imposture, stratagem, hypocrisy, treachery. *Ant.* honesty, openness, candor, fair-dealing, frankness, ingenuousness, fairness, sincerity, truthfulness, uprightness, genuineness, artlessness, integrity, probity, rectitude, rightness, straightness, reliability, unaffectedness, plainness, simplicity, fealty.

guiltless, harmless, innocent, free, sinless, crimeless, faultless, upright, honest, blameless, undefiled, impeccable, spotless, pure, untainted, innocuous, truthful. *Ant.* see **guilty.**

guilty, sinful, criminal, corrupt, wicked, liable, tarnished, stained, faulty, culpable, blameworthy, censurable, wrong, unworthy, immoral. *Ant.* see **guiltless.**

guise, pose, posture, role, semblance, clothing, appearance, dress, aspect, shape, garb, manner, air, custom, practice, behavior, demeanor, mien.

gullible, naive, credulous, unwary, guileless, innocent, unsuspicious, trustful, heedless, unguarded. *Ant.* knowledgeable, perceptive, sophisticated, wise, understanding, discerning.

gush, spurt, spout, flow, issue, rave, burst, rush, flood, pour. *Ant.* slow, stop, trickle, fade, wane.

gusto, relish, pleasure, zest, ardor, delight, enthusiasm, appetite, enjoyment. *Ant.* distaste, insipidness, reluctance.

gyrate, spin, whirl, rotate, swirl, turn, spiral, revolve, circle, eddy, convolute, twirl.

H

habiliment, dress, raiment, clothing, garb, attire, vestment, uniform, costume, apparel.

habit, custom, practice, bent, tendency, fashion, form, manner, habitude, routine, addiction, use, rule, prevalence, repetition, wont, mode, method, observance, manner, way, style, continuation; garb, covering, dress, raiment, costume, clothes. *Ant.* irregularity, disuse, desuetude, uncommonness, infrequency, nonconformity, unconventionality, uncertainty, fitfulness, capriciousness, rarity.

habitation, house, abode, apartment, flat, dwelling, occupancy, home, domicile, residence, residency, sojourn, stay, habitat, lodging.

habitual, regular, ordinary, customary, usual, perpetual, familiar, accustomed, established, normal, recurrent, systematic, periodic, stated. *Ant.* rare, uncommon, unusual, seldom, unwonted, remarkable, infrequent, nonconforming, extraordinary.

hack, cut, chop, mangle, tear, split, break, mutilate, lacerate, botch, chip, drudge, toil, cough.

hackneyed, stereotyped, trite, inane, flat, vapid, stale, banal, overworked, commonplace, ordinary. *Ant.* original, fresh, novel, new, bright, clever.

haggard, gaunt, careworn, lean, wrinkled, worried, fretted, scrawny, lined, thin, emaciated, hunger-stricken, tired, exhausted, weak, weary, wasted, debilitated. *Ant.* strong, robust, healthy, blooming, exuberant, fresh, lively, playful, vigorous, active, forcible, powerful, lusty, hearty.

haggle

haggle, bargain, dicker, stickle, cavil, wrangle, negotiate, deal, palter, quibble.

hail, call, address, salute, herald, accost, greet, compliment, summon, approach, welcome, honor, acclaim, applaud, cheer, entertain. *Ant.* ignore, neglect, disregard, overlook, slight, scorn, spurn, disdain, shun, avoid, elude.

hair-raising, exciting, frightening, spine-tingling, lurid, dramatic, breath-taking. *Ant.* boring, bland, quiet, soothing.

halcyon, golden, tranquil, placid, peaceful, calm, serene, unruffled, quiet, happy. *Ant.* stormy, turbulent, rough, tempestuous, ruffled, disorderly.

hale, healthy, vigorous, well, chipper, robust, sound, lusty. *Ant.* infirm, decrepit, feeble, weak, unhealthy.

halfhearted, indifferent, uninterested, unenthusiastic, cold, cool, dull, perfunctory, discouraging, curt. *Ant.* enthusiastic, zealous, ardent, hearty, warm, wholehearted.

hall, entrance, vestibule, passage, atrium, corridor, manor, building, residence, mansion, house, castle, room, auditorium, dormitory, headquarters, edifice.

hallowed, sacred, holy, consecrated, godly, saintly, sanctified, pious, revered, respected, dedicated. *Ant.* profane, blasphemous, cursed, execrated, unholy, ungodly.

hallucination, delusion, illusion, aberration, fantasy, chimera, fancy, mirage, phantasm. *Ant.* reality, truth, existence.

halt, arrest, stand, stop, falter, limp, linger, check, hesitate, demur, doubt, pause, stammer, stutter, desist, cease, suspend, intermit, discontinue. *Ant.* go, proceed, advance, continue, walk, run, move, persevere, endure, pursue.

hamper, impede, thwart, perplex, confuse, entangle, disconcert, annoy, embroil, obstruct, delay, prevent, retard, check, shackle, clog, hinder, prevent, encumber, restrict, restrain, oppress. *Ant.* facilitate, ease, help, assist, encourage, favor, comfort, relieve, cooperate, aid, second, support, forward, promote, cheer, inspirit, embolden.

handicap, encumbrance, obstruction, drag, limitation, defect, lack, hindrance, burden, penalty, impediment; odds, allowance. *Ant.* advantage, asset, help, benefit.

handle, manipulate, finger, manage, operate, wield, feel, use, ply, direct, manage, negotiate, cope.

handsome, beautiful, graceful, lovely, pretty, elegant, attractive, good-looking, comely, fair, well-favored, well-proportioned, shapely, agreeable; large, liberal, ample, generous. *Ant.* ugly, offensive, ill-favored, ungraceful, repulsive; mean, poor, small, insignificant.

handy, near, convenient, available, useful, helpful, ready, ingenious, fitting, skilled, skillful, inventive, clever, resourceful, dexterous, adept, able, adroit, apt. *Ant.* unhandy, unskillful, clumsy, stupid.

useless, untrained, ignorant, unskilled, awkward, bungling, inept, inexpert, ineffectual, fumbling.

hang, suspend, depend, attach, hover, droop, lean, swing, dangle, drape; lynch, execute, gibbet.

hanker, yearn, crave, want, hunger, long, lust, want, wish, pine, desire, covet. *Ant.* abhor, loathe, spurn, detect, avoid, reject.

haphazard, accidental, chancy, risky, sudden, careless, irresponsible, hit-or-miss, disorderly, unplanned, unexpected, casual, fortuitous, contingent, incidental, random, aimless. *Ant.* considered, premeditated, deliberate, intentional, purposed, designed, determined, planned, intended.

hapless, unfortunate, miserable, ill-fated, luckless, unlucky, unhappy. *Ant.* fortunate, lucky, successful, fortuitous, favored, happy, prosperous, flourishing, well-off.

happen, accrue, chance, occur, fall, supervene, transpire, betide, befall, appear, come, arrive, follow, ensue, turn, result, eventuate.

happily, fortunately, contentedly, cheerfully, willingly, gracefully, luckily, successfully, felicitously. *Ant.* unfortunately, unluckily, disastrously, calamitously, unsuccessfully, ungracefully, unwillingly.

happiness, bliss, beatitude, blessedness, aptness, felicity, satisfaction, contentment, joy, ecstasy, rapture, peace, mirth, merriment, delight, gladness, exultation, transport. *Ant.* unhappiness, grief, sorrow, sadness, misery, melancholy, gloom, distress, dejection, despair, despondency, depression, calamity, misfortune, wretchedness, mournfulness, adversity, catastrophe, disaster.

happy, joyous, joyful, merry, delighted, glad, mirthful, delightful, cheerful, gay, contented, satisfied, prosperous, rapturous, blithe, felicitous, jolly, blessed, blissful, rejoicing, jovial, jocund, glad, ecstatic, propitious, favorable, pleasing, gratified, pleased, light, fortunate, peaceful, comfortable, bright, buoyant, vivacious, successful, sunny, sprightly, lucky, lively, animated, smiling, spirited, exhilarated, thrilled, elated, jubilant, laughing, satiated. *Ant.* unhappy, sad, sorrowful, moody, morose, sour, mortified, dissatisfied, discontented, disappointed, unfortunate, unlucky, gloomy, dejected, despairing, melancholy, downcast, depressed, disheartened, discouraged, poverty-stricken, wretched, weeping, embarrassed, mournful, miserable, grieved, anguished, abject, tormented, aggrieved, forlorn, pitiable, disconsolate, comfortless, cheerless, abandoned, desolate, destitute, hopeless, forsaken, distressed, afflicted, woeful, woebegone, troubled.

harangue, declaim, plead, rant, rave, orate, scold, sermonize.

harass, annoy, vex, irritate, plague, tantalize, taunt, provoke, exasperate, exacerbate, worry, molest, pester, fret, tease, agitate, ruffle, rouse, excite, anger, inflame, enrage, incense, chafe, nettle, trouble, embarrass, twit, torment, jeer, deride, revile, ridicule, defame, vilify, traduce, calumniate, sneer, disconcert, infuriate, arouse, delude. *Ant.* cheer, encourage, aid, help, assist, advise, animate, succor, befriend, comfort, compose, forward, promote, calm, console, facilitate, support, favor, cooperate, tranquilize, incite, urge, impel, stimulate, revive, gladden, enliven, refresh, abet, countenance, contribute, instigate, strengthen, embolden, solace, appease, sustain, alleviate, lighten, allay, soothe, abate, assuage, relieve.

harbor, shelter, foster, protect, nurture, cherish, house, guard, contain, cover, shield. *Ant.* eject, expel, banish, exile.

hard, firm, compact, solid, strong, resisting, unyielding, substantial, stable, stout, close, durable, dense, unimpressible, adamantine, thick, fixed, steady, compressed, pressed, concrete, condensed, impervious, stony, rocky, rigid; arduous, difficult, troublesome, toilsome, laborious, unaccommodating, harsh, stiff, unfeeling, constrained, unconventional, severe, austere, stern, demanding, pitiless, rigorous, exacting, obdurate, cruel, unrelenting, perverse, grinding, vengeful, unforgiving. *Ant.* soft, yielding, impressible, malleable, pliant, weak, light, pliable, susceptible, penetrable; easy, simple, unexacting, soft, tender, mild, gentle, kind, pitying, tender-hearted, merciful, sensitive, delicate, frail, feeble, weak, effeminate, compassionate, affectionate, indulgent, clement, tractable, gracious, tolerant.

harden, solidify, cool, stiffen, petrify, anneal, toughen, ossify, temper; confirm, fortify, brace, steel, season, inure, accustom, habituate, nerve, train, discipline. *Ant.* soften, melt, warm; pamper, spoil, indulge, coddle.

hardihood, fearlessness, boldness, courage, resolution, impudence, impertinence, temerity, insolence, audacity, presumption, daring, spirit, confidence, assurance, effrontery, shamelessness, barefacedness, intrepidity, dauntlessness, bravery, fortitude, firmness, coolness, resistance. *Ant.* weakness, faltering, cowardice, fear, pusillanimity, fearfulness, timidity, apprehension, faintheartedness, misgiving, trepidation, dismay, consternation, dread, awe, reluctance.

hardship, trial, burden, difficulty, privation, affliction, injury, misfortune, adversity, oppression, injustice, disaster, calamity, distress, unhappiness, misery, catastrophe, trouble, sorrow, grief, regret, sadness, tribulation. *Ant.* advantage, benefit, good, profit, help, vantage, utility, gain, interest, favor, blessing, benefit, improvement, aid, assistance.

hardy, strong, enduring, fearless, unyielding, tenacious, courageous, intrepid, brave, robust, tough, inured, stouthearted, vigorous, dauntless, bold, confident, assured, spirited, daring, audacious, impudent, resistant, valorous, firm, forcible, undaunted. *Ant.* weak, yielding, soft, tender, timid, delicate, puny, feeble, debilitated, impaired, enervated, infirm, invalid, sickly, cowardly, fearful, apprehensive, timid, shrinking, craven, pliant, submissive.

harm, injury, wrong, detriment, hurt, infliction, damage, dishonor, evil, mischief, deterioration, impairment, loss, deprivation, abuse, destruction. *Ant.* good, benefit, boon, favor, advantage, advancement, interest, boost, benefit, gain, blessing, profit.

harmless, innocuous, inoffensive, safe, innocent, blameless, guiltless, faultless, irreproachable, simple, artless, unblemished, spotless, undefiled, incorrupt, impotent, manageable, pure, good, gentle, obedient, docile. *Ant.* harmful, hurtful, injurious, noxious, bad, evil, poisonous, malicious, malignant, wicked, pernicious, sinful, noisome, unwholesome, pestiferous, deleterious, damaging, detrimental, prejudicial.

harmonious, agreeable, accordant, concordant, suitable, congruous, corresponding, fit, adapted, melodious, musical, euphonious, dulcet, attuned, pleasing, mellifluent, similar, like. *Ant.* discordant, disagreeable, incongruous, opposed, unlike, unsuitable, dissonant, harsh, disagreeing, inharmonious, jarring, clashing, jangling, noisy, displeasing, incompatible, inappropriate.

harmony, concord, alliance, accord, unison, agreement, concordance, concurrence, euphony, union, unanimity, consonance, congruity, unity, uniformity, symmetry, consistency, conformity, amity, compatibility, suitableness, agreeableness. *Ant.* dissonance, change, discord, jangle, noise, disagreement, discordance, opposition, inconsistency, variance, clashing, strife, difference, incongruity, disunion, changeableness, wavering, variation, deviation, mutation, alteration, interchange, innovation, alternation, conflict, antagonism, contention, dissension.

harp, repeat, dwell, reiterate, nag, renew, bother, annoy, drum, pester, hammer, din.

harry, harass, hector, chase, pursue, persecute, snipe, afflict, annoy, badger, hound, nag, worry, torment, pester, trouble. *Ant.* relieve, comfort, console, assuage.

harsh, rough, rigorous, severe, austere, stern, gruff, sharp, cutting, keen, acrimonious, bitter, ungracious, uncivil, hard, brutal, ill-tempered, strict, rigid, censorious, jarring, unrelenting, pitiless, inexorable, unfeeling, merciless, abusive, exacting, surly, sour, grating, snarling, heartless, rude, cross, overbearing, caustic. *Ant.* gentle, mild, forbearing, placid, meek, unselfish, easy, even, good-tempered, sweet-tempered, kind, indulgent, moderate, quiet, peaceful, unassuming, courteous, benevolent, merciful, patient, calm, polite, humble, unostentatious, soft, yielding, unpretentious, tender, commiserating, sympathetic, feeling, agreeable, pleasant, consoling, compassionate, congenial, encouraging.

harvest, produce, reaping, fruitage, profit, product, proceeds, crop, return, yield, store, intake, growth, storage, ingathering, amount, increment; effect, result, consequence, outcome.

hassle, argument, controversy, dispute, fight, quarrel, disagreement, brawl, wrangle, melee, scrap. *Ant.* agreement, harmony.

haste, hurry, dispatch, rapidity, nimbleness, speed, swiftness, bustle celerity, fleetness, quickness, speediness, acceleration, exertion flurry, promptness, expedition, velocity, agility, scramble, scurry urgency, rush, activity, briskness. *Ant.* slowness, tardiness, drag laziness, lagging, loitering, lingering, delay, tarrying, lateness indolence, procrastination, inaction, leisure, ease, rest, postpone ment, dilatoriness.

hasten, accelerate, dispatch, speed, advance, spur, expedite, hurry drive, hustle, quicken, push, rush, run, sprint, dash, race, skip scamper, scurry. *Ant.* delay, procrastinate, postpone, idle, loiter linger, defer, slow, prolong, retard, impede, hamper, creep, crawl lag, saunter, plod, slouch, dawdle, drag, trudge, shuffle, shamble hobble, limp.

hasty, hurried, ill-advised, cursory, abrupt, inopportune, eager, rash quick, speedy, excited, precipitate, headlong, rushing, sudden headstrong, thoughtless, foolhardy, heedless, indiscreet, impul sive, imprudent, improvident, careless, adventurous, incautious reckless. *Ant.* patient, slow, deliberate, careful, cautious, inten tional, considerate, heedful, watchful, circumspect, provident anxious, wary, serious, judicious, discreet, prudent, thoughtful meditative, contemplative, scrupulous, politic, calculating, wily strategic, planned, plotted.

hatch, devise, invent, originate, plot, concoct, scheme, project, plan breed, incubate, brood, contrive.

hateful, odious, detestable, revolting, repugnant, repulsive, disgust ing, nauseating, disagreeable, distasteful, uncongenial, annoying shocking, unpopular, repellent, offensive, sickening, obnoxious execrable, corrupt. *Ant.* lovable, likable, friendly, appealing amiable, attractive, estimable, agreeable, engaging, delightful charming, enticing, alluring, fascinating, captivating, seductive pleasing, bewitching, entrancing, satisfying, enchanting, chaste moral, incorrupt.

hatred, enmity, hate, ill will, rancor, antipathy, abhorrence, dislike aversion, detestation, hostility, loathing, disaffection, malevolence spite, malignity, grudge, pique, umbrage, malice, resentment acrimony, execration, implacability, abomination, bitterness, re pugnance, odium, animosity. *Ant.* love, kindness, benevolence preference, friendship, fondness, admiration, devotion, rapture fervor, enthusiasm, worship, infatuation, enchantment, affection reverence, sympathy, appreciation, approbation, acclamation, ap proval, endorsement.

haughty, arrogant, disdainful, supercilious, proud, high-minded, im perious, lordly, pompous, cavalier, condescending, egotistical insolent, bumptious, swaggering, scornful, superior, prim, strait laced, affected, contemptuous, stiff. *Ant.* lowly, unassuming humble, bashful, submissive, timid, afraid, groveling, abashed unobtrusive, unpretentious, unpretending, ashamed, humiliated confused, mortified, browbeaten, crushed, subservient, crestfallen

haul, drag, pull, tug, deliver, lug, tow, trail, draw. *Ant.* push, shove, thrust, drive, impel.

haunt, frequent, visit, attend, return (to) ; obsess, frighten, disturb, terrorize, persecute; resort, follow, importune.

hauteur, haughtiness, arrogance, pomp, pride, loftiness, disdain, scorn, sauciness, superciliousness, contempt. *Ant.* humility, lowliness, condescension, plainness, humbleness.

have, hold, own, possess, carry, get, obtain, take, include, keep, maintain. *Ant.* want, lack, exclude, need.

haven, shelter, refuge, harbor, port, retreat, asylum, anchorage.

hazard, risk, venture, peril, accident, danger, chance, casualty, fortune, jeopardy, luck, fate, adventure, contingency, fluke, gamble, possibility, uncertainty, likelihood, presumption, hope, fear. *Ant.* certainty, surety, assurance, fact, decision, determination, proof, reality, confidence, conviction, trust, reliance, security, actuality, truth, realization, plan, necessity, protection, safeguard, safety.

hazy, cloudy, foggy, murky, gauzy, filmy, nebulous, misty, smoky, vaporous, obfuscated, thick, dim, dull, obscure, unclear, vague, uncertain, wavering. *Ant.* clear, bright, translucent, transparent, luminous, light, plain, open, vivid, distinct, perspicuous, radiant, lucid, illuminated, pellucid, shining, obvious, manifest, understandable.

head, summit, top, crown, apex, acme, cap, crest, peak, culmination, pinnacle, tip, termination; guide, leader, commander, ruler, chief, boss, foreman, master, director, president, manager, superintendent, principal; source, fountainhead, beginning, intellect, mind, brain, skull, judgment, faculty, reason, understanding, mentality, reasoning, intelligence, cognition, capacity, instinct. *Ant.* base, bottom, foot, foundation, substructure, substratum, basis, level, groundwork, support, rest; disciple, pupil, attendant, clerk, private, worker, valet, footman, adherent, dependent, imitator; weakness, ineptitude, idiocy, shallowness, silliness, incapacity, incompetence, stupidity.

headlong, precipitate, imprudent, thoughtless, heedless, foolhardy, reckless, hasty, hurried, reckless, impetuous, rash. *Ant.* cautious, wary, careful, deliberate, circumspect, planned.

headstrong, ungovernable, self-willed, wayward, domineering, cantankerous, unruly, obstinate, willful, stubborn, bullheaded. *Ant.* submissive, docile, tractable, obedient, biddable.

heal, cure, repair, knit, fix, remedy, restore, soothe, mend, harmonize, reconcile. *Ant.* harm, injure, break, damage.

healthy, sound, salubrious, wholesome, strong, robust, hale, vigorous, virile, well, hearty, unimpaired, lusty, invigorating, bracing, beneficial, nutritious, innocuous, harmless, sanitary, healing, hygienic. *Ant.* bad, insalubrious, unhealthy, corrupt, mephitic, rotten, noisome, pestilential, septic, deadly, noxious, unsound, invalid, deleterious, wasted, weak, worn, emaciated, frail, fragile, ill, unsound, sick, enervated, diseased, delicate, fainting, sickly, exhausted, indisposed, infirm, ailing, disordered, languishing, distempered.

heap, pile, aggregate, accumulate, amass, collect, gather, increase, bank, load, stock, hoard, add, augment, enlarge, swell, expand; cast, give, bestow. *Ant.* lessen, abate, diminish, reduce, decrease, curtail, minimize, lower, melt, withdraw, dwindle, shrivel, shrink, constrict, contract, compress.

hear, listen, heed, attend, regard, audit, consider, note, monitor, try, learn, judge.

hearsay, gossip, rumor, talk, report, word of mouth. *Ant.* statement, declaration, proclamation, testimony, evidence.

heart, core, center, pith, essence, nub, kernel, nucleus, focus. *Ant.* outside, exterior, periphery.

heartache, anguish, woe, misery, sadness, sorrow, affliction, misfortune, grief, distress, bitterness, heartbreak. *Ant.* happiness, joy, blitheness.

heartbroken, disconsolate, wretched, disheartened, desolate, miserable, forlorn, discouraged. *Ant.* happy, consoled, joyful, encouraged.

hearty, cordial, warm, cheerful, cheery, sincere, zealous, vivacious, gay, healthy, robust, sturdy, vigorous, animated, jovial, jolly friendly, ardent, genial, fervid, glowing, enthusiastic; earnest genuine. *Ant.* insincere, deceitful, dissembling, false, hypocritical, deceptive, sanctimonious, smug, mincing, mealy, unctuous affected, make-believe, simulating, pretending, counterfeit, mock spurious, feigned, sham, perfidious; weak, feeble, slight.

heat, warmth, caloric, burning, torridity, hot weather, flame, blaze furnace, bonfire, fireworks, incandescence; ardor, passion, fever excitement, temperature, intensity, fervor, zeal, agitation, emotion, vehemence, violence, glow, bloom, blush, redness. *Ant.* cold gelidity, coolness, wintriness, chilliness, frigidity; apathy, cold heartedness, unconcern, unfeelingness, impassiveness, dullness stoicism, lethargy, repression, heedlessness, carelessness, boredom.

heathen, pagan, infidel, unconverted, unbelieving, godless. *Ant.* believer, Christian, Moslem, Jew.

heave, raise, elevate, throw, hoist, rise, lift, toss, surge, swell, bulge billow, vomit. *Ant.* recede, ebb, lower.

heavy, weighty, ponderous, cumbersome, massive, burdensome, un wieldy, bulky, stormy, rough; troublesome, dull, stupid, embar rassing, pressing, vexatious, oppressive, onerous, afflicting, griev ous, severe; sad, depressed. *Ant.* light, slight, trivial, inconse quential, trifling, inconsiderable, unimportant, smooth, calm shallow, insignificant, little, small, paltry, immaterial, petty happy, gay, joyous.

heckle, bait, challenge, hector, harass, pester, badger, annoy, hound, molest, pursue, tease, taunt, jeer. *Ant.* console, help, encourage, applaud, promote, uphold, support.

hectic, feverish, restless, nervous, unsettling, agitated, excited, flustered. *Ant.* calm, cool, unhurried, serene.

hector, intimidate, bully, plague, torment, domineer, provoke, worry, threaten, browbeat. *Ant.* help, encourage, persuade, aid, comfort.

hedge, temporize, dodge, equivocate, evade, hide, disappear; fence, enclose, shelter, fortify, shield, guard, block, trim. *Ant.* meet, face, answer, confront, stand firm; unfence, free, open, neglect.

heed, care, attention, devotion, attachment, circumspection, notice, observation, application, consideration, concentration, watchfulness, concern, anxiety, solicitude, caution, precaution, regard, cognizance, vigilance, supervision. *Ant.* heedlessness, carelessness, neglect, negligence, disregard, default, omission, thoughtlessness, inattention, oversight, absent-mindedness, unconcern, inconsiderateness, recklessness, inadvertence, disinterestedness, indifference, apathy, nonchalance.

hegemony, ascendancy, leadership, predominance, authority, domination, influence, control, empire, rule, supremacy.

height, elevation, eminence, prominence, altitude, stature, loftiness. *Ant.* depth, lowness.

heighten, enhance, emphasize, increase, strengthen, intensify, augment, aggravate, amplify, advance, exaggerate, magnify, raise, elevate, exalt, improve, acclaim. *Ant.* lower, weaken, lessen, deprecate, depreciate, disapprove, diminish, alleviate, impair, decrease, reduce, abate, decry, disparage, underrate, debase, traduce, detract.

heinous, atrocious, dreadful, flagrant, awful, terrible, infamous, wicked, nefarious, hateful, depraved, profligate, immoral, bad, outrageous, vile, evil, monstrous, grievous, criminal, shameful, villainous, satanic, devilish, infernal, odious, sinful, vicious, corrupt, iniquitous, dissolute, disgraceful, disreputable, loathsome, notorious, unnatural, degrading, aggravated, abominable, detestable, abhorrent, execrable, foul. *Ant.* virtuous, moral, righteous, good, meritorious, deserving, worthy, creditable, praiseworthy, laudable, fine, excellent, commendable, admirable, exemplary, ideal, ethical, spiritual, perfect, sterling, approved, acceptable, fit, proper, glorious, high, noble, honorable, elevated, dignified, splendid, magnificent, grand, upright, just.

heir, inheritor, beneficiary, legatee, successor, scion.

help, assist, aid, succor, sustain, uphold, support, relieve, improve, second, encourage, advise, befriend, abet, foster, cooperate, prop, maintain, nourish, nurture, lift, ameliorate, alleviate, instigate, incite, countenance, favor, benefit, invigorate, intercede. *Ant.* hinder, oppose, obstruct, impede, impose (on), check, retard, injure, annoy, bother, clog, arrest, stop, embarrass, combat, withstand, resist, prevent, contradict, contravene, thwart, frustrate, hamper, counteract, discourage.

herald, announce, proclaim, declare, inform, warn, introduce, precede, publish. *Ant.* suppress, silence, stifle.

herd, group, flock, gathering, throng, multitude, drove, mob, shoal, school, assemblage, horde.

hereditary, inherited, constitutional, congenital, innate, inherent, transmitted, genetic, patrimonial. *Ant.* acquired, earned, bought, received, won.

heretic, schismatic, sectary, sectarian, dissenter, nonconformist, secularist, nonjuror, deserter, separatist, apostate, renegade, pervert, traitor. *Ant.* believer, loyalist.

heritage, inheritance, legacy, patrimony, birthright, ancestral culture.

hermetic, air-tight, sealed; mysterious, cabalistic, emblematic, occult. *Ant.* open, plain, clear, obvious.

heroic, fearless, intrepid, gallant, courageous, brave, valiant, bold, daring, undaunted, valorous, chivalrous, spirited, resolute, hardy, large, majestic, noble. *Ant.* cowardly, craven, timid, timorous, fearful, pusillanimous, mean, base, small, weak, dastardly, cringing, crawling, slinking, effeminate, spiritless.

hesitate, doubt, falter, pause, scruple, stammer, stutter, fluctuate, waver, fear, vacillate, question, ponder, think, debate, meditate, defer, delay, wait, demur, shrink, stall, dodge, shirk. *Ant.* embrace, act, attack, hasten, go, jump, tackle, continue, persevere, try, hustle, decide, resolve, carry on.

heterodox, unorthodox, heretical, free-thinking, uncanonical, pantheistic, apocryphal, dissenting, unbelieving, infidel, agnostic, pagan. *Ant.* orthodox, religious, faithful, trusting, canonical, faithful, loyal.

heterogeneous, unlike, mixed, miscellaneous, variant, discordant, nonhomogeneous, mingled, dissimilar, conglomerate, confused, various, different, contrary, contrasted. *Ant.* homogeneous, like, same, pure, uniform, similar, identical, agreeing, conforming, unvarying, unchanging.

hew, chop, cut, cleave, slash, lop, fell, trim; shape, fashion, form.

hide, conceal, secrete, mask, disguise, protect, dissemble, screen, cover, bury, veil, suppress, sequester, camouflage, shroud, curtain, shield, shade, shelter. *Ant.* expose, lay bare, uncover, show, exhibit, display, offer, present, open, disclose, reveal, make known, divulge, unveil, impart, discover, admit, advertise, avow, exhume, unmask, tell, manifest, publish, disinter, promulgate, betray, confess.

hidebound, conservative, traditional, old-fashioned, bigoted, narrow, intolerant, unchanging. *Ant.* liberal, tolerant, charitable, moderate, broad-minded.

hideous, ghastly, grisly, frightful, horrible, terrible, fierce, revolting, dreadful, awful, abominable, abhorrent, disgusting, grim, shocking, terrifying, repellent, forbidding, repulsive, monstrous, nauseating, loathsome, putrid, foul. *Ant.* pleasing, lovely, attractive, handsome, appealing, satisfying, nice, exquisite, fine, alluring, charming, fascinating, captivating, compelling, grand, soothing, assuaging, comforting, agreeable, softening, delightful, enticing, gratifying, lovable, graceful, splendid.

high, lofty, tall, elevated, towering, raised; eminent, exalted, noble; haughty, proud, arrogant, boastful, ostentatious, bumptious, conceited, self-assertive; expensive, costly; intense, strong, shrill, acute, strident; happy, merry, intoxicated. *Ant.* low, short, stunted, dwarfed; depressed, deep, inferior, weak, mean, contemptible, despicable, groveling, base, degraded, worthless, dishonorable, vile, ignoble, lowminded, poor; sober.

hilarious, mirthful, lighthearted, jocund, merry, loud, blithe, gay, gleeful, jolly, joyful. *Ant.* glum, morose, somber, cheerless, sad.

hinder, impede, obstruct, prevent, check, retard, block, trammel, thwart, bar, clog, embarrass, oppose, counteract, encumber, balk, inhibit, repress, interrupt, arrest, delay, restrain, curb, baffle, resist, prolong, foil, frustrate, hamper, deter, postpone. *Ant.* help, assist, aid, encourage, facilitate, further, advance, promote, urge, expedite, speed, hurry, dispatch, drive, hasten, press on, impel, stimulate, instigate, forward, incite, cheer, spur (on), hearten, inspirit, animate, accelerate, push, hasten.

hint, allude, refer, suggest, insinuate, intimate, imply, give (inkling of), notify, tell, warn, apprise, inform, acquaint, mention, impart. *Ant.* conceal, cover, veil, mask, refrain, disguise, camouflage, stifle, reserve, withhold, ignore, suppress.

hire, employ, engage, rent, lease, use, let, contract (for). *Ant.* discharge, buy, purchase, fire, retire.

history, story, recital, chronicle, account, narrative, narration, annals, register, record, archives, muniments, report, lore, saga, log, memoir, memorial, biography, autobiography, events, facts; past. *Ant.* legend, romance, myth, novel, invention, imagination, figment, fabrication, allegory, falsehood, fable, apologue, parable, fiction, mythology, Apocrypha; future.

hit, find, reach, gain, win, achieve, contact, attain, succeed; knock, strike, rap, beat, batter, slap, punch.

hitch, hindrance, roadblock, catch, check, obstacle, impediment. *Ant.* aid, help, assistance, opening, opportunity.

hoard, store, accumulation, savings, collection, stock, investments, bonds, pile, heap, treasure, supply, lot.

hoarse, husky, gruff, discordant, rough, guttural, throaty, thick, rasping, grating, croaking, strident. *Ant.* smooth, normal, melodious, lilting, tuneful.

hoary, gray, frosty, silvery, white, grizzled; old, aged, ancient, faded, venerable. *Ant.* dark, black, lustrous; young, virile, lusty.

hoax, trick, deception, cheat, swindle, fraud, imposture, delusion, fakery, canard, humbug, spoof, joke.

hobble, limp, falter, totter, stagger, hesitate; limit, handicap, bind, hold, shackle, restrain, fetter, impede. *Ant.* run, walk, move, speed, travel, go, progress; release, unfasten, free, assist, expedite, help, aid.

hobby, avocation, pursuit, amusement, fad, game, interest, recreation, pastime, diversion, enjoyment.

hoist, raise, lift, elevate, jack, heave, rear, uprear. *Ant.* lower, let down, drop.

hold, have, retain, keep, own, continue, detain, maintain, occupy, sustain, consider, regard, think, judge, reserve, restrain, control, attest, grip, cherish, grasp, suspend, assemble, convene, observe, celebrate, confine, contain, persevere, resist, affirm. *Ant.* lose, let go, drop, adjourn, give up, relinquish, release, dismiss, cede, convey, part with, bestow, present, confer, free, renounce, leave, quit, abandon, forsake, desert.

holiness, sanctity, piety, sacredness, godliness, devotion, consecration, unction, veneration, grace, reverence, blessedness, purity, humility. *Ant.* ungodliness, wickedness, sin, profanation, cant, blasphemy, hypocrisy, sanctimoniousness, irreverence, profanity, impiety, infidelity, materialism, rationalism, agnosticism, atheism, desecration.

hollow, incomplete, concave, void, cavernous, sunken, empty, vacant, depressed, insincere, unsound, unsubstantial, superficial, specious, weak, infirm, flimsy, artificial, transparent, faithless, rounded, false, curved, unfilled. *Ant.* full, solid, convex, raised, material, hard, firm, stable, strong, sincere, dependable, substantial, truthful, genuine, unreserved, hearty, earnest, faithful, honest, upright, frank, elevated, upraised, high.

holy, devout, pious, religious, blessed, divine, saintly, consecrated, hallowed, devoted, sacred, pure, immaculate, unstained, sinless, unspotted, righteous, virtuous, incorrupt, godly, dedicated, devout, reverent, devotional, spiritual, angelic, sanctified. *Ant.* unholy, wicked, sinful, depraved, vicious, evil, vile, contaminated, obscene, immoral, impure, lewd, profane, blasphemous, sacrilegious, impious, fiendish, infernal, reprobate, abandoned, graceless, desecrated, secular, iniquitous, nefarious, godless, irreverent, unsanctified, unregenerate, abominable, polluted, cursed, diabolical, culpable.

homage, fealty, devotion, loyalty, fidelity, deference, faithfulness, tribute, adoration, duty, honor, respect, reverence, submission, worship, obeisance. *Ant.* disrespect, disloyalty, treason, dishonor, treachery, faithlessness, disobedience, scorn.

home, house, abode, residence, dwelling, domicile, apartment, habitation, quarters, hearth, hearthstone; haven, rest, refuge, retreat, asylum, sanctuary; birthplace, country, native land; heaven; family.

omely, plain, rough, rude, coarse, awkward, uncouth, ugly, common, unadorned, ordinary, thick, vulgar, blunt, unpretentious, home-like, unattractive, inelegant, uncomely, unromantic. *Ant.* beautiful, handsome, pretty, comely, adorned, ornamental, decorative, foreign, romantic, refined, polished, suave, polite, nice, attractive, dignified, graceful, agreeable, inviting, charming.

omogeneous, uniform, alike, consonant, same, similar, harmonious, identical. *Ant.* heterogeneous, miscellaneous, mixed, variegated, unharmonious.

one, sharpen, grind, whet, file, strop, strengthen, *Ant.* make dull, roughen.

onest, frank, open, truthful, sincere, upright, straightforward, true, reliable, candid, trustworthy, honorable, trusty, ingenuous, fair, equitable, just, genuine, faithful, good, above-board, incorrupt, scrupulous, reputable, creditable, estimable, pure, chaste, principled; unmixed, unadulterated, full value. *Ant.* dishonest, dishonorable, unjust, unfair, tricky, deceptive, deceitful, fraudulent, faithless, ignoble, unfaithful, perfidious, misleading, artful, shifty, delusive, false, traitorous, untrustworthy, lying, hypocritical, treacherous, disingenuous, corrupt, unprincipled.

onesty, integrity, probity, rectitude, uprightness, honor, straightforwardness, self-respect, trustiness, trustworthiness, confidence, responsibility, faithfulness, fairness, justice, rectitude, frankness, veracity, candor, openness, sincerity. *Ant.* dishonesty, duplicity, double-dealing, double-crossing, cheating, trickery, chicanery, perfidy, roguery, cajolery, fraud, deceit, artifice, theft, deception, imposition, swindle, swindling, stealing, thieving, larceny, treachery.

onor, respect, reverence, esteem, admiration, dignity, reputation, renown, adulation, laudation, praise, commendation, principles, probity, glory, deference, recommendation, regard, trust, confidence, faith, reliance, glorification, worship, adoration. *Ant.* dishonor, disgrace, degradation, derision, contumely, opprobrium, shame, ignominy, reproach, blemish, censure, scandal, stigma, turpitude, disrespect, abasement, debasement, contempt, denunciation, humiliation, corruption, venality.

onorary, titular, gratuitous, commemorative, emeritus, *Ant.* true, full, complete, earned, won, deserved.

ope, confidence, expectation, trust, belief, assurance, desire, anticipation, prospect, aspiration, optimism, presumption, reliance, assumption. *Ant.* hopelessness, despair, despondency, dejection, pessimism, depression, low spirits, gloom, sadness, disbelief, discouragement, disappointment, fear.

opeless, despairing, desperate, reckless, rash, irretrievable, gone, abandoned, lost, inconsolable, brokenhearted, dejected, condemned, undone, futile, useless, ruined, remediless, irreparable, irrecoverable, irredeemable, irrevocable, immitigable, incurable. *Ant.* encouraging, hopeful, cheering, reassuring, confident, expectant, sanguine, elated, dauntless, enthusiastic, propitious, promising, probable, bright, sunny, trusting, believing, glowing, plucky, daring, expectant, courageous, animating, emboldening, stimulating, inciting.

horde, host, multitude, army, gang, troop, pack, mass, band, crew, throng, crowd, mob, assemblage.

horizontal, level, flat, even, plane, parallel, straight, linear; supine, prone. *Ant.* rough, rugged, uneven, irregular, broken, hilly, lumpy, slanting, sloping, rolling, inclined; erect, vertical, upright.

horrible, hateful, repulsive, loathsome, abominable, dreadful, horrid, detestable, hideous, dire, appalling, awful, fearful, terrible, frightful, alarming. *Ant.* pleasing, attractive, lovable, alluring, satisfying.

horror, dismay, consternation, dread, loathing, disgust, terror, aversion, awe, antipathy, fear, fright. *Ant.* delight, pleasure, fascination, consolation, comfort.

hospitable, receptive, companionable, welcoming, gregarious, convivial, friendly, sociable, neighborly, cordial, kind. *Ant.* inhospitable, unwelcoming, grudging, solitary, reserved, unsociable.

hospital, clinic, sanitarium, asylum, infirmary, pesthouse, sick bay, sanatorium, lazaretto.

host, landlord, publican, entertainer, innkeeper, tavernkeeper, army, horde, multitude. *Ant.* guest, visitor, patron, lodger, boarder, caller.

hostile, unfriendly, contrary, opposed, antipathetic, adverse, inimical, antagonistic, rancorous, belligerent, malevolent, *Ant.* friendly, devoted, loyal, agreeable, amicable, neutral, uncommitted.

hot, ardent, burning, fiery, flaming, incandescent, blazing, glowing, torrid, fervid, searing, heated, passionate, excited, eager; peppery, spicy. *Ant.* cold, frigid, freezing, chilling, chilly, gelid, bleak, biting, stiff, distant, rigid, affected, insensitive, calm, cool, apathetic; bland, sweet.

hotel, inn, tavern, hostel, hostelry, guest house, motel, pension, hospice, caravansary, roadhouse.

hotheaded, impetuous, ardent, unthinking, headstrong, unruly, precipitate, hasty, fiery, peppery, rash, quarrelsome. *Ant.* steady, deliberate, cool, equable, peaceable.

hound, pursue, harass, persecute, hector, pester, chase, dog, harry, track, hunt. *Ant.* leave alone, ignore, abandon.

hover, fly, librate, poise, hang, linger, waver, vacillate, wait, delay, flutter, doubt, stall, remain, swarm, lurk, flit, supervise, protect. *Ant.* go, leave, avoid, abandon, rest, settle.

however, nevertheless, notwithstanding, though, still, yet, although, but, albeit.

hubbub, tumult, noise, bedlam, din, disturbance, riot, disorder, clashing. *Ant.* quiet, peace, order, silence.

hubris, arrogance, insolence, pride, haughtiness, lordliness, conceit, egotism, vanity, self-importance. *Ant.* humility, lowliness, abasement, simplicity, reserve, restraint, self-deprecation.

huge, immense, great, giant, bulky, vast, colossal, monstrous, tremendous, enormous, gigantic. *Ant.* tiny, miniature, small, little, diminutive.

humane, kind, benevolent, pitying, merciful, sympathetic, compassionate, kind-hearted, civilized, human, forgiving, gracious, charitable, benignant, gentle, benign, indulgent, lenient. *Ant.* uncivilized, atrocious, savage, pitiless, inhuman, cruel, barbaric, merciless, brutal, dangerous, rude, uncouth, untamed, wild, fierce, brutish, ferocious, degrading, harsh, unmerciful.

humble, lowly, meek, submissive, unassuming, docile, mild, unpretentious, unpretending, simple, polite, courteous, homely, unadorned, bashful, modest, retiring, unselfish, diffident, unobtrusive, restrained, reserved, shy, coy, timid, shrinking, yielding, hesitating, unostentatious, forbearing, enduring, plain, poor, unimportant. *Ant.* proud, haughty, boastful, ostentatious, arrogant, masterful, tyrannical, overbearing, sneering, domineering, sarcastic, egotistical, self-important, censorious, presumptuous, conceited, pretentious, vain, insolent, imperious, blustering, assuming, rich, powerful, fancy, self-assertive, arbitrary, dogmatic.

humbug, counterfeit, sham, falseness, fake, feint, deception, imposition, trick, hoax, fraud, pretense, cheat, dodge, hypocrisy. *Ant.* truth, validity, correctness, honesty, reality.

humdrum, tedious, routine, monotonous, dull, prosaic, ordinary, usual, boring, tiresome, commonplace, everyday. *Ant.* lively, exciting, stimulating, gay.

humid, moist, wet, watery, damp, dank, moldy, warm, tropical, steamy, misty, foggy. *Ant.* dry, arid, sear.

humiliate, humble, hurt, abash, demean, sadden, disgrace, lower, debase, shame, abase, mortify, embarrass, insult, degrade. *Ant.* exalt, elevate, praise, help, raise, improve, gladden, please, encourage, glorify, approve.

humor, *n.* wit, pleasantry, temper, disposition, temperate, mood, caprice, fancy, badinage, banter, drollery, raillery, jesting, chaff, jocosity, jocularity, waggery, comicality, whimsicality, facetiousness, jest, joke, quip; *v.* indulge, favor, placate, oblige, satisfy, yield (to), pamper, spoil, pet, please. *Ant.* dullness, heaviness, stupidity, moroseness, slowness, taciturnity, obtuseness, depression, sadness, gloom, sullenness, melancholy, low spirits; refuse, disagree, disoblige, deny, irritate, provoke, affront, exasperate, enrage, defy, resist.

hunch, premonition, impression, feeling, presentiment, suspicion, omen, intuition.

hungry, avid, greedy, thirsting, voracious, ravenous, starving, covetous, famished. *Ant.* replete, sated, surfeited, satisfied, well fed, stuffed.

hunt, seek, chase, follow, probe, pursue, search, investigate, ferret, stalk, inquire.

hurl, throw, pitch, project, toss, impel, cast, shoot, spring, release, fling, dart, push, expel, explode.

hurricane, storm, gale, tempest, cyclone, typhoon, whirlwind, sirocco, blizzard. *Ant.* calm, peace, doldrum.

hurry, hasten, rush, accelerate, force, press, move, scurry, speed, impel, drive, quicken. *Ant.* delay, dawdle, dally, procrastinate, stall, impede, wait, slow.

hurt, wound, injure, damage, harm, bruise, cut, tear, spoil, impair, deteriorate, pain, abuse, tarnish, mar, maltreat, maul, victimize, molest, wrong, beat, strike, burn, whip, outrage; pain, ache, throb, smart. *Ant.* heal, cure, remedy, restore, benefit, relieve, serve, reward, assist, succor, comfort, aid, assuage, alleviate, soothe, abate, please.

husband, store, save, conserve, economize, manage, cultivate. *Ant.* waste, squander, misspend, misuse, dissipate, destroy.

husbandry, agriculture, cultivation, culture, farming, tillage, land management, crop production, floriculture, farm management, gardening, arboriculture, horticulture, field-culture, agronomy, cattle-raising, stock-feeding; frugality, thrift, good management, economy. *Ant.* waste, destruction, prodigality, misuse, mismanagement, loss, squandering, decrement.

hush, stifle, quiet, muffle, still, calm, relieve, silence. *Ant.* excite, encourage, amplify, incite.

hustle, hurry, rush, fly, run, push, move, crowd, dash, race, spur, act, drive, scurry, hasten, expedite, bustle, accelerate. *Ant.* slow, delay, dawdle, trifle, lag, postpone, procrastinate, idle, lounge, defer, dissipate, loll, stall.

hybrid, crossbred, mixed, mutant, mongrel, half-blooded, half-bred. *Ant.* purebred, thoroughbred, pure stock, unmixed, pedigreed.

hygienic, sanitary, wholesome, cleanly, salutary, healthful, germ-free, uncontaminated. *Ant.* unhygienic, unsanitary, contaminated, foul, sickening, contagious, noxious, infectious, unhealthful.

hypnotic, mesmeric, irresistible, quieting, lethargic, soporific, influential, impelling, narcotic, magnetic. *Ant.* stimulating, exciting, reviving, disturbing.

hypochondriacal, worrying, pessimistic, atrabilious, melancholic, melancholy, morbid. *Ant.* robust, healthy, happy, well-adjusted.

hypocritical, dishonest, deluding, deceptive, dishonorable, insincere, unprincipled, bigoted, canting, unctuous, glib, mendacious, deceiving, Pharisaical, double-dealing, assuming, pretending, pretentious, false, sanctimonious, dissimulating, dissembling, feigning, specious. *Ant.* honest, just, reputable, reliable, truthful, fair, righteous, upright, square, honorable, principled, on the level, trustworthy, faithful, steadfast, frank, ingenuous, dependable, sincere, straightforward, unimpeachable, candid, earnest, artless.

ypothesis, theory, supposition, conjecture, system, scheme, postulate, inference, deduction, assumption, presumption, thesis, condition, proposal. *Ant.* evidence, fact, proof, demonstration, conviction, certainty, discovery, confirmation, assurance, affirmation, ratification, settlement, result, consequence.

ypothetical, supposed, imaginary, suppositious, postulated, conditional, guessed, symbolic, academic, theoretical, conjectural, assumed, vague, problematical, indefinite, contingent, speculative, indeterminate. *Ant.* proved, affirmed, confirmed, demonstrated, approved, real, true, factual, exact, literal, indisputable, reliable, authentic, credible, veritable, undoubted, tested, unquestionable.

ysterical, over-excited, wild, overwrought, convulsive, uncontrolled, frenzied, emotional, raving. *Ant.* calm, composed, easy, sane, unemotional, tranquil, serene, controlled.

I

conoclast, destroyer, insurgent, nihilist, materialist, antichrist. *Ant.* believer, zealot, convert, disciple.

cy, cold, frigid, forbidding, frosty, frozen, polar, chilled, chilling; distant, cool, unemotional. *Ant.* fiery, torrid, warm, tropical, hot; passionate, ardent, fervent.

dea, image, impression, concept, conception, conceit, imagination, thought, notion, opinion, belief, principle, theory, inspiration, brainstorm, fancy, fantasy, supposition, ideal, scheme, inkling, abstraction, representation, essence, kernel. *Ant.* actuality, fact, reality, body, substance, matter, element, stuff, material, compound, thing, person, object.

deal, imaginary, fancied, illusory, impractical, visionary, fanciful, unreal, subjective, intellectual, mental, metaphysical, psychical, spiritual, psychological; excellent, perfect, complete, exemplary, consummate, fitting, supreme. *Ant.* actual, common, material, real, commonplace, pragmatic, practical; ordinary, imperfect, disappointing, vulgar, mean.

dentical, same, equal, coincident, indistinguishable, uniform, duplicate, alike, coalescent, one, equivalent, synonymous. *Ant.* unlike, different, distinct, diverse, separate, disparate, opposite.

dentify, recognize, point out, name, distinguish, characterize, note, catalog, determine, analyze, classify; brand, label, tag, mark. *Ant.* mix up, confuse, mistake, misinterpret, misname.

idiocy, imbecility, insanity, folly, foolishness, madness, senselessness, fatuity, vapidity, vacuity, stupidity, feeblemindedness, paranoia, dementia, mania, alienation, derangement, lunacy, frenzy, delirium, monomania, retardation, half-wittedness. *Ant.* wisdom, sense, acuteness, sharpness, intelligence, genius, sagacity, brilliance, perception, astuteness, soundness, understanding, acumen, shrewdness, judgment, penetration, discernment, sapience, common sense, knowledge, prudence.

idiomatic, colloquial, peculiar, vernacular, dialectal, regional, substandard, special, stylized. *Ant.* standard, classic, cultured.

idiosyncrasy, peculiarity, oddity, singularity, caprice, fad, quirk, fixation, whim, way, foolishness.

idle, unemployed, inactive, aimless, unused, unoccupied, untilled, fallow, barren, defunct, dormant, uncultivated, lazy, shiftless, sluggish, trifling, slothful, indolent, listless, inert, useless, pointless, vain, frivolous, futile, unprofitable, unimportant. *Ant.* busy, industrious, hustling, ambitious, employed, diligent, working, active, occupied, settled, fruitful, cultivated, in use, productive, assiduous, sedulous, laborious, untiring, unremitting, relevant, important.

idolize, adore, worship, admire, love, venerate, deify, revere, glorify. *Ant.* hate, abase, degrade, profane, doubt, scoff, desecrate, defile.

ignite, kindle, enkindle, fire, detonate, burn, spark, light, inflame; inspire, goad, spur, incite, urge, inspirit, help, aid, show the way, animate, encourage, foster. *Ant.* dampen, quench, extinguish; discourage, repress, dissuade, dull, slow, stop, halt, prevent.

ignoble, mean, base, despicable, dishonorable, debased, contemptible, degraded, reproachful, cowardly, scandalous, shameful, worthless, immodest, abject, disgraceful, degenerate, depraved, scurrilous, ribald, coarse, vulgar; low-born, humble, poor, plebian, unworthy. *Ant.* noble, illustrious, high, stately, dignified, majestic, august, magnanimous, generous, honorable, modest, exalted, grand, ennobled, decent, decorous, respectable, venerable, reputable, proud, worthy, charitable, refined, haughty, rich.

ignominious, shameful, infamous, disgraceful, scandalous, heinous, execrable, offensive, opprobrious, vile, hateful, despicable, low, mean, base, cowardly, discreditable, flagrant, atrocious, nefarious, abhorrent, abominable, detestable, disgusting, humiliating, dishonorable, revolting, ignoble, unworthy, disreputable, inglorious, shocking, ribald, debasing, outrageous, notorious. *Ant.* reputable, dignified, stately, glorious, creditable, gracious, worthy, praiseworthy, noble, commendable, illustrious, fine, laudable, commendatory, eulogistic, popular, estimable, distinguished, splendid, good, meritorious, exemplary, brave, courageous, excellent, honorable, respectable, admirable, pleasing, gratifying, virtuous, exalted, grand, lofty, high, magnificent.

ignoramus, illiterate, dunce, fool, dolt, novice, beginner, simpleton, greenhorn. *Ant.* scholar, intellectual, student, savant, teacher, sage, expert, pedant.

ignorant, uneducated, uncultured, obtuse, dense, stupid, uncultivated, untaught, unacquainted, unknowing, unlearned, uninstructed, unlettered, superficial, shallow, illiterate, unenlightened, nescient, benighted, gross, coarse, vulgar. *Ant.* enlightened, learned, cultivated, cultured, scholarly, schooled, taught, educated, trained, instructed, disciplined, acquainted, knowledgeable, well-informed, skilled, lettered, literate, sage, wise, erudite, efficient, competent, able, talented, accomplished, well-read.

ignore, disregard, overlook, slight, omit, reject, snub, shun, forget. *Ant.* notice, regard, heed, acknowledge, recognize, accept.

ilk, kind, character, type, genus, breed, sort, nature, class.

ill, *adj.* sick, unwell, complaining, indisposed, distempered, ailing, afflicted, unhealthy, morbid, feeble, weak, impaired, diseased, sickly, infirm; *n.* evil, wickedness, hardship, loss, danger, mischief, harm, misfortune, mishap, calamity, pain, trouble, misery, sorrow, distress, grievance, vexation. *Ant.* well, fine, healthy, bright, robust, strong, powerful, whole, sound, muscular, hale, hearty, vigorous, forcible, sprightly, lively, lusty, good, pleasing, comforting, consoling; luck, fortune, privilege, welfare, advantage, benefit, happiness, prosperity, success, gain, blessing, profit, attainment, benediction, favor, achievement.

illegal, unlawful, illicit, unauthorized, dishonest, criminal, contraband, prohibited, banned, proscribed, outlawed, illegitimate, proclaimed, interdicted. *Ant.* legal, sanctioned, permissible, confirmed, allowed, lawful, right, judicial, conformable, authorized, approved, countenanced, moral, good, right, honest.

illegitimate, illegal, unlawful, illicit, dishonest, counterfeit, immoral, lawless, wicked, wrong, bad, unlicensed, improper, unauthorized, bastard. *Ant.* legal, right, licit, correct, accepted, proper, moral, ethical.

illicit, illegitimate, unlawful, clandestine, forbidden, guilty, wrong, illegal, wicked, bad, immoral, unethical, impure, adulterous. *Ant.* right, legal, moral, worthy, sanctioned, authorized, blessed, pure, noble, wholesome, good.

illimitable, infinite, unlimited, vast, boundless, unbounded, eternal. *Ant.* finite, bounded, limited, ended, circumscribed, restricted.

illiterate, untaught, ungrammatical, unlettered, ignorant, unlearned, uneducated, nescient. *Ant.* taught, schooled, lettered, literate, grammatical.

illogical, fallacious, unreasoned, incorrect, specious, absurd, foolish, deceptive, invalid, untenable, incoherent, inconsistent, spurious, unsound. *Ant.* logical, right, true, correct, sensible, valid, conforming, reasoned.

ill-treatment, abuse, mistreatment, maltreatment, neglect, cruelty, unfeelingness, carelessness, roughness, brutality, viciousness, inhumanity. *Ant.* care, concern, gentleness, mildness, attention, consideration.

illuminate, enlighten, illustrate, elucidate, brighten, clarify. *Ant.* darken, obscure, obfuscate, complicate, cloud, dull.

illusion, fantasy, phantom, image, imagination, vision, dream, delusion, fallacy, error, chimera, deception, misapprehension, mirage, fancy, apparition; specter, spirit, ghost, ghoul, sprite, poltergeist, fairy. *Ant.* reality, fact, actuality, occurrence, happening, certainty, event, circumstance, incident, episode, materiality, corporeality.

illustration, example, comparison, case, instance, specimen, picture.

illustrious, celebrated, famous, exalted, eminent, noble, renowned, brilliant, conspicuous, distinguished, acclaimed, applauded, great, superlative, superior. *Ant.* lowly, mean, obscure, humble, poor, unassuming, unpretentious, meek, abject, debased, ignoble, spiritless, pitiable, despicable, degenerate.

image, reflection, counterpart, double, representation, form, appearance, similitude, show, perception, likeness, portrait, picture, figure, effigy, photograph, copy, imitation, resemblance, statue, drawing, facsimile, counterpart, duplication, model, pattern, impression, illustration, reproduction.

imaginary, ideal, fanciful, fabulous, legendary, fictional, illusory, unreal, nonexistent, shadowy, visionary, fancied, supposititious, hypothetical, pictured, conceived, assumed, false, deceptive, fantastic, whimsical, chimerical, dreamy. *Ant.* real, true, factual, physical, substantial, genuine, corporeal, material, existing, tried, known, proved, tested, historic, nonfiction, visible, cosmic, evident, natural, sensible, tangible, palpable, definite, perceptible.

imagination, fancy, conception, fantasy, thought, mental image, idea, notion, impression, reflection, conceit, concept, supposition, contemplation. *Ant.* reality, actuality, existence, materiality, substance, being, entity, certainty, dull-wittedness, thoughtlessness, realism.

imagine, conceive, fancy, presume, think, apprehend, assume, suppose, guess, foretell, infer, conclude, realize, believe, visualize, picture, conjure, envision.

imbecility, feeble-mindedness, brainlessness, idiocy, foolishness, incapacity, hebetude, dullness, stupidity, cretinism, incompetency, dotage, simplicity, fatuousness, childishness, senility, dementia, fatuity, ineptitude. *Ant.* wisdom, sagacity, intelligence, understanding, comprehension, capacity, sanity, sense, subtlety, sapience, judgment, perspicacity, acuteness, profundity, discernment, discrimination.

imbue, pervade, color, inspire, saturate, animate, suffuse, infuse, instill, impregnate, permeate, penetrate.

imitate, copy, mimic, ape, duplicate, counterfeit, mock, reproduce, paraphrase, parody, transcribe, travesty, impersonate, simulate, quote, caricature, burlesque, parallel, match, represent, follow, admire, mirror, forge, emulate. *Ant.* differ, modify, change, alter, vary, diverge, disagree, despise, dislike, reject, conflict, oppose, dispute, bicker, wrangle, clash, reverse.

immaculate, unstained, spotless, unsullied, untainted, chaste, pure, impeccable, undefiled, incorrupt, innocent, untarnished, sinless. *Ant.* defiled, spotted, tarnished, unclean, dirty, filthy, impure, corrupt, sullied, soiled, vile, sinful, tainted, stained, blackened, defamed.

immanent, inborn, innate, inherent, natural, internal, intrinsic, subjective; universal (as God). *Ant.* learned, acquired, extrinsic, external, objective.

immaterial, irrelevant, trifling, insignificant, inessential, unimportant; incorporeal, unsubstantial, impalpable, impertinent, disembodied, spiritual, trivial. *Ant.* material, relevant, substantial, bodily, real, essential, important.

immature, unripe, callow, undeveloped, green, unready, raw, precocious, imperfect. *Ant.* mature, ripe, mellow, adult, grown.

immeasurable, illimitable, boundless, immense, infinite, measureless, vast, unbounded, bottomless, unfathomable, abysmal. *Ant.* measureable, limited, bounded.

immediately, instantly, forthwith, straight-away, presently, directly, right away, abruptly, at once, quickly, now, instantaneously, next, promptly, speedily.

immemorial, dateless, timeless, immemorable, old, early, ancient, prehistoric. *Ant.* recent, new, memorable, young.

immense, colossal, huge, enormous, vast, bulky, large, great, titanic, mighty, gigantic, tremendous, monstrous, stupendous. *Ant.* small, little, trifling, petty, insignificant, pigmy, dwarfish, diminutive, puny, unimportant, trivial, light, minute, tiny, stinted, paltry, midget, miniature, microscopic, infinitesimal.

immerse, submerge, inundate, soak, flood, sink, dip, douse, plunge, involve, overwhelm, duck, bury, engage, bathe, engulf, engross, absorb. *Ant.* regain, recover, release, uncover, restore, retrieve.

imminent, impending, threatening, menacing, abeyant, overhanging, ominous, inevitable, coming, nigh, approaching, near, destined, pressing, brewing. *Ant.* distant, afar, receding, retiring, regressing, withdrawing, retreating, departing, unsettled, unsteady, fluctuating, wavering, doubtful, unlikely, changing, unexpected, problematical.

immoderate, excessive, extreme, intemperate, extravagant, inordinate, exorbitant, intensive, overdone, unreasonable. *Ant.* moderate, reasonable, ordered, limited, restrained.

immodest, indelicate, boastful, lewd, licentious, shameless, indecent bold, coarse, brazen, obscene, unreserved, unconstrained. *Ant* reserved, shamefaced, decorous, bashful, prudish, restrained, deli cate, wholesome, humble, modest.

immoral, unprincipled, wrong, evil, corrupt, loose, indecent, profli gate, depraved, vicious, licentious, abandoned, lecherous. *Ant* moral, chaste, pure, high-minded, noble, virtuous, good, pious holy, godly.

immortal, undying, deathless, permanent, eternal, perpetual, ever lasting, abiding, imperishable, spiritual, noble, infinite. *Ant* fleeting, transitory, mortal, ephemeral, perishable, evanescent.

immovable, steadfast, immobile, anchored, fused, cemented, stable rooted, fixed, constant, firm, obdurate. *Ant.* plastic, yielding movable, inconstant, wavering, fickle, mobile.

immunity, exemption, privilege, exoneration, release, prerogative discharge, exculpation, respite, clearance, acquittal, reprieve freedom, license, dispensation, protection. *Ant.* conviction, con demnation, proscription, sequestration, attainder, disapproba tion, blame, charge, indictment, censure, interdiction, debarment exclusion, susceptibility, vulnerability, liability.

immutable, unchanged, invariable, stable, permanent, unalterable fixed, constant. *Ant.* changeable, movable, fluctuating, variable

impact, collision, shock, concussion, percussion, clash, contact, slam *Ant.* recoil, rebound, reflex; miss, avoidance.

impair, injure, diminish, weaken, deteriorate, decrease, taint, infect contaminate, vitiate, degrade, defile, corrupt, pollute, demoralize damage, adulterate, debauch, harm, hurt, blemish, deface, break incapacitate, despoil, ravage, disfigure, mar, corrode, blight cripple. *Ant.* renew, restore, better, improve, strengthen, hearten revive, revivify, redress, heal, renovate, rally, cure, repair, mend rectify, redeem, reclaim, resuscitate, reanimate, remedy, refresh reestablish, regenerate, rejuvenate, aid, assist, help.

impart, confer, grant, give, transmit, disclose, divulge, reveal convey, bestow, notify, enlighten, tell, inform, specify, mention acquaint, communicate, advise, instruct. *Ant.* conceal, mystify deny, hide, secrete, puzzle, keep, hold, stifle, suppress, camouflage withhold.

impartial, neutral, nonpartisan, nonsectarian, equitable, just, fair unbiased, unprejudiced, reasonable, indifferent, disinterested equal. *Ant.* prejudiced, one-sided, biased, unjust, unequal favoring, unfair, interested, involved.

impasse, end, obstacle, limit, bar, deadlock. *Ant.* opening, clearance solution, victory, gain.

impassioned, burning, glowing, passionate, patriotic, fiery, intense vehement, thrilling, fervid, ardent, stirring. *Ant.* calm, cool, un disturbed, unruffled, unconcerned, impassive, uninvolved, unin terested, placid, composed, restrained, tranquil.

impassive, phlegmatic, apathetic, imperturbable, insensitive, cool, dull, tranquil, calm. *Ant.* responsive, emotional, concerned, sensitive, excitable, sympathetic.

impatient, eager, restless, fussy, fidgety, fretful, abrupt, brusque, expectant, nervous. *Ant.* cool, calm, patient, controlled, enduring, long-suffering, forbearing, tolerant.

impeccable, spotless, immaculate, faultless, innocent, incorrupt, perfect. *Ant.* messy, stained, sullied, defective, imperfect.

impecunious, destitute, penniless, poor, poverty-stricken, broke, needy, bereft. *Ant.* wealthy, rich, affluent, moneyed, opulent, prosperous, well-to-do.

impede, hinder, retard, counteract, offset, prevent, obstruct, delay, check, hamper, thwart, arrest, stop, interrupt, block, encumber, oppose, repress, restrain. *Ant.* help, assist, speed, hasten, support, facilitate, stimulate, encourage, advance, endorse, further, cooperate, expedite.

impediment, obstruction, obstacle, hindrance, disability, encumbrance, barrier, difficulty, restriction, block, wall, inhibition, weakness. *Ant.* aid, support, help, assistance, cooperation, encouragement, collaboration.

impel, instigate, drive, actuate, induce, force, move, urge, compel, goad, influence, prod. *Ant.* balk, rebuff, repulse, repress, suppress, slow, delay, stop.

impenetrable, impervious, adamant, stolid, dense, dark, undiscernible, abstruse, obtuse, esoteric. *Ant.* comprehensible, clear, permeable, intelligible, transparent, soft, penetrable.

imperative, required, unavoidable, vital, critical, inescapable, commanding, urgent, compulsory, mandatory, obligatory, dominant, peremptory, inexorable, absolute, necessary, preponderant, exigent, pressing, indispensible, requisite, essential. *Ant.* voluntary, free, discretionary, optional, unconstrained, intentional, planned, unrestrained, secondary, unnecessary, inessential, dispensable.

imperceptible, slight, gradual, subtle, indistinct, inconspicuous, insignificant, negligible, inappreciable. *Ant.* obvious, ostentatious, distinct, perceptible, conspicuous, significant, apparent, striking.

imperfection, blemish, fault, deficiency, drawback, failing, defect, stain, frailty, snag, flaw, inadequacy, infirmity, transgression, wrong. *Ant.* perfection, goodness, completeness, purity, faultlessness, excellence.

imperil, jeopardize, hazard, endanger, risk, expose, threaten, uncover. *Ant.* protect, safeguard, secure, defend, watch, shield.

imperious, commanding, dictatorial, authoritative, overbearing, exacting, domineering, arrogant, harsh, despotic. *Ant.* obsequious, fawning, subservient, sycophantic, humble, obedient, dispirited, dismal, weak, servile, groveling, pliant, parasitical, abject.

impersonate, imitate, personify, mimic, ape, act, portray, represent, pose, enact, copy, assume, feign, pretend.

impertinent, irrelevant, inapplicable, trivial, absurd, inane, rude, impudent, insolent, officious, intrusive, meddling, forward, bold, insulting, brazen, audacious, contemptuous. *Ant.* humble, refined, courteous, civil, respectful, polished, obliging, affable, pleasant, pertinent, serious, momentous, significant, important, relevant, polite.

imperturbable, calm, placid, unruffled, serene, unexcitable, composed. *Ant.* excitable, irritable, touchy, irascible.

impervious, impermeable, obdurate, impenetrable, hard, dense, resistant, frustrating. *Ant.* open, penetrable, permeable, exposed, susceptible, sensitive.

impetuous, impulsive, boisterous, violent, rash, hasty, passionate, fiery, ungovernable, obstinate, intractable, unruly, heedless, incautious, reckless. *Ant.* cautious, considerate, calm, steady, mild, thoughtful, patient, placid, tranquil, retiring, composed, unobtrusive, contemplative, cool.

impetus, momentum, impulse, force, stimulus, motive, pressure.

impinge, strike, touch, hit, clash, collide, infringe, encroach, violate, trespass. *Ant.* miss, pass, avoid, respect, defer.

impious, irreligious, profane, blasphemous, wicked, sacrilegious, disrespectful, irreverent, desecrating, unsanctified, reprobate, unrighteous, atheistic, fiendish. *Ant.* inspired, pious, devout, consecrated, prayerful, spiritual, blessed, religious, saintly, pure, angelic, righteous, sanctified, redeemed.

implacable, pitiless, inexorable, unrelenting, vindictive, vengeful, cruel, rigid, stern, ruthless, obdurate, uncompromising, inflexible. *Ant.* kind, merciful, lenient, tolerant, appeasable.

implant, plant, graft, fix, set in, sow, insert, engraft, inculcate, infuse, embed, instill. *Ant.* remove, eliminate, excise, uproot.

implement, perform, effectuate, effect, execute, achieve, fulfill, do, accomplish, realize, expedite. *Ant.* defer, restrict, cancel, hinder.

implicate, incriminate, accuse, charge, involve, impute, entangle, stigmatize, embroil, trap, concern, enfold, indict, blame, arraign, inculpate, imply, challenge, cite. *Ant.* assist, free, defend, condone, pardon, absolve, release, support, excuse, minimize, ratify, authorize, approve, sanction, endorse.

implicit, tacit, implied, presupposed, inferred, known, understood, recognized, accepted, unspoken. *Ant.* explicit, specific, stated, expressed, declared.

imply, infer, connote, mean, hint, signify, suggest. *Ant.* define, express, describe, state.

import, bring in, introduce, transport, convey, imply, purport, signify. *Ant.* export, send out, ship out.

important, influential, significant, grave, weighty, material, vital, appreciable, leading, authoritative, relevant, momentous, essential, serious, great, substantial, critical, decisive, prominent, powerful, determining, imposing, urgent, primary, paramount, chief, foremost, principal. *Ant.* paltry, petty, trivial, slight, un important, frivolous, subordinate, nonessential, commonplace, weak, worthless, cheap, meager, powerless, nugatory, picayune, insignificant, small, little, foolish, inappreciable.

importunate, urgent, impelling, insistent, pressing, persistent, demanding, pertinacious. *Ant.* unimportant, not pressing.

imposing, striking, impressive, grand, majestic, grandiose, arresting, resplendent, noble, towering, lofty, sublime, august, commanding, superlative, supreme, solemn, surpassing, magnificent, leading, stately, illustrious, eminent, imperial, splendid, awe-inspiring. *Ant.* small, mean, poor, meager, ridiculous, plebian, petty, unimportant, paltry, absurd, insignificant, subordinate, ordinary, trivial, crude, wretched, primitive, modest, unprepossessing, weak.

imposture, deception, impersonation, masquerade, fake, hoax, pretense, ruse, counterfeit, fraud, cheat. *Ant.* honesty, reality, fairness, genuineness, actuality.

impotent, powerless, feeble, weak, harmless, defenseless, useless, disabled, incapacitated, infirm, frail, debilitated, enervated, delicate, inefficient, sterile, exhausted, incapable, ineffectual, barren. *Ant.* forceful, intense, influential, strong, potent, powerful, virile, efficient, puissant, effectual, energetic, vigorous, efficacious, productive, manly, fertile, capable, masterful, dominating.

impoverish, make poor, deprive, reduce, drain, beggar, pauperize, rob, weaken, ruin. *Ant.* enrich, aid, help, elevate, raise, assist.

impracticable, unrealistic, unattainable, unachievable, impractical, unfeasible, unworkable, inexpedient, visionary. *Ant.* practicable, pragmatic, possible, workable, reasonable, feasible, practical, realistic.

impregnable, invincible, invulnerable, secure, formidable, unassailable, insuperable. *Ant.* liable, exposed, open, susceptible, unprotected, defenseless.

impressionable, easily influenced, overawed, suggestible, susceptible, vulnerable. *Ant.* stable, insusceptible, rigid, unimpressionable, immovable, obstinate, resolute.

impressive, arresting, forcible, exciting, stirring, moving, thrilling, deep, penetrating, profound, absorbing, touching, imposing, awesome, considerable, prominent, remarkable, notable, momentous, commanding, vital, serious. *Ant.* unimpressive, trivial, paltry, petty, unimportant, shallow, silly, inconsequential, ineffective, common, ordinary, insignificant, disappointing, slight, frivolous, trite, inane, ridiculous, commonplace, pitiable, uninteresting, cheap, shallow.

imprison, incarcerate, cage, restrain, confine, lock up, impound, hold, detain, enclose, limit, constrain. *Ant.* free, liberate, release, discharge, dismiss, acquit, extricate, reprieve.

improbable, unlikely, implausible, unexpected, unreasonable, rare, inconceivable, questionable. *Ant.* probable, possible, likely, usual, plausible, believable, normal, ostensible.

impromptu, extemporaneous, spontaneous, improvised, ad lib, off-hand, unplanned, unrehearsed, impulsive. *Ant.* rehearsed, prepared, planned, premeditated, considered, deliberate, devised.

improper, unbecoming, unsuitable, discourteous, wrong, offensive, daring, lewd, immodest, incorrect, indelicate, indecent. *Ant.* fitting, considerate, proper, right, seemly, good, correct.

improve, mend, reform, amend, rectify, better, edit, upgrade, revise, ameliorate, advance, correct, purify, refine. *Ant.* deteriorate, degrade, injure, damage, impair, mar, worsen, depreciate, decay, decline, degenerate, fade, sink, weaken.

improvident, incautious, careless, imprudent, prodigal, spendthrift, reckless, wasteful, unconcerned, heedless, extravangant, lavish, thriftless, dissipated, squandering. *Ant.* niggardly, penurious, miserly, thrifty, careful, stingy.

improvise, invent, extemporize, ad lib, concoct, compose, arrange, adapt, revise, devise, contrive.

imprudent, indiscreet, rash, unwise, unforeseeing, incautious, careless. *Ant.* prudent, discreet, circumspect, cautious, careful, wary.

impudent, brazen, saucy, audacious, impertinent, bold, forward, insolent, rude, uncivil, presumptuous, caustic, pert, officious, sarcastic, arrogant, insubordinate, haughty, self-assertive, flippant, supercilious, sassy, fresh, discourteous, blustering, swaggering. *Ant.* retiring, polite, genteel, modest, civil, humble, courteous, gracious, thoughtful.

impulsive, hasty, rash, violent, forcible, excitable, impatient, fiery, vehement, precipitate, daring, incautious, uninhibited, careless, indiscreet, heedless, imprudent, reckless, headstrong, foolhardy. *Ant.* cautious, thoughtful, steady, prudent, careful, cool, discreet, watchful, restrained, circumspect, sensible, patient, deliberate, heedful, politic.

impunity, license, freedom, immunity, exemption, permission, liberty, security. *Ant.* liability, danger, culpability, answerability, responsibility.

impure, unclean, corrupt, smutty, defiled, sullied, mixed, coarse, adulterated, mingled, loose, polluted, obscene, foul, indecent. *Ant.* spotless, clean, immaculate, pure, cleansed, filtered, strained, refined, perfect, impeccable.

impute, attribute, charge, ascribe, blame, implicate, allege, assign, trace (to), indict, inculpate, brand. *Ant.* defend, palliate, excuse, advocate, help, protect, extenuate, justify, exonerate, exculpate, clear, vindicate, countenance, endorse.

inactive, idle, inert, latent, quiescent, passive, motionless, stagnant, sedentary, resting, dormant, lazy, inanimate, torpid, indolent. *Ant.* active, working, acting, moving, bustling, energetic, live, dynamic.

inadequate, wanting, unfit, insufficient, lacking, partial, scanty, incompetent, deficient. *Ant.* adequate, enough, sufficient, plenty, suitable, competent.

inadvertent, unintentional, accidental, chance, thoughtless, careless, heedless, negligent, unconscious, unobservant. *Ant.* planned, intentional, careful, attentive.

inane, pointless, insipid, banal, silly, absurd, frivolous, foolish. *Ant.* expressive, important, meaningful, significant.

inappropriate, unsuitable, inapt, discordant, unfitted, infelicitous, incongruous, tasteless, improper. *Ant.* appropriate, suitable, apt, becoming, fitting, proper.

inarticulate, mute, speechless, voiceless, dumb, silent, stammering, mumbling, whispering; unjointed, unattached. *Ant.* articulate, vocal, clear speaking, fluent, glib; jointed, hinged, pivoted.

inaugurate, begin, start, found, install, open, institute, originate, initiate, introduce, commence. *Ant.* terminate, finish, deactivate, conclude, close, adjourn, discontinue.

inauspicious, unfavorable, unpromising, ill-omened, untoward, adverse, unpropitious, unlikely, discouraging. *Ant.* favorable, lucky, promising.

incarnate, embodied, exemplified, personified, materialized.

incentive, motive, spur, impulse, inducement, provocation, enticement, compulsion, allurement, stimulus, bribe, temptation, bait, lure, invitation.

inception, inauguration, origin, start, beginning, initiation, birth, commencement, founding, opening, onset. *Ant.* termination, end, finish, close, demise, death.

incessant, ceaseless, constant, perpetual, uninterrupted, endless, continual, interminable, unremitting. *Ant.* intermittent, sporadic, periodic, now and then, recurrent, interrupted, occasional.

incident, event, episode, occasion, chance, happening, occurrence.

incidental, subordinate, fortuitous, occasional, minor, contingent, concomitant, secondary, nonessential, associated. *Ant.* cardinal, fundamental, essential, elementary, basic, vital.

incite, instigate, excite, encourage, urge, stimulate, impel, stir up, provoke, rouse, enrage, arouse, prompt, animate, inflame, fire, actuate, goad, persuade, exhort, force, coax, sway, influence, induce, taunt. *Ant.* deter, repress, dishearten, defend (against), dissuade, check, admonish, discourage, expostulate, restrain, cool, dampen, calm, depress, subdue, dispirit, temper, frustrate, stop, prevent.

inclination, leaning, gradient, slope, bias, bent, tendency, disposition, wish, desire, liking, preference, fancy, allurement, attraction, fascination, hobby, proneness, prejudice, aptness, wont, habit, predilection, propensity, partiality, penchant. *Ant.* unconcern, neutrality, indifference, disinterest, nonchalance, inappetence, apathy, supineness, inattention, coldness, impotence, heedlessness, insouciance, uprightness, level.

include, contain, encompass, embody, incorporate, comprise, take in, involve, surround, embrace, consist of, number among. *Ant.* exclude, reject, eliminate, prohibit, omit, preclude.

incognito

incognito, disguised, camouflaged, masked, veiled, deceptively, privately, bogusly. *Ant.* openly, obviously, unhidden, identified, unmasked.

income, earnings, gain, revenue, proceeds, receipts, profits, interest, rents, tolls, salary, wages, stipend, emolument, annuity, dividends, winnings. *Ant.* loss, cost, charge, expense, outgo.

incommode, annoy, plague, displease, molest, distress, disturb, inconvenience, inhibit, disarrange, vex, trouble, worry, disquiet, bother, harass, pester. *Ant.* please, help, satisfy, console, gratify, appease, indulge, convenience, humor, enliven, assist, amuse, regale, refresh, comfort, gladden, attract, benefit.

incompatible, inharmonious, discrepant, discordant, incongruous, inconsistent, contrary, ill-matched, opposing, unsuited, inconsonant, unloving, unsympathetic, quarrelsome. *Ant.* compatible, attuned, well-matched, congenial, loving, harmonious.

incompetent, incapable, unfit, inadequate, inefficient, ineffectual, bungling, unhandy, unqualified, maladroit, stupid, unable, irresponsible, floundering, unskilled, ignorant, stumbling, inept, clumsy, heavy-handed, inexpert, untalented, unsuitable. *Ant.* competent, skillful, expert, dexterous, deft, proficient, talented, adroit, clever, capable, skilled, erudite, experienced, informed, efficient, facile, effectual, qualified, apt, handy, adept.

incongruous, inconsistent, incompatible, absurd, inappropriate, inharmonious, inapposite, unsuitable, disagreeing, contrary, irreconcilable, repugnant, mismatched, incommensurable, discrepant, discordant, incoherent, contradictory, divergent, different, conflicting, disparate, modified, paradoxical, diversified. *Ant.* congruous, accordant, suitable, harmonious, matched, consistent, agreeing, unified, compatible, coinciding, uniform, fitted, same, homologous, fluctuating, consonant, analogous, cognate, apposite, congeneric, allied, corresponding.

inconsiderate, thoughtless, tactless, unfeeling, unsympathetic, selfish, undiscerning, indiscreet, careless. *Ant.* considerate, sympathetic, thoughtful, generous, sensitive, discreet, helpful.

inconsistent, unsteady, fluctuating, vacillating, inconstant, varying, contrary, incompatible, unsuitable, inconsonant. *Ant.* consistent, steady, uniform, suitable, consonant.

inconstant, fickle, unstable, mutable, changing, inconsistent, uncertain, vacillating, capricious, perfidious. *Ant.* constant, reliable, fixed, loyal, steadfast.

incorporate, form, amalgamate, merge, unite, consolidate, mix, embody, establish, blend. *Ant.* dissolve, disperse, divide, separate, remove.

incorrigible, intractable, refractory, abandoned, delinquent, irreclaimable, hardened, resistant. *Ant.* educable, tractable, mild, obedient, gentle, reclaimable.

increase, augmentation, enlargement, accession, addition, growth, extension, development, increment, inflation, accretion, gain, intensification, multiplication, aggrandizement, accrual, expansion, amplification, swelling, dilation, filling, spread, intumescence, distension. *Ant.* decrease, shrinkage, contraction, deflation, loss, decrement, attenuation, leakage, diminution, curtailment, lessening, depletion, reduction, atrophy, decimation, abridgment, subtraction, abstraction, abbreviation, deterioration.

ncredible, unbelievable, astonishing, fantastic, far-fetched, suspicious, implausible. *Ant.* credible, believable, creditable, realistic, plausible.

ncrement, addition, increase, enlargement, raise (in value). *Ant.* decrease, loss, decline, diminution.

nculcate, instill, teach, implant, imbue, impress, impart, instruct, urge, discipline, drill (into), indoctrinate, brainwash.

ncumbent, *adj.* pressing, binding, obligatory, urgent, coercive, necessary, behooving, stringent, imperative, peremptory, inescapable; *n.* officeholder, occupant. *Ant.* free, unobligated, immune, unencumbered, exempt, excusable, released, absolved, unaccountable, liberated, unamenable, privileged.

ncursion, raid, robbery, infringement, attack, foray, violation, invasion, trespass.

ndebted, owing, obligated, obliged, bound, beholden, unpaid. *Ant.* paid, cleared (up), squared (with), settled (accounts).

ndecent, improper, offensive, unbecoming, indelicate, immodest, shocking, immoral, lewd, coarse, shameless. *Ant.* decent, chaste, pure, courteous, respectful, virtuous, modest.

ndefatigable, tireless, assiduous, pertinacious, diligent, persevering, unremitting, vigorous, hard-working, determined.

ndefinite, vague, uncertain, indeterminate, lax, loose, unsettled, indistinct, hazy, undefined, unclear, unlimited, unfixed, inexact, dim, inconclusive, obscure, confused, equivocal, ambiguous. *Ant.* clear, certain, conclusive, definite, indubitable, exact, indisputable, apparent, unquestionable, tested, evident, well-marked, reliable, limited, infallible, absolute, positive, assured, decided, well-known, ascertained.

ndemnify, recompense, compensate, guarantee, repay, secure, remunerate, repair, reimburse, requite, satisfy.

ndependent, free, unrestricted, separate, unconfined, unallied, self-reliant, sovereign, single, autonomous, alone, self-sufficient, self-governing, wealthy, rich. *Ant.* dependent, subservient, relative, subordinate, auxiliary, reliant.

ndeterminate, uncertain, indefinite, unmeasured, unfixed, vague, unsettled, wavering, flexible, faltering, inconclusive, vacillating. *Ant.* firm, sure, determinate, definite, certain, measurable, fixed, settled, established.

ndicate, show, disclose, designate, point out, tell, mark, register, denote, reveal, manifest, testify, differentiate, evidence, specify, signal, imply, hint, signify, connote. *Ant.* conceal, hide, confuse, discompose, perplex, disconcert, bewilder, mislead.

ndict, arraign, accuse, charge, blame, incriminate, impeach. *Ant.* absolve, release, acquit, exonerate, reward, honor.

indifference, apathy, carelessness, insensibility, inattention, non-chalance, coldness, insouciance, unconcern, impassivity, supine-ness, detachment, callousness, disinterest, neutrality, insuscep-tibility. *Ant.* concern, eagerness, feeling, involvement, caring, warmth, enthusiasm, sensitiveness, sympathy, compassion, senti-mentality, heed, desire, carefulness, inclination, vivacity, atten-tion, impressibility, sincerity, liveliness, passion.

indigence, poverty, want, need, penury, hunger, destitution, priva-tion, misery, starvation, insufficiency, scantiness, dearth, pauper-ism, scarcity, distress, tenuity, famine. *Ant.* plenty, repletion, independence, affluence, opulence, wealth, competence, substance, riches, abundance, sufficiency.

indigenous, native, inborn, aboriginal, domestic, natural, inherent, endemic, innate. *Ant.* imported, introduced, naturalized, alien, foreign, nonnative.

indignation, anger, scorn, wrath, fury, ire, displeasure, resentment, rage, exasperation, passion, huff, animosity, pique, temper, acri-mony, irascibility, virulence, annoyance, bitterness, excitement, agitation. *Ant.* calmness, benignity, gentleness, humility, imper-turbability, modesty, patience, toleration, forbearance, serenity, evenness, composure, tranquility, restraint, self-control, self-possession, equanimity, self-restraint, passiveness, poise.

indignity, insult, dishonor, disrespect, affront, outrage, humiliation, embarrassment, injury, opprobrium, disparagement, reproach, irreverence, ignominy, scurrility, discourtesy, scoffing, jeering, mockery, vituperation, taunt, slight. *Ant.* esteem, courtesy, dig-nity, honor, praise, consideration, reverence, admiration, regard, obeisance, deference, respect, approbation, admiration, venera-tion, obsequiousness.

indirect, circuitous, devious, crooked, oblique, roundabout, tortuous, implied, inferred. *Ant.* straightforward, straight, direct, blunt, unswerving, candid, explicit.

indiscreet, unwise, foolish, heedless, rash, thoughtless, foolhardy, imprudent, reckless. *Ant.* discreet, careful.

indiscriminate, unselective, heterogeneous, promiscuous, uncritical, mixed. *Ant.* selective, chosen, homogeneous, critical.

indispensable, requisite, essential, imperative, necessary, required, fundamental, needed, basic, prerequisite, expedient. *Ant.* super-fluous, unnecessary, useless, dispensable, redundant, inessential, needless, unwanted, uncalled-for.

indisputable, incontestable, undeniable, indubitable, undoubted, un-questionable, irrefutable, unassailable, incontrovertible, obvious, positive, evident, unmistakable, plain, certain, proved, sure, un-equivocal, definite, assured, infallible. *Ant.* doubtful, dubious, uncertain, vague, questionable, unreliable, untested, equivocal, indeterminate, undefined, unproved, unauthentic, undetermined, controvertible, cryptic, indefinite, ambiguous, untrustworthy, dis-putable, open to question.

ndistinct, vague, indefinite, obscure, blurred, uncertain, indistinguishable, ambiguous, confused, shadowy, dim, darkened, misty, nebulous, hazy, imperceptible, cloudy, faint, inaudible. *Ant.* clear, conspicuous, definite, distinct, manifest, obvious, plain, visible, perceptible, discernible, palpable, lucid, luminous, intelligible, explicit, positive, evident, apparent.

ndividual, peculiar, different, special, unique, distinct, original, particular, characteristic, singular, specific, idiosyncratic, personal, separate. *Ant.* general, conventional, universal, usual, regular, common, ordinary.

ndoctrinate, teach, imbue, train, instruct, discipline, drill, initiate. *Ant.* neglect, mislead, misguide, confuse, fail.

ndolent, lazy, sleepy, idle, drowsy, slothful, slack, sluggish, supine, inert, ineffectual, remiss, dull, torpid, inactive, somnolent, listless, lethargic, lackadaisical, languid, soporific. *Ant.* vivacious, active, lively, quick, prompt, keen, ardent, eager, anxious, industrious, laborious, bustling, alert, busy, smart, earnest, sharp, intent, spry, indefatigable, energetic, enthusiastic, diligent, persevering.

ndomitable, unyielding, firm, unconquerable, untameable, invincible. *Ant.* weak, feeble, yielding.

ndorse, see **endorse.**

nduce, impel, instigate, cause, bring about, persuade, actuate, encourage, move, influence, urge, stimulate, incite, motivate, spur. *Ant.* repress, discourage, repel, hinder, hamper, dissuade.

nduct, lead into, initiate, invest, introduce, install; infer, conclude, generalize. *Ant.* lead away, expel, reject; end, withdraw.

ndulge, foster, please, cherish, pamper, fondle, humor, gratify, favor, placate, spoil, concede, satisfy, permit, endear, nurture, pet, sustain, coddle. *Ant.* torment, annoy, trouble, disquiet, deny, pester, molest, displease, plague, mortify, bother, harass, sadden, disallow, faze, afflict, grieve, distress, hurt, repress, thwart, disappoint, tease, discipline, tire, punish, worry, vex.

ndustrious, diligent, sedulous, busy, engaged, active, occupied, indefatigable, assiduous, intent, zealous, plodding, laboring, hardworking, business-like. *Ant.* inactive, careless, lethargic, inert, idle, slothful, slack, languid, indolent, sluggish, remiss, supine, otiose, laggard, lazy, drowsy, unoccupied, lackadaisical, shiftless, unemployed, worthless.

ndustry, activity, assiduity, exertion, attention, sedulousness, diligence, laboriousness, persistence, effort, application, patience, intentness, constancy, perseverance, plodding, indefatigability, pursuit; enterprise, business, undertaking, production, commerce, manufacturing. *Ant.* sloth, idleness, sluggishness, fickleness, inertness, indolence, neglect, changeableness, laziness, negligence, inattention, inconstancy, dawdling, languor, lethargy, heaviness, drowsiness, torpor, procrastination, shirking.

inebriated, drunk, intoxicated, tipsy, tight; exhilarated, stimulated, refreshed, heartened. *Ant.* sober, abstinent; unmoved, calm.

ineffective, inadequate, impotent, vain, ineffectual, futile, useless, unproductive, feeble, idle, weak, unfruitful. *Ant.* effective, successful, efficacious, powerful, forceful, efficient, useful, potent.

inefficient, unproductive, wasteful, incapable, inept, unskillful, maladroit, feeble, fumbling. *Ant.* efficient, capable, able, potent, practical.

inept, awkward, unhandy, inappropriate, maladroit, clumsy, unfit, foolish. *Ant.* apt, adroit, competent, fit, skillful, able, suitable.

inert, inactive, lifeless, dead, dull, lazy, powerless, impotent, stolid, impassive, idle, slothful, torpid, dormant, dilatory, phlegmatic, supine, quiescent. *Ant.* active, alert, alive, awake, operational, working, living, moving, watchful, vigilant.

inevitable, unavoidable, certain, irresistible, indefeasible, necessary, sure, avoidless, ineluctable, imminent, inescapable, predestined, fated. *Ant.* uncertain, vague, unlikely, indeterminate, doubtful, avoidable, contingent, preventable, incidental, avertable, fortuitous, problematical, indefinite, questionable.

inexhaustible, never-ending, illimitable, indefatigable, untiring, unwearied, limitless, infinite. *Ant.* limited, ending, short-lived, tiring, finite, wearying, consumable.

inexorable, implacable, inflexible, firm, pitiless, grim, severe, resolute, obdurate, adamant, unalterable, unyielding. *Ant.* merciful, lenient, yielding, compassionate, relenting, forbearing.

inexpensive, cheap, low-priced, a bargain. *Ant.* expensive, dear, costly, valuable, high-priced.

inexperienced, untrained, unpracticed, unskilled, unsuited, artless, inexpert, unready, green, raw, beginning, rude, unpolished, unprepared, undisciplined. *Ant.* skilled, experienced, suited, ready, expert, trained, practiced.

infamous, wicked, atrocious, execrable, disreputable, heinous, abhorrent, ignominious, despicable, disgraceful, shameful, outrageous, ill-famed, shocking, dark, notorious, profligate, base, vile, scandalous, perfidious, corrupt, malevolent, vicious, immoral, sinful, depraved, iniquitous, demoralized, dissolute, foul, villainous, evil. *Ant.* virtuous, faultless, meritorious, noble, good, righteous, pure, worthy, moral, fine, incorruptible, perfect, exalted, innocent, true, sublime, admirable, glorious, constant, exemplary, clean, honest, straightforward, frank, undefiled, candid, conscientious, high-principled, likeable, just, honorable, trustworthy, respectable, dignified, beloved, reputable.

infantile, childish, babyish, immature, puerile, young, weak. *Ant.* mature, adult, grown up, of age.

infatuated, fascinated, enamored, in love, deceived, doting, fond, foolish, beguiled, enthralled, besotted, deluded, captivated, silly. *Ant.* sensible, prudent, wise, calm, cool, fancy-free, judicious.

nfectious, contagious, catching, contaminating, defiling, polluting, pestilential, noxious, vitiating, sickening, communicable. *Ant.* harmless, safe, non-infectious, sanitary, antiseptic.

nference, deduction, assumption, corollary, conclusion, judgment, result, consequence, sequence, reason, argument, solution, guess, upshot, derivation, implification, surmise, application. *Ant.* test, preconception, statement, prejudgment, evidence, anticipation, predilection, foreboding, foretelling, presentiment, forethought, foresight.

nferior, substandard, subordinate, shoddy, poorer, lesser, lower, inadequate, secondary, deficient. *Ant.* superior, first-class, better, best, prime, grade A, upper, foremost.

nfernal, diabolical, devilish, demoniacal, horrible, hellish, satanic, atrocious, fiendish, malicious, flagitious, accursed, wicked, unspeakable, damnable. *Ant.* heavenly, angelic, divine, pure, hallowed, celestial, rapturous, consecrated, sanctified, holy, sacred, sacrosanct, glorious, predestined, saintly, godlike.

nfinite, unlimited, immeasurable, unbounded, boundless, interminable, eternal, illimitable, inexhaustible, countless, endless, innumerable, indefinite, timeless, incalculable, everlasting, incomprehensible, continual, termless, continuing, perpetual. *Ant.* finite, limited, definite, numbered, particular, terminable, measurable, circumscribed, confined, bounded, momentary, comprehensible, restricted, narrow, transient, brief, transitory, ephemeral, small, little, fleeting, moderate, determinate, short, evanescent, shallow, positive, fixed.

nfirm, weak, decrepit, invalid, enervated, languid, feeble, sickly, debilitated, enfeebled, tottering, drooping, exhausted, frail, doddering, spent, worn, lacking, fragile, unstable, ailing, unhealthy. *Ant.* strong, sturdy, potent, robust, husky, stout, lusty, vigorous, powerful, forceful, active, hale, brisk, healthy, muscular, hearty, sound, tough, energetic, sinewy, virile.

nflame, anger, incense, irritate, nettle, exasperate, enrage, aggravate, chafe, arouse, provoke, kindle, incite, excite, vex, stir, roil, taunt, ruffle, heckle, infuriate, blaze, madden, ignite, craze, burn, blush. *Ant.* soothe, calm, compose, mollify, assuage, still, lull, pacify, appease, alleviate, palliate, allay, quell, smooth, quiet, repress, dampen, suppress, reconcile, mitigate, restrain, please, cool down, placate, tranquilize.

nflate, distend, dilate, expand, exaggerate, swell, enlarge, elate, fill, bloat, blow up, stuff, pad, over-lend (money), over-issue (currency). *Ant.* deflate, shrink, compress, condense, trim, edit.

nflexible, stiff, stubborn, firm, obstinate, obdurate, rigid, strict, unyielding, tenacious, inexorable, intractable. *Ant.* flexible, soft, elastic, reasonable, resilient, gentle, yielding, pliable, plastic.

nfluence, *n.* power, weight, control, supremacy, sway, superiority, authority, patronage, reputation, importance, credit, character, favor, ascendancy, prominence, predominance, prestige, leadership, command, despotism, absolutism, mastery, domination, pres-

sure, attraction, magnetism, effect, domination, prerogative, rule
v. sway, modify, direct, rule, prejudice, act upon, regulate, control, bias, counteract, restrain, compel, affect, predominate, actuate, outweigh, dominate, carry weight, draw, pull, move, drive, rouse, spur. *Ant. n.* unimportance, impotence, uselessness, inefficacy, subserviency, pettiness, inferiority, servility, worthlessness, meanness, contemptibleness, lowliness, weakness, submissiveness, feebleness, dullness, timidity, futility, inefficiency, incapacity, subjection.

informal, natural, regular, customary, unofficial, unceremonious, unconventional, easy, offhand, unconstrained. *Ant.* formal, rigid, ceremonious, stiff, punctilious, perfunctory, academic, methodical, precise, official.

information, news, data, knowledge, learning, lore, fact, intelligence. *Ant.* ignorance, rumor, guesswork, conjecture.

infraction, violation, break, trespass, transgression, non-fulfillment, illegality, breach, contravention. *Ant.* obedience, conformity, compliance, submission, legality.

infrequent, rare, sporadic, odd, irregular, unusual, isolated, scarce. *Ant.* frequent, common, ordinary, usual, customary, scheduled, often.

infringe, transgress, break, intrude, violate, encroach, trespass, infract, invade, contravene, disregard, poach, disobey, repudiate, aggress, attack, assault. *Ant.* observe, comply, obey, fulfill, retreat, perform, discharge, satisfy, redeem, request, promise, acquiesce, concur, resist, agree, repulse, repel, submit, withdraw, surrender.

infuriate, enrage, incense, anger, inflame, exasperate, madden, roil, vex, taunt, tease, incite. *Ant.* soothe, placate, appease, pacify, calm, gladden, cheer.

infuse, instill, inspire, steep, permeate, inoculate, macerate, imbue, implant, animate.

ingenious, skillful, ready, productive, clever, original, fertile, resourceful, inventive, handy, imaginative, expert, witty, apt, keen, deft, talented, proficient, competent, capable, qualified, trained, able, adroit, gifted, sagacious, endowed, dexterous. *Ant.* inept, unskilled, incompetent, bungling, unable, inapt, ungainly, stupid, clumsy, inexperienced, awkward, amateurish, childish, ignorant, careless, backward, fumbling, maladroit, unhandy, unfit, green, unqualified, immature.

ingenuous, open, candid, artless, frank, sincere, fair, undisguised, honest, plain, unsophisticated, unsuspicious, generous, guileless, natural, naive, unreserved, simple, childish, direct, literal, unworldly, inexperienced, trusting, credulous, straightforward, outspoken, unaffected, aboveboard, blunt, simple-minded. *Ant.* sly, crafty, cunning, tricky, subtle, shifty, intriguing, artful, scheming, wily, insincere, smart, sharp, untrusting, worldly, wise, suspicious, artificial, designing, shrewd, politic, insidious, strategic, deceptive, underhand, diplomatic, crooked, deceitful, stealthy.

ingratiate, disarm, charm, captivate, blandish, coax, flatter, cajole, attract. *Ant.* repel, deter, displease.

ingratitude, ungratefulness, unappreciation, thanklessness, lack of response, unconcern. *Ant.* gratitude, responsiveness, thankfulness, gratefulness, appreciation.

ingredient, component, element, part, factor, material, substance.

inhabit, dwell, remain, room, occupy, abide, nestle, sojourn, reside, stay, live, make home at, lodge, establish residence. *Ant.* vacate, be absent, give up, withdraw, retreat, exit, stay away, retire, go away, desert, forsake, abandon, visit.

inherent, inbred, natural, native, inborn, inseparable, internal, innate, indwelling, latent, intrinsic, wrought, congenital, ingrained, subjective, indispensable, instinctive, inherited, genetic, connatal, inbred. *Ant.* superficial, extrinsic, supplemental, superimposed, incidental, supplementary, environmental, added, transient, fortuitous, unconnected, ulterior, external, accidental, infused, acquired, learned.

inheritance, legacy, bequest, heritage, patrimony, birthright.

inhibit, restrain, suppress, hinder, curb, check, repress, thwart, interdict, cramp, prohibit, hold back, obstruct, interfere, veto, impede, prevent, oppose, block, obtrude, discourage, restrict, forbid, circumscribe, arrest, proscribe, exclude, bar, suspend, disallow, sublimate. *Ant.* permit, approve, empower, warrant, accord, allow, authorize, encourage, abet, spur, incite, release, ignite, consent, grant, assent, charter, yield, affranchise, license, liberate, free, unharness, adopt, unchain, succor, unleash, help, deliver, aid, unbind, help, support, maintain, patronize, commend.

inhuman, cruel, pitiless, ruthless, brutal, savage, barbarous, bloodthirsty, unfeeling, malevolent, remorseless, bestial, ferocious, truculent, venomous, cold-blooded, rancorous, stern, hateful, diabolical, harsh, fiendish, hellish, infernal. *Ant.* humane, feeling, indulgent, kindhearted, considerate, sympathetic, tender, obliging, mild, compassionate, gracious, amiable, brotherly, helpful, affectionate, kind, noble, thoughtful, charitable, benignant, generous, philanthropic, bounteous, beneficent, accommodating, refined, humanitarian, comforting.

iniquitous, wicked, sinful, unjust, nefarious, unrighteous, wrong, vicious, criminal, dissolute, profligate, unprincipled, lawless, immoral, heinous, transgressing, disreputable, shameful, degrading, reprobate, villainous, fiendish, foul, diabolical, infamous, infernal. *Ant.* good, innocent, decent, virtuous, moral, worthy, upright, pure, honest, creditable, exemplary, chivalrous, praiseworthy, blameless, admirable, lovable, noble, kind, holy, true, exalted, harmless, just, saintly, equitable, religious, reputable, respectable, worthy.

initiate, begin, start, introduce, commence, institute, originate, indoctrinate, establish, inaugurate, invest. *Ant.* end, raze, close down, terminate, finish, destroy.

initiative, leadership, energy, acceleration, drive. *Ant.* lethargy, dullness, timidity, service, cowardice, shyness.

injunction, order (of a judge), law, command, mandate, rule, bidding, ordinance, canon, regulation, directive.

injurious, hurtful, harmful, pernicious, wrongful, prejudicial, defamatory, libelous, mischievous, deleterious, detrimental, disadvantageous, destructive, damaging. *Ant.* beneficial, good, wholesome, helpful, salutary, advantageous, profitable, useful, healing, constructive, inoffensive, favorable, serviceable.

injury, hurt, wrong, harm, injustice, damage, disadvantage, detriment, prejudice, wound, cut, burn, fracture, abrasion, evil, loss, impairment, mischief, blemish, injustice. *Ant.* good, benefit, gain, emolument, recompense, advantage, favor, utility, blessing, aid, service, assistance, relief, remedy.

injustice, wrong, violation, grievance, unfairness, injury, partiality, prejudice, bias, inequity, favoritism, encroachment, nepotism, inequality, partisanship, infringement, illegality. *Ant.* fairness, justice, equity, propriety, honesty, morality, ethics, equality, rectitude, integrity, sanction, recompense, lawfulness, uprightness, impartiality, righteousness, decency, reward.

inkling, hint, suggestion, inference, clue, whisper, suspicion, notion, idea, impression, innuendo, tip.

innocent, good, blameless, pure, immaculate, artless, faultless, sinless, guiltless, undefiled, virtuous, spotless, harmless, righteous, inoffensive, guileless, clear, upright, exemplary, irreproachable, clean, virginal, innocuous, stainless, simple, uninvolved, plain, inexperienced, unsophisticated, sincere, straightforward, unsuspicious, frank, honest, candid, unaffected, open. *Ant.* guilty, culpable, blameworthy, unrighteous, blamable, criminal, sinful, bad, reprehensible, corrupt, villainous, devilish, evil, hardened, wild, delinquent, dissolute, impenitent, sensual, licentious, involved, debauched, iniquitous, vicious, experienced, voluptuous, immoral, intemperate, treacherous, sly, foul, impure, artful, cunning, lewd, evasive, lascivious.

innocuous, harmless, gentle, mild, safe, undetrimental, pallid, inoffensive, insipid, uninjurious. *Ant.* harmful, dangerous, offensive, ravaging, corrosive, eroding, rotting, atrophying, bad, injurious, detrimental, blighting, unhealthy, pestilential, baneful, tainted, noisome, unwholesome, damaging, prejudicial, destructive.

innovation, change, novelty, alteration, invention, introduction, variation, newness. *Ant.* old (way), custom, habit, tradition, rut.

innuendo, implication, double-meaning, hint, allusion, insinuation, intimation, aspersion, suggestion. *Ant.* statement, evidence, observation, assertion, declaration.

innumerable, countless, numberless, unnumbered, uncountable, infinite, myriad. *Ant.* numbered, counted, registered, known, reported, listed, accounted for.

nopportune, inconvenient, ill-timed, unpropitious, ill-omened, untimely, unfavorable, disadvantageous, inexpedient, unseasonable, premature. *Ant.* timely, suitable, opportune, auspicious, well-timed, propitious.

nordinate, excessive, intemperate, unlimited, undue, immoderate, redundant, superabundant, overwhelming, extravagant, profuse, unreasonable, prodigal. *Ant.* moderate, sufficient, adequate, deficient, meager, scanty, incomplete, exhausted, enough, expended, reasonable, depleted, measured, short, weighed.

nquest, investigation, inquisition, probe, inquiry, research, examination, inspection, scrutiny, interrogation, audit.

nquire, ask, search, interrogate, seek, question, examine, solicit, sift, scout, pursue, detect, analyze, catechize, probe, sound, pry, demand, hunt, reconnoiter, request, research, scan, explore, scrutinize. *Ant.* answer, rebut, neglect, respond, counterstate, ignore, retort, reply, contradict, rejoin, admit, silence, disregard, discard, shun, shelve, defer, abandon.

nquisitive, searching, prying, curious, scrutinizing, inquiring, intrusive, meddlesome, peeping, peering, sniffing, intruding, aggressive. *Ant.* careless, inattentive, absent-minded, unheeding, backward, abstracted, indifferent, undiscerning, bashful, neglectful, supine, regardless, negligent, incurious, uninterested, apathetic, unconcerned, lackadaisical.

nsane, mad, delirious, frenetic, lunatic, deranged, unsound, crazy, demented, frenzied, daft, fanatical, maniacal, possessed, rabid, wild, giddy, muddled, distraught, idiotic, driveling, paranoiac, furious, raging, orgiastic, manic, bewitched, unbalanced, feeble-minded, mentally ill, aberrant, psychopathic, psychotic, incoherent, irrational. *Ant.* sane, whole, right-minded, sound, sober, lucid, normal, rational, reasonable, stable, healthy, calm, level, well-adjusted, imperturbable, unruffled, wholesome, correct, vigorous, sedate, natural, unimpaired, sensible, intelligent, wise, practical, settled, solemn.

nsatiable, ravenous, hungry, gluttonous, unappeasable, greedy, unquenchable, voracious, intemperate, rapacious. *Ant.* temperate, moderate, satisfied, full, fulfilled, pleased, sated.

nscription, engraving, lettering, carving, legend, caption, impression, printing, writing, cutting.

nscrutable, mysterious, impenetrable, incomprehensible, hidden, inexplicable, baffling, secret, unfathomable, enigmatic. *Ant.* plain, obvious, manifest, clear, evident, open, overt.

nsecure, unsafe, unstable, in danger, in peril, ill-protected, shaky, unguarded, exposed, hazardous, worried, concerned, troubled, fearful. *Ant.* safe, secure, settled, strong, fortified, guarded, assured, protected, serene, well-adjusted, certain, confident, self-sufficient, sane, sound.

nsensible, stuporous, impassible, unfeeling, stolid, torpid, apathetic, numb, insentient, indifferent, unconcerned. *Ant.* conscious, feeling, aware, awake, alert, alive.

insensitive, unimpressionable, unresponsive, obtuse, dull, unaffected thick-skinned, unexcitable, unemotional, phlegmatic, callous, coo unconscious, remote. *Ant.* sensitive, empathetic, affected, impres sionable, responsive, touchy, susceptible, thin-skinned, tempera mental.

insertion, introduction, inlay, implantation, interpolation, injection inoculation, infusion, installation. *Ant.* removal, withdrawal, ex traction, transfer.

insidious, crafty, designing, guileful, elusive, cunning, intriguing wily, illusory, artful, deceitful, tricky, treacherous, subtle, sly gradual, seductive, entrapping, corrupting, deceptive. *Ant.* oper frank, sincere, honest, candid, upsophisticated, manifest, honor able, revealed, fair, unhidden, clear, overt.

insight, discernment, introspection, perspicacity, judgment, penetra tion, acumen, cleverness, shrewdness, intuition, inspection, keen ness, consciousness, inspiration, perception, understanding, com prehension. *Ant.* ignorance, unconsciousness, shallowness, unen lightenment, perplexity, confusion, incomprehensibility, doubt, in experience, stupidity.

insignificant, meaningless, trivial, unimportant, inconsequential valueless, minute, cheap, worthless. *Ant.* significant, important valuable, consequential, large, meaningful, momentous.

insinuate, suggest, intimate, hint, ingratiate, instill, infuse, infer connote, denote, signify, purport, mean, imply, convey, allude mention, insert, introduce, indicate. *Ant.* conceal, veil, hide evade, camouflage, cloud, mask, cloak, disguise, stifle, dissemble withhold, cover, keep secret, suppress, shade.

insipid, tasteless, flavorless, characterless, mawkish, flat, bland, un seasoned, unimaginative, vapid, dull, uninteresting, lifeless, unsavory inanimate, vapid, stale, slow. *Ant.* tasty, savory, flavored, deli cious, palatable, pleasing, appetizing, tempting, sharp, interest ing, lively, quick, innovative, exciting, thrilling, exhilarating enterprising, brisk.

insistent, demanding, urgent, pressing, assertive, importunate, im perative, clamorous, exigent. *Ant.* acquiescent, tolerant, lenient agreeable, indifferent, disinterested.

insolent, impudent, offensive, overbearing, impertinent, rude, un mannerly, arrogant, saucy, defiant, presumptuous, bold, haughty contemptuous, bumptious, swaggering, discourteous, snobbish, in sulting, disdainful, threatening, self-assertive, supercilious, im perious, domineering, flippant, audacious, blustering, brazen. *Ant* fawning, obsequious, sycophantic, sponging, abject, poor, cour teous, cringing, truckling, servile, base, humble, parasitic, beg garly, mean, slavish, sneaking, groveling, sniveling, abased, shy timid, cowardly.

insolvent, bankrupt, indigent, indebted, ruined, beggared, poverty stricken, impoverished, penniless, owing, indebted, fortuneless destitute, reduced, fleeced, impecunious, moneyless, straitened stripped, poor. *Ant.* solvent, independent, substantial, well-off, opulent, wealthy, rich, warm, affluent, well-to-do, moneyed, comfortable, propertied.

insouciant, careless, reckless, heedless, unconcerned, gay, carefree, indifferent, woolgathering, giddy, light-hearted, thoughtless, abstracted, supine, dreamy, absent-minded, flighty, nonchalant, indiscreet, free-spending, hare-brained. *Ant.* careful, observant, serious, circumspect, cautious, heedful, prudent, alert, watchful, mindful, preoccupied, vigilant, attentive, thoughtful, wary, concerned, cognizant, engrossed, advertent, absorbed, contemplative, thrifty, deliberate, reserved, cool, self-possessed, discreet.

inspection, examination, scrutiny, survey, supervision, investigation, inquiry, overseeing, study, observation, checking, comparison, scanning, measuring.

inspiration, stimulation, revelation, fire, incitement, exaltation, animation, predilection, arousal, enthusiasm; inhalation. *Ant.* lethargy, hebetude, apathy; exhalation.

instability, inconstancy, changeability, fickleness, insecurity, variability, mutability, wavering, unbalance. *Ant.* stability, steadfastness, constancy, unwaveringness, fixedness, evenness.

instance, case, point, occurrence, type, precedent, illustration, example, exemplification, specimen, object lesson, pattern, elucidation, antecedent, sample, application, impulse.

instantaneous, at once, abrupt, prompt, immediate, sudden, direct. *Ant.* slow, delayed, deliberate, gradual, late.

instantly, immediately, suddenly, directly, now, abruptly.

instigate, incite, encourage, influence, abet, foment, force, animate, sway, stimulate, persuade, prevail upon, arouse, entice, press, inspirit, predispose, impel, insist, overcome, induce, tempt, exhort, actuate, provoke, spur, urge, initiate, plan, plot, scheme. *Ant.* discourage, remonstrate, deter, expostulate, warn, dampen, dissuade, threaten, admonish, delay, avert, slow, prevent, hold back, dishearten, constrain, restrain, suppress, repress, check.

instill, train, impart, infuse, drill, diffuse, teach, suffuse, discipline, transfuse, intermix, combine, imbue, inject, infiltrate, inoculate, introduce, indoctrinate, impregnate, inculcate, disseminate, implant, insinuate. *Ant.* eliminate, extract, eradicate, take out, remove, draw, uproot, extirpate, expel, dislodge, exclude, clear, purify, excrete, eject, retain, replace, discard, effuse, spill, extrude, boil off.

instinctive, innate, inborn, inherent, congenital, constitutional, ingrained, spontaneous, automatic, reflexive, mechanical, natural, normal, typical, regular, habitual, accustomed, usual. *Ant.* reasoned, voluntary, willed, deliberate, planned, meditated, learned, acquired.

institute, establish, found, build, erect, plan, finance, organize, enact, begin, originate, start, invent, introduce, initiate, order, fix, ordain, settle, invest. *Ant.* terminate, close, finish, end, complete, conclude, raze, destroy.

instruct

instruct, teach, initiate, advise, inform, enlighten, tutor, educate
guide, train, direct, order, prepare, warn, qualify, prime, school
tell, exhort, convey, coach, counsel, impart, compel, correct, com
mand, drill, control, manage, regulate, proclaim, model, form
announce, promulgate, indoctrinate, review, expound, discipline
criticize, notify. *Ant.* misrepresent, misdirect, misinform, pervert
misinstruct, misguide, falsify, deceive, delude, mislead, misinter
pret, ignore, withhold, withdraw, dispute, impugn, repudiate, re
fuse, deny.

instrumental, contributory, promoting, conducive, helpful, auxiliary
serving, accessory, serviceable, subsidiary, assisting, expeditious.

insubordination, disobedience, intractability, contumacy, perversity
contrariness, rebellion, revolt, defiance, mutiny. *Ant.* obedience
tractability, loyalty.

insufferable, unbearable, unendurable, painful, agonizing, intoler
able, grievous, insupportable, dreadful, harrowing, heartrending
shocking, frightful, crushing, excruciating, frightening, depress
ing. *Ant.* pleasant, refreshing, agreeable, comfortable, delightful
healing, enjoyable, palliative, satisfying, easing, pleasurable, in
vigorating, healthful, restorative, ameliorating, salutary, salubri
ous, wholesome, salutary, uplifting, joyful, happy, gay.

insufficient, sparse, inadequate, lacking, deficient, scant, meager
incompetent, scarce, bare, rare, incomplete, imperfect, slack
drained. *Ant.* sufficient, enough, plentious, rich, ample, copious.

insulate, separate, cover, protect, wrap, seclude, segregate, discon
nect, sequester, isolate, part, sunder, detach, disengage. *Ant.* ex
pose, neglect, mingle, mix, integrate, connect, join, unite.

insult, indignity, abuse, contumely, impertinence, affront, contempt
impudence, outrage, insolence, disdain, discourtesy, snub, slight
incivility, slur, disrespect, rudeness, libel, acerbity, slander, slap
bitterness, gall, scurrility, sarcasm, mockery, derision, jeer, taunt
scoffing, sneering. *Ant.* respect, tribute, obeisance, humility, cor
diality, homage, fealty, courtesy, reverence, admiration, regard
deference, friendship, fellowship, politeness, urbanity, culture
gentility, suavity, amenity, benignity, sympathy, benevolence, es
teem, kindness, affection, mildness.

intact, whole, entire, perfect, complete, sound, untouched, unbroken
undamaged, unmarked, unscratched. *Ant.* defective, incomplete
spoiled, impaired, broken, marred.

intangible, untouchable, impalpable, immaterial, indefinite, inappre
ciable, imponderable, insubstantial, vague, dim, misty, elusive
evasive. *Ant.* real, hard, definite, plain, solid, touchable, tangible
perceptible, material, corporeal.

integral, complete, whole, entire, one, unitary, consummate, perfect
uncut, constituent, centralized. *Ant.* part, fractional, segmental
divisional.

integration, unification, joining, consolidation, merger, blending
mingling, amalgamation, fusion. *Ant.* separation, segregation
seclusion, isolation.

integrity, uprightness, correctness, honesty, incorruptness, moral soundness, purity, probity, candor, honor, rectitude, faithfulness, righteousness, constancy, trustworthiness, worth, loyalty, merit, morality, wholeness, completeness, entirety, virtue, fidelity. *Ant.* improbity, dishonesty, corruption, pretension, sham, falsity, turpitude, infidelity, treason, deceit, disloyalty, perfidiousness, faithlessness, unfairness, double-dealing, disgrace, shame.

intellectual, cerebral, mental, inventive, accomplished, cogitative, learned, talented, metaphysical, cultured, creative, ideal, reflective, thoughtful, contemplative, meditative, studious, speculative, thinking, intelligent, cognitive, keen, skilled, sharp, learned, precocious, scientific, acute. *Ant.* dull, thoughtless, vacuous, stupid, inane, silly, brainless, fatuous, foolish, unreasoning, irrational, simple, illiterate, ignorant.

intelligence, acumen, penetration, aptitude, astuteness, mental ability, knowledge, wit, sense, intellect, perspicacity, discernment, brains, grasp, insight.

intelligible, comprehensible, distinct, unequivocal, graphic, obvious, lucid, expressive, clear, perceptible, vivid, definite, plain, positive, explicit, precise, understandable. *Ant.* unintelligible, perplexing, bewildering, enigmatic, cryptic, coded, difficult, obscure, inscrutable, puzzling, abstruse, incomprehensible, muddled, ambiguous, equivocal.

intemperate, drunken, immoderate, dissipated, unrestrained, excessive, inordinate, extravagant, extreme, inclement. *Ant.* sober, temperate, conservative, abstinent, moderate, abstemious, steady, sedate, serious, dependable, reliable, self-denying, nonindulgent, ascetic, rigorous.

intend, mean, propose, design, try, conceive, destine, aim, purpose, scheme, plan, continue, hope, want, wish, desire, try (to do).

intensity, eagerness, attention, strain, vehemence, ardor, rush, concentration, earnestness, tension, force, hustle, pressure, vigor, strength, power, degree, voltage, heat, loudness, bustle, ferment, perturbation, stir. *Ant.* inactivity, inertness, inaction, laziness, listlessness, sloth, lassitude, lethargy, passivity, latency, languor, moderation, torpor, dullness, slowness, flatness, apathy, coolness, carelessness, weakness, indolence, feebleness, idleness.

intent, intention, motive, meaning, design, desire, object, purpose, plan, aim, wish, hope, ambition, effort.

intentional, intended, deliberate, studied, designed, contemplated, purposed, premeditated, meant, determined, aimed at, projected, planned, calculated. *Ant.* speculative, undesigned, purposeless, tentative, unpremeditated, causeless, accidental, fortuitous, aimless, random, indiscriminate, unintentional, chance, contingent, undesired, haphazard, casual, incidental, occasional, unforeseen.

intercept, check, interrupt, catch, stop, prevent, arrest, hinder, interpose, waylay, obstruct, avert. *Ant.* help, forward, aid, back, boost, assist, succor, abet, uphold.

intercourse, communication, connection, commerce, sociability, conversation, correspondence, fellowship, intercommunion, fraternity acquaintance, comradeship, intimacy, sociability, companionship familiarity, conversation, dealings, association, negotiations, sociableness. *Ant.* unfriendliness, hatred, estrangement, bitterness animosity, hostility, enmity, malice, alienation, seclusion, aversion, hermitism, separation, barrier, isolation, solitude, aloofness loneliness.

interest, *n.* profit, benefit, share, portion, advantage, gain, concern business, attention, curiosity, appeal, fascination, charm, behalf inquisitiveness, stake, right, title, claim, premium; *v.* hold attention, amuse, entertain, intrigue, please, enliven, gratify, divert delight, cheer, appeal to, absorb, enthrall, occupy, beguile, concern, fascinate. *Ant.* apathy, carelessness, default, indifference loss, insouciance, nonpayment, insolvency; bore, displease, weary bother, vex, stupefy, tire, worry.

interfere, conflict, meddle, oppose, interpose, clash, collide, mediate impede, obstruct, bar, hinder, intrude, thwart, frustrate, inconvenience, block, obtrude, stall, hamper, delay. *Ant.* help, stand aside, clear, aid, abet.

interim, interval, meantime, interlude, lapse, break, hiatus, gap meanwhile.

interior, inside, heart, middle; inland, hinterlands, core, bowels enclosure. *Ant.* exterior, facade, visible portion, skin, walls, coast, periphery, boundary.

interminable, endless, immeasurable, tedious, infinite, perpetual, incessant, eternal, continuous, boundless, limitless, everlasting, permanent. *Ant.* intermittent, finite, terminable, periodic, ending.

intermittent, broken, infrequent, fluttering, recurrent, periodic, interrupted, discontinuous, occasional, spasmodic, fitful, cyclic, alternate, flickering. *Ant.* incessant, constant, continual, regular, usual, perpetual.

internal, interior, intrinsic, domestic, inward, inner, inherent, enclosed, innate, ingrained. *Ant.* external, superficial, outer, alien, foreign.

interpolate, insert, introduce, interpose, intercalate, add, enlarge, alter, introduce, insinuate, interject. *Ant.* remove, take out, extract, expunge, erase, withdraw.

interpose, interfere, meddle, mediate, intervene, intercede, tamper, sandwich, intercalate, inject, obtrude, interpolate, interrupt, arbitrate, intercept, interject, intrude, intersperse, negotiate. *Ant.* refrain, withhold, ignore, overlook, withdraw, neglect, forbear, disregard, omit, retire, extract, expunge, erase, shun, avoid.

interpret, translate, decipher, expound, elucidate, unravel, explain, unfold, solve, construe, manifest, disentangle, render, describe paraphrase, define, illuminate, reveal, decode, clarify. *Ant.* misinterpret, distort, misapprehend, misconstrue, burlesque, twist misapply, misunderstand, caricature, confuse, misstate, parody, tangle, pervert, garble, mystify, subvert, jumble, scramble.

interrogation, examination, interpellation, inquiry, investigation, inquisition, test, probe. *Ant.* reply, answer, acknowledgement, response, rejoinder.

interrupt, suspend, obstruct, break, interfere, disconnect, check, discontinue, cut, disturb, stop, hinder, divide, delay, sever, arrest. *Ant.* continue, prolong, sustain, maintain.

intervene, intercede, arbitrate, interfere, mediate, intrude, befall, happen, occur, sever, part, divide, interlope. *Ant.* ignore, assist, help, stand aside.

intimate, *adj.* close, loving, personal, affectionate, private, secret, near, internal, friendly, confidential, familiar. *Ant.* formal, distant, cool, correct, remote, conventional, ceremonious.

intimate, *v.* see **insinuate.**

intimidate, cow, subdue, scare, terrify, browbeat, abash, threaten, daunt, frighten, dismay, bully, domineer, overawe, unnerve, alarm, astound, terrorize, coerce, abuse, drive, bluster, menace, shout, roar. *Ant.* encourage, inspire, mollify, hearten, comfort, soften, inspirit, console, embolden, assuage, help, assist, buoy up, gratify, cheer, praise, animate, rouse, laud, incite, inspire, please, stimulate, heal, assure, reassure.

intolerable, insufferable, unbearable, unendurable, insupportable. *Ant.* tolerable, passable, bearable, endurable, supportable, satisfying.

intolerant, bigoted, prejudiced, unyielding, unfair, biased, discriminatory. *Ant.* tolerant, fair, lenient, nondiscriminatory, unbiased, impartial, open-minded.

intrepid, brave, courageous, valiant, fearless, dauntless, bold, unafraid, strong, powerful, mighty, daring, lionhearted, valorous, heroic, nervy, unshrinking, plucky, unflinching, self-reliant. *Ant.* afraid, skulking, craven, timid, awestruck, cringing, shrinking, cowardly, nervous, faint-hearted, frightened, weak, feeble, intimidated, humble, scared, trembling, discouraged, hesitant.

intricate, complex, tangled, involved, difficult, mixed, confused, convoluted, irregular, disarranged, knotted, labryrinthine, complicated, raveled, inextricable. *Ant.* tidy, systematic, methodical, regulated, arranged, shipshape, clear, plain, not difficult, easy, trim, proper, understandable, simple, direct, straightforward, uniform, normal, untangled, ordinary, unmixed.

intrigue, plot, complication, scheme, secret, conspiracy, wire-pulling, dodge, connivance, plan, craft, ruse, design, arrangement, cabal, stratagem, collusion, maneuvering, duplicity, machination, cunning, craftiness, chicanery, double-dealing, finesse, subtlety, trickery, circumvention.

intrinsic, true, honest, fundamental, real, native, genuine, esential, vital, subjective, indigeous, inherent, innate, inbred, congenital, inborn, ingrained. *Ant.* extrinsic, extraneous, casual, objective, incidental, subsidiary, without, accidental, adventitious, external, contingent, foreign, fortuitous, dependent, exterior, occasional.

introduction, presentation, overture, commencement, interjection, prelude, beginning, inception, preface, preamble, interpolation, foreword, meeting, prologue. *Ant.* end, conclusion, epilogue, postlude, parting.

intrusive, interfering, meddlesome, inquisitive, obtrusive, invading, snooping, trespassing, infringing, encroaching.

intuitive, instinctive, involuntary, guessing, unreflecting, discerning, unreasoning, impulsive, heedless, knowing, perceptive, emotional. *Ant.* reasoned, calculated, planned, ratiocinated, meditated.

invalidate, nullify, negate, annul, null, void, abrogate, counteract, cancel, stop, recall, quash, neutralize. *Ant.* validate, endorse, enforce, accept, implement, sign, countersign.

invaluable, priceless, valuable, dear, inestimable, precious. *Ant.* worthless, useless, nugatory, cheap.

invasion, entrance, inroad, aggression, intrusion, attack, foray, raid, incursion, outbreak, irruption, ingress, take-over, ingression. *Ant.* defense, safeguard, stronghold, protection, fortification, repulsion, guard, release.

invective, blasphemy, epithets, vituperation, raillery, censure, denouncement, scurrility, condemnation, opprobrium, reproach, disapprobation, sarcasm, abuse, contumely, disparagement, deprecation, reprehension, reprimand, obloquy, denunciation, disapproval, remonstrance, reproof. *Ant.* approbation, admiration, eulogy, approval, sanction, commendation, encomium, acclaim, appreciation, praise, applause, tribute, laudation, glorification, decoration.

inveigle, lure, charm, entice, decoy, attract, beguile, dupe, trick, entrap, seduce, draw, deceive, captivate, wheedle. *Ant.* repel, disgust, fend, parry, avert, annoy.

invent, devise, fabricate, contrive, discover, design, outline, form, frame, fashion, plan, improvise, coin, manufacture, sketch, machinate, draft, lie, project, falsify, scheme, concoct, misrepresent, imagine, mystify, stimulate, misstate, deceive, equivocate, fancy, conjure, visualize, originate, conceive.

inventory, list, table, register, schedule, catalog, roll, roster; contents, stock, store, supply.

investigation, inquiry, exploration, research, review, examination, scrutiny, interrogation, search, inquisition, discussion, exploitation, catechism, quest, pursuit. *Ant.* solution, results, answer, reply, neglect, overlooking, hiding, covering.

invidious, odious, provoking, vexatious, hateful, provoking, envious, galling, heart-breaking, troublesome, harmful, irksome, painful, irritating, defamatory, galling, unsettling, annoying, obnoxious. *Ant.* pleasurable, satisfying, comforting, delectable, charitable, soothing, refreshing, benevolent, delightful, consoling, cordial, attractive, gratifying, pleasing, calming.

invigorate, strengthen, vitalize, harden, animate, brace, refresh, energize, fortify, vivify, stimulate, spur, urge, hearten, embolden. *Ant.* weaken, enervate, enfeeble, depress, dull, dishearten, discourage, sap, debilitate, impair, attenuate, injure, cripple, reduce, devitalize.

invincible, insuperable, insurmountable, indomitable, mighty, resistless, irresistible, incontestable, impregnable, unvanquishable, unconquerable, invulnerable, inseparable, unyielding, overpowering, formidable, sovereign. *Ant.* weak, frail, faint, crippled, sickly, spent, puny, fragile, enervated, languishing, feeble, pregnable, deficient, flimsy, unnerved, wasted, defective, languid, emaciated, impotent, powerless.

invitation, summons, call, bid, request, challenge, solicitation, attraction, proposition, allurement, provocation. *Ant.* refusal, denial, repulsion, rejection.

invoke, ask, appeal, beseech, conjure, beg, pray, implore, adjure, crave, invite, call, petition, solicit, supplicate, attest, enlist, summon. *Ant.* insist, refuse, deny, submit, comply.

involuntary, forced, unwilling, reflex, compulsory, instinctive, reluctant, unintentional, uncontrolled, obligatory, automatic, spontaneous, unplanned. *Ant.* voluntary, willed, designed, controlled, by choice, intentional, volitional.

involve, entangle, embarrass, contain, implicate, compromise, overwhelm, include, imply, signify, denote, entail, enwrap, envelop, cover, comprehend. *Ant.* separate, remove, free, disengage, disentangle, explicate, extricate, disconnect, distinguish, unravel, clear, untwist, untie, exclude.

irascible, bad-tempered, gruff, fractious, irritable, fretful, splenetic, cranky, cross, edgy, surly. *Ant.* calm, imperturbable, tolerant, good-humored, congenial, pleasant, cordial, kind, amiable, affable, agreeable, gracious, cheerful.

irate, angry, raging, wrathful, incensed, nettled, infuriated, mad, enraged, irritated, piqued, provoked. *Ant.* calm, cool, pleased, appeased.

irk, annoy, vex, perturb, upset, trouble, discompose, fret, bother. *Ant.* please, cheer, comfort, console, gladden, amuse, soothe, attract, delight, elate, oblige, satisfy.

irony, sarcasm, ridicule, satire, mockery, raillery. *Ant.* respect, regard, veneration, courtesy, attention, deference, homage, obsequiousness, esteem, praise, admiration, obeisance, approbation, consideration, approval.

irrational, unreasonable, foolish, absurd, stupid, illogical, demented, feeble-minded, queer, ridiculous, fatuous, evasive, unconsidered, odd, unwise, strange, crazed, injudicious, crazy, preposterous, perverted, weak-minded, daft, unsound, vacuous. *Ant.* rational, reliable, judicial, meditative, logical, intellectual, thoughtful, studious, sound, reasoned, reflective, cultured, considered, sane, lucid, wise, self-possessed, sober, sensible, normal, ordinary.

irreconcilable, incompatible, unappeasable, incongruous, implacable inconsequent, inexorable, quarrelsome, divergent. *Ant.* reconcilable, congruous, compatible, appeasable, solvable.

irrefutable, indisputable, unanswerable, invincible, incontestable, undeniable, unquestionable, incontrovertible, irrefragable. *Ant.* uncertain, doubtful, questionable, disputable, debatable.

irregularity, abnormality, unevenness, aberration, disorderliness unruliness, inconstancy, deviation, anomaly, fitfulness, caprice variation, eccentricity, tardiness, inordinateness. *Ant.* stability regularity, order, rule, method, system.

irrelevant, unrelated, foreign, inconsequent, immaterial, inapposite inappropriate, inapplicable, extraneous, unessential. *Ant.* fitting relevant, apt, pertinent.

irreligious, impious, profane, irreverent, unholy, hardened, wicked sacrilegious, blasphemous, unregenerate, perverted, agnostic ungodly, desecrating, reprobate. *Ant.* pious, reverent, godly, devout, prayerful, saintly, spiritual, consecrated, pietistic, regenerated, sacred, solemn, holy, angelic.

irremediable, incurable, hopeless, irreparable, useless, irrevokable irrecoverable, irretrievable, beyond help. *Ant.* curable, reparable recoverable.

irrepressible, insuppressible, uncontrollable, unconfined, independent unfettered, free, irresistible, unconstrained, unshackled, unrepressible, excitable, unrestricted, uninhibited, bubbling, unpredictable. *Ant.* passive, inhibited, calm, placid, cold-blooded, flat quiet, grave, dull, serious, solemn, melancholy, cool, patient, resigned, collected, tolerant, composed, submissive, meek, obedient predictable.

irresolute, wavering, shaky, fickle, unsettled, doubting, uncertain undetermined, undecided, vacillating, fluctuating, lukewarm, hesitant, hesitating, undecided, unsteady, irresponsible, drifting, unstable, half-hearted, wobbling, volatile. *Ant.* resolute, purposed unflinching, firm, unvarying, decided, determined, resolved, brave enduring, stubborn, definite, indomitable, unhesitating, unyielding, courageous, inexorable, willful, tenacious, obstinate, relentless.

irresponsible, arbitrary, irresolute, wobbly, unsteady, careless, immature, thoughtless, heedless, purposeless, unstable, fluctuating wavering, unreliable, undecided, unsettled, excusable, hesitating faltering, vacillating, weak, reckless, daring, foolish, inefficient exempt, capricious, frothy, light, light-minded, giddy, rash, feeble-minded, flighty. *Ant.* responsible, firm, answerable, amenable accountable, steady, trustworthy, liable, susceptive, dependable solvent, sure, mature, reliable, subject, resolute, determined, self-reliant, strong-willed, earnest.

irritable, sensitive, excitable, fidgety, testy, susceptible, thin-skinned, ill-tempered, irascible, fretful, touchy, querulous, petulant, fractious, captious, cantankerous, peevish, snappy. *Ant.* pleasant mild, composed, agreeable, cool, enduring, suave, passive, good-tempered, gentle, tranquil, tolerant, imperturbable, forbearing, dispassionate, polite, patient, serene, self-possessed, amenable.

irritate, provoke, excite, agitate, exasperate, foment, ruffle, exacerbate, sting, pique, embitter, fluster, annoy, nettle, bother, disturb, tease, taunt, madden, aggravate, harass, infuriate, anger, worry, inflame, enrage, vex, chafe, irk. *Ant.* soothe, console, mitigate, calm, ease, palliate, mollify, alleviate, assuage, comfort, salve, allay, soften, conciliate, ameliorate, appease, please, moderate, placate, delight, pacify.

isolate, separate, disconnect, seclude, segregate, dissociate, insulate, quarantine, sequester, exclude. *Ant.* mix, mingle, join, unite, include, integrate.

issue, *n.* subject, topic, question, point, result, aftermath, event, incident, consequence, denouement, eventuality, occurrence, circumstance, effect, contingency, upshot, culmination, progeny, conclusion, finish, publication, termination, product, offspring, children, outpouring, egression, fruits, emanation, effusion, flow, currency, family, exudation; *v.* flow, emerge, begin, ensue, arise, result, proceed, eventuate, exude, spring, start, originate, promulgate, emanate, emit, leave, depart, spread, sprout, spew, express, utter, circulate money, publish, distribute, deliver. *Ant.* retain, contain, repress, suppress.

item, entry, topic, piece, unit, story, article, listing, subject, feature, object.

itinerant, nomadic, vagrant, migratory, unsettled, roving, roaming, wandering, journeying, straying, ranging, moving, shifting, wayfaring, peripatetic. *Ant.* permanent, habitational, located, settled.

itinerary, route, course, guidebook, trip, plan, record, log, flight plan, map, circuit.

J

jam, crowd, push, cram, mass, press, squeeze, pack, block, wedge, force, crush, tamp, interfere, impede, improvise (music). *Ant.* spread, disperse, diffuse, separate, scatter, expand, free, open, release.

jar, jolt, jangle, vibrate, shock, rattle, clash, jounce, shake, quake. *Ant.* quiet, still, dampen.

jargon, cant, lingo, slang, argot, patois, jive, dialect, trade talk, shop talk.

jealous, envious, suspicious, distrustful, doubting, covetous, jaundiced, mistrustful, doubtful, dubious, invidious, resentful, angry; solicitous, vigilant, watchful. *Ant.* trusting, true, loyal, trustworthy, faithful, satisfied, serene, content, lenient.

jeer, sneer, scoff, taunt, mock, deride, hoot, gibe, flout, ridicule. *Ant.* laud, praise, honor, cheer, applaud.

jeopardize, endanger, risk, menace, threaten, expose, compromise, chance, imperil, hazard. *Ant.* protect, shield, secure, safeguard.

jest, joke, quip, banter, witticism, humor, wisecrack, prank.

jocular, humorous, funny, witty, joking, merry, pleasant, waggish, facetious, comical, droll, sportive. *Ant.* serious, morose, dull.

join, connect, cement, affiliate, tie, unite, associate, merge, knit, bind, consolidate, link, combine, marry, unify, enter, couple, add. *Ant.* separate, divide, sever, divorce, sunder, leave, detach, resign, withdraw.

joint, *n.* union, connection, juncture, junction, link, articulation, pivot, hinge, seam, welding, meeting, combination, cooperation, collaboration; *adj.* shared, associated, divided. *Ant.* separate, single.

jolly, merry, jocular, blithe, cheerful, humorous, jocund, witty, gay, jovial, frolicsome, jocose, joyous, playful, happy. *Ant.* solemn, serious, sober, melancholy, grave, morose, dour, dull.

jostle, push, crowd, ram, jog, press, squeeze, jar, bump, shove, elbow, shake, prod, disturb, jolt.

journal, daybook, diary, log, account, chart, newspaper, gazette, periodical, magazine, record, register.

journey, trip, tour, pilgrimage, course, voyage, expedition, passage, peregrination, travel, excursion, safari, cruise, trek, jaunt.

jovial, merry, jolly, lively, lighthearted, gay, frolicsome, animated, happy, cheerful, hilarious, vivacious, joyous, blithe, genial, mirthful, hearty, pleasant, sparkling, jocund, debonair, sprightly, rollicking, buoyant, sportive. *Ant.* sad, solemn, serious, morbid, drab, morose, dull, angry, doleful, dejected, cheerless, sorrowful, heavy, spiritless, melancholy, gloomy, dismal, depressed, somber, pensive, downcast, lugubrious, grim, sober, demure, disconsolate.

joy, gladness, rapture, enjoyment, ecstasy, delight, exultation, happiness, glee, cheerfulness, cheer, contentment, bliss, pleasure, merriment, gratification, gaiety. *Ant.* sorrow, displeasure, dejection, distress, heartache, gloom, tribulation, affliction, unhappiness, despair, sadness, misery, wretchedness, misfortune.

jubilant, gay, boastful, exultant, happy, delighted, rejoicing, joyous, cheerful, buoyant, celebrating, rollicking, glad, victorious, elated, high-spirited, triumphant. *Ant.* downcast, broken, defeated, sad, forlorn, cheerless, sorrowful, dejected, despondent, disappointed, gloomy, joyless, melancholy, unhappy.

judge, referee, arbiter, magistrate, interpreter, custodian, umpire, adjudicator, judiciary, guardian, arbitrator, justice, protector, reviewer, censor, critic, expert, connoisseur.

judgment, discernment, penetration, discrimination, decision, ruling, decree, sagacity, intellectuality, injunction, verdict, sentence, award. *Ant.* thoughtlessness, misunderstanding, fatuity, vacuity, inanity, indiscrimination, foolishness, stupidity, ignorance, misjudgment, misconception.

judicious, discerning, prudent, well-guided, cautious, wise, sensible, thoughtful, just, well-advised, discreet, sagacious, considered, intelligent, politic, weighed, sensible, wary, circumspect, vigilant, careful. *Ant.* injudicious, foolish, driveling, irrational, senseless, nonsensical, fatuous, reckless, hasty, idiotic, inane, unwise, indiscreet, silly, maudlin, shallow, ill-advised, puerile, asinine, inept, ill-judged.

jumble, mix up, muddle, confuse, mess, disarrange, shuffle. *Ant.* file, arrange, straighten, rectify, classify, systematize.

jump, skip, bound, leap, vault, hop, spring, bounce, caper, start, jerk, twitch, pounce.

junction, connection, fusion, joint, attachment, linkage, meeting, seam, union, merger, coupling; station, crossing. *Ant.* detachment, separation, severance, divergence, break.

just, honest, upright, good, equitable, impartial, proper, reasonable, exact, precise, fair, right, equable, blameless, innocent, unbiased, judicious, legal, merited, earned, fair and square, righteous, lawful, even, true, legitimate, rightful. *Ant.* wrong, partial, iniquitous, unjust, unequal, unfair, unjustified, inequitable, unwarrantable, one-sided, unreasonable, selfish, corrupt, biased, illegal, dishonest, base, villainous.

justice, lawfulness, fairness, impartiality, fair play, equity, propriety, uprightness, reasonableness, justness, righteousness, rectitude, legality. *Ant.* injustice, foul play, unfairness, partiality, favoritism, corruption, dishonor, unlawfulness, unreasonableness, inequity.

justify, vindicate, excuse, clear, warrant, defend, exonerate, maintain, acquit, absolve, free, advocate, support, countenance, extenuate, overlook, forgive. *Ant.* accuse, charge, reproach, impute, blame, denounce, incriminate, tax, impeach, stigmatize, condemn, indict, involve, arraign, implicate, sue, punish, inculpate.

jut, stick out, protrude, overhang, extend, bulge, project. *Ant.* indent, cave, collapse, disappear.

juvenile, young, youthful, immature, puerile, boyish, childish, newborn, vernal, girlish, adolescent, callow, infantile, tender, growing, underage, babyish, undeveloped, green, juvenescent. *Ant.* mature, aged, adult, grown-up, old, senile, senescent, withered, sere, wrinkled, doddering, waning, antiquated, hoary, doting, venerable, superannuated, decrepit, declining.

K

kaleidoscopic, multicolored, varied, colorful, patterned, variegated, variant, changing. *Ant.* steady, unchanging, plain, dull, constant, quiet.

keen, sharp, acute, bitter, enterprising, eager, piercing, acrid, energetic, penetrating, poignant, intense, cutting, stinging, caustic, mettlesome, vivid, cute, quick, incisive, lively, perspicacious, witty,

keep

sagacious, pointed, discerning, fervid, ardent, zealous. *Ant.* blunt, pointless, insensate, dull, lazy, insipid, stolid, thick, fatuous, obtuse, stupid, loutish, depressed, slothful, morose, sour, flat, dilatory, driveling, sluggish, slow, tardy, reluctant, lethargic, careless, apathetic, heedless, uninterested.

keep, hold, save, fulfill, defend, retain, guard, detain, carry, preserve, support, confine, conceal, maintain, suppress, clutch, supply, conserve, adhere, commemorate, sustain, conduct, uphold, persevere, reserve, withhold, protect, tend, imprison, obey, observe, refrain, continue, secure, restrain. *Ant.* relinquish, lose, release, resign, cede, drop, abandon, forego, dispose of, renounce, surrender, discard, stop, forsake, desist, quit, end, destroy, depart, leave, desert, withdraw, consume, exhaust, vacate, spend, disperse, deplete, retire, waste, retreat, trade, sell.

keepsake, souvenir, token, memento, memorial, reminder, emblem, testimonial.

kill, slay, destroy, murder, massacre, assassinate, butcher, end (life of), decimate, extinguish, obliterate, overcome, immolate, stifle, strangle, dispatch, choke, smother, veto, annul, suppress, delete. *Ant.* preserve, protect, defend, guard, uphold, safeguard, save, free, deliver, pardon, sustain, vindicate, succor, restore, revive.

kin, family, relatives, tribe, kinsfolk, siblings, kith, kinsmen, kindred, clan.

kind, *adj.* mild, benign, tender, clement, gentle, benevolent, loving, generous, amiable, obliging, kind-hearted, good, caring, charitable, gracious, indulgent, humane, cordial, beneficent, affectionate, warm-hearted, lenient, helpful, sympathetic, accommodating, considerate; *n.* class, category, strain, relation, sort, family, progeny, breed, genus, connection, offspring, ilk, make, brand, race, kin, species, order, type. *Ant.* unkind, harsh, bitter, cruel, malevolent, acrimonious, inhuman, malignant, grinding, ill-disposed, rancorous, ill-intentioned, spiteful, uncharitable, unfriendly, cold-hearted, invidious, cold-blooded, ruthless, mean, sadistic, vicious, virulent, truculent, brutal, barbarous, ferocious, overbearing, hard-hearted.

kindle, ignite, arouse, stir, inflame, awaken, provoke, excite, light, incite, fire, stimulate, spur, animate. *Ant.* quench, discourage, douse, smother, suppress, stifle.

kindness, generosity, benevolence, cordiality, grace, sympathy, hospitality, friendliness, goodness, benignity, complaisance, mildness, mercy, graciousness. *Ant.* harshness, viciousness, malevolence, cruelty, heartlessness.

kindred, like, sympathetic, related, empathetic, parallel, analogous, similar, corresponding. *Ant.* unlike, dissimilar, heterogeneous, unrelated, foreign.

kingdom, dominion, country, nation, monarchy, domain, empire, rule, realm.

knack, skill, talent, experience, art, proficiency, dexterity, aptitude, facility, adeptness, faculty, expertness, ability. *Ant.* ineptitude, awkwardness, clumsiness, incompetence.

knit, weave, interlace, unite, intertwine, link, bind, join, loop, tie. *Ant.* untie, unravel, separate, divide.

knot, bond, snarl, tie, bunch, perplexity, ligature, connection, collection, protuberance, entanglement, tangle, gathering, difficulty, assemblage.

know, perceive, understand, realize, comprehend, think, memorize, hold, fathom, remember, appreciate, recognize, interpret, discern, conceive. *Ant.* doubt, discredit, reject, mistrust, suspect, forget, question, disregard, test, query, differ, dispute, dissent, demur, misapprehend, deny, misunderstand, misinterpret, misconstrue.

knowledge, revelation, education, information, lore, comprehension, wisdom, skill, scholarship, science, erudition, understanding, experience, learning, cognition, intuition, recognition, perception, cognizance, light, notice, data, familiarity, enlightenment, conscience, acquaintance, consciousness, apperception. *Ant.* ignorance, stupidity, incapacity, darkness, incomprehension, blindness, inexperience, unenlightenment, obscurity, illiteracy, benightedness, unconsciousness, misconception, incomprehensibility, misunderstanding, enigma, misapprehension, unfamiliarity.

L

labor, toil, undertaking, travail, employment, work, effort, task, execution, exertion, drudgery, pains, achievement, painstaking, exercise, performance, operation, striving, industry, transaction, occupation, struggle, plodding, diligence. *Ant.* idleness, inertia, indolence, sloth, inactivity, laziness, incompetence, weakness, ease, lethargy, begging, dawdling, relaxation, loafing, inaction, inertness, unemployment, remissness, loitering.

laborious, arduous, heavy, backbreaking, tedious, hard, toilsome, crushing, difficult, stiff, wearisome, pressing, tiresome, wearing, indefatigable, assiduous, burdensome, grinding, cruel, painstaking, oppressive, plodding, strenuous, irksome, troublesome, tough, onerous, uphill, complex, discouraging, time-consuming. *Ant.* easy, smooth, facile, petty, light, simple, trivial, quick, unexacting, effortless.

labyrinthine, complicated, maze-like, confused, puzzling, intricate, involved, perplexed, winding, tortuous. *Ant.* simple, easy, plain, clear, open, explicit, straightforward.

lacerate, cut, tear, mangle, gash, maim, wound, injure, rip, rend, distress, harrow, disturb, hurt, worry. *Ant.* heal, soothe, assuage, calm, bandage, cure, treat.

lack, *n.* deficiency, scarcity, insufficiency, shortage, dearth, depletion, scantiness, privation, inadequacy, neediness, requirement,

lackadaisical

distress, poverty, fault, demerit, failing; *v.* need, want. *Ant.* surplus, plenty, excess, abundance, sufficiency, enough, profusion, supply.

lackadaisical, languishing, apathetic, carefree, indolent, inert, indifferent, spiritless, lethargic, listless, nonchalant, uncaring. *Ant.* energetic, enthusiastic, lively, zealous, spirited.

laconic, pithy, terse, condensed, succinct, curt, brief, concise, exact, pointed, sententious, epigrammatic, short. *Ant.* talkative, wordy, loquacious, voluble, verbose, diffuse, profuse, long-winded, prolix, rambling, copious, dilated.

lacuna, gap, hole, cavity, interval, opening, discontinuity, vacancy, hiatus. *Ant.* continuity, solidness, closing.

lag, delay, retard, slacken, linger, plod, loiter, tarry, idle, dawdle, dally, trudge, falter, stagger. *Ant.* hasten, hurry, quicken, hustle, bound, scamper, race, run, dash, spurt, dart, outstrip, accelerate.

lambent, radiant, shimmering, bright, brilliant, luminous, flickering, beaming, flaming, gleaming, twinkling.

lame, crippled, disabled, faltering, defective, hesitating, impotent, deformed, hobbling, limping, feeble, weak, ineffective, imperfect. *Ant.* agile, perfect, unimpaired, forceful, dashing, efficient, active, impetuous, speedy, quick, swift, healthy, well-formed, able-bodied, satisfactory.

lament, grieve, mourn, regret, sorrow, bewail, cry, anguish, weep, moan, bemoan, wail, deplore, commiserate, fret, worry, rue. *Ant.* rejoice, laugh, cheer, exult, celebrate, enjoy, delight in.

laminate, plate, veneer, overlay, layer, stratify, cover, coat.

lampoon, satire, mockery, ridicule, invective, abuse, contumely, obloquy, censure, disparagement, reproach, calumny, taunt, insinuation, libel, innuendo, diatribe. *Ant.* approbation, praise, tribute, commendation, applause, flattery, acclaim, panegyric, approval, plaudit, adulation, acclaim, sanction, admiration, support, defense, explanation, encomium.

language, speech, words, brogue, expression, vocabulary, diction, vernacular, utterance, tongue, idiom, jargon, voice, dialect, style, patois, terminology, phraseology, philology, letter, linguistics, literature.

languid, drooping, weak, dull, inert, remiss, pensive, flagging, heartless, slow, weary, feeble, listless, torpid, sluggish, lethargic, slow, apathetic, inactive, leisurely, languorous, faint, pining, sickly, debilitated, laggard, heavy, drowsy, slack. *Ant.* brisk, vigorous, nimble, smart, eager, vivacious, sharp, animated, quick, spry, lively, alert, quick, active, strong, enthusiastic, energetic, agile, restless, bustling, indefatigable, hustling, unwearying, zealous, assiduous, spirited.

lanky, tall, wiry, slim, narrow, lank, gaunt, lean, spare, bony, rawboned, thin, gangling. *Ant.* husky, fat, brawny, obese, burly, sturdy, portly.

lapse, delay, gap, passing, error, fault, mistake, blunder, slip, sin, boner, oversight, omission, flaw, fumble.

larceny, theft, appropriation, abstraction, embezzlement, thievery, pillage, peculation, pilfering, robbery, plunder, purloinment, shoplifting, burglary. *Ant.* restoration, return, reimbursement, repayment, compensation, replacement, indemnification, reversion, restitution, recoupment, atonement.

large, big, great, capacious, bulky, vast, huge, extensive, massive, colossal, spacious, wide, immense, gigantic, grand, roomy, plentiful, sizeable, copious, comprehensive, liberal, giant, monstrous, abundant, diffuse, towering, ample, titanic, mighty, commodious, swollen, magnificent, broad, bloated, tumid, long, enormous, extended, turgid, puffy, substantial, overgrown, inflated, pompous, corpulent, obese. *Ant.* small, tiny, little, thin, slight, microscopic, insignificant, attenuated, petty, minute, paltry, infinitesimal, diminutive, mean, slender, limited, scanty, short, brief, trifling, narrow, meager, trivial, wasted, dwarfish, petite, pygmy, abbreviated, miniature, puny, diminished, minuscule, emaciated.

lascivious, lewd, wanton, immoral, lustful, loose, lecherous, impure, unchaste, sensual, lubricous, unclean, polluted, ribald, bawdy, immodest, prurient, sadistic, carnal, concupiscent, masochistic, coarse, indelicate, improper, adulterous, risqué, salacious, pornographic, nymphomaniacal, libidinous, fleshly, licentious, gross, dissolute, rakish, obscene, fornicative, incestuous, shameless. *Ant.* good, uncontaminated, unstained, virginal, pure, modest, undefiled, virtuous, unsullied, retiring, continent, clean, chaste, decent, ethical, innocent, immaculate, sinless, unblemished, untarnished, holy, spotless, abstinent, celibate, incorrupt, exemplary, ascetic, moral, faultless, self-denying, righteous, restrained.

lash, whip, beat, drive, flail, goad, scourge, spur, strike, spank, pummel, abuse, impel, urge, press. *Ant.* reward, soothe, appease, refrain, restrain.

lassitude, languor, tiredness, stupor, faintness, fatigue, dullness, exhaustion, weariness, heaviness, drowsiness, listlessness, indolence, sluggishness, prostration, torpidity, phlegm, drooping, lethargy, hebetude, torpor, apathy, ennui, supineness, inertia. *Ant.* vigor, vivacity, energy, joy, vitality, vivaciousness, quickness, agility, sprightliness, briskness, activity, liveliness, agility, mirth, gaiety, refreshment, alertness, lightness, animation, nimbleness, cheerfulness, keenness, levity.

last, latest, conclusive, ultimate, hindmost, final, least, utmost, supreme, crowning, concluding, finishing, terminal, closing. *Ant.* introductory, initial, inaugural, incipient, beginning, commencing, first, primary, preparatory, foremost, leading, front.

lasting, stable, continuing, enduring, durable, protracted, unceasing, unremitting, permanent, persistent, staying, unending. *Ant.* temporary, transitory, fleeting, short-term, ephemeral, transient, impermanent, passing.

late

late, tardy, slow, dilatory, delayed, lagging; deceased, demised, departed; extinct, gone, defunct, bygone, lapsed; recent, new. *Ant.* early, punctual, prompt, ready; alive, living, animated; old, antique, ancient, aged.

latent, concealed, invisible, implied, dormant, unknown, secret, undeveloped, involved, hidden, inherent, unobserved, unperceived, passive, imperceptible, vestigial, lurking, implicit, rudimentary, unseen, quiescent, allusive, uncomprehended, recondite, potential. *Ant.* apparent, evident, unconcealed, conspicuous, active, exposed, developed, perceptible, manifest, clear, overt, visible, prominent, conclusive, obvious, distinct, known, indubitable, open, plain, undisguised, public, unmistakable, bare, definite.

latitude, range, extent, breadth, sweep, compass, scope, space, width, freedom, length, reach, distance, room, leeway.

laudable, praiseworthy, commendable, worthy, deserving, honorable, righteous, creditable, meritorious, estimable, exemplary, moral, ideal, model, dutiful, admirable, excellent. *Ant.* vile, corrupt, bad, vicious, dishonest, depraved, base, dishonorable, dissipated, mean, blameworthy, sinful, censurable, reprehensible, odious, damnable, wicked, criminal, unrighteous, demoralized, villainous, lawless, iniquitous, immoral, unprincipled, degraded, worthless, dissolute, disorderly, contemptible.

laughable, ludicrous, comical, absurd, ridiculous, funny, waggish, quaint, comic, droll, jocose, whimsical, eccentric, asinine, inane, amusing, foolish, facetious, farcical, bizarre. *Ant.* serious, awe-inspiring, sad, funereal, morbid, impressive, depressive, sorrowful, shocking, solemn, fearful, melancholy, painful, lugubrious, wretched, pitiful, morose, mournful.

laughter, mirth, gaiety, chuckle, giggle, snicker, hysteria, guffaw, amusement, derision, ridicule. *Ant.* gloom, sadness, depression, dejection, tears, crying, melancholy.

launch, start, initiate, begin, commence, inaugurate, open, project, dispatch, throw, cast, dart, float, enlarge, expatiate. *Ant.* end, close, finish, splash down, land.

lavish, *adj.* profuse, inordinate, exorbitant, superabundant, prodigal, abundant, luxuriant, wasteful, profligate, unstinted, liberal, generous, replete, exuberant, free, costly, dear, exhaustive, wild, unrestrained, excessive, improvident; *v.* squander, waste, gorge, glut, inundate, load, deluge, overload, flood, overrun, bestow, indulge, spend, expend, dissipate, deplete, disperse. *Ant.* scarce, lessened, stinted, sparse, deficient, scanty, meager, empty, lacking, inadequate, curtailed, insufficient, jejune, diminished, skimpy, wanting, little, stingy; hoard, treasure, save, economize, stint, conserve, lower, withhold, skimp, preserve, pinch, starve, curtail, limit, begrudge, reduce.

law, order, legislation, code, formula, rule, enactment, canon, ordinance, statute, decree, regulation, edict, command, precept, commandment, mandate, polity, equity, principle, constitution, jurisprudence, covenant, constitutionality, legality, rite, justice. *Ant.* lawlessness, felony, malfeasance, transgression, violation, illegality, outlawry.

lawful, legitimate, legal, permitted, allowable, permissible, licit, allowed, valid, righteous, authorized, right, recognized, granted, constitutional, admitted, judicial, statutory, conceded, warranted, juridical, sanctioned, approved, canonical, official, regular, legislative. *Ant.* illegal, arbitrary, unauthorized, prohibited, unofficial, unlicensed, unlawful, taboo, despotic, lawless, invalid, unconstitutional, unwarrantable, tyrannical, summary, oppressive, informal.

lax, remiss, vague, negligent, lawless, flaccid, derelict, relaxed, limp, careless, unobservant, unconscientious, insouciant, dishonorable, undutiful, depraved, unprincipled, weak, immoral. *Ant.* stern, rigorous, rigid, tight, upright, determined, faithful, honest, moral, reliable, observant, honorable, dutiful, conscientious, righteous, hard, true, firm.

lay, popular, common, secular, nonprofessional, profane, noncleric, nonecclesiastical, laic. *Ant.* professional, clerical, ecclesiastical, spiritual, ordained.

layer, fold, tier, stratum, veneer, lamina, plate, sheet, lap, thickness, bed, ply.

lazy, slow, sluggish, remiss, dormant, flagging, supine, indolent, idle, torpid, comatose, otiose, lackadaisical, slothful, inactive, dull, inert, lethargic, laggard, slack, tired, rusty, drowsy, dozy, weary, dronish, reluctant, sleepy, negligent, worn, shiftless, weak, leaden, impotent, dreamy. *Ant.* lively, prompt, assiduous, unwearied, fit, brisk, spry, hard-working, keen, alert, quick, diligent, sedulous, sharp, active, bustling, industrious, painstaking, vigorous, energetic, forcible, persevering, impetuous, indefatigable.

lead, guide, conduct, precede, manage, control, oversee, regulate, influence, direct, supervise, survey, steer, command, shepherd, induce, convey, pioneer, handle, govern, superintend, overlook, pilot, order, open, begin, start. *Ant.* follow, accede, concede, obey, consent, assent, attend, conform, concur, perform, comply, acquiesce, imitate, submit, attend, serve, help, assist.

leaden, heavy, dull, uninterested, spiritless, sullen, gray, gloomy, somber, funereal, sluggish; made of lead. *Ant.* gay, light, vivacious, bright, enthusiastic, cheerful.

leader, chief, director, head, master, superior, conductor, guide, commander, captain, vanguard. *Ant.* follower, henchman, soldier, disciple, worker, imitator, adherent, devotee.

league, alliance, association, pool, entente, union, confederation, coalition, cartel, club, fraternity, society.

leak, drip, exude, seep, ooze, percolate, pass, filter, escape, trickle, dribble, overflow, spill.

lean, incline, decline, crook, tend, shelve, cant, bend, slope, sidle, hang, slant, sag, tip, careen, dip, swing, list, tilt, heel, deviate, deflect.

leap

leap, spring, gambol, frolic, skip, frisk, caper, romp, vault, jump, bound, trip, dance.

learn, acquire, receive, imbibe, gain, gather, read, study, hear, ascertain, discover.

learned, scholarly, educated, academic, instructed, bookish, erudite, accomplished, philosophic, lettered, profound, solid, omniscient, well-informed, pedantic, knowledgeable, literate. *Ant.* ignorant, gross, stupid, shallow, empty-headed, incapable, illiterate, dull, uninformed, crass, incompetent, benighted, nescient, careless, uncultured, uninterested.

lease, rent, let, hire, contract, demise, charter, engage.

leave, *n.* permission, allowance, absence, holiday, license, consent, vacation, liberty, withdrawal, furlough, freedom, concession; *v* permit, depart, vacate, desert, let, quit, abandon, allow, resign, relinquish, forsake, withdraw, retire, decamp; *Ant.* retention, injunction, prohibition, confinement, restriction, limitation, proscription, interdiction, taboo, hindrance, disallowance, veto; stay, remain, persist, endure, tarry, rest, maintain, abide, hold, continue, keep.

lecherous, see **lascivious.**

leaven, *n.* ferment, yeast; *v.* generate, imbue, inspire, influence, excite, elevate, vitiate, taint, pervade, infect.

lecture, speech, discourse, address, sermon, talk, homily, lesson.

leftist, radical, communist, revolutionary, progressive, liberal, red, pink, socialist, left-winger, anarchist, rebel, reformer, fellow-traveler. *Ant.* rightist, right-winger, reactionary, conservative, tory.

legal, permissible, allowable, legitimate, warranted, permitted, allowed, licit, admitted, sanctioned, authorized, lawful, warranted, prescribed, fair, admitted, right, ordained, just, equitable, valid, constitutional, correct. *Ant.* unfair, unsanctioned, disallowed, unconstitutional, prohibited, unjust, illegal, wrong, illicit, unlawful, restricted, interdicted, invalid, illegitimate.

legendary, fictitious, fabulous, fanciful, romantic, tradional, mythical. *Ant.* historical, factual, actual, real, true.

legitimate, legal, lawful, genuine, logical, justifiable, true, correct, real, sanctioned, valid, warranted. *Ant.* illegal, illegitimate, invalid, untrue, unreal, wrong, incorrect.

leisure, rest, freedom, ease, vacation, idleness, relaxation, leave, sparetime, liberty, convenience, retirement. *Ant.* work, duty, toil, job, travail, drudgery.

lengthen, elongate, draw out, dilate, extend, prolong, increase, protract, stretch. *Ant.* shorten, speed, cut, curtail, abbreviate.

lenient, indulgent, kind, compassionate, tender, reasonable, soft, kind-hearted, merciful, tolerant, emollient, soft-hearted, mild, forbearing, moderate, assuaging, easy-going, gentle, clement. *Ant* harsh, brutal, overbearing, rigorous, acrimonious, cruel, unfeeling, severe, hard, rough, tyrannical, austere, exacting, coarse, intolerant, demanding, stern.

166

lessen, decrease, abate, dwindle, curtail, diminish, abridge, shorten, shrink, reduce, contract, narrow, trim, pare. *Ant.* increase, add, extend, enlarge, strengthen, heighten, intensify, magnify.

let, permit, tolerate, grant, authorize, concede, bear, allow, admit, empower, sanction, lease, suffer, warrant, privilege, accord, rent, yield. *Ant.* prevent, keep, preclude, debar, circumvent, hinder, inhibit, contravene, frustrate, hold, obstruct, counteract, retain, impede, oppose, defeat, halt, restrain, stop.

lethal, deadly, poisonous, virulent, mortal, fatal, baleful, murderous, killing, exterminating, destructive. *Ant.* curing, restoring, harmless, helpful, beneficial, good.

lethargy, listlessness, passiveness, torpor, lassitude, apathy, stupor, languor. *Ant.* vigor, vim, vitality, energy, liveliness, activity.

level, uniform, smooth, flush, horizontal, equal, regular, flat, balanced; genuine, honest. *Ant.* rough, irregular, unequal, uneven, hilly, rugged, mountainous, lumpy, vertical, plumb, slanting, perpendicular, leaning, upright; dishonest.

levity, lightness, frivolity, volatility, jocularity, liveliness, flightiness, gaiety, flippancy, buoyancy, merriment, hilarity, joy, inconstancy. *Ant.* gravity, austerity, sobriety, sternness, solemnity.

liable, responsible, subject, likely, answerable, accountable, apt, bound, chargeable, amenable, susceptible. *Ant.* excusable, irresponsible, clear, unbound, exempt, unamenable, absolved, freed, released, immune, unlikely.

libel, defame, slander, villify, asperse, detract, damage, lampoon, satirize, injure. *Ant.* praise, extol, elevate, help, advertise, explain, justify, defend.

liberal, generous, lavish, munificent, bountiful, open-handed, free, princely, ample, bounteous, unselfish, magnanimous, lenient, noble-minded, broad-minded, leftist, tolerant, extravagant, profuse, prodigal. *Ant.* conservative, narrow, miserly, parsimonious, thrifty, intolerant, penurious, sordid, greedy, mean, grasping, mercenary, close, shabby, stingy, venal, sparing, illiberal, avaricious.

liberate, free, loose, release, emancipate, deliver, unshackle, ransom, rescue, save, unchain, extricate, redeem, unfetter, untie, dismiss, pardon, reprieve, acquit, enfranchise, clear, discharge, absolve, quit, disenthrall. *Ant.* hold, shackle, fetter, debar, keep, bind, manacle, restrict, confine, restrain, handcuff, suppress, chain, enchain, hobble, cage, pin, arrest, imprison, prohibit, constrain, incarcerate, leash, detain, arrest, limit, immure.

liberty, freedom, right, privilege, immunity, enfranchisement, liberation, exemption, emancipation, license, leisure, leave, furlough, opportunity, permission, dismissal, independence, absolution, release, acquittance, allowance. *Ant.* slavery, serfdom, servitude, constraint, tyranny, necessity, oppression, captivity, compulsion, bondage, subjugation, obligation, detention, incarceration, duress, imprisonment, restraint, arrest, confinement, thralldom.

libidinous, lewd, wanton, licentious, lecherous, lustful, obscene, carnal, lascivious, salacious, abandoned. *Ant.* pure, chaste, good, moral, holy.

license, permit, authorize, approve, commission, warrant, sanction, endorse, allow. *Ant.* limit, refuse, withhold, disenfranchise, ban, prohibit, forbid, check.

licentious, wanton, libidinous, loose, profligate, lustful, lascivious, libertine, debauched, corrupt, dissolute, promiscuous. *Ant.* good, pure, pious, continent, innocent, chaste, moral, virtuous.

lie, falsify, deceive, prevaricate, fib, exaggerate, equivocate, evade, stretch, deviate, misrepresent; rest, recline, repose, lie (down), stay, remain, set.

life, existence, source, manner, principle, animation, essence, conduct, nature, custom, breath, vitality, origin, longevity, survival, being, entity, duration. *Ant.* death, passing, rest, cessation, dying, departure, release, destruction, dissolution, decease, mortality, demise, dullness, inaction, end, finish.

lifeless, dead, defunct, deceased, heavy, dormant, departed, inert, inanimate, gone, demised, slow, stagnant, dull, sluggish, inactive, lazy, extinct, insipid, flat, cold, frigid, lethargic, passive, latent. *Ant.* alive, animated, vigorous, lively, cheerful, living, spirited, brisk, gay, cheery, breathing, vital, active, merry, vivified, lighthearted, sprightly, alert, awake, warm, eager.

lift, raise, intensify, hoist, exalt, boost, elevate, uplift, heighten, steal, purloin, take. *Ant.* lower, depress, decline; return, repay.

light, *n.* illumination, radiation, lucency, gleam, brightness, beam, flame, blaze, glow, effulgence, luminosity, scintillation, phosphor, essence, flash, shimmer, brilliancy, incandescence, flare, gleam, shine, lustre, twinkling, sheen, sparkle, flicker, glimmer, glitter, instruction, reasoning, instinct, knowledge, understanding, comprehension, elucidation, aspect, approach, viewpoint; blanched, pale, blond, whitish; *adj.* buoyant, slight, airy, volatile, scanty, feathery, nimble, agile, lithe, imponderable, small, easy, gossamer, lissome, ethereal, imponderous, portable, shining, floating, sublimated, weightless, bright, scintillating, frothy, fluffy, downy, luminous, sparkling, shallow, flippant, lively, frivolous, giddy, unbalanced, empty, gay, unsteady, wanton, short, capricious, merry, frolicsome, vain, thoughtless, inadequate. *Ant.* darkness, shadow, blackness, shade, murkiness, dimness, gloom, murk, dusk, eclipse, somberness, duskiness; depression, benightedness, sadness, heaviness, ignorance, sorrow; heavy, weighty, clumsy, solid, sad, massive, burdensome, dense, depressed, ponderous, cumbersome, unwieldy, dejected, thick, somber, sober, serious, sorrowful, sullen, tedious, difficult, weary, morose, laborious, wearied, dull, dim, tired, dark, gloomy, concealed, unenlightened, opaque, dusky, hidden, ignorant, obscured, murky, obscurity.

lighten, ease, alleviate, cheer, appease, moderate, mitigate, temper, diminish, relieve, qualify; illuminate. *Ant.* oppress, burden, injure, sadden, aggravate, add, load.

likable, pleasant, friendly, enjoyable, good-natured, amiable, companionable. *Ant.* offensive, unlikable, unpleasant, disagreeable, unattractive.

like, similar, parallel, allied, comparable, akin, related, resembling, cognate, analogous, equivalent. *Ant.* different, divergent, dissimilar, unlike, diverse.

likely, credible, feasible, conceivable, conjectural, probable, presumable, apt, practicable, possible, reasonable, liable, suitable. *Ant.* impracticable, unlikely, improbably, unachievable, insurmountable, unobtainable, insuperable, unattainable.

likeness, similarity, portrait, analogy, representation, resemblance, illustration, counterpart, equivalence, photograph, copy.

limber, flexible, supple, springy, bouncy, pliant, pliable, bendable, lithe, lissome, lithesome. *Ant.* stiff, rigid, hard, brittle.

limit, boundary, end, terminus, brink, extreme, frontier, border, rim, edge, bound, line.

limp, limber, drooping, soft, flaccid, lax, flabby, weak, slack, enervated, exhausted, supple. *Ant.* stiff, rested, rigid, tense, fresh, hard.

limpid, clear, transparent, pure, bright, lucid, crystalline, crystal, glassy, translucent, pellucid. *Ant.* opaque, dark, turbid, muddy, cloudy.

line, cord, length, succession, thread, row, string, direction, outline, sequence, course, rope, band, streak, crease, wrinkle, occupation, career, boundary, span, measure, rank, extent, extension, descent, lineage, continuation, ancestry, stroke.

lineage, ancestry, genealogy, descent, family, extraction, forebears, line, house, forefathers, birth, breed, offspring, children, progeny, succession, descendants, pedigree.

linger, tarry, hesitate, dawdle, loiter, delay, falter, lumber, saunter, plod, totter, lag, trudge, stagger, rest, remain, cling, stay, shuffle, hobble. *Ant.* hasten, scamper, bustle, drive, quicken, spurt, sprint, hurry, dash, speed, scurry, dart, flurry, run, hustle, flutter.

link, join, connect, conjoin, bond, pin, associate, fasten, tie, unite, couple, bind. *Ant.* divide, sever, cut, separate.

liquid, fluid, sappy, solvent, deliquescent, serous, juicy, flowing, liquefied, dissolved, splashing, watery, succulent, molten, melted. *Ant.* solid, imporous, firm, undissolved, dense, impenetrable, hard, compact, solidified, impervious, close, condensed, coagulated, unchangeable, frozen, substantial, gaseous.

liquidate, settle, discharge, convert, pay, adjust, close, clear; abolish, extinguish, kill.

lissome, limber, flexible, agile, supple, pliable, energetic, active, airy, graceful, lithe. *Ant.* stiff, slow, rigid, clumsy.

list, roll, index, record, catalog, schedule, arrangement, enrollment, calendar, plan, tabulation, tape, series, roster, invoice, account, file, bulletin, register, table, manifest, directory, inventory, syllabus, tally, prospectus.

listen, hark, hear, harken, overhear, attend, heed, audit, monitor; observe, obey, follow, grant. *Ant.* ignore, shun, neglect, scorn, slight, reject, disregard.

listless, apathetic, inattentive, drowsy, supine, slack, careless, indolent, inert, sleepy, forgetful, indifferent, languid, torpid, spiritless, sluggish, heedless, leaden, lethargic, dull, heavy, laggard, uninterested, dreamy, dilatory. *Ant.* quick, spry, active, alert, agile, brisk, sharp, nimble, prompt, energetic, healthy, fresh, eager, acute, bustling, indefatigable, hustling, unweary, attentive, restless, ardent, assiduous, diligent, sedulous.

literal, verbatim, strict, rigorous, verbal, exact, conformable, veritable, accurate, real, true, precise, regular, actual, veracious, undeviating, undisputed, unerring. *Ant.* wrong, mistaken, deceiving, erring, false, untrue, misinterpreted, mistranslated, misleading, erroneous, delusive, unsound, groundless, beguiling, distorted, figurative, fallacious, metaphorical, mythical, idiomatic, unreal, symbolical, fantastic.

literature, written word, writings, translations, compilations, books, treatises, publications, literary productions, literary works, letters, poetry.

lithe, pliant, flexible, graceful, supple, lissome, resilient, limber, agile. *Ant.* stiff, awkward, rigid, clumsy.

litigation, lawsuit, case, suit, contest, arraignment.

little, small, dwarfish, scanty, diminutive, minute, inconsiderable, meager, light, miniaturized, miniature, inappreciable, trifling, short, petite, mean, selfish, petty, infinitesimal, condensed, abbreviated, trivial, puny, elfin, tiny, runty, undersized, microscopic, stunted, exiguous, pygmy. *Ant.* large, big, mighty, bulky, great, huge, immense, capacious, enormous, towering, roomy, massive, ample, magnificent, monstrous, titanic, comprehensive, gigantic, spacious, unwieldy, colossal, vast.

live, dwell, continue, remain, prevail, exist, tenant, abide, occupy, reside, stay, sojourn, lodge, room, inhabit, survive, subsist, endure, last, be, breathe, act, do, perform. *Ant.* die, pass away, depart, pass, wither, vanish, expire, fade, perish, dissolve, disappear.

livelihood, job, trade, career, maintenance, sustenance, support, subsistence, employment, resources, provision, substance, independence.

lively, gay, happy, animated, spirited, jolly, active, bustling, brisk, gleeful, exhilarated, vigorous, busy, ebullient, sparkling. *Ant.* dull, gloomy, despondent, lethargic, weary, limp, dejected, sleepy, dispirited, yawny.

livid, black-and-blue, lead-colored, grayish, discolored, bruised, pale, ashen, lurid, ghastly; enraged, infuriated, angered. *Ant.* radiant, brilliant, effulgent.

load, oppression, incubus, incumbrance, cargo, freight, shipment, lading, pack, weight, contents, burden, onus, millstone, pressure, responsibility, mass.

oath, reluctant, disinclined, unwilling, averse, indisposed. *Ant.* willing, eager, inclined, ready, enthusiastic, amenable.

oathe, abhor, detest, oppose, abominate, despise, disapprove, hate, denounce, condemn, dislike, imprecate. *Ant.* love, desire, want, delight in, like, respect, foster, esteem, admire, revere, indulge, appreciate, approve, cherish, nourish, honor, prize, nurture.

ocality, region, district, place, site, position, spot, town, city, block, community, neighborhood.

ocation, place, site, locale, situation, neighborhood, locality, region, post, position, spot.

ock, fastening, hasp, connection, link, grapple, hook, clasp, bolt, catch, bar, attachment, barrier, tuft, latch, fixture, floodgate, canal gate, grip; curl, strand, tress (hair).

odging, abode, dwelling, house, apartment, room, habitation, position; protection, harbor, security.

ofty, high, elevated, exalted, prideful, noble, majestic, proud, dignified, soaring, arrogant, eminent, vain, bombastic, stately, towering, conceited, inflated, haughty, tall, pretentious. *Ant.* low, repressed, beneath, below, modest, timid, diffident, timorous, retiring, coy, bashful, sheepish, humble, poor, plebeian, unobtrusive, shy, unpretentious, reserved, unassuming.

ogical, rational, reasonable, sound, sensible, coherent, valid, discriminating, cogent, reasoned, dialectical. *Ant.* illogical, foolish, wild, fantastic, silly, crazy, unreal, invalid, incoherent, irrational, incongruous.

oiter, linger, lag, stall, tarry, dally, wait, dawdle, loaf, delay, idle, poke, saunter, stroll. *Ant.* hasten, move, rush, hurry, speed.

one, sole, alone, lonely, lonesome, solitary, unattached, secluded, apart, retired, deserted; unique, single, only. *Ant.* accompanied, together, joined, in company.

onesome, lonely, forsaken, alone, isolated, desolate, cheerless, secluded, solitary, forlorn. *Ant.* cheerful, befriended.

ong, lengthy, elongated, protracted, enduring, lasting, extended, endless, drawn out, perpetual, prospective, outstretched, interminable, stretched, attenuated, prolonged, eternal, eventual, continued, repetitious, tedious, profuse, stretched out, diffuse, far-off, distant, far-away, remote. *Ant.* short, abbreviated, evanescent, shortened, transient, ephemeral, abridged, fleeting, cursory, curt, terse, pithy, brief, laconic, concise, curtailed, compact, condensed, epitomized, compressed.

ook, *n.* appearance, expression, manner, deportment, face, aspect, behavior, bearing, condition, air, front, mien, conduct, carriage; *v.* see, stare, descry, inspect, glimpse, distinguish, view, behold, watch, discern, speculate, observe, gaze, contemplate, survey, perceive, recognize, glance, scan, regard, spy, note, mark, investigate, peek, peer, leer. *Ant.* ignore, miss, pass by, disregard, overlook.

ookout, sentry; awareness, vigil, watch, surveillance, alertness.

loose, free, lax, unconfined, untied, separate, flowing, indefinite, unattached, relaxed, wanton, immoral, independent, careless, slack, vague, diffuse, rambling, dissolute, licentious. *Ant.* tight, taut, precise, strict, moral.

loquacity, volubility, talkativeness, verbosity, babbling, fluency, glibness, garrulity, facility. *Ant.* quietness, taciturnity, reticence, reserve, silence.

lose, miss, drop, mislay, forfeit, squander, waste, fail, falter, fold, flunk, fumble, flounder, blunder, botch, stumble, miscarry. *Ant.* gain, acquire, obtain, recover, procure, win, achieve, collect, reap, get, accomplish, conquer, master, inherit, increase, expand, regain, extend, profit, advance, progress, proceed, improve, rally, mend, surmount, overcome.

loss, injury, deprivation, privation, mishap, damage, forfeiture, bereavement, misfortune, detriment, disadvantage, death, casualty, failure, deterioration, degeneration, retardation, retrogression, impairment, decline. *Ant.* gain, acquisition, elevation, profit, improvement, advancement, emolument, procurement, capture, return, amendment, achievement.

lot, portion, fortune, fate, doom, luck, destiny, heritage, chance, award; group, assemblage, gathering, batch; land parcel.

loud, clamorous, sonorous, deafening, piercing, noisy, blatant, earsplitting, high-sounding, uproarious, clangorous, shrill, blaring, stunning, powerful, vociferous, ringing, crashing, resonant, thundering, vulgar, ill-bred, coarse, gaudy, bright. *Ant.* low, faint, tinkling, soothing, inaudible, soft, whispering, subdued, purring, sweet, stifled, sighing, dulcet, muffled, murmuring, silent, quiet, tasteful.

lounge, recline, loll, lie, idle, loaf, sprawl, wallow, relax. *Ant.* be active, work, sit up, be alert.

love, affection, passion, tenderness, attachment, emotion, feeling, liking, charity, sentiment, gratification, fondness, friendship, devotion, warmth, infatuation, ardor, yearning, joy, attraction, delight, worship, regard, benevolence, fervor, rapture, adoration. *Ant.* hate, estrangement, pique, repugnance, hatred, disinterest, enmity, grudge, revulsion, disaffection, bitterness, antipathy, malice, loathing, aversion, contumely, umbrage, detestation, execration, abhorrence, abomination, scorn, dislike, animosity, indifference, rancor, odium, disdain.

lovely, beautiful, inviting, fascinating, enticing, attractive, captivating, charming, delightful, winsome, pretty, sweet, amiable, adorable, enchanting, satisfying, graceful, lovable, exquisite, handsome, comely. *Ant.* ugly, unsightly, ill-favored, ungraceful, forbidding, plain, repellent, homely, unprepossessing, repulsive, hard-featured, grim, unseemly, unlovely, drab, awful, horrible, odious, hideous, shocking, repugnant, disgusting, revolting.

low, below, beneath, under, deep, prostrate, depressed, sunken, inferior, nether, flat, prone, supine, squat; faint, soft, hushed, muffled; small, short; mean, debased, vulgar, disreputable, shameless, coarse, disgraceful, unbecoming, dishonorable, despicable, degraded; feeble, weak, ill, sick; cheap, moderate, inexpensive. *Ant.* high, elevated, above, lofty, tall, exalted, eminent, towering, prominent; loud, clamorous, deafening, noisy, blatant, crashing, thunderous; honest, honorable, noble, upright, decent, respectable, worthy, estimable, respected; well, healthy, vigorous, strong.

owly, humble, self-abasing, poor, unassuming, unimportant, mean, submissive, self-abnegating, withdrawing, timid, reluctant, reserved. *Ant.* important, elevated, rich, high, worthy, noble, arrogant, proud.

oyal, faithful, steadfast, constant, trustworthy, true, devoted, unfailing, unswerving, patriotic. *Ant.* faithless, false, treacherous, seditious, perfidious, disloyal.

ubricate, grease, oil, lather, wax, anoint.

ubricious, oily, greasy, smooth, unsteady, shifty, wavering, uncertain; lewd, lustful, salacious, unchaste. *Ant.* dry, greaseless; chaste, pure.

ucent, bright, shining, lighted, beaming, brilliant, luminous, glittering, effulgent, respendent, gleaming, reflecting. *Ant.* dull, dim, dark, gloomy.

ucid, bright, shining, resplendent, incandescent, pellucid, serene, transparent, refulgent, luminous, radiant, pure, clear, plain, diaphanous, translucent, glassy, limpid; sane, rational, sound; explicit, distinct, understandable, obvious, reasonable, plain, evident. *Ant.* dark, murky, gloomy, obscure, dim, nebulous, dusky, shadowy, shady, cloudy; deranged, demented; unreasonable, confused, unintelligible, cryptic, incomprehensible, puzzling, enigmatic.

ucky, fortunate, successful, prosperous, auspicious, fortuitous, victorious, triumphant, thriving, flourishing, conquering, fateful, overcoming, winning, gaining. *Ant.* unlucky, unfortunate, unsuccessful, ill-starred, ill-fated, crushed, downtrodden, persecuted, wrecked, ruined, overwhelmed, defeated.

ucrative, profitable, worthwhile, self-supporting, gainful, advantageous, remunerative, self-sustaining. *Ant.* failing, losing, nonpaying, costly, wasteful, troublesome.

udicrous, comical, odd, farcical, ridiculous, droll, incongruous, humorous, funny, waggish, whimsical, laughable, sportive, amusing, queer, bizarre, quaint, outlandish, grotesque, eccentric, fantastic, burlesque, absurd. *Ant.* logical, reasonable, normal, lugubrious, serious, solemn, grievous, terrible, pitiful, tragic, grave, depressing, doleful, grim, sedate, earnest, demure, forlorn, disconsolate, downtrodden, careworn.

ugubrious, sad, morose, doleful, dreary, sorrowful, serious, melancholy, tearful, funereal, depressing, grim. *Ant.* happy, joyous, gay, light, bright, uplifting, exhilarating.

ull, quiet, still, tranquilize, appease, compose, mollify, calm, hush, pacify. *Ant.* incite, disturb, animate.

173

luminous, radiant, lucid, glowing, lit, bright, alight, shining, incandescent. *Ant.* dark, dull, dim, stupid, unclear, obscure.

lunacy, madness, furor, dementia, insanity, aberration, psychosis, mania, frenzy, imbalance, delirium, brainstorm, delusion, hallucination. *Ant.* sanity, normality, rationality, common sense, self-possession, lucidity, soundness, right-mindedness, steadiness, intelligence, reason, balance, reasonableness.

lure, attract, magnetize, deceive, flatter, delude, pull, cajole, bait, entice, decoy, inveigle, ensnare, entangle, draw, charm, coax, trap, enmesh, entrap, tempt, infatuate, trick, prevail, fascinate, induce, wheedle, persuade, bewitch, seduce, overcome, lead astray, mesmerize. *Ant.* repel, revolt, repulse, disgust, antagonize, dissuade, disenchant, dishearten, damp, deter, discourage, remonstrate, warn, admonish, deprecate.

lurid, pale, ashen, livid, sensational, horrible, gruesome, exciting, provocative, vivid. *Ant.* dark, brilliant, modest, quiet, banal, unimaginative.

lurk, skulk, sneak, ambush, hide, snoop, prowl, steal, slink.

luscious, sweet, pleasing, tasty, delectable, toothsome, savory, palatable, satisfying, agreeable, juicy, sweet, delightful, flavorful, delicious, gustatory, appetizing, exquisite, ambrosial. *Ant.* acrid, unsavory, sour, tart, bitter, sharp, unpalatable, nasty, nauseous, sickening, insipid, acidulous, repulsive, savorless, disagreeable, cloying, astringent, sourish, vapid, flat.

lush, luxuriant, succulent, fresh, exuberant, abundant, profuse, opulent, juicy, teeming. *Ant.* sparse, barren, sterile, dry, meager, arid.

lust, concupiscence, desire, carnality, greed, lechery, passion, craving, avarice, appetite, hankering, cupidity, wantonness. *Ant.* chastity, purity, restraint.

luster, brightness, brilliancy, glossiness, splendor, shimmer, glow, glare, sheen, effulgence, luminosity, dash, élan, repute, renown, fame, distinction. *Ant.* darkness, gloom, obscurity, murkiness, shade, shadow, matte-finish, drabness, dullness, dimness, somberness, cloudiness, duskiness, disrepute, dishonor, disgrace, shame, baseness, stigma, reproach, turpitude, notoriety, infamy.

luxuriant, exuberant, abundant, superabundant, profuse, teeming, opulent, excessive, fruitful, rich, abounding, rank, dense, lush, copious, plenteous, proliferous, fertile. *Ant.* meager, stunted, dwarfed, thin, shriveled, barren, withered, scarce, scanty, jejune, unproductive, infertile, fallow, sterile, arid, useless, dry, poor.

luxurious, sumptuous, rich, opulent, ornate, delicate, splendid, comfortable, voluptuous, self-indulgent, sensual, epicurean, pampered, pleasureable, wanton. *Ant.* harsh, plain, rigorous, drab, hard, simple, spartan, poor, bare, ascetic, monastic, self-denying.

lying, untruthful, mendacious, false, deceitful, prevaricating, fabricating, feigning, fraudulent, dishonest, faithless, insincere, disingenuous, forsworn, evasive, hollow, deceptive, hypocritical, dissembling, contemptible, perfidious, recumbent, resting. *Ant.* true, truthful, open, frank, sincere, candid, honest, guileless, unreserved, ingenuous, honorable, dependable, direct, trustworthy, reliable, straightforward, veracious, scrupulous, standing, sitting.

lyric, melodious, poetic, harmonious, rapturous, musical, emotional, singing. *Ant.* tuneless, harsh, grating, cacophonous, jarring, noisy.

M

macabre, gruesome, horrid, weird, morbid, fearful, grim, deathly, lurid, appalling, ghastly, grisly, repulsive. *Ant.* delightful, nice, pleasant, attractive, pretty, gay.

macerate, soak, digest, steep, wear (away), grind, mortify, torture, injure, discipline.

Machiavellian, intriguing, sly, subtle, insidious, equivocal, unscrupulous, artful, arch, designing, astute, perfidious, cunning, deceitful, wily, tricky, crafty. *Ant.* honest, direct, straightforward, sincere, trustworthy.

machination, scheme, plot, design, purpose, conspiracy, intrigue, dodge, plan, project, device, ruse, trick, maneuver, stratagem.

machine, engine, apparatus, utensil, implement, robot, motor, appliance, instrument, contrivance, tool, mechanism, automatism; organization, system, agent, puppet, cabal.

mad, insane, crazy, deranged, distracted, wild, raging, frenzied, frantic, rabid, furious, violent, lunatic, maniacal, frenetic, raving, psychotic, paranoid, fierce, convulsed, unhinged, daft, delirious, unbalanced, demented, moonstruck, unsettled, scatterbrained, imprudent, reckless, foolish, absurd, angry, upset. *Ant.* normal, steady, settled, calm, self-possessed, sober, rational, serene, cool, balanced, lucid, sane, clear-headed, perspicacious, self-controlled, acute, sharp, smart, quiet, reserved, astute, keen-minded, shrewd, incisive, reasonable, rational, sound, sensible, sagacious, strong-minded.

madden, infuriate, exasperate, inflame, enrage, craze, irritate, provoke, anger. *Ant.* calm, appease, soothe, cool.

magazine, periodical, pamphlet, newspaper; storehouse, warehouse, depot, store, depository, repository.

magic, occultism, legerdemain, witchcraft, superstition, jugglery, conjuring, sorcery, presagement, black art, voodoo, necromancy, omen, prediction, horoscopy, astrology, astromancy, divination, palmistry, trickery, illusion, hexing, rune, wizardry, demonology, hocus-pocus.

magnanimous, high-minded, exalted, noble, generous, honorable, dignified, lofty, forgiving, liberal, charitable, unselfish, princely, noble-minded, great-hearted, chivalrous, heroic, sublime. *Ant.* selfish, mean, corrupt, depraved, revengeful, vindictive, unforgiving, base, small, ungenerous, venal, mercenary, covetous, miserly, narrow-minded, self-seeking, egotistical, illiberal, close, doubting, suspicious, self-interested, grasping, greedy, self-indulgent.

magnate, tycoon, industrialist, entrepreneur, eminent person, baron capitalist.

magnificent, grand, splendid, noble, gorgeous, sublime, excellent august, splendiferous, rich, lofty, overwhelming, immense, vast princely, kingly, royal, surpassing, superb, glorious, stately, brilliant, transcendant, radiant, beautiful, fine, ostentatious, showy flashy, majestic, elegant, vast, sumptuous, spectacular. *Ant* plain, common, ordinary, normal, informal, unpretentious, dull ugly, inartistic, misshapen, dowdy, gross, dingy, uncouth, misproportioned, ungraceful, offensive, repellent, forbidding, plebeian small, cheap, humble, modest, unassuming, hideous, grim, blurred disfigured, dim, unshapely, smeared, blotted, discolored.

magnify, enlarge, amplify, hyperbolize, romanticize, aggrandize, enhance, increase, expand, augment, exaggerate. *Ant.* diminish, reduce, decrease, understate.

magnitude, size, volume, bulk, extent, greatness, extension, bigness, mass, highness, quantity, measure, amplitude, multitude, range, circumference, girth, brightness, loudness, vastness, might, intensity, power, grandeur, importance, dignity, expanse, proportions *Ant.* littleness, smallness, thinness, paucity, slenderness, dimness, insignificance, mediocrity, quietness.

maiden, unexperienced, virginal, vestal, youthful, pure, first, innocent, launching, immature, fresh, untouched, untried, unused, unmarried. *Ant.* experienced, tried, tested, used, seasoned, married, veteran, sophisticated.

maim, cripple, damage, mangle, lame, disfigure, mutilate, spoil, injure, mar, hurt.

main, principal, chief, leading, necessary, prime, cardinal, primary, foremost, central. *Ant.* secondary, minor, unimportant, inessential, subordinate.

mainstay, prop, key support, supporter, chief hope, foundation, brace, buttress, strut.

maintain, support, sustain, aid, retain, justify, aver, contend, hold, defend, uphold, assert, preserve, carry, bear, prove, vindicate, continue, keep, confirm, secure. *Ant.* deny, reject, refuse, forsake, abandon, depart, desert, retire, leave, withdraw, quit, withhold, denounce, condemn, discard, spurn, disdain.

majestic, stately, grand, august, noble, impressive, dignified, splendid, sublime, imposing, important, affecting, solemn, kingly, great imperial, inspiring, magnificent, moving, towering, high, mighty, eminent, illustrious, distinguished renowned, prominent, exalted *Ant.* mean, low, small, diminutive, subordinate, humble, inferior, little, shabby, petty, insignificant, obscure, common, trifling, unpretentious, paltry, low-class, uncouth, unrefined, clumsy, flimsy, imperfect, unadorned, contemptible, poor, second-rate, defective, dilapidated.

major, greater, main, preponderant, dominant, first, principal, chief salient, larger, superior. *Ant.* minor, small, unimportant, lesser, secondary, inferior.

make, do, form, construct, contrive, forge, fabricate, compose, produce, perform, execute, constitute, effect, build, create, shape, invent, originate, establish, frame, manufacture, generate, perfect, complete, fashion, write, carve, mold, cause, drive, impel, urge, force, get, obtain, achieve, accomplish. *Ant.* break, end, ignore, destroy, demolish, wreck, scatter, abolish, ruin, overthrow, smash, batter, ravage, dismantle, raze, level, mutilate, deform, distort, twist, undo, mar, injure, deface, impair, shatter, damage, crack, subvert, eradicate, obliterate, exterminate, annihilate, remove, extirpate, crush, split, sunder, spoil, forget, neglect.

makeshift, short-term, provisional, substitute, momentary, stopgap, expedient, temporary. *Ant.* permanent, abiding, fixed.

maladroit, clumsy, bungling, inept, awkward, inexpert, unhandy, unskilled, tactless, gauche. *Ant.* tactful, expert, adroit, clever, adept, skillful.

malady, illness, disorder, infirmity, affliction, ailment, disease, indisposition, sickness. *Ant.* health, well-being.

malcontent, *n.* grumbler, rebel, objector, faultfinder, insurgent, agitator, rioter, complainer; *adj.* dissatisfied, discontented, unhappy. *Ant.* zealot, mediator, negotiator, appeaser, supporter, defender; contented, satisfied, agreeable.

male, masculine, virile, mannish, manlike, manly, potent. *Ant.* female, womanly, effeminate, maidenly, unmanly.

malediction, curse, execration, imprecation, anathema, proscription, abuse, expletive, excoriation, revilement, fulmination, damnation, denunciation, vituperation, wrath, condemnation, commination, vilification, disparagement. *Ant.* blessing, benediction, commendation, approval, endorsement, appreciation, testimonial, adoration, approbation, praise, esteem, estimation, admiration.

malefactor, evildoer, wrongdoer, transgressor, criminal, scoundrel, rascal, villain, convict, thief, robber, forger, mugger, wretch, jailbird, culprit, murderer, delinquent, outlaw, felon, scamp, outcast, scapegrace, vagabond, highwayman, knave, rapscallion, rowdy, rogue, ruffian, hoodlum, sinner. *Ant.* model, example, pattern, hero, helper, philanthropist, paragon, ideal, saint, humanitarian, good citizen, altruist, pillar of society, innocent, benefactor, good man, good woman.

malevolent, malignant, spiteful, malicious, evil, evil-minded, hostile, ill-disposed, virulent, ill-intentioned, malign, rancorous, invidious, misanthropic, recriminatory, bitter, envenomed, caustic, spiteful, treacherous. *Ant.* amiable, cordial, soft-hearted, kind, kindly, hospitable, tolerant, affable, charitable, tender, considerate, indulgent, warm-hearted, gracious, kind-hearted, good-natured, sympathetic, beneficent, benevolent.

malice, hate, ill will, spite, rancor, animosity, grudge, enmity, implacability, malevolence, spite, virulence, cruelty, bitterness, abhorrence, hatred, antipathy, repugnance, dislike, resentment, venom, acerbity, malignity. *Ant.* benevolence, sympathy, good will, unselfishness, charity, kindliness, philanthropy, friendliness, generosity, affection, goodness, consideration, benignity, kindness, indulgence, compassion, amiability, cordiality.

malign, slander, besmirch, libel, calumniate, detract, disparage, defame, traduce, discredit, vilify. *Ant.* praise, extol, acclaim, laud, compliment, celebrate, applaud, support.

malignant, malign, spiteful, pernicious, virulent, hostile, bitter, mischievous, deadly, perilous, fatal, evil, malevolent. *Ant.* benign, good, helpful, peaceful.

malleable, plastic, yielding, shapeable, changeable, ductile, pliant, moldable, impressionable. *Ant.* stiff, unyielding, firm, resolute, fixed, indomitable.

malodorous, bad-smelling, stinking, rank, foul, fetid, noisome, gamy, rancid, musty, putrid, mephitic, noxious. *Ant.* sweet-smelling, perfumed, fragrant, aromatic.

maltreat, see **mistreat**

mammoth, huge, gigantic, tremendous, colossal, vast, mountainous, immense, enormous, elephantine, titanic. *Ant.* small, tiny, little, minute, diminutive.

manage, regulate, govern, conduct, control, show, direct, administer, wield, influence, hoard, husband, watch, rule, actuate, dominate, sway, master, prevail, accomplish, do, effect, superintend, supervise, steer, advise, guide, oversee, manipulate, contrive, execute, run, head, officiate. *Ant.* mismanage, bungle, blunder, misdirect, fumble, muff, misapply, misconduct, misguide, boggle, spoil, fail.

mandate, order, command, behest, fiat, law, edict, commission, injunction, compulsion, charge, decree, ruling, requirement, ukase, requisite, prerequisite, rule, statute, ordinance.

maneuver, artifice, tactic, wile, plot, ruse, feint, movement, action, procedure, plan, design, stratagem, scheme.

mangle, tear, mutilate, lacerate, maim, wound, rend, injure, cut, cripple, hamstring, disfigure, disjoint, fracture, slash, crush, dislocate, bruise.

manifest, clear, visible, open, apparent, plain, evident, aboveboard, obvious, definite, defined, conspicuous, patent, displayed, declared, bare, unveiled, divulged, unmistakable, self-evident, explicit, undisguised. *Ant.* buried, concealed, hidden, disguised, obscure, withheld, latent, covered, obscured, puzzling, mystifying, complex, involved, intricate, hard, difficult, twisted, warped, abstruse.

manifold, diverse, numerous, multifarious, multitudinous, several, various, many, sundry. *Ant.* single, simple, direct, few, sole, one.

manipulate, operate, feel, finger, handle, control, direct, guide, rule, lead, bribe, compel, threaten.

mankind, humanity, man, men, human race, mortality, people.

manly, brave, courageous, firm, fearless, undaunted, staunch, honorable, masculine, dignified, stately, noble, valiant, valorous, lion-hearted, high-spirited, plucky, intrepid, straightforward, virile, gallant, resolute, bold, audacious, confident, gentlemanly, independent, self-reliant. *Ant.* cowardly, timid, afraid, nervous, restless, shaky, apprehensive, faint-hearted, bashful, retiring, diffident, vacillating, hesitant, craven, unmanly, sissy, effeminate, weak, cringing, fawning.

man-made, artificial, invented, synthetic, unnatural, contrived, concocted, manufactured, fabricated. *Ant.* natural, honest, native, unadulterated.

manner, habit, custom, aspect, appearance, behavior, look, way, air, style, type, kind, sort, form, conduct, mien, mode, expression, character, stamp, wont, demeanor, method, guise, fashion, carriage, bearing, approach.

manners, morals, conduct, behavior, habits, routine, etiquette, courtesy, deportment, practice, suavity, vanity, breeding, urbanity, politeness, mode, propriety, vogue, conventionality, decorum, formality, taste, form. *Ant.* vulgarity, rudeness, boorishness, misconduct, grossness, misbehavior, ill-breeding, coarseness, rowdyism, barbarism, discourtesy, crudity, ruffianism.

many, numerous, multitudinous, myriad, several, manifold, diverse, various, countless. *Ant.* few, scarce, uniform, uncommon.

map, *v.* chart, plot, scheme, diagram, plan, design, outline; *n.* graph, representation, program, projection.

mar, deform, distort, impair, spoil, botch, hurt, injure, deface, disfigure, mutilate, twist, damage, harm, warp, stain, scratch, sear, scar, despoil, dilapidate, waste, bungle. *Ant.* beautify, adorn, repair, decorate, ornament, improve, restore, replace, garnish, refresh, mend, vivify, embellish, enrich, paint, varnish, gild, polish, furbish, lacquer, cover, brighten, clean.

marauder, raider, pillager, brigand, looter, plunderer, pirate, freebooter, sacker, invader, thief, attacker, robber, ravager.

march, walk, step, move, advance, proceed, parade, file, journey, tread, tramp, travel, patrol, range, promenade, progress. *Ant.* rest, pause, halt, stand, stay, stop, remain, recede, retreat, back, retrograde, return, revert.

margin, brink, edge, border, verge, confines, leeway, boundary, limit, wall, fence, brim, lip, rim, fringe, bank, shore, strand. *Ant.* area, interior, surface, background, extension, width, breadth, depth, heart, center, thickness.

marine, nautical, naval, oceanic, pelagic, hydrographic, seagoing, seafaring, aquatic, natatorial, oceanographic, maritime. *Ant.* midland, earthly, terrestrial, ashore, geodetic, inland, continental, landlocked, tellurian, alluvial.

marital, connubial, nuptial, matrimonial, wedded, conjugal. *Ant.* single, celibate.

mark, *v.* effect, mar, bruise, dent, scratch, smear, stain, sign; *n.* symbol, token, design, brand, badge, line, trace, tracing, drawing, stamp, impression, note, engraving, device, representation, type, emblem, stroke, character, score, stripe, figure, imprint, indication, letter, signature, notation, goal, target.

market, marketplace, bazaar, shop, supermart, shopping center, agora, bourse, stall, booth, emporium, exchange, mart, store.

marriage, espousal, union, wedlock, conjugality, wedding, nuptials, matrimony, match, contract, oath, sacrament. *Ant.* celibacy, virginity, bachelorhood, spinsterhood, singleness, widowhood, maidenhood, separation, spouselessness, divorce.

marsh, swamp, fen, bog, wash, quicksand, morass, slough, quagmire.

marshal, arrange, assemble, order, organize, mobilize, activate, convoke, collect, rank, systematize. *Ant.* derange, disorder, scatter, muss (up), dislocate, demobilize.

martial, warlike, soldierly, courageous, brave, hostile, military, belligerent, militant, combative, bristling, embattled, armed. *Ant.* peaceful, quiet, pacific, meek, submissive, non-combatant, mild, conciliatory, humble, yielding, unresisting, pliant, neutral, non-violent.

martyr, sacrifice, scapegoat, victim, saint, sufferer, messiah, volunteer.

marvel, miracle, prodigy, freak, phenomenon, wonder, monster, monstrosity, sensation, portent, oddity, genius, rarity, curiosity.

marvelous, wonderful, wondrous, miraculous, phenomenal, fabulous, extraordinary, curious, amazing, astonishing, unexpected, surprising, astounding, stupendous, mysterious, incredible, awesome, awful, overwhelming, prodigious, indescribable, remarkable, inexpressible, superb, ineffable. *Ant.* plain, ordinary, normal, common, simple, conventional, usual, commonplace, matter-of-fact, insignificant, unimportant, undistinguished, little, inconsiderable, trifling, trivial, paltry, petty, worthless, unremarkable, shallow, shabby, meager, miserable, contemptible.

masculine, manly, mannish, male, virile, aggressive, husky, strong, robust, brave, bold, daring. *Ant.* feminine, womanish, delicate, effeminate, female, modest, tender, timorous, weak, timid.

mask, conceal, cloak, cover, shield, falsify, hide, screen, disguise, dissemble, veil, muffle, camouflage, hoodwink, mystify, stifle, suppress, hush. Ant. unmask, uncover, unveil, reveal, bare, clarify, inform, tell, enlighten, explain, announce, disclose, relate, report, record, declare, proclaim, expose, publish.

masquerade, mummery, disguise, cover, deception, trickery, mask, pretense, veil, hiding.

mass, bulk, heap, totality, whole, sum, total, amount, aggregate, quantity, density, gravity, lump, pile, size, volume, magnitude, fullness, body, dimension, people, assemblage, amplitude, proportions, majority, wad, weight, solidity, consistence, accumulation, viscosity, thickness. *Ant.* part, portion, individual, factor.

massacre, slaughter, killing, extermination, slaying, murder, butchery, annihilation, genocide, carnage, bloodshed, decimation.

massage, rub, knead, manipulate, stroke, pound.

massive, huge, heavy, dense, large, weighty, ponderous, cumbrous, colossal, majestic, imposing, unwieldy, cumbersome, bulky, solid. *Ant.* small, delicate, slender, light, airy, imponderable, buoyant, sublimated, volatile, foamy, soft, pliant, flexible.

master, chief, leader, ruler, governor, president, conqueror, victor, champion, captain, potentate, employer, foreman, director, lord, principal, overseer, superintendent, supervisor, boss, teacher, instructor, preceptor, guide, mentor, judge, arbiter, sage, savant, patriarch, chieftain, commander, commandant. *Ant.* servant, follower, slave, attendant, valet, subject, tyro, apprentice, menial, henchman, dependent, amateur, greenhorn, private, vassal, serf, subordinate, disciple, learner, pupil, beginner, novice, retainer, neophyte, operative, laborer, drudge, bondman, servitor, hireling, mercenary.

masterpiece, greatest accomplishment, monument, magnum opus, forte, chef d'oeuvre, masterwork, paragon, peak.

mastery, ascendancy, dominance, skill, command, dominion, control, power, influence, superiority, rule, success, government, sway, advantage, expertise, supremacy, conquest, victory, triumph, exultation. *Ant.* failure, miscarriage, inefficiency, impotence, defeat, incapacity, blunder, stumble, breakdown, mishap, defeat, subjugation, downfall, wreck, ruin, loss, collapse, bankruptcy.

masticate, chew, crunch, crush, champ, eat, grind, munch, ruminate. *Ant.* gulp, bolt, swallow whole.

matchless, peerless, incomparable, consummate, inimitable, surpassing, unparalleled, unrivaled, supreme, unequaled, topmost, best, unmatched, finest, excellent, exquisite, superior. *Ant.* common, ordinary, commonplace, mean, meager, petty, paltry, second-rate, cheap, poor, imperfect, mediocre, middling, inept, impaired, inferior, damaged, mutilated, faulty, defective, secondary.

mate, companion, spouse, assistant, friend, intimate, pal, chum, associate, associate, consort, husband, wife, ship's officer.

material, *adj.* corporeal, bodily, physical, sensible, tangible, solid, concrete, temporal, substantial, ponderable, palpable, somatic; *n.* substance, matter, provision, equipment, constituent, gear, stuff, outfit, fabric. *Ant.* immaterial, incorporeal, airy, bodiless, misty, shadowy, ethereal, spectral, unsubstantial, intangible, unearthly, spiritual, spiritistic, disembodied, ghostly.

maternal, motherly, tender, caring, affectionate, matronly. *Ant.* unfeeling, cold, paternal, fatherly.

mathematical, exact, certain, regular, definite, precise. *Ant.* careless, inexact, irregular, loose, random.

matter, substance, substantiality, body, corporeality, stuff, element, materiality, materialization, object, article, thing, business, subject, topic, affair, content, interest. *Ant.* nihility, nothingness, immateriality, incorporeality, spirit, soul, ego, ghost, apparition, phantasm, vision, phantom, intellect, mind, thought, fancy, imagination.

mature, ripe, adult, full-grown, full-blown, matronly, experienced, hardened, toughened, aged, pubescent, fertile, productive, virile, womanly, marriageable, ready, fit, perfect, prime, complete, prepared, seasoned, developed, mellow, man-like, settled, maturated. *Ant.* immature, unripe, green, undeveloped, fresh, new, incom-

maudlin

plete, unprepared, premature, rudimentary, callow, raw, unfitted unready, imperfect, juvenile, puerile, fledgling, unseasoned, weak deficient, inexperienced.

maudlin, sentimental, mawkish, emotional, mushy, effusive, silly *Ant.* cold, unfeeling, unromantic, unimaginative, brusque.

mawkish, flat, insipid, stale, vapid, dull, nauseous, loathsome, disgusting, emotional, maudlin, sentimental, foolish, effusive. *Ant* tasty, flavorsome; lively, exciting, sensible, calm, serious, sober.

maxim, aphorism, precept, byword, proverb, apothegm, adage, saw saying, epigram, motto, dictum, tenet, bromide, platitude, teaching, moral, theorem, truism, axiom.

maximum, most, greatest, ultimate, biggest, largest, farthest, highest, utmost, supreme. *Ant.* minimum, least, smallest.

maze, tangle, twist, intricacy, winding, confusion, convolution, torsion, sinuosity, meandering, labyrinth, perplexity, coil, network bewilderment, difficulty, enigma, riddle, puzzle, ignorance, benightedness. *Ant.* simplicity, ease, easiness, plainness, flatness smoothness, roundness, circularity, direct route, order, facility clearness, disencumbrance, perception, knowledge, enlightenment

meager, thin, poor, lank, emaciated, slender, small, scanty, starved barren, diminutive, withered, inconsiderable, dry, short, incomplete, deficient, slight, flimsy, puny, sparse, lean, unfertile, gaunt insufficient, skimpy, sparing, stinted. *Ant.* sufficient, ample, lavish, abundant, plenteous, luxuriant, copious, abounding, plump replete, stuffed, chock-full, liberal, unstinted, wide, running over expanded, outspread, outstretched, large, fat, corpulent, big, full complete, excessive, unlimited, generous.

mean, *adj.* low, base, degraded, despicable, vile, debased, contemptible, ignoble, abject, disgraceful, nasty, bad-tempered, grouchy unobliging, common, humble, disgusting, shameful, dishonorable deceitful, pitiful, shabby, beggarly, stingy, parsimonious, miserly penurious, scrubby, piddling, poor, miserable, squalid, sordid mercenary, discreditable, disreputable, selfish, average, medium middling, median, modal, normal; *v.* intend, ordain, indicate design, denote, express, say, state, imply, contemplate, determine predetermine, undertake, pursue, purport, connote, infer, convey suggest, signify. *Ant.* generous, unselfish, open-hearted, liberal honorable, noble, charitable, philanthropic, helpful, compassionate, indulgent, bountiful, unsparing, ungrudging, free, munificent, prodigal, extravagant, profuse, lavish, magnificent, rich improvident, distinguished, respected, high, eminent, extreme extraordinary, superior, inferior.

meander, wander, amble, stroll, wind, ramble, saunter, sinuate, veer rove, vary, drift.

means, resources, materials, wherewithal, revenue, income, money wealth, riches, capital, stock, property, provision, method, way procedure, expedient, measure, agency, instrumentality, medium factor.

measure, quantity, magnitude, amplitude, measurement, degree, extent, grade, amount, gauge, scale, mensuration, quantification, allotment, dimension, portion, standard, tempo, cadence, rhythm, beat, range, scope, reach, plan, plot, design, scheme, outline, bill, sketch, draft, proposal, project, proposition, suggestion.

measureless, unlimited, boundless, limitless, eternal, unending, vast, infinite, immeasurable, illimitable, interminable, indefinite, incomprehensible, incalculable, endless, termless, perpetual. *Ant.* precise, definite, bounded, limited, comprehensible, short, transient, ephemeral, transitory, evanescent, passing, brief, temporary, meager, little, small, inconsiderable, trivial, circumscribed, measurable, defined, dimensional.

mechanical, instinctive, reflex, machinelike, rote, automatic, unreasoned, impulsive, involuntary, routine, perfunctory, autonomic, automated, dehumanized, controlled, contrived.

meddle, interpose, interfere, mix, tamper, obtrude, impede, pry, intrude, annoy, pester, intervene. *Ant.* shun, refrain, steer clear, ignore, avoid, aid, encourage, support, oblige.

mediate, intercede, intervene, settle, conciliate, arbitrate, interpose, pacify, reconcile. *Ant.* ignore, shun, aggravate, annoy, fight, contend, wrangle.

medicine, remedy, specific, treatment, medicament, simple, cure, drug, medical profession, therapy, restorative, prophylaxis, dose, electuary.

medieval, old-fashioned, quaint, out-dated, incongruous, antiquated, obsolete, traditional, courtly, feudal. *Ant.* new, modern, fresh, avant-garde, contemporary, ordinary, commonplace.

mediocre, commonplace, indifferent, adequate, passable, middling, fair, average, normal, ordinary. *Ant.* superior, inferior, unusual, extraordinary, transcendent.

meditate, study, contemplate, resolve, consider, project, ruminate, reflect, ponder, deliberate, cogitate, speculate, pray, plan, think, reason, brood over, cerebrate, muse, concentrate. *Ant.* overlook, disregard, discard, distract, divert, dismiss, be inattentive, turn from, neglect, ignore, act.

medium, mean, average, mediocrity, normality, means, agency, surroundings, nutrients, method, artistic material, channel, means, instrument, organ, agent, oracle, operator, executor, go-between, soothsayer, fortune teller, prophet, seer, clairvoyant, intermediary, representative, interagent, substitute.

medley, mixture, mingling, variety, variance, confusion, miscellany, jumble, potpourri, combination, interlauding, diversity, disorder, diffusion, admixture, derangement, hodgepodge. *Ant.* arrangement, order, system, proportion, uniformity, separation, orderliness, simpleness, simplification, normality, regularity, method, grouping, allotment.

meek, humble, mild, gentle, unpretentious, unassuming, modest, retiring, docile, calm, obedient, bashful, soft, yielding, compliant
unprepossessing, malleable, deferential, lowly, submissive, spiritless, enduring, subdued, demure, inhibited, placid, tolerant, forbearing, resigned, patient, timid, pacific, peaceable. *Ant.* harsh
cruel, overbearing, proud, assertive, tyrannical, haughty, disdainful, vain, presumptuous, arrogant, bold, conceited, uninhibited
rash, immodest, audacious, insolent, daring, ambitious, willful
wrathful, resentful, choleric, fierce, furious, fiery, obstinate, vindictive, vengeful, stubborn, highspirited, contemptuous, contentious, lofty, impertinent, impudent, pompous, self-important
high-toned, supercilious, bumptious, consequential.

meet, encounter, find, join, connect, cross, converge, intersect, greet
gather, unite, collide, confront, touch. *Ant.* depart, separate
miss, avoid, shun.

meeting, conference, convention, assembly, gathering, reunion, convocation, conclave, interview, tryst, rendezvous, duel; confluence
crossing, junction. *Ant.* separation, division, adjournment, scattering, divergence.

melancholy, depressed, gloomy, low-spirited, dispirited, pensive, dejected, discontented, glum, sorrowful, sad, despondent, somber
downcast, funereal, dismal, heavy-hearted, spiritless, grim, joyless, mournful, dull, doleful, wistful, blue, drab, lugubrious
lackadaisical, jaundiced, discouraged, forlorn, moody, sulky. *Ant*
cheerful, gay, lively, merry, light-hearted, happy, smiling, blithe
devil-may-care, joyous, fine, buoyant, exhilarated, convivial, contented, ecstatic, light, sprightly, hilarious, jovial, jolly, jaunty
sportive, spirited, gleeful, vivacious, breezy, playful, animated
brisk, rollicking, fresh, dashing, fun-loving, frisky, agreeable,
amiable, bright, elated, jubilant, entertaining, inspiriting.

melee, fracas, row, fight, turmoil, confusion, excitement, chaos, fray,
jumble, embroilment, skirmish. *Ant.* peace, discussion, calm, concord, agreement, harmony.

mellow, ripe, mature, perfected, sweet-sounding, delicate, subdued,
seasoned, rich, full-flavored, soft, aged, pleasing, refined, relaxed,
happy, genial, gay. *Ant.* immature, hard, harsh, sour, acrid, tart,
pungent, flat, stale, dull, steady, stubborn, callous, sober, serious,
temperate, solemn.

melodious, musical, harmonious, agreeable, pleasing, sweet, tuneful,
dulcet, mellifluous, assonant, soft, clear, silvertoned, resonant, accordant, euphonious. *Ant.* harsh, grating, inharmonious, unmusical, discordant, dissonant, tuneless, cacophonous, jarring, raucous,
ear-splitting, noisy, blaring, unmelodious, jangling, shrill, strident, hollow, sepulchral.

melody, descant, tune, theme, song, chant, aria, lyric, strain, mono-
phony, euphony, mellifluence.

melt, liquefy, dissolve, liquidate, fade, dwindle, disappear, fuse, diffuse, sublimate, relax, soften, mollify, deliquesce, thaw, decrease,

render, diminish, vanish. *Ant.* freeze, densify, thicken, coagulate, solidify, congeal, condense, crystallize, harden, petrify, consolidate.

member, constituent, arm, organ, branch, follower, segment, part, unit, adherent, element, limb, component.

memento, souvenir, remembrance, memorial, token, reminder, memorandum, trophy, relic, curio.

memoir, account, report, history, life, diary, journal, record, narrative, relation, recollection, autobiography, biography, memory.

memorable, extraordinary, unforgettable, uncommon, striking, important, vivid, surpassing, crucial, critical, prominent, noticeable, remarkable, celebrated, outstanding, conspicuous, famous, illustrious, distinguished, great, particular, momentous, notable, noteworthy, historic, significant. *Ant.* unimportant, trifling, uneventful, trivial, petty, foolish, frivolous, uninteresting, absurd, ridiculous, idle, insignificant, meaningless, nugatory, light, inconsiderable, inconsequential, irrelevant.

memorial, memento, commemoration, souvenir, remembrance, monument, obelisk, monolith, mausoleum, record, inscription; scholarship, professorship, chair.

memory, recollection, remembrance, retrospect, retention, tradition, after-thought, retrospection, reminiscence, mental trace, fame. *Ant.* oblivion, forgetfulness, oversight, unconsciousness, Lethe, obliteration, amnesia, effacement, lapse.

menace, threat, intimidation, warning, danger, hazard, peril, portent, vengeance, revenge, fear, trepidation, forecast, jeopardy. *Ant.* reassurance, encouragement, inspiration, equanimity, security, safety.

mend, improve, repair, rectify, restore, amend, correct, patch, reform, ameliorate, revive, refine, revise, better, refresh, renew, touch up, heal, get well, recover, remedy, enhance. *Ant.* weaken, deteriorate, destroy, damage, impair, ruin, hurt, injure, mar, disfigure, despoil, dilapidate, fall ill, wane, retrogress, regress, rot, fade, wound, raze, mutilate, blemish, deface, deform.

mendacity, lying, falsehood, misrepresentation, prevarication, perjury, calumny, untruthfulness, dishonesty, fraudulence, crookedness, deception, falsification, invention, fabrication, suppression, distortion. *Ant.* truthfulness, veracity, openness, frankness, candor, honesty, authenticity, exactness, probity, fidelity, sincerity, ingenuousness, artlessness.

mendicant, beggar, pauper, solicitor, starveling, object of charity, sponge, codger. *Ant.* donor, benefactor, giver, contributor.

menial, servile, mean, lowly, unskilled, unimportant, abject, humble, ignoble, base, degrading. *Ant.* noble, elevated, expert, uplifting, professional.

mensuration, measuring, measurement, survey, surveying, counting, weighing, checking, noting, bounding, calculating.

mental, intellectual, psychical, psychological, metaphysical, subliminal, subjective, rational, percipient, nonphysical, cognitive, cerebral, thoughtful, subconscious, telepathic, psychic, clairvoyant. *Ant.* incogitant, incogitative, unreasoning, thoughtless, fatuous, inane, vacuous, unintelligent, idiotic, imbecile, brainless, physical, somatic, bodily, anatomical.

mention, say, refer, allude, cite, remark, impart, name, disclose, divulge, tell, reveal, specify, speak of, aver, report, communicate. *Ant.* suppress, hide, forget, ignore, overlook, avoid.

mentor, teacher, guide, instructor, monitor, counselor, advisor, leader. *Ant.* follower, disciple, student, pupil.

mercantile, commercial, trading, industrial, marketing, selling, dealing, wholesaling, buying, exchanging, factoring.

mercenary, venal, sordid, selfish, calculating, grasping, avaricious, hired. *Ant.* unselfish, nonprofit, unpaid, donated, generous.

merchandise, stock, produce, goods, wares, commodities, supplies, effects, articles, cargo, vendibles, inventory.

merchant, dealer, agent, factor, trader, businessman, hawker, shopkeeper, peddler, salesman.

merciful, kind, lenient, gentle, feeling, gracious, tender, compassionate, benignant, beneficent, clement, kind-hearted, pitying, philanthropic, sympathetic, humane, soft-hearted, forbearing. *Ant.* unkind, cruel, inhuman, ruthless, cold-blooded, barbarous, truculent, savage, tyrannical, pitiless, severe, unforgiving, inclement, unmerciful, merciless, relentless.

mercurial, changeable, variable, unsteady, inconstant, fluctuating, exhilarated, gay, active, unstable, restless, erratic, capricious, fickle, excitable, uneasy, flighty, irresolute, wavering, feverish, fidgety, unreliable, volatile. *Ant.* steady, stable, settled, patient, constant, unvarying, immutable, fixed, unchangeable, unyielding, invariable, steadfast, imperturbable, unalterable, obstinate, tranquil, calm, dispassionate, placid, dull, stolid, composed, cool.

mercy, pity, forbearance, charity, compassion, humanity, clemency, leniency, tolerance, forgiveness, kindness, pardon, benevolence, benignity. *Ant.* cruelty, severity, harshness, punishment, justice, revenge, vengeance, implacability, tyranny, domination, pitilessness, arrogance, intolerance, oppression, despotism, castigation, condemnation, proscription, banishment, inhumanity.

meretricious, spurious, dishonest, insincere, fraudulent, deceitful, showy, gaudy, tawdry, pretentious, false, deceptive, misleading, sham. *Ant.* genuine, authentic, bona fide, true, honest, real, valid.

merge, blend, unite, mix, dip, join, add to, mingle, unify, integrate, amalgamate, coalesce. *Ant.* separate, divide, divest.

meridian, midway, noon, noon-tide, summit, climax, zenith, culmination, acme, apex, apogee. *Ant.* nadir, lowest point.

merit, worth, worthiness, goodness, excellence, reward, regard, importance, probity, strength, honor, appreciation, value, credit, virtue, rectitude, stability, sincerity. *Ant.* vice, dishonor, shame, demerit, worthlessness, evil, unworthiness, weakness, shortcoming, disgrace, scandal, degradation.

meritorious, worthy, praiseworthy, commendable, generous, noble, estimable, admirable, deserving, creditable, honorable, fine, exemplary, laudable, unselfish, magnanimous, heroic, spirited, chivalrous, liberal, honest, conscientious, high-principled, righteous, self-denying, self-sacrificing, philanthropic, charitable. *Ant.* unworthy, dishonorable, dishonest, treacherous, shameless, blameworthy, reprehensible, improper, wrong, corrupt, depraved, immoral, iniquitous, dissolute, discreditable, disreputable, profligate, shameful, cowardly, despicable, unbecoming, undecorous, unprincipled, unrighteous, infamous, scandalous, flagrant.

merry, gay, cheerful, happy, mirthful, joyous, jocular, jovial, lively, sprightly, boisterous, hilarious, spirited, frolicsome, devil-may-care, animated, vivacious, rollicking, buoyant, light-hearted, uproarious, ecstatic, exuberant, glad, exhilarated, ebullient, sportive, playful, jubilant, festive, entertaining, gleeful, laughable, elated, blithe, blithesome, revelling, rejoicing. *Ant.* sorrowful, sad, doleful, gloomy, miserable, downcast, dull, melancholy, moping, wretched, mournful, unhappy, dispirited, dismal, dejected, crying, weeping, moaning, groaning, lamenting, tired, grieving, bored, weary, pessimistic, worried, drowsy, monotonous, pensive, tedious, hypochondriacal, splenetic, jaundiced, jaded, grim, forlorn, somber, solemn, saturnine, doleful, woebegone, lachrymose, listless, languid, lackadaisical, morose, moody.

mesmerize, hypnotize, charm, enchant, bewitch, fascinate, magnetize, spellbind. *Ant.* repel, fend off, reject, drive away.

mess, mixture, combination, conglomeration, melange, litter, medley, potpourri, botch, jumble, hodgepodge, dirtiness, untidiness, mussiness, disorder, disorganization, confusion, difficulty, predicament, problem, dilemma, plight, muddle, shambles; allowance, portion, ration. *Ant.* order, system, tidiness, arrangement, method, solution, plan.

message, communication, news, letter, note, dispatch, telegram, signal, report, word.

metamorphosis, transformation, transmutation, conversion, change, transfiguration, life cycle.

metaphorical, symbolical, allegorical, figurative, referential, comparative, allusive, anagogic, contrastive, euphuistic, representative, ironic, colloquial, poetic. *Ant.* literal, plain, direct, obvious.

metaphysical, ideal, mental, intellectual, abstract, subjective, speculative, visionary, unreal, immaterial, incorporeal, psychological, philosophical, ontological, transcendental. *Ant.* material, solid, earthly, concrete, physical, realistic.

mete, dole, distribute, allot, deal, divide, parcel, apportion, limit, award, share, inflict, dispense, measure, sort, assort, spread, classify. *Ant.* chance, hazard, scatter.

meter, cadence, rhythm, beat, measure, accentuation, stress, tempo; indicator, measuring device, gauge.

method, order, style, way, system, manner, rule, arrangement, regularity, vogue, custom, mode, procedure, scheme, plan, process, adjustment, form, tenor, routine, course, regulation, technique, disposition, discipline, means, fashion. *Ant.* disorder, derangement disunion, disarrangement, irregularity, confusion, discord, entanglement, complication, complexity, mess, mixture, intricacy chaos, chance, happenstance, shuffle, muddle, misplacement, involvement.

meticulous, scrupulous, punctilious, precise, fussy, fastidious, particular, finical, exacting, clean, tidy, painstaking. *Ant.* careless sloppy, remiss, casual, unconcerned, rude, untidy, cursory, haphazard, unkempt, disheveled.

mettle, spirit, stamina, courage, animation, bravery, physical endurance, character, temperament, determination, ardor, grit, liveliness, fire, pluck, fiber, nerve, valor, manliness, gallantry, dash intrepidity, vigor, resoluteness, hardihood, energy, tenacity, intensity, earnestness. *Ant.* fear, weakness, cowardice, timidity faintheartedness, shyness, effeminacy, trepidation, laziness, sloth dormancy, languor, dastardliness, inertness, passiveness, tiredness, dullness, weariness, irresolution, inactivity, sluggishness, latency, cowardliness, rashity.

mettlesome, spirited, bold, rash, animated, brave, venturesome, unafraid, dashing, gallant, active, vigorous, energetic, fiery, chivalrous, high-spirited, dynamic, lion-hearted, courageous, plucky, nervy, manly, valiant, resolute, valorous, daring, dauntless, self-reliant. *Ant.* dastardly, sneaking, timid, abject, effeminate, weak, cowardly, shrinking, faint-hearted, feeble, weary, tired, skulking, irresolute, pusillanimous, timorous, mean-spirited, weak-minded, spiritless.

microbe, germ, micro-organism, bacillus, virus, bacterium.

microscopic, infinitesimal, tiny, minimal, minute. *Ant.* large, big easily seen.

middle, central, median, mean, average, mediocre, interjacent, halfway, intermediate, equidistant, axial, pivotal. *Ant.* extreme, high low, large, small, many, few; beginning, end.

mien, manner, condition, aspect, look, appearance, air, bearing, attitude, expression, carriage, deportment, demeanor, visage.

mighty, strong, forceful, vigorous, powerful, potent, robust, great, lusty, resistless, muscular, large, vast, heavy, immense, sturdy bold, able, majestic, stupendous, momentous, hardy, indomitable, unconquerable, husky, invincible, manful, puissant, overpowering, virile, doughty, strapping, stalwart. *Ant.* weak, puny, poor, infirm, debilitated, effeminate, feeble, powerless, flaccid, small, delicate, tottering, doddering, unimportant, enervated,

migratory, wandering, roving, transient, roaming, nomadic, vagrant, unsettled, itinerant, peripatetic, changeable, casual. *Ant.* settled unchanging, permanent, stable, fixed, steady, lasting, continuing established, staying, irremovable.

mild, soft, gentle, tender, humane, kind, meek, mellow, quiet, tranquil, smooth, amiable, friendly, untroubled, calm, moderate, temperate, placid, peaceful, pacific, genial, tepid, lukewarm, clement, considerate, submissive, lenient, compassionate, indulgent, imperturbable, complaisant, tolerant, peaceable, patient, easy-going; sweet, bland, savory. *Ant.* severe, strict, sharp, fierce, bluff, forceful, rigid, stern, rough, unkind, rude, harsh, uncouth, boisterous, abrupt, tyrannical, blustering, irritating, bullying, arrogant, exacerbating, turbulent, unruly, disorderly, austere, arbitrary, domineering, despotic, ruffled, perturbed, angry, irritable, agitated, cold; bitter, acid, stringent, sour, biting.

milieu, background, surroundings, class, neighborhood, environment, medium, sphere, element.

militant, contentious, combative, fighting, warring, prepared, armed, aggressive, belligerent, pugnacious, hostile, active, combating, pushing, assertive, contending. *Ant.* peaceful, pacific, submissive, acquiescent, tolerant, amenable, compliant, compromising.

mimic, imitate, mock, repeat, ape, echo, simulate, iterate, parody, burlesque, caricature, resemble, parrot, portray, counterfeit, reproduce, copy, represent, act, impersonate, feign, forge, emulate.

mind, soul, spirit, intellect, inclination, judgment, liking, belief, sentiment, choice, will, understanding, desire, purpose, impetus, reason, remembrance, memory, faculty, recollection, thought, consciousness, intelligence, instinct, rationality, disposition, mentality, intuition, intellectuality, perception, percipience, conception, sense, apperception, brains, genius, capacity, talent, reasoning, wisdom. *Ant.* matter, substance, materiality, substantiality, corporeality, body, stuff, element.

mindful, attentive, thoughtful, careful, heedful, observant, watchful, concerned, regardful, observing, involved with, alert. *Ant.* inattentive, inadvertent, heedless, absent-minded, careless, unconcerned, distrait, bemused, day-dreaming, distracted, dreamy, engrossed, rapt, dazed, preoccupied.

mingle, blend, mix, unite, intermingle, commingle, intermix, join, conjoin, combine, merge, compound, concoct, amalgamate, fuse, associate, participate, jumble, confound, consort, fraternize. *Ant.* separate, disjoin, sort, distinguish.

miniature, diminutive, minuscule, reduced, abridged, small, minikin, little, tiny, minute, bantam. *Ant.* large, full-size, normal size, regular.

minimize, belittle, depreciate, degrade, fault, detract, disparage, derogate. *Ant.* magnify, accept, recognize, exalt, extol, praise.

minister, *n.* priest, preacher, padre, parson, divine, clergyman, monk, dominie, ecclesiastic, rector, cleric, curate, vicar, bishop, abbot, chaplain, pulpiteer, churchman, pastor, confessor, reverend, shepherd, servant, official, ambassador, delegate, envoy, diplomat, plenipotentiary, consul, representative; *v.* serve, act, help, succor, perform, aid, assist, officiate, feed, nurse, relieve, rescue, support, sustain, nurture, nourish, administer, tend, attend, wait on. *Ant.* layman, parishioner, disciple, secularist, tyro, catechumen, learner, follower, apostate, probationer, novice, student, neophyte, recruit, renegade; obstruct, stop, impede, check, bar, encumber, interdict, hinder, interfere, embarrass, incommode, counteract, hamper, restrain, oppose.

minor, lesser, subordinate, petty, inconsiderable, younger, smaller, inferior, unimportant, junior, secondary, lower; adolescent, child. *Ant.* major, greater, first, important; adult, of age.

minstrel, bard, singer, rhymer, player, musician, poet, comedian, balladeer, troubadour, minnesinger.

mint, coin, make, stamp, fabricate, manufacture, fashion, forge, invent, produce.

minute, small, little, microscopic, diminutive, insignificant, atomic, inconsiderable, miniscule, miniature, tiny, puny, infinitesimal, exiguous, petty, molecular, exact, precise, fine, particular, accurate, critical, detailed. *Ant.* large, rough, general, heavy, great, bulky, immense, unwieldy, huge, colossal, towering, vast, big, massive, enormous, considerable, stupendous, lengthy, capacious, extensive, infinite, commodious, comprehensive, spacious, ample, mighty, magnificent.

miraculous, supernatural, wonderful, prodigious, marvelous, extraordinary, curious, spectacular, outstanding, unusual, surprising, stupendous, preternatural, wondrous, astonishing, incredible, unbelieveable, strange, bewildering, overwhelming, astounding, indescribable, amazing, inexpressible, inexplicable, unimaginable, fearful, stupefying, awesome. *Ant.* common, ordinary, usual, commonplace, everyday, unimportant, expected, prosaic, matter-of-fact, trivial, habitual, prevalent, general, customary, trifling, regular, frequent, familiar, petty, natural, formal, insignificant, normal.

mirthful, merry, cheery, vivacious, frolicsome, sportive, jolly, gay, glad, hilarious, gleeful, jovial, festive. *Ant.* sad, dull, gloomy, unhappy, melancholic, morose.

misadventure, mishap, mischance, misfortune, accident, disaster, calamity, catastrophe. *Ant.* good luck, good fortune, favorable happening, mastery, success, victory, triumph.

misanthrope, cynic, pessimist, man-hater, churl, egotist, grouch, misfit. *Ant.* optimist, altruist, humanitarian, patriot.

misapprehend, mistake, misunderstand, misjudge, misconceive, misinterpret. *Ant.* understand, interpret, perceive, comprehend.

miscellaneous, mixed, mingled, combined, commingled, promiscuous, commixed, various, dissimilar, motley, confused, variant, assorted, conglomerate, heterogeneous, intermingled, indiscriminate, collective, compound, manifold, different, diverse, several, diversified. *Ant.* simple, unblended, uniform, elemental, unmixed, same, similar, like, single, homogeneous, common, unadulterated, filed, unalloyed, sorted, classified.

mischief, damage, evil, hurt, wrong, injury, ill, detriment, harm, grievance, outrage, affront, vandalism, annoyance, deviltry, misfortune, prank, trouble, roguery, disadvantage, disservice. *Ant.* good, service, benefit, profit, advantage, improvement, favor, betterment, blessing, kindness, friendship, friendliness, countenance, assistance, reparation, support, help, aid, concession, payment, good will, amity, defense, vindication.

misconstrue, misunderstand, mistake, misapprehend, misconceive, misinterpret, misjudge, misread, misrender. *Ant.* construe, solve, understand, interpret, unravel, discern.

misdeed, crime, transgression, misdemeanor, trespass, wrong, sin, breach, offense, fault, delinquency.

misdemeanor, fault, transgression, error, crime, trespass, breach, misconduct, offense, sin.

miser, curmudgeon, hoarder, skimper, scrimp, niggard, tightwad, churl, pinchpenny. *Ant.* waster, spendthrift, squanderer, showoff, lavisher, big spender, prodigal, wastrel.

miserable, unhappy, distressed, uncomfortable, pained, unfortunate, discontented, afflicted, sick, woebegone, sorrowful, sickly, ailing, crushed, sad, friendless, suffering, heartbroken, worried, disconsolate, dismal, wretched, uneasy, doleful, forlorn, small, scanty, meager, insufficient, contemptible, illiberal, mean, stingy, poor, lowly, despicable, low, abject, pitiable, lamentable, worthless. *Ant.* happy, smiling, comfortable, prosperous, cheerful, blithe, gay, debonair, satisfied, mirthful, lighthearted, contented, buoyant, high-spirited, vigorous, lively, vivacious, jocund, merry, exhilarated, jovial, jocose, hilarious, waggish, sportive, sprightly, elated, riant, rejoicing.

miserly, stingy, greedy, parsimonious, covetous, avaricious, selfish, penurious, niggardly, rapacious, acquisitive, close, tight-fisted. *Ant.* bountiful, generous, liberal, munificent, prodigal, wasteful.

misery, pain, depression, infelicity, worry, distress, wretchedness, grief, unhappiness, sorrow, despair, desolation, fear, tribulation, torment, sickness, illness, woe, suffering, trouble, agony, care, anxiety, trial, affliction, ordeal, uneasiness, anguish, bother, irritation, chagrin, annoyance, mortification, heaviness, vexation, heartache, despondency. *Ant.* pleasure, well-being, happiness, enjoyment, comfort, gratification, ease, felicity, cheerfulness, gaiety, gladness, fun, amusement, bliss, rapture, ecstasy, joy, rejoicing, jollity, mirth, merriment, joviality, levity, animation, glee, buoyancy, delight, light-heartedness, elation.

misfortune, calamity, injury, misadventure, adversity, harm, hurt, bad luck, accident, loss, privation, mishap, collapse, evil, sorrow, ill fortune, catastrophe, trial, ill luck, trouble, affliction, reverse, mischance, bereavement, disappointment, tribulation, misery, infliction, blow, chastening, hardship, stroke, chastisement, eclipse, visitation, disaster, failure, sickness, distress, casualty, ill, ruin, set-back. Ant. prosperity, joy, happiness, success, good luck, welfare, advantage, good fortune, consolation, gratification, comfort, boon, pleasure, blessing, relief, serenity, contentment, satisfaction, bliss, ease, cheerfulness, recovery, well-being, legacy, donation, bounty, profit, reward, compensation.

misgiving, doubt, distrust, suspicion, mistrust, hesitation, uncertainty. *Ant.* trust, security, certainty, sureness.

mishap, accident, contretemps, reverse, misadventure, mischance misfortune, disaster, slip. *Ant.* good fortune, luck.

misinterpret, misconstrue, misconceive, misunderstand, falsify, distort, pervert. *Ant.* understand, perceive, comprehend.

misjudge, mistake, misconstrue, misconceive, misestimate, miscalculate, err, overshoot, miss.

mislead, delude, defraud, deceive, cheat, cozen, misrepresent, hoodwink, lead astray, bilk, take in, overreach, misinform, outwit ensnare, misconduct, trick, enmesh, entangle, misguide, victimize, lure, beguile, inveigle, hoax, misdirect, dupe, gull, bait, bluff. *Ant.* advise, aid, counsel, assist, relieve, encourage, succor, help befriend, inform, guide, instruct, suggest, conduct, teach, prompt steer, direct, warn, protect, safeguard, guard, favor, defend, uphold, support, sustain, benefit.

misrepresent, falsify, pervert, exaggerate, dissemble, simulate, misstate, mislead, feign, caricature, distort, belie. *Ant.* represent, depict, delineate.

mission, errand, business, affair, activity, purpose, attack, commission; calling, work, duty, task.

missive, message, dispatch, epistle, letter, communication, report note, radiogram, telegram.

mistake, blunder, failure, error, oversight, omission, miss, fallacy slip, downfall, mishap, miscarriage, lapse, misapprehension, delusion, misconception, illusion, flaw, misprint, laxity, aberration, misstatement, misunderstanding, misinterpretation, misidentification. *Ant.* truth, fact, reality, verity, accuracy, veracity, exactitude, precision, authenticity, interpretation, explanation, proof, evidence, success, authority, understanding, perfection, surety certainty, sureness, certitude, assurance, correctness, definiteness, exactness.

mistreat, abuse, wrong, misguide, harm, neglect, injure, mishandle, pervert, outrage, oppress, misuse, cheat, desecrate, maltreat, punish, maul, bruise, persecute, tyrannize. *Ant.* treat well, care for, gratify, gladden, cheer, aid, assist, succor, benefit, befriend, favor, pet.

mistrust, doubt, misgiving, uncertainty, apprehension, presentiment, fear, suspicion. *Ant.* trust, confidence, assurance, faith.

misty, foggy, blurred, dark, dim, murky, vague, hazy, obscure, faint, clouded. *Ant.* clear, bright, cloudless, fair, dry.

misunderstanding, misapprehension, mistake, error, discord, misconception, quarrel, disagreement, misinterpretation, difference, dissension. *Ant.* agreement, understanding, concord.

mitigate, assuage, lighten, soothe, abate, moderate, calm, alleviate, soften, lessen, relieve, countervail, modify, quell, ameliorate, rebate, dilute, mollify, allay, temper, lull, appease, deaden, palliate, diminish, subdue, decrease, weaken. *Ant.* aggravate, strengthen, increase, intensify, excite, swell, augment, inflate, deepen, stimulate, enrage, heighten, provoke, accelerate, incite, exacerbate, exasperate, embitter.

mix, blend, join, commix, mingle, compound, intermix, confuse, combine, unite, integrate, jumble, fuse, commingle, confound, intermingle, incorporate, amalgamate, shuffle, associate, adulterate, infiltrate, alloy, stir, crossbreed, homogenize, coalesce. *Ant.* dissolve, purify, exclude, eliminate, regulate, sift, adjust, separate, simplify, systematize, arrange, disintegrate, disperse, unravel, untangle, untwine, sort, remove, segregate, disjoin, divide, sever, detach, part, disconnect, disengage, dissociate, disunite, assort, analyze, discriminate, classify.

mixture, compound, miscellany, melange, olio, composite, interlarding, blend, jumble, assortment, medley, variety, alloy, amalgam, fusion, union, suspension, adulteration, infusion, stew.

mob, multitude, crowd, gathering, throng, populace, people, rabble, flock, riffraff, drove, herd, assemblage, horde, gang.

mobile, movable, unstable, free, changeable, variable, loose, motile, expressive, fickle, sensitive, animated. *Ant.* fixed, stationary, immobile, quiet, permanent.

mobilize, marshal, call up, organize, adapt, unite, order, command, assemble, unify, prepare, gather, increase, transport. *Ant.* end, separate, disperse, demobilize, scatter, finish.

mock, ridicule, defy, deride, gibe, jeer, imitate, taunt, ape, insult, counterfeit, satirize, flout, mimic, sneer at. *Ant.* honor, praise, applaud, support.

modal, typical, most frequent, average, central, middling, habitual, formal, customary, structural. *Ant.* out of style, untypical, extreme, provisional, incidental, adventitious.

mode, fashion, rule, habit, style, method, condition, manner, kind, custom, sort, state, mood, decorum, convention, conventionality, vogue, practice, etiquette, usage, breeding, attitude, taste, form, wont, appearance, quality, way, precedent, prevalence, tone, procedure, course, plan, scheme.

model, archetype, standard, facsimile, prototype, example, design, original, mold, mock-up, form, gauge, paragon, image, pattern, imitation, representation, type, copy, likeness, miniature, replica, tracing, outline, structure, duplicate, shape, illustration, counterpart, figure, delineation, sketch.

moderate, *adj.* temperate, judicious, reasonable, fair, just, steady, calm, middling, abstemious, sparing, frugal, modest, ordinary, abstinent, steady, sober, regulated, cool, measured, mild, gentle, dispassionate, lenient, tolerant, tranquil; *v.* hush, check, curb, repress, dull, quell, subdue, chasten, appease, pacify, slacken, abate, decrease, deaden, tame, weaken, restrain, reduce, lessen, qualify, allay, control, temper, limit, soften, mitigate, repress, calm, regulate, blunt, govern, alleviate, tranquilize, slake, smooth, assuage, tone down, slow, cool, delay, palliate. *Ant.* large, great, considerable, excessive, extensive, extravangant, extended, exorbitant, outrageous, sufficient, full, radical, inordinate, unreasonable, unstinted, unlimited, liberal, plenty, abundant, ample, complete, fast, intemperate, indulgent, voluptuous, sensual, immoderate; incite, excite, inflame, stimulate, rouse, exacerbate, quicken, exasperate, urge, inspire, enlarge, expand, infuriate, swell, anger, madden, agitate, enrage, irritate, craze, foment, increase, intensify, strengthen, instigate, animate, goad, arouse, spur.

modern, recent, newfangled, up-to-date, fresh, new, novel, late, neoteric, contemporary, current, untried, unhandled, renovated, up-to-the-minute, improved, fashionable, latest. *Ant.* ancient, antique, old, primitive, fossil, prehistoric, obsolete, primeval, antemundane, archaic, hoary, venerable, ancestral, olden, classical, traditional, outworn, timeworn, out-of-fashion, medieval, out-of-date, passé, vintage, outmoded.

modest, bashful, reserved, shy, retiring, unobtrusive, diffident, coy, humble, insignificant, minute, inconsiderable, small, constrained, meek, nervous, blushing, timid, unpretentious, demure, sheepish, unassuming, unostentatious, timorous, decent, virtuous, decorous, continent, chaste, undefiled, pure. *Ant.* extravagant, outrageous, excessive, imposing, exorbitant, towering, glaring, mighty, impressive, grand, big, huge, magnificent, vain, bold, conceited, brazen, self-confident, presumptuous, ostentatious, flaunting, inflated, corrupt, egotistical, unabashed, arrogant, assured, proud, haughty, indecent, supercilious, obscene, indelicate, lascivious, unclean, shameless, impure, prurient, immodest, erotic, pompous, gaudy, showy, libidinous, unchaste, wanton.

modification, alteration, variation, modulation, adaptation, change, transformation, limitation, qualification, mutation.

modify, alter, vary, convert, soften, shape, transform, qualify, limit, lower, temper, change, reform, moderate, restrict, expand, adapt, reduce; reshape.

modulate, regulate, harmonize, attune, adapt, alter, inflect, tone down, vary, tune, adjust.

moist, damp, watery, saturated, humid, dank, infiltrated, aqueous, wet, fresh, soaked, muggy, dewy, vaporous, juicy, dripping, sodden, soppy, sloppy, swampy. *Ant.* dry, sandy, arid, waterless, barren, desiccative, desiccated, dehydrated, anhydrous, droughty, parched, sere, desert-like, scorched, dried up.

mold, cast, carve, create, make, shape, fashion, influence, alter, model, sculpt, modify.

molecule, particle, corpuscle, atom, monad, mite, micron.

molest, damage, disturb, pester, annoy, bother, hurt, worry, harry, injure, plague, harass, discompose, badger, displease, assail, attack, bore, irritate, confuse, vex, aggrieve, thwart, oppress, incommode, trouble, ill-treat, tease, wrong, persecute, maltreat, misuse. *Ant.* comfort, console, protect, guard, escort, soothe, aid, hearten, help, encourage, assist, cheer, befriend, benefit, praise, commend, applaud, recommend, oblige, eulogize, favor, approve, acclaim, endorse, defend.

mollify, assuage, ameliorate, soothe, soften, appease, lessen, mitigate, moderate, compose, abate, reduce, lull, tranquilize, smooth, alleviate, calm, temper, pacify, restrain, repress, reconcile, ease, placate, restrain, comfort, repress, console, reconcile, please, allay, flatter, gratify. *Ant.* anger, tempt, enrage, excite, infuriate, incite, taunt, disturb, annoy, harass, torment, agitate, vex, worry, irritate, plague, provoke, exasperate, inflame, exacerbate, incense, arouse, chafe, nettle, madden, hurt, injure.

molten, melted, liquified, fused, in liquid state. *Ant.* solid, cold, hard, cast.

moment, instant, second, minute, jiffy, trice, flash, wink, twinkling; importance, consequence, gravity, significance, weight.

momentous, important, consequential, far-reaching, grave, serious, solemn, notable, weighty, salient, memorable, eventful, influential, vital, critical, crucial, stirring, signal. *Ant.* unimportant, slight, insignificant, trivial, small, trifling, immaterial, irrelevant, unessential, commonplace, uninteresting, ordinary, boring.

monastery, convent, abbey, cloister, priory, nunnery, lamasery.

monastic, secluded, austere, cenobitic, ascetic, monkish, solitary, conventual, religious, holy, celibate, spiritual, prayerful.

monetary, financial, pecuniary, fiscal, sumptuary, nummary, nummular.

money, gold, currency, funds, wealth, cash, specie, bullion, silver, bills, capital, stock, coin, notes, property, change, assets, checks, finance, lucre, wherewithal, opulence, means, treasure, resources, riches, affluence, substance, independence, supplies, securities, bonds, legal tender.

monitor, adviser, instructor, teacher, observer, guide, overseer, counselor, sentinel, guard.

monolithic, indivisible, massive, unvarying, uniform, disciplined, controlled, intractable. *Ant.* separate, divisible, tractable, divisive.

monomania, insanity, derangement, madness, morbidity, morbidness, single idea, mania, delirium, lunacy, aberration, dementia, morosis, *idée fixé*, phrenitis, paranoia, delusion, fanaticism, hallucination, illusion, infatuation, obsession. *Ant.* sanity, lucidity, self-possession, normalcy, common sense, normality, soundness, saneness, steadiness, mental vigor, rationality, reasonableness.

monopolize, control, own, engross, absorb, corner, possess, direct.

monopoly, trust, pool, limitation, restriction, combination, cartel syndicate, corner, control.

monotonous, dull, wearying, tiresome, tedious, unvaried, irksome, wearisome, undiversified, uninteresting, boring, uniform, repetitious, humdrum, heavy, prosy, depressive, slow, flat, dry, drowsy. *Ant.* varied, versatile, interesting, witty, pleasant, amusing, en-

tertaining, brilliant, whimsical, humorous, lively, facetious, invit
ing, pleasing, attractive, appealing, refreshing, heartening.

monstrous, abnormal, atrocious, awful, horrible, frightful, dreadful
unsightly, hideous, unnatural, ugly, flagrant, grotesque, heinous
outrageous, shocking, stupendous, uncanny, preposterous, vast
wonderful, marvelous, prodigious, wondrous, inconceivable, huge
unspeakable, strange, enormous, terrifying, incredible, immense
anomalous, teratoid. *Ant.* common, commonplace, ordinary, con
ventional, diminutive, normal, formal, beautiful, natural, small
nice, little, pretty, attractive, usual, expected, graceful, simple
shapely, plain, regular, customary, habitual, standard, average.

monument, tomb, shaft, column, pillar, vault, pyramid, cairn, pile
mausoleum, headstone, memorial, cenotaph, gravestone, statue
tombstone, shrine, building, erection, tower, obelisk, plaque, slab
memento, monolith, record, tablet, scroll, stone, testimonial, reg
ister, dolmen.

mood, mode, temper, behavior, condition, vein, manner, humor, state
disposition, conduct, inclination, spirit, nature, habit, principle
constitution, character, quality, temperament, propensity, ten
dency, emotion, feeling, proclivity, susceptibility, idiosyncrasy.

moral, ethical, upright, virtuous, righteous, scrupulous, honest, just
good, noble, decent, self-righteous, chaste, logical, blameless, hon
orable, faultless, decent. *Ant.* immoral, amoral, bad, evil, un
ethical, dishonorable.

morbid, abnormal, sickly, unsound, sick, affected, diseased, ailing
unhealthy, unwholesome, tainted, corrupted, drooping, gloomy
dour, grim, glum, depressed, sensitive, flagging. *Ant.* healthy
robust, strong, sound, normal, well, vigorous, lively, wholesome
cheerful, hardy, blooming, lusty, spirited, sane, bright, salubrious

mordant, caustic, sarcastic, mordacious, acrid, scathing, biting, in
cisive, cutting, derisive, sardonic. *Ant.* complimentary, favor
able, kind, flattering, supporting.

moreover, besides, further, furthermore, too, likewise, also.

moron, imbecile, idiot, dope, fool, simpleton, dullard, dummy. *Ant*
genius, sage, intellectual, savant.

morose, gloomy, splenetic, acrimonious, sour, morbid, ill-natured
sullen, depressed, ill-humored, petulant, perverse, gruff, dolorous
melancholy, ill-tempered, surly, sulky, moody, grouchy, churlish
cantankerous, dour, glum, crabbed, frowning, cross, snappish
mournful, funereal, lugubrious, *Ant.* cheery, lively, smiling, ani
mated, debonair, cheerful, spirited, happy, bright, blithe, light
hearted, ebullient, buoyant, sprightly, vivacious, jolly, jovial
breezy, hilarious, lightsome, exhilarated, gleesome, rollicking, re
joicing, joyous, benignant, high-spirited, pleasant, amiable, sym
pathetic, tender, indulgent, mild, loving, good-natured, gentle
kind, friendly, complacent, complaisant, genial, bland.

mortal, deadly, fatal, lethal, destructive, deathly, death-dealing, ex
treme, serious, human, final, perishable, ephemeral, transient

temporal, passing. *Ant.* lifegiving, reviving, refreshing, freshening, reinvigorating, immortal, strengthening, curative, vivifying, light, revivifying, trivial, trifling, lasting, everlasting, perpetual, eternal.

mortification, chagrin, annoyance, shame, abasement, vexation, dissatisfaction, humiliation, embarrassment; gangrene, necrosis. *Ant.* satisfaction, success, praise, elevation, happiness.

motif, figure, theme, design, text, pattern, concept, leitmotif, topic, subject, matter, device.

motion, movement, transit, motility, change, move, action, transition, passage, act, restlessness, passing, mobility, changeableness, impulse, revolution, gesture, proposal, suggestion, recommendation. *Ant.* quiet, fixity, quiescence, immobility, rest, stillness, inaction, repose, deadlock, lull, stoppage, stagnation, cessation, halt.

motionless, still, inert, unmoving, quiescent, torpid, resting, immotile, dead, fixed, stationary, stable, stockstill, stagnant, calm, immovable, becalmed, unruffled, quiet, undisturbed, silent. *Ant.* moving, shifting, active, stirring, changing, motile, movable, restless, changeable.

motivate, impel, move, induce, prompt, inspire, excite, arouse, actuate, stimulate, provoke, incite, spur, drive, propel, bribe. *Ant.* repress, discourage, halt, disconcert.

motive, *n.* motivation, incitement, incentive, stimulus, spur, influence, impulse, prompting, instigation, urge, cause, reason, encouragement, determinant, ground. *adj.* movable, mobile, motile.

motley, assorted, diverse, heterogeneous, incongruous, disparate, varied, miscellaneous, speckled, dappled, parti-colored, mottled, composite. *Ant.* uniform, like, homogeneous, similar, unmixed, pure, unvaried.

mound, hill, knoll, pile, heap, elevation, fortification, defense, grave, eminence, hillock, barrow, dune, terrace, ridge, hogback, shield, protection, mole, rampart, bulwark, scarp, embankment, entrenchment. *Ant.* valley, depression, plain, ditch, moat.

mount, rise, arise, ascend, uprise, climb, aspire, tower, scramble, scale, grow, swell, increase, soar, augment, surge. *Ant.* descend, subside, decline, lapse, drop, collapse, fall, sink, slump, droop, ebb, dismount, diminish, abridge, alight, lessen, decrease, abate, curtail, dip, shrink.

mourn, lament, fret, regret, deplore, sorrow, droop, grieve, bemoan, bewail, rue, languish, repine, sob, pray, sing, sigh, cry, whimper, groan, wail. *Ant.* rejoice, exult, revel, laugh, applaud.

mournful, sorrowful, sad, doleful, lugubrious, downcast, funereal, down-hearted, melancholy, unhappy, somber, distressed, woeful, tearful, gloomy, dreary, grievous, afflicted, joyless, cheerless, dire, abandoned, disconsolate, heartsick, forlorn, afflicting, broken-hearted, calamitous, despairing. *Ant.* joyful, light, cheerful, lightsome, merry, light-hearted, gay, buoyant, lively, rejoicing,

animated, vivacious, high-spirited, enlivening, jolly, frolicsome
exhilarated, playful, gleeful, elated, hilarious, sprightly, sparkling, rollicking.

move, stir, advance, influence, actuate, convert, impel, run, budge
shift, glide, fly, walk, travel, drift, go, propel, transfer, turn, re-
locate, propel, rotate, operate, revolve, drive, march, start, transport, convey, proceed, stimulate, propose, rouse, induce, arouse
persuade, agitate, instigate, incite, excite, inspirit, wheedle, coax
lure, spur, urge. *Ant.* stand, halt, remain, pause, rest, cease
stop, relax, sleep, doze, drowse, calm, suppress, restrain, pacify
mollify, dissuade, fix, discourage, dishearten, quell, settle.

movement, motion, change, restlessness, velocity, motility, flight
transition, movableness, journey, maneuver, transit, advancement, travel, progression, progress, speed, activity, agitation
quickness, action, hustle, nimbleness, bustle, hurry, flurry, gesture, undertaking, scurry, act, work, enterprise, labor. *Ant.* inactivity, resignation, stoppage, abandonment, cessation, inaction
stop, idleness, inertness, inertia, stupor, laziness, insensibility
somnolence, hypnosis, stasis, slumber, sloth, sleep, quiescence, indolence, inaction, stagnation, passiveness.

movies, cinema, motion pictures, cinematograph, kinematograph
biograph, film, panorama, photodrama, diorama, cosmorama
photoplay.

muddle, *n.* difficulty, confusion, disarray, clutter, dilemma, mixup
chaos, maze, disorder, turmoil, jumble, perplexity, mixture, en
tanglement, disarrangement, misarrangement, snarl, intricacy
derangement, complication, mess, farrago, botch, ferment, hodge
podge, complexity; *v.* bemuddle, confuse, disturb, jumble, mis
arrange, mix, derange, perturb, disarrange, disorder, shuffle
ravel, ruffle, disorganize, mess, spoil, addle, befuddle, perplex
puzzle, mystify, foul, bewilder, upset, agitate, embarrass, en
tangle, distract, embroil, confound, involve, disconcert. *Ant*
order, plan, orderliness, arrangement, conformity, method, unity
system, ease, uniformity, disencumbrance, regulation, systemati
zation, organization; clarify, explain, enlighten, elucidate, adjust
arrange, regulate, methodize, unravel, systematize, untangle
sort, classify, group, grade, allot.

muddy, turbid, dark, clouded, opaque, miry, oozy, mucky, silty
soiled, murky, foul, unclear, obscure, vague. *Ant.* clear, trans
parent, clarified, lucid, limpid, pure, filtered.

muffle, wrap, envelop, conceal, cover, subdue, soften, deaden, mute
silence, damp, stifle, gag, hush.

mulct, fine, penalize, amerce, charge, extort.

mulish, obstinate, pertinacious, stubborn, intractable, recalcitrant
intransigent, dogged, fixed, immobile, set, headstrong. *Ant.* obe
dient, tractable, biddable, docile, reasonable.

multiply, increase, augment, enlarge, grow, reproduce, propagate
generate. *Ant.* divide, reduce, lessen, shrink, waste.

multitude, crowd, congregation, throng, swarm, aggregation, gathering, collection, assemblage, horde, mob, populace, host, legion, array, galaxy, army. *Ant.* fewness, scarcity, sparseness, part, portion, nothing, handful, paucity, nobody, part, zero, minority, fraction.

mundane, worldly, terrestrial, temporal, mortal, carnal, secular, earthly. *Ant.* heavenly, celestial, infinite, eternal, paradisiac, unearthly, supernal.

munificent, bountiful, helpful, lavish, generous, bounteous, charitable, liberal, openhanded, philanthropic, beneficent, benevolent, hospitable, unselfish, altruistic, prodigal, unsparing, princely, profuse, ample. *Ant.* miserly, penurious, selfish, close-fisted, parsimonious, chary, frugal, saving, grudging, stingy, thrifty, cold, tight-fisted, sordid, improvident, illiberal, avaricious, cautious, careful.

murder, kill, slay, slaughter, dispatch, assassinate, immolate, shoot, execute, stab, choke, poison, destroy, victimize, settle. *Ant.* restore, refresh, reanimate, animate, vitalize, vivify, reinvigorate, revive, nurse, support, propagate, produce.

murky, obscure, dull, clouded, dark, flat, somber, filmy, gloomy, overcast, dim, lowering, dismal, funereal, umbrageous, dreary, tenebrous, turbid, hazy, smoky, cheerless, shaded, dusky, dingy. *Ant.* light, lucent, effulgent, clear, lambent, shining, bright, unclouded, glittering, sunny, glistening, sparkling, radiant, unobscured, brilliant, glowing, luminous, dazzling, cloudless, lustrous, flashing, shimmering.

murmur, whisper, mutter, mumble, grouse, complain, grumble, hum, rustle, ripple, babble, meander.

muscular, vigorous, lusty, forceful, athletic, stout, husky, brawny, powerful, sinewy, sturdy, stalwart, strong, belligerent. *Ant.* infirm, puny, feeble, flabby, weak, slight.

muse, think, reflect, ponder, deliberate, meditate, study, dream, imagine, ruminate, mull, lucubrate, contemplate, consider, speculate, cogitate, reason, recall, remember, cerebrate, brood. *Ant.* relax, unbend, forget, divert.

musical, melodious, harmonious, tuneful, euphonious, lyrical, lyric, euphonic, symphonious, melodic, pleasing, agreeable, canorous, symphonic, mellow, vocal, homophonous, assonant, choral, tonal, unisonant. *Ant.* discordant, jangling, harsh, grating, disagreeable, jarring, cacophonous, clashing, clanging, tuneless, incongruous, dissonant, inharmonious, unmusical, conflicting.

muster, convoke, assemble, gather, convene, congregate, summon, call, collect, marshal, organize, arrange. *Ant.* scatter, separate, disperse, disjoin, divert.

musty, moldy, mildewed, rank, foul, fetid, rotting, decaying, putrid, spoiled, tainted, stale. *Ant.* clean, fresh, sweet, spotless.

mutable, changeable, alterable, unsettled, changing, inconstant, uncertain, flexible, unstable, unsteady, vacillating, variable, wavering, fickle, flickering, irresolute, swaying. *Ant.* constant, steady, uniform, lasting, equable, permanent, fixed.

mute, silent, speechless, inarticulate, dumb, still, hushed, noiseless, calm, aphonic, soundless, inaudible, voiceless, muffled, gagged. *Ant.* vocal, talkative, articulate, clear, distinct, accentuated, eloquent, voiced, oratorical, loquacious, garrulous.

mutilate, maim, disfigure, deface, cripple, injure, lame, disable, impair, wound, mangle, amputate, excise, scratch, dent, mar, fracture, butcher, hurt, spoil, damage, cut, despoil, truncate, mar, distort, deform. *Ant.* form, fashion, restore, trim, fix, shape, patch, replace, reconstitute, renovate, renew, remodel, revive, reconstruct, rectify, repair, mend, rehabiltate, cure, heal.

mutinous, seditious, insurgent, rebellious, riotous, insubordinate, revolutionary, turbulent, violent, insurrectionary, resistive, disobedient, resistant, recalcitrant, tumultuous, traitorous, pugnacious, contumacious, unruly, treacherous, argumentative, faithless, lawless, ungovernable, refractory. *Ant.* obedient, submissive, subjective, loyal, resigned, passive, subordinate, patriotic, compliant, devoted, supportive, obsequious, faithful, peaceful, contented, observant, satisfied, true, constant, firm, consistent, trustworthy, stanch, incorruptible, attached, yielding, orderly, dutiful, subservient, docile.

mutter, mumble, murmur, rumble, grouse, complain, moan, grumble.

mutual, reciprocal, joint, convertible, interchangeable, common, coincident, identical, correlative, shared, equivalent, correspondent, self-same, analogous, similar, like. *Ant.* individual, inseparable, particular, separate, dissociated, distinct, unrequited, unshared, detached, dissimilar, disconnected, unlike, different, divergent, disparate, unequal.

muzzle, bind, gag, restrain, restrict, repress, suppress, edit, bridle, check, confine, prevent, stop, silence, censor, hush, quiet. *Ant.* free, unfasten, approve, liberate, foster, stimulate, unbind, encourage.

myopic, near-sighted, short-sighted; obtuse, dull, stubborn. *Ant.* far-sighted, far-seeing; keen, alert.

mysterious, mystic, enigmatic, dark, obscure, covert, secret, occult, incomprehensible, unintelligible, cabalistic, inconceivable, hidden, incredible, inexplicable, unaccountable, mystifying, impenetrable, puzzling, transcendental, inexpressible, ineffable, ambiguous, esoteric, abstruse, equivocal, unrevealed, unfathomable, coded, unknown, recondite, mystical, clandestine, inscrutable, oracular, surreptitious, latent, cryptic, baffling. *Ant.* clear, distinct, plain, definite, obvious, apparent, unambiguous, unmistakable, lucid, unequivocal, evident, intelligible, perspicuous, explicit, straightforward, graphic, proved, tested, vivid, open, comprehensible, known, knowable, precise, indubitable, conclusive, overt, patent, manifest, undisguised, ostensible, exoteric, self-evident, incontrovertible, discernible, palpable, indisputable, axiomatic.

mystery, puzzle, enigma, conundrum, obscurity, problem, riddle, perplexity, secret.

mystical, esoteric, secret, cryptic, mysterious, bizarre, abstruse, obscure, recondite, cabalistic, hidden, occult. *Ant.* plain, overt, clear, evident, apparent, undisguised.

mystify, perplex, bewilder, distract, puzzle, confuse, hoodwink, confound, embarrass, mislead, misguide, misrepresent, equivocate, delude. *Ant.* make clear, declare, explain, report, illustrate, interpret, inform, translate, unravel, define, disentangle, render, elucidate, clarify, reveal, delineate, enlighten, communicate, tell, disclose.

mythical, fabulous, fictitious, traditional, imaginary, visionary, legendary, apocryphal, allegorical, fanciful, fantastic, invented. *Ant.* historical, real, actual, factual, true.

N

nab, catch, bag, grab, entrap, ensnare, arrest, trap, snag, snatch, snare, nail, capture, collar, seize, hook. *Ant.* miss, lose, release.

nag, irritate, annoy, harass, bother, worry, vex, scold, provoke, torment, pester, hector, harry. *Ant.* soothe, please, mollify.

naive, artless, simple, guileless, provincial, inexperienced, unsophisticated, ingenuous, spontaneous, fresh, unaffected, plain. *Ant.* sophisticated, wise, experienced.

naked, bare, exposed, uncovered, unclothed, open, nude, bald, barren, unclad, threadbare, undressed, manifest, stripped, plain, unconcealed, evident, revealed, palpable, obvious, undisguised, distinct, simple, explicit, definite, literal, divested, unsheathed, express, unarmored. *Ant.* covered, dressed, garbed, cloaked, robed, clothed, draped, clad, arrayed, attired, appareled, costumed, invested, gowned, habited, enveloped, wrapped, swathed, protected, armored, shielded, artful, complex, swaddled, hidden, secret, undisclosed, latent, covert, veiled, concealed, unexposed.

name, *n.* cognomen, designation, epithet, appellation, title, denomination, surname, reputation, repute, character, distinction, eminence, fame, sign, signature, autograph, pseudonym, *nom de plume; v.* call, title, signify, christen, entitle, denote, term, designate, list, elect, appoint, identify, mark, proclaim, dub, label, specify, denominate, head, characterize, baptize, define.

nameless, unnamed, anonymous, disreputable, unacknowledged, obscure, inglorious, despicable, unknown, shameful, unmentionable, degraded, pseudo, humiliated, forgotten, bastard. *Ant.* named, confirmed, famous, acknowledged, designated, celebrated, signed, known, renowned, distinguished, prominent, well-known, eminent.

narcissistic, self-loving, self-admiring, egocentric, self-centered. *Ant.* outgoing, adult, generous, self-sacrificing.

narcotic, *adj.* anesthetizing, tranquilizing, nepenthic, stupefying, doping, drugging; *n.* dope, tranquilizer, sedative, soporific, anaesthetic, opiate, drug, anodyne.

narrate, tell, rehearse, describe, relate, detail, recount, recite, enumerate, portray, picture, proclaim, state, second, report, unfold, disclose, recapitulate, reveal, paint. *Ant.* cover, shade, withhold, veil, hide, suppress, repress, conceal, stifle, disguise, smother, restrain.

narrow, restricted, contracted, close, shrunken, cramped, confined, compressed, slim, circumscribed, strict, limited, parsimonious, scanty, constrained, miserly, tenuous, slender, thread-like, lanky, thin, scrawny, attenuated, spindling, spare, prejudiced, bigoted, illiberal, intolerant, insular. *Ant.* wide, extended, expanded, ample, broad, expansive, turgid, tumid, corpulent, bloated, thick, fat, thickset, stubby, adipose, fleshy, plump, portly, stout, dilated, liberal, broadminded, generous, catholic, tolerant.

nascent, incipient, dawning, evolving, rudimental, initiatory, arising, beginning, emerging, budding, sprouting, unfolding, commencing, forming.

nasty, repulsive, pornographic, loathsome, obscene, dirty, filthy, foul, disgusting, offensive, contaminated, unclean, tainted, defiled, impure, slimy, soiled, gross, smutty, squalid, pediculous, putrid, fetid, mucky, rotten, putrefied, saprophytic, corrupt, polluted, stormy, sleeting, inclement, rainy, nauseating. *Ant.* clean, pure, sweet, untainted, uncontaminated, delightful, decent, pleasant, unsullied, spotless, attractive, winsome, purified, stainless.

nation, state, commonwealth, realm, republic, country, colony, territory, empire, kingdom, principality; people, population, society, populace, community, persons, public, folk, tribe, clan, race.

native, indigenous, aboriginal, original, natural, natal, congenital, inherent, innate, domestic, domesticated, inborn, home-grown, pristine, vernacular, domiciliary, local, regional. *Ant.* foreign, alien, imported, immigrant, extraneous, extrinsic, artificial, assumed, introduced, unnatural, acquired.

natural, regular, legitimate, essential, normal, true, spontaneous, consistent, probable, subjective, artless, implanted, cosmical, inborn, fundamental, unstudied, intrinsic, original, innate, inbred, ingrained, immanent, inherited, natal, congenital, incarnate, indigenous, unintentional, simple, ingenuous, unaffected, plain, unsophisticated, genetic. *Ant.* extrinsic, contingent, extraneous, adventitious, subsidiary, outward, external, contemplated, ornamented, intended, embellished, elaborated, decorated, beautified, objective, unnatural.

naturalize, acclimatize, habituate, adopt, adapt, accustom, domesticate, inure, tame.

nature, kind, sort, character, temperament, bent, humor, mood, disposition, essence, constitution; universe, creation.

naughty, perverse, bad, contrary, disobedient, corrupt, wanton, mischievous, wicked, wayward. *Ant.* obedient, good, docile.

nauseate, disgust, sicken, abhor, revolt. *Ant.* soothe, gratify, delight, please, attract.

nauseous, disgusting, nasty, detestable, abhorrent, loathsome, unsavory, abominable, unpleasant, distasteful, despicable, emetic, disagreeable, repulsive, offensive, repellent, revolting, fulsome, nasty, unpalatable, sickening. *Ant.* pleasing, sweet, pleasant, delectable, savory, agreeable, delicious, nectareous, luscious, palatable, ambrosial, tasty, satisfying, refreshing, desirous, appetizing, desirable.

navigate, guide, control, sail, conduct, steer, pilot, govern, manage, cruise, steam, plan, plot.

near, nigh, adjacent, close, bordering, intimate, neighboring, abutting, contiguous, adjoining, proximal, approaching, next, prospective, expectant, threatening, imminent, impending, looming, immediate, coming, forthcoming, brewing, approximate, converging, allied, attached, dear, familiar, miserly, penurious, stingy, niggardly, parsimonious. *Ant.* far, distant, remote, past, lavish, gone, expired, postponed, deferred, stopped, suspended, prodigal, extravagant, liberal, generous.

neat, tidy, clean-cut, shapely, trim, proportioned, spruce, compact, dainty, exact, finished, well done, skillful, clever, adroit, well-planned, orderly, suitable, ship-shape, regular, well-dressed, correct, symmetrical, uniform, methodical, systematic, spotless. *Ant.* slovenly, ragged, ungainly, untidy, unkempt, careless, awkward, irregular, disordered, disorderly, maladroit, straggling, negligent, untrimmed, sloppy, slipshod, lax, clumsy, inept, rough, ill-fitting.

nebulous, vague, cloudy, hazy, misty, smoky, uncertain, distant, indistinct, confused. *Ant.* clear, solid, definite, distinct, certain, hard, plain, obvious.

necessary, essential, needful, required, requisite, indispensable, unavoidable, expedient, needed, undeniable, imperative, urgent, prerequisite, irrevocable, inevitable, pressing, inexorable, exigent, obligatory, binding, compulsory. *Ant.* unnecessary, redundant, inexpedient, prodigal, extravagant, exorbitant, superfluous, unfit, inadmissible, unsatisfactory, disadvantageous, needless, worthless, useless, casual, contingent, optional.

necromancy, magic, witchcraft, enchantment, witchery, wizardry, thaumaturgy, sorcery, conjuration, divination, spell, voodoo.

need, want, misery, distress, destitution, privation, penury, poverty, urgency, indigence, necessity, extremity, exigency, emergency, lack, requirement. *Ant.* plenty, competence, fullness, wealth, comfort, riches, luxury, property, independence, fortune, opulence,

nefarious, wicked, abominable, sinful, atrocious, detestable, horrible, evil, dreadful, monstrous, unlawful, villainous, sinister, vile, corrupt, iniquitous, vicious, base, depraved, disgraceful, foul, shameful, gross, scandalous, outrageous, brazen, dishonorable, shameless, immodest, immoral, illegal, detestable, recreant, heinous, improper, infernal, flagrant, infamous, unpardonable, inexcusable, disreputable. *Ant.* virtuous, righteous, good, praiseworthy, innocent, noble, right, commendable, worthy, creditable, inoffensive, exemplary, blameless, irreproachable, meritorious, honest, honorable, reputable, dependable, just, scrupulous, true, noble, incorruptible, unselfish, magnanimous.

negate, controvert, deny, nullify, abrogate, cancel, confute, refuse revoke, refute, ignore, disavow, reject. *Ant.* approve, accept allow, acknowledge.

neglect, *n.* negligence, omission, failure, slight, default, remissness carelessness, indifference, thoughtlessness, oversight, disregard disrespect, scorn, inadvertence, inattention, slackness, evasion heedlessness, inexactness, recklessness, improvidence, indolence deferment, laxness, forgetfulness, apathy, procrastination, disuse, nonchalance, disusage, nonfulfilment, incompleteness, dereliction; *v.* omit, disregard, ignore, forbear, slight, overlook, fail defer, dismiss, spurn, procrastinate, discard, underestimate, suspend, depreciate, miss, skip, undervalue, forget. *Ant.* performance, perpetration, execution, achievement, vigilance, alertness watchfulness, concern, surveillance, care, heedfulness, vigil, observance, carefulness, fulfilment, attention, action, attentiveness, consideration, ardor, enthusiasm, application, perseverance, caution, forethought, circumspection, management, foresight, heed, prudence, wariness, precaution, solicitude; do, care for, act, perform, watch, safeguard, protect, accomplish, complete, finish achieve, consummate, conclude, effect, discharge, execute, work serve, try, continue.

negotiable, transferable, conveyable, assignable.

negotiate, bargain, contract, confer, consult, arrange, transact, debate, treat, dicker, deal, compromise, accomplish, overcome, sell achieve, reflect, agree.

neighborhood, environs, vicinity, locality, proximity, district, adjacency, community, region.

neophyte, novice, beginner, learner, probationer, apprentice, tyro student, trainee, cub, recruit.

nerve, courage, hardihood, audacity, fortitude, intrepidity, pluck, strength, vigor, vitality, resolution, determination.

nervous, timid, shaky, timorous, excitable, high-strung, apprehensive, quivering, restless, shaking, afraid, trembling, perturbed, frightened, aghast, panic-stricken, fidgety, hysterical, tremulous, alarmed, flighty, uneasy, jittery, tense, fearful, sensitive, terror-stricken, agitated, neurotic, weak. *Ant.* brave, inured, fearless, bold, strong, seasoned, hardy, courageous, plucky, resolute, daring, stout-hearted, dauntless, audacious, confident, spirited, unshirking, heroic, strongwilled.

nestle, cuddle, snuggle, nuzzle, lodge, embed, settle.

nettle, irk, vex, irritate, fret, tease, harrass, trouble, chafe, ruffle, incense, exasperate, sting, provoke, annoy, agitate. *Ant.* mollify, please, appease, help, aid.

neutral, indifferent, indeterminate, nonpartisan, disinterested, unconcerned, impartial, unallied. *Ant.* positive, decided, biased, involved, predisposed.

neutralize, cancel, annul, nullify, counteract, invalidate, affect, undo, counterbalance, countervail, offset.

new, novel, fresh, recent, original, late, untried, modern, up-to-date, unaccustomed, unfamiliar, strange. *Ant.* old, ancient, worn, deteriorated, medieval, worn-out, time-worn, antique, venerable, prehistoric, primeval, primordial, antiquated, archaic, obsolete, old-fashioned, outmoded.

news, information, tidings, intelligence, advice, report, message, communication, bulletin.

newspaper, publication, press, fourth estate, journal, magazine, periodical, review.

next, nearest, adjacent, bordering, succeeding, following, ensuing, contiguous, beside, adjoining, later, after.

nice, exact, precise, accurate, correct, critical, discerning, definite, strict, fine, delicate, exquisite, dainty, attractive, pleasing, fastidious, punctilious, scrupulous, neat, trim, tidy, tender, savory, pleasant, delicious, palatable. *Ant.* ugly, repulsive, coarse, revolting, repellent, abhorrent, displeasing, rude, unpleasant, rough, scarred, misshapen, grim, unseemly, disfigured, shabby, hulking, deformed, ungainly, horrid, hideous, unmannerly, slovenly.

nickname, sobriquet, pet name, diminutive, appellation, pseudonym, alias, monicker, agnomen.

niggardly, miserly, stingy, parsimonious, sparing, penurious, close, cheap, ungenerous, tight-fisted, chary, tight, grudging, penny-pinching, avaricious, illiberal, mercenary, mean, sordid. *Ant.* generous, prodigal, profuse, open-handed, unsparing, liberal, extravagant, lavish, wasteful, bounteous, munificent.

nimble, alert, spry, hustling, lively, active, speedy, quick, prompt, rapid, brisk, swift, bustling, flexible, supple, agile, sprightly, expeditious, fast. *Ant.* slow, dull, slack, dilatory, languid, heavy, clumsy, inert, wearisome, weary, apathetic, sluggish, lumbering.

nobility, rank, distinction, eminence, condition, birth, blood, preeminence; greatness, dignity, nobleness, gentility, grandeur, magnanimity; aristocracy, peerage, gentry, royalty. *Ant.* commonalty, public, proletariat, people.

noble, grand, august, princely, high, stately, generous, exalted, imperial, magnanimous, courtly, majestic, illustrious, famous, regal, worthy, royal, lofty, elevated, eminent, lordly, dignified, genteel, sublime, superior, honorable, titled, distinguished, patrician, aristocratic, loyal, incorrupt *Ant.* ignoble, plebeian, servile, abject.

noise, clamor, clatter, din, tumult, uproar, sound, sonance, clangor, hubbub, racket, pandemonium, blare. *Ant.* silence, stillness, calm, hush, quiet, tranquility.

noiseless, silent, still, soundless, inaudible, hushed, lulled, calm, muted, quiet, smothered, stifled, dead, muffled, deadened, gagged, stilled, stopped. *Ant.* sounding, sonorous, sonant, noisy, audible, resonant, clangorous, shrill, raucous.

noisome, noxious, stinking, putrid, rotten, mephitic, decaying, disgusting, offensive, malodorous, fetid, foul, strong-smelling, unpleasant, musty, tainted, rank, fulsome, moldy. *Ant.* good, fragrant, redolent, aromatic, sweet-smelling, scented.

nomad, wanderer, itinerant, rover, gypsy, vagabond, roamer, migrant, vagrant.

nomenclature, terminology, glossary, name, appellation, designation, head, title, epithet, nomination, cognomen, term, expression, cant.

nominate, present, propose, elect, suggest, choose, appoint, offer, propound. *Ant.* reject, blackball.

nonchalant, careless, unconcerned, neglectful, indifferent, negligent, uncaring, trifling, insouciant, heedless, untroubled, thoughtless, inconsiderate; unruffled, casual, collected, composed, cool, imperturbable. *Ant.* careful, considerate, thoughtful, cautious, anxious, wary, eager, solicitous, spirited, enthusiastic, heedful, emotional, earnest, attentive, fervent, fervid, zealous, ardent, impressionable, prudent, excitable, quick, agitated, active, perturbed, vigilant, watchful, alert.

nonconformity, dissent, rebellion, heresy, disagreement, individuality, heterodoxy. *Ant.* conformity, orthodoxy, obedience, uniformity, compliance.

nondescript, strange, odd, peculiar, indescribable, unclassifiable, amorphous. *Ant.* regular, usual, common, standard, superior.

nonentity, upstart, nobody, cipher, non-subsistence, nonexistence.

nonplus, confuse, disturb, worry, annoy, puzzle, perplex, mystify, confound, disconcert, astonish, vex, discomfit, embarrass, bewilder. *Ant.* satisfy, affirm, please, strengthen, aid, enlighten, tell, advise, assure.

nonsense, silliness, absurdity, pretense, folly, jest, joke, jargon, gibberish, imbecility, inanity, drivel, tomfoolery, mummery, muddle, jabber, foolishness, shallowness, senselessness, rigmarole, babble, babbling, rant, froth, frippery, inconsistency. *Ant.* sense, wisdom, truth, fact, common sense, reality, veracity, exactness, significance, substance, exactitude, evidence, actuality, accuracy, certainty, sureness, reliability, intelligibility, clarity, lucidity, comprehensibility, import.

normal, regular, ordinary, general, conventional, common, usual, rational, typical, reasonable, natural, average, sane, standard, customary, commonplace. *Ant.* irregular, unnatural, unusual, queer, extraordinary, atypical, eccentric, odd, abnormal, unconventional, anomalous, exceptional, strange, singular, peculiar, uncommon, unprecedented, rare.

nosy, inquisitive, curious, snoopy, intrusive, meddling, prying. *Ant.* uninterested, incurious, correct, decorous, polite, restrained.

notable, remarkable, well-known, famous, celebrated, unusual, noteworthy, renowned, distinguished, eminent, illustrious, significant, outstanding, uncommon, memorable, noticeable, exceptional, rare, striking, manifest, pronounced, extraordinary, eventful, worthy, conspicuous, prominent, great, heroic, foremost, honored, exalted, imposing. *Ant.* unknown, obscure, humble, low, lowly, unworthy, false, common, plebeian, unimportant, trivial, insignificant, inconsequential, petty, immaterial, ordinary, commonplace, usual, uneventful, slight, uninteresting.

ote, *n.* sign, symbol, token, comment, indication, explanation, commentary; letter, acknowledgment, missive, message, memorandum, notice, notation, postcard, dispatch, epistle; repute, fame, renown, distinction, reputation; *v.* notice, remark, discern, see, perceive, observe, view, contemplate, survey, heed.

oteworthy, significant, important, prominent, newsworthy, unusual, historical, exceptional, rare, memorable, extraordinary, remarkable, momentous, salient. *Ant.* unimportant, insignificant, incidental, trivial, common, inconsequential, dull, tiresome, regular, usual, ordinary.

othing, nonexistence, nullity, nihility, nonentity, naught, blank, zero, nullification, bagatelle, cipher.

otice, *n.* announcement, notification, bulletin, poster, placard, sign, warning, note, cognizance, comment, mention, recognition, heed, civility, attention, respect, consideration, observation, regard; *v.* note, observe, detect, discover, perceive, heed, discern, mind, examine, regard, mark, see, distinguish, warn. *Ant.* neglect, omission, evasion, forgetfulness, laxity, unmindfulness, exemption; overlook, miss, disregard, ignore, shun, avoid.

otify, inform, warn, alert, advise, call, apprise, tell, acquaint, express, intimate, impart, communicate, signify, specify, convey, disclose, indicate, proclaim, advertise, circulate, spread, diffuse, disseminate, divulge, reveal, report. *Ant.* conceal, hide, screen, cover, mask, secrete, camouflage, withhold, reserve, cloak, evade, suppress, smother, dissemble, disguise, mystify, confuse.

otion, thought, idea, conception, belief, theory, opinion, sentiment, understanding, inkling, whim, caprice, conceit, inclination, fancy, imagination, knowledge, impression, view, judgment, perception, reflection, viewpoint, presumption, conviction, persuasion.

otorious, ill-famed, infamous, shameful, opprobrious, disreputable, disgraceful, discreditable, inglorious, arrant, glaring, flagrant, blatant, shocking, scandalous, dishonorable, iniquitous, dissolute.

ourish, feed, supply, sustain, nurture, minister, administer, nurse, serve, attend, tend, succor; strengthen, encourage, help, aid, support, back, foster. *Ant.* starve, deprive, exhaust, weaken, enervate, debilitate, enfeeble, sap, reduce, neglect, attenuate, impair, abandon.

ourishment, nutriment, sustenance, aliment, food, meal, refreshment, maintenance, support, provisions. *Ant.* starvation, hunger, deprivation, destitution, detriment, want, deficiency.

ovel, new, unusual, different, original, unique, neoteric, uncommon, rare, modern, recent, fresh, untried, unprecedented, odd, wonderful, unparalleled, dissimilar. *Ant.* old, ancient, primitive, antiquated, old-fashioned, out-of-date, hoary, known, familiar, usual, habitual, customary, frequent, common, ordinary, similar.

ovice, beginner, learner, student, amateur, newcomer, neophyte, tyro, pupil, intern, cadet, postulant, follower, disciple, recruit, apprentice, probationer, tenderfoot, greenhorn. *Ant.* master, instructor, trainer, tutor, teacher, professor, preacher, guide, director, mentor, adviser, old hand, expert.

noxious, harmful, noisome, injurious, baneful, pestiferous, deadly deleterious, pernicious, poisonous, pestilential, dangerous, virulent, unwholesome, venomous, toxic, rotten, stinking, mephitic smelling, tainted, offensive, malodorous, contaminated, putrid septic, miasmic, zymotic, foul, bad, rank, nocuous, unhealthy hurtful, destructive. *Ant.* good, salubrious, curative, wholesome bracing, healthy, strengthening, prophylactic, invigorating, hygienic, harmless, innoxious, innocuous, restorative, helpful, preservative, healing, nutritious, remedial, beneficial, advantageous useful, healthful, profitable, energizing, valuable, forceful, antiseptic, stimulating, inoffensive, harmless.

nucleus, core, focus, hub, center, heart, middle, kernel, basis.

nude, bare, undraped, stripped, naked, uncovered, disrobed, unclothed, denuded, bald, barren, divested, undressed, exposed. *Ant.* clothed, clad, cloaked, dressed, screened, robed, draped, covered habited, costumed, invested, garbed, liveried, arrayed, attired appareled.

nudge, push, jog, shove, touch, elbow, poke, urge, spur, incite, aid encourage, prod. *Ant.* avoid, repress, suppress, prevent.

nugatory, useless, vain, abortive, fruitless, futile, hopeless, unavailing, trivial, petty, paltry, ineffectual, insignificant, inoperative trifling. *Ant.* successful, vital, useful, effectual, important.

nuisance, trouble, plague, bore, pest, vexation, irritation, bother infliction, offense, annoyance, expense. *Ant.* aid, comfort, delight pleasure.

nullify, invalidate, annul, negate, void, destroy, abolish, abrogate counteract, upset, suppress, obliterate, erase, countermand, neutralize, dispel, overthrow, revoke, rescind, discard, repeal, cancel *Ant.* affirm, ratify, confirm, corroborate, uphold, support, conform, consent, concur, agree, observe, execute, perform.

numb, dull, stupefied, torpid, insensitive, deadened, unfeeling, insensible, unaware, paralyzed, dazed, frozen, lifeless, inert. *Ant.* alert, sensitive, aware, alive, responsive, lively.

number, count, reckon, check, enumerate, compute, tell, list, score calculate, muster, aggregate, include, figure. *Ant.* guess, estimate

numerous, many, various, multifarious, divers, profuse, multitudinous, sundry, multifold, teeming, manifold, crowded, populous abundant, numberless, plentiful, myriad, thick. *Ant.* few, lacking scarce, reduced, sparse, diminished, scant, small, thin, fractional deficient, decimated.

nurse, cherish, foster, minister, tend, feed, encourage, nurture succor, suckle, nourish, pamper. *Ant.* neglect, slight, ignore deprive.

nurture, nourish, foster, nurse, support, train, rear, feed, tend, educate, discipline, instruct, cherish, uphold.

nutriment, food, provision, sustenance, nourishment, aliment.

nutritious, nutritive, wholesome, alimental, nourishing, invigorating

O

oath, affirmation, declaration, vow, pledge, promise, imprecation, affidavit, assertion, malediction, blasphemy, anathema, curse, execration, denunciation, swearing, profanity, cursing, reprobation, adjuration, ban, fulmination. *Ant.* benediction, approval, blessing, sanction, benison, approbation, commendation, acclaim, laudation, acclamation, praise.

obdurate, stubborn, unyielding, obstinate, callous, self-willed, immovable, hard, adamant, hardened, headstrong, dogged, relentless, firm, unshakeable, harsh, unbending, impenitent, perverse, unregenerative, dogmatic, tenacious, opinionative, sulky, mulish, resolute, inflexible, inexorable, sullen. *Ant.* susceptible, fitful, amenable, tractable, gentle, yielding, relenting, submitting, careless, changing, changeful, erratic, whimsical, flighty, capricious, inconsistent.

obedient, compliant, respectful, faithful, dutiful, law-abiding, devoted, submissive, loyal, deferential, docile, observant, tractable, regardful, malleable, resigned, passive, sycophantic, acquiescent, yielding, conformable, submitting, surrendering. *Ant.* unwilling, obstinate, disobedient, mischievous, obdurate, contumacious, infringing, mutinous, insubordinate, insurgent, lawless, unruly, riotous, intractable, rebellious, obstreperous, seditious, defiant, recalcitrant, contrary, unyielding, impertinent, insolent, stubborn, impudent, dour.

obeisance, homage, salutation, fealty, salute, allegiance, reverence, bow, deference, curtsy, genuflection.

obese, fat, plump, chubby, corpulent, fleshy, adipose, rotund, stout, unwieldy, burly, lumpish, bulky, lusty, ponderous, portly, puffy, swollen. *Ant.* scrawny, spare, angular, slim, slight, raw-boned, lean, lanky, thin, slender, attenuated, emaciated, delicate, skinny, gaunt, skeletal.

obey, conform, answer, comply, respond, submit, assent, accede, act, concur, perform, surrender, yield, follow, keep, mind, heed, observe, serve. *Ant.* disobey, scorn, rebel, mutiny.

obfuscate, muddle, bewilder, darken, obscure, adumbrate, stupefy, cloud, confuse, perplex. *Ant.* clarify, brighten, enlighten, clean, explain, purify.

object, oppose, protest, remonstrate, resist, balk, reject, refuse, contravene, demur, disapprove, gainsay, hesitate, scruple. *Ant.* acquiesce, accept, accede, admit, approve, concur, comply, consent, sanction, applaud, welcome, admire.

objection, disapproval, opposition, dislike, exception, scruple, cavil, censure, doubt, argument, protest, criticism. *Ant.* acceptance, affirmation, agreement, approval, concurrence, accord.

objective, *n.* object, purpose, scheme, goal, end, aim, intention, aspiration, design, result, mark, target, destination, motive, intent; *adj.* unbiased, impartial, impersonal, disinterested, dispassionate, just, fair, equitable. *Ant.* subjective, personal, partial, introspective, emotional.

objurgation, rebuke, condemnation, abuse, execration, vituperation, reprobation, criticism. *Ant.* praise, applause, approval, commendation, acclaim, recognition.

obligation, responsibility, duty, stipulation, indebtedness, bond, contract, accountability, requirement, pledge, liability, agreement, promise.

oblige, accommodate, gratify, benefit, help, favor, please, constrain, drive, prevent, compel, enforce, necessitate, force, hinder, coerce, insist, impel, serve, restrain, command, commandeer. *Ant.* free, acquit, unshackle, release, unbind, exempt, discharge, grant, excuse, dissolve, absolve, renounce, spare, accede.

oblique, indirect, askew, devious, crooked, tilted, transverse, slanting, diagonal, sidelong, sloping. *Ant.* direct, straightforward, forthright, immediate, parallel, upright, vertical.

obliterate, erase, cancel, raze, expunge, efface, delete, nullify, expurgate, annihilate, destroy.

obloquy, reproach, disgrace, defamation, calumny, revilement, invective, abuse, aspersion, slander, disapprobation, debasement, dishonor, stigma, scandal, brand, infamy, humiliation, turpitude, villification, opprobrium. *Ant.* approbation, commendation, praise, plaudit, credit, laudation.

obnoxious, offensive, displeasing, hurtful, reprehensible, detestable, blameworthy, pernicious, loathsome, objectionable, hateful, repugnant, invidious, unpleasant, abhorrent, abominable, odious, repulsive, shocking, repellent, irritating, revolting. *Ant.* pleasing, beneficial, attractive, inviting, pleasant, fascinating, delightful, satisfying, gratifying, welcome, delectable, refreshing, sweet.

obscene, impure, lewd, pornographic, vulgar, lubricious, ribald, indecent, coarse, immoral, dirty, filthy, immodest, lascivious, foul, licentious, wanton, smutty, abominable, offensive, defiled, corrupt, polluted, contaminated. *Ant.* pure, upright, honorable, virtuous, unsullied, immaculate, innocent, decent, well-behaved, modest, particular, respectable.

obscure, dim, cloudy, dark, complex, mysterious, blurred, dusky, shadowy, inconspicuous, misty, hazy, nebulous, abstruse, hidden, indistinct, concealed, veiled, ambiguous, dense, incomprehensible, deep, complicated, unintelligible, enigmatic, involved, uncertain, difficult, dubious, vague, confused, indeterminate, cryptic, indefinite, unknown. *Ant.* plain, undisputed, clear, unquestionable, evident, apparent, axiomatic, obvious, conclusive, definite, intelligible, unequivocal, comprehensible, explicit, positive, lucid, absolute, perspicuous, graphic, distinct, manifest, unmistakable, visible, known, perceptible, distinguished, famous, celebrated.

obsequious, cringing, slavish, menial, sycophantic, deferential, flattering, compliant, servile, subordinate, parasitic, fawning, truckling, groveling, spineless, abject, beggarly, sniveling, sneaking, submissive. *Ant.* insolent, defiant, impudent, swaggering, bold, presumptuous, presumptive, contemptuous, saucy, mutinous, intractable, factious, headstrong, bullying, haughty, arrogant, assertive, imperious, overbearing, assuming, brazen, confident, audacious.

bservant, attentive, heedful, regardful, watchful, mindful, careful, listening, alert, perceptive, obedient, submissive, aware. *Ant.* heedless, indifferent, careless, abstracted, unmindful, neglectful, inattentive, lax, preoccupied, thoughtless, nonobservant.

bsolete, disused, archaic, old-fashioned, antique, outdated, outmoded, ancient, out-of-date, antiquated, rare, obsolescent, old, neglected, outworn, forgotten, rejected, hoary, primitive, extinct, timeworn. *Ant.* new, novel, recent, modern, current, up-to-date.

bstacle, impediment, barricade, difficulty, bar, check, hindrance, barrier, snag, stumbling block, interruption, obstruction. *Ant.* help, clearance, aid, boost, blessing.

bstinate, stubborn, opinionated, pertinacious, headstrong, contumacious, inflexible, resolute, immovable, unaffected, determined, indomitable, unimpressible, resolved, intractable, firm, willful, self-willed, recalcitrant, recusant, dogged, obdurate, persistent, unflinching, refractory, mulish, unyielding, decided, fixed. *Ant.* complaisant, yielding, submissive, courteous, tractable, docile, pliant, obedient, pliable, malleable, compliant, agreeable, amenable, controllable, acquiescent, manageable, governable.

bstreperous, troublesome, boisterous, turbulent, noisy, uncontrolled, tumultuous, vociferous, clamorous, blatant, riotous, recalcitrant, refractory, unruly, uproarious. *Ant.* quiet, peaceful, silent, harmonious, genial.

bstruct, impede, oppose, retard, restrain, curb, inhibit, block, prevent, hinder, bar, occlude, choke, dam, stop, interfere, interrupt, frustrate, counteract, circumvent, barricade, contravene, thwart, cramp, hamper, handicap, cripple. *Ant.* aid, favor, assist, succor, help, support, encourage, sustain, abet, advance, further, uphold, promote, forward, reinforce, facilitate.

btain, acquire, win, collect, attain, gain, recover, procure, secure, gather, get, achieve, earn. *Ant.* lose, forgo, forsake, sacrifice, forfeit, award.

btrusive, interfering, intrusive, impertinent, officious, meddling, curious, forward, meddlesome, prying. *Ant.* shy, diffident, retiring, modest.

btuse, blunt, stolid, stupid, insensitive, dull, impassive, slow, heavy, phlegmatic, unintelligent, dense. *Ant.* acute, sensitive, sharp, imaginative, keen, quick, brilliant.

bviate, avoid, remove, prevent, evade, forestall, elude, avert, preclude, counteract, anticipate. *Ant.* permit, allow, help.

bvious, plain, self-evident, apparent, clear, conclusive, distinct, evident, manifest, lucid, unmistakable, visible, patent, intelligible, definite, comprehensible, unequivocal, precise, unambiguous, explicit. *Ant.* complex, confused, puzzling, indefinite, esoteric, unintelligible, ambiguous, obscure, occult, muddy, latent, abstruse, mysterious.

occasional, incidental, irregular, contingent, rare, scattered, scarce, random, sporadic, infrequent, unstable, unsettled, indefinite, indeterminate, uncommon. *Ant.* frequent, customary, often, usual, invariable, regular, constant, steady.

occult, latent, esoteric, unrevealed, hidden, secret, mysterious, unintelligible, ambiguous, obscure, enigmatic, metaphysical, recondite, concealed, supernatural, cabalistic, transcendental, mystical, inexplicable, veiled, undisclosed. *Ant.* obvious, natural, manifest, clear, scrutable.

occupation, calling, vocation, work, trade, craft, profession, employment, pursuit, business, mission, position, job.

occupy, inhabit, dwell, tenant, fill, employ, use, hold, possess, own, engage, absorb, engross, entertain; invade, capture, seize, keep. *Ant.* leave, vacate, surrender, empty.

occurrence, happening, incident, event, occasion, circumstance, episode, affair, proceeding, eventuality, transaction.

odd, uneven, single, unmatched, alone, lone; strange, queer, occult, weird, mysterious, peculiar, quaint, curious, rare, different, extraordinary, exceptional, unique, erratic, eccentric, awkward, droll, laughable, bizarre, unnatural, grotesque, unusual, uncommon, abnormal. *Ant.* uniform, even, conformable, normal, usual, customary, typical, natural, regular, habitual, ordinary, common, conventional, standard, sane, lucid, sober, steady, reasonable, reliable, rational.

odious, hateful, disgusting, foul, abhorrent, abominable, detestable, repellent, offensive, loathsome, disagreeable, forbidding, invidious, objectionable, repugnant, unpleasant, despicable, revolting, execrable, horrible, repulsive, hideous, obnoxious, shocking, distasteful, putrid, rotten, purulent. *Ant.* pleasing, attractive, inviting, delightful, cheerful, lovable, likable, pleasant, refreshing, clean, pure, wholesome, moral, agreeable.

odor, scent, smell, essence, redolence, perfume, fragrance, aroma, reek, fume, fetor, stench.

offense, misdeed, transgression, trespass, misdemeanor, fault, sin, affront, scandal, resentment, attack, crime, assault, insult, onset, onslaught, wrong, aggression, harm, hurt, misconduct, atrocity, malfeasance, outrage, injury, felony, corruption, siege.

offensive, insolent, impudent, combative, annoying, insulting, loathsome, revolting, vexing, discourteous, aggressive, impertinent, disagreeable, abusive, fetid, obnoxious, disgusting, displeasing, rude, opprobrious, scurrilous, reprehensible, abhorrent, hateful, detestable, foul, vulgar, indecent, unclean, coarse, ribald, filthy, odious. *Ant.* agreeable, pleasing, clean, decent, defensive.

offer, present, tender, propose, submit, suggest, advance, hand, bid, volunteer, proffer, move. *Ant.* withdraw, withhold, retain, deny, reject, refuse.

offhand, extemporaneous, impromptu, unpremeditated, extemporary, improvised; casual, impulsive, hasty, abrupt, careless, impetuous, curt, cavalier, unceremonious. *Ant.* studied, considered, advised, deliberate.

official, authoritative, authentic, genuine, authorized, proper, unquestionable, certain, reliable, assured, absolute, unequivocal, unmistakable, undeniable, governmental, indisputable, definite. *Ant.* dubious, doubtful, indeterminate, disputable, equivocal, questionable, indefinite, confused, unauthorized, unreliable, uncertain, problematical, contingent, unofficial.

officious, meddling, obtrusive, presumptuous, nosy, pushing, bossy, impertinent, forward, intrusive, interfering. *Ant.* shy, backward, timid, retiring.

offset, balance, compensate, counteract, countervail, counterpoise, counterbalance; nullify, negate, redeem, reclaim, neutralize, cancel.

offspring, progeny, issue, descendants, children, posterity, brood, family, heirs, sons, daughters, successors. *Ant.* ancestry, forefathers, ancestors, fathers, progenitors, forebears.

often, frequently, recurrently, commonly, repeatedly, ofttimes. *Ant.* seldom, rarely, infrequently.

old, ancient, antique, antiquated, old-fashioned, pristine, obsolete, immemorial, early, prehistoric, venerable, antediluvian, hoary, superannuated, patriarchal, remote, faded, experienced, aged. *Ant.* new, modern, up-to-date, current, recent, late, inexperienced, fresh, young, contemporary, unhandled, neoteric.

old-fashioned, old, outmoded, obsolete, antique, passé, archaic, out-of-date. *Ant.* new, up-to-date, current, stylish, modern, fashionable, late, recent, modish, natty.

omen, portent, foreshadow, auspice, augury, warning, harbinger, sign, indication, prediction, foreboding, token, precursor, presage.

ominous, threatening, portentous, unpropitious, foreboding, imminent, premonitory, suggestive, inauspicious, precursive, presaging, significant, ill-fated, fateful, unlucky, menacing.

omit, exclude, overlook, disregard, bar, except, preclude, repudiate, skip, spare, miss, evade, drop, forget, reject, eliminate, discard. *Ant.* insert, enter, include, introduce, inject, add, enroll, accept.

onerous, burdensome, difficult, heavy, troublesome, distressed, oppressive, serious, overpowering, exacting, wearing, discouraging, ponderous, weighty, laborious, arduous, cumbersome, toilsome, formidable, irksome. *Ant.* easy, light, trivial, agreeable, normal, pleasant, insignificant, unessential, common, ordinary, inconsiderable.

one-sided, unilateral, partial, biased, unjust, distorted, slanted, unfair, prejudiced, loaded, bigoted, inequitable. *Ant.* fair, honest, judicial, equitable, just, impartial, balanced.

onlooker, spectator, bystander, witness, viewer, beholder, observer, watcher, loiterer. *Ant.* participant, player, actor, doer.

only, exclusively, simply, solely, singly, merely, just, but, barely.

onus, burden, liability, load, shame, difficulty, oppression, chore, job responsibility, debt, fear, threat. *Ant.* freedom, irresponsibility prize, gain.

opaque, dark, darkened, non-transparent, dim, dull, shady, smoky obfuscated, misty, nubilous, cloudy, shadowy, murky, unintel ligible, obscure, fuliginous, sooty, cloudy, dusky, filmy. *Ant.* clear pellucid, diaphanous, transparent, lucid, limpid, lustrous, hyaline translucent, serene, glassy, vitreous, undimmed, crystalline, un clouded, luminous.

open, *adj.* unclosed, public, free, accessible, unrestricted, unsealed unobstructed, perforated, unstopped, passable, apart, ajar, un barred, gaping, expanded, agape, full-blown, pervious, exposed susceptible, permeable, clear, definite, manifest, plain, apparent evident, ostensible, candid, unmistakable, disclosed, conspicuous explicit, frank, unreserved, undisguised, straightforward, simple sincere, patent, unaffected, unsophisticated, ingenuous, artless outspoken, naïve, bare, undefended; *v.* unbar, unlock, unclose expand, uncover, clear, unfold, expose, spread, reveal, exhibit disclose, show, split, discover, divide, rend, separate, explain initiate, start, commence, begin, inaugurate, admit. *Ant.* closed blocked, shut, obstructed, barred, tight, stopped, contracted, com pressed, buried, hidden, latent, concealed, secret, underhand cryptographic, enigmatical, covert, cryptic, equivocal, insincere cunning, intriguing, hypocritical, crafty, clandestine, subtle designing, deep, artful, tricky, shrewd, deceptive, shifty, canny deceitful, astute, wily, sharp; bar, lock, shut, close, deny, cover stop, hide, block, secrete, plug, conceal, screen, finish, terminate reject, conclude, repudiate, end, preclude, exclude, prevent, inter dict, hinder, inhibit, restrain, disallow, prohibit, debar.

operate, work, act, perform, execute, run, conduct, direct, manage manipulate, transact, practice, go, function, react.

operation, action, execution, performance, act, process, procedure manipulation, maneuver, proceeding, transaction. *Ant.* faineance inaction, inutility, uselessness, inefficiency, ineffectiveness.

operative, efficacious, efficient, effective, effectual, serviceable, act ing, active, performing, moving, working. *Ant.* useless, inactive inefficient, ineffective, unimportant, still, quiet.

opine, suppose, think, believe, judge, presume, surmise. *Ant.* know confirm, prove, ascertain.

opinion, notion, sentiment, view, judgment, belief, thought, verdict persuasion, theory, consensus, determination, conception, convic tion, estimation, impression, conclusion, principle, inference, view point, tenet, evaluation.

opponent, rival, antagonist, adversary, competitor, disputant, assail ant, emulator, challenger, invader, claimant, attacker, encroach er, contestant, foeman, violator, foe, infringer, enemy, intruder *Ant.* associate, companion, colleague, comrade, assistant, ally helper, mate, partner, consort.

opportunity, chance, contingency, occasion, situation, timeliness, advantage, occurrence, time, opening, possibility.

oppose, resist, obstruct, check, contravene, combat, withstand, deny, oppugn, restrain, thwart, counteract, retaliate, rebuff, snub, interfere, contrast, confront, cross, contradict, protest, face, dare, brave, defy, cross, overpower, antagonize, impede, frustrate, neutralize, hinder, overcome, invert, reverse. *Ant.* cooperate, concur, combine, fraternize, conspire, federate, ratify, confirm, endorse, sanction, certify, commend, attest, recommend, support, sustain, laud, collude, acclaim, participate, praise, eulogize, connive, approve, applaud, coalesce, join.

opposite, antonymous, contrary, antithesis, contradictory, reverse, inverse. *Ant.* counterpart, same, like, identical, compatible.

oppress, afflict, overbear, burden, crush, overwhelm, tyrannize, persecute, maltreat, aggrieve, harass, grieve, subdue, load, depress. *Ant.* relieve, aid, support.

opprobrium, scurrility, abuse, infamy, calumny, contumely, odium, contempt, obloquy, dishonor, ignominy, reproach. *Ant.* praise, aid, honor, favor, glorification, eulogy.

oppugn, dispute, resist, oppose, argue, assail, criticize, combat, attack, withstand, doubt, battle, fight. *Ant.* favor, endorse, assist, support, help, aid.

optimistic, hopeful, cheerful, cheering, sanguine, comforting, confident, assured, bright, happy, elated, encouraging, expectant, enthusiastic, heartening, arousing, promising, inspiriting. *Ant.* pessimistic, doleful, despairing, afraid, gloomy, doubtful, depressed, hopeless, dejected, inconsolable, melancholy, mournful, broken-hearted.

option, choice, preference, discretion, alternative, selection, election, right, prerogative.

opulent, rich, wealthy, affluent, moneyed, profuse, abundant, luxuriant, plentiful, sumptuous. *Ant.* poor, deprived, destitute, scarce, limited, depressed, indigent, squalid.

oracular, ambiguous, cryptic, esoteric, obscure, vague, unintelligible, mystical, hazy, equivocal, obscured, portentous, ominous, incomprehensible, mysterious, mystifying, prophetic, occult, abstruse, dubious, doubtful. *Ant.* plain, lucid, distinct, intelligible, clear, unequivocal, explicit, positive, definite.

oral, spoken, vocal, articulate, mouthed, uttered, said. *Ant.* written, printed.

oration, speech, discourse, address, talk, declamation, lecture, sermon.

orbit, circuit, ambit, path, gamut, sweep, scope, range, purview, reach, track.

ordain, install, decree, institute, dictate, appoint, order, enact, command, prescribe, invest, determine, predestine, destine, select, impose, assign, commission, delegate. *Ant.* abrogate, rescind, cancel, repeal, depose, revoke, dismiss, disallow, disqualify, invalidate, annul, prohibit, abolish, countermand, nullify, disestablish, void, retract.

ordeal, trial, strain, test, tribulation, judgment, scrutiny, hardship experience, cross, pain, assay, agony.

order, *n.* command, injunction, mandate, instruction, precept, canon prescription, law, directive, direction, regulation, requirement rule, regularity, system, plan, method, economy, symmetry, ar rangement, succession, sequence; *v.* command, dictate, instruct appoint, enjoin, request, require, direct, bid, rule, demand, align array, regulate, arrange, adjust, methodize, systematize, manage conduct, direct, decree, proclaim, ordain, impose, prescribe, exact charge. *Ant.* allowance, consent, leave, liberty, license, permis sion, permit, disorder, chaos, disorganization, derangement, con fusion, irregularity, mixture, perplexity, snarl, muddle, maze labyrinth.

orderly, methodical, peaceable, tidy, regular, quiet, systematical, cor rect, arranged, systematic, neat, business-like, trim, adjusted regulated, ship-shape, symmetrical, formal, unconfused, normal classified. *Ant.* disorderly, chaotic, disordered, tangled, confused disorganized, irregular, promiscuous, intricate, gnarled, snarled complex, untidy, straggling, slovenly.

ordinance, statute, regulation, enactment, law, prescript, ceremony decree, rule, order, injunction, command.

ordinary, common, regular, commonplace, usual, customary, normal conventional, typical, accustomed, consistent, habitual, medium average, inferior, low, workaday, middling, familiar, simple trite, unaffected, prevalent, natural, stereotyped, unadorned, vul gar, plain. *Ant.* uncommon, extraordinary, unconventional, ex ceptional, anomalous, irregular, eccentric, strange, curious, un natural, wonderful, unique, unusual, unaccustomed, egregious exclusive, peculiar, rare, odd, bizarre.

organic, systematic, innate, structural, inherent, constitutional, vital radical, essential, fundamental, natural. *Ant.* inorganic, external extraneous, nonessential.

organization, construction, constitution, arrangement, establishment institution, association.

organize, arrange, systematize, form, establish, classify, institute co-ordinate, plan, shape, found, frame, constitute, regulate. *Ant* disorganize, divide, destroy, disband, disperse.

orgy, debauchery, carousal, revelry, bacchanal, saturnalia.

orifice, opening, hole, aperture, perforation, window, mouth, vent interstice, inlet, outlet.

origin, rise, beginning, commencement, source, cause, outset, start incipience, inception, derivation, root, birth, nativity, foundation origination. *Ant.* end, result, termination, consequence, effect issue, conclusion, outcome, finish, outgrowth, finality, close, com pletion, eschatology, determination, goal, destiny, destination death, burial.

original, first, primary, new, fresh, rudimentary, causal, etiological formative, aboriginal, inceptive, novel, unique, initial, model, pat tern, archetypal. *Ant.* dependent, consequential, deriving, result ing, following, accruing, emanating, evolved, derivative, copied, imitated, secondary, issuing.

ornamental, decorative, embellishing, garnishing, ornate, beautifying, adorning, gilt.

ornate, decorated, opulent, florid, ornamented, embellished, figured, rich, adorned. *Ant.* simple, chaste, austere, unadorned, drab, dull.

orthodox, conventional, strict, conforming, sound, true, correct, accepted, standard, approved. *Ant.* heterodox, unconventional, untrue, doubting, disloyal, diversive, heretical, apocryphal, dissenting, agnostic, secular.

oscillate, waver, sway, vary, vibrate, fluctuate, vacillate, undulate, swing. *Ant.* stay, stand, halt, stop, remain, settle.

ostensible, apparent, avowed, outward, professed, manifest, illusory, seeming, exhibited, pretended, demonstrative, striking, expected, notable, probable, anticipated, pronounced, likely, seeming, plain, plausible, visible, obvious, evident. *Ant.* improbable, unlikely, unexpected, vague, obscure, latent, shadowy, concealed, secret, invisible, implausible, covert, veiled, hidden, indirect, abeyant.

ostentation, show, display, bravado, vaunting, boasting, pomp, gloss, tinsel, glitter, veneer, vanity, vulgarity, pomposity, flourish, array, pageantry, parade, magnificence, pretension, spectacle, exhibition. *Ant.* modesty, diffidence, humility, unobtrusiveness, retirement, timidity, quietness, coyness, reserve, bashfulness, demureness, backwardness, restraint, constraint, shyness.

ostracize, banish, bar, expel, exile, blackball, deport, exclude. *Ant.* accept, embrace, include, welcome, praise.

oust, eject, dislodge, dispossess, remove, evict, dismiss, proscribe, deprive, expel, reject, exile, depose, distrain, dethrone, disinherit, banish, discharge. *Ant.* restore, retain, reinstate, depute, commission, install, delegate, induct, authorize, welcome, receive, empower, admit, appoint, ordain, constitute.

outbreak, eruption, violence, ebullition, fury, outburst, explosion, fray, commotion, flare-up, row, riot, disturbance, revolt, mutiny, rebellion, insurrection, uprising. *Ant.* peace, quiet, order.

outcast, exile, expatriate, vagabond, reprobate, castaway, tramp, hobo, blasphemer, sinner, derelict, pariah, criminal, outlaw, fugitive, loner, reject.

outcome, result, effect, outgrowth, conclusion, upshot, consequence, issue, end, termination, sequel.

outcry, exclamation, shout, yell, scream, screech, clamor, noise, protest, tumult, uproar. *Ant.* silence, acceptance, assent.

outdo, excel, exceed, outstrip, surpass, outdistance, overcome, top, beat, eclipse, outshine, overshadow, outwit, frustrate, transcend.

outlaw, criminal, fugitive, outcast, brigand, excommunicant, bandit, desperado, robber, mugger, murderer.

outline, delineation, plan, profile, sketch, contour, silhouette, drawing, boundary, draft, skeleton, perimeter, periphery, form, configuration, synopsis, graph, framework, shape, figure, formation, representation, design, tracing, copy, alignment.

outrage, insult, injury, abuse, indignity, affront, offense, grievance, mortification, oppression, transgression, persecution, maltreatment, shock, violation, annoyance, disturbance, maliciousness, atrocity, enormity.

outrageous, wanton, abusive, monstrous, flagrant, heinous, violent, nefarious, excessive, scandalous, atrocious, infamous, disgraceful, abominable, wicked, shocking, notorious, disreputable, shameful, opprobrious, despicable, ignominious, exorbitant, extravagant, turbulent, wild, villainous, disorderly, insulting, frenzied, unbearable, furious, frantic, desperate, fierce. *Ant.* calm, peaceful, quiet, tranquil, dispassionate, mild, favorable, pleasant, passive, self-controlled, cool, submissive, imperturbable, composed, untroubled, peaceable, soothing.

outspoken, blunt, direct, plain, forthright, plain-spoken, candid, frank, free, open, unreserved, unceremonious, abrupt. *Ant.* reserved, cautious, insincere, circumspect, timid, misleading, subtle, taciturn.

outstanding, prominent, eminent, distinguished, dominant, notable, foremost, important, remarkable, superior, striking, salient, exceptional, noticeable, conspicuous, unpaid, unsettled, owing. *Ant.* ordinary, commonplace, inconspicuous, usual, regular, average, paid, settled, cleared.

outward, external, exterior, extraneous, outside, outer, foreign, outermost, superficial. *Ant.* inward, inner, interior, inside, internal, innermost, interstitial.

overbearing, tyrannical, haughty, oppressive, domineering, disdainful, lordly, imperious, proud, despotic, dictatorial, arrogant, insolent, magisterial, brazen, supercilious, swaggering, blustering, intimidating, pedantic, egotistic, audacious. *Ant.* meek, humble, mild, submissive, deferential, docile, subservient, sycophantic, retiring, bashful, modest, obsequious.

overcome, subdue, beat, conquer, outdo, subjugate, overthrow, overpower, crush, defeat, vanquish, exceed, overwhelm, master, suppress, surmount. *Ant.* yield, lose, fail, surrender, succumb.

overflow, redundancy, abundance, superabundance, congestion, glut, oversupply, plethora, superfluity, inundation, exuberance, deluge, engorgement, avalanche. *Ant.* scarcity, insufficiency, sparseness, deficiency, meagreness, reduction, curtailment, retrenchment, inadequacy, shortage, want, depletion, dearth, emptiness, scantiness.

overlook, ignore, skip, miss, neglect, omit, slight, excuse, condone, forgive, pardon, disregard, forget; oversee, supervise, inspect, examine, dominate. *Ant.* note, watch, regard, observe, see; indict, charge, punish.

overpower, subdue, overcome, vanquish, defeat, conquer, crush, subjugate, overwhelm, beat, rout, overreach, outwit. *Ant.* lose, fail, surrender, withdraw, retreat.

verrule, reject, revoke, nullify, cancel, rescind, repeal, recall, repudiate, abrogate, override, annul, veto, defeat, supersede; control, sway, influence, govern. *Ant.* endorse, accept, approve.

versee, supervise, manage, direct, superintend, command, order, guide.

versight, supervision, inspection, direction, management, superintendence, guidance, custody, charge, control, watchfulness, watch, government, surveillance, regulation; failure, blunder, neglect, lapse, miss, omission, inadvertence, mistake, inattention, abstraction, error, slip, heedlessness, preoccupation, aberration, misconception, misapprehension, fault, stumble.

vert, manifest, undisguised, patent, open, obvious, unconcealed, apparent, plain, public. *Ant.* covert, latent, concealed, hidden, private, closed, secret.

verthrow, destroy, ruin, overcome, subvert, demolish, overturn, rout, upset, defeat, beat, conquer, depose, invert, reverse, abolish, disrupt, extirpate, disorganize, obliterate, crush, master, subjugate, subdue, overpower. *Ant.* construct, rehabilitate, restore, support, aid, preserve, assist, maintain, develop.

verwhelm, overcome, inundate, ruin, crush, defeat, destroy, rout, submerge, vanquish, ravage, drown, disrupt, overpower, triumph, demolish, master, upset, suppress, conquer, override, swamp, subdue, subjugate. *Ant.* fail, lose, miss, flounder, weaken, falter, restore, assist, succor, help, befriend, save, rescue.

verwork, overburden, overtask, overdo, exhaust, overtax, misuse. *Ant.* rest, loaf, stall, shirk, malinger.

verwrought, excited, exhausted, impassioned, tired, perturbed, agitated, worn out, inflamed, spent, ruffled, disturbed, flustered, hysterical, shaken. *Ant.* unruffled, composed, peaceful, content, tranquil, quiescent, self-possessed, undisturbed, rested, restrained, unimpassioned, satisfied, complacent, resigned, patient, stoical.

wn, possess, retain, reveal, hold, confess, disclose, control, admit, have, concede, avow, recognize, allow. *Ant.* have not, deny, disavow, lack, need, lose, reject, loose.

P

ace, speed, gait, velocity, rate, step, stride.

acific, peaceful, untroubled, gentle, placid, smooth, calm, halcyon, tranquil, conciliatory, nonviolent, quiet, still, composed, restful, unruffled, easygoing. *Ant.* rough, turbulent, quarrelsome, aggressive, hostile, militant, contentious, combative, belligerent, bellicose, disturbed, tempestuous.

acify, compose, reconcile, mollify, appease, allay, tranquilize, propitiate, placate, relieve, alleviate, calm, ameliorate, subdue, quell, assuage, settle. *Ant.* antagonize, anger, roil, stir.

pack, n. bundle, kit, package, roll, knapsack, burden, parcel, load, baggage, grip, bag, duffle bag, valise, trunk, luggage, lot, amount, assemblage, concourse, gathering, number, group, band, company, crew, collection, flock; v. prepare, stuff, squeeze, tie, bind, brace, girdle, gather, collect, store, cram, condense, compress, press, arrange, stow. *Ant.* unpack, scatter, loosen, sort, unbind, dispose, untie, disperse, distribute, allot, allocate, apportion, strew.

package, parcel, bundle, box, carton, bale, pack, packet.

pact, agreement, compact, treaty, bond, covenant, concord, bargain, alliance, deal, union, entente, cartel, league, contract, arrangement, understanding.

pagan, idolater, pantheist, heathen, doubter, scoffer, heretic, unbeliever, skeptic, infidel, freethinker, atheist, agnostic. *Ant.* Christian, Jew, Muslim, believer.

pageantry, pomp, exhibition, parade, show, display, flourish, spectacle, ostentation, pretension, extravaganza, masque, procession, magnificence, glitter, splendor, revel, revelry, carnival, festivity.

pain, suffering, affliction, paroxysm, pang, throe, discomfort, ache, twinge, misery, torture, anguish, torment, distress, agony, woe, grief, worry, anxiety. *Ant.* health, comfort, well-being, pleasure, enjoyment.

painstaking, laborious, careful, scrupulous, particular, sedulous, precise, diligent, assiduous, strenuous, correct. *Ant.* careless, negligent, thoughtless, reckless, unmindful.

paint, color, daub, stain, delineate, picture, describe, portray, reveal, express, explain, adorn, decorate, ornament.

pal, comrade, buddy, associate, chum, mate, companion, fellow, crony, friend. *Ant.* foe, enemy, adversary.

pale, pallid, spectral, wan, ghastly, blanched, white, faded, colorless, bleached, achromatic, ashen, cadaverous, obscure, dim. *Ant.* florid, roseate, flushed, bright, glowing, colorful, luminous, radiant, lambent, gleaming, rosy, ruddy, inflamed.

pall, cloy, jade, dispirit, satiate, sicken, deject, surfeit. *Ant.* excite, intrigue, interest.

palliate, extenuate, screen, hide, qualify, excuse, assuage, conceal, cover, veil, cloak, mitigate, temper, ease, relieve, quell, diminish, allay, abate, gloss, soften, moderate, vindicate, defend, justify, alleviate. *Ant.* charge, check, impute, blame, denounce, reproach, accuse, implicate, tax, censure, brand, incriminate, indict, disapprove, arraign, impeach, condemn, reprove, upbraid, reprehend.

pallid, wan, pale, colorless, ashen, sallow, waxen. *Ant.* ruddy, pink, flushed, glowing.

palmy, prosperous, sunny, pleasant, glorious, victorious, thriving, delightful, flourishing, halcyon, bright, golden, fortunate, enjoyable, auspicious, pleasurable, captivating, joyous, exhilarating, entrancing, happy. *Ant.* sad, irksome, dreary, melancholy, deplorable, gloomy, annoying, pensive, woeful, doleful, comfortless, disagreeable, tiresome, intolerable, distressing, wearisome, insufferable, heartbreaking, dire, unfortunate.

palpable, plain, perceptible, sensible, appreciable, manifest, unmistakable, obvious, discernible, tactile, tangible, apparent, visible, clear, conspicuous, evident, open, distinct, definite, intelligible, patent, well-defined, prominent, real, corporeal, material, salient, indubitable, ostensible, self-evident, explicit. *Ant.* latent, hidden, puzzling, occult, mystic, obscure, concealed, doubtful, dubious, questionable, involved, inferential, complicated, complex, veiled, indirect, intricate, symbolic, implied, covert, mysterious, secret, anagogic, cryptic, recondite.

palpitation, throbbing, beating, fluttering, pulsation, vibration, quivering. *Ant.* stillness, quiescence, immobility, fixity.

paltry, insignificant, petty, trifling, picayune, inconsequential, puny, trivial, measly, small, poor, pitiful, minor, unimportant, worthless. *Ant.* important, large, rich, momentous.

pamper, indulge, caress, gratify, spoil, pet, humor, coddle, fondle, baby, please, satisfy, satiate. *Ant.* deny, chastise, suppress, correct, refuse, chasten, punish, spank, whip, neglect, withhold, discipline, reprimand.

pandemonium, uproar, racket, ado, din, hubbub, noise, shouting, chaos, bedlam, tumult. *Ant.* quiet, peace, silence.

pander, procure, gratify, subserve, truckle, cater, cringe, pimp. *Ant.* refuse, deny, suppress.

panegyric, praise, eulogy, tribute, encomium, commendation, citation, laudation. *Ant.* censure, blame, disdain, scorn.

panic, alarm, fright, horror, terror, dread, consternation, apprehension, dismay, awe, fear, tremor, perturbation, trepidation, nervousness. *Ant.* peace, peacefulness, quiet, tranquility, pacification, contentment, calm, placidity, repose, calmness, assurance, reassurance, hopefulness, confidence, security, trust, bravery, optimism, cheerfulness, courage, intrepidity, boldness, firmness, invincibility, nerve, pluck, dauntlessness, fearlessness, stamina, daring, stout-heartedness.

par, level, balance, equality, parity, norm, mean, standard.

parade, display, publish, flaunt, show, vaunt, expose; march, strut.

paradox, contradiction, ambiguity, absurdity, mystery, enigma, inconsistency, puzzle, perplexity.

paragon, pattern, ideal, nonpareil, standard, model, phoenix, criterion, paradigm.

paragraph, item, clause, verse, article, notice, passage, section, sentence, subdivision.

parallel, correspondent, congruent, alike, congruous, analogous, concurrent, concentric, correlative, similar, like, uniform, regular. *Ant.* irregular, crooked, sloped, distorted, skewed, diagonal, slanting, askew, oblique, zigzag, unique, different, dissimilar, unlike, divergent.

paralyze, stun, daze, benumb, deaden, demoralize, bemuse, prostrate, shock, dumbfound, unnerve, petrify, daunt, disable, cripple, incapacitate, astound. *Ant.* stimulate, vitalize, excite, revive.

paramount, supreme, eminent, all-important, chief, superior, excellent, principal, transcendent, greatest, utmost, dominant, preponderant, capital, unequaled, unsurpassed, unique, inimitable, unparalleled, foremost, peerless, culminating, matchless. *Ant.* inferior, lesser, deficient, subordinate, unimportant, least, minor, secondary, smallest, less, second-rate, commonplace, poor, trifling, paltry, trivial, ordinary, insignificant, common, normal, petty, inconsequential, meager, slight, inconsiderable, unessential, light, low, weak, worthless.

paraphernalia, equipment, accessories, apparatus, trappings, impedimenta, belongings, property, gear, accoutrements, tackle.

paraphrase, restate, explain, translate, render, interpret, rephrase, metaphrase.

parasite, sycophant, flatterer, fawner, flunky, sponger, dupe, freeloader, hanger-on, courtier, devotee, dependent, panhandler, mendicant, cadger, loafer; leech, louse, tick. *Ant.* master, leader, director, ringleader, ruler, driver, taskmaster, superior, blusterer, dictator, swaggerer, bully, tyrant, swashbuckler, daredevil, detractor, rowdy, desperado, reviler, cynic, critic, muckraker, castigator, defamer, reprover, traducer.

pardon, *n.* forgiveness, absolution, amnesty, discharge, forbearance, remission, release, exoneration, acquittal, respite, immunity, reprieve, parole, exculpation, condonation, deliverance, freedom, commutation; *v.* forgive, absolve, release, remit, exonerate, quash, reprieve, acquit, exculpate, forget, excuse, condone, overlook, wipe out, efface, liberate. *Ant.* condemnation, punishment, conviction, proscription, penalty, retaliation, vengeance, chastisement; avenge, castigate, boycott, punish, banish, censure, blame, retaliate, expel, ostracize, correct, scourge, chastise, convict, damn, imprison, sentence, transport, condemn, proscribe, doom, exile, indict.

pare, skin, strip, peel, trim, bark, decorticate, shave, flay, lessen, reduce, remove, clip, diminish, plane. *Ant.* increase, add, augment, stretch, extend, expand.

parentage, ancestry, descent, birth, extraction, line, family, parenthood, lineage, origin, pedigree, stock, race.

pariah, see **outcast.**

parley, confer, discuss, palaver, dispute, argue, converse, negotiate, debate, treat, talk.

parody, travesty, take-off, mockery, burlesque, caricature, mimicry, imitation, lampoon, spoof.

paroxysm, violence, agitation, fit, attack, spasm, outbreak, convulsion, outburst, furor, fury, tremor, quiver, seizure, throe, rage. *Ant.* tranquility, restraint, equanimity, steadiness, imperturbability, dispassion, suppression, repression, passiveness, quiet, calm, self-restraint, unconsciousness, stupefaction, inexcitability, rest, impassiveness, stupor, torpor, apathy.

parry, avoid, avert, evade, elude, dodge, fence, stall; arrest, stop, prevent, preclude, halt, obviate. *Ant.* face, meet; encourage, aid, assist, further.

parsimonious, stingy, miserly, niggardly, tight, penurious, penny-pinching, mean, scrimping, covetous, greedy, extortionate, frugal, saving, sparing, ungenerous, illiberal, shabby, grudging, grasping, mercenary, avaricious. *Ant.* prodigal, profuse, lavish, open-handed, wasteful, liberal, thriftless, generous.

part, portion, section, member, fragment, constituent, share, piece, component, division, passage, sector, item, particle, partition, segment, element, subdivision, fraction, installment, allotment, slice, dividend, morsel, cut, detachment, bit, chip, chunk, lump. *Ant.* whole, sum, all, entirety, total, aggregate, completeness, mass, embodiment, totality, amount, bulk, gross, combination, surfeit, unity, integration.

partial, unfinished, imperfect, limited; one-sided, unjust, unfair, disposed, prejudiced, biased, partisan. *Ant.* whole, finished, complete; unbiased, fair, just, impartial.

partiality, bias, unfairness, bent, liking, leaning, favoritism, preference, predilection, fondness, prejudice, one-sidedness, injustice, tendency, inclination. *Ant.* fairness, justice, honor, equality, impartiality, even-handedness.

participate, share, use, enjoy, partake, join, cooperate, mingle.

particle, atom, mite, iota, bit, jot, corpuscle, speck, scrap, shred, molecule, scintilla, whit, tittle, grain, element. *Ant.* mass, whole, quantity, entirety, lot, aggregate, sum, total.

particular, exact, specific, actual, exclusive, precise, distinct, definite, appropriate, careful, discrete, individual, scrupulous, notable, discriminating, watchful, attentive, demanding, painstaking, unbending, rigid, severe, methodical, punctilious, singular, fastidious, fussy, squeamish, finicky, meticulous, querulous, prudish, prim, straitlaced. *Ant.* general, indefinite, inexact, imprecise, ordinary, fallacious, careless, heedless, unwary, unwatchful, unguarded, reckless, imprudent, neglectful, undiscriminating, insouciant, supine, nonchalant, negligent, unmethodical, slovenly, untidy, irregular.

partisan, adherent, aide, champion, disciple, henchman, ally, assistant, supporter, follower, backer. *Ant.* leader, chief.

partition, distribution, separation, enclosure, apportionment, barrier, division, compartment, detachment, apartment, segregation, wall, fence, screen. *Ant.* juncture, conjunction, unity, connection, attachment, conjugation, union, coalescence, combination.

partner, colleague, associate, sharer, ally, confederate, accomplice, consort, spouse, participant, companion, mate.

partnership, alliance, association, company, collaboration, participation, cooperation.

party, company, troop, troupe, faction, ring, cabal, club, clique, combination, junto, set, circle, band, detachment, gang, league, group, alliance, gathering, body, soiree, levee, entertainment, assembly, reception, function.

pass

pass, *n.* thrust, lunge; course, route, opening, crossing, passageway ticket, passport, license, permit; *v.* go, proceed, move, travel, advance, expire, depart, recede, vanish, die, disappear, surpass overcome, transcend, overstep, ratify, sanction, approve, undergo ignore, skip, overlook, disregard.

passable, tolerable, endurable, adequate, acceptable, admissible, fair mediocre, middling, ordinary, so-so, allowable, penetrable, traversable, navigable. *Ant.* impassable, intolerable, unendurable unacceptable, superior, excellent, inferior, below par.

passage, corridor, gateway, hallway, arcade, aisle, channel, pass course, hall, way, road, path, avenue.

passion, intensity, emotion, desire, ardor, zeal, frenzy, lust, fervor excitement, fury, love, craving, agony, distress, ecstasy, yearning, feeling, suffering, anguish, anger.

passionate, ardent, intense, fervid, burning, vehement, extreme, fervent, feverish, earnest, impetuous, warm, excited, violent, precipitate, intemperate, quickened. *Ant.* stolid, apathetic, cool, dull impassive, phlegmatic, frigid.

passive, submissive, inactive, idle, supine, resigned, dull, cold, inert quiescent, receptive, unresisting, indifferent, quiet. *Ant.* active dynamic, live, resistant, impassive, operative.

pastoral, rural, bucolic, simple, idyllic, arcadian, provincial, georgic rustic. *Ant.* urban, suburban.

patch, mend, restore, repair, correct, remodel, rebuild, remedy, revamp, amend, fix, renew. *Ant.* damage, rip, dent, smash, tear break, crack, injure, impair, ravage.

patent, plain, manifest, open, obvious, clear, evident, apparent public, conspicuous, indisputable, unconcealed, unmistakable *Ant.* hidden, obscure, concealed, covered.

path, sidewalk, pathway, footway, runway, track, trail, lane, route avenue, course, passage, access.

pathetic, touching, sad, plaintive, heartrending, distressing, pitiful, poignant, affecting, moving. *Ant.* cheering, joyful, happy.

patience, resignation, fortitude, endurance, forbearance, composure calmness, submission, sufferance, long-suffering, tolerance, diligence, passivity, leniency, moderation, perseverance, persistence constancy, equanimity, poise, imperturbability. *Ant.* impatience uneasiness, restlessness, excitability, petulance, excitement, disquietude, fretfulness, perturbation, hurry, rage, fuss, flurry, passion, fluster, anger.

patient, passive, composed, long-suffering, submissive, cool, calm, quiet, meek, lenient, enduring, serene, imperturbable, unruffled placid, resigned, dispassionate, easygoing, grave, kindly, gentle philosophic, unimpassioned, tolerant. *Ant.* impatient, vehement, excitable, irritable, boisterous, fidgety, flustered, hotheaded, fiery, feverish, clamorous, hysterical, rampant, turbulent, nervous, ungovernable, chafing, irrepressible, furious, raging, high-strung hasty, violent, passionate.

patron, benefactor, encourager, advocate, helper, upholder, defender, protector, supporter, guide, contributor, backer, guardian, ally, leader, champion, friend, well-wisher, sympathizer, partisan, employer, customer, buyer, client, purchaser. *Ant.* enemy, detractor, opponent, adversary, foe, traitor, assailant, competitor, rival, seller, antagonist, contender, disputant, vendor, salesman, preemptor.

pattern, model, exemplar, prototype, standard, ideal, paragon, mold, conformation, plan, outline, archetype, norm, sample, guide, blueprint, paradigm.

paucity, sparseness, scantiness, dearth, scarcity, fewness, smallness, rarity, lack, need, insufficiency, poverty. *Ant.* plenty, abundance, profusion, affluence, wealth.

pauperism, poverty, penury, indigence, beggary, destitution, privation, paucity, deficiency, need, want. *Ant.* wealth, plenty, luxury, affluence, opulence, solvency, independence.

pause, rest, cessation, stop, halt, intermission, suspension, hesitation, delay, wait, discontinuance, truce, stay, hitch, respite, lull, interregnum, standstill, deadlock, inaction, hiatus, waiver, stillness, break, interlude, interruption, recess. *Ant.* continuance, persistence, constancy, incessancy, prolongation, repetition, extension, continuity, progression.

pay, *n.* compensation, reward, recompense, salary, payment, wages, remuneration, commission, royalty, subsidy, fee, earnings, allowance, stipend, honorarium, indemnity, acknowledgment, retribution, reparation, atonement, redress, meed, emolument, perquisite, tribute, consideration, defrayment, satisfaction, reciprocation, recokoning, clearance, settlement, liquidation; *v.* compensate, expend, reward, defray, recompense, offer, punish, remunerate, liquidate, discharge, refund, settle, reimburse. *Ant.* penalty, fine, confiscation, amercement, damages, seizure, forfeiture, forfeit, execution, default, nonpayment, failure, repudiation, insolvency, dispersion, expense, disbursement, distribution, bankruptcy, expenditure, outlay, waste; cheat, victimize, defraud, bilk, circumvent, swindle, overreach, embezzle, steal.

peace, calm, order, repose, pacification, conciliation, concord, harmony, quiet, amity, composure, accord, pacifism, contentment, agreement, unanimity, equanimity, concordance, silence, congeniality, stillness, armistice. *Ant.* discord, dissension, disruption, variance, division, disunion, difference, split, rupture, fight, fracas, riot, scrimmage, disturbance, disagreement, battle, enmity, contention, skirmish, anger, conflict, sound, clamor, roar, racket, uproar, clatter, noise, belligerency, war, warfare.

peaceful, calm, quiet, serene, undisturbed, complacent, mellow, composed, unruffled, gentle, placid, tranquil, mild, pacific, still. *Ant.* turbulent, violent, perturbed, noisy, upset, agitated.

peak, top, spire, acme, zenith, apex, pinnacle, crest, summit, arete, high point. *Ant.* bottom, nadir, lowest point, base, abyss.

peculate, embezzle, steal, cheat, deceive, defraud, rob, purloin, pilfer, appropriate.

peculiar, particular, especial, characteristic, proper, specific, singular, indigenous, individual, uncommon, distinctive, odd, queer strange, abnormal, bizarre, eccentric, idiosyncratic, unusual. *Ant* common, regular, usual, normal.

peculiarity, feature, singularity, idiosyncrasy, eccentricity, oddity irregularity. *Ant.* normality, regularity, uniformity, usualness.

pecuniary, monetary, financial, fiscal, nummular.

pedantic, scholarly, professorial, learned, scholastic, bookish, conceited, fussy, officious, ostentatious, showy, precise, pompous particular, affected, impractical, stuffy, dry, dull, tedious, stilted *Ant.* clear, practical, concise, short, simple, interesting, lively.

pedigree, genealogy, family, ancestry, descent, heritage, race, line stock, patrimony, breed, descent.

peer, equal, fellow, colleague, companion, mate, match, compeer; nobleman, lord, knight, aristocrat. *Ant.* commoner, inferior superior.

peerless, unequaled, perfect, nonpareil, supreme, glorious, unique best, transcendent, unrivaled, inimitable, unexampled, superior indomitable, maximum, paramount, preeminent, matchless, prime, superlative, exquisite, outstanding, priceless, faultless, incomparable, transcendental. *Ant.* inferior, subordinate, imperfect secondary, unimportant, common, minor, commonplace, secondrate, ordinary, petty, worthless, inconsiderable, deficient, defective, faulty, mediocre. obscure, indifferent, unknown, average, valueless, inadequate, deteriorated, worn-out, useless.

peevish, fretful, perverse, fretting, obstinate, captious, acrimonious, cantankerous, cross, ill-natured, ill-humored, pessimistic, critical, grumbling, faultfinding, growling, repining, censorious, irascible, splenetic, irritable, ungracious, uncivil, grouchy, gruff, fractious, touchy, petulant, fidgety, thin-skinned, querulous, morose, sullen, moody, sulky. *Ant.* courteous, amiable, kind, agreeable, gentle, pleasant, civil, polite, good-mannered, well-behaved, refined, winning, gentlemanly, winsome, unctuous, mild, bland, complaisant, soft-spoken, mannerly, complacent, benevolent, affable, well-bred, polished, sympathetic, gracious, cordial, conciliatory, captivating, good-humored, charming, engaging, attractive, soothing.

pejorative, disparaging, declining, degrading, deprecatory, opprobious. *Ant.* elevating, complimentary, flattering.

pellucid, limpid, crystalline, translucent, lucid, transparent, pure, bright, clear. *Ant.* turbid, muddy, roiled, dark, opaque.

pelt, beat, strike, hit, batter, throw, cast, hurl, assail, rattle, smack, spank, whip.

penalize, punish, mulct, fine, discipline, chasten, handicap. *Ant.* reward, pay, praise.

penalty, punishment, disadvantage, forfeit, damages, fine, handicap. *Ant.* reward, prize, pay, benefit, medal, forgiveness, pardon.

penchant, leaning, tendency, bias, inclination, fondness, liking, taste, prediliction, yearning, hankering, desire, need, want, urge, proclivity, propensity, proneness, flair, knack, prejudice. *Ant.* unconcern, dislike, aversion, antipathy.

penetrate, bore, pierce, perforate, infiltrate, enter, permeate, insert, pervade, probe, invade, entrench, encroach, interfere, trespass, puncture, burrow, touch, affect, impress, excite. *Ant.* withdraw, exit, vacate, recede, evacuate, emerge, exude, recede, depart, retreat, slump, misinterpret, misconstrue, miscomprehend, doubt, misapprehend.

penetrating, sharp, acute, pointed, keen, shrewd, piercing, astute, subtle, sagacious, discriminating, boring, wide-awake, quick, farseeing, clever, clearheaded, trenchant, critical, farsighted, canny, incisive, discerning. *Ant.* dull, heavy, inept, stupid, silly, obtuse, shallow, fatuous, thick, idiotic, blunt, foolish, muddled, stolid, confused, doltish, asinine, senseless, nonsensical.

penetration, entrance, infiltration, discernment, ingress, insertion, invasion, discrimination, acuteness, comprehension, perception, intelligence, understanding, judgment, capacity, sagacity, grasp, acumen, subtlety, perspicacity. *Ant.* egression, emergence, exit, emanation, evacuation, indiscrimination, lethargy, shallowness, incapacity, dullness, shortsightedness, simplicity, ineptitude, incomprehensibility.

penitence, contrition, remorse, regret, suffering, atonement, mortification, compunction, qualms, repentance, sorrow. *Ant.* obduracy, impenitence, contumacy, rejoicing, joy.

pensive, thoughtful, speculative, solemn, grave, musing, reflective, contemplative, meditative, melancholy, serious, dejected. *Ant.* careless, happy, active, unconcerned.

penurious, miserly, stingy, close, mean, parsimonious, ungenerous, sordid, greedy, sparing, saving, grasping, avaricious, covetous, indigent, mercenary, cheap. *Ant.* generous, liberal, charitable, philanthropic, unstinting, bountiful, prodigal, wasteful.

penury, indigence, privation, poverty, destitution, need, lack, want, distress. *Ant.* luxury, abundance, plenty, opulence, affluence, wealth, solvency.

people, persons, humanity, mankind, human race, populace, individuals, population, inhabitants, community, public, tribe, nation, state, multitude, crowd, commonwealth, mass, mob, herd, folk, residents, mortals, clan, family, kin, generation, society.

pep, zest, energy, keenness, fervor, initiative, vim, gusto, vitality, enthusiasm, spirit, animation, vigor, liveliness. *Ant.* languor, apathy, lethargy, lassitude, sloth, torpor.

perceive, note, sense, observe, comprehend, conceive, discern, distinguish, appreciate, notice, espy, understand, apprehend, see, realize, discover, descry, recognize. *Ant.* mistake, misunderstand, misconceive, misjudge, overlook, misapprehend, confuse, jumble, muddle, ignore, miss, lose.

perceptible, visible, tangible, discernable, perceivable, sensible, palpable, ponderable, appreciable, noticeable, apparent, touchable, audible. *Ant.* imperceptible, inaudible, silent, invisible, obscure, impalpable.

perception, apprehension, discernment, cognizance, sensation, recognition, insight, feeling, acumen, sharpness, keenness, acuteness.

percolate, seep, ooze, filter, permeate, strain, brew, exude, drip, trickle.

percussion, collision, concussion, shock, encounter, impingement, jar, jolt, clash, impact.

perdition, destruction, defeat, loss, downfall, overthrow, wreckage, failure, ruin, Hell, Hades, Gehenna, damnation. *Ant.* success, victory, happiness, salvation, Heaven, Paradise, eternal joy, blessedness.

peremptory, imperative, arbitrary, harsh, assertive, absolute, overbearing, authoritative, dictatorial, decisive, firm, domineering, certain, conclusive, compulsory, dogmatic, final, rigorous, dominant, stringent, imperious, commanding, strict, uncompromising, stern, positive, rigid, coercive, oppressive, inexorable, unsparing, relentless, inflexible, exacting, tyrannical, austere, insistent, unmistakable, determined, emphatic, binding, obligatory, distinct, compelling, explicit, express, precise, unavoidable. *Ant.* mild, indulgent, lenitive, clement, moderate, easygoing, tolerant, lax, compassionate, loose, slack, careless, weak, feeble, wavering, light, uncertain, inconclusive, unexacting, indeterminate, irresolute, indecisive, fluctuating, negligible, hesitating, vacillating, indefinite, half-hearted, optional, discretionary, inconsistent.

perennial, enduring, constant, continual, unfailing, perpetual, recurrent, consecutive, successive, incessant, stable, long-lived, imperishable, eternal, immortal, endless, permanent, lasting, ceaseless, persistent, everlasting. *Ant.* fleeting, fugitive, temporary, inconstant, annual, mortal, transient, evanescent.

perfect, complete, consummate, thorough, conclusive, faultless, unblemished, crowning, flawless, prime, uninjured, impeccable, immaculate, intact, spotless, culminating, absolute, august, plenary, grand, full, dignified, unqualified, sublime, supreme, ideal. *Ant.* imperfect, flawed, deficient, unfinished, incomplete, defective, wanting, lacking, short, mutilated, damaged, spoiled, faulty, middling, stained, mediocre, spotted, tainted, inferior, secondary, second-rate, worthless, useless, corrupt, deformed, ruined.

perfidious, treacherous, traitorous, false, untrustworthy, deceitful, venal, disloyal, faithless. *Ant.* loyal, faithful, true.

perforate, pierce, bore, permeate, punch, puncture, drill, prick.

perform, do, act, play, effect, conduct, achieve, fulfill, execute, complete, accomplish. *Ant.* fail, neglect, rest, loaf, refrain.

performance, accomplishment, achievement, completion, action, deed, stunt, production, fulfillment, exploit, feat, entertainment, consummation, show, turn. *Ant.* failure, incompletion, defeat.

perfume, scent, fragrance, aroma, redolence, cologne, attar, sachet, incense.

perfunctory, indifferent, half-hearted, reckless, thoughtless, careless, negligent, slovenly, heedless, superficial, hasty. *Ant.* careful, serious, concerned, detailed, precise, fussy, diligent, thoughtful.

perhaps, possibly, peradventure, maybe, mayhap, perchance, haply, probably, conceivably. *Ant.* incredibly, improbably, untruly, impossibly, unlikely, certainly, definitely.

peril, danger, jeopardy, pitfall, hazard, snare, exposure, risk, insecurity, menace, threat, liability, apprehension. *Ant.* safety, protection, safekeeping, impregnability, security.

perimeter, circumference, girth, periphery, circuit, ambit, compass, border, edge, boundary. *Ant.* center, heart, core, hub, middle, midst.

period, epoch, term, age, duration, era, cycle, limit, circuit, lifetime, interval, spell, season, generation, semester.

periodical, regular, intermittent, cyclic, recurrent, alternate, serial, recurring, occasional, incidental. *Ant.* irregular, uncertain, fitful, sporadic, erratic, variable, capricious, anomalous, unsystematic, constant, perpetual, continuing, lasting, permanent.

periphery, see **perimeter.**

perish, die, expire, waste, fade, pass away, wither, decease, vanish, decay, shrivel. *Ant.* last, endure, continue, live, thrive.

perjure, forswear, recant, abjure, disavow, deceive, lie, prevaricate. *Ant.* attest, certify, prove.

permanent, durable, constant, unchangeable, lasting, unchanging, abiding, indelible, enduring, persistent, perpetual, irremovable, indestructible, everlasting, imperishable, chronic, continual, unalterable, established, fixed, immutable, confirmed, ineradicable, habitual, customary, invariable, unfailing, invariant, stable, steadfast. *Ant.* fleeting, short, evanescent, brief, passing, changing, changeable, transitory, uncertain, fugitive, temporary, momentary, unstable, ephemeral, temporal, transient, short-lived, impermanent, inconstant, unsettled, variable, erratic, mutable, fitful, alternating, spasmodic, vacillating, fluctuating, unsteady, alterable, capricious.

permeate, saturate, steep, soak, pervade, penetrate, infiltrate, infuse, imbue, ingrain, drench, impregnate.

permission, leave, permit, liberty, allowance, consent, license, law, enfranchisement, authority, toleration, tolerance, authorization, dispensation, warranty, grace. *Ant.* prohibition, injunction, inhibition, proscription, restraint, debarment, interdiction, embargo, opposition, circumscription, veto, refusal, taboo, exclusion, restriction, hindrance.

permit, *v.* allow, let, authorize, admit, empower, grant, tolerate, concede, endure, recognize, accord, approve, endorse, enfranchise, sanction; *n.* law, license, permission, warrant, pass, passport, charter, patent. *Ant.* forbid, prohibit, prevent, enjoin, disallow, deny, refuse, interdict, inhibit, oppose, restrict, stop, preclude, restrain, veto, exclude, bar, debar; interdiction, injunction, inhibition, embargo, ban, restriction, prevention, proscription.

pernicious, destructive, deadly, hurtful, evil, noxious, malevolent, wicked, virulent, ruinous, harmful, injurious, detrimental, deleterious, malign, prejudicial, lethal, venomous, dire, damnable, grievous, toxic. *Ant.* good, healthy, salubrious, invigorating, innocuous, wholesome, hygienic, pure, restorative, helpful, advantageous, harmless, inoffensive, beneficial, propitious, profitable, benign, favorable, unobjectionable, salutary, tonic, remedial, curative, healing, therapeutic, useful, serviceable, efficacious.

perpendicular, vertical, upright, plumb, erect, upstanding. *Ant.* horizontal, level, slanting, oblique.

perpetrate, commit, do, inflict, enact, execute, accomplish.

perpetual, continual, incessant, uninterrupted, constant, lasting, unceasing, permanent, illimitable, interminable, everlasting, enduring, continuing, infinite, eternal, endless, ceaseless, imperishable, undying, immortal. *Ant.* momentary, brief, fleeting, short, transient, temporary, inconstant, passing, fugitive, ephemeral, evanescent, transitory, impermanent, short-lived.

perplex, puzzle, confound, mystify, bewilder, baffle, complicate, snarl, involve, worry, annoy, trouble, entangle, nonplus, confuse, mislead, fluster. *Ant.* clarify, disencumber, assure, convince, inform, please, satisfy, enlighten, acquaint.

perplexity, doubt, distraction, bewilderment, embarrassment, disturbance, astonishment, amazement, confusion, intricacy, error, uncertainty, doubtfulness, dilemma, suspense, wonder, quandary, contingency, predicament, emergency, crisis, exigency. *Ant.* certainty, sureness, disentanglement, feasibility, assurance, intelligibility, understanding, sense, lucidity, enlightenment, precision.

perquisite, privilege, prerogative, birthright, due, right; reward, gratuity, bribe, bonus, tip.

persecute, oppress, annoy, victimize, torment, harass, abuse, afflict, inflict, worry, aggrieve, bother, tease, vex, trouble, maltreat, chastise, torture, punish, castigate, imprison, scourge, pester, badger, irritate, provoke, roil, rile, gall, enrage, plague, crush, banish. *Ant.* reward, recompense, protect, remunerate, recommend, serve, please, benefit, gratify, comfort, aid, satisfy, support, gladden, refresh, help, sustain, indulge, assist, nourish, accommodate, nurture, cheer, oblige, encourage, patronize, endorse, approve, relieve, inspirit, soothe, enliven, console, solace, assuage, stimulate.

perseverance, steadfastness, constancy, persistence, tenacity, effort, application, firmness, push, indefatigability, perpetuation, continuance, pursuance, continuation, endurance, resolution, determination, stamina, doggedness. *Ant.* slothfulness, inactivity, idleness, languor, torpidity, otiosity, irresolution, indolence, sluggishness, ennui, stupor, lethargy, cessation, stoppage, suspension, laziness, rest.

persiflage, banter, jesting, frivolity, badinage, raillery, chaffing, pleasantry, flippancy.

personality, character, ego, temperament, individuality, identity, self; notable, celebrity.

perspicacious, penetrating, discerning, discriminating, astute, acute, shrewd, sharp, keen, sharp-witted, clear-sighted.

perspicuity, clearness, distinctness, lucidity, plainness, explicitness, clarity, intelligibility, preciseness. *Ant.* obscurity, vagueness, unintelligibility, incomprehensibility, uncertainty, perplexity, mystification, confusion, intricacy, complexity.

persuade, coax, entice, urge, allure, impel, lead, influence, incite, move, wheedle, exhort, prompt, instigate, lure, inspire, bribe, induce, provoke, arouse, actuate, inspirit, stimulate, rouse, reason, inveigle, cajole, satisfy, assure, convince. *Ant.* dissuade, restrain, discourage, remonstrate, curb, dishearten, check, deter, prevent, dampen, repress, hinder, stop, suppress, constrain, restrict, prohibit, divert, admonish, dispirit, depress, frighten, terrify.

pert, bold, rude, presumptuous, impudent, forward, brisk, obtrusive, impertinent, saucy, smart, lively, sprightly. *Ant.* bashful, shy, demure, modest, diffident, humble, unobtrusive.

pertinacious, tenacious, constant, unyielding, obstinate, persevering, resolute, firm, headstrong, persistent, dogged, inflexible, stubborn. *Ant.* tractable, flexible.

pertinent, relevant, apropos, appropriate, fit, germane, fitting, relating, apt, suited, proper, applicable. *Ant.* irrelevant, improper, unsuited.

perturbation, trepidation, disorganization, worry, excitation, agitation, derangement, effervescence, excitement, disorder, turmoil, tumult, disturbance, ado, alarm, disquiet, commotion, flurry, confusion, distraction, fluster, consternation. *Ant.* peace, quietness, tranquility, dispassion, calmness, composure, silence.

pervade, diffuse, affect, penetrate, impenetrate, impregnate, fill, overspread, permeate, saturate, extend, spread, infiltrate, imbue.

perverse, obstinate, contrary, reactionary, stubborn, unyielding, wayward, contumacious, forward, ungovernable, fractious, seditious, willful, obdurate, self-willed, irascible, resolute, sullen, intractable, sulky, dogged, petulant, ill-tempered, cross, troublesome, cantankerous, querulous, splenetic, contentious, grouchy, quarrelsome, vexatious, faultfinding, cranky, headstrong. *Ant.* tractable, gentle, docile, irresolute, mild, yielding, amenable, accommodating, genial, complacent, soft, willing, capricious, changeable, obedient, agreeable, conformable, cooperative, harmonious, acquiescent, condescending, pliant, assenting, compliant, conceding, consenting, submissive, manageable, governable, shy, wavering, timid, timorous.

pessimistic, gloomy, blue, foreboding, cynical, depressed, despairing, despondent, misanthropic. *Ant.* bright, assured, enthusiastic, optimistic, hopeful, sanguine, confident.

pester, harass, bait, harry, molest, torment, annoy, tease, disturb, vex, chafe, provoke, heckle, fret, bother, badger, plague, trouble. *Ant.* please, divert, delight, entertain.

pestilential, infectious, malignant, noxious, contagious, destructive, communicable, virulent, contaminating, venomous, poisonous, pernicious, deleterious, deadly, septic, toxic, epidemic, endemic, pandemic. *Ant.* wholesome, hygienic, healthful, salubrious, sanitary innocuous, uninfectious, healthy, beneficial, advantageous.

petition, appeal, entreaty, application, request, prayer, supplication requisition, invocation, proposal, solicitation.

petrify, lapidify, fossilize, ossify, calcify, mineralize, harden, deaden benumb, amaze, stupefy, paralyze, astonish, astound, confound dumbfound, stun, frighten, shock.

petty, small, puny, trivial, insignificant, trifling, lesser, poor, nugatory, negligible, weak, mean, ignoble, childish, meager, puerile paltry, contemptible, frivolous, little, shallow, slight, worthless unimportant, cheap, miserable, tawdry, beggarly, trashy, shabby. *Ant.* important, leading, significant, salient, prominent, generous, beneficial, profitable, useful, necessary, salutary, principal, valuable, advantageous, essential, serious, vital, commanding, consequential, absorbing, impressive, paramount, worthy, eminent, remarkable, foremost, considerable, broad-minded, extraordinary.

petulant, peevish, fretful, ill-humored, cranky, cross, querulous, irritable, touchy. *Ant.* temperate, pleasant, congenial, good-natured.

phantom, ghost, shade, specter, apparition, vision, illusion, spook, revenant, wraith, phantasm.

phenomenon, manifestation, occurrence, event, prodigy, marvel, object, wonder, thing, incident, emanation, miracle, circumstance, anomaly, paradox.

philanthropic, kind, benevolent, humanitarian, considerate, generous, eleemosynary, liberal, loving, gracious, chivalrous, cosmopolitan humane, good, helpful, charitable, beneficent, benignant, munificent, altruistic, sympathetic, friendly, compassionate. *Ant.* misanthropic, egotistical, antisocial, selfish, cynical, morose, grouchy, merciless, pitiless, harsh, hard-hearted, cruel, miserly, stingy tyrannical, parsimonious, oppressive, sordid, penurious, beggarly, unpitying, greedy.

philosophical, calm, rational, imperturbable, contemplative, deliberative, unmoved, reflective, studious, staid, steady, stoical, tranquil, tolerant, wise, prudent, considerate, sagacious, judicious, sensible. *Ant.* imprudent, rash, precipitate, headlong, thoughtless, shallow, careless, irrational, unphilosophical, injudicious, inconsistent, frivolous, narrow-minded, unreasonable, fatuous.

phlegmatic, dull, indifferent, lethargic, impassive, unemotional, inert, incurious, stoical, cold, sluggish, inexcitable, stolid, slow, apathetic, languid, dispassionate. *Ant.* lively, quick, keen, acute, sharp, eager, aggressive, excitable, restless, passionate, fiery, demonstrative, hot-headed, enthusiastic, urgent, turbulent, tempestuous, uproarious, boisterous, assertive, self-assertive, domineering, impetuous.

phobia, fear, aversion, dread, dislike, distaste, hatred. *Ant.* liking, love, attraction, tolerance, endurance.

phraseology, language, expression, speech, vocabulary, diction, style, phrasing.

232

physical, material, natural, corporeal, visible, tangible, substantial, sensible, bodily, somatic, palpable, carnal, materialistic, real, anatomical, mortal. *Ant.* immaterial, incorporeal, insubstantial, spiritual, mental, ethereal, intellectual, subjective, metaphysical, psychical, psychological, discarnate, disembodied, intangible, asomatous, abstract, moral, imaginary, visionary, unreal, fanciful, ideal, dreamy, ghostly.

pick, select, choose, gather, cull, take, prefer, single, acquire, get, gather. *Ant.* reject, refuse, decline.

picturesque, artistic, pictorial, quaint, beautiful, graphic, scenic, attractive, compelling, pleasing, lucid, vivid, bright, striking, lively, intense, charming, clear, alluring, elegant, pretty, aesthetic. *Ant.* ugly, repulsive, ungainly, repellent, forbidding, grim, squalid, dingy, distorted, inartistic, unsightly, unseemly, coarse, misshapen, hideous.

piece, *n.* part, bit, segment, shred, chunk, portion, fragment, section, morsel, fraction, hunk, scrap; *v.* combine, repair, unite, patch. *Ant.* whole, entire, all.

piercing, shrill, keen, biting, cutting, high, piquant, acute, sharp, deafening, penetrating, ear-splitting, perforating, boring, stabbing, harsh, strident, cacophonous, metallic, discordant, cold, chilling, freezing, thrilling, exciting. *Ant.* soft, low, modulated, faint, stifled, muffled, whispered, soothing, lulling, gentle, mute, melodious, soundless, nonresonant, silent, inaudible, dull, warm, undiscerning.

pile, *n.* stack, heap, collection, mass, load, bank, structure, building; *v.* load, amass, assemble, heap, furnish, accumulate.

pillage, damage, spoliation, desecration, robbery, devastation, plundering, destruction, looting, depredation, confiscation. *Ant.* restitution, restoration, recompense, satisfaction, remuneration, return, amends, indemnification, reparation, replacement, requital, retribution, repayment, expiation, indemnity, reimbursement, refund, recoupment, redress.

pinch, crisis, difficulty, strain, plight, emergency, pressure, plight, predicament, stress, vicissitude. *Ant.* good fortune, ease, prosperity.

pine, *n.* tree, shrub; *v.* droop, flag, yearn, long, want, wish, desire, languish, waste, grieve, decline, decay.

pinnacle, peak, culmination, top, zenith, summit, apex, climax, acme. *Ant.* bottom, base, foot, depths, nadir.

pious, religious, devotional, pure, reverent, righteous, holy, devout, godly, saintly, spiritual, saintlike, dedicated, prayerful, sanctified, sacred, solemn, seraphic, consecrated, unworldly. *Ant.* impious, blasphemous, irreverent, wicked, sacrilegious, evil, sinful, profane, perverted, defiled, unhallowed, unholy, irreligious, hypocritical.

piquant, spirited, charming, clever, racy, interesting, lively, sparkling, smart, bright, sharp, stimulating, savory, pungent, high-flavored, biting, strong, keen, tart, spicy, trenchant, impressive, incisive, caustic. *Ant.* unsavory, insipid, unpalatable, tasteless, flat, sweet, cloying, nauseating, prosaic, dull, vapid, dry, monotonous, languid, mawkish.

pitiful, doleful, mournful, sorrowful, wretched, miserable, piteous, sad, distressing, woeful, rueful, lamentable, distressed, deplorable, pathetic, mean, disreputable, abject, base, low, vile, contemptible; merciful, compassionate, tender, sympathetic. *Ant.* exalted, superb, beneficent, mighty, dignified, superior, sublime, grand, commanding, noble, august.

pitiless, merciless, unfeeling, malevolent, hard-hearted, revengeful, ruthless, obdurate, incompassionate, unpitying, unmerciful, relentless, inclement, unconcerned, callous, inexorable, tyrannical, unkind, rigorous, austere, spiteful, harsh, unfeeling, cruel, cold-blooded, savage, ferocious, truculent, diabolical, atrocious, fiendish, barbarous, bloodthirsty. *Ant.* merciful, kind, benevolent, indulgent, charitable, compassionate, sympathetic, warm-hearted, gentle, cordial, philanthropic, bountiful, kindhearted, beneficent, unselfish, good-natured, soft-hearted, amiable, tender, considerate, tender-hearted, humane, altruistic, friendly, bounteous, well-intentioned, clement, benignant, comforting, kindly.

pity, compassion, sympathy, kindness, charity, philanthropy, tenderness, lamentation, empathy, condolence, commiseration, clemency, mercy. *Ant.* severity, malevolence, hard-heartedness, harshness, mercilessness, truculence, ruthlessness, ferocity, cruelty, brutality, vindictiveness, sternness, revenge, vengeance, inhumanity, barbarity.

place, *n.* locality, point, situation, site, post, premises, spot, station, position, area, quarters, abode, region, section, residence, dwelling, home, habitation, encampment; *v.* put, set, arrange, lay, allocate, locate, group, dispose, assign, allot, distribute, deposit, install, plant, store, lodge, stow, invest. *Ant.* displace, misplace, remove, disestablish, dislodge, empty, disarrange, unload, discompose, disorganize, dismiss, disturb, unsettle, eject, jumble, shuffle.

placid, quiet, gentle, equable, unmoved, undisturbed, calm, serene, tranquil, unruffled, peaceful. *Ant.* agitated, disturbed, excited.

plain, open, obvious, perceptible, evident, clear, exposed, manifest, visible, conspicuous, distinct, simple, discernible, apparent, notable, definite, recognizable, unmistakable, indubitable, explicit, patent, intelligible, comprehensible, lucid, unequivocal, severe, neat, unadorned, undisguised, level, flat, even, smooth. *Ant.* complex, obscure, intricate, difficult, complicated, enigmatical, unintelligible, puzzling, illegible, inscrutable, cryptic, cloudy, mystical, occult, hazy, incomprehensible, indistinct, imperceptible, latent, unperceivable, hidden, concealed, involved, esoteric, mysterious, cabalistic, impenetrable, secret, profound.

plaintive, melancholy, doleful, grievous, sorrowful, sad, mournful, lugubrious, wistful, pathetic, woeful. *Ant.* rejoicing, happy, gay.

plan, *n.* arrangement, design, drawing, sketch, blueprint, diagram, chart, draft, delineation, map, project, view, plot, proposal, outline, model, prospectus, proposition, policy, method, device, contrivance, program; *v.* devise, delineate, shape, depict, outline, sketch, design, represent, map, illustrate, chart, conspire, invent, prepare, scheme, contrive, plot, draft.

plant, *n.* factory, mill, shop, complex, distillery, refinery, foundry, establishment, works; flower, vegetable, herb, tree, organism, shrub, vine, bush, sprout, shoot; *v.* place, put, implant, set, sow, bed, transplant.

plastic, ductile, formable, impressible, resilient, pliant, flexible, malleable. *Ant.* hard, rigid, brittle, stiff.

platitude, banality, truism, nonsense, cliché, commonplace, inanity, bromide, flatness, triteness.

plausible, credible, acceptable, probable, reasonable, defensible, justifiable, likely, believable, specious. *Ant.* implausible, unlikely, incredible.

playful, sportive, gay, jolly, frisky, prankish, sprightly, roguish, lively, frolicsome, mischievous. *Ant.* dull, morose, listless, sullen, humorless, sedate.

plead, implore, argue, beseech, beg, advocate, entreat, ask, urge, request, solicit, press, petition, appeal, crave, supplicate.

pleasant, agreeable, pleasing, enjoyable, enlivening, obliging, pleasurable, kind, attractive, good-natured, welcome, cordial, refreshing, acceptable, glad, delectable, engaging, winning, enticing, fascinating, captivating, good-humored, gay, lively, humorous, amusing, merry, sportive, witty, charming, jovial, jolly, frolicsome, entertaining, diverting, flattering, comforting. *Ant.* dull, unpleasant, disagreeable, painful, irritating, vexing, annoying, disturbing, hurtful, sorrowful, disquieting, displeasing, bothersome, saddening, troublesome, mortifying, harassing, distressing, tormenting, unsatisfactory, exasperating, glum, ill-humored, unkind, arrogant, harsh, cruel, offensive, repellent, hateful, afflicting, gloomy, mournful, deplorable, bitter, unwelcome, undesirable, depressing, melancholy, forbidding, dismal, dreary, woeful, grim, rueful, comfortless, grievous, pitiful, irksome, dreadful, fearful, dire.

pleasantry, banter, joke, sport, jollity, badinage, merriment, humor, jest, witticism, drollery, facetiousness, raillery.

pleasure, gratification, enjoyment, satisfaction, indulgence, delight, joy, gladness, happiness, rapture, ecstasy, diversion, entertainment, exhilaration, felicity, contentment, bliss. *Ant.* displeasure, sorrow, woe, grief, suffering, dissatisfaction, uneasiness, pain, vexation, affliction, grievance, anguish, disappointment, despair, tribulation, hopelessness, misery, wretchedness, desolation, care, burden, anxiety, responsibility, discontent, distress, mortification, adversity, trouble, unhappiness.

plebian, common, mean, ordinary, base, unrefined, coarse, ignoble, commonplace, vulgar, lowborn, obscure. *Ant.* aristocratic, high born, elevated, wealthy, noble, patrician.

pledge, *n.* guarantee, vow, promise, contract, affirmation, bond, oath troth; candidate; *v.* hypothecate, deposit, wage, engage, vow promise, guarantee.

plentiful, abundant, copious, ample, profuse, lavish, full, sufficient adequate, enough, liberal, unsparing, replete, plethoric, luxuriant rich, overflowing, inexhaustible, teeming, complete, bountiful generous, large, exuberant, affluent, bounteous. *Ant.* scarce, insufficient, deficient, scant, scanty, exhausted, impoverished, sparing, stingy, inadequate, drained, poor, skimpy, depleted, denuded stripped, lacking, sparse.

pleonasm, wordiness, verbosity, verbiage, diffuseness, repetition tautology, redundancy, circumlocution. *Ant.* terseness, curtness plainness, succinctness, condensation, directness.

pliable, flexible, pliant, adjustable, wavering, lithe, limber, docile ductile, manageable, supple, tractable, yielding, compliant, adaptable. *Ant.* rigid, unyielding, stiff, rigorous, intractable.

plot, see **plan.**

plumb, perpendicular, upright, vertical, straight, square. *Ant.* flat, horizontal, level, oblique, slanting.

plump, fleshy, portly, chubby, round, fat, obese, stout, corpulent buxom, puffy, swollen. *Ant.* lean, thin, emaciated, puny, spindly, skeletal, shrunken, spare, withered, wrinkled, wasted, shriveled attenuated, atrophied.

plunder, see **pillage.**

plush, luxurious, sybaritic, affluent, sumptuous, rich, elegant, prodigal. *Ant.* wretched, miserable, poor, scanty.

poignant, keen, piercing, distressing, penetrating, acute, pungent biting, sharp, intense, bitter, painful, trenchant. *Ant.* dull, blunt, obtuse, numb, insipid, painless, easy, pleasant.

point, *n.* tip, end, prong, peak, apex, acme, promontory, summit, part, place, location, position, goal, meaning, gist, intent, juncture, significance, suggestion, characteristic, trait, object, purpose; *v.* aim, direct, sharpen, level, indicate, designate, show, punctuate.

poisonous, toxic, noxious, harmful, dangerous, malignant, virulent, venomous, vicious, corrupt, deleterious, noisome, morbid, evil, bad, fatal, pestilential, deadly, destructive. *Ant.* good, healthful, invigorating, stimulating, salubrious, wholesome, nourishing, tonic, sanitary, hygienic, preservative, curative, innocuous, harmless.

policy, plan, strategy, tactic, contract, system, course, platform, plank, scheme, outline, handling, management.

polish, *n.* gloss, smoothness, finish, luster, glaze, sheen, glossiness, elegance, politeness, courtesy, culture, grace, breeding, training, refinement, tact, suavity, skill, art; *v.* burnish, smooth, rub, wax, refinish, brighten, shine, refine, civilize, train, discipline. *Ant.* roughen, mar, spoil, neglect, dull, debase, deface, ruin.

olite, civil, courteous, genteel, polished, refined, well-bred, urbane, accomplished, amiable, tactful, decorous, mannerly, attentive, obliging, cultivated, affable, agreeable, chivalrous, gallant, well-behaved, courtly, cordial, diplomatic, obsequious. *Ant.* rude, uncivil, rough, gruff, unmannerly, discourteous, ill-bred, abusive, ungracious, impudent, brusque, coarse, opprobrious, obscene, low, offensive.

olitic, cunning, discreet, diplomatic, wary, judicious, wise, adroit, foxy, sagacious, provident, prudent, expedient strategic, tricky, wily, watchful, calculating, sapient, sage, crafty, subtle, artful, intriguing, designing, Machiavellian, unscrupulous, shifty, deceptive, shrewd, sharp, astute, acute, canny. *Ant.* dull, stolid, stupid, blundering, simple, unsophisticated, blunt, slow, shallow, obtuse, ingenuous, sincere, honest, candid, unreserved, rash, foolhardy, hasty, careless, heedless, hot-headed, indiscreet, reckless, specious, headstrong, stubborn.

ollute, contaminate, adulterate, pervert, vitiate, defile, taint, soil, infect, poison, demoralize. *Ant.* purge, purify, clean, sanitize.

omp, glory, splendor, style, ostentation, display, flourish, state, magnificence, grandeur, pageantry. *Ant.* plainness, simplicity, shabbiness, tawdriness.

ompous, arrogant, domineering, vain, haughty, boastful, grandiose, vainglorious, proud, ostentatious, swaggering, blustering, showy, bombastic, egotistical, inflated, grandiose, flashy, flamboyant, affected, stilted, disdainful, bumptious, supercilious, imperious, magisterial, superb, pretentious, theatrical, gaudy, dashing, spectacular, jaunty, flaunting, garish. *Ant.* unobtrusive, mild, retiring, shy, unpretentious, diffident, timid, bashful, unassuming, humble, meek, modest, reserved, submissive, plain, ordinary, obsequious, common, demure.

onder, weigh, contemplate, think, deliberate, reflect, ruminate, calculate, meditate, plot, plan, devise. *Ant.* ignore, forget.

onderous, dull, heavy, massive, weighty, burdensome, bulky, cumbersome, unwieldy. *Ant.* light, imponderable, volatile, ethereal, fluffy, buoyant, airy.

oor, indigent, penniless, impecunious, destitute, impoverished, distressed, needy, poverty-stricken, insolvent, defective, mediocre, substandard, imperfect, underprivileged, meager, miserable, dejected, wretched, pitiable, scanty, insignificant. *Ant.* well-to-do, rich, wealthy, affluent, solvent, opulent, strong, robust, vigorous.

opular, plebeian, public, lay, familiar, comprehensible, ordinary, common, current, universal, prevalent, general, accepted, desired, favorite, accredited, admired, approved, liked. *Ant.* unpopular, disliked, disreputable, shunned, esoteric, recondite.

ort, harbor, shelter, anchorage, haven, berth, bay, cove, inlet, door, entrance, gateway, portal; bearing, demeanor, air, mien, manner, behavior, presence, carriage.

portent, omen, sign, token, wonder, meaning, marvel, foreboding, foreshadowing, presage, warning, phenomenon.

portion, share, part, fraction, parcel, allotment, dividend, fragment, subdivision, section, ration, measure, morsel, quota, piece, slice, cutting, consignment. *Ant.* whole, all, aggregation, entirety, embodiment, sum, total, mass.

portray, show, picture, draw, paint, copy, reveal, sketch, delineate, describe, represent, depict, impersonate, act, figure.

position, place, condition, attitude, station, circumstance, rank, state, posture, office, job, occupation, employment, standing, situation, post, status, caste, environment, site, ground, seat, locality, spot, location, whereabouts, point, bearings.

positive, affirmative, certain, absolute, decided, peremptory, unqualified, unequivocal, assertive, obstinate, stiff, precise, strict, actual, stubborn, factual, substantive, rigid, uncompromising, sure, genuine, unquestionable, inescapable, assured, clear, unmistakable, dogmatic, definite, dictatorial, obvious, distinct, incontrovertible, sanguine, firm, explicit, emphatic, immovable, inexorable, exact, obdurate, veritable, arbitrary, imperative. *Ant.* negative, doubtful, uncertain, questionable, fallible, ambiguous, puzzling, vague, obscure, indefinite, incomprehensible, contradictory, disputable, irresolute, veiled, changeable, inexplicable, confused, indistinct, enigmatic, hazy, equivocal, indeterminate, problematical.

possible, feasible, practicable, likely, contingent, potential, performable, liable, credible, conceivable, accessible, obtainable, achievable, attainable. *Ant.* impossible, unattainable, unlikely, insurmountable, impracticable, improbable, incredible, foolish, unreasonable, fantastic, inconceivable.

posterity, children, descendants, offspring, progeny, issue, family, brood, heirs.

postpone, defer, delay, procrastinate, adjourn, suspend, retard, remand, waive, protract, temporize, pigeonhole, stall, neglect, forget, shelve, table. *Ant.* proceed, continue, accelerate, expedite, hasten, solve, hurry, persist, uphold, pursue, persevere, maintain, prolong, extend, conclude.

potent, powerful, strong, forceful, forcible, efficacious, influential, able, effective, mighty, vigorous, sturdy, robust, intense, capable, irresistible, puissant, virile. *Ant.* weak, delicate, fragile, disabled, impotent, incompetent, inept, powerless, inefficient, invalid, unfit, effeminate, enervated, emasculate, exhausted, helpless, unimportant.

pound, strike, thump, buffet, batter, beat, drum, drive, pulverize, hit, hammer.

poverty, distress, want, penury, deficiency, indigence, destitution, need, pauperism, dearth, inadequacy, scarcity, exigency, insufficiency, privation, starvation, famine. *Ant.* wealth, riches, plenty, affluence, opulence, abundance.

powder, pulverize, crumble, abrade, crush, grind, crunch, pound, grate, sift, mill, triturate, granulate, bray, comminute.

power, efficacy, strength, energy, vigor, force, forcefulness, might, potentiality, effectiveness, potency, capacity, capability, sway, authority, dominion, influence, susceptibility, jurisdiction, government, ability, qualification, skill, talent, expertness, dexterity, competence, efficiency, pressure, domination, mastery, control, predominance. *Ant.* weakness, infirmity, impotence, debility, disability, ineptitude, inability, incapacity, inefficiency, impairment.

practicable, practical, useful, possible, workable, performable, feasible, achievable, attainable, sensible, bearable. *Ant.* impractical, impossible, useless, outlandish, foolish, fantastic.

practical, operative, efficient, sound, sensible, useful, workable, balanced, pragmatic, judicious, effective. *Ant.* impractical, foolish, senseless, impossible, unreal, useless, unworkable, unserviceable.

praise, *n.* laudation, adulation, plaudit, eulogy, encomium, applause, blandishment, exaltation, esteem, commendation, approval, approbation, appreciation, admiration, tribute, compliment, homage, prayer, benediction, grace, thanksgiving; *v.* laud, extol, commend, applaud, recommend, magnify, glorify, acclaim, exalt, sanction, admire, endorse, approve, eulogize, compliment, boost. *Ant.* condemnation, disapproval, censure, blame, obloquy, contempt, disparagement, denunciation, hatred, vituperation, detraction, umbrage, accusation, vilification, disfavor, repudiation, rebuke, remonstrance, scorn, slander, reproach, reprimand, reproof, execration; censure, disapprove, reprehend, condemn, dislike, disparage, decry, blame, reproach, admonish, berate, impugn, upbraid, defame, denounce, deprecate.

precarious, doubtful, uncertain, unsettled, dangerous, critical, risky, unstable, unsteady, equivocal, hazardous, insecure, perilous. *Ant.* certain, assured, unquestionable, undeniable, sure, steady, stable, settled, immutable, incontestable, firm, strong.

precept, doctrine, maxim, mandate, law, instruction, commandment, rule, principle, injunction, charge, command, canon, code, rubric, direction, regulation, form, adage, model, aphorism.

precious, valuable, costly, dear, inestimable, high-priced, expensive, superior, important, excellent, select, worthy, invaluable, priceless, fine, first-class, unequaled, superlative, exquisite, precise, overnice, beloved, darling, dear. *Ant.* worthless, insignificant, valueless, trashy, trifling, useless, unimportant, immaterial, commonplace, ordinary, cheap, faulty, imperfect, defective, impaired, deficient.

precipitate, *adj.* headlong, impetuous, rash, sudden, hasty, abrupt; *v.* hasten, accelerate, speed, quicken. *Ant.* deliberate, willful, intentional; retard, check, slow, moderate, delay, preclude.

precise, accurate, exact, definite, punctilious, scrupulous, rigorous, well-defined, strict, meticulous, rigid, prim, fastidious, unbending, particular, obdurate, uncompromising, exacting, strait-laced, inflexible, austere, prudish. *Ant.* inexact, slipshod, stumbling, careless, loose, negligent, faulty, erroneous, misleading, fallacious, false, jumbled, uncertain, paradoxical, questionable, ambiguous, contradictory.

preclude, prevent, exclude, forestall, bar, avert, stop, prohibit, hinder, check, obviate. *Ant.* include, recognize, embody, embrace, allow, permit.

prediction, prophecy, prognostication, foretelling, presage, forecast, warning, foreboding, fortunetelling, divination, omen, augury, prognosis, horoscope.

predilection, preference, leaning, favor, desire, yearning, bias, bent, inclination, partiality, prejudice, predisposition. *Ant.* dislike, disfavor, disinclination, aversion.

predominant, prevailing, prevalent, reigning, controlling, notable, distinguished, ruling, supreme, dominant, preponderant, compulsory, paramount, imperious, peremptory, sovereign. *Ant.* insignificant, slight, rare, obscure, subordinate, dependent, impotent, unimportant, ineffective, inefficient.

preeminent, conspicuous, renowned, leading, surpassing, eminent, superior, distinguished, excellent, unequalled, paramount, consummate, predominant, supreme. *Ant.* inferior, humble, low, common, average, usual.

preface, introduction, foreword, prelude, preamble, prologue, overture, beginning. *Ant.* epilogue, afterword, addendum, supplement, conclusion, ending.

prefer, desire, approve, select, choose, favor, pick, promote, advance, adopt. *Ant.* dislike, reject, spurn, exclude.

prejudice, partiality, bias, prepossession, prejudgment, objection, dislike, aversion, antipathy, predilection, intolerance, pique, animosity, contemptuousness. *Ant.* appreciation, tolerance, regard, respect, approval, approbation, consideration, confidence, benevolence, kindness, benignity.

preliminary, preparatory, introductory, preceding, prefatory. *Ant.* concluding, final, ending, finishing.

prelude, see **preface.**

premature, untimely, unseasonable, crude, precipitate, hasty, rash, unauthenticated, precocious, early, impending, incomplete, green, unfinished, anticipatory, unripe, sudden, unprepared, immature, raw. *Ant.* detained, delayed, ripe, retarded, mature, ready, finished, prepared, anticipated, expected, seasonable, appropriate, arranged, belated, deferred, backward, tardy, slow, dilatory, overdue, behindhand.

premeditated, intended, intentional, voluntary, calculated, studied, predetermined, prearranged, planned, designed, plotted, deliberate. *Ant.* spontaneous, unforeseen, accidental, casual.

premium, *n.* prize, bonus, gift, award, bounty, present, favor, bribe, appreciation, enhancement, recompense, remuneration, gratuity, boon, guerdon; *adj.* first, best, choicest, top grade, highest quality. *Ant.* poor, low grade, third rate, low quality.

premonition, omen, foreboding, portent, presage, warning, sign.

preoccupied, abstracted, reflective, engrossed, absorbed, musing, intent, inattentive, unobservant, oblivious.

prepare, arrange, fix, concoct, provide, form, plan. *Ant.* neglect, forget, overlook, ignore.

prepossessing, charming, winning, pleasing, attractive, fascinating, inviting, engaging. *Ant.* ugly, homely, displeasing, repulsive, repellent, unpleasant.

preposterous, absurd, extravagant, nonsensical, unreal, unreasonable, ridiculous, fantastic. *Ant.* sensible, realistic, practical, true.

prerogative, right, privilege, perquisite, birthright, claim, liberty, immunity. *Ant.* obligation, duty, limitation.

prescribed, destined, decreed, established, assigned, ordained, urged, advised, suggested, allotted.

present, bestow, tender, deliver, award, confer, show, give, proffer, endow, assign, grant. *Ant.* accept, receive, take.

preserve, maintain, protect, support, keep, uphold, save, secure, sustain, guard, hold, conserve. *Ant.* abolish, destroy, abrogate, forego, lose, waste.

prestige, ascendancy, honor, rank, influence, authority, weight, repute, power, credit, supremacy, glory. *Ant.* insignificance, weakness, unimportance, impotence.

pretense, subterfuge, pretext, sham, pomposity, show, seeming, semblance, simulation, affectation, make-believe, misrepresentation, falsification, ostentation, disguise, deceit, dissimulation, prevarification, evasion, perversion, equivocation, wile, fabrication, trickery, ruse. *Ant.* candor, honesty, truth, probity, sincerity, truthfulness, veracity, straightforwardness, guilelessness, trustworthiness, exactness, frankness, simplicity, naivete, reality, fact.

pretext, plea, alibi, justification, excuse, pretense, affectation, simulation, cloak, veil, guise, mask. *Ant.* truth, honor, realism, reality.

prevailing, prevalent, predominant, catholic, general, universal, world-wide, ubiquitous, reigning, sweeping, all-embracing, controlling, comprehensive, widespread, rife. *Ant.* isolated, sporadic, individual, spotty, irregular, infrequent, uncertain, peculiar, exclusive, private, restricted.

prevaricate, lie, falsify, equivocate, evade, elude, misrepresent, fib, quibble, cavil, shift, deviate.

prevent, preclude, obviate, forestall, block, stop, interrupt, avert, repress, check, debar, impede, thwart, halt, hinder, foil, retard, prohibit, obstruct, restrain, counteract, intercept, inhibit, override, circumvent, corner. *Ant.* allow, permit, aid, support, abet, sustain, encourage, uphold, accommodate, further, assist, back, stimulate.

previous, antecedent, prior, former, preceding, anterior, foregoing, preliminary, preparatory, aforesaid, earlier, prefatory. *Ant.* succeeding, pursuant, following, concluding, posterior, after, latter, subsequent, later, hindmost, ensuing.

pride, vanity, egotism, vainglory, conceit, self-satisfaction, egoism self-respect, self-esteem, haughtiness, arrogance, presumption pomposity, disdain, assumption, self-conceit, self-complacency reserve, loftiness. *Ant.* humility, lowliness, self-effacement, obsequiousness, abasement, bashfulness, self-distrust, meekness, modesty, timidity.

primary, principal, original, leading, chief, basic, fundamental, first, primitive, prime, important, initial, elementary, main. *Ant.* following, secondary, subordinate, subsequent.

prime, first, primary, principal, chief, leading, primal, pristine, best, main, excellent, primordial, primitive, beginning, opening. *Ant.* later, secondary, inferior.

princely, royal, regal, august, grand, splendid, magnificent, superb, majestic, supreme, noble, munificent, exalted, imperial, titled, aristocratic, highborn, generous, patrician, magnanimous, chivalrous, lofty, dignified, stately. *Ant.* mean, contemptible, lowly, underbred, vulgar, coarse, gross, plebeian, rude, base, graceless, ill-mannered, scurrilous, abusive, abject, worthless.

principal, leading, main, essential, chief, foremost, prime, first, head, cardinal, paramount, greatest, preeminent, highest, dominant, supreme, prominent, predominant. *Ant.* inferior, secondary, accessory, negligible, supplemental, minor, auxiliary, added, helping, contributory, subsidiary, additional, inconsiderable, dependent, subordinate, nonessential, subject, trivial, nugatory, unimportant, immaterial, insignificant.

principle, law, doctrine, precept, tenet, rule, basis, premise, theory, postulate, foundation, nature, disposition, conviction, integrity, equity, uprightness, rectitude, conviction.

priority, precedence, ascendancy, pre-existence, antecedence, supremacy, preeminence, seniority.

privacy, seclusion, isolation, solitude, withdrawal, secrecy, concealment. *Ant.* company, publicity, sociality, association.

privation, want, deprivation, indigence, need, destitution, poverty, exigency, penury. *Ant.* plenty, abundancy, affluence, wealth, opulence, riches.

probable, likely, presumable, plausible, rational, reasonable, apparent, credible. *Ant.* improbable, unlikely, incredible.

probity, honesty, honor, integrity, loyalty, trustworthiness, fairness, rectitude, uprightness, impartiality, virtue, respectability, faith, fidelity, justice, righteousness, principle, incorruptibility. *Ant.* dishonor, dishonesty, infidelity, deception, perfidy, unfaithfulness, injustice, treachery, turpitude, improbity.

problem, difficulty, perplexity, dilemma, plight, mystery, enigma, riddle, puzzle, conundrum. *Ant.* certainty, solution, explanation.

proceeds, income, profits, receipts, earnings, gain, yield, return, produce, net, gross. *Ant.* costs, expenses, outlay.

proclaim, announce, voice, promulgate, publish, advertise, broadcast, circulate, declare, divulge, reveal.

proclivity, leaning, flair, penchant, propensity, tendency, bent, bias, proneness, inclination, aptitude, faculty. *Ant.* aversion, dislike, inaptitude, antipathy.

procrastinate, delay, lag, dawdle, prolong, extend, postpone, adjourn, protract, defer, suspend, dally, retard, loiter, stall, tarry. *Ant.* hurry, hasten, accelerate, quicken, persevere, decide.

prodigious, huge, extraordinary, wonderful, immense, enormous, monstrous, vast, amazing, marvelous, astonishing, stupendous, indescribable, inconceivable, abnormal, incredible, phenomenal, impressive, overwhelming. *Ant.* common, small, petty, meager, commonplace, ordinary, insignificant, trivial, usual, normal, inconsiderable, trifling, unimpressive, minor, slight.

produce, *n.* product, fruit, harvest, yield, goods; *v.* bear, yield, impart, give, afford, make, breed, sire, originate, constitute, create, manufacture, form, fabricate, issue, institute.

production, output, product, work, performance, erection, creation, project, harvest, yield.

profane, secular, temporal, worldly, earthly, sacrilegious, impious, idolatrous, unholy, lay, vulgar, unconsecrated. *Ant.* sacred, holy, spiritual, hallowed.

proficient, competent, adept, accomplished, adroit, skilled, dextrous, able, expert, practiced. *Ant.* incompetent, unskilled, incapable, inept, maladroit.

profit, gain, improvement, proceeds, benefit, return, receipts, advantage, returns, earnings, interest, remuneration. *Ant.* loss, failure, hurt, indebtedness, ruin, injury, bankruptcy, disadvantage, harm, waste, destruction.

profound, deep, abysmal, mysterious, solemn, abstruse, heavy, erudite, scholarly, recondite, learned, undisturbed, heartfelt, intense, penetrating, great, consummate, enlightened, discerning, comprehensive, fathomless, serious. *Ant.* shallow, slight, superficial, unsettled, simple, trifling, unlearned, unenlightened, absurd, frivolous, fatuous.

profuse, lavish, abundant, excessive, prodigal, liberal, plentiful, extravagant, improvident, wasteful, copious, overflowing, superfluous, redundant. *Ant.* scarce, meager, insufficient, inadequate, scanty, wanting, lacking, deficient, barren, incomplete.

progress, advancement, development, advance, progression, growth, improvement, locomotion, proficiency, attainment, motion, movement, increase, headway. *Ant.* rest, standstill, stagnation, immobility, retrogression, stay, stop, stoppage, delay, relapse, check, decrease, cessation, decline.

prohibit, bar, block, preclude, debar, check, hinder, forbid, prevent, interdict, circumscribe, inhibit, proscribe, restrict, ban, restrain, taboo, exclude, veto, refuse, deny, withhold. *Ant.* allow, concede, permit, tolerate, warrant, license, endorse, sanction, empower, encourage, legalize, authorize, recognize, admit, enjoin, command, direct, order, let.

projection

projection, extension, plan, project, working draft, outline, design
protrusion, protuberance, bulge, prominence.

prolific, fertile, productive, fecund, swarming, breeding, propagat
ing, teeming, fruitful. *Ant.* barren, unfruitful, sterile.

prologue, prelude, introduction, preface, foreword, exordium, pre
amble, beginning. *Ant.* epilogue, conclusion, end.

prolong, protract, lengthen, extend, sustain, elongate, continue, in
crease, augment, amplify, stretch. *Ant.* shorten, curtail.

prominent, convex, raised, notable, leading, eminent, distinguished
renowned, jutting, conspicuous, extended, remarkable, protruding
projecting, well-known, popular, famous, celebrated, marked
salient, important. *Ant.* depressed, sunken, flat, level, concave
obscure, unknown, humble, common, ordinary.

promote, advance, encourage, organize, endow, further, forward
prefer, push, aid, assist, cultivate, dignify, urge, foster, help
encourage, foment, exalt, contribute. *Ant.* impede, obstruct, de
grade, dishonor, discredit, impair, wreck, pervert, injure, harm
demoralize, damage.

prompt, quick, alert, vigilant, keen, immediate, swift, ready, instant
punctual, active. *Ant.* tardy, late, remiss, lax, slow, negligent.

promulgate, see **proclaim.**

prone, tending, open, liable, disposed, subject, inclined, predisposed
sensitive, prostrate, recumbent, flat.

propagate, breed, engender, raise, grow, create, procreate, originate
generate, disseminate, increase, diffuse, spread, publish, multiply
develop, produce, inculcate, reproduce, imbue, teach, implant
graft. *Ant.* destroy, exterminate, kill, waste, suppress, extirpate
crush, slaughter, annihilate, devastate, eradicate, ravage.

propel, thrust, impel, move, start, force, urge, push, drive. *Ant*
hinder, hold, delay, drag, discourage, stop.

propensity, leaning, proclivity, flair, prejudice, knack, predilection
gift, aptitude, inclination, penchant. *Ant.* antipathy, dislike
aversion.

proper, just, right, fair, decent, suitable, fit, appropriate, pertinent
equitable, legitimate, fitting, correct, seemly. *Ant.* improper, in
congruous, unfit, inapplicable, inappropriate, incorrect, inaccu
rate, objectionable, unsuitable, inopportune, unseemly.

propitiate, conciliate, calm, satisfy, appease, assuage, soothe, pacify
mollify, placate, moderate, reconcile, allay, soften, mitigate, expi
ate. *Ant.* annoy, anger, aggravate, scoff, enrage, infuriate, irri
tate, provoke, agitate, offend, displease, harass, thwart, vex
worry, bother, distress.

proposal, scheme, plan, design, offer, suggestion, overture, motion
statement, outline, prospectus, proposition, request, advance, bid
application. *Ant.* deprecation, refusal, remonstrance, denuncia
tion, denial, negation, rejection, repulse.

propriety, decency, righteousness, appropriateness, aptness, fitness
correctness, decorum, conventionality, dignity. *Ant.* impropriety
misconduct, unseemliness, unlawfulness, immorality, unfitness.

prosperity, success, welfare, well-being, good fortune, attainment, happiness, achievement, affluence, riches, opulence, independence, money, profits, income, wealth. *Ant.* adversity, failure, poverty, misfortune, calamity, loss, ruin, penury, destitution, privation, distress, neediness.

prostrate, flat, down, powerless, abject, recumbent, prone, helpless, humbled, fallen. *Ant.* upright, erect, proud, exalted, solvent, self-sufficient.

protect, safeguard, defend, shield, guard, preserve, conserve, shelter, harbor. *Ant.* neglect, forget, ignore, expose, attack.

protract, postpone, prolong, extend, defer, lengthen, procrastinate, elongate, continue, delay, stretch. *Ant.* shorten, curtail, conclude, abbreviate, contract, hurry, abridge, limit, reduce, hasten, condense, lessen, epitomize, shrink.

protrude, jut, bulge, extend, overhang, swell, distend, expand, project.

proud, imperious, lordly, exalted, arrogant, lofty, majestic, dignified, haughty, supercilious, stately. *Ant.* humble, meek, lowly, modest.

prove, show, verify, corroborate, demonstrate, confirm, justify, substantiate, establish. *Ant.* disprove, deny, expose, refute.

proverb, see **maxim.**

proverbial, current, unquestioned, notorious, acknowledged, familiar, well-known, recognized, established, traditional, common, circulating, axiomatic, accustomed, routine.

provide, furnish, supply, prepare, replenish, store, stock, equip, arm, contribute, cater, purvey. *Ant.* withhold, deprive, remove.

provident, prudent, thoughtful, foresighted, cautious, economical, careful, discreet, wise, saving, frugal, thrifty. *Ant.* extravagant, prodigal, wasteful, profuse.

province, domain, office, district, function, department, field, sphere, territory.

provoke, arouse, incite, enrage, excite, exasperate, anger, inflame, stir, move, annoy, taunt, irritate, foment, vex, pique, incense, infuriate, aggravate, exacerbate, agitate, perturb. *Ant.* mollify, pacify, comfort, please, calm, placate, soothe, gratify, appease, cheer, propitiate, tranquilize, assuage, restrain, quell, conciliate, moderate, lull, allay, quiet, soften, abate, alleviate, mitigate, ameliorate.

prowess, bravery, gallantry, valor, heroism, chivalry, intrepidity, courage, skill, competence, drive. *Ant.* fear, vacillation, trepidation, pusillanimity, cowardice, effeminacy, weakness, timidity.

proximity, nearness, contiguity, propinquity, vicinity, neighborhood. *Ant.* distance, remoteness.

prudence, discretion, circumspection, caution, judgment, restraint, judiciousness, foresight, forethought, consideration, care, carefulness, frugality, common sense, discrimination, vigilance. *Ant.* negligence, imprudence, improvidence, carelessness, folly, indiscretion, thoughtlessness, heedlessness, recklessness, prodigality, wastefulness.

prune, trim, thin, shear, lop, clip, crop, rid, clear, remove.

prurient, craving, desiring, wishful, longing, eager, avid, ardent lecherous, debauched, fervent, lewd, depraved, impure, wanton dissolute, salacious, lustful, concupiscent, erotic, carnal, voluptuous, foul, licentious, lascivious, gross, beastly, adulterous. *Ant* cold, indifferent, phlegmatic, frigid, neutral, supine, lukewarm listless, half-hearted, impotent, lacking desire, self-controlled, unfeeling, modest, chaste, pure, continent, immaculate, unspotted pious, religious, God-fearing.

pseudo, false, counterfeit, bogus, spurious, fake, sham, phony, mock, simulated. *Ant*. real, true, honest, correct, sound, genuine.

publish, communicate, impart, utter, circulate, issue, promulgate disseminate, declare, print, disclose, broadcast, publicize, reveal post, proclaim, divulge, announce.

puerile, boyish, inexperienced, immature, youthful, childish, petty fatuous, juvenile, trivial, hopeless, irrational, idle, simple, senseless, frivolous. *Ant*. adult, mature, experienced, wise, sensible veteran, patriarchal, aged, sage, rational, judicious, discerning shrewd, forcible, impressive, great, important, grave, serious.

pugnacious, belligerent, aggressive, petulant, irascible, contentious combative, disputatious, irritable, quarrelsome, militant. *Ant*. peaceful, pacific, placid, peaceable, timid, weak.

pulchritude, beauty, grace, attractiveness, loveliness, comeliness. *Ant*. ugliness, repulsiveness, loathsomeness.

pull, draw, drag, tug, tow, pluck, pick, haul. *Ant*. push, thrust, drive, propel.

pulse, throb, vibration, beat, palpitation, oscillation.

punctual, prompt, exact, timely, strict, early, scrupulous, meticulous, punctilious. *Ant*. careless, unreliable, inconstant, tardy, irregular, variable, fluctuating.

pungent, sharp, acid, tart, biting, racy, hot, keen, stinging, penetrating, severe, burning, acute, painful, poignant, sour, acrid, peppery, bitter, mordant, trenchant, piquant, gamy, rough, caustic, strong. *Ant*. mild, pleasant, painless, soothing, agreeable, insipid, tasteless, vapid, watery, weak, dull, flat, stale, flavorless, unseasoned.

punish, chastise, correct, discipline, flog, castigate, inflict, afflict, chasten, scold, imprison, fine. *Ant*. free, acquit, exonerate, forgive, defend, applaud, pardon, praise, commend, release, laud, reward, redress, comfort, humor, encourage, endorse, relieve, cheer, rescue, indulge, benefit, guard, protect.

puny, feeble, small, undeveloped, diminutive, stunted, undersized, dwarfish, frail, inferior, tiny, weak, little, slight. *Ant*. robust, sturdy, strong, mighty, big, large.

pure, unmixed, unadulterated, spotless, stainless, undefiled innocent, virtuous, guiltless, unblemished, untainted, unsullied, chaste, immaculate, clean, incorrupt, holy, virginal, virtuous, upright, perfect, clear. *Ant.* impure, polluted, adulterated, libidinous, unclean, gross, dirty, coarse, filthy, foul, immodest, unclean, indecent, unchaste, obscene, corrupt, rotten, tainted, spotted, mixed, mingled, sullied, ribald, immodest, indelicate, vulgar, lustful, licentious, dissolute.

purge, clear, purify, unburden, eliminate, cleanse, exclude, debar, eject, oust, dismiss, expunge, excrete, erase, efface, delete. *Ant.* keep, retain, hold.

purify, cleanse, wash, deodorize, chasten, disinfect, clear, refine, fumigate, clarify, purge, filter, revise, correct, improve. *Ant.* soil, corrupt, debase, tarnish, stain, pollute, contaminate, defile, putrefy, taint, sully, debauch, vitiate.

puritanical, prim, rigid, rigorous, prudish, prissy, strict, severe, strait-laced, moralistic, harsh, narrow, hidebound, bigoted, intolerant, austere. *Ant.* liberal, loose, bold, spirited, uninhibited, careless, tolerant.

purport, gist, meaning, import, trend, substance, drift, significance, tendency, sense, intent.

purpose, intention, goal, end, object, objective, view, aim, resolve, inclination, determination.

pursue, shadow, follow, seek, track, chase, hound, hunt, trail. *Ant.* abandon, stop, ignore.

pursuit, calling, occupation, vocation, work, business, job, avocation, adventure, activity, hobby, craft, trade; chase, race, search, hunt.

purvey, supply, cater, bring, provide, deliver, nourish, feed.

purview, range, reach, dimension, field, compass, sweep, gamut, orbit, extent, limit, sphere, scope.

push, impel, propel, shove, press, urge, thrust, drive, expedite, butt, force, advance, compel, elbow, nudge, encourage, hearten. *Ant.* discourage, pull, drag, retreat.

pusillanimous, timorous, cowardly, spiritless, weak, timid, craven, dastardly, afraid, vacillating, feeble, sorry, fearful. *Ant.* brave, courageous, bold, fearless.

put, place, lay, set, deposit, settle, lodge, locate, assign, install, establish, plant, insert, imbed. *Ant.* remove, displace, misplace, take, transfer, oust.

putative, reputed, supposed, deemed, suppositious, conjectural, reported, hypothetical. *Ant.* known, true, confirmed, certain, observed, recognized.

putrid, corrupt, rotten, decayed, polluted, contaminated, disgusting, purulent. *Ant.* clean, pure, wholesome, uncontaminated, fresh, healthy, sanitary, incorrupt, pleasing, fragrant.

puzzle, *n.* perplexity, mystery, mystification, conundrum, enigma, poser, labyrinth, intricacy, complexity, riddle, maze; *v.* perplex, confuse, confound, mystify, bewilder, disconcert, baffle, distract, entangle. *Ant.* clarify, illustrate, explain, demonstrate, inform, prove, confirm, elucidate, exemplify, reveal, interpret, unravel, unfold, solve.

pygmy, *adj.* diminutive, small, tiny, little, undersized, dwarfish runty, miniature, stunted; *n.* midget, dwarf, manikin, homun culus, runt. *Ant.* large, huge, giant, enormous, vast, great colossal.

Q

quack, impostor, charlatan, mountebank, humbug, sophist, empiric pretender, phony, fraud, counterfeiter, boaster, deceiver, faker swindler, knave, cheat, rogue.

quagmire, swamp, bog, marsh, fen, morass, slough.

quail, cower, recoil, falter, flinch, hesitate, wince, quake, shrink tremble. *Ant.* confront, defy, face, battle.

quaint, odd, unique, strange, queer, curious, old-fashioned, fanciful antique, whimsical, unconventional, anomalous. *Ant.* up-to-date ordinary, common, normal, conformable, regular, usual, conventional, fashionable.

quake, *v.* tremble, shiver, shake, totter, flutter, shudder, quiver vibrate, quail; *n.* earthquake, temblor.

qualified, capable, able, adequate, competent, efficacious, efficient fit, eligible, accomplished, experienced, equipped, modified, tempered, limited, moderated. *Ant.* inept, incapable, incompetent, unfit, ineffectual, inefficient, unsuitable, impotent, unskilled, helpless, unqualified, inefficacious, ignorant, powerless.

quality, nature, characteristic, character, attribute, peculiarity, condition, qualification, property, status, brand, grade, faculty, rank nobility.

qualm, compunction, twinge, uncertainty, pang, scruple, misgiving apprehension, remorse, pain, fear. *Ant.* relief, solace, comfort.

quandary, dilemma, plight, perplexity, puzzle, predicament, pickle bewilderment.

quarrel, wrangle, strife, bickering, dispute, altercation, argument feud, brawl, contention, fuss, disagreement, dissension, affray misunderstanding, fray, clash, contradiction, disruption, hostility squabble, row, tiff, animosity, embroilment, fracas, riot, disturbance, breach, disagreement.

quarrelsome, factious, unruly, contentious, fractious, pugnacious, turbulent, irascible, irritable, snappish, hot-tempered, fiery, excitable, petulant, bickering, churlish, ugly, bad-tempered, touchy hasty, huffy, quick, rash, hotheaded, impassioned, tempestuous, tumultuous, violent, impetuous, vehement, furious. *Ant.* peaceful, quiet, inoffensive, agreeable, good-natured, affable, friendly, patient, good-tempered, pacific, tolerant, submissive, imperturbable easygoing, placid, calm, composed, steady, cool, tranquil, dispassionate, level-headed, forbearing, unresisting, indulgent, forgiving.

quash, terminate, end, stop, suppress, quell, crush, subdue, repress, nullify, annul, abrogate, extinguish, veto, destroy, abolish. *Ant.* initiate, begin, start, support, incite, urge, revive, rebuild.

quaver, see **quake.**

queer, odd, abnormal, unique, strange, extraordinary, peculiar, uncommon, erratic, eccentric, unusual, ridiculous, ludicrous, fantastic, curious, anomalous, bizarre, irregular, freakish, unnatural. *Ant.* commonplace, usual, natural, normal, ordinary, customary, regular, familiar, conventional, conformable, consistent, prevalent, widespread, typical, established, recognized, accepted, orthodox.

quell, subdue, allay, disperse, reduce, silence, quiet, scatter, check, moderate, assuage, placate, overcome, vanquish, stem, defeat, conquer, pacify, calm, subjugate, crush, tranquillize, demolish, hush, curb, restrain, overthrow, still. *Ant.* foment, encourage, excite, incite, inflame, urge, stimulate, foster, endorse, promote, aggravate, infuriate, agitate, perturb, disturb, irritate, rouse, arouse, instigate, embitter, anger, incense, roil, enrage, rile.

quench, extinguish, suppress, destroy, quash, crush, check, slake, repress, stifle, allay, end, chill, damp, satisfy. *Ant.* ignite, incite, excite, start, acerbate, fuel, foster, endorse, abet.

querulous, fretful, peevish, touchy, carping, caviling, discontented, complaining, faultfinding, murmuring, resentful, disagreeable, dissatisfied, irascible, irritable, petulant, contentious, testy, cross, disputatious, perverse, obstinate, whining, grumbling, plaintive, finicky. *Ant.* contented, cheerful, happy, joyous, carefree, calm, satisfied, content, easygoing, serene, unperturbed, light-hearted.

query, question, ask, interrogate, examine, quiz, inquire, challenge, dispute, doubt. *Ant.* answer, reply, retort, respond.

quest, expedition, seeking, adventure, journey, pursuit, trek, search, enterprise.

questionable, uncertain, equivocal, obscure, dubious, disputable, indecisive, doubtful, suspicious, controvertible, unsettled, debatable, indeterminate, unproved, unconfirmed, problematical, mysterious, occult, apocryphal, cryptic, enigmatic, hypothetical, ambiguous, indefinite, paradoxical, contingent, provisional, curious, incredible, unbelievable. *Ant.* certain, obvious, positive, sure, assured, indubitable, unequivocal, reliable, definite, plain, proven, decisive, determinate, unmistakable, unquestionable, evident, undoubted, credible, satisfactory, believable, aboveboard, axiomatic, straight forward, self-evident, logical, unimpeachable, clear, veracious, precise, convincing, dependable, exact, authentic, true, genuine, correct, legitimate.

quibble, evade, cavil, pretend, prevaricate, dodge, equivocate, sidestep, shuffle, straddle, shift, trifle. *Ant.* accept, agree, concur, admit, approve.

quick, swift, fast, rapid, brisk, active, alert, lively, sharp, ready, prompt, expeditious, fleet, speedy, mercurial, instantaneous, agile, hasty, winged, clever, keen. *Ant.* slow, tardy, dilatory, languid, phlegmatic, sluggish, apathetic, listless, lazy, indolent, slothful, drowsy, doltish.

quiescent, still, resting, abeyant, placid, undisturbed, smooth, peaceful, tranquil, serene, motionless, silent, unruffled, inactive, quiet, latent, calm, dormant. *Ant.* active, dynamic, stirring, vivacious, spirited.

quiet, peaceful, still, placid, tranquil, pacific, calm, pleased, contented, mild, meek, peaceable, secluded, retired, sequestered, halcyon, silent, quiescent, hushed, motionless, soundless, muffled, mute, noiseless, solemn. *Ant.* noisy, sonorous, loud, clangorous, blatant, thunderous, deafening, earsplitting, shrill, uproarious, warlike, explosive, ringing, jingling, reverberating.

quip, sally, retort, taunt, gibe, jest, witticism, sarcasm.

quirk, oddity, eccentricity, mannerism, accident, peculiarity, trick, quibble, evasion, flourish. *Ant.* normality, reality, regularity, sense.

quit, abandon, relinquish, leave, cease, forsake, stop, withdraw, remove, yield, surrender, resign, desert. *Ant.* remain, retain, hold, keep, begin, stay, start, continue, persevere, stand.

quiver, shiver, shudder, agitate, shake, oscillate, vibrate, quake, tremble, flutter, quaver.

quixotic, chimerical, fantastic, visionary, fanciful, imaginary, mad, wild, romantic, sentimental, idealistic, abstract.

quiz, test, examination, interrogation, puzzle, riddle, questionnaire.

quota, ration, allotment, proportion, portion, share, percentage.

quotation, extract, citation, excerpt, quote, passage, selection, reference, blurb, repetition, price, estimate, rate.

quotidian, daily, diurnal, circadian, regular.

R

rabble, mob, canaille, scum, horde, populace, poor, proletariat, riff raff, trash, herd, crowd.

rabid, insane, infuriated, mad, berserk, frantic, furious, raging, fanatical, deranged, crazy, maniacal, frenzied, bigoted, intolerant, irrational. *Ant.* sane, normal, lucid, rational, reasonable, sound, clearheaded.

race, breed, stock, family, tribe, nation, people, lineage.

rack, torture, punish, torment, harass, strain, pain, distress, afflict, irritate, harry, rend, oppress, stretch, lacerate, wring, agonize. *Ant.* cheer, support, encourage, enliven, sustain, inspirit, stimulate, soothe, comfort, assuage, alleviate, calm, entertain, refresh.

racket, see noise.

racy, pungent, flavorous, bright, piquant, clever, spicy, sharp, keen, lively, rich, interesting, saucy, entertaining, spirited, smart, provocative, stimulating, savory, appetizing, caustic, tasty, palatable, incisive, gusty, poignant, trenchant. *Ant.* dull, vapid, insipid, unsavory, tasteless, flavorless, flat, acrid, nauseating, bitter, disgusting, sour, stale, repulsive, heavy, nasty, coarse, offensive, phlegmatic, morose, doltish, languid, languorous.

radiant, bright, brilliant, luminous, lustrous, beaming, glowing, shimmering, effulgent, shining, sparkling, glittering, resplendent. *Ant.* dull, dark, dim, cloudy, obscure.

radiate, shine, gleam, emanate, spread, diffuse, circulate, glitter, propagate, dissipate, emit. *Ant.* concentrate, absorb, gather, converge.

radical, *adj.* basic, native, natural, innate, fundamental, organic, essential, ingrained, original, complete, entire, thorough, extreme, constitutional, total, intrinsic, inherent, inborn, deep-rooted, indigenous, genetic, inherited, congenital, internal, extreme, violent, fanatical, excessive; *n.* Red, Communist, Socialist, insurgent, leftist, liberal, reformer, fellow traveler. *Ant.* incomplete, partial, slight, tentative, superficial, weak, inadequate, palliative, trivial, extrinsic, casual, nonessential, incidental, deficient, imperfect, conservative, stable, moderate; rightist, conservative, reactionary, right-winger, traditionalist, John Bircher.

raid, *n.* foray, assault, invasion, incursion; *v.* attack, invade, forage, pillage, steal, assault.

raillery, chaff, jest, persiflage, banter, satire, badinage, ribbing, ragging, joking, teasing, irony, taunting. *Ant.* geniality, friendliness.

raiment, dress, array, attire, garb, clothes, clothing, habit, apparel, costume, vestments, garments.

raise, lift, heighten, uplift, elevate, boost, hoist, erect, exalt, honor, grow, aggrandize, increase, rear, produce, stir, arouse, excite, cause, heave, construct, build, cultivate, gather, appropriate, stimulate, advance, animate, intensify, inspire, magnify, amplify, augment. *Ant.* lower, reduce, abate, decrease, lessen, curtail, diminish, depress, depreciate, ravage, demolish, overthrow, level, destroy, raze, depress, debase, upset, pacify, quell.

rally, reassemble, meet, assemble, reunite, concentrate, muster, regroup, collect, recuperate, revive, recover, stir, rouse, arouse, awaken, alert, ridicule, banter, tease, twit, chaff. *Ant.* disperse, scatter, retreat, surrender, quit, lose, weaken, regress.

ram, crowd, jam, butt, tamp, crowd, cram, stuff, press, pack, poke, beat, compress, squeeze. *Ant.* release, expand, swell, relieve, loosen.

ramble, rove, stroll, roam, stray, wander, range, saunter, traverse, straggle, drift, digress, rave, meander, prowl.

ramification, complication, division, expansion, branching, offshoot, subdivision, forking, multiplicity. *Ant.* unification, simplification, clarification.

rampart, parapet, breastwork, bulwark, bastion, mound, barricade, embankment, wall, fortification, fence, defense, guard, elevation, railing.

rancor, malignity, enmity, spite, ill will, hatred, resentment, malice, venom, malevolence, animosity, unfriendliness, hostility, antagonism, bitterness, vindictiveness. *Ant.* friendship, love, regard, respect, sympathy, affection, confidence, benevolence, benignity, kindness, charity.

random

random, casual, haphazard, fortuitous, unplanned, vagrant, stray, chance, irregular, wandering, desultory, aimless. *Ant.* planned, definite, specific, designed, intentional, particular, invariable, systematic.

rankle, irritate, inflame, annoy, bother, disturb, fester, gall, ulcerate. *Ant.* please, assuage, calm, sooth, satisfy, ease, reassure, help.

ransack, pillage, rummage, plunder, overhaul, ravish, scour, loot, explore, search, strip, seek, spoil, sack, raid, rifle.

rapid, quick, flying, swift, expeditious, speedy, accelerated, fast, fleet, brisk, hasty, mercurial. *Ant.* slow, tardy, slack, dilatory, sluggish, inert, leaden, laggard.

rapture, ecstasy, delight, joy, bliss, gladness, felicity, beatitude, happiness, cheer, exultation, enjoyment, gratification, enchantment, pleasure, passion, infatuation, enthusiasm, devotion. *Ant.* sorrow, suffering, misery, distress, melancholy, disillusion, complaint, grumbling, worry, discontent, languor, lassitude, bitterness, pain, annoyance, irritation, grief, affliction.

rare, uncommon, infrequent, unprecedented, scarce, unique, singular, unparalleled, unusual, odd, peculiar, curious, precious, extraordinary, strange, incomparable, choice, remarkable, inimitable, exceptional, anomalous. *Ant.* common, general, typical, commonplace, normal, ordinary, universal, formal, usual, habitual, profuse, regular, various, manifold, recurring, frequent, current, constant, incessant, cheap, worthless.

rarefied, thin, attenuated, ethereal, expanded, tenuous, refined, purified, diluted. *Ant.* dense, thick.

rascal, knave, rogue, trickster, villain, cheat, scamp, scalawag, miscreant, rapscallion, reprobate, ruffian, scoundrel, renegade.

rash, hasty, reckless, headstrong, precipitate, careless, impetuous, foolhardy, thoughtless, heedless, audacious, wild, inconsiderate, incautious, imprudent, headlong, adventurous, impulsive, indiscreet. *Ant.* careful, thoughtful, cautious, vigilant, prudent, slow, deliberate, guarded, discriminating, heedful, considerate, mindful, observant, scrupulous, discerning, wise, calculating, sensible.

rasp, file, scrape, grate, abrade, chafe, excoriate, fret, aggravate, annoy, vex, irk, bother, irritate. *Ant.* soothe, please, amuse, gratify.

ratify, confirm, sanction, warrant, endorse, establish, approve, substantiate, validate, verify, sign, seal, certify, attest, support, second, corroborate, uphold, acquiesce, accede, consent. *Ant.* refuse, oppose, renounce, denounce, counteract, deny, ignore, protest, refute, dissent, disagree, differ, recant, revoke, abjure, disclaim, forswear, disavow, abrogate, veto, negate, repudiate, rebut, confute.

ratio, proportion, quota, percentage, comparison, rate.

ration, *n.* portion, dole, share, measure, pittance, quota, allotment, allowance; *v.* apportion, allot, parcel, divide, prorate.

ational, wise, sane, sound, sensible, reasonable, intelligent, judicious, sagacious, conscious, subjective, logical, deductive. *Ant.* absurd, ridiculous, erratic, eccentric, senseless, irrational, unreasonable, nonsensical, blundering, incompetent, inconsistent, stupid, wandering, visionary.

attle, confuse, embarrass, disconcert, discomfit, fluster, distract, upset, muddle. *Ant.* calm, ease, settle, clarify, cheer.

aucous, harsh, loud, hoarse, husky, strident, stentorian, coarse, rough. *Ant.* soft, smooth, melodious, quiet, calm, tuneful.

avage, see **devastate.**

ave, rant, storm, fume, rage, bluster.

avenous, rapacious, omnivorous, grasping, ferocious, gluttonous, insatiable, voracious, greedy. *Ant.* temperate, abstemious, forbearing, honest, gentle.

aw, green, callow, unprepared, inexperienced, immature, boorish, undisciplined, rude, unripe, rough, crude. *Ant.* mature, adult, ripe, seasoned, courteous, polished.

aze, destroy, ruin, demolish, dismantle, overthrow, level, overturn, obliterate, fell, efface, topple. *Ant.* build, raise, erect, construct, restore, repair.

each, arrive, accomplish, attain, achieve, gain, earn, touch; extend, stretch. *Ant.* leave, start, fail, miss, bungle.

ead, peruse, con, scan, study, browse, leaf, interpret, decipher, perceive, discern, understand; register, indicate; foresee, foretell. *Ant.* misread, misinterpret.

eady, prompt, prepared, suitable, equipped, available, apt, ripe, adroit, willing, disposed, active. *Ant.* unprepared, unsuitable, improper, unfit, tardy, slow, deficient, immature, raw, unripe, green, undeveloped, unseasoned, unready, disqualified.

eal, actual, genuine, true, certain, substantive, sure, positive, intrinsic, absolute, veritable, substantial, unquestionable, essential, authentic, existing. *Ant.* nonexistent, false, unreal, mythological, imaginary, supposititious, fallacious, deceptive, erroneous, hypothetical, untrue, illusive, fancied, mythical, fantastic, visionary, unsubstantial, illusory, theoretical, feigned, fictitious, supposed.

eality, truth, verity, existence, actuality, entity. *Ant.* fantasy, fiction, imagination, nonentity.

eap, gain, cut, collect, get, win, acquire, obtain, gather, mow, earn, merit, realize, draw, harvest. *Ant.* sow, lose, scatter, miss, disperse, forfeit, fail.

eason, *n.* motive, view, cause, end, aim, object, consideration, purpose, ground, principle, account, judgment, sake, basis, argument, inducement, intuition, understanding, foundation, source; *v.* conclude, trace, deduce, question, contend, discuss, establish, debate, speculate, analyze, converse, think, reflect, consider, contemplate, meditate, ponder, study.

reasonable, fair, right, equitable, logical, rational, agreeable, tolerable, fit, credible, plausible, sensible, moderate, inexpensive, low-priced, justifiable, just. *Ant.* excessive, immoderate, unreasonable, outrageous, extreme, inordinate, excessive, preposterous, prodigious, unconscionable, expensive, costly, exorbitant, extortionate.

rebellion, insurrection, revolt, revolution, uprising, mutiny, riot, upheaval, sedition, outbreak, disorder, tumult, disturbance, insubordination. *Ant.* peace, calm, law, order, tranquility, resignation, quiet, tolerance, submission, patience, forbearance, endurance, conciliation.

rebellious, mutinous, recalcitrant, revolutionary, unmanageable, uncontrollable, pugnacious, quarrelsome, resistant, ungovernable, refractory, intractable, seditious, disobedient, insubordinate, contumacious. *Ant.* docile, submissive, yielding, dutiful, subservient, manageable, obedient, tractable, gentle, deferential, agreeable, compliant, respectful, loyal, controlled, controllable, willing, contented, satisfied.

rebound, see **recoil.**

rebuff, repel, check, snub, defeat, refuse, oppose, resist, discourage. *Ant.* accept, include, encourage, aid, help, surrender.

rebuke, reproach, berate, reprove, criticize, admonish, chide, scold, censure, reprimand, remonstrate, punish. *Ant.* approve, praise, reward, laud.

rebut, disprove, refute, confute, controvert, retort, oppose, repel, rebuff. *Ant.* accept, surrender, approve, endorse.

recalcitrant, obstinate, refractory, unruly, intractable, rebellious, stubborn, disobedient, ungovernable. *Ant.* amenable, docile, obedient.

recall, remember, review, reminisce, recollect, remind, revoke, annul. *Ant.* forget, restore, reestablish.

recant, recall, retract, retreat, abjure, deny, cancel, renounce, disavow, disclaim, withdraw, rescind, abrogate, forswear, repudiate, abnegate, nullify, void. *Ant.* acknowledge, admit, proclaim, endorse, accredit, confirm, strengthen, persevere, support, persist, maintain, uphold, affirm, emphasize, insist, avow, sustain, defend.

recapitulate, repeat, restate, review, recite, recount, reiterate, summarize.

recast, alter, change, remodel, revise, remold, reconstruct.

recede, withdraw, retreat, revert, ebb, regress, fade, wane, retire. *Ant.* approach, advance, gain, near.

receive, accept, admit, take, acquire, get, gain, win, obtain, catch. *Ant.* give, deliver, contribute, bequeath, donate, bestow, grant, restore, return, disburse, expend.

recent, late, modern, new, novel, fresh, young, latter, retiring, deceased, foregoing, preceding. *Ant.* old, former, aged, obsolete, old-fashioned.

recite, repeat, state, deliver, report, recapitulate, enumerate, tell, narrate, relate, recount.

reckless, rash, careless, impetuous, foolhardy, heedless, wild, daring, precipitate, desperate. *Ant.* cautious, circumspect, calculating, prudent, wary.

reclaim, restore, renovate, redeem, regenerate, save, ransom, rescue, renew, regain, correct. *Ant.* abandon, neglect, forget.

recognize, perceive, acknowledge, accede, distinguish, concede, admit, realize, accept, know. *Ant.* ignore, forget.

recoil, rebound, return, bounce, reflect, kick, react, ricochet, echo, carom.

recommend, commend, approve, endorse, advocate, suggest, acclaim, extol, applaud, sanction, prescribe, praise, counsel, advise. *Ant.* disapprove, denigrate, condemn.

reconcile, accommodate, conform, adjust, adapt, rectify, correct, regulate, placate, pacify, conciliate.

recondite, see **abstruse.**

reconnoiter, survey, inspect, view, inquire, scan, search, examine.

record, *n.* chronicle, schedule, history, document, register, registry, docket, archive, report, inventory, inscription; *v.* list, register, enroll, report, file, tape, catalogue, enter, note.

recoup, regain, balance, recover, restore, retrieve, reimburse, indemnify, remunerate.

recover, regain, renew, restore, renovate, recoup, redeem, salvage, retrieve, recuperate, heal, mend, rally. *Ant.* lose, mislay, forfeit, deteriorate, degenerate, decline, wane, sink, perish, die.

recreant, cowardly, craven, false, base, low, faithless, unfaithful, apostate, erring, dastardly, perfidious, treacherous, vile. *Ant.* truthful, brave, courageous, gallant, straightforward, conscientious, bold, honorable, honest, just, loyal, incorruptible, noble, reliable, trustworthy, upright, daring, good, faithful.

recreation, pastime, game, relaxation, amusement, play, sport, fun, diversion, refreshment, relief, entertainment, frolic. *Ant.* toil, work, labor.

rectify, remedy, improve, correct, revise, adjust, fix, refine, purify, repair, regulate, amend, reform. *Ant.* debase, falsify, adulterate, damage, ruin.

recumbent, prone, supine, reclining, prostrate, couchant, leaning, dormant, resting. *Ant.* erect, upright, standing.

recuperate, improve, recover, heal, mend, regain, strengthen, fortify, invigorate, energize, restore. *Ant.* decline, weaken, fail, sink.

recur, return, reappear, recrudesce, revert, revive.

redeem, ransom, repurchase, rescue, liberate, recover, deliver, free, reclaim, recoup, atone, expiate, propitiate, repair, retrieve, extricate, emancipate, regain, save. *Ant.* abandon, forfeit, neglect, shun, ignore, overlook, disregard.

redress, restoration, amendment, restitution, repair, remedy, relief, reparation, abatement, replacement, rehabilitation, reform, propitiation, compensation, amends, atonement, indemnification, payment, satisfaction, reward, indemnity, remuneration, retribution, recompense.

reduce, lower, diminish, curtail, lessen, abate, subdue, decrease, abridge, conquer, modify, impoverish, thin, shorten, decimate, degrade, eliminate, weaken, debilitate, enervate, attenuate, condense, contract, abbreviate, defeat, override, conquer, raze, rebate, discount. *Ant.* increase, expand, augment, swell, enlarge, spread, extend, amplify, inflate, stretch, develop, magnify, distend, strengthen, invigorate, reinforce, refresh, raise, heighten, inspirit, aggrandize, advance, intensify, enrich, enhance, improve.

redundant, extra, excessive, superfluous, wordy, profuse, copious, verbose, repetitious, prolix, diffuse. *Ant.* concise, terse, succinct, laconic.

refer, allude, consult, cite, quote, appeal, point, commit, consign, deliver, advert, apply, submit, concern, appeal.

refinement, culture, civilization, elegance, cultivation, clarification, purification, polish, poise, breeding, finesse, delicacy, finish, purity. *Ant.* rudeness, coarseness, crudity, rusticity, barbarism, vulgarity.

reflect, consider, ponder, muse, contemplate, think, reason, cogitate, meditate, study, speculate, ruminate, deliberate; mirror, copy, reproduce.

reform, correct, better, restore, improve, mend, revise, amend, reorganize, repair, transmute, renovate, redress, reconstruct, renew, freshen.

refractory, see recalcitrant.

refrain, *v.* abstain, forbear, withhold, desist, curb, avoid, govern; *n.* chorus, undersong, burden.

refresh, revive, renovate, animate, stimulate, strengthen, renew, brace, invigorate, restore, freshen, air, rest, enliven, cheer. *Ant.* fatigue, tire, bore, exhaust, weary.

refrigerate, chill, cool, freeze, refresh. *Ant.* warm, calefy, tepefy, heat.

refuge, privacy, solitude, seclusion, sanctuary, home, fortress, stronghold, protection, hideway, harbor, haven, asylum, retreat, shelter. *Ant.* danger, risk, pitfall, exposure, peril, jeopardy.

refuse, *n.* remains, waste, trash, garbage, scoria, rubbish, dross, residue, litter, rubble, sweepings, junk; *v.* reject, decline, disown, withhold, protest, renounce, negate, veto, disavow, repudiate, deny, disown, rebuff, repel, spurn, decline. *Ant.* effects, goods, supplies, valuables, property, belongings, assets, resources; accede, acquiesce, accept, acknowledge, assent, admit, comply, acquire, conform, consent, concede, yield, grant, sanction, approve, proffer, dispose, offer, present, bestow, allow, give.

refute, disprove, confute, overthrow, confound, repel, rebut, parry, invalidate, stultify, controvert, expose. *Ant.* support, sustain, endorse, encourage, defend, sanction, establish, prove, approve, assist, aid, confirm, affirm, ratify, commend, praise, uphold, corroborate, strengthen.

regal, royal, stately, imperial, imposing, majestic, sublime, queenly, autocratic, kingly, noble, magnificent, splendid. *Ant.* servile, lowly, plebian, common.

regarding, about, re, respecting, concerning, apropos, touching, anent.

regenerate, reproduce, revive, renovate, convert, change, renew, reform, inspire.

register, *v.* list, enroll, table, enter, record, admit, insert, fix, save, establish, chronicle, note, declare, express, indicate; *n.* archive, catalog, annal, list, roll, schedule, roster.

regression, reversion, recession, deterioration, retrogression, withdrawal, return, ebb, recidivism, backsliding.

regret, *n.* grief, remorse, sorrow, repentance, lamentation, concern, penitence, repining, contrition, compunction, self-reproach, bitterness, heartache, nostalgia, dissatisfaction, worry, disappointment, vexation; *v.* deplore, lament, rue, repine, repent, sorrow, bewail. *Ant.* contentment, satisfaction, serenity, tranquillity, cheerfulness, impenitence, induration, obduracy.

regular, customary, ordinary, orderly, uniform, homologous, homogeneous, consistent, constant, steady, natural, invariable, methodical, systematic, symmetrical, normal, habitual, punctual, conventional, cyclic, usual, successive, serial, periodic, recurrent. *Ant.* irregular, inconstant, inconsistent, variable, heterogeneous, infrequent, extraordinary, changing, sporadic, rare, uncommon, anomalous, eccentric, unusual, strange, peculiar, unsteady.

regulate, arrange, govern, direct, adjust, rule, organize, fix, correct, rectify, legislate, control, classify, systematize, allocate, readjust, adapt, reconcile. *Ant.* disarrange, confuse, mix, disarray, muss, jumble, entangle, scatter, misplace, commingle, disjoin, dissociate, disconnect, divide, disrupt, sunder, detach, separate, disorganize, disunite.

rehabilitate, restore, repair, reinvigorate, renew, reconstruct, reconstitute, reinstate.

reimburse, see **remunerate.**

reinforce, fortify, energize, invigorate, strengthen, augment. *Ant.* weaken, detract.

reject, exclude, deny, discard, refuse, spurn, veto, repudiate, eliminate, dismiss, eject, renounce. *Ant.* accept, admit, choose, select.

rejoice, exult, celebrate, triumph, delight, glory, revel, gloat. *Ant.* grieve, sulk, lament, mourn.

rejoinder, answer, rebuttal, retort, riposte, defense, reply, response.

relate, recount, tell, narrate, detail, recite, describe, report, state.

related, allied, correlative, akin, associated, analogous, kindred, leagued, germane, cognate, connected, affiliated. *Ant.* dissociated, dissimilar, alien, unrelated, foreign.

relative, *adj.* dependent, contingent, conditional, respecting, referable, comparative, special, particular, definite, appositive, germane, cognate, pertinent, relevant; *n.* kin, relation, connection.

relaxation, rest, leisure, mitigation, diversion, loosening, ease, comfort, amusement, abatement, recreation, relief, repose.

release, freedom, discharge, liberation, surrender, absolution, deliverance, exoneration, dispensation, emancipation, acquittal, relinquishment.

relegate, entrust, commit, confide, assign, consign, transfer, remove, refer, dispatch, remand, table, banish, expel, expatriate. *Ant.* assume, accept, keep, withhold.

relent, abate, soften, yield, subside, defer, forbear, bend, comply, relax, submit, bow, refrain. *Ant.* stiffen, harden, persist, persevere.

relentless, implacable, rigorous, pitiless, hard, stringent, obdurate, inexorable, strict, unyielding, ruthless, fierce, vindictive, rigid, inflexible. *Ant.* merciful, compassionate, lenient, gentle.

relevant, suitable, appropriate, pertinent, apt, applicable, fitting, congruous, germane, apropos, apposite, cognate, associated, affinitive. *Ant.* disparate, separate, discrepant, irrelevant, unrelated, inconsistent.

relief, succor, alleviation, help, support, assistance, ease, mitigation, redress, consolation, extrication, remedy, aid, comfort, exemption, deliverance, release, refreshment, softening, moderation, encouragement, reenforcement, palliation, easement, rescue. *Ant.* inhibition, hindrance, impediment, interference, obstruction, burden, aggravation, restriction, incumbrance, discouragement, incubus, disapproval, restraint.

relinquish, renounce, quit, forego, resign, abandon, forsake, yield, cede, spare, dismiss, revoke, reject, surrender, abjure, forswear, desert, deny, secede, discard, drop, desist, disclaim, abdicate, vacate. *Ant.* hold, keep, persevere, continue, persist, pursue, retain, maintain, perpetuate, prolong.

relish, gusto, zest, gratification, appreciation, satisfaction, enjoyment, inclination, preference, partiality, appetizer, seasoning, spice. *Ant.* distaste, disfavor.

reluctant, disinclined, opposed, loath, slow, averse, backward, tardy, unwilling, unready, doubtful, demurring, concerned, afraid, indisposed. *Ant.* willing, eager, disposed, inclined, ready, amenable, enthusiastic, predisposed, agreeable, hopeful, unhesitating, voluntary, anxious.

rely, depend, trust, confide, count, bank, lean. *Ant.* distrust, doubt.

remain, continue, endure, last, abide, dwell, stay, survive, inhabit, reside. *Ant.* decamp, depart, go, leave, vanish, fade, move, run, bolt.

remainder, rest, balance, remnant, surplus, dregs, excess, leavings, leftovers, remains, residue, residuum.

remarkable, notable, memorable, striking, peculiar, rare, extraordinary, famous, important, prominent, conspicuous, salient, wonderful, uncommon. *Ant.* usual, common, normal, regular, inconspicuous.

remedy, *n.* cure, reparation, specific, restorative, redress, antidote, counteractive, relief, corrective, medication, panacea, nostrum, help, bracer; *v.* repair, redress, renew, correct, fix, amend, cure, relieve, heal, restore. *Ant.* worsen, aggravate, intensify, neglect, ignore.

remember, recall, recollect, remind, review, retrace, reminisce, retain, memorize. *Ant.* forget, obliterate, disregard, repress, suppress.

reminiscence, remembrance, mind, recollection, memory, memoir, souvenir, token. *Ant.* forgetfulness, oblivion, nirvana.

remiss, careless, lax, slack, negligent, lazy, dilatory, slow, backward, thoughtless, forgetful, inattentive, derelict. *Ant.* careful, scrupulous, mindful, dutiful, vigilant, thorough, observant.

remit, release, relax, absolve, pardon, forgive, surrender, relinquish, discontinue, postpone, defer, moderate, mitigate, excuse, alleviate, overlook, soften, exempt, relent, restore. *Ant.* hold, reserve, keep, withhold, persist, retain, continue, exact, dominate, control, command, avenge, bind, enjoin, repress, suppress, restrain, restrict, prohibit.

remnant, remainder, balance, residue, strip, leavings, piece, rest, fragment, relic, scrap, vestige, trimming, waste, reject, surplus, refuse. *Ant.* whole, entire, total, all, completeness, entirety, bulk, mass.

remodel, change, renew, alter, improve, rebuild, renovate, repair, recreate. *Ant.* restore, reinstate.

remonstrate, expostulate, check, criticize, animadvert, censure, object, scold, upbraid, reprimand, discourage, recriminate, blame, objurate, decry, protest, disapprove, chide, reproach. *Ant.* commend, laud, sustain, support, endorse, favor, praise, eulogize, assist, encourage, defend, admire, appreciate, advocate, recommend, uphold, acclaim, applaud, compliment.

remorse, see **repentance.**

remote, distant, foreign, alien, faraway, unconnected, separate, unrelated, indirect, inappropriate, secluded, inaccessible, beyond, far-fetched, out-of-the-way, uttermost. *Ant.* near, proximate, nigh, close, neighboring, adjoining, contiguous, adjacent, intimate, bordering, abutting, related, touching, connected, approximate.

remove, move, transport, dislodge, displace, separate, eject, transfer, abstract, eliminate, dismiss, evict, oust, depart, displant, migrate, take, shift, unseat, leave, withdraw, vacate, evacuate, retire, eliminate, kill, destroy, quit, extract, draw, wrench, pull, uproot. *Ant.* place, stop, settle, replace, remain, establish, stay, fix, root, imbed, plant, stow, deposit, dwell, linger, maintain, conserve, preserve.

remunerate, compensate, recompense, reimburse, reward, repay, pay, requite, satisfy, indemnify, atone, return, redress, acknowledge, give. *Ant.* deprive, amerce, confiscate, withhold, mulct, charge, fine, penalize, forfeit, levy, tax, extort, appropriate, seize.

renaissance, revival, rebirth, awakening, reappearance, restoration, regeneration.

rend, rip, lacerate, burst, tear, sever, mangle, break, slit, rupture, sunder, cleave, harrow, fracture, split, dislocate, dissect, crack, mince, dismember, separate. *Ant.* join, mend, reunite, secure, fasten, brace, replace, renew, connect, conjoin, fuse, cement, fix, graft, splice, tighten, attach.

render, give, present, return, restore, apportion, assign, dispense, distribute, pay, requite, surrender, deliver, contribute, afford, produce, furnish, yield, supply, impart, allot, communicate, interpret, translate, explain, state, specify, perform, express, define, *Ant.* withhold, retain, appropriate, hold, seize, withdraw, secure, receive, keep, take, get, obtain, abstract, deduct, curtail, refuse, hoard, neglect, scrimp, ignore, store, forget, garner, save, amass, misinterpret, accumulate, misconstrue, blunder, confuse.

rendezvous, *n.* tryst, meeting, date, arrangement, assignation, appointment; *v.* meet, assemble, join, gather.

renew, refresh, renovate, restore, revive, continue, repeat, resume, reestablish, replace, reiterate, regenerate, replenish, resuscitate. *Ant.* exhaust, deplete, diminish, enfeeble.

renounce, repudiate, reject, disavow, recant, abjure, revoke, refuse, abandon, forswear, deny, disclaim, disown, abdicate, drop, abrogate, rescind, relinquish, desert, quit, discard, secede, surrender, forsake, forego, abnegate. *Ant.* persist, remain, conserve, stay, keep, maintain, continue, uphold, persevere, own, praise, prize, retain, value, commend, defend, sustain, advocate, support, assert, preserve, cherish, vindicate, claim, acknowledge, avow, proclaim.

repair, mend, refit, remodel, renew, renovate, patch, replace, amend, fix, restore, mend, remedy, correct, rectify. *Ant.* damage, spoil, neglect, wreck, ruin, injure, mar, break, tear, destroy, replace.

reparation, atonement, repair, satisfaction, remuneration, return, compensation, recompense, indemnity, restoration, restitution, indemnification, amends, redress, propitiation, expiation, retribution, emolument, payment. *Ant.* confiscation, penalty, appropriation, extortion, seizure, acquisition, deprivation, theft, plunder, swindle.

repay, recompense, remunerate, refund, reimburse, requite, reward, indemnify, retaliate, avenge, pay, compensate, satisfy, restore. *Ant.* cheat, default, defraud, swindle.

repeal, revoke, recall, annul, rescind, abolish, abrogate, cancel, abolish, veto. *Ant.* continue, maintain, renew, validate, keep.

repeat, iterate, recite, recapitulate, reproduce, echo, duplicate, tell, quote, relate, recur.

repel, repulse, reject, disgust, disperse, rebuff, sicken, parry, resist, refuse, scatter. *Ant.* draw, attract, surrender, succumb.

repentance, remorse, penitence, sorrow, compunction, contrition, self-reproach, regret. *Ant.* impenitence, callousness, obduracy, recusancy, complacency, comfort, shamelessness.

eplace, restore, repay, substitute, reinstate, rehabilitate, refund, reconstruct, reconstitute, succeed, supplant, supersede. *Ant.* exchange, bandy, shuffle, change, alternate, shift, alter, turn, vary, modify, transform, diversify.

eplete, full, sated, exuberant, fraught, stuffed, charged, abundant, gorged, surfeited, glutted. *Ant.* poor, needy, starved, hungry, empty.

eply, answer, rejoin, respond, counter, retort, echo, acknowledge. *Ant.* ask, question, demand, plead.

eport, *n.* story, description, recital, statement, narrative, narration, account, record, tale, hearsay, rumor, tidings, announcement, communication, news, chronicle, publication, intelligence, dispatch, message; *v.* announce, describe, declare, relate, detail, record, tell, communicate, recite, proclaim, chronicle, advertise, inform, write, state, publish, disclose, impart, express, mention, specify, broadcast. *Ant.* concealment, secrecy, reserve, suppression, evasion, cancellation, reticence, deletion; conceal, screen, hide, secrete, veil, cloak, withhold, mask, suppress, delete, muzzle.

epose, rest, comfort, leisure, ease, calm, tranquility, relaxation, peacefulness, respite, quiet, serenity. *Ant.* activity, disturbance, agitation, noise, alertness.

epresent, depict, portray, describe, picture, delineate, imitate, draw, personate.

epress, suppress, subdue, quell, choke, dull, overpower, silence, smother. *Ant.* let alone, ignore, permit, allow, assist, approve, help, aid.

eprieve, suspend, delay, relieve, pardon, forgive, absolve; remission, commutation, suspension.

eprimand, admonish, berate, reprehend, reprove, rebuke, censure, scold, reproach, chide, blame, punish. *Ant.* praise, laud, forgive, reward.

eproduction, copy, print, casting, imitation, representation, ectype, facsimile, replica, transcript, propagation, generation. *Ant.* pattern, original, model, archetype, prototype.

eprove, disapprove, disparage, rebuke, berate, lecture, reproach, scold, chide, condemn, blame, objurgate, censure, snub, correct, criticize, upbraid, reprimand, admonish, chasten, punish, check, warn. *Ant.* approve, applaud, acclaim, sanction, endorse, encourage, cheer, reward, inspirit, embolden, comfort, praise, promote, inspire, congratulate, eulogize, flatter.

epudiate, disavow, renounce, disown, reject, exclude, abjure, disclaim, discard, expel, contradict, banish, dissent, protest, demur, disagree, spurn, deny, withdraw, revoke, dismiss, cancel, abrogate, repeal, rescind, annul, retract, reverse, veto, void, nullify, quash, countermand, overrule, abolish, recall, evade, dodge, omit, ignore. *Ant.* acknowledge, asseverate, avow, profess, affirm, assert, admit, embody, ratify, incorporate, own, approve, concede, accept, assent, acquiesce, select, yield, choose, countersign, comply, prefer, adhere, observe, perform, defend, discharge, settle.

repugnant, antagonistic, disagreeable, inimical, antipathetic, disgusting, hostile, distasteful, repellent, incompatible, disobedient contrary, unwilling, inconsistent, opposed, offensive, abhorrent offensive, invidious, revolting, obnoxious, unbearable. *Ant.* compatible, agreeable, pleasant, harmonious, pleasing, conformable suitable, concordant, accordant, concomitant, sympathetic, compliant, congenial, apt, conciliatory, fit.

repulsive, odious, ugly, horrible, repellent, horrid, disagreeable, revolting, hideous, detestable, distasteful, repugnant, obnoxious detestable, abhorrent, nauseating, abominable, gruesome, frightful, terrible, offensive, disgusting, loathsome. *Ant.* pleasing, attractive, inviting, delicate, enticing, refined, agreeable, alluring captivating, fascinating, enchanting, entrancing, bewitching.

reputable, honorable, worthy, respectable, estimable, trustworthy famous, creditable, celebrated, dignified, distinguished, straightforward, popular, notable, illustrious, righteous, just, reliable dependable, virtuous, noble. *Ant.* base, foul, dishonorable, disloyal, arrant, dishonest, treacherous, unscrupulous, depraved undignified, untrustworthy, debased, abject, contemptible, recreant, inglorious, shameless, disreputable, despicable, infamous, unworthy, vile, notorious, scandalous.

request, ask, entreat, importune, beg, sue, pray, appeal, implore invite, petition, apply, solicit, plead, demand, bid, summon, supplicate, beseech.

requirement, claim, demand, need, want, requisition, urgency, call necessity, exigency, pinch, mandate, charge, bidding, decree, injunction, behest.

requisite, necessary, needful, pressing, required, demanded, essential, urgent, imperative, indispensable. *Ant.* unnecessary, useless, excessive, dispensable, worthless, superfluous.

requite, remunerate, recompense, reward, reciprocate, exchange, repay, satisfy, compensate, pay, avenge, retaliate, return, revenge punish, quit. *Ant.* pardon, forgive, absolve, overlook, excuse acquit, neglect, extenuate, release, justify, discharge, exempt clear, exonerate, exculpate, remit, vindicate.

rescind, abrogate, cancel, revoke, reverse, annul, vacate, void, disclaim, veto, withdraw, retract, nullify, abolish, quash, repeal, dissolve, recall, countermand. *Ant.* command, appoint, inaugurate propose, permit, advance, allow, present, ordain, order, validate renew, retain, propose, establish.

rescue, save, recover, free, deliver, recapture, preserve, liberate redeem, reclaim, extricate, release, ransom, retrieve. *Ant.* incarcerate, impede, hinder, constrict, prosecute, inhibit, hamper, obstruct, preclude, bind, abandon, ignore, enslave.

resemblance, likeness, similarity, match, semblance, effigy, double facsimile, correspondence, agreement, analogy, affinity, simile similitude. *Ant.* difference, variance, dissimilarity, distinction discrepancy, oppositeness, heterogeneity, contrast, inconsistency disparity, dissimilitude, diversity, contrast, deviation, contradiction, disagreement.

resentment, anger, perturbation, displeasure, wrath, indignation, animosity, ire, annoyance, sullenness, vexation, exasperation, rancor, moroseness, exacerbation, acerbity, bitterness, acrimony, umbrage, huff, pique, asperity, rankling. *Ant.* affection, amity, concord, harmony, pleasure, endearment, patience, happiness, geniality, enthusiasm, compliance, good humor.

reserved, restrained, shy, modest, undemonstrative, formal, cold, reticent, cautious, diffident, secretive, unsociable, aloof, close, demure, taciturn, detached, saved, hoarded, preserved, booked, distant, bashful. *Ant.* affable, friendly, uninhibited, expansive, unreserved, blatant.

residue, see **remainder.**

resign, quit, yield, vacate, surrender, eschew, renounce, retract, abdicate, relinquish, waive, forgo, abjure, abandon, withdraw, cede. *Ant.* assume, accept, stay, remain, retain, receive.

resilient, elastic, springy, supple, buoyant, flexible, spirited. *Ant.* rigid, stiff, tense, inflexible, unbending.

resist, oppose, withstand, hinder, obstruct, check, thwart, stem, refuse, counteract, impede, frustrate, contest, conflict, antagonize, impugn, neutralize. *Ant.* comply, collaborate, contribute, concur, help, conform, cooperate, assist, submit, consent, obey, observe, defer, yield, surrender, accede, bend, capitulate, abandon, cede, waive, assent, acquiesce, ratify, confirm.

resolute, steadfast, decided, persevering, unshaken, constant, determined, bold, resolved, earnest, serious, unyielding, fixed, unwavering, intransigent, uncompromising, courageous, enduring, unalterable, intrepid, valiant, audacious, fearless, dauntless, confident, grim, stubborn, unflinching, indomitable. *Ant.* irresolute, vacillating, afraid, weak, unsteady, cautious, wavering, timorous, unstable, cowardly, hesitant, undecided, fickle, yielding, vague, uncertain, changeable.

resolution, decision, determination, resolve, firmness, constancy, courage, fortitude, stamina, zeal, devotion. *Ant.* irresolution, uncertainty, indecision, caprice, hesitation, vacillation, instability.

resound, reverberate, echo, reecho, vibrate, ring, sound.

resources, capital, funds, money, wealth, property, reserve, income, riches, supplies, means, contrivances, appliances, instrumentality.

respect, deference, admiration, consideration, esteem, reverence, regard, fealty, recognition, veneration, honor. *Ant.* contempt, disdain, scorn, contumely, irreverence, disparagement.

respectable, estimable, honorable, decent, proper, reputable, presentable, good, upright, mediocre, fair, moderate. *Ant.* dishonorable, improper, unworthy, scandalous, inglorious, undignified.

respective, individual, specific, particular, special.

resplendent, shining, bright, glorious, radiant, lustrous, brilliant, splendid, beaming, glittery, effulgent, refulgent. *Ant.* dull, drab, inglorious, dark, dreary, somber.

responsible, accountable, liable, answerable, subject, amenable, dependable, obligatory, trustworthy. *Ant.* irresponsible, exempt, excusable, unrestrained, immune, uncontrolled, unfettered, unbound, lawless, arbitrary, free, unconditioned, supreme, absolute, unlimited.

restful, serene, peaceful, still, easy, quiet, cozy, comfortable, tranquil, soothing. *Ant.* disturbing, annoying, alarming.

restitution, restoration, return, compensation, amends, indemnification, satisfaction, repayment, atonement, reimbursement.

restless, agitated, fidgety, disturbed, nervous, uneasy, sleepless, fitful, unsettled, worried, anxious, excited, changeable, transient, moving, roving, wandering. *Ant.* unmoved, tranquil, calm, composed, quiet, placid, unperturbed, imperturbable, undisturbed, resigned, content.

restrain, check, suppress, curb, keep, bridle, restrict, constrain, confine, circumscribe, hold, control, subdue, govern, hamper, hinder, limit, shackle, tie, hobble, withhold, repress, prevent, stop. *Ant.* loosen, unbind, free, liberate, release, emancipate, arouse, aid, animate, encourage, impel, dismiss.

restrict, limit, check, fence, restrain, obstruct, inhibit, impede, confine, bind, curb. *Ant.* widen, expand, extend, enlarge, release, free.

result, *n.* effect, outcome, issue, end, termination, conclusion, upshot, product, fruit, consequence; *v.* proceed, come, follow, flow, issue, arise, spring, eventuate, resolve, originate, accrue. *Ant.* cause, origin, source, root.

résumé, abstract, statement, synopsis, summary, recapitulation.

resume, reassume, recommence, renew, continue. *Ant.* stop, quit, forget.

retain, hold, maintain, preserve, keep, employ, detain, hire, withhold, secure, engage, reserve. *Ant.* relinquish, dismiss, surrender, cede, dispense, lose, jettison, discard, forego, surrender.

retaliate, requite, reciprocate, return, repay, avenge, retort. *Ant.* pardon, forgive, forget, ignore.

retard, hinder, check, interrupt, delay, arrest, postpone, hamper, clog, impede. *Ant.* assist, advance, speed, hasten.

retract, abjure, disown, forswear, revoke, recall, deny, withdraw, recant, annul, cancel, reverse, nullify, abrogate, rescind, ignore, renounce, disclaim, contradict, abnegate. *Ant.* affirm, confirm, asseverate, assert, declare, reassert, state, depose, advance, emphasize, corroborate, endorse, ratify, approve, acknowledge, commend, admit, praise, uphold.

retrieve, recapture, redeem, regain, reclaim, recover, restore, recoup, rescue, reestablish, recall, revive. *Ant.* lose, surrender, relinquish.

retrogress, regress, decline, retrograde, retreat, degenerate, backslide, deteriorate, relapse, revert. *Ant.* improve, advance, proceed, progress, develop.

return, recur, restore, revert, reciprocate, reappear, yield, reply.

reveal, divulge, impart, unmask, unveil, discover, open, disclose, expose, show, confess, betray, uncover, inform, unfold, publish, announce, impart, explain, express. *Ant.* hide, conceal, cover, blind, mask, secrete, dodge, evade, deceive, disguise, delude, mystify.

revenge, vengeance, retribution, retaliation, requital, vindictiveness, implacability, malevolence. *Ant.* forgiveness, pardon, amnesty, reprieve, conciliation, forbearance, indulgence, reconciliation, excuse, acquittal.

reverence, honor, homage, veneration, respect, regard, approbation, awe, adoration, admiration, esteem, worship. *Ant.* disrespect, contumely, dishonor, irreverence, discourtesy, mockery, contempt, execration, indignity.

reverse, transpose, upset, rescind, retract, invert, alter, undo, nullify, repeal, revoke, overturn, annul.

review, reconsider, rehearse, analyze, inspect, retrace, survey, edit, criticize, judge, examine.

revive, refresh, renew, renovate, resuscitate, awaken, revivify, reanimate, reinforce, reproduce, recall, rouse, invigorate, freshen, improve, repair. *Ant.* weaken, wither, waste, lessen, decay, deteriorate, decline, perish, droop, fade, sink, shrink, crumple, rot, shrivel.

revoke, see **repeal.**

revolting, nauseating, offensive, loathsome, objectionable, odious, abominable, repugnant, obnoxious, repulsive, sickening. *Ant.* attractive, gratifying, pleasing, charming.

revolve, rotate, turn, eddy, circulate, roll, circle, spin, whirl, orbit, ponder, study, consider.

reward, remuneration, gain, retribution, recompense, compensation, amends, bounty, prize, bonus, gratuity, return, requital, satisfaction, indemnity, recoupment, redress, atonement, acknowledgment, consideration, payment. *Ant.* penalty, fine, punishment, amercement, damages, confiscation, appropriation, deprivation, divestment, attachment, seizure, forfeiture, levy, toll, tax, loss.

rhythm, cadence, meter, beat, regularity, periodicity, tempo, swing, measure, lilt, pulsation.

ribald, low, base, lewd, lascivious, vulgar, indecent, loose, obscene, gross, scurrilous, uncouth, indecorous, coarse, vile, contemptible. *Ant.* clean, decent, pure, undefiled, chaste, virtuous, modest, wellbred, decorous, genteel.

rich, wealthy, ample, abundant, opulent, copious, plentiful, affluent, sumptuous, moneyed, independent, generous, luscious, exuberant, fruitful, fertile, superb, independent, profuse, luxuriant, vivid, strong, intense. *Ant.* poor, impoverished, indigent, mendicant, squalid, penniless, destitute, depleted, needy, plain, drab, barren.

ridicule, mockery, persiflage, derision, satire, sarcasm, irony. *Ant.* praise, honor, respect, approval.

ridiculous, ludicrous, preposterous, absurd, farcical, funny, odd, droll, nonsensical, comic, bizarre. *Ant.* correct, sensible, wise, conventional.

rigid, stiff, inelastic, indurate, inflexible, hard, petrified, firm, stony, unyielding, unbending, exact, scrupulous, stern, exacting, precise, austere, rigorous, severe, strict, relentless. *Ant.* soft, pliant, ductile, flexible, mobile, elastic, yielding, limber, tolerant, indulgent, lenient, complaisant, forbearing, considerate.

rigorous, stern, harsh, stiff, exacting, inflexible, oppressive, rigid, severe, stringent, strict. *Ant.* lax, easygoing, lenient, easy.

ring, *n.* circle, hoop, round, band, arena, set, clique, coterie, faction, league, confederation, gang, reverberation, resonance, chime, clangor; *v.* encircle, circle, orbit, enclose, surround, girdle, resound, tinkle, jingle, toll, knell, clang, chime, peal.

riot, outbreak, insurgence, rebellion, disturbance, tumult, fray, row, commotion, melee, altercation, turmoil, broil, uprising, quarrel, strife, pandemonium, revelry, excess, confusion, violence. *Ant.* peace, quiet, order, tranquility, regularity.

rip, rend, tear, lacerate, cut, split, slit, burst.

ripe, mature, mellow, complete, finished, ready, developed, seasoned, consummate. *Ant.* immature, young, green, raw, unripe, unready, unseasoned, budding, unfit, undeveloped.

rise, arise, ascend, mount, climb, scale, spring, begin, increase, grow, progress, commence, originate, start, thrive, prosper. *Ant.* decline, settle, recede, fall, return, descend, drop, sink, regress, retrograde, tumble, slump.

risky, hazardous, chancy, precarious, dangerous, uncertain, perilous. *Ant.* safe, sure, certain.

rite, ceremony, liturgy, ritual, ordinance, formality, solemnity, duty, observance, sacrament, service.

rival, *n.* opponent, competitor, antagonist, emulator, adversary, disputant, combatant; *v.* oppose, compete, challenge, contest, dispute, emulate, conflict, counteract, resist, confront, oppugn, battle, antagonize, attack, repel, contend, encounter, struggle, combat, wrestle, fight. *Ant.* patron, helper, assistant, mate, partner, confrère, auxiliary, ally, supporter, advocate; aid, assist, uphold, support, champion, cooperate, sustain, second, abet, back, favor, encourage, patronize, defend.

roam, ramble, range, rove, wander, stray, prowl, saunter.

rob, steal, purloin, rifle, burglarize, forge, cheat, defraud, pilfer, appropriate, embezzle, plunder, loot, despoil.

robber, thief, plunderer, burglar, marauder, raider, pirate, pillager, bandit, despoiler, forager, poacher, rustler, forger, swindler.

robust, strong, vigorous, sturdy, muscular, tough, sound, brawny, strapping, powerful, hardy. *Ant.* weak, feeble, debilitated, frail, infirm, sickly, flabby, soft.

roll, *n.* list, catalog, document, scroll, register, schedule, rota, inventory; *v.* revolve, rotate, whirl, wheel, turn, wallow, tumble, wrap, enfold, swathe, bind, press, level, smooth, flatten, bowl, resound, reverberate, rumble, undulate, fluctuate.

romantic, sentimental, chimerical, imaginative, extravagant, improbable, fanciful, idealistic, fictional, poetic, imaginary. *Ant.* real, pragmatic, solid, definite, practical, realistic.

roster, list, catalog, roll, table, register, schedule, inventory, directory.

rot, decay, spoil, defile, decompose, waste, disintegrate, degenerate, putrefy. *Ant.* bloom, grow, flourish, thrive.

rotate, spin, circulate, circle, revolve, swirl, wheel, turn, eddy, gyrate, whirl.

rough, uneven, coarse, irregular, bumpy, harsh, rugged, jagged, serrated, unrefined, crude, austere, rude, gruff, blunt, impolite, unpolished, indecent. *Ant.* smooth, polished, even, level, courteous, refined.

round, globular, spherical, circular, rotund.

rouse, animate, awaken, whet, inspire, agitate, motivate, provoke, inflame, stir, excite, stimulate. *Ant.* lull, calm, tranquilize, pacify.

rude, uncouth, coarse, vulgar, rough, churlish, uncivilized, saucy, barbarous, insolent, impudent, impertinent, surly, insulting, curt, brusque, gruff, unpolished, disrespectful, scurrilous, scornful, discourteous, boorish, impolite, ungracious. *Ant.* polite, refined, cultured, genteel, courteous, suave, civil, cordial, gracious, amiable, civilized, pleasant, gentle, gallant, chivalrous, respectful, courtly, decorous, dignified, considerate, sociable, affable, tactful, congenial, mannerly, engaging.

rueful, melancholy, lugubrious, sorrowful, dejected, regretful, penitent, depressed, sad, plaintive, mournful, despairing. *Ant.* happy, cheerful, nonchalant, content, hopeful, insensitive, insouciant.

rugged, rough, craggy, irregular, furrowed, broken, jagged, corrugated, uneven, difficult, arduous, harsh, hardy, brawny, husky. *Ant.* smooth, even, level, polished, refined, courteous, gentle, weak, feeble, delicate.

rural, country, pastoral, bucolic, agricultural, agrarian, rustic, nonurban. *Ant.* urban, citified, suburban.

ruse, artifice, shift, deception, wile, stratagem, expedient, trick, subterfuge, dodge, imposture, hoax, maneuver, sham.

rustic, countrified, agricultural, bucolic, rural, pastoral, rude, unadorned, unpolished, verdant, awkward, inelegant, crude, simple, unsophisticated. *Ant.* accomplished, elegant, cultured, refined, urbane, polished, stylish, sophisticated, dignified.

rut, track, furrow, groove, channel, crevice, routine, rote, habit, tedium.

ruthless, brutal, cruel, remorseless, tyrannical, relentless, merciless, inhuman, pitiless, harsh, unkind, vengeful, vindictive, rancorous, implacable, unforgiving, malevolent. *Ant.* kind, forgiving, amiable, compassionate, sympathetic, lenient, merciful, benevolent, humane, charitable, considerate.

S

sack, pillage, devastate, despoil, plunder, ravage, ruin, demolish, waste, loot, strip.

sacred, holy, hallowed, consecrated, sanctified, inviolable, blessed, divine, venerable, sacrosanct. *Ant.* lay, temporal, worldly, blasphemous.

sacrifice, *n.* offering, oblation, libation, abnegation, self-denial, loss, atonement; *v.* forgo, give up, lose, offer, surrender, immolate, destroy.

sacrilegious, impious, profane, blasphemous, irreverent, desecrating. *Ant.* pious, holy, reverent.

sad, unhappy, dejected, gloomy, sorrowful, despondent, disconsolate, blue, depressed, woeful, dismal, melancholy. *Ant.* happy, cheerful, blithe, glad, gay, joyful.

safeguard, *n.* protection, defense, security, escort, guard, convoy, palladium, passport, shield, guardian; *v.* watch, protect, defend, secure, escort, support, preserve, shield.

safety, security, refuge, preservation, surety, escape, asylum, custody. *Ant.* danger, peril, risk, hazard, jeopardy.

sag, sink, bend, droop, strain, weaken, settle, sway, decline.

sage, savant, intellectual, scholar, authority, professor, pundit, philosopher.

salient, outstanding, marked, important, conspicuous, impressive, prominent, signal, striking, notable, significant. *Ant.* minor, unimportant, inconspicuous, insignificant.

salubrious, healthful, healthy, wholesome, helpful, safe, hygienic, sanitary, beneficial. *Ant.* unwholesome, noisome, unhealthy, detrimental.

sample, *n.* model, specimen, cutting, example, slice, part, illustration, instance, prototype, case, pattern; *v.* test, try, check, taste, smell, inspect, judge.

sanction, *n.* approval, authority, permit, commendation, ratification, permission, support, allowance, warrant, authorization, liberty, privilege, license, approbation, countenance; *v.* confirm, sustain, encourage, ratify, support, authorize, approve, countenance, favor, endorse, commend, allow, promote, proclaim. *Ant.* disapproval, disapprobation, denunciation, disparagement, refusal, stricture, objection, prohibition, injunction, interdiction, inhibition, restraint, hindrance, exclusion; denounce, disparage, disapprove, prohibit, inhibit, veto, disallow, refuse, ban, forbid, exclude, prevent.

sane, rational, sensible, normal, wholesome, lucid, healthy, steady, reasonable, self-possessed, sound. *Ant.* insane, idiotic, irrational, demented, mad, deranged, unsound, lunatic, crazy, psychotic, maniacal.

sap, undermine, tunnel, impoverish, debilitate, drain, enfeeble, weaken, exhaust, enervate, impair, deplete.

apient, sagacious, knowing, acute, judicious, sage, discerning, prudent, learned, wise, shrewd. *Ant.* ignorant, stupid, obtuse, dull.

arcastic, scornful, satirical, sardonic, mocking, taunting, bitter, ironical, derisive, hostile, sneering, caustic. *Ant.* pleasant, courteous, pleasing, civil, polite, agreeable, amiable, deferential, respectful, complimentary, ingratiating, affable, gracious, cordial, flattering.

ate, satiate, satisfy, cloy, saturate, quench, slake, gorge, glut, stuff.

atire, ridicule, sarcasm, derision, mockery, irony, humor, abuse, lampoon, burlesque, wit, invective, parody, travesty.

aturate, permeate, wet, drench, impregnate, soak, imbrue, fill. *Ant.* dry, desiccate, dehydrate, wipe.

aunter, stroll, ramble, rove, loiter, amble, linger, meander, wander, dawdle, waver, tarry, dally.

avory, palatable, piquant, pleasing, pungent, appetizing, spicy, tasty, tangy, tempting, delectable, luscious, toothsome. *Ant.* unsavory, vapid, offensive, tasteless, sickening, insipid, flat, bland.

aying, byword, proverb, saw, maxim, aphorism, apothegm, adage, quotation, epigram, dictum, citation, remark, observation, statement.

can, scrutinize, inspect, examine, survey, investigate, audit, skim.

canty, scarce, meager, small, ragged, insufficient, inadequate, thin, sparse, skimpy, limited. *Ant.* ample, sufficient, plentiful, profuse, prevalent, unstinted, abundant.

care, frighten, intimidate, terrorize, alarm, startle, terrify, affright. *Ant.* inspirit, entice, encourage, revive.

cathing, mordant, scorching, trenchant, cutting, fierce, caustic, searing, harsh, bitter, injurious, savage.

catter, see **disperse.**

cene, show, sight, view, display, exhibition, spectacle, representation, scenery, panorama, pageant, setting, tableau.

coff, jeer, scout, sneer, gibe, mock, taunt, fleer, deride, flout, ridicule. *Ant.* praise, laud, commend.

corn, disdain, spurn, reject, slight, contemn, despise, abhor, detest.

creen, winnow, sift, sort, examine, separate, inspect, shield, protect, guard, hide, camouflage, conceal.

crupulous, punctilious, careful, cautious, exact, meticulous, precise, conscientious. *Ant.* remiss, negligent, careless, unscrupulous.

crutiny, inspection, examination, search, probe, investigation, inquiry, observation, review, study.

currilous, abusive, vituperative, vulgar, coarse, offensive, opprobrious, insulting, ribald, low, indecent, foul.

search, examine, investigate, explore, ransack, scrutinize, sift, inspect, probe, seek, scour, hunt, comb, rummage.

ecluded, hidden, sequestered, private, secret, retired, withdrawn, covert, embowered, isolated, segregated, solitary, screened, separated.

secret, concealed, private, clandestine, secluded, hidden, latent, confidential, mystic, unexplained, inscrutable, covert, cabalistic, unknown, veiled, esoteric, cryptic. *Ant.* open, apparent, evident, conspicuous, obvious, indubitable, plain, unmistakable, express, undisguised, explicit, manifest, transparent, clear, defined.

sedate, sober, staid, dignified, serious, proper, grave, serene, calm, solemn, tranquil, earnest, composed, demure. *Ant.* flighty, gay, mercurial, excitable, frivolous, lively.

seditious, insubordinate, factious, mutinous, rebellious, insurgent, perfidious, faithless, treacherous, disloyal. *Ant.* loyal, firm, faithful, obedient, dependable.

sedulous, assiduous, unremitting, industrious, diligent, painstaking, avid, persistent, persevering, ardent. *Ant.* careless, insouciant, indifferent, lethargic, somnolent, uninterested, unmotivated, indolent, languid, sluggish, remiss, shiftless, listless, lackadaisical.

seeming, apparent, ostensible, external, superficial, pretending, specious. *Ant.* real, true, certain, specific, definite.

seize, grasp, take, catch, comprehend, appropriate, grip, clasp, clutch, commandeer, grab, snatch, capture, confiscate, impound, maraud. *Ant.* restore, return, free, liberate, forgive, avoid, shun, spare, leave, relinquish, release, withdraw.

select, choose, prefer, nominate, pick, elect, opt, specify, designate, cull. *Ant.* reject, refuse, eliminate, rebuff.

send, transmit, delegate, fling, dispatch, depute, hurl, project, emit, forward, propel, ship, toss, sling, throw, impel, drive, cast, transfer, mail, consign, carry, convey, deliver. *Ant.* give, retain, get, receive, hold, keep, withhold.

senile, doddering, superannuated, ancient, decrepit, aged, infirm. *Ant.* young, strong, alert.

senior, *adj.* older, elder, advanced, superior; *n.* dean, chief.

sensibility, feeling, sense, sensation, impressibility, susceptibility, taste, discernment, insight. *Ant.* indifference, apathy, obtuseness, lethargy, numbness, insensibility.

sensitive, predisposed, conscious, alert, aware, susceptible, prone, perceptive, impressionable, subject, liable, tender, responsive. *Ant.* impassive, heartless, unfeeling, obdurate, unconscious, indifferent, inert.

sensual, voluptuous, carnal, salacious, earthy, licentious, lewd, dissolute, fleshly, unspiritual, intemperate. *Ant.* chaste, temperate, ascetic, rigorous, moderate, abstemious, austere, self-controlled.

sentiment, feeling, perception, tenderness, sympathy, emotion, remark, thought, opinion, affection, passion.

sentimental, romantic, effusive, maudlin, gushing, mawkish, languishing, emotional, overemotional, mushy, tender. *Ant.* cynical, reserved, unromantic, realistic, pragmatic, sardonic, objective.

separate, *adj.* apart, disunited, disjoined, divergent, radial, private, distinct, unique, independent, unconnected, alone, parted; *v.* disjoin, divide, disunite, sever, disengage, detach, disconnect, disentangle, dismember, disperse, dissect, scatter, isolate. *Ant.* united, connected, joined, mixed, associated, together; combine, consolidate, assemble, connect, attach, mix, fuse, blend, intertwine.

sequence, series, succession, following, gradation, order, arrangement, train, string, chain.

serene, see **tranquil.**

serious, solemn, grave, somber, sedate, staid, thoughtful, earnest, sober, profound, critical, austere, important, deep, momentous, weighty. *Ant.* flippant, trivial, insignificant, slight.

set, *n.* group, cluster, collection, arrangement, series, class, party, sect, knot, company, coterie, circle, club, association, attitude, position, posture; *v.* place, station, locate, lay, fix, put, stand, mount, establish, settle, stake, regulate, adjust, appoint, predetermine, expose, congeal, solidify, harden, coagulate; *adj.* regular, formal, established, settled, firm, unyielding, fixed, positive, immovable, placed, located.

settle, regulate, adjust, straighten, decide, determine, conclude, fix, reconcile, stabilize, set, dispose, arbitrate, establish, confirm, colonize, domesticate, sink, drop, fall, coalesce, subside, gravitate. *Ant.* disturb, disorganize, disarrange, displace, unsettle, confuse, muddle, shift, distort, remove, depart, migrate, move, forsake, quit, leave, stir, mix, blend, mingle, intermingle.

sever, divide, split, separate, disunite, part, sunder, detach, disconnect, cleave. *Ant.* unite, join, assemble, connect, fuse.

several, diverse, sundry, various, some, few. *Ant.* none, one.

severe, harsh, rigid, strict, forbidding, stringent, unyielding, stiff, rigorous, relentless, unmitigated, grim, unrelenting, inflexible, austere, uncompromising, hard, exacting, domineering, despotic, oppressive, obdurate, plain, simple, unadorned, inclement, extreme, violent. *Ant.* lenient, gentle, tractable, yielding, pliable, indulgent, courteous, clement, genial, kind, merciful, bland, compassionate, affable, tolerant, moderate, easygoing, forbearing, placid, mild, pleasant, temperate, calm.

shackle, chain, hobble, handcuff, tether, fetter, limit, bind, trammel, curb, check, manacle, restrict, impede. *Ant.* release, unbind, free, liberate, extricate.

shake, tremble, quiver, shiver, shudder, flutter, quake, oscillate, waver, intimidate, dissuade, dishearten, discourage.

sham, imitation, pretense, fraud, counterfeit, wile, fake, trick, deceit, dissimulation, humbug, ruse, stratagem.

shame, mortify, abash, embarrass, discomfit, humiliate, dishonor, degrade, discredit. *Ant.* encourage, glorify, honor, uphold, respect.

shape, *n.* form, mold, image, pattern, figure, cut, guise, aspect, appearance, configuration, conformation, construction, frame, outline, trim, contour, cast; *v.* form, mold, cast, model, fabricate, forge, regulate, fashion, make, produce, develop, adjust, direct, discipline, cut, sketch.

shapeless, amorphic, misshapen, formless, amorphous, unshapely, deformed, disfigured, irregular. *Ant.* shapely, symmetrical, trim, neat, regular, proportionate, well-formed, proportioned.

sharp, acute, keen, piercing, fine, barbed, biting, cutting, pointed, pungent, piquant, acrid, stinging, sour, spicy, intelligent, wise, sagacious, brilliant, discerning. *Ant.* dull, blunt, rough, flat, insipid, tasteless, bland, unsavory, vapid, dull-witted, unintelligent, stultified, insensitive, shallow, stupid, inept.

shelter, *v.* screen, shroud, cover, hide, guard, house, harbor, defend, protect, shield, secure, preserve, safeguard; *n.* refuge, asylum, sanctuary, harbor, haven, retreat. *Ant.* expose, endanger, ignore, jeopardize, neglect, imperil, uncover.

shield, protect, shelter, cover, defend, guard, preserve, repel, forbid, safeguard, avert. *Ant.* neglect, ignore, desert, expose, endanger, uncover, bare, imperil.

shine, glare, scintillate, shimmer, glitter, glow, radiate, beam, buff, sparkle, gleam, glisten, glimmer, illumine, irradiate, illuminate, polish, burnish.

ship, transport, transmit, forward, route, send, dispatch, remit.

shoal, reef, bank, bar, sandbar, shallow; horde, crowd, throng, swarm, multitude, mass, flock, school.

shock, *n.* concussion, collision, percussion, assault, impact, onset, attack, clash, jolt, outrage, violence, fury, outburst, agitation, tumult, disturbance; *v.* agitate, horrify, frighten, alarm, embarrass, offend, distress, disturb, scandalize, nauseate, terrify, startle, astound, appall, abash, overawe, terrorize. *Ant.* soothe, calm, lull, pacify, mitigate, quiet, comfort, tranquillize, allay, assuage, alleviate, console, please, inspirit, relieve, humor, reconcile, compose.

shoot, *v.* discharge, fire, emit, hurl, cast, eject, dart, propel, expel, catapult, kill, wound, hit, sprout, bloom, burgeon, bud, germinate, project, protrude; *n.* sprout, offshoot, scion, sucker, branch, twig, channel, trough, chute.

shore, *n.* beach, strand, bank, margin, border, brink, coast; *v.* support, brace, prop, stabilize.

short, brief, succinct, abridged, condensed, little, compact, laconic, curt, abbreviated, stunted, squat. *Ant.* long, lengthy, prolonged, endless, elongated, protracted, interminable, perpetual.

showy, flashy, garish, gaudy, pompous, sumptuous, resplendent, opulent, loud, pretentious, flaunting, proud, ostentatious, tawdry, brilliant, ornate. *Ant.* dull, lusterless, dim, colorless, pale squalid, dismal, gloomy, dingy, grim, drab, monotonous.

shrewd, knowing, sharp, acute, cunning, clever, discerning, astute, sagacious, alert, sapient, reflective, cautious, prudent, careful, observant, mindful, wily, crafty, artful, perspicacious, circumspect, sly. *Ant.* unthinking, unreasoning, impetuous, ignorant, dull, foolish, stultified, obtuse, dense, undiscerning, frivolous, indifferent, simple, stupid, unintelligent, absurd, senseless.

shrink, dwindle, diminish, lessen, wither, contract, shrivel, deflate, decrease, wince, cringe, balk, flinch, quail, withdraw, recoil. *Ant.* expand, grow, enlarge, extend, puff, dilate.

shun, see **avoid.**

shy, bashful, fearful, reserved, modest, diffident, wary, timid, chary, timorous. *Ant.* bold, brazen, obtrusive, audacious, self-possessed, confident.

sick, ill, diseased, ailing, unwell, impaired, sickly, unhealthy, infirm, invalid, confined, bedridden, nauseated, satiated. *Ant.* healthy, hearty, fine, well, vigorous, healthful, blooming, hale, hardy, unimpaired, wholesome.

sift, screen, probe, analyze, separate, discuss, winnow, examine, sort.

sign, omen, emblem, signal, symbol, symptom, indication, portent, token, badge, mark, manifestation, presage, identification, notice, suggestion, proof, wonder, miracle, augury, representation.

signal, *adj.* conspicuous, important, salient, striking, outstanding, momentous, famous, remarkable, memorable, prominent; *n.* indicator, alarm, mark, cue, sign, gesture, message.

significant, important, momentous, critical, prominent, outstanding, weighty, meaningful, expressive, indicative, emphatic, worthy, suggestive, notable, remarkable, serious, paramount, vital. *Ant.* unimportant, trivial, petty, shallow, inconsequential, worthless, insignificant.

silent, taciturn, reticent, reserved, uncommunicative, secretive, mute, tight-lipped, quiet, noiseless. *Ant.* voluble, talkative, glib, communicative, loquacious, noisy, clamorous.

silly, foolish, ridiculous, absurd, vacuous, stupid, witless, preposterous, simple, fatuous, asinine, inane, unreasonable, shallow, dense. *Ant.* sensible, wise, prudent, sagacious, practical, intelligent.

similar, resembling, like, analogous, alike, akin, corresponding, comparable, reciprocal. *Ant.* unlike, disparate, alien, opposite, dissimilar, different.

similitude, resemblance, likeness, analogy, comparison, affinity, similarity. *Ant.* dissimilarity, disparity, difference, divergence.

simple, pure, absolute, sheer, easy, effortless, light, uninvolved, uncomplicated, natural, artless, unaffected, naïve, unadorned, plain, unpretentious, foolish, ignorant. *Ant.* complex, compound, complicated, exacting, difficult, sophisticated, involved, intricate, contrived, ornate, embellished, fancy, wise, sagacious, intelligent.

simultaneous, concurrent, concomitant, contemporaneous, accompanying, coeval, synchronous, coincident. *Ant.* preceding, subsequent, following, foregoing.

sincere, honest, truthful, frank, unreserved, veracious, candid, unaffected, trustworthy, whole-souled, ingenuous, unfeigned, undisguised, conscientious, plain, guileless, direct, straightforward, earnest, serious. *Ant.* false, insincere, hypocritical, deceitful, dishonest, mendacious, two-faced, tricky, untruthful, evasive, deceptive, fraudulent, unreliable, malicious, disreputable, untrustworthy.

sinewy, brawny, strong, wiry, firm, muscular, stalwart, strapping, burly, powerful, sturdy, robust, husky, able-bodied, steely, energetic. *Ant.* weak, puny, thin, feeble, delicate, scrawny.

single, one, only, sole, solitary, individual, separate, unique, elemental, unaccompanied, isolated, pure, unmixed, simple, unmarried, celibate, unwed. *Ant.* numerous, attended, mixed, associated, accompanied, coupled, combined, double, multiple, compounded, composite, united, married, wedded.

singular, extraordinary, unusual, exceptional, particular, unique, strange, odd, uncommon, remarkable, eccentric, rare, abnormal, erratic, outlandish, diverse. *Ant.* common, usual, regular, ordinary, familiar, habitual.

sinister, evil, corrupt, perverse, dishonest, foreboding, disastrous, harmful, hostile, dire, pernicious, mischievous, malefic, deleterious, ominous, threatening, adverse, unlucky, unfavorable. *Ant.* auspicious, opportune, lucky, hopeful, propitious, fortunate, encouraging, favorable, promising, heartening, good, expedient, desirable, befitting, suitable, gracious, beneficent, wholesome.

situation, position, location, place, case, whereabouts, circumstances, state, spot, site, status, plight, predicament, condition.

size, magnitude, expanse, bigness, dimension, bulk, volume, extent, greatness, space, quantity, amplitude, area.

skeleton, sketch, outline, draft, structure, shell, frame, framework.

skeptic, doubter, unbeliever, infidel, idolator, atheist, agnostic, dissenter, schismatic, nihilist, apostate. *Ant.* believer, devotee, worshiper, monotheist, evangelist, disciple.

skillful, skilled, efficient, ingenious, handy, apt, adroit, proficient, clever, dexterous, trained, masterful, deft, adept, expert, ready, talented, accomplished, capable. *Ant.* unskillful, blundering, inept, fumbling, inexpert, maladroit, unhandy, lubberly, unfit, unqualified, incompetent, green, ignorant, untrained, clumsy, awkward, inexperienced.

skin, epidermis, husk, surface, hide, veneer, rind, pelt, bark, peel, integument, plating, lining, lamina.

skip, omit, neglect, disregard, pass, overlook, intermit, leap, spring, hop, jump, bound, trip, caper, cavort, gambol, prance, frisk, lope, richochet, skim.

skit, lampoon, satire, sketch, playlet.

skittish, restive, restless, fidgety, nervous, jumpy, feverish, jittery, timorous, uneasy, impatient, volatile. *Ant.* calm, cool, serene, self-possessed, brave.

slack, lax, indifferent, careless, negligent, remiss, stagnant, tardy, backward, dilatory, slow, loose, limp, relaxed. *Ant.* taut, drawn, alert, disciplined, shipshape, careful, dutiful.

slake, extinquish, assuage, quench, sate, satisfy, slacken.

slant, *n.* pitch, angle, slope, list, declivity, acclivity, inclination, grade, tile, bias, divergence, leaning, obliquity; *v.* tilt, lean, tip, turn, slope.

slavery, servitude, drudgery, thralldom, bondage, captivity, subjection, peonage, serfdom, subjugation. *Ant.* freedom, liberty, liberation, emancipation, manumission, independence.

sleazy, flimsy, tenuous, fragile, poor, thin, limp, feeble, worthless, flabby, trashy, flaccid, weak. *Ant.* fine, strong, excellent.

sleek, glossy, lustrous, shiny, smooth, silky, satiny, oily, velvety, bland. *Ant.* dull, rough, coarse, dry, harsh, blunt.

sleep, slumber, snooze, doze, hibernate, drowse, nap, nod, coma, stupor.

slender, slight, feeble, trivial, slim, flimsy, meager, thin, skinny, tenuous, lean, spare, lank, narrow. *Ant.* thick, strong, fat.

slide, *v.* slip, skim, slither, glide, skate, skip, skid; *n.* chute, ramp, incline.

slight, little, puny, small, tenuous, petty, trivial, frail, slim, scant, trifling. *Ant.* robust, sturdy, heavy-set, important, momentous, serious.

sling, hurl, throw, cast, pitch, toss, throw, propel, heave, hoist, impel, drive, shove, suspend, hang, dangle.

slip, error, blunder, fault, indiscretion, mistake, misstep, boner, lapse, fluff.

slope, see **slant.**

slothful, see **lazy.**

sluggish, lazy, slothful, inactive, dull, torpid, slow, indolent, inert, comatose, sleepy, dozing, lethargic, apathetic. *Ant.* swift, alert, quick, brisk, active, energetic.

sly, crafty, cunning, underhand, shrewd, furtive, wily, stealthy, insidious, covert, clandestine, artful, foxy, tricky, subtle, mischievous. *Ant.* candid, simple, artless, open.

small, little, minute, petty, tiny, diminutive, miniature, pygmy, inconsiderable, microscopic, scanty, slender, slight, puny, weak, young, feeble, ungenerous, mean, lowly, humble. *Ant.* large, big, strong, powerful, immense, important, considerable, momentous, rich, generous, large-hearted, distinguished, famous, excellent, fine.

smart, clever, keen, bright, quick-witted, intelligent, adroit, alert, sharp, acute, shrewd, modish, stylish, chic, dapper. *Ant.* dull, dense, crass, stupid, unintelligent, dowdy, shabby, frowzy.

smooth, *adj.* even, level, mild, plain, unruffled, uniform, regular, unvarying, flat, plane, flush, sleek, glossy, polished, silky, tranquil, unwrinkled, calm, easy, still. *Ant.* rough, rugged, uneven, hairy, notched, bristly, jagged, crinkled, corrugated, prickly, furrowed, gnarled, rumpled, craggy, rocky; *v.* level, even, flatten, press, file, plane, sand, grind, polish, palliate, calm, quiet, settle, mollify, assuage, allay. *Ant.* roughen, ruffle, crumple, corrugate, wrinkle, crinkle, aggravate, torment, annoy, incite, irritate, provoke.

snag, obstacle, bar, hindrance, block, obstruction, impediment, diffi culty, hitch.

snappy, acute, animated, piquant, crisp, pungent, quick, poignant prompt, spicy, keen, lively, smart, dashing, chic. *Ant.* dull, slow stupid, insipid, bland, dowdy, shabby.

snare, trap, ambush, net, subterfuge, pitfall, ruse, lure, decoy.

snub, abash, ignore, crush, cut, slight, humble, rebuke, discomfit humiliate.

snug, cozy, comfortable, convenient, concealed, compact, neat, trim firm, warm, close.

soak, drench, immerse, imbrue, steep, wet, impregnate, water, sat urate. *Ant.* dry, wring, desiccate, drain, dehydrate, evaporate.

sober, temperate, calm, serious, moderate, reasonable, quiet, solemn unruffled, abstemious, austere, dispassionate, unintoxicated, se date, steady. *Ant.* drunk, excited, overwrought, passionate, dis sipated, immoderate.

social, sociable, friendly, communicative, companionable, convivial hospitable, pleasant, courteous, agreeable, affable, urbane, genial gracious. *Ant.* unsociable, discourteous, disagreeable, secluded inhospitable, cynical, morose, sullen, hermitical, solitary, stern estranged, severe, captious, austere, scowling, acrimonious, un gracious, ill-mannered, impolite, crude.

soft, pliant, yielding, impressible, elastic, malleable, downy, silky smooth, pliable, bland, gentle, meek, mild, wooly, fluffy, mellow flexible, tolerant, flaccid, indulgent, spongy, easy, lenient, merci ful, clement, sensitive, compassionate, tender-hearted, unmanly weak, effeminate, tractable, docile, easygoing, amenable, irreso lute, fainthearted, credulous, silly, sentimental. *Ant.* hard, rigid rocky, stubborn, stiff, unyielding, indurate, brittle, severe, cruel tyrannical, domineering, callous, strict, stern, harsh, arbitrary absolute, pitiless, merciless, unsympathetic, brutal hard-hearted determined, insensible, strong-willed, resolute, indomitable, self possessed, rough, obstinate.

sojourn, lodge, live, stay, tarry, remain, dwell, reside.

solace, see **console.**

solemn, grave, staid, earnest, serious, sober, notable, formal, devout outstanding, ceremonial, important, weighty, momentous, impres sive, imposing, distinguished, august, majestic, stately, liturgical ceremonious, ritualistic. *Ant.* slight, uneventful, transitory, light insignificant, petty, lively, cheerful, ordinary, frivolous, animated boisterous, rejoicing.

solicit, ask, importune, desire, request, implore, beseech, petition beg, entreat, invoke, supplicate. *Ant.* protest, deprecate, reject remonstrate, disapprove, veto, oppose.

solid, dense, sound, stable, compact, hard, firm, substantial, unyield ing, rigid. *Ant.* fluid, liquid, gaseous, vaporous, thin, weak, open porous, vulnerable, tenuous, permeable.

solution, answer clue, key, explanation, elucidation, disentanglement, unraveling, liquefaction, mixture, dissolution melting, infusion.

solve, unfold, explain, resolve, decipher, untangle, discover, interpret, elucidate. *Ant.* tangle, involve, complicate.

somber, cloudy, overcast, dusky, dim, gloomy, murky, depressing, melancholy, grim, dismal, sober, grave, subdued, dejected, depressed. *Ant.* bright, brilliant, clear, happy, cheerful, blithe, gay.

soothe, calm, compose, tranquilize, lull, quiet, pacify, mollify, allay, alleviate, please, assuage, relieve, ease. *Ant.* awaken, alert, distress, annoy, stimulate, afflict.

sophisticated, worldly, wise, experienced, astute, polished, blasé, knowledgeable. *Ant.* naive, simple, artless, ingenuous, green, young.

sorcery, see **magic.**

sordid, mean, ignoble, contemptible, squalid, dirty, base, foul, vile, abject, degraded. *Ant.* elevated, pure, noble, honorable.

sorrow, sadness, heartache, distress, remorse, contrition, affliction, penitence, regret, anguish, grief, misfortune. *Ant.* happiness, joy, pleasure, delight.

sound, healthy, unimpaired, whole, entire, vigorous, hale, satisfactory, solvent, intact, stable, durable, substantial, genuine, reliable, faithful, legal, valid. *Ant.* impaired, defective, deficient, broken, affected, diseased, infirm, dilapidated.

sour, acid, tart, sharp, bitter, astringent, spoiled, curdled, rancid, vinegary, morose, ill-natured, embittered, discontented, grouchy, sullen, dissatisfied, querulous, complaining. *Ant.* sweet, sugary, bland, pleasant, agreeable, cheerful, courteous, polite, kind, suave, cordial, affable, friendly, gracious, amiable.

source, origin, beginning, primogenitor, cause, root, commencement, incipience, rise, foundation. *Ant.* issue, outcome, accomplishment, end, termination, conclusion, finish.

souvenir, keepsake, memento, token, reminder, remembrance, relic.

sovereign, paramount, dominant, preponderant, transcendent, predominant, ruling, supreme, absolute, authoritative, royal, regal, princely, free, autonomous, independent. *Ant.* subordinate, subservient, secondary.

speak, talk, utter, tell, say, express, pronounce, declare, vocalize, declaim, converse, chatter, announce, articulate, communicate, proclaim, report, voice, lecture, debate, discuss.

special, specific, particular, distinctive, exceptional, peculiar, extraordinary, exclusive, restricted, singular, proper, uncommon, individual, determinate, definite, unique, rare, choice. *Ant.* general, comprehensive, commonplace, usual, regular, prevalent, worldwide, broad, ecumenical, universal.

specific, particular, special, individual, definite, explicit, categorical, limited, characteristic, express, especial, exact, concrete, precise. *Ant.* vague, general, indefinite, uncertain, generic.

spell, turn, interval, period, term, season, round; jinx, charm, incantation, witchery, allurement, fascination.

spend, expend, use, exhaust, consume, waste, dissipate, squander disperse, scatter, dispense. *Ant.* save, hoard, collect, pocket, keep retain, hold, bank, cache.

sphere, globe, ball, spheroid, orb, compass, province, scope, realm department, domain.

spirit, mood, temper, nature, disposition, life, soul, mind, psyche vivacity, vitality, vigor, energy, fervor, liveliness, meaning, intent.

spiteful, vindictive, malicious, mean, antagonistic, rancorous, vengeful, venomous, malevolent, malign, hostile. *Ant.* forgiving, helpful, merciful, friendly, generous.

splendid, glorious, gorgeous, brilliant, bright, showy, resplendent excellent, refulgent, eminent, grand, superb, magnificent, sumptuous. *Ant.* mean, drab, plain, dull, humble.

spoil, *v.* ruin, damage, harm, mar, injure, disfigure, impair, destroy decay, rot, corrupt, decompose, pervert, debase, vitiate; *n.* booty loot, plunder.

sponsor, advertiser, patron, subscriber, backer, surety.

spontaneous, involuntary, unintentional, instinctive, impulsive, unbidden, automatic. *Ant.* deliberate, intended, voluntary, designed determined, premeditated, considered, volitional.

sporadic, infrequent, irregular, occasional, uncertain, scattered, isolated, separate. *Ant.* frequent, habitual, constant, prevalent continual, general, dependable, sure, regular.

spread, disperse, extend, diffuse, propagate, scatter, disseminate expand, unroll, unfold, circulate, strew, dispense, distribute, sow stretch, radiate, publish, promulgate. *Ant.* assemble, collect unite, crowd, concentrate, cluster, compress, condense, tighten circumscribe, gather, fold, suppress, conceal.

sprout, bud, shoot, germinate, burgeon, develop, grow.

spruce, trim, clean, smart, tidy, neat, dapper, jaunty, trig. *Ant* sloppy, careless, dirty, neglected, shabby.

spry, nimble, quick, frisky, active, agile, vivacious, lively, brisk alacritous, spirited, blithe, sprightly. *Ant.* torpid, lethargic, sluggish, inactive, feeble.

spurious, counterfeit, false, artificial, make-believe, feigned, pretended, fraudulent, deceptive, sham, fabricated, misrepresented illegitimate, bastard. *Ant.* genuine, real, true, actual, accurate authentic, valid, veritable, sound, certain, trustworthy, authorized, legitimate, lawful, justified, correct.

squabble, see quarrel.

squalid, dirty, filthy, unclean, miserable, wretched, foul, sordid, unkempt. *Ant.* clean, attractive, neat, tidy, trim, appealing, inviting, comfortable, pleasant, suitable.

squander, waste, misuse, expend, scatter, lavish, dissipate. *Ant* save, invest, retain, hoard, preserve, redeem.

stable, fixed, durable, firm, enduring, regular, steady, constant, steadfast, immutable, settled, balanced, resolute, equable. *Ant.* unsteady, shaking, unsettled, wavering, fluctuating, mutable, variable, restless, fickle, erratic, mercurial, unstable.

staid, serious, sober, sedate, stuffy, unimaginative, solemn, steady, earnest, grave, complacent. *Ant.* flighty, impulsive, nervous, boisterous, frivolous, volatile.

stain, blot, speck, spot, tarnish, blotch, mark, tinge, color, soil, tint, dye, disgrace, dishonor, taint, blemish.

stake, bet, wager, pledge, risk, hazard, investment, venture, chance, share, interest; prize, reward; pole, post.

stately, see **grand.**

status, condition, state, position, standing, situation, rank.

steady, see **stable.**

sterile, barren, unfruitful, unproductive, fallow, infecund, impotent, fruitless, worthless, infertile, arid. *Ant.* fertile, productive, fruitful, prolific, fecund, proliferous, generative.

stern, severe, austere, rigid, stiff, hard, formal, rigorous, harsh, unrelenting, determined, unbending, resolute, grim, unyielding, resolved, forbidding, inexorable, earnest, firm, strict, exacting, inflexible, uncompromising. *Ant.* lenient, indulgent, easygoing, tolerant, merciful, amiable, complacent, agreeable, affable, compliant, sociable.

still, silent, soundless, noiseless, motionless, calm, quiet, mute, unruffled, tranquil. *Ant.* noisy, tumultuous, loud, stirring, moving.

stilted, affected, bombastic, pompous, turgid, swelling, pretentious, high-sounding, fustian, grandiose, magniloquent. *Ant.* humble, plain, reserved, shy, simple, honest, candid.

stimulate, stir, excite, instigate, rouse, energize, animate, awaken, provoke, invigorate, pique, urge, incite, impel, kindle. *Ant.* tranquilize, deaden, unnerve.

stingy, see **miserly.**

stop, cease, halt, check, discontinue, quit, stay, block, impede, defer, interrupt, desist. *Ant.* start, begin, commence, initiate.

storm, *n.* agitation, disturbance, commotion, turmoil, turbulence, upheaval, tumult, violence, rage, fury, paroxysm, outbreak, hurricane, cyclone, whirlwind, tornado; *v.* attack, bombard, assault, assail, rant, rage, fume, boil, blow, hail, rain, snow. *Ant.* tranquility, calm, quietness, silence, repose, stillness, peace, placidity, serenity.

stormy, tempestuous, excitable, raging, angry, violent, furious, passionate, agitated, frenzied, turbulent, raving. *Ant.* calm, patient, composed, quiet, peaceful, tranquil, repressed, unexcited, grave, demure, steady, sedate, meek, tolerant, gentle, forbearing, content.

stout, fat, corpulent, fleshy, obese, rotund, burly, thickset, portly, large, stocky, plump, chubby, sturdy, stalwart, brave, firm, undaunted, courageous. *Ant.* lean, spare, lanky, scrawny.

straight, direct, rectilinear, vertical, undeviating, perpendicular, unswerving, erect, reliable, unbent; honorable, regular, honest, upright, candid, trustworthy. *Ant.* crooked, bent, distorted, curved, twisted, deviating, swerving, sloping, angular, deformed, grotesque, misshapen; dishonest, unreliable, devious, fraudulent, deceptive.

strange, unrelated, irrelevant, foreign, alien, remote, far-fetched, inapplicable, dissociated, abnormal, anomalous, irregular, unaccustomed, peculiar, misplaced, queer, nondescript, extraordinary, unfamiliar, grotesque, bizarre, fantastic, odd, inconceivable, incredible, eccentric, bewildering, stupefying, indescribable, ineffable. *Ant.* ordinary, trite, expected, unimportant, trifling, usual, well-known, plain, regular, conventional, typical, simple, matter-of-fact, natural, habitual, customary, general, frequent, familiar, normal, average, prevailing.

strict, exact, accurate, precise, severe, rigorous, stern, inflexible, rigid, stringent, austere, unyielding. *Ant.* lax, flexible, loose, vague, lenient, slack, careless.

strong, robust, sturdy, powerful, forceful, mighty, sinewy, vigorous, stout, tough, solid, virile, firm, energetic, hardy, stalwart, lusty, brawny, indomitable, strapping, strenuous, invincible, forcible, resistant, resolute, self-reliant, plucky, determined, potent, hale, courageous, healthy, sound, hearty, durable. *Ant.* weak, feeble, delicate, infirm, emaciated, fragile, sickly, enervated, debilitated, spent, wasted, languishing.

stubborn, obstinate, adamant, refractory, intractable, pertinacious, headstrong, recalcitrant, unyielding, ungovernable, dogged, mulish, obdurate. *Ant.* yielding, tractable, reasonable, compliant, amenable.

stupid, dull, foolish, obtuse, witless, senseless, vapid, inane, crass, feeble-minded, asinine, inept, moronic. *Ant.* comprehending, perspicacious, wise, sapient, sagacious, acute, sage, discerning, smart, witty, brilliant, bright, keen-witted, clearheaded, intelligent, cunning, thoughtful, solid.

stupor, insensibility, lethargy, apathy, daze, coma, unconsciousness, numbness, torpor, narcosis, inertness. *Ant.* feeling, susceptibility, consciousness, sensibility, activity, vivacity.

sturdy, see strong.

suave, gracious, polite, urbane, gallant, pleasing, tactful, courteous, amiable, debonair, glib, bland, smooth, adroit. *Ant.* crude, rude, ignorant, inept, awkward, displeasing, discourteous, brusque, bluff.

subdue, overcome, subjugate, tame, conquer, vanquish, master, control, temper, restrain, soften, moderate, beat, suppress, defeat. *Ant.* awaken, rouse, stimulate, incite, enrage.

submit, defer, yield, obey, abide, surrender, capitulate, bend, bear, resign, relent, succumb, suffer; offer, propose, suggest. *Ant.* resist, defy, withstand, obstruct.

subordinate, *adj.* inferior, minor, unimportant, secondary, subsidiary, dependent, ancillary, subject; *v.* control, subdue, subjugate. *Ant.* chief, leading, dominant, superior.

subsequent, succeeding, successive, following, consequent, after, secondary, next, posterior, ensuing, later. *Ant.* preceding, prior, anterior, antecedent, earlier, former.

subvert, overthrow, supplant, destroy, extinguish, invert, pervert, overwhelm, overturn, depress, upset, demolish, topple, reverse. *Ant.* elevate, establish, support, perpetuate, preserve, conserve, sustain, uphold.

succeed, prevail, accomplish, gain, achieve, attain, prosper, win, triumph, thrive, surmount, conquer, vanquish, defeat. *Ant.* fail, lose, forfeit, miss, blunder.

suffer, feel, bear, endure, undergo, sustain, permit, allow, tolerate, submit, support, abide, admit, ache, smart, grieve, agonize.

sufficient, enough, adequate, suitable, satisfying, plenty, commensurate, proper, ample, fitting, abundant, satisfactory. *Ant.* insufficient, inadequate, wanting, deficient, lacking.

suggestion, hint, insinuation, implication, allusion, intimation, innuendo, thought, recommendation, indication, implication, connotation, note, trace. *Ant.* expression, declaration, revelation, statement, assertion.

suitable, proper, appropriate, fitting, seemly, becoming, meet, just, applicable, relevant, eligible, adapted, accordant, consonant, conformable, congruous, pertinent, agreeable, expedient.

sullen, morose, glum, cross, sour, ill-humored, churlish, cynical, gloomy, dismal, dull, baleful, sulky, stubborn, surly, somber. *Ant.* cheerful, jovial, sociable, amiable, genial, good-natured

superficial, cursory, hasty, desultory, shallow, outward, surface, short-sighted, flimsy. *Ant.* deep, careful, thorough, deliberate, profound.

superfluous, unnecessary, excessive, redundant, spare, useless, extra, overmuch, abounding, inordinate, needless, profuse, luxuriant, inexhaustible, lush, lavish. *Ant.* scarce, scanty, insufficient, inadequate.

superior, higher, above, greater, major, upper, excellent, unsurpassed, supreme, distinguished, sovereign. *Ant* inferior, below, under, minor.

supplicate, see **beg.**

support, prop, maintain, uphold, sustain, keep, bear, carry, bolster, hold, shore, aid, assist, contribute, advance, expedite, second, verify, abet, endure, confirm, corroborate, advocate, defend. *Ant.* abandon, desert, betray, destroy, hinder, impede, obstruct, counteract, encumber, block, frustrate, dishearten, circumvent, discourage, cripple, check, inhibit, oppose, disconcert, block, undermine, prevent, defeat.

supreme, paramount, transcendent, chief, highest, foremost, dominant, peerless, principal, ultimate, final, greatest.

surrender, sacrifice, yield, capitulate, cede, give, relinquish, abandon, submit, comply.

surround, encompass, circle, encircle, environ, enclose, circumscribe.

suspend, discontinue, cease, desist, interrupt, delay, postpone, defer; hang, swing, sling, hitch, append. *Ant.* continue, persist, maintain, extend, prolong, expedite, accelerate, support, sustain.

swallow, absorb, engulf, devour, envelop, consume, believe, accept, tolerate, stomach, bear, endure, bolt; recant, retract, withdraw, suppress. *Ant.* reject, protest, object, contradict, doubt.

sweep, *v.* brush, clean, whisk, graze, touch, rake, remove, traverse, clear, win, achieve; *n.* swing, range, scope, reach, compass, extent, stretch, amplitude, contour, curve, bend.

swell, *v.* expand, dilate, distend, intensify, bulge, tumefy, increase, amplify, rise, protrude, inflate, puff, heave; *n.* protuberance, bulge, swelling, curve, elevation, intensity, power, crescendo. *Ant.* shrink, contract, diminish, deflate, shrivel, compress.

swindler, thief, cheat, impostor, fraud, embezzler, forger, counterfeiter, charlatan.

symmetry, proportion, equality, arrangement, regularity, order, conformity, harmony, agreement, finish, form, shapeliness, balance, centrality, equivalence, evenness. *Ant.* disproportion, disparity, inequality, irregularity, difference, disagreement, imbalance, misproportion, distortion, unevenness, unconformity.

sympathy, commiseration, compassion, condolence, harmony, alliance, pity, accord, concord, tenderness, pity, consolation, affection, empathy, warm-heartedness.

synchronous, concomitant, coeval, coetaneous, concurrent, together, simultaneous, coexistent, contemporary.

syndicate, pool, trust, association, league, monopoly, alliance, union.

system, method, plan, order, regularity, manner, network, mode, scheme, way, policy, organization, operation, arrangement, procedure, program. *Ant.* chaos, disorder, confusion, jumble, disarray, clutter.

T

table, *n.* catalog, inventory, syllabus, file, chart, list, roll, tabulation, compendium, schedule, register, index, synopsis, roster, desk, board, counter; *v.* defer, postpone, shelve.

taciturn, reserved, reticent, uncommunicative, silent, mute, speechless, mum, close-mouthed, laconic. *Ant.* sententious, garrulous, talkative, loquacious, chatty, communicative, fluent, voluble, gossiping, verbose, wordy.

tackle, *v.* undertake, attempt, try, catch, attack, seize, capture, grapple; *n.* equipment, gear, rigging, cordage, harness, tools, apparatus.

tact, diplomacy, perception, discrimination, judgment, discretion, insight, acuteness, penetration, intelligence, poise, skill, acumen, perspicacity, subtlety, discernment, finesse. *Ant.* tactlessness, maladroitness, blundering, thoughtlessness, stupidity, folly, indiscrimination, incompetence, fatuity.

alent, aptitude, knack, endowment, capacity, genius, bent, skill, faculty, gift, power, craft, ability, forte, cleverness. *Ant.* stupidity, awkwardness, incapability, inability, weakness.

all, high, towering, soaring, lofty, elevated, stretched. *Ant.* low, small, short, stubby, squat.

ame, submissive, pliant, amenable, domesticated, subdued, broken, obedient, tractable, timid, docile, meek, boring, tedious, vapid. *Ant.* wild, fierce, spirited, unruly, bright, interesting.

amper, meddle, interfere, bribe, suborn, intervene, seduce, discommode, inconvenience, trouble.

angle, *v.* complicate, spoil, hinder, perplex, interfere, snarl, involve, confuse, entrap, intertwine, jumble, ensnare, muddle; *n.* perplexity, puzzle, quandry, embarrassment, dilemma, muddle, disorder, snarl.

antalize, vex, torment, tease, lure, tempt, provoke, bait, badger, irritate, torture, afflict, test, try, tempt. *Ant.* appease, sooth, please, assuage.

ardy, late, overdue, delayed, retarded, slow, detained, slack, lax. *Ant.* prompt, punctual, quick, ready, early.

arnish, stain, smudge, blemish, taint, soil, dishonor, besmirch, defame, sully, discolor, blot. *Ant.* clean, brighten, restore, honor, clear, defend.

ask, burden, stint, function, duty, charge, assignment, office, mission, pursuit, chore, business.

aunt, mock, jeer, deride, rally, insult, ridicule, revile, upbraid, reproach, censure, offend, scoff, twit, gibe, scorn. *Ant.* praise, honor, respect, uphold.

awdry, see **gaudy.**

each, educate, school, indoctrinate, instruct, enlighten, tutor, train, inculcate, advise, direct, guide, interpret, lecture, instill, inform, nurture, imbue, expound, prepare, coach, explain. *Ant.* learn, follow, imbibe, understand.

edious, wearisome, irksome, tiresome, fatiguing, boring, uninteresting, dull, humdrum, monotonous, soporific, drowsy. *Ant.* lively, exhilarating, inspiring, animating, refreshing, relieving, entertaining, amusing, diverting, interesting, charming, fascinating, enthralling.

eem, abound, swarm, overflow, exuberate, produce.

ell, reveal, divulge, discern, impart, communicate, relate, declare, disclose, inform, describe, narrate, acquaint, explain, testify, state, betray, recount. *Ant.* withhold, conceal, suppress.

emerity, audacity, boldness, rashness, presumption, over-confidence, effrontery, recklessness, hastiness, heedlessness, thoughtlessness, foolhardiness, carelessness, indiscretion, imprudence, impetuosity. *Ant.* caution, forethought, prudence, deliberation, discretion, care, vigilance, circumspection, wariness, heed, prescience, restraint, delay, hesitation, timidity.

temper, *n.* disposition, mood, humor, composure, type, composition, quality, structure, nature; rage, anger, passion; *v.* harden, anneal, modify, moderate, qualify, change, soothe, assuage, soften, mollify.

temperament, character, constitution, personality, nature, temper, disposition, make-up, spirit, propensity.

temperate, mild, moderate, reasonable, unruffled, self-restrained, sober, frugal, abstinent, abstemious. *Ant.* immoderate, excessive, tempestuous, stormy, uncontrolled, passionate, impetuous.

temporal, mundane, secular, worldly, transient, fleeting, temporary, transitory, short-lived, ephemeral. *Ant.* spiritual, ecclesiastical, perpetual, everlasting, eternal.

temporary, transitory, short, transient, ephemeral, fleeting, passing, evanescent, shifting, summary, momentary, recurring, cyclical, acting, provisional, impermanent, changeable, vicarious. *Ant.* lasting, permanent, fixed, durable, persistent, chronic, eternal, immortal, undying, unperishing, endless, perpetual.

tempt, invite, attract, charm, fascinate, entice, allure, lure, inveigle, court, test, try. *Ant.* repel, discourage, disenchant, repulse.

tenacious, tough, stubborn, purposeful, pertinacious, obstinate, persistent, unyielding, adhesive, retentive, cohesive, sticky, gummy, inseparable, resisting, cartilaginous, leathery, viscous, glutinous, dogged, persevering, uncompromising, resolute, determined, intransigent. *Ant.* loose, lax, immiscible, nonadhesive, detached, slack, brittle, delicate, crumbling, fragile, splitting, wavering, splintery, vacillating, irresolute, feeble, fickle, unstable, timid, easygoing, cowardly, faltering.

tend, lean, lead, gravitate, dispose, incline, verge, trend, contribute, attend, watch, keep, guard, manage, protect, nurse.

tendency, conatus, tone, propensity, drift, bent, susceptibility, turn, leaning, bias, mood, predisposition, trend, inclination, disposition, temperament, direction, aptness, aptitude, course, proclivity, proneness, prejudice, purpose. *Ant.* contrariety, opposition, aversion, antipathy, apathy, inanity.

tender, *adj.* gentle, lenient, loving, kind, warm, merciful, compassionate, humane, mild, benevolent, responsive, soft, delicate, sympathetic, young, immature, weak, fragile, feeble; *v.* offer, propose, suggest, present. *Ant.* harsh, severe, unfeeling, callous.

tenet, view, conviction, belief, position, doctrine, system, dogma, principle, precept.

tense, tight, taut, rigid, stiff, strained, intent, rapt. *Ant.* loose, relaxed, limp, tranquil, lax, slack, calm.

tension, strain, stress, effort, pull, drag, pressure, torsion, worry, nervousness, fear, apprehension, excitement.

tentative, provisional, temporary, experimental, probationary. *Ant.* definitive, decisive, conclusive, final, permanent.

terminal, final, concluding, ultimate, last, ending, limiting, terminating. *Ant.* initial, first, beginning, opening.

errestrial, earthly, mundane, worldly, terrene, sublunary.

errible, frightful, terrific, dire, horrible, alarming, appalling, fearful, terrifying, dreadful, awful, horrid, shocking, gruesome.

erse, short sententious, neat, succinct, compact, concise, laconic, compendious, crisp, brief, exact, summary, incisive, pointed, trenchant. *Ant.* tedious, wearisome, tiresome, profuse, verbose, wordy, lengthy, diffuse, confused, loose, meaningless, redundant, roundabout, ambiguous, rambling, long-winded, discursive.

est, *v.* try, assay, inspect, examine, prove, scrutinize, substantiate, verify, experiment; *n.* trial, proof, essay, criterion, standard, demonstration, examination.

estimony, affirmation, confirmation, affidavit, evidence, indication, proof, witness, attestation, deposition, declaration, certification, warrant, credentials.

ext, topic, theme, subject, passage, sentence, verse, wording, matter.

exture, structure, make, composition, organization, fiber, fabric, firmness, feel, nap, tissue, grain, smoothness, coarseness, roughness, flexibility, rigidity, character, disposition, constitution, makeup, organization.

hankful, grateful, gratified, contented, satisfied, beholden, pleased, appreciative. *Ant.* ungrateful, careless, forgetful, thankless, unsatisfied, insensible, unmindful, grumbling, faultfinding, critical, censorious, dissatisfied, morose, discontented.

haw, melt, run, liquefy, deliquesce, dissolve, liquate, flow. *Ant.* freeze, solidify, congeal, chill, petrify.

heatrical, dramatic, showy, ceremonious, histrionic, meretricious, affected, spectacular, ostentatious, melodramatic, scenic, pretentious, stagy, unreal, unnatural, flaunting, flashy, demonstrative, pompous, swaggering, arrogant, overbearing. *Ant.* humble, retiring, modest, bashful, reserved, diffident, unassuming, demure, unaffected, unpretentious, unobtrusive, unostentatious, unpretending.

heft, robbery, pillage, plunder, holdup, spoliation, swindle, embezzlement, fraud, larceny, misappropriation, plagiarism, burglary, rapine, piracy. *Ant.* restoration, return, amends, recoupment, restitution, compensation, indemnification indemnity.

theme, subject, dissertation, thesis, topic, proposition, discourse, text, essay, writing, composition, idea, tenor, trend, motive, report, statement, narrative, description.

theory, hypothesis, scheme, surmise, conjecture, plea, attribution, thesis, speculation, supposition, ascription, perception, apperception, intuition, viewpoint, apprehension, condition, precognition, presumption, assumption, guess. *Ant.* certainty, practice, proof.

therefore, accordingly, consequently, hence, so, then, wherefore, for, since.

thesis, dissertation, theme, essay, composition, doctrine, proposition, affirmation, study, report, dictum, position, argument.

thick, dense, close, crowded, solid, compact, solidified, muddy, miry, heavy, turbid, gelatinous, viscous, glutinous, gummy, opaque, ropy, vitrified, numerous, swarming, populous, heaped, profuse, multitudinous, squat, broad, stubby, dumpy, chunky, thickset, stupid, obtuse, crass, gross, coarse, ignorant, stultified, dull, stolid. *Ant.* thin, rarefied, airy, ethereal, tenuous, subtle, filmy, gossamery, unsubstantial, light, porous, clear, transparent, slim, slender, diaphanous, limpid, pellucid, gaseous, shadowy, imponderable, vaporous, fragile, frail, flimsy, few, scarce, sparse, scant, smart, sharp, acute, intelligent.

thin, slight, slender, slim, threadlike, fine, flimsy, lean, scraggy, skeletal, wasted, lank, gaunt, haggard, tenuous, emaciated, rare, attenuated, gossamer, meager, spare, scarce, scanty. *Ant.* thick, fat, profuse, heavy, dumpy, abundant, plethoric, ponderous, full, ample, solid, plenteous, massive, squat, pudgy, obese, swollen, inflated, puffed.

think, cogitate, imagine, guess, muse, suppose, conjecture, ponder, consider, fancy, meditate, contemplate, regard, reckon, opine, believe, conceive, deem, reflect, apprehend, surmise, judge, picture, determine, hold, speculate, esteem, reason, study, deliberate, ruminate.

thirst, desire, craving, hankering, longing, yearning.

thorough, complete, perfect, accurate, finished, unmitigated, total, plenary, absolute, entire, consummate, exact, painstaking, sweeping, scrupulous, exhaustive, radical, thoroughgoing. *Ant.* shallow, superficial, incomplete, inadequate, inefficient, sketchy, crude, perfunctory, deficient, imperfect.

thought, conception, consideration, reflection, idea, notion, deliberation, cogitation, cerebration, meditation, speculation, lucubration, impression, perception, contemplation. *Ant.* vacuity, fatuity, vacancy, inanity, incogitability, emptiness, heedlessness.

thoughtful, thinking, cogitative, absorbed, meditative, engrossed, wistful, pensive, philosophic, contemplative, rapt, preoccupied, studious, deliberative, introspective, museful, reflective, speculative, acute, level-headed, perspicacious, quick, sharp, cautious, rational, intelligent, farsighted, keen, absorbed, calculating, discerning, wise, discriminating, sagacious, politic, cunning, penetrating, shrewd, heedful, provident, careful. *Ant.* thoughtless, heedless, careless, indifferent, inattentive, neglectful, unthinking, unreasoning, inconsiderate, inadvertent, foolhardy, lax, remiss, negligent, rash, reckless, stupid, obtuse, dull, stolid, senseless, senile, fatuous, idiotic, foolish.

thrift, economy, prudence, saving, providence, frugality, parsimony, conservation. *Ant.* waste, prodigality, shiftlessness, extravagance.

thrill, *n.* sensation, excitement, tingling, shock, flutter, tremor; *v.* affect, agitate, penetrate, move, touch, strike, stir, inspire, rouse, stimulate, electrify, tremble, vibrate, tingle.

thrive, flourish, prosper, grow, increase, advance, luxuriate, bloom, improve, succeed. *Ant.* fail, lose, decline, fall.

hrob, *v.* palpitate, pulsate, beat, vibrate, oscillate; *n.* beating, palpitating, pulsing, vibrating.

hrong, multitude, assembly, host, mass, assemblage, concourse, crowd, army, legion, gathering, congregation, group, company, horde, aggregation, flock, body, gang, swarm, band, mob, herd, collection, cluster, pack. *Ant.* scarcity, sparsity, paucity, handful, scattering, dispersion.

:hrow, cast, impel, toss, project, propel, chuck, fling, thrust, shy, sling, pitch, hurl, push, drive, launch.

thrust, *v.* shove, push, pierce, penetrate, fling, propel, throw, move, drive, enter, cast, stab, extend, tilt; *n.* push, propulsion, force, explosion, pressure, impact.

:hwart, baffle, oppose, impede, block, outwit, hinder, curb, frustrate, balk, prevent, defeat, foil, check, contravene. *Ant.* help, support, aid, favor, back, further.

:idy, neat, clean, spruce, orderly, methodical, shipshape, snug, trim, systematic. *Ant.* slovenly, sloppy, messy, unkempt, disorderly, chaotic, confused, deranged, disheveled, disorganized, irregular, jumbled, shabby, littered.

:ie, *n.* band, yoke, connection, ligament, fastening, bond, ligature, security, coupling, link, cord, rope, string, strap, tackle, bandage, brace; *v.* bind, restrain, confine, constrain, restrict, shackle, fasten, join, fetter, unite, hitch, secure, tether, link, obligate, handcuff, fix, engage, moor, attach. *Ant.* separation, break, disjunction, sunderance, division, detachment, severance, looseness; loose, unbind, displace, free, unfasten, untie, loosen, unloose, detach, disunite, separate.

:ight, taut, constricted, compact, snug, close, tense, compressed, firm, strict, condensed, narrow. *Ant.* loose, free, easy, lax, comfortable, wide, slack, tolerant.

:ilt, slope, incline, cant, slant, lean, list, tip, forge, point, thrust, joust, pitch, sway.

:ime, *n.* duration, eon, while, age, epoch, course, period, term, era, succession, season, sequence, date, interim, span, cycle, spell, stage, interval, measure, tempo; *v.* set, regulate, measure, adjust.

:imely, opportune, well-timed, appropriate, proper, suitable, happy, seasonable, providential, convenient, propitious. *Ant.* untimely, late, early, inopportune, inexpedient, premature, immature, dilatory, tardy.

:imid, fearful, afraid, cowardly, shy, faint-hearted, spiritless, timorous, diffident, weak, unspirited, effeminate, fearful, skulking, frightened, nervous, shaky, apprehensive, retiring, discouraged, terrified, hesitant, daunted, sheepish, irresolute, shamefaced, scared, vacillating, wavering, faltering. *Ant.* brave, bold, resolved, unflinching, courageous, determined, undaunted, resolute, unbending, unyielding, daring, unafraid, valiant, valorous, gallant, intrepid, stout-hearted, lion-hearted, indomitable, fearless, chivalrous, unshrinking, dauntless, self-reliant, venturous, self-possessed, venturesome, hardy, reckless.

tiny, small, miniature, little, diminutive, minute, wee, microscopic. *Ant.* large, great, big, huge, gigantic, enormous, vast, immense, mammoth, monstrous.

tire, weary, fatigue, bore, exhaust, fag, irk, jade, strain, harass, worry, drain, overwork, overtax, prostrate, pall, disgust. *Ant.* refresh, embolden, brace, invigorate, inspire, regale, incite, enliven, energize, amuse, freshen, inspire, entertain, stimulate, encourage, divert, cheer, relax, rouse, comfort, relieve, animate, solace, rest, interest, restore.

title, name, appellation, heading, caption, inscription, legend, designation, epithet, cognomen, denomination, dignity, honor, right, birthright, claim, ownership, possession, prerogative, privilege.

toil, work, grind, occupation, labor, drudgery, trouble, travail, task, pains. *Ant.* leisure, rest, relaxation, repose.

token, mark, sign, evidence, note, emblem, badge, symbol, index, trace, manifestation, trait, memorial, keepsake, reminder, memento, souvenir.

tolerate, permit, admit, concede, allow, let, recognize, suffer, abide, endure, indulge, accord, license, sanction, authorize, submit, bear, warrant, bide, stand, swallow, pocket, stomach. *Ant.* prohibit, inhibit, forbid, interdict, bar, disallow, veto, hinder, disapprove, prevent, deprecate, restrict, censure, decry, remonstrate, protest, reprehend, check, restrain, obstruct, curb, discountenance, stop, preclude, oppose.

tool, implement, instrument, mechanism, utensil, device, apparatus, appliance, equipment.

top, summit, crown, head, culmination, surface, apex, vertex, tip, crest, peak, pinnacle, acme, zenith. *Ant.* bottom, nadir, foot, base.

topic, question, text, proposition, theme, theorem, resolution, subject, material, motion argument, point, matter, problem, affair, issue.

torment, afflict, annoy, trouble, torture, badger, provoke, rack, grill, try, pain, harass, agonize, bait, harry, gull, distress, plague. *Ant* soothe, mollify, help, please, comfort, console, relieve, ease.

torpid, dull, numb, sluggish, inert, lethargic, sleepy, indolent, apathetic, listless, benumbed, inactive, dormant, stuporous, motionless idle, phlegmatic, impassive. *Ant.* agile, nimble, spry, active, quick, sprightly.

torture, pain, rack, martyrdom, anguish, agony, torment, cruelty, excruciation, persecution, torment, suffering. *Ant.* gratification, comfort, ease, relief, consolation.

total, *adj.* whole, complete, all, entire, absolute, undivided, full; *n.* aggregate, sum, lump, mass, all, quantity, totality, whole.

touch, *v.* handle, stroke, brush, feel, finger, graze, glance, concern, hint, allude, regard, affect, impress, soften, melt, mollify, strike, stir, pat, tap, distress, impair, sting, mar; *n.* feeling, sensation, tangency, palpability, tinge, trace, infusion, dash, sprinkling, taste.

tough, stubborn, unmanageable, firm, hardened, tenacious, seasoned, refractory, strong, stalwart, intractable, obstinate, dogged, wiry, resisting, coherent, hard, unyielding, difficult, adhesive, fibrous, inseparable, cohesive, turbulent, rampant, bullying, uproarious, unruly, impetuous, immitigable, boisterous, savage, fierce, raging, laborious, desperate, ferocious, rigorous, brutal, ruffianly, troublesome, onerous, intricate, puzzling. *Ant.* mild, amenable, tractable, compliant, obedient, yielding, submissive, docile, complaisant, dutiful, controllable, subservient, affable, quiet, passive, bland, deferential, peaceable, soft, genial, delicate, weak, puny, vulnerable, defenseless, easygoing, fragile.

trace, sign, footprint, remains, mark, impression, vestige, trail, clue, touch, tinge, hint, memorial, token, indicator, track, record, symbol, remnant, indication, index, scent. *Ant.* obliteration, extinction, oblivion, deletion, suppression, nonexistence, effacement, cancellation.

tractable, amenable, docile, obedient, pliant, manageable, compliant, submissive, governable, willing, yielding, acquiescent, adaptable. *Ant.* unruly, intractable, ungovernable, stubborn, refractory, obstinate.

trade, *n.* business, speculation, dealing, exchange, sales, traffic, employment, barter, commerce, metier, livelihood, office, profession, position, occupation, line, trading, job, calling, situation, undertaking, pursuit, vocation, matter, province, affair, art, function, concern, handicraft, craft, case, work, transaction, duty, avocation; *v.* exchange, deal, sell, buy, bargain, barter, swap.

traduce, calumniate, slander, revile, defame, libel, asperse, vilify, malign, disparage.

traffic, *n.* commerce, trade, sale, business, barter, deal, bargain, selling, buying, contracting; *v.* buy, sell, trade, exchange, deal.

trail, *n.* track, trace, mark, footprint, scent, path, course, way; *v.* pull, draw, drag, track, hunt, follow, lag, straggle, crawl, climb, creep, grow.

train, *n.* series, procession, succession, sequel, sequence, retinue, line, trail, chain, staff, suite, string; *v.* lead, innure, discipline, rear, drill, instruct, accustom, exercise, habituate, practice, bend, teach, educate, prepare, aim, qualify, direct, initiate, inculcate, indoctrinate, infuse, school, inform, imbue, enlighten, implant, prime, guide, coach.

traitorous, perfidious, treacherous, faithless, disloyal, treasonable, seditious, recreant, apostate, insidious, mutinous, rebellious, false, renegade. *Ant.* loyal, faithful, constant, steadfast.

trammel, impede, hamper, hobble, hinder, shackle, restrain, obstruct, fetter, clog, curb, check, encumber, cramp, retard, oppose, thwart, confine, frustrate, circumvent, restrict. *Ant.* help, animate, aid, encourage, stimulate, succor, inspirit, assist, incite, advance, relieve, sustain, uphold, support, serve, nurture, accommodate, befriend, tend, second, oblige, cheer, countenance, favor, liberate, free, release, enfranchise, unbind, extricate, unloose.

tranquil, calm, still, restful, peaceful, hushed, composed, unruffled, undisturbed, quiet, smooth, pacific, sedative, untroubled, gentle, moderate, soft, low, reposeful, serene, soothing, temperate, placid, halcyon, quiescent, whispering, faint, stifled, murmuring, muffled, softened, pleasing, solacing, unstirred, comforting, dulcet, agreeable. *Ant.* noisy, tumultuous, unquiet, violent, clamorous, rough, uproarious, troubled, disturbing, loud, raging, blatant, raving, clangorous, furious, tempestuous, excited, agitated, distracting, raving, ruffled, disturbed, distressing, frenzied, rampant, perturbed, flaming, flustered, turbulent, frantic, hysterical.

transact, do, treat, act, negotiate, perform, dispatch, accomplish, conduct, achieve, execute, prosecute, enact, practice, perpetrate, conclude, settle, manage, work, operate, officiate, exercise.

transaction, doing, proceeding, deed, business, action, act, event, affair, step, matter, happening, negotiation, deal, purchase, sale, activity, selling, purchasing, performance, buying, disposal, execution, undertaking.

transcendental, transcendent, intuitive, primordial, intellectual, innate, original, vague, supernatural, abstract, exceeding, consummate, metaphysical, extraordinary, visionary, idealistic, obscure, fantastic, supereminent. *Ant.* plain, intelligible, perspicuous, evident, clear, manifest, unequivocal, obvious, distinct, transparent, definite, simple, comprehensible, unmistakable, positive.

transform, convert, change, evolve, develop, modify, transmute, vary, transfigure, metamorphose, alter.

transgression, infringement, breach, misdeed, error, fault, trespass, violation, sin, infraction, invasion, crime, iniquity, misdemeanor, disobedience, nonobservance, delinquency, slip, encroachment.

transient, brief, fugitive, ephemeral, fleeting, transitory, passing, momentary, flying, temporary, evanescent, short, temporal, provisional, flitting, cursory, impermanent, vanishing, short-lived, volatile. *Ant.* lasting, enduring, protracted, permanent, durable, persistent, perpetual, chronic, ceaseless, imperishable, everlasting, incessant, unending, interminable, deathless, undying, never-ending, immortal, eternal.

translate, transmute, transform, interpret, construe, decode, render, decipher, repeat, retransmit.

transparent, clear, obvious, glassy, diaphanous, pellucid, serene, translucent, lucid, crystalline, explicit, evident, manifest, patent, limpid, guileless. *Ant.* turbid, muddy, opaque, roiled, hidden, dark.

trap, snare, plot, ambush, net, pitfall, intrigue, ruse, stratagem, wile.

trash, waste, rubbish, garbage, refuse, dross, dregs, trumpery, junk, scourings, leavings, sweepings, rubble, debris, slag, litter, rabble, riffraff. *Ant.* goods, valuables, benefits, advantages, perquisites, acquisitions.

ravel, *n.* journey, excursion, tour, pilgrimage, voyage, trip, expedition, ramble, cruise, sojourn, ride, walk, peregrination, wandering, march, circuit, migration, wayfaring, exodus, course; *v.* go. move sail, fly, drive, walk, wander, journey.

ravesty, caricature, parody, burlesque, imitation, ridicule, distortion, farce, mockery, mimicry, derision.

reacherous, false, traitorous, false-hearted, faithless, treasonable, unfaithful, perfidious, untrustworthy, unreliable, deceitful, ill-intentioned, malign, malicious, malevolent, rancorous, evil, spiteful, base, vile, foul, ignominious, venomous, inglorious, recreant, disloyal. *Ant.* true, reliable, faithful, dependable, trustworthy, magnanimous, fraternal, charitable, kind, well-intentioned, sympathetic, loving, loyal, affectionate, considerate, honorable, frank, honest, constant, aboveboard, straightforward, staunch, conscientious, upright, high-principled, candid.

treason, sedition, betrayal, deception, subversion, treachery, perfidy. *Ant.* allegiance, loyalty, fidelity, fealty, homage, devotion, support.

treat, handle, arrange, attend, manage, manipulate, comment, doctor, interpret, prescribe, explain, criticize, discuss, review, negotiate, bargain, indulge, satisfy, amuse, divert. *Ant.* mismanage, neglect, deny, disappoint.

tremble, shake, pulsate, vibrate, shiver, totter, shudder, oscillate, rock, quake, quail, quiver, wobble, teeter.

tremendous, huge, great, enormous, vast, prodigious, colossal, monstrous, enormous, appalling, stupendous, monumental, startling, astounding, awesome, alarming, amazing, immense, gigantic. *Ant.* small, tiny, miniature, unimportant, trivial, insignificant.

trenchant, sharp, critical, emphatic, keen, unsparing, assertive, severe, energetic, cutting, vigorous, ironical, strong, censorious, forcible, powerful, sarcastic, strenuous, dynamic, impressive, intense, incisive, vivid, poignant, positive, graphic, dogmatic, unmistakable, explicit, salient, express, decided, weighty, grave, penetrating, distinct, clear-cut, acute, biting, crisp, caustic, sardonic, pointed, piercing, effective, serious, pungent, significant, piquant, spirited. *Ant.* weak, unimportant, unimpressive, light, simple, ambiguous, vacillating, shallow, obscure, feeble, diffuse, pointless, languid, insipid, rambling, inflated, senseless, paltry, mollifying, gentle, nonsensical, silly, frivolous, frothy, nonessential, worthless, trite, petty, trifling, dull, ineffective, inane, futile, insignificant, objectionable, inopportune, ridiculous.

trespass, encroach, intrude, invade, infringe, enter, poach, intrude, entranch, violate, transgress, interlope, interfere.

trial, test, touchstone, effort, experiment, examination, demonstration, attempt, scrutiny, endeavor, proof, ordeal, assay, trouble, tribulation, affliction, woe, lawsuit, case, cause.

tribulation, suffering, distress, trial, oppression, wretchedness, hardship, misery, affliction, agony, trouble, adversity, grief. *Ant.* joy, happiness, peace, success, consolation.

trick, artifice, maneuver, swindle, deception, cheat, subterfuge, ruse, illusion, humbug, wile, imposture, deceit, fraud, stratagem, leger demain, caper, stunt.

trifle, *n.* nothing, triviality, bagatelle, particle, bit, modicum, fig, bauble, morsel, iota, jot, trace; *v.* dally, toy, play, flirt, deceive, fib, coquet.

trim, *adj.* neat, compact, tidy, clean, orderly, well-adjusted, well proportioned, shapely, spruce, smart; *n.* dress, gear, ornaments, edging, trappings, state, condition; *v.* balance, equalize, adjust, adorn, garnish, deck, array, fit, dress, clip, decorate, lop, cut, smooth, scold, beat, thrash, chide, rebuke, punish, defeat, cheat.

trite, hackneyed, ordinary, oft-repeated, common, dull, wearisome, commonplace, stupid, old, ancient, stale, out-of-date, familiar, well-known, hoary, banal, conventional, venerable, archaic, worn out, stereotyped, bromidic, obvious, shopworn, uninteresting, driveling. *Ant.* original, uncommon, fresh, interesting, keen, fit ting, sharp, pointed, suitable, up-to-date, new, novel, appealing, opportune, desirable, moving, becoming, expedient, proper, seem ly, rousing, bracing, agreeable, germane, heartening, apposite, felicitous, enlightening, pertinent, seasonable, apt, applicable, effectual, relevant, impressive.

triumph, *n.* victory, achievement, exultation, conquest, jubilation, mastery, ovation, joy, subjugation, routing, success, ascendancy, boast, celebration, gain, advantage, trophy, prize; *v.* flourish, rejoice, exult, celebrate, win, master, succeed, thrive, surpass, prevail, glory. *Ant.* defeat, subjection, loss, failure, subjugation, ruin, vanquishment, repulse, destruction, downfall, catastrophe, adversity, misfortune, reverse, calamity, setback, disaster; lose, fail, succumb.

trivial, petty, trifling, small, little, unimportant, scanty, frivolous, diminutive, insignificant, mean, scanty, meager, inappreciable, dribbling, minute, unessential, paltry, beggarly, inconsiderable, valueless, worthless, useless. *Ant.* important, consequential, big, powerful, ample, grave, mighty, valuable, serious, far-reaching, precious, large, massive, heavy, weighty, paramount, necessary, significant, useful, grand, essential, serviceable, vital, material, advantageous, beneficial, momentous.

troop, company, party, band, legion, host, unit, group, lot, herd, flock, army, multitude.

trophy, prize, memorial, palm, token, memento, wreath, medal, loving cup, laurel, crown, citation.

trouble, *v.* distress, upset, distract, perturb, annoy, vex, plague, agitate, bother, embarrass, concern, worry, disquiet, irk, pester, tease, afflict, disarrange, disorder; *n.* grief, distress, illness, ailment, hardship, difficulty, effort, pains. *Ant.* soothe, assist, calm, ease.

truculent, savage, ruthless, cruel, barbarous, belligerent, inhuman, fierce, ferocious, rude, harsh, mean. *Ant.* harmless, tame, mild, inoffensive, gentle, peaceable.

rue, real, reliable, honorable, accurate, trustworthy, honest, exact, veracious, dependable, straight, sincere, correct, authentic, actual, veritable, loyal, literal, genuine, positive, precise, absolute, natural, typical, factual, legitimate, uncontradictable, unimpeachable, definite, valid, well-founded, truthful, faithful, punctilious, legal, rightful, scrupulous, just, incorrupt, upright, righteous. *Ant.* false, disloyal, fabulous, fickle, unreal, mythical, fictional, treacherous, lying, imaginary, spurious, unauthentic, incorrect, illusive, wrong, erroneous, illusory, astray, inaccurate, inexact, mistaken, ridiculous, nonsensical, contradictory, absurd, self-contradictory, fantastic, fraudulent, sham, preposterous, untrue, misrepresented, deceptive, mock, illegitimate, counterfeit, unbelievable, visionary, deceitful, shadowy, baseless, perfidious, perjured, faithless, evasive, dishonorable, evil, dishonest, untrustworthy, trustless.

runk, chest, box, coffer, portmanteau, stem, stalk, stock, body, bole, shaft, torso, compartment, casing, proboscis, snout.

rust, *n.* belief, confidence, dependence, credit, assurance, faith, reassurance, credence, certitude, certainty, expectation, conviction, holding, opinion, estate, reliance, security, monopoly, benefit, interest; *v.* believe, rely, credit, consider, esteem, confide, depend, allow, suppose, expect, hope, count, bank, entrust. *Ant.* mistrust, unbelief, misgiving, distrust, doubt, discredit, disbelief, suspicion, incredibility, skepticism; distrust, impugn, dispute, doubt, suspect, disbelieve, assail, discredit, hesitate, waver, challenge.

rustworthy, reliable, true, sincere, honest, veracious, honorable, candid, loyal, faithful, dependable, steady, constant, steadfast, truthful, decent, upright, incorrupt, reputable, right, righteous, conscientious, respectable, staunch, high-principled. *Ant.* deceitful, faithless, unreliable, corrupt, inconstant, false, underhand, unfaithful, undependable, contemptible, sneaking, irregular, unsteady, bribed, venal, weak, dubious, perfidious, disloyal, base, treacherous, unfriendly, dishonorable, ignominious, traitorous, inimical, infamous.

ruth, truthfulness, honor, candor, veracity, ingenuousness, openness, probity, sincerity, honesty, fidelity, frankness, orthodoxy, verity, accuracy, authenticity, fact, correctness, exactness, rectitude, constancy, exactitude, uprightness, precision, faithfulness, incorruptibility, trustworthiness. *Ant.* untruth, lie, falsehood, mendacity, lying, fabrication, deception, prevarication, falsification, invention, misrepresentation, suppression, equivocation, perversion, exaggeration, evasion, duplicity, improbity, apostasy, double-dealing, hypocrisy, insincerity, dishonesty, perfidy.

ry, attempt, aim, tackle, essay, strive, test, assay, experiment, endeavor, risk, venture, speculate, use, ply, handle, manipulate, judge, inquire, examine, undertake, fit, struggle, seek, adjudicate, hear, adjudge, investigate, render, refine, extract, purify.

tug, *v.* tow, drag, pull, haul, draw, labor, struggle, strive; *n.* pull, effort, haul, towboat, trace.

tumble, roll, heave, toss, plunge, pitch, fall, wallow, trip, sprawl stumble, topple, disturb, rumple, derange, dishevel, disarrange.

tumid, turgid, protuberant, ostentatious, swollen, distended, inflated pompous, bloated, full, bulging, expanded, grandiloquent, dilated pretentious, bombastic. *Ant.* shrunken, deflated, reduced, concise

tumult, disorder, disturbance, turbulence, confusion, uproar, bustle hubbub, commotion, activity, ferment, trouble, riot, agitation *Ant.* quiet, tranquility, peace.

tumultuous, agitated, violent, uproarious, disturbed, boisterous, disorderly, turbulent, lawless, rowdy, rude, riotous, vehement, noisy obstreperous, excited, blustering, tempestuous, stormy, rampant clamorous, rough, perturbed, passionate, raging, wild, foaming uncontrolled, seditious, mutinous, rebellious, demonstrative, vociferous. *Ant.* peaceful, gentle, unexcited, easygoing, subdued, unperturbed, restful, tame, quiet, law-abiding, muffled, restrained modest, tranquil, silent, pacific, mild, still, quiescent, moderate soft, calm, unruffled, repressed, passive, inexcitable, resigned cool, orderly, sedate, obedient, placid, undemonstrative, patient staid, dispassionate, composed, temperate, meek, unimpassioned grave.

turbid, muddy, roiled, mixed, muddled, impure, unsettled, unclean mired, befouled, cloudy, opaque, murky, dirty. *Ant.* transparent clear, crystal, limpid, purified, pellucid, translucent, pure, clarified, filtered, unsoiled, settled, unsullied, strained, cleared.

turbulent, disturbed, blustery, obstreperous, tumultuous, wild, insurgent, restless, brawling, agitated, violent, boisterous, stormy riotous. *Ant.* peaceful, quiet, orderly, calm, placid.

turn, *v.* rotate, gyrate, oscillate, swing, whirl, reel, revolve, pivot wheel, twirl, reverse, spin, circle, divert, deflect, avert, swerve deviate; *n.* revolution, spin, twist, aptitude, bent, knack, cast fashion, bias, inning, shift.

twist, wind, rotate, writhe, contort, distort, pervert, complicate convolve, gnarl, crook, turn, twine, screw, bend, coil, wring wreathe, encircle, knot.

type, symbol, character, representation, emblem, letter, sign, figure sort, kind, standard, pattern, form, nature, class, model, genus species, phylum, variety, breed, caste, assortment, cast, mold shape. *Ant.* amorphism, monstrosity, deviation, misproportion abnormality, malformation, deformity, distortion, unconformity anomaly, peculiarity, anomalousness, shapelessness; *v.* typify represent, classify, categorize, determine, typewrite.

typical, common, usual, average, modal, illustrative, normal, model good, middling, figurative, emblematical, representative, true indicative, symbolic, exemplary, ideal. *Ant.* abnormal, unusual superior, rare, distinctive, inferior, aberrant, atypical, deviant.

tyrant, despot, dictator, oppressor, autocrat, sovereign, emperor slavedriver, martinet.

tyro, novice, beginner, learner, neophyte, amateur, rooky, tenderfoot, dabbler. *Ant.* expert, master, professional, teacher, guide leader, veteran.

U

ugly, homely, unsightly, repulsive, ill-favored, unseemly, hideous, plain, deformed, horrible, unpleasant, revolting, offensive, objectionable, threatening, unshapely, hulking, tough, bullying, quarrelsome, ill-grained, stiff-necked, rude, rough, pugnacious, vile, corrupt, disagreeable, disorderly. *Ant.* beautiful, handsome, fair, comely, charming, graceful, pretty, captivating, elegant, lovely, fascinating, good-looking, blooming, appealing, magnificent, refined, radiant, attractive, delicate, splendid, gorgeous, exquisite, dainty, symmetrical, tidy, shapely, neat, trim, well-formed, sleek, well-developed, grand, gorgeous, dazzling, gentle, law-abiding.

ultimate, extreme, maximum, last, final, terminal, absolute, decisive, eventual, farthest, concluding. *Ant.* first, beginning, preliminary, primary.

umbrage, dissatisfaction, offense, contempt, resentment, hatred, displeasure, suspicion, estrangement, anger, indignation, wrath, huff, grudge, resentment, enmity, antipathy, aversion, pique, malice, bitterness, alienation, detestation, animosity, repugnance, spite, rancor. *Ant.* love, esteem, regard, sympathy, admiration, pleasure, affection, respect, tenderness, attachment, infatuation, cordiality, devotion, benevolence, friendliness, fervor, friendship, fraternalism, brotherhood, amity, harmony, unselfishness, consideration.

umpire, arbiter, justice, negotiator, arbitrator, moderator, peacemaker, referee, mediator, judge, propitiator, settler, censor, compromiser, inspector, assessor. *Ant.* partisan, client, parasite, adherent, sycophant, follower, player, sympathizer, patron, litigant, backer, opponent, advocate, antagonist, enemy, foe.

unanimity, accord, unison, sympathy, agreement, concord, concert, harmony, congruence, unity, concordance, conformity, apposition, correspondence, compatibility. *Ant.* discord, disagreement, break, dissonance, dissidence, difference, variance, disruption, division, dispute, quarrel.

unbecoming, improper, undecorous, indecent, unseemly, unsuitable, inappropriate, unfit, unbefitting, inept, gauche, maladroit. *Ant.* fitting, proper, becoming, suitable, appropriate, decent.

unbiased, just, impartial, impassionate, unprejudiced, judicial, fair-minded, equitable, objective. *Ant.* prejudiced, partial, unfair, slanted.

uncertain, doubtful, undecided, equivocal, insecure, irresolute, precarious, vacillating, dubious, unsure, questionable, irregular, vague, aimless, unstable, perilous, indistinct, problematical, indefinite, unsettled, ambiguous. *Ant.* certain, sure, definite, fixed, settled, regular.

uncivilized, rude, barbarous, ignorant, superstitious, uncultured, simple, boorish, heathenish, crude, cruel, discourteous, low, unenlightened, savage. *Ant.* civilized, cultured, courteous, educated, polished, refined, cultivated.

unclean

unclean, dirty, slimy, impure, filthy, unwashed, foul, vile, smutty, grimy, nasty, soiled, unwashed, offensive, squalid, beastly, repulsive, obscene, fetid, sooty, abominable. *Ant.* clean, pure, chaste.

uncommon, scarce, rare, strange, odd, unique, unusual, queer, noteworthy, unwonted, singular, occasional, infrequent, remarkable. *Ant.* usual, common, regular, expected, customary, conventional, typical.

uncompromising, obstinate, stiff, rigid, unyielding, strict, orthodox, determined, narrow, firm, hard, tough, confirmed, fixed, stable, dependable, intransigent. *Ant.* flexible, easy-going, yielding, soft, mild, submissive, amenable, adaptable.

unconforming, aberrant, erratic, singular, abnormal, peculiar, odd, irregular, eccentric, offbeat, exceptional, incongruous. *Ant.* conforming, lawful, regular, normal.

unconstrained, free, spontaneous, unsophisticated, voluntary, easy, natural, primitive, willful, impulsive, autonomous. *Ant.* limited, bounded, constrained, forced, obliged, unnatural, compelled.

uncouth, clumsy, strange, ungraceful, ungainly, gawky, awkward, graceless, vulgar, boorish, rude, rough, unrefined, homely, rustic. *Ant.* handsome, well-proportioned, graceful, attractive, well-built, easy, becoming, symmetrical, shapely, pleasing, neat, elegant, refined, mannerly, courteous.

understand, comprehend, know, conceive, note, apprehend, recognize, learn, discern, interpret, perceive, imply, experience, see, assume, appreciate, accept, believe, hear, gather, grasp. *Ant.* mistake, misunderstand, misinterpret, misconstrue.

understanding, intellect, rationality, comprehension, intelligence, reason, knowledge, capacity, reasoning, perception, conception, penetration, grasp, sapience, discernment, perspicacity, insight, wisdom, intuition, inspiration. *Ant.* noncomprehension, vacancy, incapacity, anility, senility, dotage, stupidity, simplicity, fatuity.

undertaking, venture, enterprise, project, task, business, attempt, effort, work.

undisguised, open, honest, sincere, real, true, ingenuous, plain, frank, genuine, unadulterated, uncovered. *Ant.* covered, hidden, dishonest, adulterated, false, masked, veiled, concealed.

undoing, ruin, reversal, trouble, ruination, destruction, grief, downfall, misfortune, defeat, calamity, accident, catastrophe, mishap, casualty, infliction, adversity, defeat, reverse, blow, affliction, trial, loss, mischance, failure, collapse, misadventure. *Ant.* prosperity, fortune, blessing, wealth, happiness, pleasure, joy, fame, success, advantage, renown, triumph, ascendancy, glory, victory, delight, exaltation, honor, emolument, gain, mastery.

uneasy, unquiet, disturbed, fearful, restless, anxious, fidgety, uncomfortable, troubled, alarmed, afraid, apprehensive, nervous, shaky, frightened, watchful, wakeful, suspicious, petulant, harried, unsettled, peevish, irritable, fretful, worried. *Ant.* steady, firm, undismayed, peaceful, sober, calm, quiet, constant, reserved, staid, secure, serene, settled, stable, content, satisfied, joyful, pleased, resigned, glad, happy, cheerful.

unequal, uneven, irregular, unlike, inequitable, unjust, unparallel, unfair, ill-matched, unbalanced, different, top-heavy, disparate, lop-sided, wanting, one-sided, lacking, short, deficient. *Ant.* equal, balanced, same, homologous, even, matched, synonymous, full, equivalent, coequal, sufficient, identical, uniform, invariable, steady, regular, constant.

unfair, prejudiced, partial, unjust, biased, dishonest, one-sided, oblique, inequitable, slanted, disingenuous, unethical, uncandid, hypocritical, unequal, inequitable. *Ant.* honest, just, judicial, impartial, candid, honorable, fair, unbiased, ethical.

unfeeling, callous, unkind, inconsiderate, insensate, cruel, numb, unsympathetic, insensible, senseless, hard-hearted, merciless, cold, stony, adamantine, pitiless, torpid, apathetic, unconscious. *Ant.* kind, merciful, sympathetic, helpful, alert, awake, tender, conscious, tolerant, responsive, compassionate.

unfit, unsuitable, inappropriate, unhealthy, improper, unqualified, unconditioned, incompetent, inexpert, objectionable, incapable. *Ant.* fit, suitable, ready, competent, skilled, capable.

unfortunate, unlucky, ill-fated, miserable, disastrous, unhappy, lost, calamitous, wretched, abandoned, deserted, unsuccessful, ruined, overwhelmed, down-hearted, inexpedient, untimely, doomed, unprosperous, unfavorable, ill-starred, unpropitious, inopportune, prostrate, desolate, ill, sick, poverty-stricken. *Ant.* fortunate, happy, successful, prosperous, healthy, triumphant, affluent, victorious, conquering, advantageous, beneficial, thriving, opportune, flourishing, timely, providential, propitious, auspicious, satisfied, comfortable, contented, delighted, pleasurable, joyous, cheerful, blithe.

ungainly, clumsy, inexpert, unfit, awkward, unskilled, uncouth, ungraceful, lumbering, hulky, incompetent, unhandy, unwieldy, bungling, gawky, cumbersome, inexperienced, inapt, stupid, inept, green, ugly, unseemly, slouching, ungracious, discourteous, stiff, ill-mannered, rude, rough, gruff, vulgar, churlish, impolite, clownish, boorish. *Ant.* smart, attractive, handsome, quick, refined, appealing, active, trim, skillful, neat, expert, symmetrical, fair, beautiful, dainty, graceful, elegant, delicate, fit, comely, lovely, good-looking, acute, experienced, handy, shapely, alert, skilled, bright, keen, well-proportioned, lively, polished, suave, qualified, courteous, cultured, gentle, well-bred, polite, civil, bland, adroit, clever, talented, expert, proficient, masterly, capable, competent, efficient, trained, artistic, nimble, accomplished, apt, deft, able.

ungovernable, uncontrollable, wild, refractory, intractable, rampant, rebellious, mutinous, unbridled, frantic, furious, raging, violent, headstrong, impetuous, vehement, unmanageable, irrepressible, unruly. *Ant.* tractable, controllable, docile, manageable, calm, peaceable, mild, obedient, submissive, amenable.

unhappy, sad, dolorous, miserable, dejected, wretched, distressed, sorrowful, gloomy, despondent, disconsolate, dismal, unfortunate, calamitous. *Ant.* happy, joyful, gay, fortunate, lucky.

uniform, even, equal, agreeing, alike, regular, conformable, normal, symmetrical, unvaried, consistent, homogeneous, unvarying, unchanging, homologous, undiversified, equable, undeviating, constant, stable, steady, agreeable, solid, plain, harmonious, proportionate, proportional. *Ant.* irregular, awry, grotesque, askew, uneven, crooked, distorted, misproportioned, jumbled, contorted, confused, twisted, unconformable, diversified, heterogeneous, dissimilar, disjoined, divergent, indiscriminate, chaotic, anomalous, deranged, tangled, unsystematic, formless, disordered, misshapen, amorphous, straggling, shapeless.

unify, unite, consolidate, concentrate, rally, join, organize, connect, combine. *Ant.* divide, disrupt, split, disperse, separate, part.

unimportant, trivial, small, frivolous, ordinary, unessential, slight, mediocre, inferior, poor, immaterial, irrelevant, incidental, commonplace, picayune, nugatory, petty, trifling, paltry, inconsequential, indifferent, insignificant. *Ant.* important, grave, momentous, large, serious, notable.

union, unity, unification, unison, coalition, junction, conjunction, concert, combination, cooperation, connection, concord, marriage, confederacy, alliance, association, harmony, attachment, agreement, annexation, blending, compound, absorption, alloy, affinity, amalgamation, commixture. *Ant.* disunion, opposition, discord, difference, disagreement, discordance, divergence, dissidence, incongruity, disproportion, disunity, disparity, variance, unconformity, inequality, clash, conflict, irregularity, split, rebellion, irrelevancy, disconnection, separation, disjunction, dissociation, division, rupture, break, severance, segregation, contrariety, disintegration, dispersion, counteraction, antagonism.

unique, sole, single, only, one, matchless, unmatched, original, different, unprecedented, unparalleled, unlike, novel, unexampled, unrivaled, individual, unusual, strange, remarkable, rare, bizarre, uncommon, outlandish. *Ant.* common, normal, commonplace, everyday, ordinary, regular, usual, standard, agreeing, conventional, universal, accordant, customary, congruous, general, conformable, well-known, familiar, trite, formal, hackneyed, prevailing.

unity, oneness, singleness, union, solidarity, agreement, concord, unification, constancy, continuity, uniformity, concert, harmony. *Ant.* diversity, variety, multiplicity, discord, dissimilarity.

universal, general, all-embracing, total, entire, complete, unlimited, whole, comprehensive, pandemic, broad, generic, cosmic, cosmopolitan, boundless, catholic, world-wide, exhaustive, sweeping, ecumenical, all, widespread, prevailing. *Ant.* special, sectional, local, limited, private, distinctive, narrow, individual, unique, particular, definite, restricted, small, certain, bounded, partial, circumscribed, singular, confined, terminable, walled, defined, ringed, curtailed.

universe, cosmos, macrocosm, earth, creation, world, heavens, sky, firmament, galaxy.

nlimited, boundless, limitless, illimitable, immeasureable, infinite, interminable, unrestrained, unrestricted, unconstrained, absolute, unconfined, full, undefined, indefinite, vast. *Ant.* limited, defined, constricted, confined, bounded, definite, restricted.

nnerve, upset, weaken, unman, confound, discourage, enfeeble, enervate, fluster, shake, disarm. *Ant.* encourage, nerve, steel, inspirit, strengthen, invigorate.

nruly, fractious, ungovernable, recalcitrant, disobedient, willful, obstreperous, headstrong, refractory, wanton, mutinous, violent, rebellious, lawless, stubborn. *Ant.* law-abiding, obedient, docile, tractable, manageable.

nscrupulous, ruthless, reckless, unprincipled, unrestrained, dishonest. *Ant.* honest, careful, just, kind, merciful, scrupulous, conscientious.

nseemly, unbecoming, unsuitable, objectionable, unfit, ill-advised, undesirable, inept, inappropriate, ugly, inopportune, forbidding, improper, inexpedient, imprudent, unsightly, vulgar, ungraceful, inartistic, indecorous, slovenly, homely, ribald, gross, dowdy, unkempt, boorish, brutish, uncouth, clownish, depraved, unpolished, rowdy, disorderly, dissolute, immoral, disgraceful, worthless. *Ant.* desirable, convenient, seemly, expedient, fitting, practicable, becoming, acceptable, good-looking, handsome, cultured, attractive, refined, comely, shapely, polished, cultivated, decorous, praiseworthy, artistic, proper, courteous, correct, worthy, suave, right, commendable, well-intentioned, excellent, righteous, admirable, meritorious, moral, deserving, unexceptionable.

nsettled, restless, wavering, fickle, vacillating, unsteady, unstable, changeable, unhinged, inconstant, unequal, transient, inequable, stirred, turbid, muddy, roily, uninhabited, wild, adrift, tentative, open, unpaid, outstanding, owing, unnerved, troubled, perturbed, nervous, apprehensive. *Ant.* calm, secure, certain, peaceful, paid, steady, stable, settled, cleared, clarified.

nskilled, unpracticed, inexperienced, awkward, clumsy, ill-qualified, incompetent, unfit, inept, rusty, maladroit, ignorant. *Ant.* skilled, experienced, proficient, competent, efficient, expert, trained, qualified, capable, accomplished.

nsophisticated, guileless, ignorant, simple, unaffected, natural, artless, ingenuous, innocent, genuine, pure, true, real, naive, fresh, unstudied, undesigning, unspoiled, unpolluted, unvitiated. *Ant.* knowledgeable, wise, worldly, guileful, hard, sophisticated, experienced, trained, initiated.

nutterable, ineffable, indescribable, incommunicable, inexpressible, unpronounceable, unspeakable.

upright, vertical, erect, perpendicular, standing, honest, honorable, true, virtuous, faithful, incorruptible, pure, straightforward, just, scrupulous, ethical, moral, trustworthy, straight, conscientious. *Ant.* prone, devious, horizontal, dishonest, unjust, inequitable, unfair, immoral, lax, loose, corruptible, crooked, fraudulent.

urgent, pressing, imperative, serious, compelling, important, momentous, necessary, required, demanded, solemn, earnest, impressive, grave, weighty, chief, salient, crucial, exigent, insistent, critical, essential, primary, principal, vital, absorbing, hasty, precipitate, breathless, importunate. *Ant.* unnecessary, desultory, trifling, trivial, slight, unimportant, nonessential, unessential, irrelevant, petty, frivolous, immaterial, farcical, insignificant, nonsensical, inconsiderable, useless, uneventful, inferior, commonplace, mere, common, ordinary, subordinate.

use, employ, manipulate, manage, apply, exploit, utilize, wield, ply, handle, occupy, operate, work, try, consume expend, exhaust, wear, absorb.

useful, serviceable, helpful, suitable, advantageous, valuable, practical, applicable, beneficial, gainful, remunerative, pragmatic, profitable, utilitarian.

useless, worthless, valueless, ineffectual, futile, unproductive, idle, unserviceable, unavailing, inadequate, empty, fruitless.

usual, ordinary, general, habitual, normal, accustomed, frequent, familiar, prevalent, common, prevailing, regular, commonplace, customary, everyday, public, conventional, prosaic, trite, current, formal, well-known, stereotyped, recognized, expected. *Ant.* rare, unusual, infrequent, strange, extraordinary, peculiar, unique, unconventional, odd, uncommon, wonderful, noteworthy, remarkable, unexpected, queer, abnormal, arbitrary, quaint, exceptional, informal, singular, anomalous, unaccustomed.

usurp, assume, seize, claim, arrogate, take, appropriate, assume, preempt, confiscate, encroach, exact, wrest, violate, commandeer, infringe. *Ant.* renounce, abdicate, relinquish.

utility, use, advantage, serviceableness, usefulness, convenience, expediency, service, benefit, avail, efficacy, productiveness, benefit, efficiency, utilitarianism, profit, adequacy, favor, value, worth. *Ant.* inutility, futility, inanity, unprofitableness, inexpediency, disadvantage, folly, impolicy, unfitness, ineptitude, uselessness, inefficiency, inaptitude, unfruitfulness, disservice, worthlessness, inefficacy.

utmost, last, farthest, main, highest, greatest, uttermost, extreme, most. *Ant.* least, nearest, closest.

utter, *adj.* extreme, pure, consummate, complete, unqualified, total, perfect, entire, sheer, absolute, thorough, exorbitant, excessive, outrageous, extravagant, preposterous; *v.* speak, pronounce, say, express, issue, assert, articulate, declare, talk, voice, enunciate, ejaculate, announce, deliver, emit, vocalize, recite, blurt, proclaim, declaim, acclaim, disclose, reveal, divulge, breathe, inform, publish, circulate, diffuse, disseminate, tell. *Ant.* little, small, inconsiderable, diminutive, paltry, trifling, insignificant, partial, incomplete, relative, limited, inappreciable, meager, infinitesimal, simple.

utterly, completely, wholly, exclusively, entirely, altogether, absolutely, thoroughly, totally, fully, quite, unreservedly, assuredly, positively.

V

vacant, empty, void, unoccupied, hollow, depleted, untenanted, idle, uncrowded, unencumbered, thoughtless, unfilled, free, silly, inane, daft, unemployed, dreaming, foolish, vacuous, empty-headed, unused, blank, waste, deserted, uninhabited, tenantless. *Ant.* filled, tangible, inhabited, occupied, corporeal, peopled, substantial, congested, solid, thoughtful, bright, cultured, meditative, clever, wise, tenanted, learned, accomplished, scholarly, studious, reflective, contemplative, replete, introspective, crowded, cogitative, busy, overflowing, full.

vacate, leave, resign, depart, quit, relinquish, surrender, abandon, desert, evacuate, empty. *Ant.* remain, stay, occupy, fill, settle, assume.

vacillation, wavering, rocking, swaying, uncertainty, faltering, hesitation, indecision, inconstancy, reeling, oscillation, irresolution, unsteadiness, fluctuation. Ant. constancy, certainty, dependability, firmness.

vagary, caprice, whim, fancy, humor, eccentricity, whimsey, crotchet, impulse, fantasy, oddity. *Ant.* plan, rule, regulation, duty.

vagrant, *adj.* idle, wandering, roaming, traveling, roving, ranging, itinerant, nomadic, discursive, digressive, divergent, straying, loose, erratic, inconstant, unstable, unsteady, peripatetic, fickle, fluctuating, changeable, irresolute, unsettled, homeless; *n.* beggar, wanderer, vagabond, tramp, rogue, truant, bum, idler, rambler, rover, loafer, hobo, straggler. *Ant.* fixed, steady, stable, settled, stationary, immovable, restful, still, unchangeable, rooted, unerrant, constant, established, invariable, permanent, untraveled, irremovable, stuck, anchored.

vague, uncertain, visionary, casual, unsettled, undetermined, doubtful, indefinite, unsure, dubious, confused, problematic, indeterminate, obscure, questionable, undefined, enigmatic, contingent, provisional, dim, nebulous, indistinct, loose, lax, imprecise, dark, formless, unknown, cryptic, ambiguous, mysterious. *Ant.* certain, sure, definite, specific, real, undoubted, true, authoritative, lucid, evident, undisputed, incontestable, unquestioned, unquestionable, incontrovertible, express, clear, perspicuous, unobscured, positive, manifest, unequivocal, tested, proved, unmistakable, dogmatic, absolute.

vain, trifling, visionary, delusive, trivial, unavailing, frivolous, shadowy, valueless, unreal, ineffective, unprofitable, ineffectual, useless, fleeting, hollow, idle, futile, unsatisfactory, deceitful, vapid, unsatisfying, unsubstantial, nugatory, unimportant, null, unserviceable, inconstant, abortive, profitless, empty, fruitless, worthless, inflated, proud, conceited, arrogant, egotistical, showy, ostentatious, vainglorious. *Ant.* solid, useful, advantageous, substantial, sound, worthy, beneficial, valid, serviceable, expedient, effective, potent, valuable, efficient, competent, adequate, serious, sufficient, retiring, profitable, humble, bashful, real, modest, demure, earnest, meek, unpretending, shy, unassuming, unpretentious.

vainglorious, conceited, proud, vain, haughty, boastful, vaunting, bragging, pretentious, pompous, arrogant, disdainful, insolent. *Ant.* modest, humble, restrained, silent, reserved, unpretentious.

valiant, brave, daring, undismayed, bold, unafraid, intrepid, dauntless, courageous, puissant, gallant, spirited, vigorous, valorous, high-spirited, heroic, chivalrous, plucky, assertive, manly, mettlesome, doughty, audacious, unflinching, self-reliant, undaunted, unshrinking, strong-willed, indomitable, fearless, adventurous, venturesome. *Ant.* cowardly, fearful, afraid, shy, timorous, weak, effeminate, craven, frightened, pusillanimous, skulking, slinking, soft, sneaking, trembling, shaking, quivering, unnerved, terrified, faint-hearted, despicable, contemptible, scared, terror-stricken.

valid, sound, weighty, powerful, cogent, substantial, efficient, sufficient, strong, conclusive, operative, binding, solid, true, genuine, real, actual, well-founded, authentic, tested, legitimate factual, accurate, efficacious, forceful, effective. *Ant.* misleading, erroneous, erring, fallacious, invalid, weak, deceptive, defective, untrue, worthless, unauthentic, deficient, spurious, counterfeit, fraudulent, insufficient, fictitious, sham.

valor, bravery, intrepidity, heroism, courage, boldness, fearlessness, prowess, gallantry, daring, chivalry, defiance, pluck, dash, manliness, spiritedness, spirit, determination, hardihood, firmness. *Ant.* fear, cowardice, cowardliness, fright, consternation, effeminacy, dismay, alarm, timidity, faint-heartedness.

value, *n.* worth, price, esteem, excellence, importance, usefulness, consideration, estimation, price, appreciation, utility, approbation, consideration, goodness, valuation, advantage, desirability, merit, remuneration, benefit, quality, tint, tone, shade, tinge; *v.* esteem, prize, rate, estimate, appraise, figure, assess, treasure, appreciate, compute. *Ant.* undesirableness, disadvantageousness, inexpediency, inutility, unfitness, worthlessness, inexpedience, uselessness; despise, relinquish, abrogate, discard, repudiate, surrender, condemn, disuse, drop, forego, renounce, abandon, neglect.

vandalism, destruction, wrecking, spoliation, damage, burning, looting, wasting, barbarism. *Ant.* preservation, repair, replacement, care, protection.

vanish, disappear, sink, depart, die, evaporate, dissolve, fade. *Ant.* appear, reappear, emerge.

vanity, ostentation, self-esteem, self-laudation, display, conceit, self-glorification, show, self-applause, pretension, vainglory, assurance, conceitedness, affectation, self-love, arrogance, selfishness, egotism, pride. *Ant.* modesty, diffidence, bashfulness, humility, unpretention, demureness, self-abasement, unobtrusiveness, submission, timidity, self-distrust, reserve, shyness.

vanquish, defeat, conquer, beat, subdue, outwit, suppress, master, quell, crush, rout, subjugate, overpower, overcome. *Ant.* yield, surrender, retreat withdraw, abandon.

apid, flat, lifeless, spiritless, insipid, banal, gentle, mild, prosaic, inane, bland, tasteless, tame, feeble, dull, dry, uninteresting. *Ant.* spicy, racy, pungent, piquant, tasty, interesting, sharp, bright.

apor, mist, smoke, gas, fog, steam, cloud, spray.

ariation, change, deviation, oscillation, fluctuation, modification, mutation, variety, diversity, disagreement, difference, incongruity, inconsistency, heterogeneity, disagreement, dissimilarity, discrepancy, aberration, innovation, departure, rotation, alteration, distinction, nonconformity, arrangement, contrast, discord, dissent, disparity, dissidence, contrariety, unfitness, proportion, dissimilitude. *Ant.* equality, agreement, permanence, stability, constancy, sameness, concord, harmony, consistency, conformity, congruity, accord, concordance, uniformity, homogeneity.

ariegated, diversified, multicolored, motley, mottled, marbled, particolored, versi-color, spotted, striped, speckled, checkered, polychromatic, banded, prismatic. *Ant.* monochromatic, monochoic, plain.

ariety, diversity, mixture, variance, difference, miscellany, medley, change, diversification, dissimilarity, assortment, array, division, genus, class, species, kind, race, sort, brand. *Ant.* sameness, unchangeableness, monotony, unity.

arious, diverse, different, divergent, disparate, many, several, assorted, manifold, numerous, miscellaneous. *Ant.* same, uniform, identical, equal, equivalent, alike.

ast, huge, enormous, colossal, mighty, spacious, bulky, boundless, immense, infinite, measureless, unbounded, great, large, gigantic, wide, unlimited, extensive, far-flung, uncircumscribed, expansive, widespread, world-wide. *Ant.* small, limited, little, bounded, petty, narrow, confined, insignificant, slight, inconsiderable, trifling, circumscribed, trivial.

ault, *n.* tomb, crypt, mausoleum, sepulcher, cell, cellar, dungeon, safe, repository, arch, dome, span; *v.* leap, bound, jump, spring, tumble, turn.

aunt, boast, brag, swagger, exaggerate, glory, strut, bluster, exult, flaunt, gloat. *Ant.* cringe, bow, hide, shrink, retire.

ehemence, violence, warmth, ardor, keenness, passion, vigor, force, zeal, fire, enthusiasm, fervor, impetuousness. *Ant.* calmness, restraint, coolness, apathy, dullness, quietness.

ehicle, carriage, conveyance, train, automobile, bus, wagon, cycle, cart, instrument, agency, intermediary, medium, channel.

elocity, speed, rapidity, impetus, alacrity, pace, celerity, swiftness.

enal, sordid, mean, mercenary, corrupt, nefarious, vicious, ignoble. *Ant.* honest, certain, loyal, sure, clean, noble.

enerable, old, aged, antique, antiquated, hoary, time-worn, time-honored, superannuated, patriarchal, revered, adored, venerated, worshipped, honored, erudite, respected, esteemed. *Ant.* young, youthful, callow, inexperienced, immature, modern, new, recent.

venerate, worship, cherish, honor, revere, respect, adore, regard, reverence, esteem, admire.

vengeance, revenge, revengefulness, spitefulness, retribution, vindictiveness, retaliation, reprisal. *Ant.* forgiveness, forgetfulness, mercy, unconcern, pardon, condonation.

venial, excusable, allowable, defensible, pardonable, trivial, forgivable, justifiable, exculpatory, slight, extenuatory, vindicatory, warrantable. *Ant.* mortal, indefensible, unpardonable, deadly, vicious, serious, inexcusable, grave, unjustifiable, flagrant, inexpiable, grievous, heinous, atrocious, wicked.

venom, poison, bane, malice, spite, malignity, malevolence, enmity, bitterness, acerbity, contempt, resentment, rancor, virulence, gall, hate. *Ant.* antidote, benevolence, kindness, benignity, charity, love, praise, goodness, warm-heartedness, fellowship.

vent, *n.* opening, hole, spout, tap, overflow, orifice, mouth, airhole, plug, spiracle, nostril, loophole, crenel, inlet, outlet, emission, passage, escape, valve, petcock; *v.* discharge, emit, expel, ventilate, explode.

ventilate, air, aerate, oxygenate, freshen, purify, express, explain.

venture, *n.* adventure, risk, hazard, peril, stake, chance, gamble, speculation, dare, experiment, trial, attempt, business, project, work, undertaking, enterprise, investment; *v.* attempt, undertake, test, experiment, grope, stake, try, feel, hazard, assay, speculate, bet, gamble, wager, risk, dare, brave, advance, invest.

veracity, truth, reality, truthfulness, exactitude, verity, accuracy, credibility, sincerity, honesty, candor, frankness, fidelity, probity. *Ant.* falsehood, falsification, lying, chicanery, equivocation, misrepresentation, lying, falsity, falseness, deception, imposture, deceit, guile, delusion, fiction, duplicity.

verbal, oral, spoken, vocal, unwritten, textual, lingual, nuncupative.

verdict, judgment, finding, decision, opinion, determination, decree, result, conclusion, adjudication, arbitrament.

verge, brink, rim, edge, margin, lip, boundary, border, brim, limit, confine, skirt, end, extreme. *Ant.* center, inside, body, bulk, whole.

verify, confirm, prove, test, corroborate, certify, substantiate, attest, affirm, check, investigate, authenticate, identify, validate. *Ant.* contradict, disprove, invalidate, deny, repudiate.

versatile, variable, ready, apt, changeable, adaptable, many-sided, varied, movable. *Ant.* limited, unadaptable, awkward, unchanging.

vertical, erect, perpendicular, standing, upright, plumb, straight. *Ant.* horizontal, prone, supine.

vexation, chagrin, trouble, mortification, harassment, irritation, infliction, annoyance, anxiety, worry, ordeal, sadness, torment, unhappiness, heartache, distress, desolation, misery, discontent, wretchedness. *Ant.* pleasure, peace, felicity, satisfaction, amusement, cheerfulness, contentment, happiness, ecstasy, enjoyment, delight, comfort, gladness, well-being.

vibrate, swing, undulate, wave, sway, oscillate, quiver, fluctuate, alternate, flicker, quaver, shake, tremble, shiver, echo, resound, pulsate.

vice, vileness, depravity, evil, corruption, immorality, iniquity, blot, guilt, crime, blemish, defect, sinfulness, fault, sin, wickedness, carnality, debauchery, excess, depravation, perversity, impurity, lewdness, impropriety, profligacy. *Ant.* virtue, morality, honor, decency, rectitude, integrity, innocence, sinlessness, propriety, chastity, righteousness, purity, honorableness, uprightness.

vicious, corrupt, degenerate, unruly, bad, base, demoralized, sinful, depraved, profligate, debased, vile, evil, harmful, reprehensible, obnoxious, abandoned, hurtful, malignant, destructive, impure, mischievous, virulent, pernicious, wicked. *Ant.* virtuous, good, harmless, moral, innocent, honorable, upright, decent, helpful, noble, charitable, temperate, righteous, admirable, excellent, laudable, praiseworthy, exemplary.

victim, prey, quarry, sufferer, martyr, dupe, tool, hireling, gull, puppet, scapegoat. *Ant.* malefactor, evil-doer, criminal, culprit, law-breaker, felon, swindler.

victor, champion, conqueror, vanquisher, master, winner. *Ant.* vanquished, loser.

victory, conquest, success, ascendancy, triumph, mastery, achievement, supremacy, superiority, win, winning, advantage, exultation. *Ant.* defeat, retreat, rout, disaster, destruction, overthrow, failure, frustration, disappointment, collapse, miscarriage, fiasco, blunder, breakdown.

view, *n.* scene, sight, panorama, vista, vision, prospect, look, survey, glance, glimpse, examination, inspection, observation, regard, impression, theory, judgment, conception, opinion, object, aim, goal, sketch, picture, photograph; *v.* see, look, behold, observe, survey, scan, eye, watch, inspect, scrutinize, examine, consider.

vigilant, wary, watchful, wide-awake, cautious, careful, guarded, alert, heedful, circumspect, attentive. *Ant.* careless, negligent, inattentive, heedless, neglectful, oblivious, unwary, dull, reckless, drowsy, indiscreet, impulsive, rash, foolhardy.

vigorous, energetic, powerful, strenuous, strong, vital, healthy, spirited, robust, virile, lively, active, lusty, flourishing, forceful. *Ant.* debilitated, inactive, feeble, weak, frail, languorous, lethargic.

vile, evil, base, depraved, odious, repulsive, brutish, ugly, abject, contemptible, ignoble, wicked, sinful, impure, foul gross, disgusting, iniquitous, cheap, worthless. *Ant.* fine, good, noble, pure, excellent, elevated, important, valuable.

vindicate, extenuate, advocate, acquit, excuse, exonerate, support, justify, defend, maintain, uphold, clear, avenge, retaliate. *Ant.* blame, denounce, accuse, convict, charge, indict, impute.

vindictive, avenging, vengeful, resentful, malicious, rancorous, unforgiving, malevolent, grudgeful. *Ant.* forgiving, excusing, placable, conciliatory.

violate, transgress, invade, infringe, disobey, encroach, disregard, profane, ravish, outrage, dishonor, defile, rape, desecrate.

violent, impetuous, angry, boisterous, furious, raging, riotous, fiery, vehement, frenzied, ungovernable, wild, acute, disorderly, fuming, uproarious, obstreperous, rampant, frantic, intense, extreme, turbulent, convulsive, savage, hysterical, desperate. *Ant.* gentle, mild, kind, moderate, peaceful, quiet, pacific, smooth, tranquil, sober, untroubled, tame, unruffled, peaceable, undisturbed, composed.

virtue, excellence, chastity, morality, uprightness, purity, righteousness, sanctity, goodness, rectitude, honor, honesty, decency, temperance, integrity, fortitude, innocence, incorruption, guiltlessness, sinlessness, impeccability, prudence, justice, effectiveness, power. *Ant.* vice, wickedness, vileness, evil, dishonor, dishonesty, misconduct, wrongdoing, flagrancy, perversity, sinfulness, immorality, depravity, corruption, impurity.

vision, phantom, shadow, specter, apparition, ghost, dream, image, phantasm, fancy, chimera, hallucination, illusion, manifestation, appearance, sight, seeing, perception, discernment, imagination, conception, hope. *Ant.* reality, actuality, fact, corporality, substantiality, materiality, blindness, sightlessness.

vital, necessary, essential, cardinal, important, basic, requisite, radical, fundamental, indispensable, paramount, living, existing, animate, alive. *Ant.* unimportant, trivial, insignificant, external, excessive, dispensible, unnecessary.

vitiate, spoil, degrade, injure, impair, ruin, debase, corrupt, infect, deprave, deteriorate, defile, adulterate, poison, pollute, pervert, damage, contaminate, void, annul, nullify, invalidate. *Ant.* save, restore, repair, revive, reanimate, clean, purify, rebuild.

vituperate, vilify, abuse, revile, berate, scold, reproach, censure, rebuke, denounce, curse, calumniate, upbraid, objurgate, condemn, rate. *Ant.* praise, laud, reward, honor, commend.

vivid, striking, pictorial, graphic, picturesque, realistic, lifelike, fresh, brilliant, bright, quick, strong, vibrant, intense, telling, sprightly, real. *Ant.* cloudy, dull, slow, tame, weak.

vocal, spoken, eloquent, voluble, verbal, expressive, oral, articulate, fluent. *Ant.* silent, quiet.

vociferous, blatant, loud, obstreperous, uproarious, clamorous, noisy, strident, vehement, shouting, unruly, ranting, boisterous. *Ant.* quiet, silent, peaceful, pacific.

voice, *n.* speech, enunciation, accent, utterance, pronunciation, intonation, vocalization, articulation, sound, noise, expression; *v.* speak, utter, say, declaim, declare, express, announce.

void, empty, blank, unoccupied, vacuous, lacking, hollow, destitute. *Ant.* full, useful.

volatile, light, airy, lively, gay, giddy, buoyant, gaseous, vaporous, evaporable, vapory, fleeting, weak, irresolute, wavering, changeable, inconstant, capricious, vacillating. *Ant.* heavy, ponderous, weighty, massive, unwieldy, durable, lasting, permanent, soluble, resolute, stable, steadfast, unflinching, firm, persevering.

voluntary, intentional, deliberate, unconstrained, spontaneous, uncompelled, volitional, free, unbidden, unasked, willful, optional, gratuitous. *Ant.* forced, involuntary, obligatory, instinctive, compelled.

voluptuous, sensual, sensuous, luxurious, hedonic, carnal, opulent, sumptuous, sybaritic. *Ant.* ascetic, austere, puritanical, gloomy, dull, abstinent, abstemious, self-sacrificing, moral, modest, chaste.

voracious, greedy, insatiable, grasping, covetous, ravenous, gluttonous, rapacious.

vouch, assert, attest, warrant, affirm, confirm, guarantee, declare, certify, testify, depose, avow, swear, guarantee, uphold, support. *Ant.* deny, contradict, confute, repudiate, recant, controvert, discard, rebut, negate, impugn, dispute, disavow, reject, disclaim, renounce, abnegate, deprecate, disapprove, disprove.

vow, *n.* promise, pledge, oath; *v.* pledge, swear, affirm, promise, certify, devote, dedicate, consecrate, assert.

vulgar, common, uncultured, ignorant, ordinary, unpolished, inelegant, rude, rough, uncouth, unpolished, offensive, impertinent, ill-bred, impudent, profane, tawdry, gaudy, rowdy, abusive, crass, cheap, undignified, coarse, indecent, ribald, obscene, nasty, boorish, plebeian, low-minded, brutish, disgusting, loathsome, odious. *Ant.* refined, polite, accomplished, polished, civil, cultured, well-spoken, agreeable, elegant, chaste, graceful, proper, artistic, pleasing, charming, well-bred, aesthetic, decorous, fashionable, decent, conventional, gentlemanly, ladylike.

vulnerable, unprotected, defenseless, assailable, exposed, unsafe, insecure. *Ant.* secure, protected, safe.

W

wag, *n.* joker, comic, comedian, jester, wit, humorist, punster, droll, banterer; *v.* sway, swing, waddle, waggle.

wager, *v.* bet, risk, play, gamble, punt, stake, hazard, gage, chance; *n.* betting, gambling, speculation, risk.

wages, pay, salary, fee, payment, stipend, compensation, income, remuneration, earnings.

wait, tarry, linger, await, stay, bide, expect, delay, abide, serve, attend. *Ant.* proceed, leave, go, act, depart.

waken, awake, rouse, stimulate, awaken, excite, enkindle, stir, wake, animate, arouse, kindle, activate.

wallow, flounder, roll, grovel, toss, indulge, revel, welter.

wander, roam, stroll, stray, walk, range, rove, ramble, drift, prowl, journey, err, digress, travel, diverge, tour, deviate, traverse, peregrinate, straggle, meander, swerve. *Ant.* stay, settle, pause, wait, remain, rest, repose, tarry, halt, stop.

want, lack, wish, desire, need, starvation, insufficiency, privation, penury, scarcity, hunger, poverty, dearth, famine, inadequacy, exigency, depletion, emptiness, pauperism, incompetence, absence, deficiency, neediness, necessity, dearth, distress, indigence. *Ant.* plenty, wealth, profusion, abundance, sufficiency, copiousness, enough, competence, adequacy, fullness, affluence, luxury, opulence.

ward, *n.* guardianship, protection, care, charge, custody, minor, dependent, precinct, section, quarter, district, division; *v.* guard, parry, watch, defend, protect, keep, safeguard.

warfare, war, combat, operations, fighting, struggle, battle, conflict, hostilities, battle, mobilization, contest. *Ant.* peace, truce, harmony, accord, pacification, armistice.

warm, *adj.* tepid, heated, mild, snug, cozy, feverish, flushed, affable, cordial, fervent, genial, affectionate, ardent, compassionate, sympathetic, heartfelt, tender, warmhearted, loving, gracious, responsive, enthusiastic, passionate, sincere; *v.* heat, tepefy, calefy, melt, thaw, chafe, foment. *Ant.* cool, cold, indifferent, insensitive, unfriendly, dispirited, frigid, austere, aloof; freeze, refrigerate, chill, soothe, temper, calm.

warn, caution, apprise, forewarn, advise, admonish, forebode, call, inform, summon, notify, alert, counsel, threaten.

warning, caution, omen, augury, prediction, notice, admonition, advice, alarm, portent, summons, premonition, sign, indication, signal, threat.

warrant, *n.* writ, summons, voucher, permit, order, subpoena, surety, authentication, verification, guarantee, warranty, pledge, license, attestation, authorization, justification; *v.* attest, guarantee, assure, secure, certify, vouch, avouch, authorize, declare, affirm, state, justify, sanction, uphold, sustain.

wary, circumspect, cautious, alert, heedful, guarded, provident, careful, vigilant, chary, watchful, mindful, calculating, scrupulous, discreet. *Ant.* careless, incautious, rash, precipitate, unwary, thoughtless, impetuous, imprudent, impulsive, foolish, brash, rash, heedless, reckless, foolhardy, negligent.

waste, squander, dissipate, consume, corrode, destroy, lavish, scatter, spend, dwindle, wither, pine, expend, decay, spoil, abuse, misuse, lose, ravage, devastate, exhaust, damage, pillage, misapply, misspend. *Ant.* save, hoard, conserve, preserve, achieve, accomplish, erect, establish, provide, supply, furnish, improve, restore, repair, revive, use, operate, utilize, acquire, recover, gain, win, procure, get, collect.

wasteful, extravagant, prodigal, squandering, profligate, thriftless, profuse, dissipated, lavish, unthrifty, careless, improvident, reckless, ruinous, wild, destructive. *Ant.* saving, petty, sordid, close, miserly, mercenary, hoarding, tight-fisted, avaricious, ungenerous, chary.

watchful, vigilant, wary, wakeful, alert, heedful, careful, prudent, circumspect, cautious, attentive. *Ant.* negligent, oblivious, careless.

water, wet, soak, irrigate, immerse, moisten, dilute, wash, bathe, sprinkle, deluge, steep, douse, flood, drench. *Ant.* dry, dehydrate, desiccate, drain, wipe, parch, sear.

wave, *n.* undulation, surge, ripple, roller, billow, swell, breaker; *v.* swing, beckon, shake, signal, sway, oscillate, stir, flutter, flap.

waver, vacillate, fluctuate, reel, totter, tremble, quiver, oscillate, twitch, shake, flicker, flutter, vibrate, hesitate, falter, boggle, equivocate.

way, path, roadway, avenue, track, route, thoroughfare, driveway, highway, street, road, pathway, alley, artery, course, pass, lane, channel, gateway, entrance, passage, approach, mode, system, form, method, means, process, design, fashion, plan, manner, procedure.

weak, feeble, infirm, soft, timorous, helpless, faint, exhausted, unnerved, effeminate, flaccid, relaxed, tender, vulnerable, strengthless, exposed, unguarded, impotent, ineffectual, fragile, delicate, enervated, unsound, languid, shaky, nervous, worn, effete, wasted, aged, valetudinary, shattered, unstrung, powerless, decrepit, defenseless, unsubstantial. *Ant.* strong, stout, vigorous, muscular, robust, athletic, sturdy, husky, manly, able-bodied, virile, potent, powerful, stalwart, hard, hardy, healthy, strapping, brawny, forceful, lusty, mighty, dynamic, energetic, courageous.

weaken, debilitate, enervate, exhaust, enfeeble, devitalize, undermine, sap, reduce, attenuate, impair, incapacitate, cramp, relax, cripple, dilute, thin, diminish. *Ant.* strengthen, revitalize, aid, brace, improve, fortify, invigorate, energize, reinforce.

wealth, money, assets, opulence, riches, belongings, possessions, competence, property, affluence, prosperity, substance, means, goods, fortune, plenty, luxury, resources, estate, profusion, amplitude, abundance. *Ant.* poverty, scarcity, lack, want, pauperism, need, privation, indigence, destitution, penury, dearth, shortage, insufficiency, incompetence, inadequacy.

wear, *v.* bear, consume, endure, use, carry, display, diminish, waste, impair, erode, abrade; *n.* use, service, utilization.

weariness, fatigue, tiredness, annoyance, pall, disgust, tedium, lassitude, exhaustion, ennui, lethargy, languor, prostration, faintness. *Ant.* alertness, energy, vim, strength, amusement.

wearisome, tedious, vapid, slow, apathetic, tiresome, insipid, slack, phlegmatic, uninteresting, dull, stupid, laborious, hard, heavy, toilsome, difficult, troublesome, strenuous, arduous, irksome, boring, monotonous, humdrum, burdensome, fatiguing, plodding, overpowering, exhausting, backbreaking, grinding, merciless. *Ant.* exhilarating, refreshing, exciting, bracing, stimulating, invigorating, restorative, interesting, inspiring, comforting, happy, consoling, amusing, entertaining, genial, pleasing.

weary, fatigue, pain, vex, tire, disgust, anger, irritate, bother, jade, annoy, bore, distress, exhaust, fret, displease, overtax, grieve, irk, overburden, depress, discourage, dishearten, deject, prostrate, sadden, strain, enfeeble, dispirit. *Ant.* refresh, regale, animate, comfort, brace, gladden, invigorate, inspirit, inspire, brighten, please, arouse, strengthen, enliven, revive, cheer, elate, energize, vitalize, exhilarate, entertain, encourage, delight, ease, divert, amuse, calm, console.

weather, bleach, dry, rot, shrink, fade, discolor, split, expand, tan, disintegrate, toughen, endure, stand, resist, overcome, sustain, bear.

weave, mat, lace, intertwine, braid, twist, knit, construct, crochet, lace, form, compose, design, fabricate, imagine.

weight, heaviness ponderousness, load, ballast, burden, mass, contents, influence, domination, power, control, favor, authority, gravity, importance, seriousness, moment, significance, consequence, import, preponderance.

weird, eerie, spooky, ghostly, unearthly, wild, supernatural, strange, odd, mysterious, uncanny, curious, peculiar. *Ant.* usual, common, normal, plain, ordinary, regular.

wheedle, cajole, flatter, coax, inveigle, lure, entice, intimidate, seduce, flatter.

wheel, *n.* circle, disk, roller, bicycle; *v.* revolve, rotate, gyrate, roll, whirl, spin, swirl, veer, twist, transport, wind, twist, turn, eddy, pirouette.

whim, notion, idea, whimsey, caprice, impulse, vagary, inclination, fancy, fantasy, dream, vision, motive, tendency.

whole, entire, all, complete, total, absolute, integral, plenary, undivided, full, unbroken, gross, integral, all-embracing, inclusive. *Ant.* part, fractional, partial, sectional, incomplete, divided, insufficient, short, deficient, broken, reduced.

wicked, iniquitous, sinful, erring, nefarious, wayward, dissolute, vile, vicious, unrighteous, wrong, criminal, disorderly, immoral, disreputable, impure, evil, corrupt, malevolent, shameful, base, scandalous, foul, infamous, gross, villainous, atrocious, unholy, irreligious, fiendish. *Ant.* good, innocent, spotless, decent, noble, virtuous, worthy, chaste, undefiled, unsullied, righteous, upright, exemplary, pure, praiseworthy, meritorious, commendable, laudable, deserving, well-intentioned, excellent, admirable.

will, volition, resolution, desire, intent, wish, mind, inclination, willingness, pleasure, determination, decision, choice, preference, purpose.

winding, twisting, sinuous, writhing, devious, bending, twining, meandering, turning, coiling, crooked, involuted, curving. *Ant.* straight, plain, direct.

wisdom, prudence, farsightedness, intelligence, foresight, acumen, comprehension, sagacity, astuteness, acuteness, perspicacity, discrimination, ability, discernment, cunning, profundity, reason, attainment, understanding, reasonablness, insight, sense, depth, discretion, skill, prudence, judiciousness, learning, information, prescience, enlightenment, erudition, knowledge, experience, judiciousness, reasoning. *Ant.* foolishness, absurdity, nonsense, folly, stupidity, senselessness, error, silliness, fatuity, misjudgment, miscalculation, vacuity, indiscretion, simplicity, frivolity, imprudence, irrationality, incapacity, rashness, ineptitude, impetuosity, shallowness, trifling, lightness, inexperience, incompetence, short-sightedness.

wise, sagacious, sensible, rational, discerning, enlightened, shrewd, profound, intelligent, astute, alert, calculating, foresighted, sane, smart, discreet, sound, informed, sage, deep, judicious. *Ant.* silly, simple, ignorant, foolish, stupid.

wish, *v.* desire, hanker, hope, pine, hunger, crave, long, yearn; *n.* craving, yearning, want, desire, need, petition, plea, request, bid.

wit, humor, jest, drollery, fun, burlesque, facetiousness, jocularity, banter, raillery, witticism, pleasantry, waggishness, playfulness, repartee, badinage, satire, irony, joking, sally, epigram, pun, wittiness, intellect, understanding, perception, sense, humorist, wag. *Ant.* dullness, solemnity, stupidity, sobriety, stolidity, heaviness, gravity, flatness, moroseness, prosiness, monotony, gloom, melancholy, dejection, depression, pessimism, despondency.

withdraw, retreat, remove, separate, deduct, retract, draw, sequester, retire, abstract, part, disengage, wean, secede, shrink, recall, revoke, relinquish, abjure, recant, depart, vacate, dissociate. *Ant.* remain, return, introduce, bring.

withhold, restrain, retain, check, detain, suppress, reserve, keep, conceal, hide, refuse, hinder. *Ant.* yield, release, open, accord, grant, concede, award.

witness, *n.* testifier, watcher, observer, beholder, spectator, onlooker, eyewitness, deponent, corroborator; *v.* observe, see, confirm, mark, attest, vouch, corroborate, note, watch.

wonder, *n.* amazement, bewilderment, awe, admiration, perplexity, fascination, astonishment, surprise, prodigy, marvel, miracle, rarity, curiosity, phenomenon, spectacle, portent, sign, sight; *v.* query, ponder, doubt, marvel. *Ant.* expectation, anticipation, steadiness, commonness, perturbability, calmness, coolness, hardheadedness, stolidity.

wordy, verbose, diffuse, rambling, prolix, digressive, long-winded, loquacious, redundant, voluble, talkative. *Ant.* terse, concise, succinct, summary, brief, laconic.

work, *n.* labor, performance, achievement, task, accomplishment, deed, toil, action, job, profession, duty, office, function, calling, pursuit, business, product, drudgery, employment, production, exertion, occupation; *v.* perform, function, labor, operate, make, do, struggle, toil, achieve, react, act.

worn, used, shabby, threadbare, exhausted, wasted, weary. *Ant.* new, unused.

worry, *v.* disturb, harry, annoy, torture, plague, irritate, tease, harass, trouble, gnaw, grieve, fret, torment, pester, vex; *n.* concern, care, anxiety, agitation, doubt. *Ant.* soothe, calm.

worth, value, virtue, estimation, merit, price, importance, excellence, advantage, benefit.

worthless, valueless, insignificant, useless, unimportant, meritless, inane, empty, futile, poor, unproductive, unserviceable, barren, profitless, sterile. *Ant.* valuable, serviceable, beneficial, precious, important, remunerative, useful, advantageous, profitable, fertile, gainful, essential, productive, primary, excellent, superior.

worthy, good, honorable, dependable, reliable, noble, dutiful, trustworthy, charitable, virtuous, moral, pure, decent, righteous, fit, suitable, reputable, incorrupt, meritorious, incorruptible, model, creditable, deserving, exemplary. *Ant.* unworthy, reprehensible, bad, evil, untrustworthy, sinful, dishonorable, deceitful, immoral, treacherous, dishonest, vicious, wicked, dissolute, disreputable, iniquitous, profligate, villainous, corrupt, infamous.

wrangle, quarrel, argue, dispute, brawl, contest, bicker, debate, fight, struggle, squabble, cavil. *Ant.* agree, accept, cooperate, concur.

wrap, *n.* cloak, cape, coat, overcoat, blanket, shawl, coverlet; *v.* lap, enfold, roll, enclose, cover, swathe, furl, wind, muffle, envelop, hide, conceal, package, bundle. *Ant.* unwrap, open, unfold.

wreck, *n.* ruins, loss, smash, crash, accident, desolation, perdition, destruction, shipwreck; *v.* smash, injure, ruin, destroy, demolish, founder, break, shatter, damage, blight, raze. *Ant.* repair, save, rebuild, preserve, conserve.

write, record, compose, pen, scrawl, inscribe, draft, draw, engross.

writing, penmanship, handwriting, calligraphy, manuscript, document, inscription, composition.

wrong, evil, sin, baseness, injury, sinfulness, turpitude, spite, vice, immorality, wickedness, indecency, oppression, hurtfulness, hate, transgression, persecution, virulence, tyranny, cruelty, outrage, malignity, inhumanity, misusage, malevolence, abuse, imposition, damage, tort, hatred, unfairness, iniquity, malice, partiality, depravity, injustice, partisanship, corruption, wrongdoing, flagrancy, profligacy. *Ant.* right, righteousness, honesty, goodness, uprightness, justice, decency, virtue, morality, innocence, integrity, sinlessness, charity, benevolence, kindness, kindliness, benignity, sympathy, impartiality, nobleness, loyalty, sincerity, devotion, truth, faithfulness, rectitude.

wry, twisted, crooked, warped, askew, contorted, distorted, contrary, awry, perverse. *Ant.* straight, correct, erect.

X

xanthic, yellow, yellowish, fulvid, fulvose, saffron.

xanthous, yellow, yellow-haired, blonde, light-complexioned, light, fair.

xylography, woodengraving, woodcutting.

Y

yard, court, patio, enclosure, courtyard, playground.

yardstick, rule, measure, criterion, standard, test, gauge, touchstone.

yaw, veer, shift, deviate, turn, alter.

yearn, desire, crave, long, hanker, grieve, mourn, pine, languish, wish, thirst, hunger. *Ant.* reject, ignore, avoid, shun, deprecate, surrender.

yeasty, foaming, frothy, excited, energetic, vigorous, bubbling, light, superficial, unsettled, restless.

yell, cry, scream, shout, yelp, bawl, squall, roar, vociferate, whoop, howl, screech, shriek, shrill, squeal, bellow.

yet, nevertheless, however, notwithstanding, hitherto, furthermore, although, now, still, but, though.

yield, surrender, acquiesce, resign, waive, accede, abdicate, relax, relinquish, quit, succumb, forego, submit, cede, confer, allow, grant, comply, bestow, communicate, impart, defer, capitulate, concede, produce, return, sacrifice, tolerate, permit, suffer, bear, abandon, sanction. *Ant.* deny, protest, withstand, forbid, debar, resist, disallow, reject, disapprove, hinder, refuse, inhibit, negate, interdict, rebuff, preclude, repulse, prevent, oppose, counteract, counter, overcome, clash, overpower, antagonize, cross, master, frustrate, impede, interfere, withhold, contravene, retain, assert, conflict, withdraw, claim, dissent, struggle, strive.

yielding, producing, teeming, accommodating, submissive, pliant, unresisting, conceding, surrendering, soft, spongy, resilient, ductile, flexible, plastic, limber, malleable, tender, lithe, supple, acquiescent, weak, extensible, obedient, cringing, nonresistant, unresisting. *Ant.* unproductive, barren, brittle, sterile, hard, non-productive, waste, tough, fallow, stubborn, defiant, brave, rigid, courageous, intrepid, masterful, stiff, unbending, callous, stony, unyielding, unbending, obdurate, obstinate, intolerant, tenacious, dogmatic, unchangeable, inexorable, stiff-necked, bigoted, head-strong, hidebound, impervious.

yoke, couple, harness, bind, link, splice, attach, connect, associate, join, unite, pair, tie, hitch, fasten, secure. *Ant.* sever, disunite, untie, disconnect, release, free, disengage, detach, disjoin, unbind, dissociate, divide, sunder, separate.

young, youthful, juvenile, immature, adolescent, puerile, green, in-experienced, fresh. *Ant.* old, aged, mature.

youthful, young, juvenile, puerile, budding, blooming, vigorous, active, strong, vibrant. *Ant.* old, aged, elderly, hoary, senile, tired, mature, decrepit, withered, worn, out-of-date, weary.

Z

zany, clown, comedian, fool, comic, jester, madcap, buffoon, dolt, simpleton, half-wit, harlequin, stooge, entertainer.

zeal, ardor, enthusiasm, eagerness, fervor, energy, activity, inclination, willingness, involvement, passion, intentness, industry, determination, dedication, assiduity, diligence, perseverance, philanthropy, concentration, vigilance, single-mindedness, warmth, glow, devotion, passion, courage. *Ant.* indifference, coldness, apathy, carelessness, torpor, laziness, reluctance, indisposition, idleness, indolence, languor, lethargy, slackness, nonchalance, unconcern, timidity.

zealot, partisan, visionary, opinionist, bigot, enthusiast, fanatic, patriot, devotee, dogmatist, martyr, adherent, votary, dreamer. *Ant.* idler, slacker, shirker, dawdler.

zealous, fervent, intense, enthusiastic, earnest, eager, ardent, alert, willing, hustling, animated, diligent, bustling, vivacious, brisk, desirous, assiduous, steadfast, indefatigable, sedulous, resolute. *Ant.* apathetic, lazy, languid, careless, idle, inactive, listless, sluggish, indifferent, inert, unconcerned, lethargic, slack, phlegmatic, dull, indolent.

zenith, top, culmination, maximum, pinnacle, height, climax, peak, summit, apogee, eminence, pitch, apex, acme, tip, crest, crown, cap. *Ant.* base, foundation, nadir, floor, foot, root, pedicle, depth, bottom, minimum.

zero, nothing, nobody, unsubstantiality, naught, unreality, cipher, nonentity, nullity, blank, nil, void. *Ant.* something, material, substantiality, matter, body, anything, substance, corporeality, person, object, thing, existence.

zest, relish, desire, gusto, taste, savor, pleasure, savoriness, flavor, exhilaration, enhancement, enjoyment, pungency, tang, sharpness, piquancy, zeal, enthusiasm, spirit, energy, ardor, passion, delight. *Ant.* distaste, disgust, tastelessness, staleness, acerbity, flatness, vapidness, unsavoriness, mawkishness, dullness, apathy.

zigzag, oblique, awry, sinuous, inclined, crooked, twisted, sloping, wry, askew, curved, serrated, transverse, bent, diagonal, forked, crinkled, jagged, devious, oscillating, straggling, erratic, spiral, fluctuating, meandering, rambling, waggling, indirect, tortuous, undulatory, vibratory. *Ant.* straight, concentric, even, direct, collateral, unbent, parallel, rectilineal, horizontal, vertical, unswerving, plumb, right, true, regular, perpendicular, undeviating, uniform, level, unvarying, flat, undistorted, conventional, rectilinear, symmetrical, inflexible, normal.

zone, belt, section, terrain, region, quarter, commune, district, area, precinct, territory, circuit, sector, tract, locality, segment, ward, country, enclosure, dominion, ground, band.

zymotic, fermentative, bacterial, germinating, infectious, rotting, decomposing, spoiling.

How to Order
Extra Copies of this book

This book is one of a series if books which make up the *Instant Reference Library*. Titles currently included in the series are as follows. Other titles may be added from time to time.

Instant Spelling Dictionary
Instant English Handbook
Instant Quotation Dictionary
Instant Synonyms and Antonyms
Instant Medical Spelling Dictionary
Instant Business Dictionary
Instant Medical Adviser
Instant Secretary's Handbook
Instant Sewing Handbook
Instant Home Repair Handbook

You may order any of the above books from your local bookstore, or send your order directly to Career Institute, Dept. 267, 1500 Cardinal Drive, Little Falls, New Jersey 07424. Individuals, send check or money order. Minimum order $10. No COD's. Business firms or other organizations must send cash with order if 5 or fewer books. For larger orders, use purchase order and we will bill you on open account. Each book $2.95 plus shipping, less the following quantity discounts:

Quantity	Discount
1 to 5 books	None
6 to 15 books	15¢ per book
16 to 49 books	25¢ per book
50 to 149 books	35¢ per book

Orders for different titles may be combined to take advantage of the above quantity prices. Postage and handling $1 for 1st book plus 25¢ for each additional book. New Jersey residents add Sales Tax. Prices subject to change.